Macmillan/McGraw-Hill READING

Mc Graw Hill Macmillan McGraw-Hill

Contributors

The Princeton Review, Time Magazine, Accelerated Reader

The Princeton Review is not affiliated with Princeton University or ETS.

RFB&D learning through listening

Students with print disabilities may be eligible to obtain an accessible, audio version of the pupil edition of this textbook. Please call Recording for the Blind & Dyslexic at 1-800-221-4792 for complete information.

The McGraw-Hill Companies

Macmillan McGraw-Hill

Published by Macmillan/McGraw-Hill, of McGraw-Hill Education, a division of The McGraw-Hill Companies, Inc., Two Penn Plaza, New York, New York 10121.

Printed in the United States of America

4 5 6 7 8 9 006/043 09 08 07 06 05 04

Macmillan/McGraw-Hill READING

Authors

James Flood
Jan E. Hasbrouck
James V. Hoffman
Diane Lapp
Donna Lubcker
Angela Shelf Medearis
Scott Paris
Steven Stahl
Josefina Villamil Tinajero
Karen D. Wood

Macmillan
McGraw-Hill

Managing the

Classroom

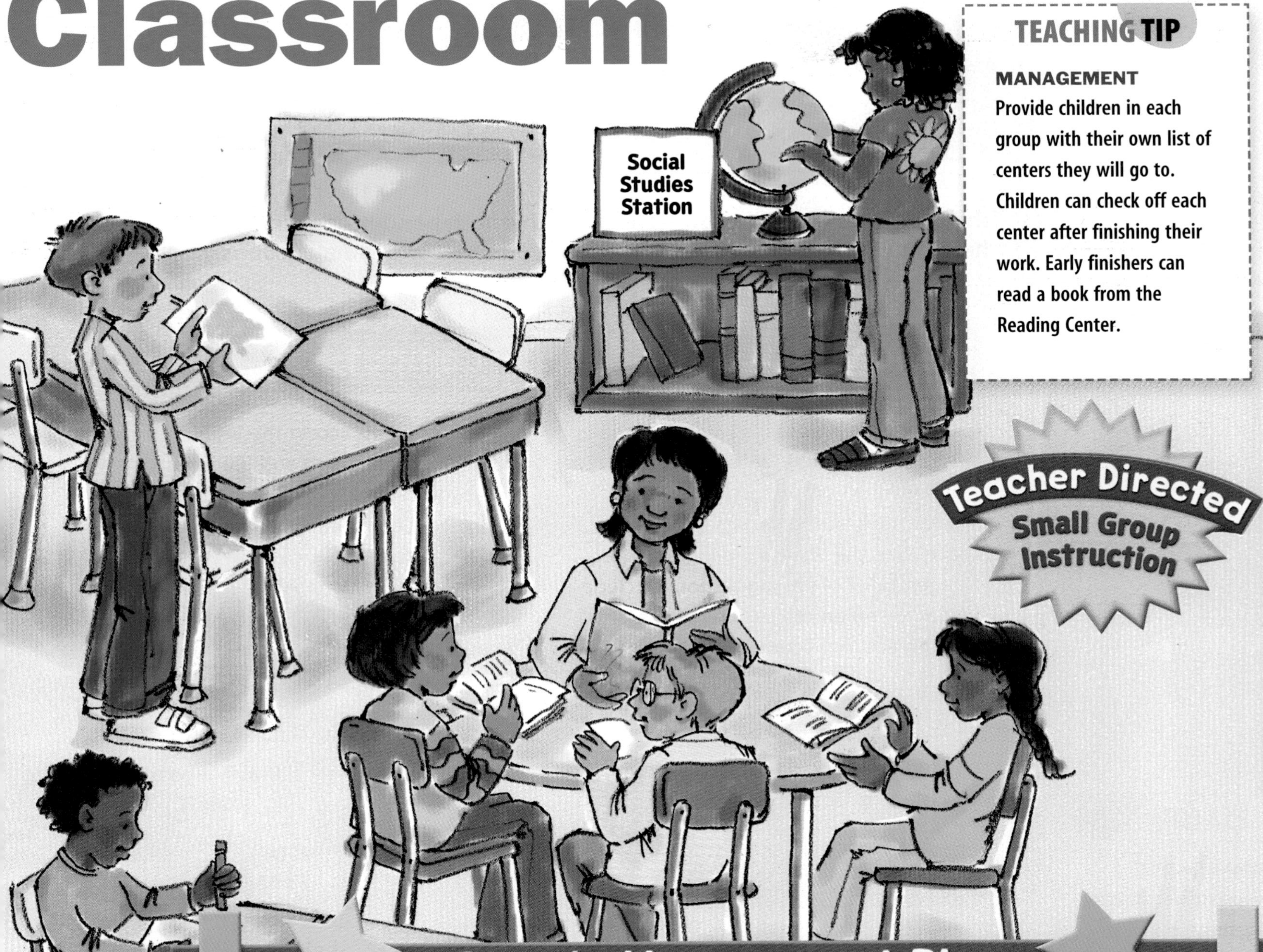

TEACHING TIP

MANAGEMENT
Provide children in each group with their own list of centers they will go to. Children can check off each center after finishing their work. Early finishers can read a book from the Reading Center.

Sample Management Plan

Group 1	Group 2	Group 3	Group 4
With Teacher	Reading or Writing Workstation	Working with Words Station	Cross-Curricular or Computer Station
Reading or Writing Workstation	**With Teacher**	Cross-Curricular or Computer Station	Working with Words Station
Working with Words Station	Cross-Curricular or Computer Station	**With Teacher**	Reading or Writing Workstation
Cross-Curricular or Computer Station	Working with Words Station	Reading or Writing Workstation	**With Teacher**

Creating WORKSTATIONS

Establishing independent workstations and other independent activities is the key to helping you manage the classroom as you meet with small groups.

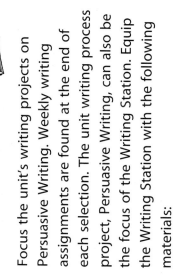

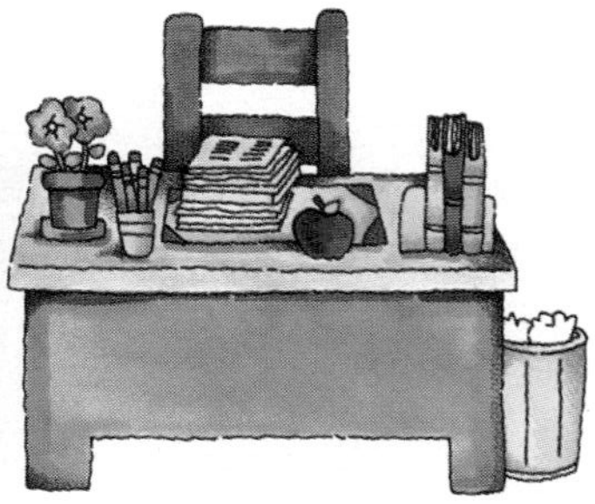

Reading

Set up a classroom library for independent reading. Add Leveled Books as read during small-group instruction. Add other titles, also grouped by reading level. See the Theme Bibliography on pages T78-T79 for suggestions. Include titles based on discussions of students' fiction and nonfiction preferences.

- Self-Selected Reading
- Paired Reading
- Student Anthology selection from the Listening Library

Computer

Students can access the Internet to complete the Research and Inquiry activities suggested throughout the unit. Look for Internet connections in the following Research and Inquiry projects:

- Find Out More project at the end of each selection
- Cooperative Theme Project: The Talent Pool
- Cross-Curricular Activities
- Bringing Groups Together project

TEACHING TIP

MANAGEMENT
Incorporate workstation suggestions into a class assignment chart.

If classroom space is limited, shelve materials for each project in the classroom and distribute them as you assign an activity.

Have students work in groups, pairs, or independently.

Writing

Focus the unit's writing projects on Persuasive Writing. Weekly writing assignments are found at the end of each selection. The unit writing process project, Persuasive Writing, can also be the focus of the Writing Station. Equip the Writing Station with the following materials:

- Samples of published persuasive writing
- Persuasive Writing samples, available in the Teacher's Writing Resource Handbook, pages 20-21

healthy inspire teammates

Working with Words

Selection Vocabulary
Have students create a crossword puzzle using the selection vocabulary words. They should number and block off spaces for the words on graph paper and then shade in the remaining boxes. They should also write a numbered clue for each word. Students can exchange puzzles.

High-Frequency Words
Create cards for the words: *clothes, while, box, thanks, high*, and *brown*. Have students create word puzzles by switching the first and last letters or each word. Have students switch puzzles and solve.

Cross-Curricular STATIONS

Set up Cross-Curricular Stations to help extend selection concepts and ideas. Suggestions for Cross-Curricular activities can be found in the Teacher's Edition.

Science

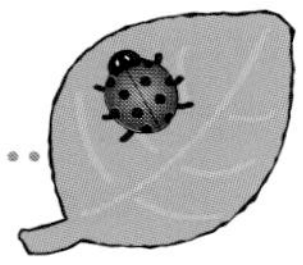

- Parchment and Quills, 264
- Cats, 290
- Natural Dyes, 320
- Constellations, 338

Social Studies

- Historical Landmarks, 268
- Map Skills, 286, 324
- The Underground Railroad, 340

Math

- Multiplication, 274
- Moon Watch, 318
- People and Mules, 344

Art

- Hat Styles, 272
- Japanese Art, 302

Additional Independent Activities

The following independent activities are offered as a means to practice and reinforce concepts and skills taught in the unit.

PUPIL EDITION: READER RESPONSE

Story Questions to monitor the student's comprehension of the selection. The questions are leveled progressing from literal to critical thinking.

Story Activities related to each selection. Four activities are provided: one writing activity, two cross-curricular activities, and a research and inquiry activity in the Find Out More project. Students are encouraged to use the Internet for research.

LEVELED PRACTICE

Each week, Reteach, Practice, and Extend pages are offered to address the individual needs of students as they learn and review skills.

Theme Chart

McGraw-Hill Reading

GRADE LEVEL	Experience	Connections
	Experiences can tell us about ourselves and our world.	Making connections develops new understandings.
Kindergarten	**My World** We learn a lot from all the things we see and do at home and in school.	**All Kinds of Friends** When we work and play together, we learn more about ourselves.
Sub-theme 1	At Home	Working Together
Sub-theme 2	School Days	Playing Together
1	**Day by Day** Each day brings new experiences.	**Together Is Better** We like to share ideas and experiences with others.
2	**What's New?** With each day, we learn something new.	**Just Between Us** Family and friends help us see the world in new ways.
3	**Great Adventures** Life is made up of big and small experiences.	**Nature Links** Nature can give us new ideas.
4	**Reflections** Stories let us share the experiences of others.	**Something in Common** Sharing ideas can lead to meaningful cooperation.
5	**Time of My Life** We sometimes find memorable experiences in unexpected places.	**Building Bridges** Knowing what we have in common helps us appreciate our differences.
6	**Pathways** Reflecting on life's experiences can lead to new understandings.	**A Common Thread** A look beneath the surface may uncover hidden connections.

MULTI-AGE Classroom

Using the same global themes at each grade level facilitates the use of materials in multi-age classrooms.

Themes: Kindergarten – Grade 6

Six Units IN EVERY GRADE

Expression	Inquiry	Problem-Solving	Making Decisions
There are many styles and forms for expressing ourselves.	By exploring and asking questions, we make discoveries.	Analyzing information can help us solve problems.	Using what we know helps us evaluate situations.
Time to Shine We can use our ideas and our imagination to do many wonderful things.	**I Wonder** We can make discoveries about the wonders of nature in our own backyard.	**Let's Work It Out** Working as part of a team can help me find a way to solve problems.	**Choices** We can make many good choices and decisions every day.
Great Ideas	**In My Backyard**	**Try and Try Again**	**Good Choices**
Let's Pretend	**Wonders of Nature**	**Teamwork**	**Let's Decide**
Stories to Tell Each one of us has a different story to tell.	**Let's Find Out!** Looking for answers is an adventure.	**Think About It!** It takes time to solve problems.	**Many Paths** Each decision opens the door to a new path.
Express Yourself We share our ideas in many ways.	**Look Around** There are surprises all around us.	**Figure It Out** We can solve problems by working together.	**Starting Now** Unexpected events can lead to new decisions.
Be Creative! We can all express ourselves in creative, wonderful ways.	**Tell Me More** Looking and listening closely will help us find out the facts.	**Think It Through** Solutions come in many shapes and sizes.	**Turning Points** We make new judgments based on our experiences.
Our Voices We can each use our talents to communicate ideas.	**Just Curious** We can find answers in surprising places.	**Make a Plan** Often we have to think carefully about a problem in order to solve it.	**Sorting It Out** We make decisions that can lead to new ideas and discoveries.
Imagine That The way we express our thoughts and feelings can take different forms.	**Investigate!** We never know where the search for answers might lead us.	**Bright Ideas** Some problems require unusual approaches.	**Crossroads** Decisions cause changes that can enrich our lives.
With Flying Colors Creative people help us see the world from different perspectives.	**Seek and Discover** To make new discoveries, we must observe and explore.	**Brainstorms** We can meet any challenge with determination and ingenuity.	**All Things Considered** Encountering new places and people can help us make decisions.

UNIT 3

Contents

Our Voices

We can each use our talents to communicate ideas.

Unit Planner **254C**
Unit Resources **254E**
Meeting Individual Needs **254F**
Unit Assessment Resources **254G**
Unit Opener **254I**
"The Poet Pencil" a poem by *Jesús Carlos Soto Morfín* . . **254**
(translated by Judith Infante)

THE HATMAKER'S SIGN 256A

retold by ***Candace Fleming***
illustrated by ***Robert Andrew Parker***

HISTORICAL FICTION

SKILLS

Comprehension	Vocabulary	Study Skill	Phonics
• **Introduce** and **Review** Judgments and Decisions • **Introduce** Summarize	• **Introduce** Suffixes	• **Graphic Aids:** Read Signs	• **Review** /ou/ and /oi/

PAT CUMMINGS: MY STORY 282A

compiled and edited by ***Pat Cummings***

INTERVIEW

SKILLS

Comprehension	Vocabulary	Study Skill	Phonics
• **Introduce** Fact and Opinion • **Review** Fact and Opinion • **Review** Summarize	• **Review** Suffixes	• **Graphic Aids:** Read a Flow Chart	• **Review** /ù/ and /yù/

Grass Sandals: The Travels of Basho . . . 298A

written by ***Dawnine Spivak***
illustrated by ***Demi***

BIOGRAPHICAL STORY

SKILLS			
Comprehension	**Vocabulary**	**Study Skill**	**Phonics**
• **Introduce** and **Review** Author's Purpose • **Review** Judgments and Decisions	• **Introduce** Context Clues	• **Graphic Aids:** Read a Map	• **Review** Digraphs

A Place Called Freedom 332A

written by ***Scott Russell Sanders***
illustrated by ***Thomas B. Allen***

HISTORICAL FICTION

SKILLS			
Comprehension	**Vocabulary**	**Study Skill**	**Phonics**
• **Review** Fact and Opinion • **Review** Summarize	• **Review** Context Clues	• **Graphic Aids:** Read a Line Graph	• **Review** Digraphs

TIME FOR KIDS

Twisted Trails 360A

Special Report

SOCIAL STUDIES ARTICLE

SKILLS			
Comprehension	**Vocabulary**	**Study Skill**	**Phonics**
• **Review** Make Judgments and Decisions • **Review** Author's Purpose, Point of View	• **Review** Context Clues • **Review** Suffixes	• **Graphic Aids:** Read a Diagram	• **Review** /ou/ and /oi/, /ů/ and /yů/, Digraphs

Unit Closer **370**

"My Poems" a poem by *Alan Barlow*

Reading Science **371A**

Unit Writing Process: Persuasive Writing **371E**

Unit Assessment **371K**

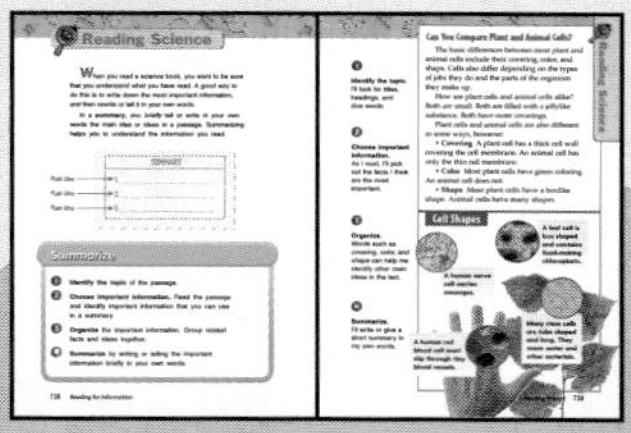

INFORMATIONAL TEXT

UNIT 3

Unit Planner

	WEEK 1 The Hatmaker's Sign	WEEK 2 Pat Cummings: My Story
Leveled Books	Easy: *George Washington and the American Revolution* **Independent:** *Paul Revere: Midnight Rider* Challenge: *The Work of Many Hands*	Easy: *Ping's Pictures* **Independent:** *How Do They Do That?* Challenge: *Wynton Marsalis: Music Man*
Tested Skills	**Comprehension** Judgments and Decisions, 257A–257B, 281E–281F; Summarize, 281G–281H **Vocabulary** Suffixes, 281I–281J **Study Skills** Graphic Aids, 280	**Comprehension** Fact and Opinion, 283A–283B, 297E–297F; Summarize, 297G–297H **Vocabulary** Suffixes, 297I–297J **Study Skills** Graphic Aids, 296
Minilessons	**Phonics and Decoding:** /ou/ and /oi/, 261 **Genre: Historical Fiction,** 259 **Prefixes,** 267 **Summarize,** 273 **Plot,** 275	**Phonics and Decoding:** /ù/ and /yù/, 287 **Genre: Autobiography,** 285 **Root Words,** 289 **Main Idea,** 291
Language Arts	**Writing:** Persuasive Writing, 281K **Grammar:** Present Tense, 281M–281N **Spelling:** Words with /ou/ and /oi/, 281O–281P	**Writing:** Persuasive Writing, 297K **Grammar:** Past and Future Tenses, 297M–297N **Spelling:** Words with /ù/ and /yù/, 297O–297P

Activities

	WEEK 1	WEEK 2
Curriculum Connections	Read Aloud: "What's the Big Idea, Ben Franklin?," 256E	Read Aloud: "Beezus and Her Imagination," 282E
	Stories in Art: *Food City,* 256	Stories in Art: *Blue Dancers,* 282
	Science: Parchment and Quills, 264	Social Studies: Map Skills, 286
	Social Studies: Historical Landmarks, 268	Science: Cats, 290
	Art: Hat Styles, 272	Science: Classifying Clouds, 295
	Math: Multiplication, 274	
	Math: Collecting and Analyzing Data, 279	
CULTURAL PERSPECTIVES	Cultural Crafts, 266	Architectural Landmarks, 288

 	 	 	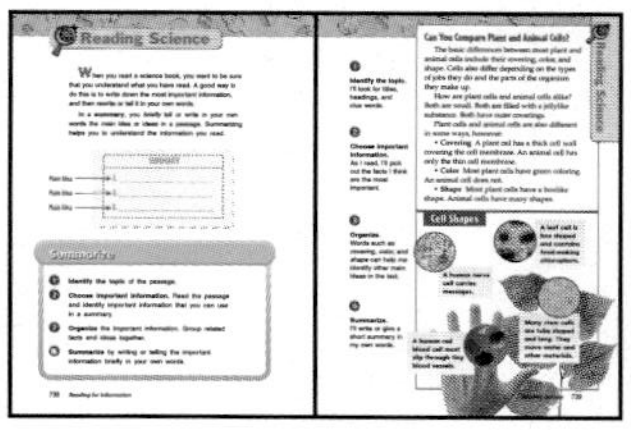
WEEK 3 Grass Sandals	**WEEK 4 A Place Called Freedom**	**WEEK 5 Twisted Trails**	**WEEK 6 Review, Writing, Reading Information, Assessment**
Easy: ***Bookworm's Band*** Independent: ***Bad Day, Glad Day*** Challenge: ***Nonsense, Mr. Lear!***	Easy: ***Walking in Beauty*** Independent: ***Teeny's Great Inventions*** Challenge: ***Aboard the Underground Railroad***	**Self-Selected Reading of Leveled Books**	**Self-Selected Reading**
✓ **Comprehension** Author's Purpose, Point of View, 299A–299B, 331E–331F Judgments and Decisions, 331G–331H ✓ **Vocabulary** Context Clues, 331I–331J ✓ **Study Skills** Graphic Aids, 330	✓ **Comprehension** Fact and Opinion, 333A–333B, 359E–359F Summarize, 359G–359H ✓ **Vocabulary** Context Clues, 359I–359J ✓ **Study Skills** Graphic Aids, 358	✓ **Comprehension** Judgments and Decisions, 361A–361B Author's Purpose, Point of View, 369E–369F ✓ **Vocabulary** Context Clues, 369G–369H Suffixes, 369I–369J ✓ **Study Skills** Graphic Aids, 368	✓ **Assess Skills** Judgments and Decisions Summarize Fact and Opinion Author's Purpose, Point of View Suffixes Context Clues Graphic Aids ✓ **Assess Grammar and Spelling** Review Verbs, 371K Review Spelling Patterns, 371L ✓ **Unit Progress Assessment** ✓ **Standardized Test Preparation** Reading Science 371A
Phonics and Decoding: Digraphs, 319 **Genre: Biographical Story,** 301 **Main Idea,** 307 **Context Clues,** 309 **Character,** 323	**Phonics and Decoding: Digraphs,** 353 **Genre: Historical Fiction,** 335 **Analyze Setting,** 337 **Main Idea,** 343 **Character,** 345 **Suffixes,** 347	**Genre: Social Studies Article,** 363	
Writing: Persuasive Writing, 331K **Grammar:** Main and Helping Verbs, 331M–331N **Spelling:** Words with Digraphs, 331O–331P	**Writing:** Persuasive Writing, 359K **Grammar:** Linking Verbs, 359M–359N **Spelling:** Adding *-ed* and *-ing*, 359O–359P	**Writing:** Persuasive Writing, 369K **Grammar:** Irregular Verbs, 369M–369N **Spelling:** Words from Art, 369O–369P	**Unit Writing Process:** Persuasive Writing, 371E–371J
Read Aloud: Four Haiku, 298E Stories in Art: *Pilgrims Going to Canterbury*, 298 Art: Japanese Art, 302 Math: Moon Watch, 318 Science: Natural Dyes, 320 Language Arts: Haiku, 322 Social Studies: Map Skills, 324 Compare Foods, 314	Read Aloud: "Follow the Drinkin' Gourd," 332E Stories in Art: *The Migration of the Negro*, 332 Science: Constellations, 338 Social Studies: The Underground Railroad, 340 Math: People and Mules, 344 Music: African American Spirituals, 357 Buildings, 348	Read Aloud: "The Needle in the Haystack," 360E Stories in Art: *Relativity*, 360 Science: Making a Soil Profile, 367	GROUP **Cooperative Theme Project Research and Inquiry:** The Talent Pool, 371

UNIT 3

Unit Resources

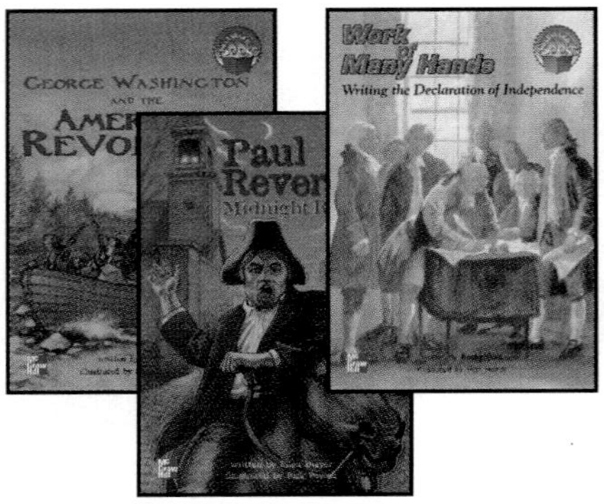

LITERATURE

LEVELED BOOKS

Easy:

- ***George Washington and the American Revolution***
- ***Ping's Pictures***
- ***Bookworm's Band***
- ***Walking in Beauty***

Independent:

- ***Paul Revere: Midnight Rider***
- ***How Do They Do That?***
- ***Bad Day, Glad Day***
- ***Teeny's Great Inventions***

Challenge:

- ***Work of Many Hands: Writing the Declaration of Independence***
- ***Wynton Marsalis: Music Man***
- ***Nonsense, Mr. Lear!***
- ***Aboard the Underground Railroad***

LISTENING LIBRARY Recordings of the student book selections and poetry. Available on **audiocassette** or **compact disc**.

Macmillan/McGraw-Hill
Intervention
Easy Leveled Books
Skills Intervention Guide
Phonics Intervention Guide

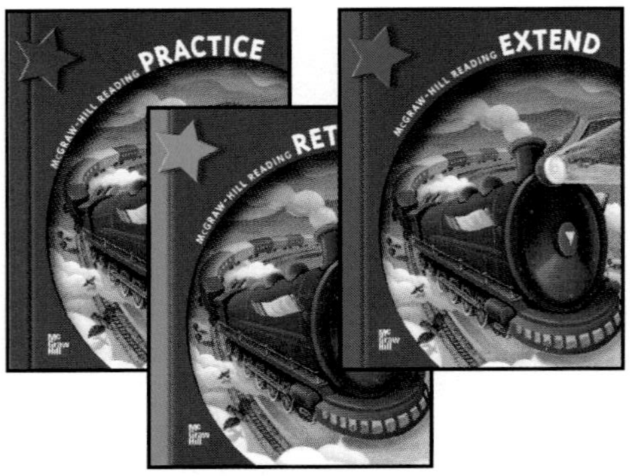

SKILLS

LEVELED PRACTICE

Practice: Practice for comprehension, vocabulary, and study skills; plus practice for instructional vocabulary and story comprehension. Take-Home Story included for each lesson.

Reteach: Reteaching opportunities for students who need more help with assessed skills.

Extend: Extension activities for vocabulary, comprehension, story and study skills.

TEACHING CHARTS Instructional charts for modeling vocabulary and tested skills. Also available as **transparencies**.

WORD BUILDING MANIPULATIVE CARDS Cards with words and structural elements for word building and practicing vocabulary.

LANGUAGE SUPPORT BOOK ESL Parallel lessons and practice for students needing language support.

PHONICS/PHONEMIC AWARENESS PRACTICE BOOK Additional practice focusing on key phonetic elements.

FLUENCY ASSESSMENT Evaluation and practice for building reading fluency.

LANGUAGE ARTS

GRAMMAR PRACTICE BOOK Provides practice for grammar and mechanics lessons.

SPELLING PRACTICE BOOK Provides practice and home involvement activities.

DAILY LANGUAGE ACTIVITIES Reinforce grammar, mechanics, and usage skills. Available as **blackline masters** and **transparencies**.

WRITING PROCESS TRANSPARENCIES Model each stage of the writing process.

HANDWRITING HANDBOOKS Offer instruction and practice.

McGraw-Hill School **TECHNOLOGY**

VOCABULARY PUZZLEMAKER Provides practice with instructional vocabulary.

HANDWRITING CD-ROM Offers instruction and practice.

MINDJOGGER VIDEOS Review grammar and writing skills.

interNET CONNECTION Extends lesson activities through Research and Inquiry Ideas.

Visit ***www.mhschool.com/reading***

Resources for
Meeting Individual Needs

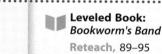

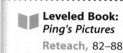

UNIT 3	EASY	ON-LEVEL	CHALLENGE	LANGUAGE SUPPORT
 *The Hatmaker's Sign*	**Leveled Book:** *George Washington and the American Revolution* **Reteach,** 75–81 **Alternate Teaching Strategies,** T60–T66 **Writing:** Thank-You Card, 281L **Intervention**	**Leveled Book:** *Paul Revere: Midnight Rider* **Practice,** 75–81 **Alternate Teaching Strategies,** T60–T66 **Writing:** Store Idea, 281L	**Leveled Book:** *Work of Many Hands: Writing the Declaration of Independence* **Extend,** 75–81 **Writing:** Newspaper Editorial, 281L **Math:** Collecting and Analyzing Data, 279	**Teaching Strategies,** 258A, 258C, 259, 262, 271, 281L **Language Support,** 81–88 **Alternate Teaching Strategies,** T60–T66 **Writing:** Write an Ad, 281K–281L
 *Pat Cummings: My Story*	**Leveled Book:** *Ping's Pictures* **Reteach,** 82–88 **Alternate Teaching Strategies,** T60–T66 **Writing:** Illustrate an Activity, 297L **Intervention**	**Leveled Book:** *How Do They Do That?* **Practice,** 82–88 **Alternate Teaching Strategies,** T60–T66 **Writing:** A Future Career, 297L	**Leveled Book:** *Wynton Marsalis: Music Man* **Extend,** 82–88 **Writing:** How Did You Do It?, 297L **Science:** Classifying Clouds, 295	**Teaching Strategies,** 284A, 284C, 285, 289, 297L **Language Support,** 89–96 **Alternate Teaching Strategies,** T60–T66 **Writing:** Write an Encouraging Note, 297K–297L
 *Grass Sandals*	**Leveled Book:** *Bookworm's Band* **Reteach,** 89–95 **Alternate Teaching Strategies,** T60–T66 **Writing:** Pack for a Trip, 331L **Intervention**	**Leveled Book:** *Bad Day, Glad Day* **Practice,** 89–95 **Alternate Teaching Strategies,** T60–T66 **Writing:** Tour Guide, 331L	**Leveled Book:** *Nonsense, Mr. Lear!* **Extend,** 89–95 **Writing:** Write a Dialogue, 331L **Social Studies:** Elevation Maps, 329	**Teaching Strategies,** 300A, 300C, 301, 306, 309, 323, 331L **Language Support,** 97–104 **Alternate Teaching Strategies,** T60–T66 **Writing:** Write a Book Review, 331K–331L
 *A Place Called Freedom*	**Leveled Book:** *Walking in Beauty* **Reteach,** 96–102 **Alternate Teaching Strategies,** T60–T66 **Writing:** Map, 359L **Intervention**	**Leveled Book:** *Teeny's Great Inventions* **Practice,** 96–102 **Alternate Teaching Strategies,** T60–T66 **Writing:** Diary, 359L	**Leveled Book:** *Aboard the Underground Railroad* **Extend,** 96–102 **Writing:** New Story, 359L **Music:** African American Spirituals, 357	**Teaching Strategies,** 334A, 334C, 335, 337, 343, 352, 359L **Language Support,** 105–112 **Alternate Teaching Strategies,** T60–T66 **Writing:** Write an Editorial, 359K–359L
 *Twisted Trails*	**Review** **Reteach,** 103–109 **Alternate Teaching Strategies,** T60–T66 **Writing:** Poster, 369L **Intervention**	**Review** **Practice,** 103–109 **Alternate Teaching Strategies,** T60–T66 **Writing:** Newspaper Article, 369L	**Review** **Extend,** 103–109 **Writing:** Interview, 369L **Science:** Making a Soil Profile, 367	**Teaching Strategies,** 362A, 362C, 363, 369L **Language Support,** 113–120 **Alternate Teaching Strategies,** T60–T66 **Writing:** Write a Letter, 369K–369L

UNIT 3

Unit Assessment

INFORMAL

Informal Assessment

- Comprehension, 257B, 276, 277, 281F, 281H; 283B, 292, 293, 297F, 297H; 299B, 326, 327, 331F, 331H; 333B, 354, 355, 359F, 359H; 361B, 365, 369F
- Vocabulary, 281J, 297J, 331J, 359J, 369H, 369J

Performance Assessment

- Scoring Rubrics, 281L, 297L, 331L, 359L, 369L, 371J
- Research and Inquiry, 254J, 371
- Writing Process, 281K, 297K, 331K, 359K, 369K
- Listening, Speaking, Viewing Activities, 256E, 256, 258A, 258–279, 281D, 281L; 282E, 282, 284A, 284–295, 297D, 297L; 298E, 298, 300A, 300–329, 331D, 331L; 332E, 332, 334A, 334–357, 359D, 359L; 360E, 360, 362A, 362–367, 369D, 369L
- Portfolio, 281L, 297L, 331L, 359L, 369L

  Writing, 281K–281L, 297K–297L, 331K–331L, 359K–359L, 369K–369L, 371E–371J
- Cross Curricular Activities, 264, 266, 268, 272, 274, 279, 286, 288, 290, 295, 302, 314, 318, 320, 322, 324, 329, 338, 340, 344, 348, 357, 367
- Fluency, 276, 292, 326, 354, 364

Leveled Practice

Practice, Reteach, Extend

- **Comprehension**
  - Judgments and Decisions, 75, 79, 94, 103
  - Summarize, 80, 87, 101
  - Fact and Opinion, 82, 86, 96, 100
  - Author's Purpose, 89, 93, 107
- **Vocabulary Strategies**
  - Suffixes: *-ful, -ous,* 81, 88, 109
  - Context Clues: Unfamiliar Words, 95, 102, 108
- **Study Skills**
  - Graphic Aids, 78, 85, 92, 99, 106

FORMAL

Selection Assessments

- **Skills and Vocabulary Words**
  - *The Hatmaker's Sign,* 21–22
  - *Pat Cummings: My Story,* 23–24
  - *Grass Sandals,* 25–26
  - *A Place Called Freedom,* 27–28
  - *Twisted Trails,* 29–30

Unit 3 Test

- **Comprehension**
  - Judgments and Decisions
  - Summarize
  - Fact and Opinion
  - Author's Purpose and Point of View
- **Vocabulary Strategies**
  - Suffixes
  - Context Clues
- **Study Skills**
  - Graphic Aids

Grammar and Spelling Assessment

- **Grammar**
  - Verbs, 95, 96
- **Spelling**
  - Unit Review, 95–96

Fluency Assessment

- Fluency Passages, 14–17

Diagnostic/Placement Evaluation

- Informal Reading Inventory
- Running Record
- Placement Tests

Test Preparation

- Test Power, 281, 297, 331, 359, 369
- Additional standardized test preparation materials available

Reading Test Generator

- Assessment Software

Assessment Checklist

Student .... **Grade** ....

Teacher ....

	The Hatmaker's Sign	Pat Cummings: My Story	Grass Sandals	A Place Called Freedom	Twisted Trails	Assessment Summary
LISTENING/SPEAKING						
Participates in oral language experiences						
Listens and speaks to gain knowledge of culture						
Speaks appropriately to audiences for different purposes						
Communicates clearly						
READING						
Uses a variety of word identification strategies, including • /ou/ and/oi/						
• /ů/and /yů/						
• Digraphs:						
• Suffixes: *-ful, -ous*						
• Context Clues: Unfamiliar Words						
Reads with fluency and understanding						
Reads widely for different purposes in varied sources						
Develops an extensive vocabulary						
Uses a variety of strategies to comprehend selections • Judgments and Decisions						
• Summarize						
• Fact and Opinion						
• Author's Purpose, Point of View						
Responds to various texts						
Analyzes the characteristics of various types of texts, including • Story Elements (Character, Setting, Plot)						
Conducts research using various sources, including • Graphic Aids						
Reads to increase knowledge						
WRITING						
Writes for a variety of audiences and purposes						
Composes original texts using the conventions of written language such as capitalization and penmanship						
Spells proficiently						
Composes texts applying knowledge of grammar and usage						
Uses writing processes						
Evaluates own writing and writing of others						

\+ Observed   – Not Observed

Introduce the Theme

Our Voices

We can each use our talents to communicate ideas.

DISCUSS THE THEME Write the theme statement on the board and read it aloud with students. Explain that a talent is a special skill or ability that someone has. Ask:

- What are some of your special talents?
- How can you use your talents to communicate or share ideas with others?
- Who are some people whose talents you admire?
- What are your favorite things to read, watch, and listen to?

PREVIEW UNIT SELECTIONS
Have students preview the unit by reading the selection titles and looking at the illustrations. Ask:

- How might the stories, poems, and the *Time for Kids* magazine article relate to the theme Our Voices?
- What may be some similarities and differences among these stories?

As students read the literature in Unit 3, return often to the theme, Our Voices. You may want to have students:

- talk about how the characters, settings, and events in the selections relate to the theme.
- discuss how different authors and cultures featured in the selections treat the theme.
- visit the Library Media Center and choose other reading material related to the theme. Have students write a few sentences on the relevance of their choices.
- relate their film, television, or theater viewing to the theme.

THEME CONNECTIONS

Each selection relates to the unit theme Our Voices as well as to the global theme Expression. These thematic links will help students to make connections across texts.

The Hatmaker's Sign A story about the wording of the Declaration of Independence.

Pat Cummings: My Story The autobiographical story of an illustrator.

Grass Sandals A journey of prose and poetry about the travels of Basho across Japan.

A Place Called Freedom The adventures of a family freed from slavery.

Twisted Trails Learn more about a man who designs mazes for a living.

Activity

Research and Inquiry

GROUP **Theme Project: The Talent Pool** Have teams of students brainstorm talents and skills they possess that could be used in the community. Then have the class plan a project to share these talents and skills.

Make a Resource Chart Have teams list their talents and skills. Help the class narrow down their list of talents and skills. Then ask students to brainstorm questions they need to answer in order to identify a project in which each of them could use their chosen talents and skills. They should also brainstorm resources for finding the answers.

Have students create a three-column chart like the one below. Remind students that they will need to identify and cite their sources properly.

Create a Presentation Allow students to explore a variety of formats to showcase their talents. They may wish to create a project for the school's Web site (if the school has one) or visit a children's center or a retirement home to present their production. Remind students that everyone has talents they can share. Suggest that they research and prepare audio and visual aids to use in their presentations.

QUESTIONS	RESOURCES	ANSWERS
• Where are our talents needed? • How could these talents best be used?	• Principal • Parents • Internet • Newspapers	

See **Wrap Up the Theme**, page 371.

Research Strategies

Students can use the Internet to find information about almost any topic. Share these tips on using the Internet. Remind students to have an adult help and supervise them.

- Make a list of key words that relate to your topic.
- Type one or two of your key words and click the *search* button.
- Click on one Web site at a time to determine if the site includes the information you need.
- Take good notes, or print out the information from the Web site.

interNET CONNECTION Have students learn more about community projects by visiting ***www.mhschool.com/reading***

Poetry

Read the Poem

READ ALOUD Read "The Poet Pencil" aloud to students. Ask:

- How do you think this poem relates to the unit theme?
- Have you ever read a poem like this before? What is unusual about this poem?

LISTENING LIBRARY The poem is available on **audiocassette** and on **compact disc.**

CHORAL READING Have the class rehearse and read the poem aloud together as a chorus. Remind students to pay attention to the punctuation.

GROUP

Learn About Poetry

FIGURATIVE LANGUAGE Explain:

- A **metaphor** is a comparison between things that are otherwise not alike.
- When a poet sees a similarity between two things and substitutes one word with the other, a metaphor is created.

Discuss with students how the words the pencil writes can have a similarity with a river (both flow). Guide students to see that the poet is comparing written words filling a page to water filling a river.

TONE Explain:

- The **tone** of a poem refers to a writer's attitude toward a subject and the feelings the poem creates.
- The poet chose a simple writer's tool, a pencil, as a subject.
- This poem reads almost like a fairy tale. The tone of the poem is light and fanciful.

Discuss with students how they think the poet feels about writing. Ask: Has writing ever seemed like a magical act to you?

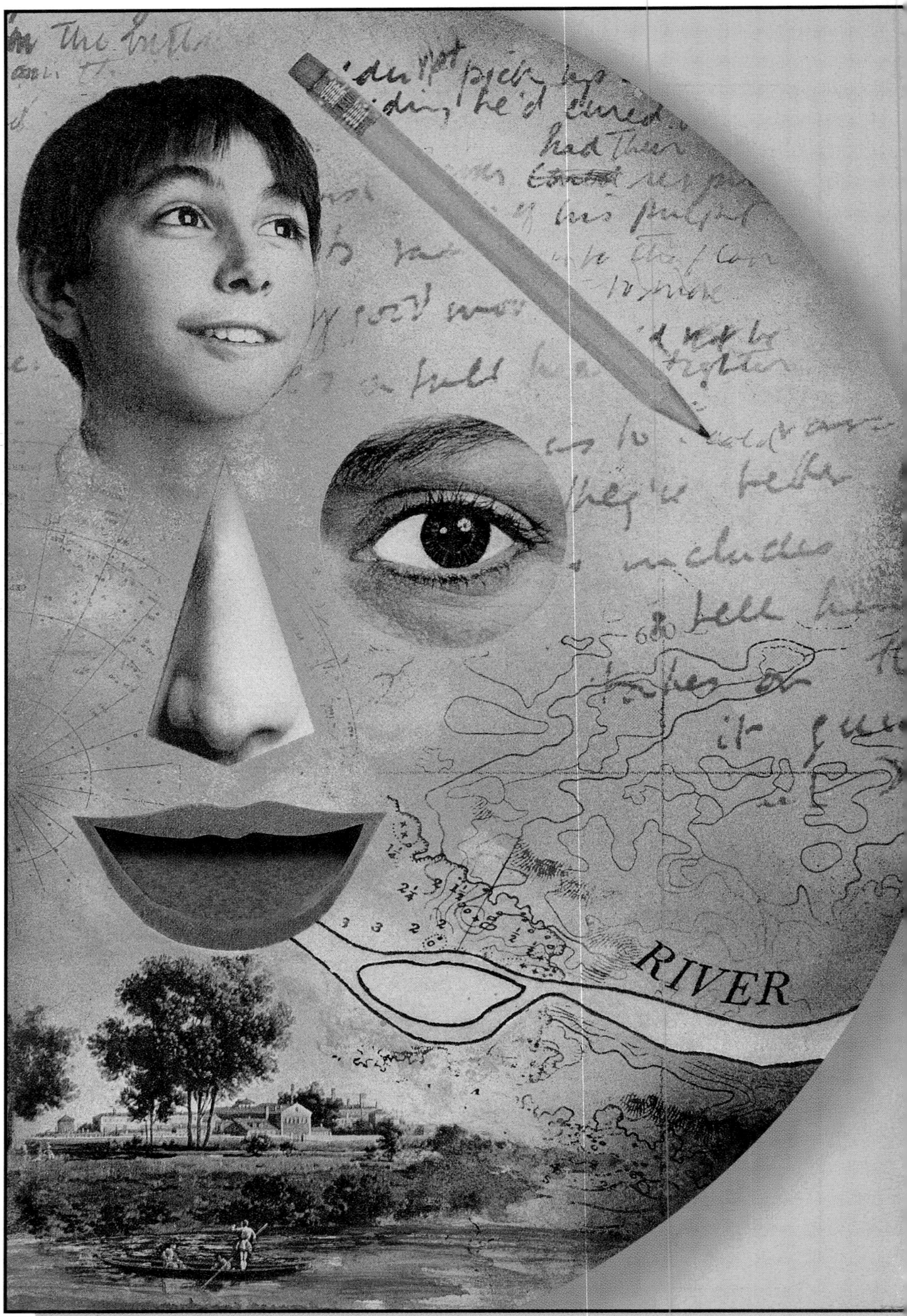

MEET THE POET

ABOUT JESÚS CARLOS SOTO MORFÍN Jesús Carlos Soto Morfín was born in 1984 and lives in Guadalajara, Mexico. Most of his childhood interests were ordinary, such as school and football. However, Jesús has written and published poetry from a very young age. The son of the writer Guadalupe Morfín Otero, Jesús seemed destined to become a writer. He wrote "The Poet Pencil" when he was eight years old. His younger brother, Daniel, is also a published poet.

UNIT 3

Our Voices

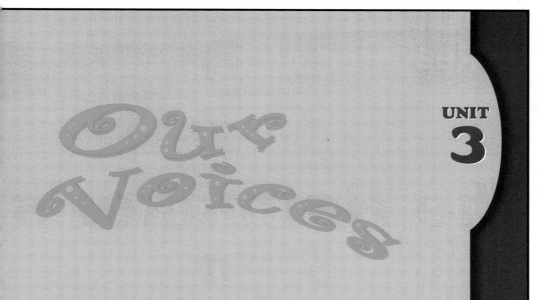

The Poet Pencil

Once upon a time a pencil wanted to write poetry but it didn't have a point. One day a boy put it into the sharpener, and in place of a point, a river appeared.

by Jesús Carlos Soto Morfín
Translated by Judith Infante

255

WRITE A POEM

Write a Similar Poem Invite students to write a similar kind of poem that tells how they feel about a topic or describes a talent or skill they possess. Have them brainstorm ideas before deciding on a topic. Suggest that students use "The Poet Pencil" as a model. Challenge them to incorporate symbols or metaphors in their work.

WRITING

Make a Bulletin Board Display Have students illustrate their poems. Create a bulletin board display of the poems and accompanying art.

Poetry

SYMBOL Read the poem aloud emphasizing the words *pencil, point,* and *sharpener.* Explain that while the pencil, its point, and the pencil sharpener are each part of the real world, the poet uses each of them as a symbol. A symbol is something that stands for, or represents, something else.

Discuss with students who or what the pencil could symbolize (the poet himself) and the double meaning of *point* (sharp end; message or goal). Suggest the sharpener is a symbol for the poet's brain. Ask students if they agree or disagree and why.

Oral Response

SMALL-GROUP DISCUSSION Have students share personal responses to the poem and discuss these questions:

GROUP

- What do you think of the poem's title? Would you suggest any other title? Why or why not?
- Why do you think the poet chose to begin with the words *Once upon a time?* How do these words make you feel?
- The poem has no rhyme and reads almost as if it were a story. How does the writing style affect the tone of the poem?
- How would you summarize what the poet is saying about writing?

Reaching All Learners

Concept
- American Revolution

Comprehension
- Judgments and Decisions

Vocabulary
- admitted
- brisk
- displaying
- elegantly
- strolling
- wharf

Anthology

The Hatmaker's Sign

Selection Summary **Benjamin Franklin tells Thomas Jefferson a story about a hatmaker. The hatmaker's struggle to find just the right words for his sign consoles Jefferson as Congress debates his wording for the Declaration of Independence.**

Stories in Art focuses on the **comprehension** skill

Reading Strategy applies the **comprehension** skill

Listening Library

INSTRUCTIONAL pages 258-281

About the Author Candace Fleming discovered the magic of words from her second grade teacher. Of her writing she says, "I want to tell you a good story. I want to tell it in a believable way. And I want to tell it with language that opens your ears to the music and magic of words."

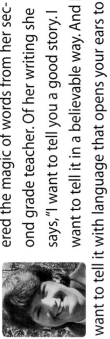

About the Illustrator Robert Andrew Parker was born in Norfolk, Virginia. He has illustrated over seventy children's books. Ironically, this father of five boys did not begin his career as an illustrator of children's books until after his sons had outgrown children's literature.

Same Concept, Skills and Vocabulary!

Leveled Books

George Washington and the American Revolution
written by Becky Gold
illustrated by Stephen Marchesi

EASY
Lesson on Pages 281A and 281D

INDEPENDENT
Lesson on Pages 281B and 281D

Take-Home version available

CHALLENGE
Lesson on Pages 281C and 281D

Leveled Practice

EASY

Reteach, 75–81 blackline masters with reteaching opportunities for each assessed skill

INDEPENDENT/ON-LEVEL

Practice, 75–81 workbook with Take-Home stories and practice opportunities for each assessed skill and story comprehension

CHALLENGE

Extend, 75–81 blackline masters that offer challenge activities for each assessed skill

Quizzes Prepared by Accelerated Reader®

WORKSTATION Activities

Social Studies	Historical Landmarks, *268*
Science	Parchment and Quills, *264*
Math	Multiplication, *274* Collecting and Analyzing Data, *279*
Art	Hat Styles, *272*
Language Arts	Read Aloud, *256E*
Cultural Perspectives	Cultural Crafts, *266*
Writing	An Ad, *278*
Research and Inquiry	Find Out More, *279*
Internet Activities	www.mhschool.com/reading

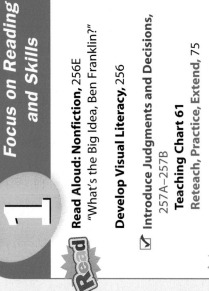

Suggested Lesson Planner

READING AND LANGUAGE ARTS	DAY 1 Focus on Reading and Skills	DAY 2 Read the Literature
Comprehension Vocabulary Phonics/Decoding Study Skills Listening, Speaking, Viewing, Representing	Read **Read Aloud: Nonfiction,** 256E "What's the Big Idea, Ben Franklin?" **Develop Visual Literacy,** 256 ☑ **Introduce Judgments and Decisions,** 257A–257B **Teaching Chart 61** **Reteach, Practice, Extend,** 75 Read **Reading Strategy: Make Judgments and Decisions,** 257 "A Vote for Independence" Intervention Program	**Build Background,** 258A Develop Oral Language **Vocabulary,** 258B–258C ***admitted*** ***displaying*** ***strolling*** ***brisk*** ***elegantly*** ***wharf*** **Teaching Chart 62** Word Building Manipulative Cards **Reteach, Practice, Extend,** 76 Read **Read the Selection,** 258–277 ☑ **Judgments and Decisions** **Genre: Historical Fiction,** 259 **Cultural Perspectives,** 266 Intervention Program
Curriculum Connections	Link **Works of Art,** 256	Link **Social Studies,** 258A
Writing	**Writing Prompt:** Good writers work hard to make sure their writing is the best it can be. Describe the steps you take to make sure your writing is the best it can be.	**Writing Prompt:** Choose a favorite illustration from the story and describe what you see. Then compare the historical images to present-day people, places, and things. **Journal Writing,** 277 Quick-Write
Grammar	**Introduce the Concept: Present Tense,** 281M Daily Language Activity 1. John Thompson like hats. likes 2. He walk to the sign maker's shop. walks 3. His wife wave to him. waves **Grammar Practice Book,** 65	**Teach the Concept: Present Tense,** 281M Daily Language Activity 1. They strolls along the wharf. stroll 2. He brush his hair from his face. brushes 3. John carrys his sign with him. carries **Grammar Practice Book,** 66
Spelling	**Pretest: Words with /ou/ and /oi/,** 281O **Spelling Practice Book,** 65, 66	**Explore the Pattern: Words with /ou/ and /oi/,** 281O **Spelling Practice Book,** 67

Intervention Program Available

Meeting Individual Needs

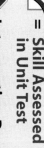

Read EVERY DAY

☑ = Skill Assessed in Unit Test

ⓘ Intervention Program Available

DAY 3 Read the Literature

Rereading for Fluency, 276

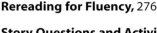

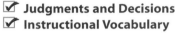

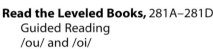

Story Questions and Activities, 278–279
Reteach, Practice, Extend, 77

Study Skill, 280
☑ **Graphic Aids**
Teaching Chart 63
Reteach, Practice, Extend, 78

Test Power, 281

Read: **Read the Leveled Books,** 281A–281D
Guided Reading
/ou/ and /oi/
☑ **Judgments and Decisions**
☑ **Instructional Vocabulary**

ⓘ Intervention Program

Activity: **Science,** 264

Writing Prompt: Pretend you have just purchased a fashionable hat from the hatmaker. Write a letter to a friend describing your new hat.

Writing Process: Persuasive Writing, 281K
Prewrite, Draft

Review and Practice: Present Tense, 281N
Daily Language Activity
1. John wish he didn't talk to everyone. wishes
2. The congressmen changes the words on the sign. change
3. He hurry to the sign maker's shop. hurries

Grammar Practice Book, 67

Practice and Extend: Words with /ou/ and /oi/, 281P
Spelling Practice Book, 68

DAY 4 Build Skills

Read: **Read the Leveled Books and Self-Selected Books**

☑ **Review Judgments and Decisions,** 281E–281F
Teaching Chart 64
Reteach, Practice, Extend, 79
Language Support, 86

☑ **Introduce Summarize,** 281G–281H
Teaching Chart 65
Reteach, Practice, Extend, 80
Language Support, 87

Minilessons, 261, 267, 273, 275

Writer's Craft, 260

ⓘ Intervention Program

Activity: **Social Studies,** 268; **Art,** 272

Writing Prompt: Make up a silly product, such as slippers for elephants. Write a TV commercial for it and list the props you'll need to film the commercial.

Writing Process: Persuasive Writing, 281K
Revise

Meeting Individual Needs for Writing, 281L

Review and Practice: Present Tense, 281N
Daily Language Activity
1. The people tries to help John Thompson. try
2. He want the sign maker's advice. wants
3. The sign maker washs his dirty brush. washes

Grammar Practice Book, 68

Proofread and Write: Words with /ou/ and /oi/, 281P
Spelling Practice Book, 69

DAY 5 Build Skills

Read: **Read Self-Selected Books**

☑ **Introduce Suffixes,** 281I–281J
Teaching Chart 66
Reteach, Practice, Extend, 81
Language Support, 88

Listening, Speaking, Viewing, Representing, 281L

Minilessons, 267, 273, 275

Phonics Review,
/ou/ and /oi/, 261

Phonics/Phonemic Awareness Practice Book, 33–36

ⓘ Intervention Program

Activity: **Math,** 274, 279

Writing Prompt: Look at the picture on page 263. Write what Ben Franklin is saying to Thomas Jefferson before telling him the story.

Writing Process: Persuasive Writing, 281K
Edit/Proofread, Publish

Assess and Reteach: Present Tense, 281N
Daily Language Activity
1. Jefferson crunchs up the paper. crunches
2. He toss it into the wastebasket. tosses
3. Franklin smile at his friend. smiles

Grammar Practice Book, 69, 70

Assess and Reteach: Words with /ou/ and /oi/, 281P
Spelling Practice Book, 70

Link
Language Arts

Read Aloud

What's the Big Idea, Ben Franklin?

biography by Jean Fritz

Benjamin Franklin lived on High Street, the busiest and noisiest street in Philadelphia. On one end of the street was the Delaware River to jump into when he felt like swimming. On the other end of the street was Debbie Read, whom he courted and married.

Benjamin and Debbie were married in 1730. Benjamin was 24 years old. He had his own printshop and owned his own newspaper.

Yet no matter how busy he was, Benjamin found time to try out new ideas.

Sometimes Benjamin's ideas were for the improvement of Philadelphia. He formed the first circulating library in America. He helped organize Philadelphia's fire department. He suggested ways to light the streets, deepen the rivers, dispose of garbage, and keep people from slipping on ice in winter.

Sometimes his ideas turned into inventions. At the head of his bed he hung a cord which was connected to an iron bolt on his door. When he wanted to lock his door at night, he

Continued on page T2

Oral Comprehension

LISTENING AND SPEAKING Read the biographical essay aloud. Encourage students to picture the inventions described in the essay. Afterward, ask:

- Which of Franklin's inventions would you like to know more about?
- Many of his inventions are still used in one form or another. Why do you think these inventions are still in use?

GENRE STUDY: BIOGRAPHY Discuss the genre. Explain that a biography tells about the life of a real person, quite often an important historical figure. Ask:

- Who is the subject of this biography? What do you learn about him?
- Does the author portray Benjamin Franklin positively or negatively? What examples from the selection helped you reach that conclusion?
- Franklin made many contributions to the city of Philadelphia. Which of his improvements do you think was the most valuable? Why?

Activity Ask partners to come up with a "big idea" of their own that might improve life in some way. Have students draw a picture or design of their invention. Then hold an "invention convention" where students display their work and present their ideas. ▶ **Logical/Spatial**

Develop Visual Literacy

Link
Works of Art

Stories in Art

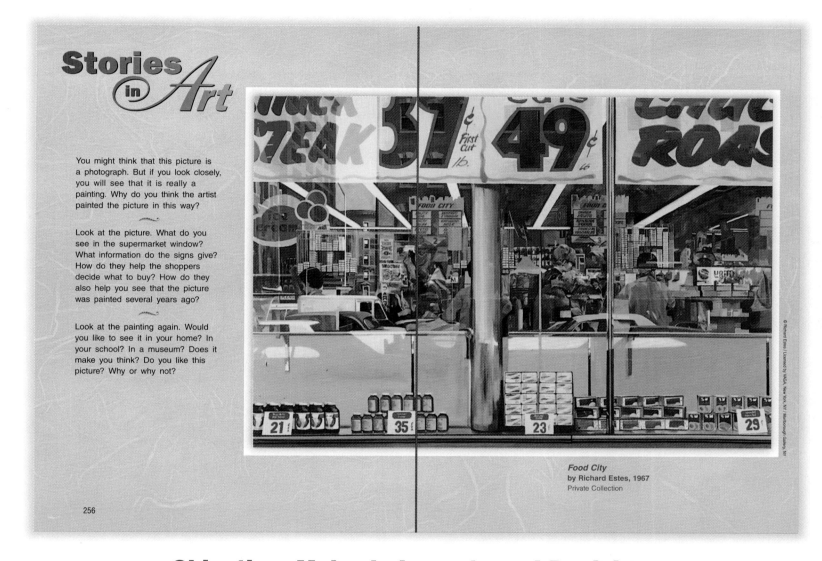

Food City
by Richard Estes, 1967
Private Collection

You might think that this picture is a photograph. But if you look closely, you will see that it is really a painting. Why do you think the artist painted the picture in this way?

Look at the picture. What do you see in the supermarket window? What information do the signs give? How do they help the shoppers decide what to buy? How do they also help you see that the picture was painted several years ago?

Look at the painting again. Would you like to see it in your home? In your school? In a museum? Does it make you think? Do you like this picture? Why or why not?

256

Objective: Make Judgments and Decisions

VIEWING In his paintings, Richard Estes uses color, shadows, and mirror-like images to make his painting look like a photograph. Point out details, such as the reflection of the parking lot in the window. Ask students to describe other details that the artist includes in his photo-realistic painting.

Read the page with students, encouraging individual interpretations of the painting.

Ask students to make judgments and decisions. For example:

- A photograph would show even more details than the painting.
- The artist decided to make the scene look as real as possible.

REPRESENTING Have students draw a classroom object, focusing on the details that would make the drawing look like a photograph.

Introduce Judgments and Decisions

TESTED OBJECTIVES

Students will make judgments and decisions about a character's actions.

Skills Finder

Judgments and Decisions	
Introduce	257A-B
Review	281E-F, 331G-H, 361A-B, 631G-H, 665A-B, 691E-F
Test	Unit 3, Unit 6

LANGUAGE SUPPORT

Use situations like this one to help students understand how their own experiences help them make judgments and decisions:

- You find a wallet with one hundred dollars. What do you do? Why?
- You have invitations to go to two parties on the same day. What do you do? Why?

PREPARE

Discuss Daily Decisions Have students think about and discuss decisions or choices they have already made today. Ask: What decisions have you made for yourself today? How have these decisions affected you?

TEACH

Read the Story and Model the Skill Tell students: Making judgments and decisions involves using your own values and experiences as well as evidence from the story to help you decide how to react toward people, events, and ideas.

The Young Soldier

Robert was only seventeen years old in 1775 when the men from his town decided to fight the British. He had a big decision to make. Should he leave his family and risk his life for his country? Robert felt it was unfair of King George to control the Americans. Robert knew that if his new country wanted to be free from Great Britain, people would have to take a stand.

As the troops marched past his house, Robert kissed his mother good-bye and walked proudly with the other soldiers.

Teaching Chart 61

Display **Teaching Chart 61**. Have students make judgments about whether or not Robert made the right decision.

MODEL Robert is very young to be a soldier. However, he knows that if he doesn't stand up to the British, they will take away his freedom. I think Robert made the right decision.

Make Judgments Have students underline phrases in the passage that help them support their judgments about Robert.

PRACTICE

Create a Judgments and Decisions Chart

GROUP

Have students create a Judgments and Decisions chart to record their thoughts about Robert's actions. ▶ **Logical**

JUDGMENTS AND DECISIONS	EVIDENCE FROM THE STORY
• I think Robert made the right decision to join the other men and fight the British.	• King George is asking for too much money from the Americans. • People in the new country need to take a stand against Great Britain to gain their freedom.

ASSESS/CLOSE

Make Judgments and Decisions

Ask students to suppose they are Robert's mother. How might she feel about his decision to leave home to fight in a war? (Sample answer: She thinks Robert is too young and she needs him to help out at home. She would want Robert to stay.)

ALTERNATE TEACHING STRATEGY

JUDGMENTS AND DECISIONS

For a different approach to teaching this skill, see page T60.

Intervention ▶ Skills

Intervention Guide, for direct instruction and extra practice with judgments and decisions

Meeting Individual Needs for Comprehension

EASY

Name__________ Date______ **Reteach 75**

Make Judgments and Decisions

Making judgments and decisions is a natural part of storytelling and story reading. When you read a story you read about characters who think about what they will do in difficult situations. As a reader, you too, can think about what you may do in similar situations.

Read the story. Then answer the questions. **Answers may vary.**

Lucinda was excited as she finished writing her story. She thought she had a good chance to win the story contest. She had read the rules carefully, and had thought a lot about what her story was going to be about. Then she had written it, choosing her words carefully. When she finished writing the story she read it and thought it was great. Then she showed it to her best friend, Pam. Pam told her to change several things about the story to make it different. Lucinda liked Pam, but was confused by her advice.

1. What decision does Lucinda have to make?
Possible answer: She has to decide whether or not to take Pam's advice and change a story she thinks is good as it is.
2. What things should Lucinda think about before she makes a decision?
She should think about why Pam made her comments. She should think about which changes she agrees with and which changes she will not make.
3. Suppose you were Lucinda. What might you say to Pam?
"How do you think these changes will help my story?"
4. Who else might help Lucinda decide what to do?
a teacher, her parents, an adult friend

4 Book 4/Unit 3 **The Hatmaker's Sign** **At Home:** Have students discuss a decision they have made and how they came to it. 75

Reteach, 75

ON-LEVEL

Name__________ Date______ **Practice 75**

Make Judgments and Decisions

Read the story below about Keeshawn and the **judgments and decisions** he makes. Then answer each question.

Entering the soapbox derby, Keeshawn knew he had to build the soapbox car himself. It was the most important rule of the derby. He worked hard all day. Then he went to see his friend, Charles. Charles' older brother was helping Charles build his car. Keeshawn was angry because Charles was cheating. You weren't supposed to have help. Tomorrow he'd report Charles to the judges.

The next morning Keeshawn practiced racing his car. Later, he went to the library to research building cars. He found two ideas to make his car lighter, and therefore faster.

That night, Keeshawn thought again about Charles. Maybe other kids had help building their cars, too. Was Keeshawn going to report everyone? No. Instead he would compete against himself and try his best to win.

1. Who is the main character? **Keeshawn**
2. How did he feel when he saw Charles getting help? **It made him angry.**
3. What did Keeshawn decide to do when he saw Charles' brother helping him? **He decided to report Charles.**
4. What did Keeshawn do to make his car better? **He practiced racing and by doing research, he figured out how to build a faster car.**
5. What new decision did Keeshawn make about Charles, and why did he make it? **Answers will vary, but should mention Keeshawn's decision not to report Charles because of the possibility that other racers had help also.**

5 Book 4/Unit 3 **The Hatmaker's Sign** **At Home:** Have students write about a decision they have made to work at doing something better. 75

Practice, 75

CHALLENGE

Name__________ Date______ **Extend 75**

Make Judgments and Decisions

A statement in a conversation may be a **judgment**, or the speaker's opinion about something. Another statement may be a **decision**, or what the speaker has decided to do. Read each statement below. Then write **J** if it is a judgment, **D** if it is a decision, or **N** if it is neither a judgment nor a decision.

1. The clothes in that store don't look good on me. J
2. I am going to go to another store. D
3. I think this is the best looking sweater in the whole world. J
4. I already have a blue sweater. N
5. This sweater would look great in red. J
6. I will buy this sweater for my cousin. D

Write a statement that is a judgment about a store in which you have shopped.
Answers will vary.

Write a statement that is a decision about shopping for something you want to buy.
Answers will vary.

Book 4/Unit 3 **The Hatmaker's Sign** **At Home:** Identify statements made during family conversations that are judgments or decisions. 75

Extend, 75

TESTED OBJECTIVES

Students will make judgments and decisions about an author's or character's ideas and actions.

Apply Judgments and Decisions

READING STRATEGY

Judgments and Decisions

Develop a strategy for making judgments and decisions.

1. **Decide what the story** is about.
2. **Think about the characters' actions.** What are the reasons for their actions?
3. **Decide what you would do** in a similar situation.
4. **Make a judgment.** Did the colonists who signed the document make the right decision?

257

READING STRATEGY

A Vote for Independence

Over two hundred years ago, America was made up of thirteen colonies ruled from a distance by the king of England.

But some of the colonists wanted to stop being a part of England and to become a free nation.

So they had a debate with those who wanted to remain a part of England.

"We ought to be independent," said the people on one side.

"But England is good for us. We owe our loyalty to England," said the others.

"England treats us unfairly and is not fit to rule us," said the first group.

"But cutting ourselves off from England is a serious step and should not be taken lightly," the other group answered.

The debate went on for days. Finally, someone suggested that a committee should be formed to draw up a list of demands. This document, which became the Declaration of Independence, stated the colonists' wish to be freed from English rule.

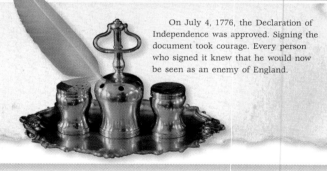

On July 4, 1776, the Declaration of Independence was approved. Signing the document took courage. Every person who signed it knew that he would now be seen as an enemy of England.

PREVIEW Have students preview "A Vote for Independence." Point out that the selection is based on historical events. Ask: Based on the title and first paragraph, what do you predict the selection will be about? (how the 13 American colonies broke away from England)

SET PURPOSES Tell students to apply what they have learned about judgments and decisions as they read.

APPLY THE STRATEGY Discuss the strategy and help students apply it to the passage.

- Identify the subject of the story.
- Think about the reasons for characters' actions. For example, can you understand why some people wanted to remain loyal to England?
- Put yourself in a character's shoes. Think: What would I do in the same situation?
- Use your own knowledge and beliefs to judge the characters' actions or ideas.

Activity Have each student create a Judgments and Decisions chart for the passage.

Build Background

Link
Social Studies

Concept: American Revolution

Evaluate Prior Knowledge

CONCEPT: AMERICAN REVOLUTION These stories tell about the American Revolution. Have students share information about the setting, events, and people who lived during this time in America's past.

MAKE A WORD WEB Have students use what they know about the American Revolution to make a word web.

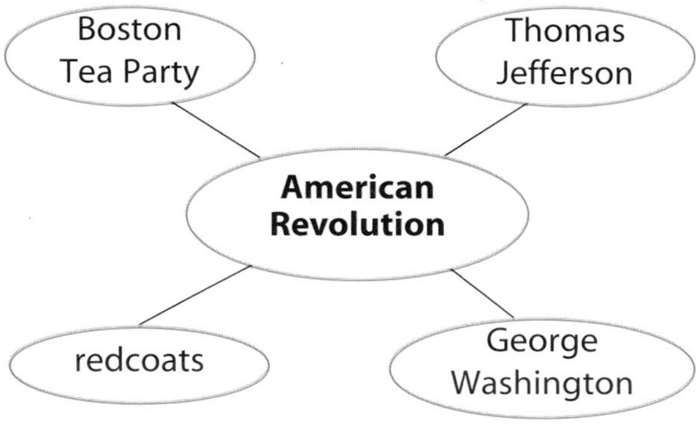

Graphic Organizer 29

WRITE A JOURNAL ENTRY WRITING ONE Ask students to suppose they are participating in the American Revolution. Have them decide what role they would have played, such as a soldier, a doctor, a spy, or a troop leader. Then have them write a page in their journals, as they pretend to be American Revolution participants.

Develop Oral Language

DISCUSS THE AMERICAN REVOLUTION Encourage students to ESL discuss the American Revolution. Introduce and if necessary explain terms such as revolution, colonies, taxation, democracy, monarchy, and representation.

If possible, display a map of the thirteen colonies as well as pictures of famous American and British people involved in the Revolution, encouraging students to identify and discuss people they know. Have volunteers help you list names, places, and events associated with the Revolution as well as some of the reasons it occurred.

Divide the group into two teams and ask each one to prepare a short statement outlining their point of view on the American Revolution. Then have team leaders present the statements to the whole group.

Anthology and Leveled Books

TEACHING TIP

MANAGEMENT Have small groups work together to make separate word webs before bringing the groups together to make a class word web. Provide books about the American Revolution for students to browse through.

LANGUAGE SUPPORT

See the **Language Support Book**, pages 81–84, for teaching suggestions for Build Background.

TESTED OBJECTIVES

Students will use context clues to determine the meanings of vocabulary words.

strolling
wharf
admitted
elegantly
brisk
displaying

Vocabulary

Teach Vocabulary in Context

Identify Vocabulary Words Display **Teaching Chart 62** and read the passage with students. Have volunteers circle each vocabulary word and underline other words that are clues to its meaning.

A Walk Through Town

1. The hatmaker's wife asked him to put on his boots so they could go strolling through town. **2.** She wanted to walk to the wharf to see where the British ships were docked. **3.** In a tired voice, the hatmaker admitted to her that he could use some fresh air. **4.** The wife was elegantly dressed in her finest clothes. **5.** As they walked, the brisk wind from the sea cooled their faces. **6.** Before they went home, they stopped to watch a shop owner who was displaying fresh flowers in his shop window.

Teaching Chart 62

Discuss Meanings Ask questions like these to help clarify word meanings:

- If you were in a hurry, would you be walking fast or strolling?
- Would you see boats at a wharf?
- Have you ever admitted to doing something wrong?
- Do you see elegantly dressed people at school or at a party?
- Do you wear gloves in brisk weather?
- If you were walking in a mall, what might you see shop owners displaying in store windows?

Definitions

strolling (p. 267) walking in a slow, relaxed way

wharf (p. 274) a structure built along a shore as a landing place for boats and ships; dock

admitted (p. 274) made known that something is true; confessed

elegantly (p. 268) manner of being rich and fine in quality

brisk (p. 271) refreshing; keen; bracing

displaying (p. 272) showing or exhibiting

Story Words

These words from the selection may be unfamiliar. Before students read, have them check the meanings and pronunciations of the words in the Glossary, beginning on page 756, or in a dictionary.

- quibbled, p. 261
- coonskins, p. 264
- tricorns, p. 264
- halfpenny, p. 271

Activities

Practice

Demonstrate Word Meaning (PARTNERS)

Have each student choose a vocabulary card and draw a picture that demonstrates the meaning of the word. Have partners choose the word card that corresponds to each other's illustrations.

▶ **Spatial/Logical**

elegantly | wharf | brisk

Word Building Manipulative Cards

Write a Story (WRITING)

Have partners work together to write fill-in-the-blank stories that leave out the vocabulary words. Have partners exchange papers with other pairs and then fill in the blanks.

▶ **Interpersonal/Linguistic**

Assess Vocabulary

Use Words in Context (PARTNERS)

Ask students to write a letter that uses all the vocabulary words. The recipient of the letter should be a historical figure. Have students share letters with partners for checking.

SPELLING/VOCABULARY CONNECTIONS

See Spelling Challenge Words, pages 281O–281P.

LANGUAGE SUPPORT

See the **Language Support Book**, pages 81–84, for teaching suggestions for Vocabulary.

Vocabulary PuzzleMaker

Provides vocabulary activities.

Meeting Individual Needs for Vocabulary

EASY

Name_______ Date_______ Reteach 76

Vocabulary

Read each clue. Then find the vocabulary word in the row of letters and circle it.

admitted brisk displaying elegantly strolling wharf

1. quick — n b r i s k d a q t e c f
2. richly or beautifully — p r w s c e l e g a n t l y i
3. showing — t r v m d i s p l a y i n g f e
4. confessed — w u n a d m i t t e d k o l
5. landing place for boats — a l d p i r w h a r f k n d s
6. walking slowly and in a relaxed way — l e s t r o l l i n g r c b n k

6

Reteach 77

Story Comprehension

Write a complete sentence to answer each question about "The Hatmaker's Sign."

1. Who is the main character of the story? The main character is John Thompson.
2. How did the hatmaker feel about his sign before he talked to others? He liked the sign the way he had planned it.
3. How did everyone want him to change the sign? Each person wanted him to take something off of the sign.
4. What did the sign maker suggest about changing the sign? He suggested that John's sign read as he had planned it originally.
5. Why did Ben Franklin share this story with Jefferson? He wanted Jefferson to know he was not the only one who had to deal with people's suggestions.

76–77 At Home: Have students retell the main events of "The Hatmaker's Sign." Book 4/Unit 3 The Hatmaker's Sign 5

Reteach, 76

ON-LEVEL

Name_______ Date_______ Practice 76

Vocabulary

Fill in each blank with the correct vocabulary word from the list.

admitted brisk displaying elegantly strolling wharf

1. Many ships were docked at the wharf.
2. Some people were strolling slowly down the sidewalk.
3. The queen held her head high and walked elegantly.
4. My dad was in a rush, so he walked at a brisk pace.
5. She admitted that she was late.
6. We were displaying our art collections so that other classes could view them.

76 At Home: Have students use the vocabulary words in new sentences. Book 4/Unit 3 The Hatmaker's Sign 6

Practice, 76

ON-LEVEL

The Wharf Fundraiser

Karla and her mother were active with the community fundraiser to rebuild the *wharf* at the lake. Karla and her mother decided to make huge cardboard cutouts of pirates. The cutouts had no faces, so people could pose as pirates. One pirate was a captain with a hook and was dressed very *elegantly*. The other pirate had a parrot perched on his shoulder.

Business was *brisk*. Many of the people *strolling* on the wharf stopped to have their pictures taken. Laughing, most people *admitted* they looked silly, but they were having fun! *Displaying* their sense of humor and generosity, the people in the community raised enough money to rebuild the wharf.

1. Who was dressed *elegantly*? the captain with a hook
2. Where did Karla and her mother set up the cardboard cutouts? on the wharf
3. What word in the story describes Karla's business? brisk
4. What is another word for people walking slowly? strolling
5. Why did Karla and her mother do this project? To help the community raise money.

5 Book 4/Unit 3 The Hatmaker's Sign — At Home: Have students use the vocabulary words to describe a pirate they have read about or have seen in the movies. 76a

Practice, 76a
Take-Home Story

CHALLENGE

Name_______ Date_______ Extend 76

Vocabulary

admitted brisk displaying elegantly strolling wharf

Write a paragraph about going shopping, using as many vocabulary words from the box as you can. Then erase those vocabulary words or cover them with tape. Exchange paragraphs with a partner and fill in the blanks.

Extend 77

Story Comprehension

Suppose you were the first person to whom John Thompson showed his idea for a sign. Make a judgment about how he could change his sign. Then write what you would have told him to change. Explain why he should make that change.

76–77 At Home: Find an ad in a newspaper or magazine. Discuss how it could be changed to be more effective. Book 4/Unit 3 The Hatmaker's Sign

Extend, 76

Comprehension

Prereading Strategies

PREVIEW AND PREDICT Have students preview the story, looking for clues to help them make judgments and decisions.

- When and where is the story set?
- What do you notice about the sign that appears on many of the pages?
- What do you think this story will be about?
- What clues suggest this is historical fiction? (It mentions Benjamin Franklin and seems to take place in the past.) ***Genre***

Have students record their predictions about the story and the main characters.

PREDICTIONS	WHAT HAPPENED
This story takes place around the time of the American Revolution.	
The hatmaker's sign changes whenever he talks to someone.	

SET PURPOSES What do students want to find out by reading the story? For example:

- Why does the design on the hatmaker's sign keep changing?
- What do Benjamin Franklin and Thomas Jefferson have to do with the story?

Meet Candace Fleming

Candace Fleming discovered the music and magic of words when she learned the word "cornucopia" in second grade. "It sounded good. I loved the way it felt on my tongue and fell on my ears. I skipped all the way home from school that day chanting 'Cornucopia! Cornucopia!'"

Fleming has always admired Benjamin Franklin. She discovered *The Hatmaker's Sign* in a collection of Franklin's writings. She decided that young people would enjoy its humor and wisdom.

Fleming has won many awards for her writing. Besides her work as an author, she teaches at a college outside Chicago. When she is not working, she enjoys reading, camping, hiking, and traveling.

Meet Robert Andrew Parker

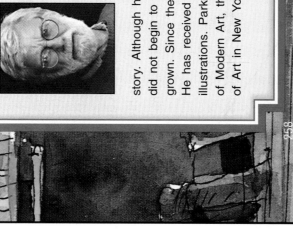

Robert Andrew Parker was born in Norfolk, Virginia. He served in the United States Army during World War II and later studied art in Chicago. Since then, he has lived in New York, Connecticut, and Ireland.

Parker's illustrations for *The Hatmaker's Sign* are an important part of the book. They help show the humor in Benjamin Franklin's story. Although he had been a painter for many years, Parker did not begin to illustrate books until after his five sons were grown. Since then, he has worked on more than fifty books! He has received many awards for his paintings and his illustrations. Parker's paintings can be found in The Museum of Modern Art, the Whitney Museum, the Metropolitan Museum of Art in New York City, and the Brooklyn Museum.

258

Meeting Individual Needs • Grouping Suggestions for Strategic Reading

EASY

Read Together Read the story together or invite students to use the **Listening Library.** Have students use the Judgments and Decisions chart from page 259. Comprehension and Intervention prompts offer additional help with decoding, vocabulary, and comprehension.

ON-LEVEL

Guided Instruction Read the selection aloud or play the **Listening Library** recording. Choose from the Comprehension questions. Have students use the Judgments and Decisions chart during reading. You may wish to have students read the story first on their own.

CHALLENGE

Read Independently Have independent readers read silently. Have them use the Judgments and Decisions chart on page 259 to record story details that help them make judgments and decisions about characters and events. After reading, have students use their chart to summarize the behaviors and actions of Thomas Jefferson.

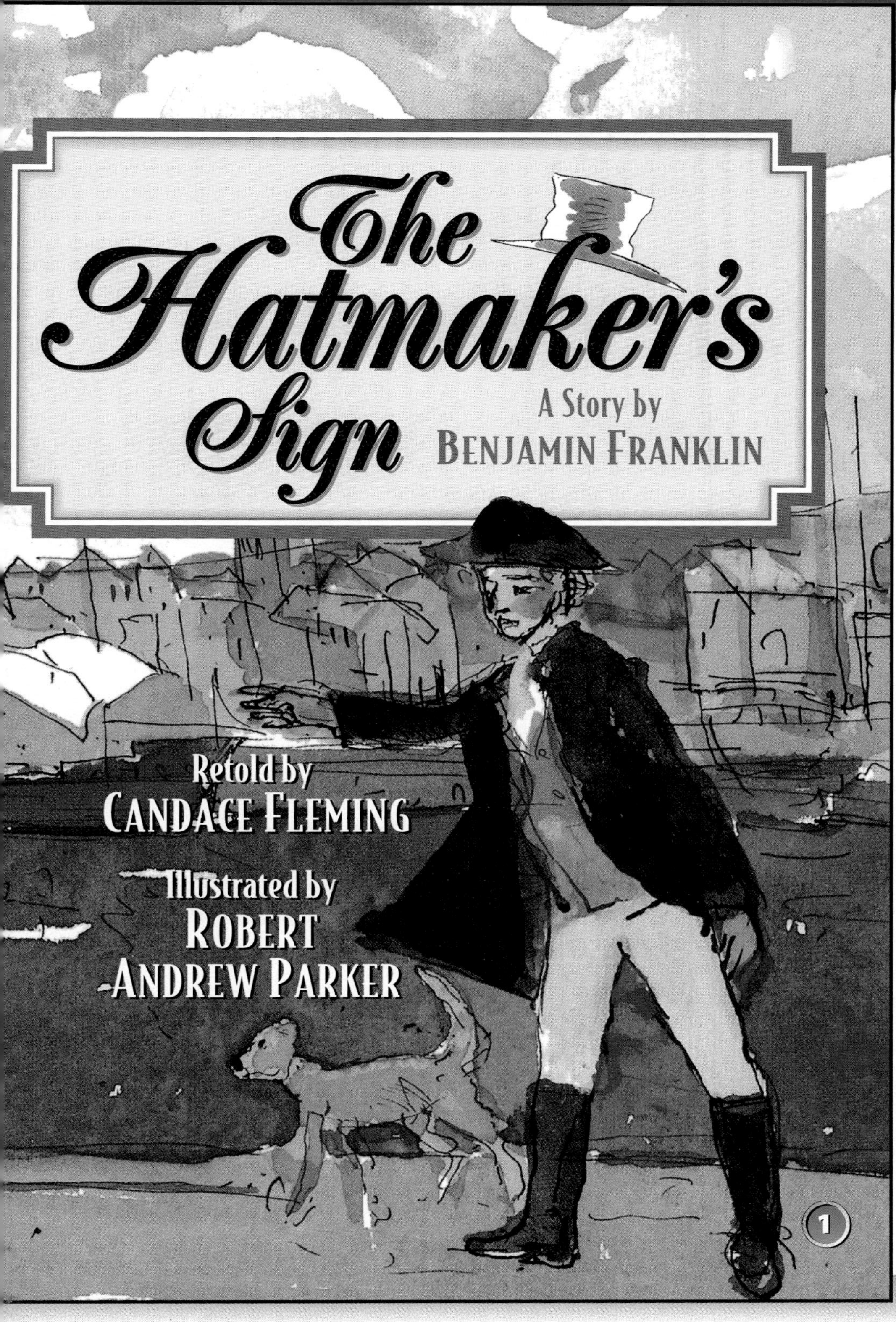

Comprehension

Apply Judgments and Decisions

STRATEGIC READING Before we begin reading, let's prepare Judgments and Decisions charts. We can write down our opinions and then find story evidence to support our judgments and decisions.

JUDGMENTS AND DECISIONS	EVIDENCE FROM THE STORY

1 JUDGMENTS AND DECISIONS Make a judgment about the man in the illustration. How do you think he is feeling? What clues can you find in the picture to support your judgment?

MODEL The man in the picture seems to be frustrated. He has a sad expression on his face. He also seems to be throwing away a piece of paper. Maybe the paper is causing him some trouble. Those two clues suggest that he is feeling a little upset.

Genre

Historical Fiction

Explain that historical fiction:

- is set in a real time and place in the past.
- may feature real-life people and events as well as made-up people and events.
- usually unfolds in time-order but may contain flashbacks.

Activity After students read *The Hatmaker's Sign*, have them identify examples of real and made-up events and characters. Ask: Which characters and events do you know are real? Which characters and events are probably made-up?

LANGUAGE SUPPORT

A blackline master of the Judgments and Decisions chart is available in the **Language Support Book.**

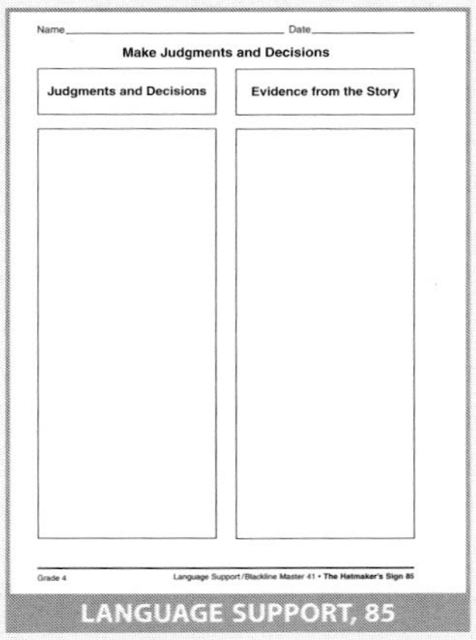
Name________ Date________

Make Judgments and Decisions

Judgments and Decisions	Evidence from the Story

Grade 4 Language Support/Blackline Master 41 • The Hatmaker's Sign 85

LANGUAGE SUPPORT, 85

Comprehension

2 JUDGMENTS AND DECISIONS Thomas Jefferson has just finished writing a document. What does he seem to think about the job he has done? (He thinks he did a good job.) How can you tell this from the story? (He worked on the document for hours. He believes the writing is perfect.) Let's record Thomas Jefferson's judgment on the chart. Remember we must also include evidence from the story.

JUDGMENTS AND DECISIONS	EVIDENCE FROM THE STORY
Thomas Jefferson thinks he did a good job.	He worked on it for hours. He believes it is perfect.

P/I MULTIPLE-MEANING WORDS Look at the last sentence on this page. What do you think it means to say "Every paragraph flowed with truth"?
Semantic Cues

Writer's Craft

TONE

Explain: **Tone** refers to the attitude the author expresses toward the readers of his or her writing or the characters that appear within it. The tone of a selection—for example, happy, sad, celebratory—is created by the words the writer chooses.

Example: Discuss examples of words that show the tone expressed about Jefferson's achievement. Ask: Which words did the author use to show that Jefferson felt he had achieved something great?

WRITING Have students write a paragraph that expresses a particular tone toward the person, place, or thing being described.

At last!

2 After endless hours of scribbling and struggling, Thomas Jefferson had written it. And it was perfect. Every word rang. Every sentence sang. Every paragraph flowed with truth.

260

P/I PREVENTION/INTERVENTION

MULTIPLE-MEANING WORDS Ask students to describe a flowing river. (Water moves along smoothly without stopping.) Ask: "Why do you think the author chose the word *flow* to describe Jefferson's writing?" (The ideas were put together so well that the reader did not have to stop and question what they meant.)

Lead students to see that their prior knowledge of *flow* along with context clues helped them to understand an unfamiliar usage of the word.

Ask students to explain the meanings of *rang* and *sang* in these sentences: *Every word rang. Every sentence sang.*
Semantic Cues

"It is exactly right," Jefferson exclaimed. "The Continental Congress will surely love it."

But the next morning, after Jefferson's wonderful words had been read aloud, the Congress broke into noisy debate.

"I do not like this word," quibbled one delegate. "Let's replace it."

"And this sentence," argued another. "I think we should cut it."

"What about this paragraph?" shouted still another. "It must be removed!" (3)

Comprehension

(3) JUDGMENTS AND DECISIONS What do you think of the delegates' decision to change Jefferson's writing? Do you think they were right or wrong? Explain. (Sample answer: I am surprised that Jefferson's writing was debated. But I suppose it was the right decision, since it ended up improving the Declaration.)

TEACHING TIP

DECLARATION OF INDEPENDENCE

Tell students that the goals of the Declaration of Independence included:

- **describing what a good government should do for its people.**
- **explaining the mistakes King George III made as the ruler of the 13 colonies.**
- **telling everyone that the 13 colonies were independent states.**

Minilesson

REVIEW/MAINTAIN

/oi/ and /ou/

Point out the word *noisy* in the second paragraph on page 261. Ask students to say the sound represented by the letters *-oi*. Then remind them that /oi/ can also be spelled *-oy*, as in *enjoy*.

Then have students find the word *out* on page 268. Ask them to say the sound represented by the letters *-ou*. Remind them that this sound is also represented by the letters *-ow* as in *frown*.

Activity Ask partners to brainstorm word pairs with /ou/ spelled *-ou, -ow* and word pairs with /oi/ spelled *-oi, -oy*.

Phonics Intervention Guide

Comprehension

4 Why do you think Ben Franklin is about to tell Thomas Jefferson a story? (Since Benjamin Franklin knows that Thomas Jefferson is upset, he is probably going to tell his friend a story to make him feel better.) ***Make Inferences***

While the Congress argued around him, Thomas Jefferson slumped into his chair. His face flushed red with anger and embarrassment.

"I thought my words were perfect just the way they were," he muttered to himself.

Just then he felt a consoling pat on his shoulder. He looked up and into the sympathetic eyes of Benjamin Franklin.

4 "Tom," Benjamin Franklin said, smiling, "this puts me in mind of a story."

262

LANGUAGE SUPPORT

ESL Write *anger* and *embarrassment* on the chalkboard. Reread sentences containing these words with students. Ask them to paraphrase it. For example, *His face flushed red with anger and embarrassment* might be reworded as *His face got red because he was mad and he was ashamed.*

Point out the sentence *This puts me in mind of a story.* Ask students what words we would use to express this idea today. (*That reminds me of a story* or *That makes me think of a story I heard.*)

263

Comprehension

5 Looking at this picture, what can you conclude about what sort of relationship Thomas Jefferson and Benjamin Franklin have? (I think they must be friends.) What makes you think so? (Ben Franklin puts a consoling hand on Thomas Jefferson's shoulder. Thomas Jefferson feels comfortable enough with Ben Franklin to express his sadness.) ***Draw Conclusions***

Comprehension

6 Up until this point, the story has taken place at a meeting of the Second Continental Congress in Philadelphia. Where is it taking place now? (Boston) Has the time period also changed? (No, it seems to be the same.) How can you tell? (The streets have cobblestones, and the hatmaker sells old-fashioned hats like tricorns and coonskins.) ***Setting***

7 John, the hatmaker, says his sign is "exactly right." Who in this story does this remind you of? (Thomas Jefferson) Based on how Jefferson's writing was received, what do think will happen if John shows his sign to other people? (Sample answer: I think other people might find fault with John's sign.) ***Make Predictions***

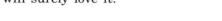

6 In the city of Boston, on a cobblestoned street, a new hat shop was opening for business.

All stood ready. Comfortable chairs had been placed before polished mirrors. Wooden hatboxes were stacked against one wall. And the front window was filled with tricorns and top hats, coonskins, and wool caps.

There was only one thing the hat shop did not have—a sign.

But the hatmaker, John Thompson, was working on it.

Knee-deep in used parchment and broken quill pens, John struggled to create a sign for his shop. And at long last, he wrote one. It read:

Beneath the words, John drew a picture of a hat.

7 "It is exactly right," John exclaimed. "Customers will surely love it."

264

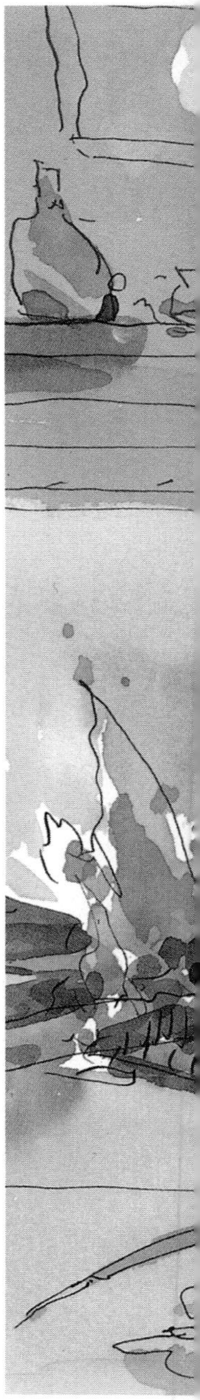

Activity

Cross Curricular: Science

PARCHMENT AND QUILLS In the 1700s, parchment was used instead of paper for special documents like the Declaration of Independence.

RESEARCH AND INQUIRY Have students research and compare the process of making written documents today versus how they were made in the 1700s.

Students can make a sign like the hatmaker did by using the tip of a tail feather, tempera paint, and white construction paper. ▶ **Spatial/Logical**

interNET CONNECTION Students can learn more about the history of paper by visiting ***www.mhschool.com/reading***

Comprehension

8 Look at the illustration on this page. How might the picture be different if it showed a modern-day man working on a sign? (The man's clothes, hairstyle, and working tools would be different. A modern-day scene might include a man dressed in jeans and sneakers working in an office with a computer to make a sign.) ***Compare and Contrast***

Comprehension

9 JUDGMENTS AND DECISIONS What judgment does Hannah make about John's sign? What caused her to make this judgment?

MODEL Hannah wanted John to remove the words "for ready money" from the sign. Let me think about why. She said that since he would not sell hats for anything else, he could remove these words. She must think that everyone knows that he would expect money for his hats. There is no need to state what is obvious.

TEACHING TIP

ROLE PLAY Suggest that the same pairs of students work together throughout the story, role-playing the different people that the hatmaker meets. Encourage partners to make up their own dialogue.

Invite volunteers to act out the meetings in front of the class.

But before hurrying to the sign maker's shop, where his words and picture would be painted onto board, John showed his parchment to his wife, Hannah.

"Oh John," Hannah giggled after reading what John had written. "Why bother with the words 'for ready money'? You're not going to sell hats for anything else, are you? Remove those words and your sign will be perfect."

9 "You're probably right," sighed John.

So John rewrote his sign. Now it read:

266

CULTURAL PERSPECTIVES

CULTURAL CRAFTS Remind students that in Colonial America most things were made by hand. Explain that people today continue to make things by hand to preserve tradition.

RESEARCH AND INQUIRY Have small groups of students choose a country or culture and research its traditional crafts. Have them make a poster that shows one of the crafts and label it with the name of the group that produces it.

▶ **Visual/Interpersonal**

interNET CONNECTION Students can learn about traditional crafts by visiting ***www.mhschool.com/reading***

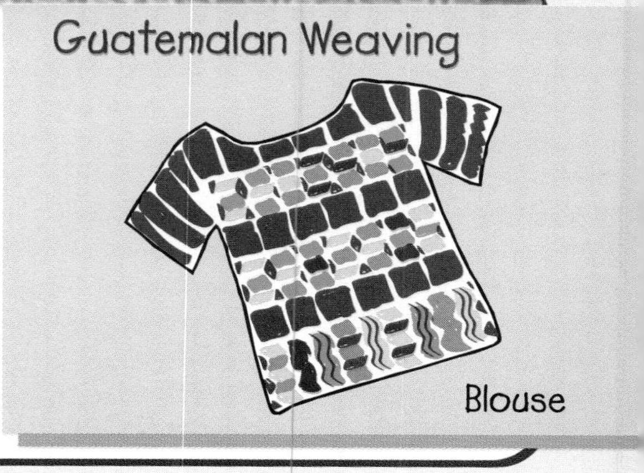

Beneath the words he drew a picture of a hat.

Parchment in hand, John headed for the sign maker's shop.

He had gone as far as the Old North Church when he met Reverend Brimstone.

"Where are you strolling on such a fine morning?" asked the reverend.

"To the sign maker's shop," replied John. He held out his parchment.

Reverend Brimstone read it.

"May I make a suggestion?" he asked. "Why don't you take out the words 'John Thompson, Hatmaker'? After all, customers won't care who made the hats as long as they are good ones."

10 "You're probably right," sighed John.

And after tipping his tricorn to the reverend, John hurried back to his hat shop and rewrote his sign. Now it read:

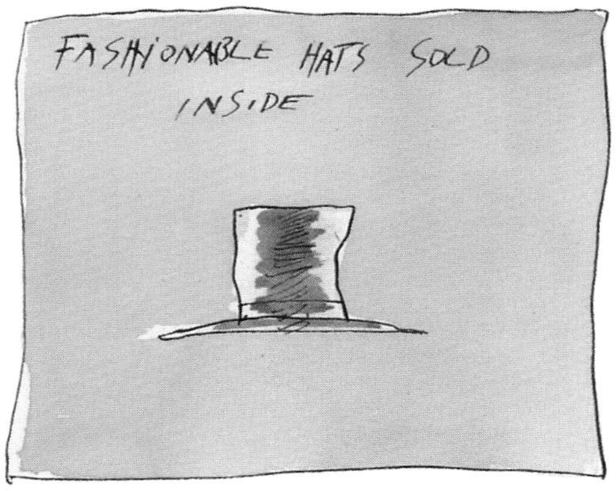

Beneath the words he drew a picture of a hat.

Parchment in hand, John headed for the sign maker's shop.

267

Comprehension

10 The hatmaker decides that the Reverend's suggestion is a good one. Let's have pairs of students play the parts of Reverend Brimstone and John Thompson. How do you think the characters would speak and interact with each other? What else might they have said if the conversation had lasted a little longer? *Role-Play*

P/I **PHONICS/DECODING** Find the word *tricorn* on page 267. Look at the vowel that precedes the letter *r*. How does the letter *r* change the vowel sound? *Graphophonic Cues*

Minilesson

REVIEW/MAINTAIN

Prefixes

Point out the word *rewrote.* Review with students the meaning of the prefix *re-*. (again) Have students practice adding the prefix *re-* to root words to create new words.

For Example:

Prefix	+ Root Word	= New Word
re-	+ copy	= recopy
re-	+ warm	= rewarm
re-	+ decorate	= redecorate

Activity Display these words: *check, attach, stitch, dye.* Have students add *re-* to these words and use them in a paragraph that tells what the hatmaker does at his shop.

P/I PREVENTION/INTERVENTION

PHONICS/DECODING Point out that when the letter *r* follows a vowel, it often changes the sound of the vowel. Write *pot* and *port* on the chalkboard. Help students see that the *o* stands for the sound /o/ in *pot* and /ô/ in *port*.

Write *tricorn* on the chalkboard and underline the letters *or*. Ask students what sound they think the letter *o* makes in this word. (/ô/) Explain that when the letter *r* follows an *o*, they usually make the sound /ôr/. Help students brainstorm other examples of words with the /ôr/ sound such as *score, stork,* and *thorn.* *Graphophonic Cues*

Comprehension

(11) What kind of person do you think Lady Manderly is? Explain your answer.
(Lady Manderly seems rude and a bit of a snob. She acts haughty, grabs John's sign without asking permission, and calls it absurd. Also, she expects nothing but fashionable hats.) ***Character***

He had gone as far as Beacon Hill when Lady Manderly stepped from her carriage and into his path.

"What have you there?" asked the haughty lady. She plucked the parchment from John's hand and read it.

"Absurd!" she snorted. "Why bother with the word 'fashionable'? Do you intend to sell unfashionable hats?"

"Absolutely not!" cried John.

"Then strike that word out," replied Lady Manderly. "Without it, your sign will be perfect."

"You are probably right," sighed John.

(11) And after kissing the lady's elegantly gloved hand, John hurried back to his hat shop and rewrote his sign. Now it read:

Beneath the words he drew a picture of a hat.

Parchment in hand, John headed for the sign maker's shop.

268

Activity

Cross Curricular: Social Studies

HISTORICAL LANDMARKS Have students use a map of Boston to find Old North Church, Boston Common, the Charles River, Beacon Hill, and Harvard College.

RESEARCH AND INQUIRY Have small groups research Boston landmarks including the role each played in the American Revolution.
▶ **Linguistic/Interpersonal**

269

Comprehension

12 What are some signs in the picture that Lady Manderly is a respected citizen in Boston? (She rides in a carriage. John kisses her hand before she leaves. She wears elegant clothes.) ***Make Inferences***

13 **JUDGMENTS AND DECISIONS** So far in the story, John has shown his sign to several different people. Do they seem to like it? (no) How can you tell? (They all suggest he change it.) Let's add this new information to our chart.

JUDGMENTS AND DECISIONS	EVIDENCE FROM STORY
Thomas Jefferson thinks he did a good job.	He worked on it for hours. He believes it is perfect.
No one likes John's sign.	Everyone he meets suggests he change it.

SELF-MONITORING STRATEGY

ASK FOR HELP Help students understand that sometimes it is necessary for them to ask someone for help if they can't find evidence to help them make a judgment about something in a story.

MODEL I'm not sure if I understand why John keeps agreeing to change his sign. Doesn't he trust his own judgment anymore? Now he's making me doubt myself, too. I'm going to ask someone else what they think.

Comprehension

14 What is the job of the magistrate? (He watches out for unlawful behavior.) Do you think he will like John's sign? (Sample answer: No, he will probably ask for a change.) ***Make Predictions***

15 What do you think about the way the magistrate talks to John? (He isn't very polite. The first thing he says to John is to threaten to put him in jail.) Do you think the magistrate is used to getting his way? Explain. (He is probably used to getting his own way because he acts like a bully.) ***Make Inferences***

Fluency

READ DIALOGUE Students can use page 270 to practice reading dialogue expressively. Have partners choose between the roles of the magistrate and John Thompson. Suggest that partners:

PARTNERS

- discuss the personalities of these two men and compare them to people they know.
- look for clues about their character's speech, such as *demanded, gulped nervously,* and *stammered.*
- trade places to appreciate the differences between the two characters.

He had gone as far as Boston Common when he met a British magistrate.

14 The magistrate, always on the lookout for unlawful behavior, eyed John's parchment.

"Hand it over or face the stockades!" demanded the magistrate.

John did. He gulped nervously as the magistrate read it.

"Tell me hatter," bullied the magistrate. "Why do you write 'sold inside'? Are you planning on selling your hats from the street? That is against the law, you know. I say delete those words if you want to stay out of jail. And **15** if you want your sign to be perfect."

"Yes, sir. No, sir. I mean I will, sir," stammered John.

And after hastily bowing to the magistrate, John hurried back to his hat shop and rewrote his sign.

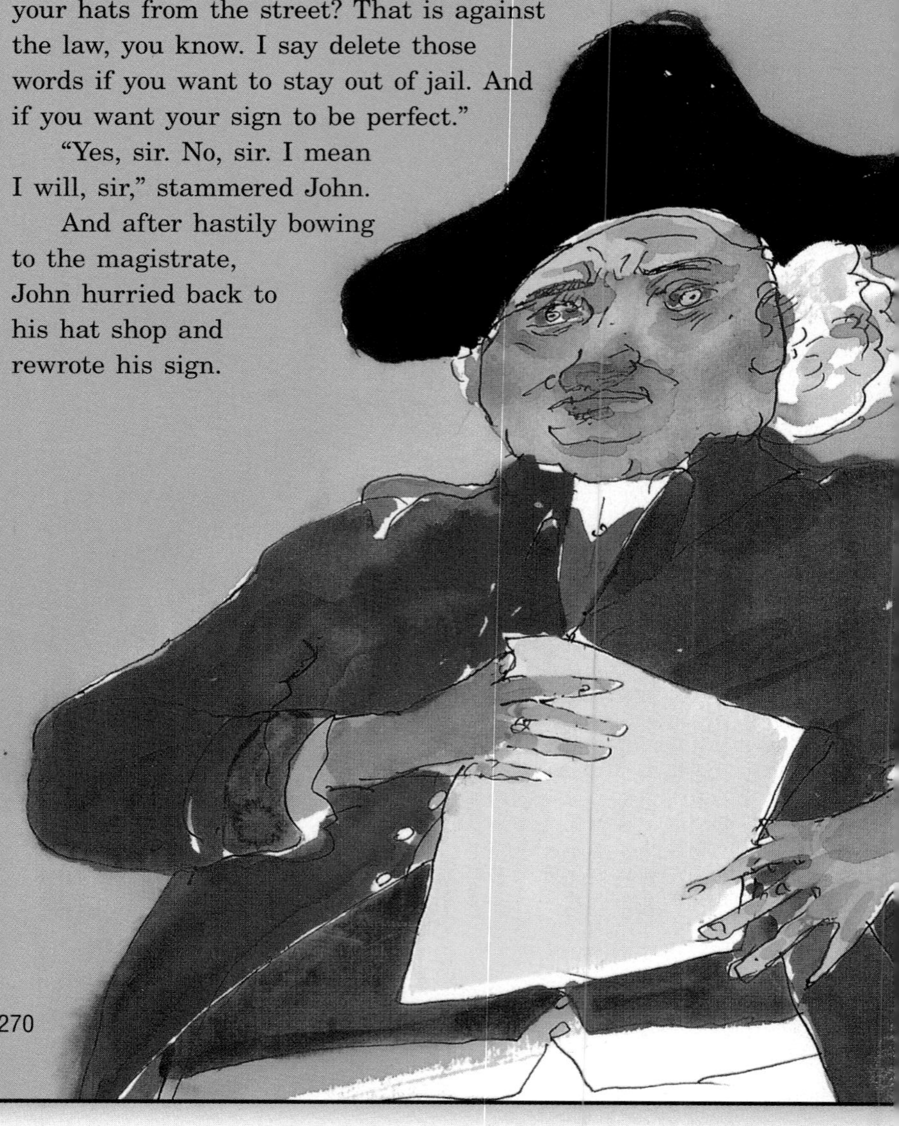

270

Now it read:

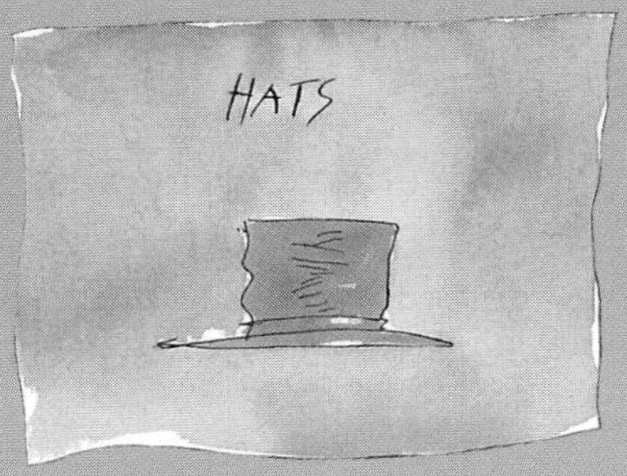

(16)

Beneath the word he drew a picture of a hat.

Parchment in hand, John headed for the sign maker's shop. He had gone as far as the Charles River when a brisk breeze snatched the parchment from his hand and dropped it at the feet of two young apprentices sitting on a crate of tea.

The first apprentice picked up the parchment and read it. "Hey, mister," he said. "Why do you write 'hats' when you already have a picture of one?"

"Yes, why?" asked the second apprentice.

"It would be a much better sign without that word," suggested the first apprentice.

"It would be perfect," added the second apprentice.

"You are probably right," sighed John.

And after tossing each boy a halfpenny, John hurried back to his hat shop and rewrote his sign. Now it read: (17)

(18)

Nothing.

He drew a picture of a hat.

271

Comprehension

(16) Look at the two hats on this page. How are they different? (They're different colors.) Why do you think John made this change? (Sample answer: Because he may have been tired of drawing the same hat over and over.)

(17) How are the two young apprentices different from the characters John has met so far? (Reverend Brimstone, Lady Manderly, and the magistrate all seem to be important members of Boston society. The apprentices are not well-known figures. John doesn't know them by name, and he gives them each a coin when he leaves.) ***Compare and Contrast***

(18) How do you think John feels now? People keep suggesting that he change his sign. Pretend you are John. Tell us what you're thinking. ***Role-Play***

TEACHING TIP

HISTORICAL CONTEXT **Remind students that this story was originally written by Benjamin Franklin in the 1700s. Explain that the customs, attitudes, and events of a certain time period influence works written during that time. Have students find clues in the story that help them see what life was like during Ben Franklin's lifetime. For example:**

- **Fashion: men wearing hats, women wearing gloves**
- **Transportation: walking or riding in a carriage on cobblestone streets**
- **Writing: using parchment and quill pens**
- **Money: donating a halfpenny**
- **Law enforcement: British magistrate threatening the stockade**

LANGUAGE SUPPORT

Explain to students that during the time of the American Revolution, young people called apprentices worked and studied for many years with master craftsmen to learn trades to make a living. Occupations that had apprentices included printers, silversmiths, and shipbuilders.

Ask students what occupation in today's world they would like to be an apprentice for. Encourage them to explain why they made that choice and what they would expect to learn as an apprentice.

Comprehension

(19) Look at the illustration on this page. Observe what the man in the hat is holding, and notice the expression on his face. Based on what you've read so far, what do you think is happening? What do you think will happen next? (The man in the hat is looking at the sign and doesn't like what he sees. He will probably suggest changing the sign.) ***Make Predictions***

(20) What was Professor Wordsworth's opinion about the sign? Was your prediction correct? (He suggested eliminating the picture of the hat.) ***Revise or Confirm Predictions***

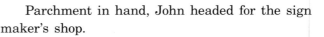

(19)

Parchment in hand, John headed for the sign maker's shop.

He had gone as far as Harvard College when he met Professor Wordsworth.

John shoved his parchment under the professor's nose. "Please, sir," he said. "Would you tell me what you think of my sign?"

The surprised professor straightened his spectacles and peered at the picture.

"Since you ask my opinion, I shall give it," said Professor Wordsworth. "However, I must ask you a question first. Are you displaying your hats in your shop's front window?"

John nodded.

"Then this picture is useless," declared the professor. "Everyone will know you sell hats simply by looking in your window. Eliminate the picture and your sign will be perfect."

"You are probably right," sighed John.

(20) And after pumping the professor's hand in thanks, John hurried back to his hat shop and rewrote his sign.

Now it read nothing.

It showed nothing.

(21) It was wordless and pictureless and entirely blank.

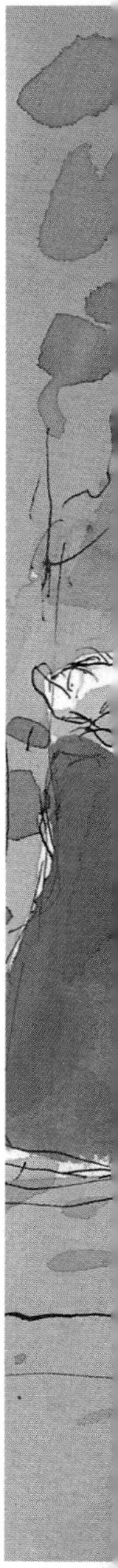

272

Activity

Cross Curricular: Art

HAT STYLES Point out the different hat styles shown in the story illustrations for this time period. Have students pretend that they are present-day owners of a hat shop. Ask them to draw a picture of a hat that they think would be popular. (You may choose to have students make the hats rather than draw them.) Suggest that students think about who would buy it and why it would be popular. When the designs are finished, have students share their ideas with the class.

▶ **Spatial/Linguistic**

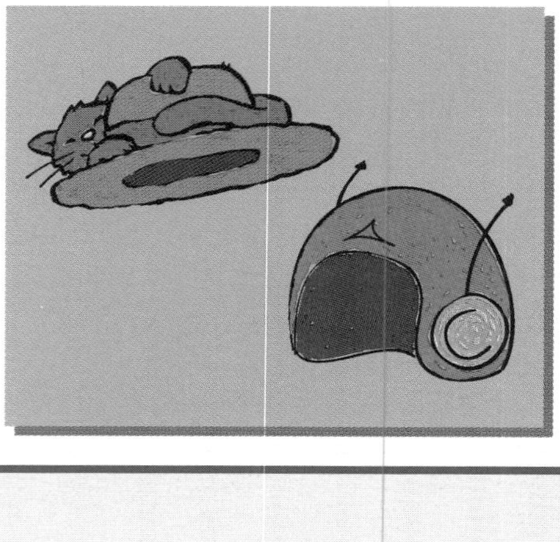

Comprehension

21 Based on events so far in the story, what do you think John should do about his blank sign? (John should change his sign back to the way it was.) Why? (He was happy with his original sign. Now he is just tired and confused.) ***Draw Conclusions***

P/I **WORD STRUCTURE** Find the word *useless* in the seventh paragraph on page 272. What is the base word? (use) How does the ending change the meaning of the word? ***Graphophonic/Syntactic Cues***

Minilesson

REVIEW/MAINTAIN

Summarize

Remind students that to summarize means to tell in a few sentences what happened in the story. Tell students to only include important information in their summaries.

- Ask students to list the events that have happened in the story so far. Help them decide if each event is important enough to include in the summary of the story.

Activity Ask students to write a one or two sentence summary of this story up to the end of page 273. Encourage them to focus on important information from the story.

P/I PREVENTION/INTERVENTION

WORD STRUCTURE Write *useless, wordless,* and *pictureless* on the chalkboard. Have a volunteer read each word and circle the suffix *-less.* Explain that *-less* is a word ending that makes a noun into an adjective and means "without." For example, if something is wordless, it is without words. Ask students to reread the sentences where each of these words is found to see if the definition for *-less* makes sense.

Then share the following words with students: *worthless, penniless, voiceless, sleepless, thoughtless.* Ask volunteers to identify the meanings of the words and to use each word in a sentence. ***Graphophonic/Syntactic Cues***

Comprehension

22 JUDGMENTS AND DECISIONS
How do think John feels about his sign now? (He is pleased with it.) How can you tell this from the story? (He says that it's perfect. The sign has everything he wanted to put on it from the beginning.) Let's put this on our chart.

JUDGMENTS AND DECISIONS	EVIDENCE FROM STORY
Thomas Jefferson thinks he did a good job.	He worked on it for hours. He believes it is perfect.
No one likes John's sign.	Everyone he meets suggests he change it.
John is pleased with his sign.	It has everything he wanted to put on it from the beginning.

Parchment in hand, John headed to the sign maker's shop.

Past the Old North Church and Beacon Hill. Past Boston Common and the wharf and Harvard College.

At long last, John arrived at the sign maker's shop. Exhausted, he handed over his parchment.

"I do not understand," said the puzzled sign maker as he stared at the empty parchment. "What does this mean? What are you trying to say?"

John shrugged. "I do not know anymore," he admitted. And he told the sign maker about his new hat shop, and his sign, and how no one had thought it was perfect enough.

When he had finished, the sign maker said, "May I make a suggestion? How about:

'John Thompson, Hatmaker
Fashionable Hats Sold Inside for Ready Money.'

"Beneath the words I will draw a picture of a hat."

22 "Yes!" exclaimed John. "How clever of you to think of it. That is exactly right! Indeed, it's perfect!"

274

Activity

Cross Curricular: Math

MULTIPLICATION Explain to students that sign makers usually charge their customers for each letter or picture. Have students calculate how much one of the hatmaker's signs would cost if he charged $3.00 per letter or picture.

Students can draw their own sign, determine a price for each letter, and exchange it with a classmate to figure out how much the sign would cost.
▶ **Mathematical/Interpersonal**

Comprehension

23 In the end, whose advice seemed to help John the most? (The sign maker's.) Why do you think the sign maker was the most helpful? (Sample answer: He makes signs for a living, so he has a better idea how to write one.) ***Character***

24 Compare John's sign now with the one he started with on page 264. What do you notice? (The signs are the same.) ***Compare and Contrast***

LANGUAGE SUPPORT

ESL Read aloud some sentences with action verbs on page 274. Ask volunteers to paraphrase them and pantomime the actions. For example, *John headed to the sign shop* means he started to go to the sign shop; *he handed over the parchment* means he gave the parchment to the sign maker; *he stared at the empty parchment* means he looked at it intently.

Then write the phrase *At long last* on the board, and read it aloud. Encourage students to tell what they think this phrase means. (after a long time, finally) Point out that the author used this phrase to emphasize the distance that John had traveled. After passing all the sites mentioned in the second paragraph, John finally got to where he was going.

Minilesson

REVIEW/MAINTAIN

Plot

Remind students that a story's plot is its organized pattern of events, which often centers on a problem. Help students define some key terms associated with plot.

- Problem—a problem or a goal of characters.
- Rising Action—events leading to the climax.
- Climax—when the problem peaks and comes to a head.
- Resolution—when the problem is solved.

Activity Have students fill in a plot time line for *The Hatmaker's Sign* that includes the problem, the rising action, the climax, and the resolution.

Comprehension

25 JUDGMENTS AND DECISIONS What decision did the delegates make about the Declaration of Independence? (Most thought it was exactly right.) Do you think Jefferson was proud of the Declaration of Independence? Let's record our judgment about Jefferson in our chart.

JUDGMENTS AND DECISIONS	EVIDENCE FROM THE STORY
Thomas Jefferson thinks he did a good job.	He worked on it for hours. He believes it is perfect.
No one likes John's sign.	Everyone he meets suggests he change it.
John is pleased with his sign.	It has everything he wanted to put on it from the beginning.
Thomas Jefferson must be proud of the Declaration of Independence.	Most delegates believed the Declaration of Independence was perfect.

RETELL THE STORY Ask volunteers to tell the major events of the story. Students may refer to their charts to help them. Then have small groups write two sentences that summarize the story. Have them focus on decisions made by the main characters. *Summarize*

STUDENT SELF-ASSESSMENT

- How did using the strategy of making judgments and decisions help me understand the story?
- How did the Judgments and Decisions chart help me?

TRANSFERRING THE STRATEGY

- When might I try using this strategy again? In what other reading could the chart help me?

"So you see, Tom," concluded Benjamin Franklin. "No matter what you write, or how well you write it, if the public is going to read it, you can be sure they will want to change it."

276

REREADING FOR *Fluency*

PARTNERS Have students choose a favorite section of the story to read aloud with a partner. Encourage them to look at the punctuation marks to guide their expression.

READING RATE When you evaluate rate, have the student read aloud from the story for one minute. Place a stick-on note after the last word read. Count words read. To evaluate students' performance, see the Running Record in the **Fluency Assessment** book.

Intervention For leveled fluency lessons, passages, and norms charts, see **Skills Intervention Guide**, Part 4, Fluency.

For several moments, Thomas Jefferson pondered Franklin's story. Then sighing with acceptance, he listened as the Congress argued over the words that rang, the sentences that sang, and the paragraphs that flowed with truth.

And surprisingly, when the debate was done, and the changes were made, most believed Thomas Jefferson's Declaration of Independence was exactly right. Indeed, they thought, it was perfect! 25

LITERARY RESPONSE

QUICK-WRITE Invite students to record their thoughts about the story. These questions may help them get started.

- What did you learn about working with other people after reading this story?
- Do you prefer working on a project by yourself or with other people? Why?

ORAL RESPONSE Have students share their journal writings and discuss what part of the story they enjoyed most.

Comprehension

Return to Predictions and Purposes

Review with students their story predictions and reasons for reading the story. Were their predictions correct? Did they find out what they wanted to know?

PREDICTIONS	WHAT HAPPENED
This story takes place around the time of the American Revolution.	This story is about the writing of the Declaration of Independence.
The hatmaker's sign changes whenever he talks to someone.	Both Thomas Jefferson and the hatmaker learned that people usually want to change someone else's written words.

INFORMAL ASSESSMENT

JUDGMENTS AND DECISIONS

HOW TO ASSESS

- Have students decide if Benjamin Franklin's story helped Thomas Jefferson.

Students should recognize that the story helped Jefferson understand that getting criticism is part of offering something to people, which helped him in the debates over the Declaration of Independence.

FOLLOW UP If students can't decide whether or not the story helped Jefferson, ask them to think about how Jefferson might have felt during the debates over the Declaration of Independence if he had never heard the story.

Story Questions

Have students discuss or write answers to the questions on page 278.

Answers:

1. The hatmaker's story takes place in Boston around the time of the American Revolution. *Literal/Setting*
2. They both want to make changes to something they have read. *Inferential/Judgments and Decisions*
3. Possible answer: He understood human nature. *Inferential/Judgments and Decisions*
4. Sample answer: Listen to others, but in the end, listen to yourself. *Inferential/Summarize*
5. Sample answer: He would like to see more information. *Critical/Reading Across Texts*

Write an Ad For a full writing process lesson, see pages 281K–281L.

Story Questions & Activities

1. When and where does the story take place?
2. How are the members of Congress like the people the hatmaker meets on his way to the sign shop?
3. What do you think made Benjamin Franklin a great storyteller?
4. What is the "message" of this story?
5. Imagine that the hatmaker became part of the picture on page 256. What do you think he would say about the signs in the picture?

Write an Ad

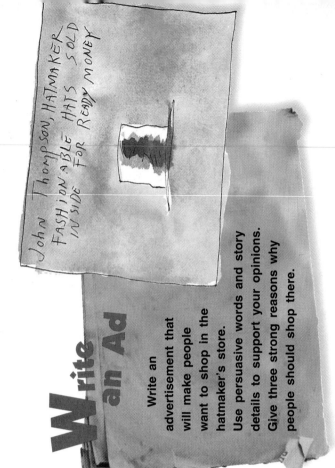

Write an advertisement that will make people want to shop in the hatmaker's store.
Use persuasive words and story details to support your opinions. Give three strong reasons why people should shop there.

Meeting Individual Needs

EASY

Name ________ Date ________ **Reteach 76**

Vocabulary

Read each clue. Then find the vocabulary word in the row of letters and circle it.

admitted	brisk	displaying	elegantly	strolling	wharf

1. quick — n b r i s k d a q t e c f
2. richly or beautifully — p r w s c e l e g a n t l y i
3. showing — t r v m d i s p l a y i n g f e
4. confessed — w u n a d m i t t e d k o l
5. landing place for boats — a l d p i r w h a r f k n d s
6. walking slowly and in a relaxed way — l e s t r o l l i n g r c b n k

6

Story Comprehension **Reteach 77**

Write a complete sentence to answer each question about "The Hatmaker's Sign."

1. Who is the main character of the story? The main character is John Thompson.
2. How did the hatmaker feel about his sign before he talked to others? He liked the sign the way he had planned it.
3. How did everyone want him to change the sign? Each person wanted him to take something off of the sign.
4. What did the sign maker suggest about changing the sign? He suggested that John's sign read as he had planned it originally.
5. Why did Ben Franklin share this story with Jefferson? He wanted Jefferson to know he was not the only one who had to deal with people's suggestions.

At Home: Have students retell the main events of "The Hatmaker's Sign."
76–77 Book 4/Unit 3 The Hatmaker's Sign 5

Reteach, 77

ON-LEVEL

Name ________ Date ________ **Practice 77**

Story Comprehension

Answer the questions about "The Hatmaker's Sign." Look back at the story to help you answer the questions.

1. At the beginning of the story, Thomas Jefferson is reading what he wrote in The Declaration of Independence. What does he think of his writing? Answers will vary but should include: He thought it was perfect and that the Congress would love it.
2. What happened when Thomas Jefferson showed The Declaration of Independence to Congress? They wanted words and paragraphs changed. Congress made 87 changes to Jefferson's draft.
3. Who tells the story of the hatmaker's sign? Benjamin Franklin
4. How did the sign change from the beginning to the end of the story? At first, it had words and pictures, then few words, then it was blank, and finally it ended as it had begun.
5. What was Benjamin Franklin's point in telling Thomas Jefferson that story? No matter how good your writing is, people will have different opinions and will want to change it. Revision is part of writing.

77 At Home: Have students retell the story. Book 4/Unit 3 The Hatmaker's Sign 5

Practice, 77

CHALLENGE

Name ________ Date ________ **Extend 76**

Vocabulary

admitted	brisk	displaying
elegantly	strolling	wharf

Write a paragraph about going shopping, using as many vocabulary words from the box as you can. Then erase those vocabulary words or cover them with tape. Exchange paragraphs with a partner and fill in the blanks.

Extend 77

Story Comprehension

Suppose you were the first person to whom John Thompson showed his idea for a sign. Make a judgment about how he could change his sign. Then write what you would have told him to change. Explain why he should make that change.

At Home: Find an ad in a newspaper or magazine. Discuss how it could be changed to be more effective.
76–77 Book 4/Unit 3 The Hatmaker's Sign

Extend, 77

Make a Sign

Follow the hatmaker's example and make a sign for a store you would like to own. Use a piece of construction paper to make your sign. Include the name of your store, a picture, and the kinds of things sold in it. Then display your sign in class.

Figure Out Prices

Storekeepers like the hatmaker have to use their math skills every day. For example, they have to add prices, make change, and keep track of how many items they have in stock. Look through a catalog or a newspaper. Choose five items you would like to have. Then add up the prices. See how much money you would spend if you bought all five items.

Find Out More

In the story, Thomas Jefferson is hurt that Congress is changing his words. After all, he thought *his* Declaration of Independence was perfect. Find out more about the Declaration of Independence. Start by checking in a social studies book or an encyclopedia. Share what you find with a group or the class.

279

Activity

MATH: COLLECTING AND ANALYZING DATA Ask partners to research the 1760 and 1775 populations of Boston, New York, and Philadelphia. Have them create a three-column chart that shows which city's population grew the most.

What to Look For Check that students:

- use correct population data (Boston: 1760, 15,600; 1775, 16,000; New York: 1760, 18,000; 1775, 25,000; Philadelphia: 1760, 23,750; 1775, 40,000).
- subtract the 1760 population from the 1775 population for each city.
- compare the three increases to find that Philadelphia grew the most.

CHALLENGE

St Activities

Make a Sign

ONE Before having students make a sign for a store, have the class brainstorm different types of stores they would be interested in owning. List their ideas on the chalkboard. Suggest that students sketch a sign and plan what information they want to include on it before they begin making their sign.

Figure Out Prices

PARTNERS Encourage partners to have contests, such as seeing who can find five different items that add up to the smallest total or the largest total. Have students add up their totals and then use calculators to check their sums.

Find Out More

ONE **RESEARCH AND INQUIRY** Students may wish to research and report on other members of the Second Continental Congress who signed the Declaration of Independence, such as John Adams and John Hancock. Suggest that students portray these characters as they give their reports.

*inter***NET CONNECTION** For more information on the writing of the Declaration of Independence, have students visit ***www.mhschool.com/reading***

FORMAL ASSESSMENT

After page 279, see the Selection Assessment.

Stud Skills

GRAPHIC AIDS

TESTED **OBJECTIVES** Students will identify symbols and interpret and use other information on signs.

PREPARE Ask students to describe some of the signs they see every day. Then, with students, read aloud the first paragraph.

TEACH Explain that signs are used to promote safety or provide directions. Display **Teaching Chart 63.**

PRACTICE Have students answer questions 1–5. Review the answers with them. **1.** 3; bike lane, no smoking, and use this exit when there is a fire **2.** The no pedestrian crossing sign; it shows a line across a person walking. **3.** It reminds them to slow down for children arriving or leaving school. **4.** because it is bright and easy to see **5.** Answers may vary.

ASSESS/CLOSE Have students create a sign to post at home.

STUDY SKILLS

Read Signs

In Benjamin Franklin's day, **signs** on the streets of cities and towns often had pictures, just as they do today. Many signs use **symbols**, simple drawings that stand for actions, objects, or directions. For example, the symbol ⃠ means "No" or "Don't."

Use the signs to answer these questions.

1. How many of the signs have both words and symbols? What do those signs mean?
2. Which sign tells walkers not to cross the street? Describe it.
3. Why should drivers notice the School Crossing sign?
4. Why is yellow a good color for some warning signs?
5. Why do you think many signs contain symbols along with, or instead of, words?

Meeting Individual Needs

EASY

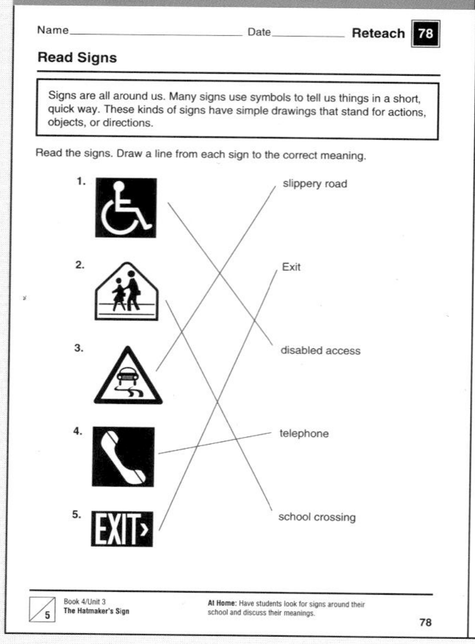
Name______________ Date__________ Reteach 78

Read Signs

Signs are all around us. Many signs use symbols to tell us things in a short, quick way. These kinds of signs have simple drawings that stand for actions, objects, or directions.

Read the signs. Draw a line from each sign to the correct meaning.

1. slippery road
2. Exit
3. disabled access
4. telephone
5. EXIT school crossing

Book 4/Unit 3 The Hatmaker's Sign
At Home: Have students look for signs around their school and discuss their meanings.
5 78

Reteach, 78

ON-LEVEL

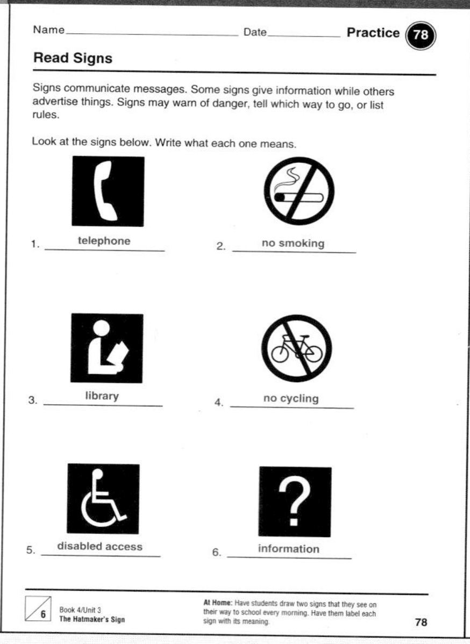
Name______________ Date__________ Practice 78

Read Signs

Signs communicate messages. Some signs give information while others advertise things. Signs may warn of danger, tell which way to go, or list rules.

Look at the signs below. Write what each one means.

1. telephone
2. no smoking
3. library
4. no cycling
5. disabled access
6. information

Book 4/Unit 3 The Hatmaker's Sign
At Home: Have students draw two signs that they see on their way to school every morning. Have them label each sign with its meaning.
6 78

Practice, 78

CHALLENGE

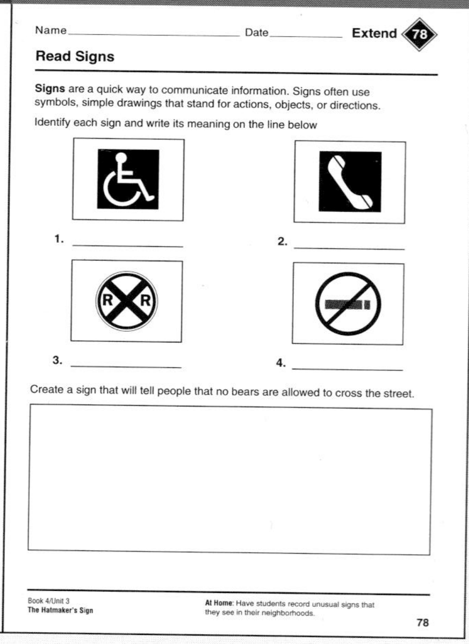
Name______________ Date__________ Extend 78

Read Signs

Signs are a quick way to communicate information. Signs often use symbols, simple drawings that stand for actions, objects, or directions.
Identify each sign and write its meaning on the line below

1. ________
2. ________
3. ________
4. ________

Create a sign that will tell people that no bears are allowed to cross the street.

Book 4/Unit 3 The Hatmaker's Sign
At Home: Have students record unusual signs that they see in their neighborhoods.
78

Extend, 78

TEST POWER

Test Tip
State the questions in your own words to make sure you understand them.

DIRECTIONS
Read the sample story. Then read each question about the story.

SAMPLE

Sally's Day at the Ballpark

Sally woke up at dawn, already grinning with excitement. She was going to a baseball game today with her cousin Jake. He was eighteen years old, and he had what seemed to Sally to be the world's best job. Jake was a hot-dog vendor.

Jake spent all summer in the park, talking with people and selling hot dogs. Sally loved the hot-dog cart. But most of all, she loved sitting with Jake—listening to him talk about funny, exciting things. She loved baseball. And she knew Jake loved baseball, too. It was no wonder Sally woke up happy. It promised to be a wonderful day.

1 The word vendor in this story means—

A friend
B brother
(C) seller
D teacher

2 Sally had the chance to go to the baseball game with Jake because—

F she pushed the hot-dog cart
G he played baseball
H she liked hot dogs
(J) he was her cousin

Did you rule out wrong answers? Tell how.

281

Test Power

THE PRINCETON REVIEW

Read the Page

Tell students to note the underlined word as they read the passage.

Discuss the Questions

Question 1: This question asks students to define a word in context. Instruct students to read each answer choice and to replace the underlined word in the sentence with each of the answer choices. Tell them to continue this process until they find the answer choice that makes the most sense.

Question 2: This question requires students to recall a supporting fact. Remind students that they should *not* rely on their memories. They should *always* refer back to the story. Ask students, "Why did Sally have the chance to go to the baseball game with Jake?" Have students support their answers with facts from the story.

Leveled Books

EASY

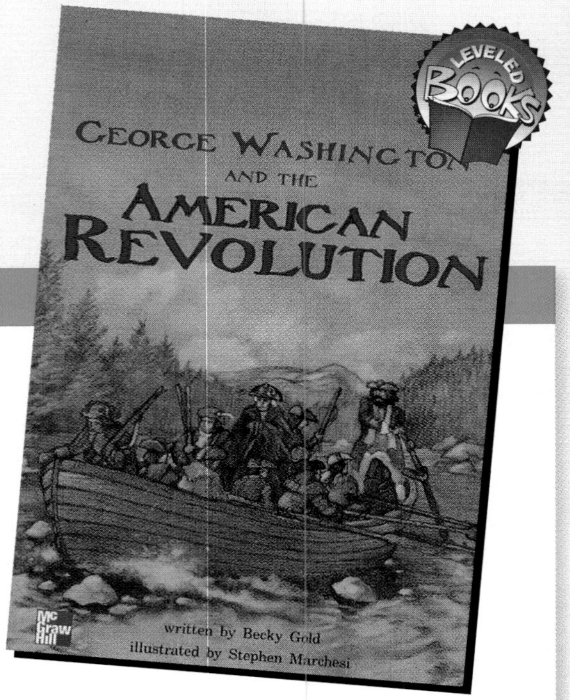

George Washington and the American Revolution

/oi/ and /ou/

☑ **Judgments and Decisions**

☑ **Instructional Vocabulary:** ***admitted, brisk, displaying, elegantly, strolling, wharf***

Guided Reading

PREVIEW AND PREDICT Have students discuss the illustrations up through page 9. Ask them to predict in their journals how they think the soldiers on page 9 will do in battle.

SET PURPOSES Have students write reasons for reading the story. For example, *I want to know more about our country's beginnings.*

READ THE BOOK Ask the following questions during guided reading or after students have read the story independently.

Pages 2–5: Do you think it was wise or unwise to have the troops travel hundreds of miles to bring cannons to Boston? Explain. (Sample answer: It was wise because the cannons scared away the British.) ***Judgments and Decisions***

Page 8: What does the word *brisk* mean? Which word in the same sentence helps explain the meaning of the word? (quick, sharp; shivering) ***Vocabulary***

Pages 9–12: Why do you think Washington and his men decided to attack the Hessians on the day after Christmas? (Sample answer: The Hessians would be tired from celebrating and not prepared to fight.) ***Judgments and Decisions***

Page 15: Find words on this page with /oi/ spelled *oi* and *oy*. (choice, joy) Then find words with /ou/ spelled *ou* and *ow*. (outside, powerful, however, powers) ***Phonics***

RETURN TO PREDICTIONS AND PURPOSES Have students compare their predictions to what happened in the story. Which predictions were accurate? Did they learn what they expected from the story?

LITERARY RESPONSE Discuss these questions:

- How might the United States be different if Washington's troops had lost?
- Why is the "father of our country" a good title for Washington?

Also see the story questions and activity in *George Washington and the American Revolution.*

Intervention ➔ Skills

Intervention Guide, for direct instruction and extra practice in vocabulary and comprehension

Answers to Story Questions

1. Some Americans wanted to break away because they were angry about Britain's strict rule and high taxes. They wanted to rule themselves.
2. The British knew they needed to leave the city, or Washington would attack.
3. Washington knew that his men were tired of being defeated, and he judged that defeating the Hessians would encourage them not to give up hope.
4. George Washington made good decisions as a general in the American Revolution and became the first president of the United States.
5. Answers will vary.

The *Story Questions and Activity* below appear in the *Easy Book*.

Story Questions and Activity

1. Why did some Americans want to break away from Britain?
2. When Washington placed cannons on a hill above Boston, what signal did it give the British?
3. Why did Washington make the decision to attack the Hessians in Trenton?
4. What is the main idea of this book?
5. If the Hatmaker from *The Hatmaker's Sign* had met George Washington along the road to the sign maker, what advice do you think George Washington would have given him?

But General...

Write a dialogue between Washington and one of his soldiers right before the Battle of Trenton. Show how Washington might have encouraged his men not to lose hope. With a partner, you can perform your dialogue as a play.

from *George Washington and the American Revolution*

Leveled Books

INDEPENDENT

Paul Revere: Midnight Rider

- ☑ **Judgments and Decisions**
- ☑ **Instructional Vocabulary:** ***admitted, brisk, displaying, elegantly, strolling, wharf***

Guided Reading

PREVIEW AND PREDICT Have students compare the settings of the illustrations up through page 8. Then ask them to predict the results of Paul Revere's ride. Chart students' predictions.

SET PURPOSES Have students write their purposes for reading the selection. For example: *I've heard of Paul Revere. I want to know why he's famous.*

READ THE BOOK Use questions such as these to guide a group reading or to check understanding after students read independently.

Page 3: What were some reasons the patriots decided to rebel against King George III? (high taxes and strict, unfair laws) ***Judgments and Decisions***

Page 6: What was Paul's mission? (to warn patriot leaders that Redcoats were coming; to have men in Concord hide the arms; to warn people along the route to prepare for the invasion) ***Summarize***

Page 13: What is the difference between *pacing* and *strolling*? (Pacing is quickly walking back and forth due to nervous energy; strolling is more casual, carefree walking.) ***Vocabulary***

Pages 15–16: In later years, do you think Paul was proud or regretful of his decision to ride? Why? (Sample answer: He was proud, because he helped make a better country for his children and grandchildren.) ***Judgments and Decisions***

RETURN TO PREDICTIONS AND PURPOSES Have students compare their predictions and purposes with actual story events. Were their predictions accurate? Did they learn what they expected from the story?

LITERARY RESPONSE Discuss these questions:

- Which version of the events gives more information—the story or the poem?
- Which version makes you feel more as if you were there? Why?

Also see the story questions and activity in *Paul Revere: Midnight Rider.*

Answers to Story Questions

1. A messenger could be caught and arrested by the Redcoats, and would probably be hung as a traitor.
2. Some citizens still thought of themselves as British because Britain had established settlements in Massachusetts over a hundred years earlier.
3. He was able to help patriot leaders Adams and Hancock flee to safety.
4. Paul Revere's ride helped to prepare people for the Redcoats and the start of the Revolutionary War.
5. Answers may include the following: Mitchell: Unfortunately, the traitor Paul Revere had to be set free on April 18, 1775; Hancock: The hero Paul Revere saved patriot leaders Hancock and Adams on April 18, 1775; Newman: Heroes Paul Revere and Robert Newman worked together to save the day on April 18, 1775.

The *Story Questions and Activity* below appear in the *Independent Book*.

Story Questions and Activity

1. Why was it so dangerous for anyone to be carrying messages for the revolutionaries?
2. Why did some citizens of Massachusetts still think of themselves as British?
3. How did Paul's decision to go back to Lexington after his capture affect the cause of freedom?
4. What is the story mostly about?
5. Keeping in mind how the sign from *The Hatmaker's Sign* was rewritten based on the ideas of others, how might the statement below be rewritten by Major Mitchell, John Hancock, and Robert Newman?

   The great American hero Paul Revere saved the day on April 18, 1775.

An Important Message

Suppose that you are a present-day Paul Revere and you have to deliver an important message to the people in your community. What would the message be? Write a paragraph describing how you would deliver it.

from *Paul Revere: Midnight Rider*

Leveled Books

CHALLENGE

The Work of Many Hands: Writing the Declaration of Independence

- ☑ **Judgments and Decisions**
- ☑ **Instructional Vocabulary:** ***admitted, brisk, displaying, elegantly, strolling, wharf***

Guided Reading

PREVIEW AND PREDICT Have students preview the story up to page 14. Then ask students to write predictions about how the other founding fathers will react to Jefferson's draft of the Declaration.

SET PURPOSES Ask students to write a purpose for reading. For example: *I want to know why the Declaration of Independence was written.*

READ THE BOOK Use these questions during guided reading or as part of a follow-up discussion.

Pages 2–3: Why were the colonists angry at Great Britain? (King George III raised taxes and made unfair laws.) ***Make Inferences***

Page 5: What were some arguments against declaring war on Britain? (It was too soon. The colonies did not have a real army.) ***Judgments and Decisions***

Page 9: The debate was *brisk*. Does this mean that the discussion was quick and lively, or were the debaters afraid to say what they meant? (The debate was quick and lively.) ***Vocabulary***

Page 14: Why do you think Jefferson agreed not to mention slavery in the document? (He wanted everyone to be united and in agreement with what the document stated.) ***Judgments and Decisions***

RETURN TO PREDICTIONS AND PURPOSES Review students' predictions and purposes for reading. Did students accurately predict the delegates' reactions? Did they learn what they expected about the Declaration of Independence?

LITERARY RESPONSE Discuss these questions:

- Why are visitors to the National Archives so anxious to see the original Declaration of Independence?
- How did the Declaration change the whole world?

Also see the story questions and activity in *The Work of Many Hands: Writing the Declaration of Independence.*

Answers to Story Questions

1. The colonists dumped tea into Boston Harbor to protest high taxes on tea.
2. Great Britain didn't want the colonies to stop buying British goods and wanted to avoid further problems.
3. Answers may include: he should not have signed a document that was so flawed; he made the right judgment in compromising to get the Declaration adopted.
4. Before the Declaration of Independence could be printed, the Congress had to agree that the colonies should be free.
5. Answers will vary.

The *Story Questions and Activity* below appear in the *Challenge Book*.

Story Questions and Activity

1. Why did a group of colonists dump tea into Boston Harbor?
2. Why did Great Britain ease up on the colonies after the First Continental Congress?
3. Did Jefferson make the right decision when he agreed to omit the wording about slavery from the declaration?
4. What is the main idea of the book?
5. If the owner of the hat shop from *The Hatmaker's Sign* had been in the room when the Declaration of Independence was being discussed, what do you think he might have suggested?

What Does It Say?

The text of the Declaration of Independence can be found in many reference sources. Read the first paragraph of the Declaration carefully, looking up the words you don't know in a dictionary. Then rewrite the Declaration in your own words. Don't forget to sign it!

from ***The Work of Many Hands: Writing the Declaration of Independence***

Bringing Groups Together

Anthology and Leveled Books

Connecting Texts

FOUNDING FATHERS WEB Many students already know a lot about colonial history. Point out that the books they read included many of the same historical characters. Have students from all reading groups work together to complete a chart that includes information about important people of the colonial era, such as George Washington, Benjamin Franklin, Paul Revere, and Thomas Jefferson.

Benjamin Franklin	George Washington	Thomas Jefferson	Paul Revere
• Friend of Thomas Jefferson • Wise man and peacemaker	• Revolutionary War general • First United States President • "Father of Our Country"	• Man of many talents • Wrote the Declaration of Independence	• Warned that the British were coming • Silversmith

Viewing/Representing

GROUP PRESENTATIONS Organize the class into groups according to the leveled books they read. (For *The Hatmaker's Sign*, combine students of different reading levels.) Tell groups to list and discuss the characters in their selection and then choose group members to play the roles of the characters in a panel discussion. Have groups present their panel discussion to the class.

AUDIENCE RESPONSE Have audience members prepare a list of questions to ask panel members. At the end of each presentation, allow time for questions and answers.

Research and Inquiry

MORE ABOUT FOUNDING FIGURES Remind students that even though most civic leaders in colonial days were men, many women played important roles in founding the United States, too. Have students find out more about "Founding Mothers" by:

- Researching famous colonial women.
- Drawing a picture that shows the role one of the women played.
- Writing a summary paragraph to go along with their picture.

interNET CONNECTION Have students log on to ***www.mhschool.com/reading*** to find out more about women in history.

TESTED OBJECTIVES

Students will make judgments and decisions about a story.

Skills Finder

Judgments and Decisions

Introduce	257A-B
Review	281E-F, 331G-H, 361A-B, 631G-H, 665A-B, 691E-F
Test	Unit 3, Unit 6

TEACHING TIP

MANAGEMENT Organize the class into two groups to help you read the Teaching Chart aloud. Ask one group to read the role of the hatmaker and the other group to be the magistrate. Discuss how pretending to be each character helps readers make judgments about the characters and events in the story.

SELF-SELECTED Reading

Students may choose from the following titles.

ANTHOLOGY

- The Hatmaker's Sign

LEVELED BOOKS

- George Washington and the American Revolution
- Paul Revere: Midnight Rider
- The Work of Many Hands

Bibliography, pages T78–T79

Review Judgments and Decisions

PREPARE

Discuss Judgments and Decisions

Review: You make judgments about characters and ideas when you read. Your judgments are based on information you have read in the story and also what you personally feel is right or wrong based on your knowledge and experience. When faced with making choices about something you read, think about all of the story evidence and your judgments before you make a decision.

TEACH

Read the Story and Model the Skill

Ask students to make judgments about the personalities of the hatmaker and the magistrate as they read **Teaching Chart 64** along with you.

Have a Good Day

John Thompson saw the magistrate coming in his direction as he was walking back with his new sign. He bowed his head so their eyes would not meet.

"Hand over that sign!" demanded the magistrate. "I must read it to see if you followed my directions!"

"Yes, sir. I ... I ... put more information on it than I needed because I wanted to make sure that I followed your rules, sir," said the hatmaker.

"Ah, yes, very well then," said the magistrate, " I have my eyes on you!"

"Yes, sir," stammered the hatmaker. "Have a good day!"

Teaching Chart 64

No, Too afraid - He listens to other people and changes his mind. A magistrate must always follow rules.

Ask students if the hatmaker would make a very good magistrate. Discuss evidence that would help them make a decision.

MODEL I don't think the hatmaker would make a very good magistrate because he is too afraid to say what he feels. He listens to other people and changes his mind. A magistrate always has to be thinking about one thing—following the rules.

PRACTICE

Make Judgments and Decisions

GROUP

Have volunteers underline words or phrases in "Have a Good Day" that support their judgment about whether the hatmaker would make a good magistrate.

Then ask students to decide if they think the magistrate would be a successful shop owner. Have them give reasons to support their judgments. ▶ **Logical**

ASSESS/CLOSE

Make Judgments in Writing

PARTNERS

Have partners work together to write a story in which the hatmaker and the magistrate trade jobs. Point out that they will have to make judgments and decisions about how the personalities of the two characters will affect them in their new roles. Have students share their stories with the class.

ALTERNATE TEACHING STRATEGY

JUDGMENTS AND DECISIONS

For a different approach to teaching this skill, see page T60.

Intervention Skills

Intervention Guide, for direct instruction and extra practice with judgments and decisions

Meeting Individual Needs for Comprehension

EASY

Name________ Date________ **Reteach 79**

Make Judgments and Decisions

It is common for readers to put themselves in the place of a character in a story. Readers who do this **make judgments and decisions** about the characters and their actions.

Read the story. Then answer the questions.

Luis was looking forward to playing soccer with his team on the weekend. He was also happy because on the playground, his friend Larry had talked about having the whole group over some time. Larry's family lived on the lake and had a big boat.

Luis had a problem, though. Larry had invited everyone to the lake on the same weekend as the game. Luis knew the team should come first. But, Lester, a friend, said if Luis didn't go to the lake, Larry would be angry and would never invite him again.

1. What should Luis do? He should probably be loyal to the team and play the game.
2. Should Luis listen to Lester's advice? Why? No. He should do what he thinks is right and not worry about what others think.
3. If you were Luis, what would you say to Larry? Luis should thank Larry for the invitation, explain his team is counting on him, and ask to be invited some other time.
4. If you were Luis and others made fun of your decision to play the game, how would you feel? a little upset, but glad to have been loyal to the team

At Home: Have students comment on a judgment or decision made by a television show character.

79 Book 4/Unit 3 The Hatmaker's Sign 4

Reteach, 79

ON-LEVEL

Name________ Date________ **Practice 79**

Make Judgments and Decisions

Making **judgments** about the actions of characters is a natural part of reading a story. That is how you make **decisions** about whether or not you like or respect a character. Read each statement, and then tell if the statement is **True** or **False**.

1. Thomas Jefferson believed the people in America should be free. True
2. Thomas Jefferson believed he was a fine writer. True
3. The other members of the Continental Congress thought The Declaration of Independence was written perfectly. False
4. Benjamin Franklin told a story to make Thomas Jefferson feel better. True
5. The story of the hatmaker and his sign proves that everyone has an opinion about hats. Explain your answer. False; they changed the sign and said nothing about hats.

Use your own ideas from "The Hatmaker's Sign" to write what you think of Thomas Jefferson and Benjamin Franklin. Answers will vary.

6. I think that Thomas Jefferson Answers will vary, but may include: believed in freedom, liked his writing, and was a smart man.
7. I believe that Benjamin Franklin Answers will vary, but may include: was a kind and smart man, cared for others, and was a good storyteller.
8. Telling stories such as "The Hatmaker's Sign" is a good way to get a point across. Choose to agree or disagree, then explain your answer. Answers will vary.

At Home: Have students discuss which of Jefferson's or Franklin's actions helped them make a judgment about the two men.

79 Book 4/Unit 3 The Hatmaker's Sign 8

Practice, 79

CHALLENGE

Name________ Date________ **Extend 79**

Make Judgments and Decisions

In "The Hatmaker's Sign," you read the **judgments** that several people made about John Thompson's sign. You also read about John's **decisions** to change the sign after hearing the judgments.

Design a sign to hang on the wall over your bed. It should say something about you. Include your first name, words or pictures that tell what you want to say, and any other important details.

Show your design to three friends. Ask them if you should make any changes to your sign. Have them explain. Record your friends' judgments below.

Friend 1 ________

Friend 2 ________

Friend 3 ________

Now decide if you will change your sign and, if so, how. Explain your decision below. Then make any changes to your sign.

At Home: Tell students to share their signs with family members and discuss the various judgments.

79 Book 4/Unit 3 The Hatmaker's Sign

Extend, 79

LANGUAGE SUPPORT

Name________ Date________

Hats Off to You!

1. Look at the hats below. 2. Describe each hat. 3. What kind of hat would you like to wear?

86 The Hatmaker's Sign • Language Support / Blackline Master 42 Grade 4

Language Support, 86

TESTED OBJECTIVES

Students will summarize a story they have read.

Skills Finder

Summarize	
Introduce	281G-H
Review	297G-H, 359G-H
Test	Unit 3
Maintain	385, 415, 461

LANGUAGE SUPPORT

To help students understand what should be included in a summary, retell *The Hatmaker's Sign*, leaving blanks for the setting, main characters, and important events. Have students say the words that belong in the blanks.

Introduce Summarize

PREPARE

Discuss Summarizing

Explain: A summary is a short retelling of a story in your own words. It describes the setting, the main characters, and the important events. When you summarize a story, it helps you find meaning and order in what you just read.

TEACH

Read the Story and Model the Skill

Read **Teaching Chart 65.** Focus students' attention on what happens in the beginning, the middle, and the end of the story.

A Good Sign

John Thompson loved hats. He loved to wear them, design them, and make them. So, he and his wife, Hannah, decided to sell them.

First, they bought a store that had large windows in front where they could display their hats. Then they cleaned the shop and built shelves. Next, they hired workers to help them make and sell their hats. Last, they added furniture and put the hats on display in the windows.

Finally they were ready to open! At first, business was slow. Then John hung a notice on the front of his store that brought people in to buy many hats. It was a good sign!

Teaching Chart 65

Say

Ask students to underline important information in this story that they would want to include in a summary.

MODEL If I retold this story, I would tell only the important information that happened at the beginning, the middle, and the end. I would keep my summary short—one or two sentences long.

PRACTICE

Create a Summary Organizer

GROUP

Have students create a summary organizer. Then ask them to use the organizer to help them summarize "A Good Sign."
▶ **Logical/Spatial**

STORY SUMMARY:
"A Good Sign"

Beginning: John and Hannah Thompson decide to open a hat shop.

Middle: The shop is ready for business, but no one comes.

End: John hangs a sign on the front of the shop, and business improves.

ASSESS/CLOSE

Summarize a Familiar Story

Have students create a summary organizer for a familiar story or show. Have them use their organizer to write a summary of the story or event.

ALTERNATE TEACHING STRATEGY

SUMMARIZE

For a different approach to teaching this skill, see page T62.

Intervention Skills

Intervention Guide, for direct instruction and extra practice in summarizing

Meeting Individual Needs for Comprehension

EASY

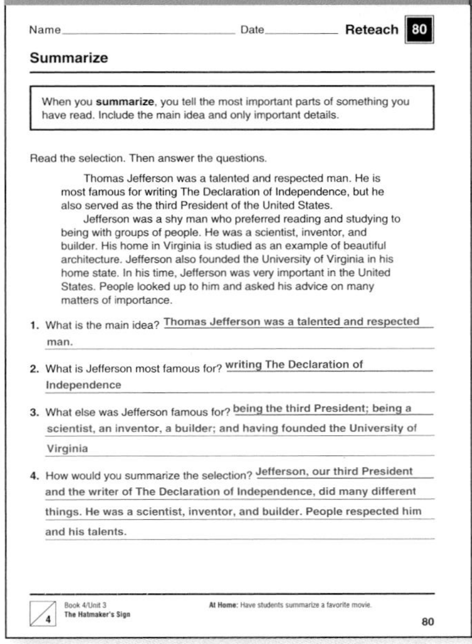
Name______________ Date__________ Reteach 80

Summarize

When you **summarize**, you tell the most important parts of something you have read. Include the main idea and only important details.

Read the selection. Then answer the questions.

Thomas Jefferson was a talented and respected man. He is most famous for writing The Declaration of Independence, but he also served as the third President of the United States.

Jefferson was a shy man who preferred reading and studying to being with groups of people. He was a scientist, inventor, and builder. His home in Virginia is studied as an example of beautiful architecture. Jefferson also founded the University of Virginia in his home state. In his time, Jefferson was very important in the United States. People looked up to him and asked his advice on many matters of importance.

1. What is the main idea? Thomas Jefferson was a talented and respected man.
2. What is Jefferson most famous for? writing The Declaration of Independence
3. What else was Jefferson famous for? being the third President; being a scientist, an inventor, a builder; and having founded the University of Virginia
4. How would you summarize the selection? Jefferson, our third President and the writer of The Declaration of Independence, did many different things. He was a scientist, inventor, and builder. People respected him and his talents.

Book 4/Unit 3 The Hatmaker's Sign 4 | At Home: Have students summarize a favorite movie. | 80

Reteach, 80

ON-LEVEL

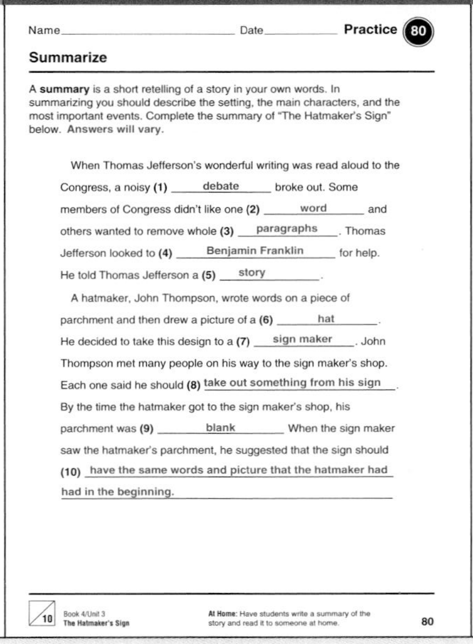
Name______________ Date__________ Practice 80

Summarize

A **summary** is a short retelling of a story in your own words. In summarizing you should describe the setting, the main characters, and the most important events. Complete the summary of "The Hatmaker's Sign" below. Answers will vary.

When Thomas Jefferson's wonderful writing was read aloud to the Congress, a noisy (1) debate broke out. Some members of Congress didn't like one (2) word and others wanted to remove whole (3) paragraphs. Thomas Jefferson looked to (4) Benjamin Franklin for help. He told Thomas Jefferson a (5) story.

A hatmaker, John Thompson, wrote words on a piece of parchment and then drew a picture of a (6) hat. He decided to take this design to a (7) sign maker. John Thompson met many people on his way to the sign maker's shop. Each one said he should (8) take out something from his sign. By the time the hatmaker got to the sign maker's shop, his parchment was (9) blank. When the sign maker saw the hatmaker's parchment, he suggested that the sign should (10) have the same words and picture that the hatmaker had had in the beginning.

Book 4/Unit 3 The Hatmaker's Sign 10 | At Home: Have students write a summary of the story and read it to someone at home. | 80

Practice, 80

CHALLENGE

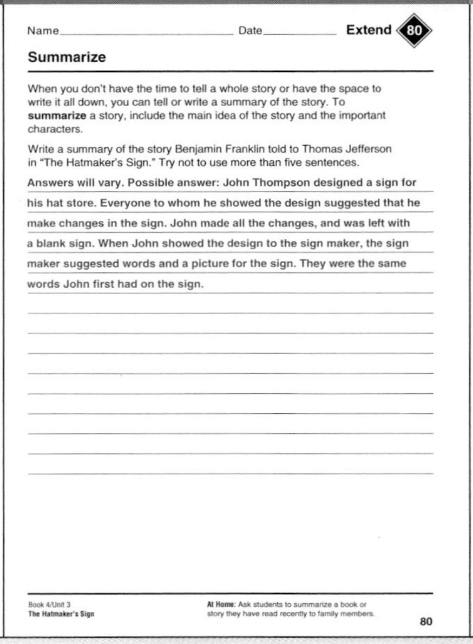
Name______________ Date__________ Extend 80

Summarize

When you don't have the time to tell a whole story or have the space to write it all down, you can tell or write a summary of the story. To **summarize** a story, include the main idea of the story and the important characters.

Write a summary of the story Benjamin Franklin told to Thomas Jefferson in "The Hatmaker's Sign." Try not to use more than five sentences.

Answers will vary. Possible answer: John Thompson designed a sign for his hat store. Everyone to whom he showed the design suggested that he make changes in the sign. John made all the changes, and was left with a blank sign. When John showed the design to the sign maker, the sign maker suggested words and a picture for the sign. They were the same words John first had on the sign.

Book 4/Unit 3 The Hatmaker's Sign | At Home: Ask students to summarize a book or story they have read recently to family members. | 80

Extend, 80

LANGUAGE SUPPORT

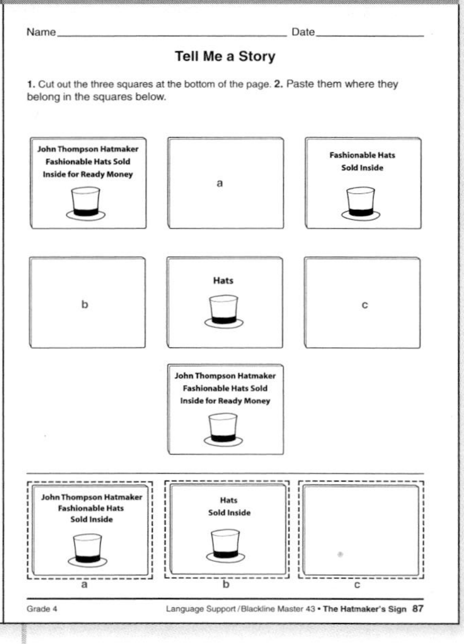
Name______________ Date__________

Tell Me a Story

1. Cut out the three squares at the bottom of the page. 2. Paste them where they belong in the squares below.

Grade 4 | Language Support /Blackline Master 43 • The Hatmaker's Sign 87

Language Support, 87

Introduce Suffixes

TESTED OBJECTIVES

Students will learn how the suffix *-ful* changes word meaning.

Skills Finder

Suffixes	
Introduce	281I-J
Review	297I-J, 369I-J
Test	Unit 3
Maintain	433, 457, 553, 681

TEACHING TIP

SUFFIXES When students come to an unfamiliar word that has a suffix, tell them to:

- cover the suffix to identify the base word.
- think about the meaning of the base word.
- think about the meaning of the suffix.
- check to see if the combined meanings make sense in the sentence.

PREPARE

Discuss Meaning of the Suffix *-ful*

Explain: Grouping words with similar parts together can make the words easier to understand and remember. For example, words with the same suffix can be grouped together. A suffix is a word part added to the end of a base word. Suffixes have their own meanings. The suffix *-ful* usually means "full of" or "having." When a suffix is added to a word, the meaning of the word changes. As you read the following passage, you will look for all the words with the suffix *-ful*.

TEACH

Read "Wonderful Words" and Model the Skill

Have students read the passage on **Teaching Chart 66.**

Wonderful Words

Thomas Jefferson sat at his desk and thought about the wonderful words he had just written.

"Surely it must be unlawful for my friends to make changes in these truthful words," he said out loud.

"Thomas, my friend," said Benjamin Franklin, "you should be joyful that they care enough to want the best possible plan for our country. Their doubts are not meant to be harmful."

Teaching Chart 66

MODEL The word *wonderful* in the first sentence ends in *-ful*. The base word is *wonder*. If *-ful* means "full of," then *wonderful* means "full of wonder." I will read the sentence again to see if that meaning makes sense.

Have students define *truthful* in the second sentence using the meaning of the suffix *-ful*. *(full of truth)* Ask them whether that meaning makes sense in the sentence.

PRACTICE

Identify Words with the Suffix -*ful*

GROUP

Have volunteers underline in "Wonderful Words" each word that ends with the suffix *-ful* and then circle the suffix of the word. Have students give the meanings of these words.

ASSESS/CLOSE

Form Words with Suffix -*ful* and Make a Suffix Book

PARTNERS

Have students write the following words: grace, delight, hurt, and hope. Then have them add the suffix *-ful* to each word. Ask students to work with a partner to create a suffix book for *-ful*. Each page should include a sentence and an illustration of a word ending in *-ful*, to show the meaning of that word. Encourage students to find other words that end with the suffix *-ful*.

ALTERNATE TEACHING STRATEGY

SUFFIXES

For a different approach to teaching this skill, see page T63.

Intervention **Skills**

Intervention Guide, for direct instruction and extra practice with suffixes

Meeting Individual Needs for Vocabulary

EASY

Name________ Date________ **Reteach 81**

Suffixes

Suffixes are word endings. They add to the meaning of a word. The suffix *-ful* adds the meaning "full of" to a word.

Add the suffix *-ful* to each word.

1. fear + ful = fearful
2. help + ful = helpful
3. hope + ful = hopeful
4. joy + ful = joyful
5. doubt + ful = doubtful
6. health + ful = healthful

Now use one of the words above with *-ful* to complete each sentence.

7. Carrot sticks are a healthful snack.
8. She was doubtful that she could finish on time.
9. My brother is fearful of dark places.
10. Birthdays are joyful occasions.
11. Can you be helpful and hand me the hammer?
12. Aaron is hopeful he will win the contest.

81 **At Home:** Have students use three words they formed in sentences of their own. Book 4/Unit 3 The Hatmaker's Sign 12

Reteach, 81

ON-LEVEL

Name________ Date________ **Practice 81**

Suffixes

A **suffix** is a group of letters, such as *-ful*, added to the end of a base word, or root word. Use the words below to complete the sentences.

wonderful	unlawful	willful	thoughtful
plentiful	handful	bountiful	surprisingly

1. The harvest was rich and bountiful.
2. The queen looked thoughtful as she read the new law.
3. The baker made a chocolate cake that was wonderful.
4. The number of apples picked was plentiful, so we shared them with our neighbors.
5. Dumping waste in the river is unlawful.
6. I could hold only a handful of those large marbles.
7. Marcus was very willful and stubborn.
8. The day looks cold, but it is surprisingly warm.

81 **At Home:** Have students write sentences using the words. Book 4/Unit 3 The Hatmaker's Sign 8

Practice, 81

CHALLENGE

Name________ Date________ **Extend 81**

Suffixes

Word parts that are added to the end of words, such as *-ed* and *-ing*, are called **suffixes**. The suffix *-ful* means "full of." When you add *-ful* to a noun, it forms an adjective. For example, *wonderful* is an adjective that means "full of wonder." Add *-ful* to each noun to create adjectives. Then write sentences using the adjectives you created. Sentences will vary.

1. thought thoughtful
Sample: It was thoughtful of her to remember my birthday.
2. use useful
Sample: A shovel is useful when working in the garden.
3. sorrow sorrowful
Sample: Saying goodbye can be sorrowful.
4. help helpful
Sample: I try to be helpful by mowing the lawn.
5. care careful
Sample: Be careful when you cross the street.
6. joy joyful
Sample: Holidays can be a joyful time.
7. hope hopeful
Sample: Shandra was hopeful that she did well on the test.

81 **At Home:** Direct students to create adjectives by adding *-ful* to nouns and use the adjectives in conversation. Book 4/Unit 3 The Hatmaker's Sign

Extend, 81

LANGUAGE SUPPORT

Name________ Date________

Full Time

1. Write the suffix **-ful** at the end of each word below. 2. Use one of the words to best describe each picture below.

wonder help thank care

wonderful careful

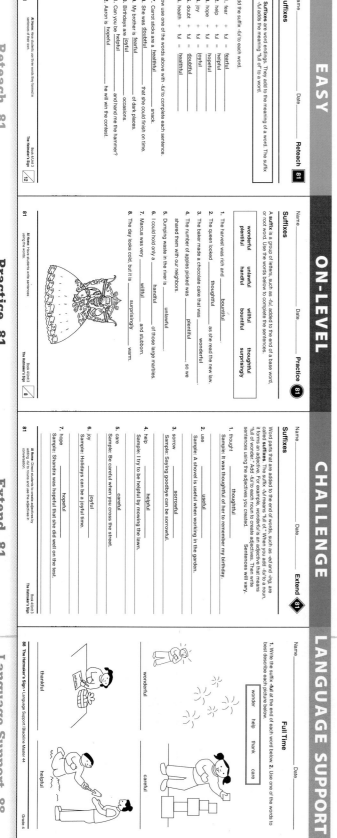

thankful helpful

88 The Hatmaker's Sign • Language Support/Blackline Master 44 Grade 4

Language Support, 88

Persuasive Writing

Prewrite

WRITE AN AD Present this writing assignment: Write an advertisement that will make people want to shop in the hatmaker's store. Use persuasive words and story details to support your opinions. Give three strong reasons why people should shop there.

BRAINSTORM IDEAS Have students brainstorm reasons why people would want to visit the hatmaker's shop. Have them consider the merchandise, prices, atmosphere, and service.

Strategy: Make a Cluster Have students write "Hatmaker's Shop" in the center of the cluster, and then list phrases about the shop that would persuade people to buy their hats there. Suggest the following:

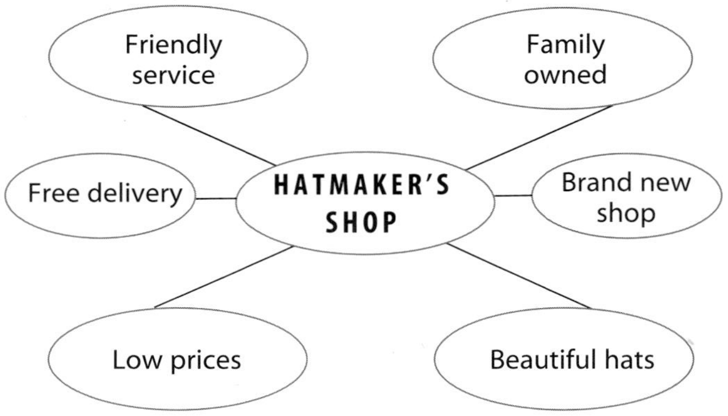

Draft

USE THE CLUSTER In their advertisements, students should use the three strongest reasons from their cluster to persuade people to shop in the store. Then they should include persuasive words and story details to support their opinions.

Revise

SELF-QUESTIONING Ask students to assess their drafts.

- Did I give strong reasons for visiting the hatmaker's shop?
- Have I included persuasive words and story details to support my opinions?
- How can I make my ad better?

PARTNERS Have partners compare word clusters and brainstorm additional persuasive devices to include in their advertisements.

Edit/Proofread

CHECK FOR ERRORS Students should reread their ads for spelling, grammar, punctuation, and proper word usage.

Publish

EXCHANGE ADS Have students exchange their ads with a classmate. Encourage them to tell what information in the ad would make them want to shop at the hatmaker's store.

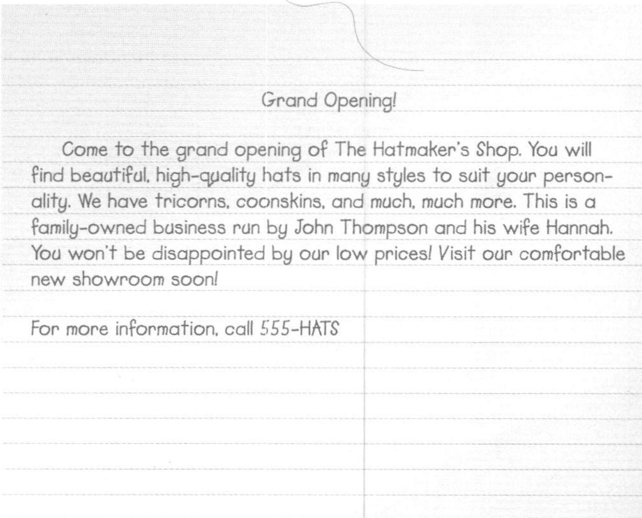

Grand Opening!

Come to the grand opening of The Hatmaker's Shop. You will find beautiful, high-quality hats in many styles to suit your personality. We have tricorns, coonskins, and much, much more. This is a family-owned business run by John Thompson and his wife Hannah. You won't be disappointed by our low prices! Visit our comfortable new showroom soon!

For more information, call 555-HATS

GRAMMAR/SPELLING CONNECTIONS

See the 5-Day Grammar and Usage Plan on present tense, pages 281M–281N.

See the 5-Day Spelling Plan on words with /ou/ and /oi/, pages 281O–281P.

TEACHING TIP

Technology Have students who design their ads on the computer experiment with different fonts and colors. Ask them how the size and color of certain words in their ads might affect the reader.

Handwriting Remind students to use their neatest handwriting when publishing. Write on one side of the paper only and leave wide margins on all sides. For specific instruction on handwriting, see pages T68–T73.

Handwriting CD-ROM

Presentation Ideas

ILLUSTRATE THE AD Have students draw a colorful picture to go along with their advertisements. ▶ **Viewing/Representing**

RADIO AD Have students record their ad as though it were a radio advertisement. Encourage them to use expression in their voices. ▶ **Speaking/Listening**

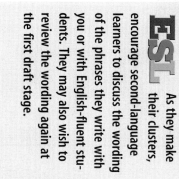

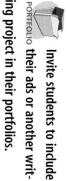

Consider students' creative efforts, possibly adding a plus (+) for originality, wit, and imagination.

Scoring Rubric

Excellent	Good	Fair	Unsatisfactory
4: The writer • states at least three reasons for visiting the hat shop. • includes story details to support statements. • uses language that would persuade a reader to visit the shop.	**3:** The writer • states at least two reasons for visiting the hat shop. • includes some supporting details. • uses language that is adequately persuasive.	**2:** The writer • gives a reason for visiting the hat shop. • presents few supporting details from the story. • uses language that is somewhat persuasive.	**1:** The writer • lists no reasons for visiting the hat shop. • includes no supporting details from the story. • does not use persuasive language.

Incomplete 0: The writer leaves the page blank or fails to respond to the writing task. The student does not address the topic or simply paraphrases the prompt. The response is illegible or incoherent.

For a 6-point or an 8-point scale, see pages T107–T108.

Meeting Individual Needs for Writing

EASY

Thank-You Card Have students design and write a thank-you card from the hatmaker to the signmaker. Ask them to include reasons from the hatmaker stating why he would use this signmaker again.

ON-LEVEL

Store Idea Ask students to think of a store they would like to see open in their community. Have them list how this store could benefit the area where they live.

CHALLENGE

Newspaper Editorial Have students pretend that the magistrate from the story has made up a new law: No one may wear hats anymore. Ask them to write a persuasive letter to the editor of the newspaper saying why they think this law is unfair. Have them list in their letter any benefits they can think of for wearing hats.

Viewing and Speaking

VIEWING STRATEGIES
Have students:
- look for the main idea of the ad.
- look for details in the ad that support the main idea.

SPEAKING STRATEGIES
As students record their ads, encourage them to:
- speak clearly and distinctly.
- vary their tone of voice.

LANGUAGE SUPPORT

ESL As they make their clusters, encourage second-language learners to discuss the wording of the phrases they write with you or with English-fluent students. They may also wish to review the wording again at the first draft stage.

PORTFOLIO **Invite students to include their ads or another writing project in their portfolios.**

5 Day Grammar and Usage Plan

LANGUAGE SUPPORT

Tell students that a verb shows action. Read these sentences aloud and ask students to demonstrate the actions: *Sabrina skips rope. The dog shakes its wet fur. Jake eats apples. Sara grins.*

DAILY LANGUAGE ACTIVITIES

Write the Daily Language Activities on the chalkboard each day or use **Transparency 11**. Have students correct the sentences orally. For answers, see the transparency.

Day 1

1. John Thompson like hats.
2. He walk to the sign maker's shop.
3. His wife wave to him.

Day 2

1. They strolls along the wharf.
2. He brush his hair from his face.
3. John carrys his sign with him.

Day 3

1. John wish he didn't talk to everyone.
2. The congressmen changes the words on the sign.
3. He hurry to the sign maker's shop.

Day 4

1. The people tries to help John Thompson.
2. He want the sign maker's advice.
3. The sign maker washs his dirty brush.

Day 5

1. Jefferson crunchs up the paper.
2. He toss it into the wastebasket.
3. Franklin smile at his friend.

Daily Language Transparency 11

DAY 1 Introduce the Concept

Oral Warm-Up Read this sentence aloud: *The dog chews the bone.* Ask students which word shows action.

Introduce Verbs A word that expresses action is a verb. Present:

Present-Tense Verbs

- An **action verb** tells what the subject does or did.
- A verb in the **present tense** tells what happens now.
- The present tense must have **subject-verb agreement**. Add *-s* to most verbs if the subject is singular. Do not add *-s* if the subject is plural or *I* or *you*.

Present the Daily Language Activity. Then have students write two sentences for *like*, *walk*, and *wave*, using a singular then a plural subject.

WRITING Assign the daily Writing Prompt on page 256C.

Name ______ Date ______ LEARN Grammar 65

Action Verbs in the Present Tense

- An **action verb** tells what the subject does or did.
- A verb in the **present tense** tells what happens now.
- The present tense must have **subject-verb agreement**. Add *-s* to most verbs if the subject is singular. Do not add *-s* if the subject is plural or *I* or *you*.

Write the correct present tense of each underlined verb on the lines provided.

1. John Thompson place hats in the window of his shop. places
2. He stack hatboxes along a wall. stacks
3. John write some words on parchment. writes
4. He draw a picture of a hat under the words. draws
5. John show his idea for a sign to his wife. shows
6. His wife giggles when she read the words. reads
7. John make changes in his sign. makes
8. The hatmaker walk to the sign maker's shop. walks
9. The hatmaker meet many people on the way. meets
10. What does the sign maker say to the hat maker? say

10 Grade 4/Unit 3 The Hatmaker's Sign — Extension: Have students write three sentences about the story, using the present tense of these verbs: *grab, rewrite, suggest.* Ask students to circle the verbs in their sentences. 65

GRAMMAR PRACTICE BOOK, PAGE 65

DAY 2 Teach the Concept

Review Present-Tense Verbs Have students explain how to form present-tense verbs.

Introduce Other Endings Tell students that some present-tense verbs get a different ending depending on how they are spelled.

Present-Tense Verbs

- Add *-es* to verbs that end in *s*, *ch*, *sh*, *x*, or *z* if the subject is singular.
- Change *y* to *i* and add *-es* to verbs that end with a consonant and *y*.
- Do not add *-es* to a present-tense verb when the subject is plural or *I* or *you*.

Present the Daily Language Activity. Then have students write sentences for *brush*, *carry*, *watch*, *bring*, and *make* using the verbs in the present tense with a singular subject.

WRITING Assign the daily Writing Prompt on page 256C.

Name ______ Date ______ LEARN & PRACTICE Grammar 66

Action Verbs

- Add *-es* to verbs that end in *s, ch, sh, x,* or *z* if the subject is singular.
- Change *y* to *i* and add *-es* to verbs that end with a consonant and *y*.
- Do not add *-es* to a present-tense verb when the subject is plural or *I* or *you*.

Read each sentence. Write the correct present tense of each underlined verb on the line provided.

1. Thomas Jefferson is angry, and his face flush red. flushes
2. Benjamin Franklin try to make Jefferson feel better. tries
3. The hatmaker kiss Lady Manderly's hand. kisses
4. The lady snatch the parchment away from the hatmaker. snatches
5. John Thompson toss coins to the boys. tosses
6. He push the parchment under a man's nose. pushes
7. John hurry home to his shop several times. hurries
8. The hatmaker fix the words on his sign. fixes
9. John rush to the sign maker's shop. rushes
10. Do you realize what happens to the hatmaker's sign? realize

66 Extension: Ask students to write five sentences, using these verbs: watch, watches; worry, worries. Grade 4/Unit 3 The Hatmaker's Sign 10

GRAMMAR PRACTICE BOOK, PAGE 66

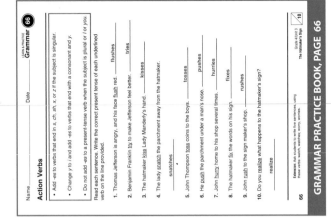

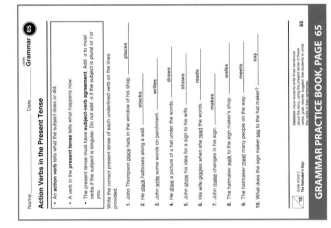

Present Tense

DAY 3 Review and Practice

Learn from the Literature Review present-tense verbs. Read the last sentence on page 262 of *The Hatmaker's Sign*:

> **"Tom," Benjamin Franklin said, smiling, "this puts me in mind of a story."**

Ask students to identify the present-tense verb and base word *put*. Have students explain how the present tense of the verb was formed and why.

Use Present-Tense Verbs Present the Daily Language Activity. Then have students make a four-column chart and write one of the rules from Days 1 and 2 at the top of each column. Ask them to brainstorm a list of present-tense verbs and then write them in the appropriate column.

WRITING Assign the daily Writing Prompt on page 256D.

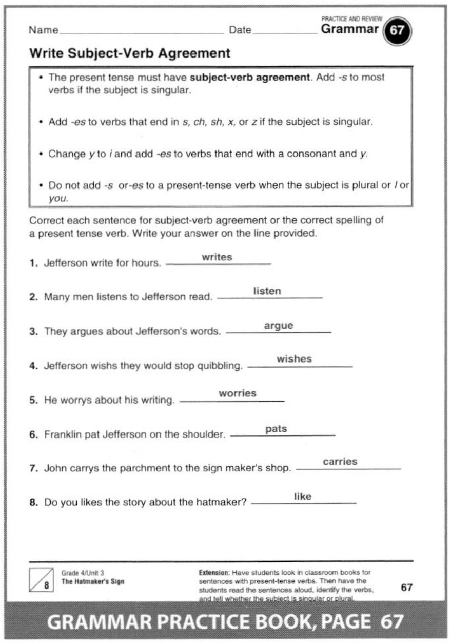

Name________ Date________ PRACTICE AND REVIEW Grammar 67

Write Subject-Verb Agreement

- The present tense must have **subject-verb agreement**. Add *-s* to most verbs if the subject is singular.
- Add *-es* to verbs that end in *s, ch, sh, x,* or *z* if the subject is singular.
- Change *y* to *i* and add *-es* to verbs that end with a consonant and *y*.
- Do not add *-s* or *-es* to a present-tense verb when the subject is plural or *I* or *you*.

Correct each sentence for subject-verb agreement or the correct spelling of a present tense verb. Write your answer on the line provided.

1. Jefferson write for hours. writes
2. Many men listens to Jefferson read. listen
3. They argues about Jefferson's words. argue
4. Jefferson wishs they would stop quibbling. wishes
5. He worrys about his writing. worries
6. Franklin pat Jefferson on the shoulder. pats
7. John carrys the parchment to the sign maker's shop. carries
8. Do you likes the story about the hatmaker? like

Grade 4/Unit 3 The Hatmaker's Sign 8

Extension: Have students look in classroom books for sentences with present-tense verbs. Then have the students read the sentences aloud, identify the verbs, and tell whether the subject is singular or plural.

67

GRAMMAR PRACTICE BOOK, PAGE 67

DAY 4 Review and Practice

Review Present-Tense Verbs Write these verbs on the board: *punch, pass, fix, drop, shake*. Ask students to tell how they would change the ending of each verb to complete the sentence *He ____ the ball*. Then present the Daily Language Activity.

Mechanics and Usage Before students begin the daily Writing Prompt on page 256D, review commas in a series.

> **Commas in a Series**
>
> - A comma tells the reader to pause between the words that it separates.
> - Use commas to separate three or more words in a series.
> - Do not use a comma after the last word in a series.

Show students this example: *The dog chews, bites, and plays with the bone.*

WRITING Assign the daily Writing Prompt on page 256D.

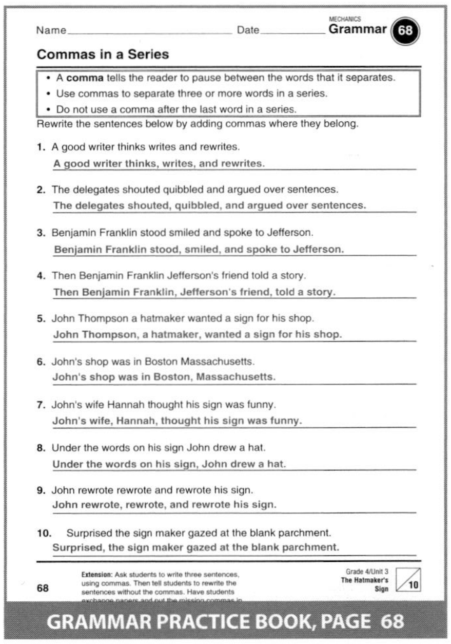

Name________ Date________ MECHANICS Grammar 68

Commas in a Series

- A **comma** tells the reader to pause between the words that it separates.
- Use commas to separate three or more words in a series.
- Do not use a comma after the last word in a series.

Rewrite the sentences below by adding commas where they belong.

1. A good writer thinks writes and rewrites.
   A good writer thinks, writes, and rewrites.
2. The delegates shouted quibbled and argued over sentences.
   The delegates shouted, quibbled, and argued over sentences.
3. Benjamin Franklin stood smiled and spoke to Jefferson.
   Benjamin Franklin stood, smiled, and spoke to Jefferson.
4. Then Benjamin Franklin Jefferson's friend told a story.
   Then Benjamin Franklin, Jefferson's friend, told a story.
5. John Thompson a hatmaker wanted a sign for his shop.
   John Thompson, a hatmaker, wanted a sign for his shop.
6. John's shop was in Boston Massachusetts.
   John's shop was in Boston, Massachusetts.
7. John's wife Hannah thought his sign was funny.
   John's wife, Hannah, thought his sign was funny.
8. Under the words on his sign John drew a hat.
   Under the words on his sign, John drew a hat.
9. John rewrote rewrote and rewrote his sign.
   John rewrote, rewrote, and rewrote his sign.
10. Surprised the sign maker gazed at the blank parchment.
    Surprised, the sign maker gazed at the blank parchment.

68

Extension: Ask students to write three sentences, using commas. Then tell students to rewrite the sentences without the commas. Have students exchange papers and put the missing commas in.

Grade 4/Unit 3 The Hatmaker's Sign 10

GRAMMAR PRACTICE BOOK, PAGE 68

DAY 5 Assess and Reteach

Assess Use the Daily Language Activity and page 69 of the **Grammar Practice Book** for assessment.

Reteach Ask pairs of students to write these verbs and present tense endings on separate index cards: *like, dress, push, fix, wash, sit, -s,* and *-es*. Have one student choose a verb card and the other select the appropriate ending. Together they should make up a sentence that shows subject-verb agreement in the present tense. Then the students switch roles.

Have students add these present-tense verbs to the classroom word wall.

Use page 70 of the **Grammar Practice Book** for additional reteaching.

WRITING Assign the daily Writing Prompt on page 256D.

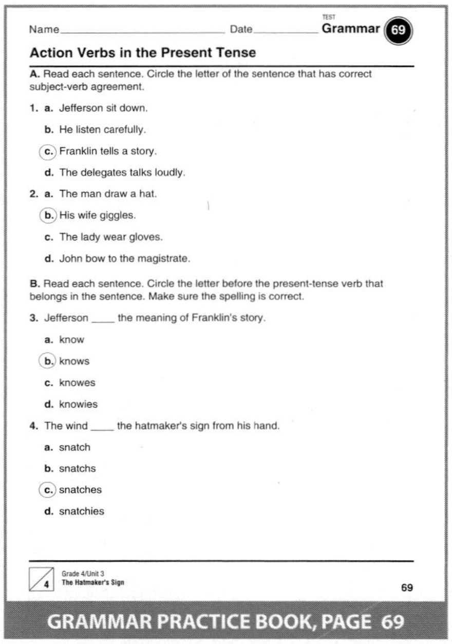

Name________ Date________ TEST Grammar 69

Action Verbs in the Present Tense

A. Read each sentence. Circle the letter of the sentence that has correct subject-verb agreement.

1. a. Jefferson sit down.
   b. He listen carefully.
   (c.) Franklin tells a story.
   d. The delegates talks loudly.
2. a. The man draw a hat.
   (b.) His wife giggles.
   c. The lady wear gloves.
   d. John bow to the magistrate.

B. Read each sentence. Circle the letter before the present-tense verb that belongs in the sentence. Make sure the spelling is correct.

3. Jefferson ____ the meaning of Franklin's story.
   a. know
   (b.) knows
   c. knowes
   d. knowies
4. The wind ____ the hatmaker's sign from his hand.
   a. snatch
   b. snatchs
   (c.) snatches
   d. snatchies

Grade 4/Unit 3 The Hatmaker's Sign 4

69

GRAMMAR PRACTICE BOOK, PAGE 69

GRAMMAR PRACTICE BOOK, PAGE 70

5 Day Spelling Plan

LANGUAGE SUPPORT

To help students distinguish the vowel sounds and spelling patterns of /oi/ and /ou/, list the following words on the chalkboard: *tower, moist, noun,* and *avoid.* Pronounce each word and have students repeat. Have students identify the vowel sound and the spelling pattern of each word.

DICTATION SENTENCES

Spelling Words

1. Do not slip on the oily spot.
2. Loud noises annoy me.
3. Run around the track.
4. Some animals growl.
5. Rain will disappoint the baseball team.
6. The jewels were fit for royalty.
7. This basketball does not bounce well.
8. The children on the stage are bowing.
9. Is the dirt moist or dry?
10. Soft music gives enjoyment.
11. Can a secret be said aloud?
12. We looked out from the high tower.
13. He wants to avoid trouble.
14. Ranches employ cowboys.
15. Birds are on the lookout for seeds.
16. Draw the house however you wish.
17. She is late for her appointment.
18. The scout rode ahead on his horse.
19. Bath powder is soft.
20. The name of a thing is a noun.

Challenge Words

21. He admitted he was wrong.
22. Stores are displaying their goods.
23. The woman is elegantly dressed.
24. We were strolling in the park.
25. Ships load at the wharf.

DAY 1 Pretest

Assess Prior Knowledge Use the Dictation Sentences at the left and **Spelling Practice Book** page 65 for the pretest. Allow students to correct their own papers. Students who require a modified list may be tested on the first ten words.

Spelling Words		Challenge Words
1. oily	11. **aloud**	21. **admitted**
2. annoy	12. tower	22. **displaying**
3. **around**	13. avoid	23. **elegantly**
4. growl	14. employ	24. **strolling**
5. disappoint	15. **lookout**	25. **wharf**
6. royalty	16. **however**	
7. bounce	17. appointment	
8. **bowing**	18. scout	
9. moist	19. powder	
10. enjoyment	20. noun	

*Note: Words in **dark type** are from the story.*

Word Study On page 66 of the **Spelling Practice Book** are word study steps and an at-home activity.

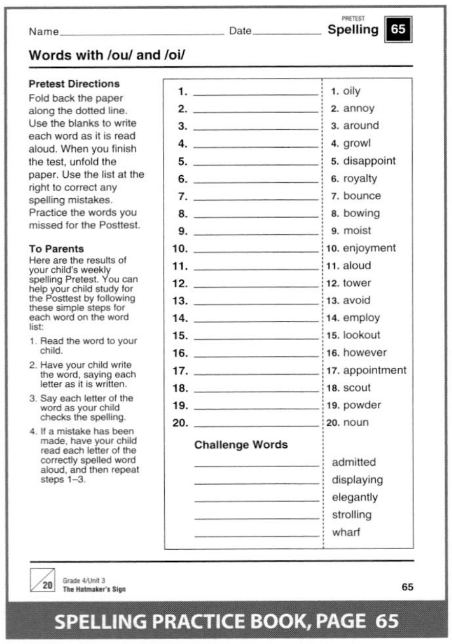
Name______ Date______ PRETEST Spelling 65

Words with /ou/ and /oi/

Pretest Directions
Fold back the paper along the dotted line. Use the blanks to write each word as it is read aloud. When you finish the test, unfold the paper. Use the list at the right to correct any spelling mistakes. Practice the words you missed for the Posttest.

To Parents
Here are the results of your child's weekly spelling Pretest. You can help your child study for the Posttest by following these simple steps for each word on the word list:
1. Read the word to your child.
2. Have your child write the word, saying each letter as it is written.
3. Say each letter of the word as your child checks the spelling.
4. If a mistake has been made, have your child read each letter of the correctly spelled word aloud, and then repeat steps 1–3.

1. oily
2. annoy
3. around
4. growl
5. disappoint
6. royalty
7. bounce
8. bowing
9. moist
10. enjoyment
11. aloud
12. tower
13. avoid
14. employ
15. lookout
16. however
17. appointment
18. scout
19. powder
20. noun

Challenge Words
admitted
displaying
elegantly
strolling
wharf

Grade 4/Unit 3 The Hatmaker's Sign 20 65

SPELLING PRACTICE BOOK, PAGE 65

WORD STUDY STEPS AND ACTIVITY, PAGE 66

DAY 2 Explore the Pattern

Sort and Spell Words Say the following word pairs, and have students listen for and identify the common vowel sound: *moist, employ* /oi/; *growl, bounce* /ou/. Have students read the Spelling Words aloud and sort them as below.

Words with /ou/ spelled		/oi/ spelled	
ou	*ow*	*oi*	*oy*
around	growl	oily	annoy
bounce	bowing	disappoint	royalty
aloud	tower	point	enjoyment
lookout	however	moist	employ
scout	powder	avoid	
noun		appointment	

Spelling Patterns Ask: Which spelling of /ou/ may appear at the end of a word or syllable? (ow) In the middle? (ou) Which spelling of /oi/ usually appears at the end of a word or syllable? (oy) In the middle? (oi)

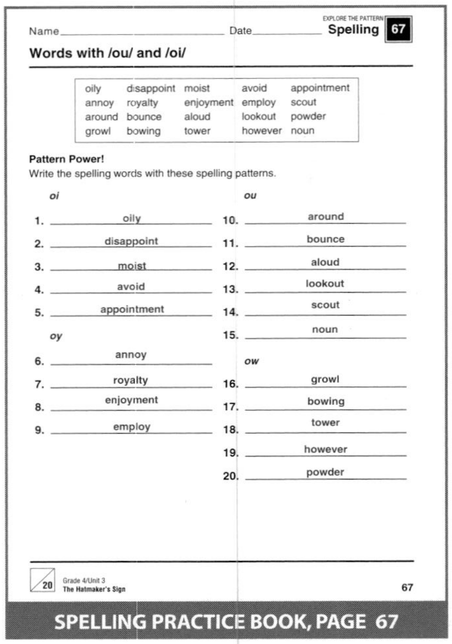
Name______ Date______ EXPLORE THE PATTERN Spelling 67

Words with /ou/ and /oi/

oily, disappoint, moist, avoid, appointment, annoy, royalty, enjoyment, employ, scout, around, bounce, aloud, lookout, powder, growl, bowing, tower, however, noun

Pattern Power!
Write the spelling words with these spelling patterns.

oi
1. oily
2. disappoint
3. moist
4. avoid
5. appointment

oy
6. annoy
7. royalty
8. enjoyment
9. employ

ou
10. around
11. bounce
12. aloud
13. lookout
14. scout
15. noun

ow
16. growl
17. bowing
18. tower
19. however
20. powder

Grade 4/Unit 3 The Hatmaker's Sign 20 67

SPELLING PRACTICE BOOK, PAGE 67

Words with /ou/ and /oi/

DAY 3 Practice and Extend

Word Meaning: Suffixes Write *appointment* on the chalkboard and underline the suffix. Tell students that *-ment* means "the act of" and *appointment* means "the act of naming or selecting for a position, office, or duty." Have students identify and define another Spelling Word with the suffix *-ment*. (enjoyment; "the act of getting pleasure or joy") Then have them add the suffix *-ment* to *disappoint* and *employ* to form two new words. (disappointment, employment)

If students need extra practice, have partners give each other a midweek test.

Glossary Tell students that a Glossary sometimes includes information about a word's history or origin. Have partners:

- write each Challenge Word.
- look up each word in the Glossary.
- identify the word with a word history (elegantly) and list facts about the word's origin.

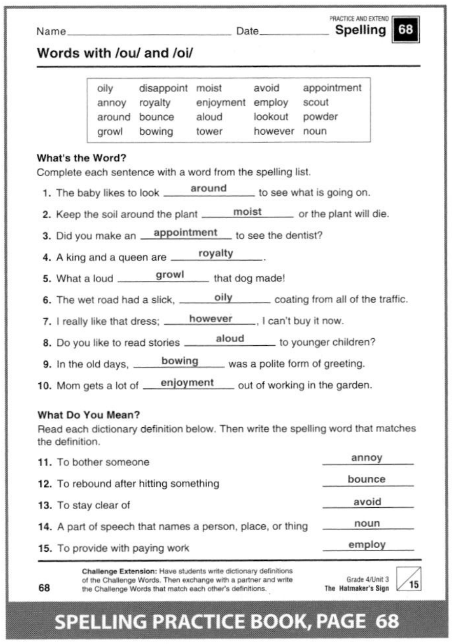

Name________________ Date__________ PRACTICE AND EXTEND Spelling 68

Words with /ou/ and /oi/

oily	disappoint	moist	avoid	appointment
annoy	royalty	enjoyment	employ	scout
around	bounce	aloud	lookout	powder
growl	bowing	tower	however	noun

What's the Word?
Complete each sentence with a word from the spelling list.

1. The baby likes to look ___around___ to see what is going on.
2. Keep the soil around the plant ___moist___ or the plant will die.
3. Did you make an ___appointment___ to see the dentist?
4. A king and a queen are ___royalty___.
5. What a loud ___growl___ that dog made!
6. The wet road had a slick, ___oily___ coating from all of the traffic.
7. I really like that dress; ___however___, I can't buy it now.
8. Do you like to read stories ___aloud___ to younger children?
9. In the old days, ___bowing___ was a polite form of greeting.
10. Mom gets a lot of ___enjoyment___ out of working in the garden.

What Do You Mean?
Read each dictionary definition below. Then write the spelling word that matches the definition.

11. To bother someone ___annoy___
12. To rebound after hitting something ___bounce___
13. To stay clear of ___avoid___
14. A part of speech that names a person, place, or thing ___noun___
15. To provide with paying work ___employ___

68 **Challenge Extension:** Have students write dictionary definitions of the Challenge Words. Then exchange with a partner and write the Challenge Words that match each other's definitions. Grade 4/Unit 3 The Hatmaker's Sign 15

SPELLING PRACTICE BOOK, PAGE 68

DAY 4 Proofread and Write

Proofread Sentences Write these sentences on the chalkboard, including the misspelled words. Ask students to proofread, circling incorrect spellings and writing the correct spellings. There are two spelling errors in each sentence.

> **It will anoy me if you miss your appontment. (annoy, appointment)**
>
> **We took a walk arond the touer. (around, tower)**

Have students create additional sentences with errors for partners to correct.

WRITING Have students use as many Spelling Words as possible in the daily Writing Prompt on page 256D. Remind students to proofread their writing for errors in spelling, grammar, and punctuation.

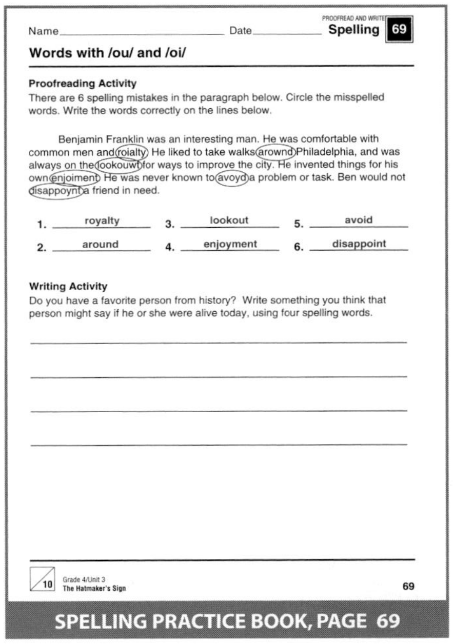

Name________________ Date__________ PROOFREAD AND WRITE Spelling 69

Words with /ou/ and /oi/

Proofreading Activity
There are 6 spelling mistakes in the paragraph below. Circle the misspelled words. Write the words correctly on the lines below.

Benjamin Franklin was an interesting man. He was comfortable with common men and roialty. He liked to take walks arownd Philadelphia, and was always on the lookouwt for ways to improve the city. He invented things for his own enjoiment. He was never known to avoyd a problem or task. Ben would not disappoynt a friend in need.

1. ___royalty___ 3. ___lookout___ 5. ___avoid___
2. ___around___ 4. ___enjoyment___ 6. ___disappoint___

Writing Activity
Do you have a favorite person from history? Write something you think that person might say if he or she were alive today, using four spelling words.

10 Grade 4/Unit 3 The Hatmaker's Sign 69

SPELLING PRACTICE BOOK, PAGE 69

DAY 5 Assess and Reteach

Assess Students' Knowledge Use page 70 of the **Spelling Practice Book** or the Dictation Sentences on page 281O for the posttest.

JOURNAL **Personal Word List** If students have trouble with any words in the lesson, have them add to their personal lists of troublesome words in their journals. Have students draw a simple picture for each word and include the word as part of the illustration.

Students should refer to their word lists during later writing activities.

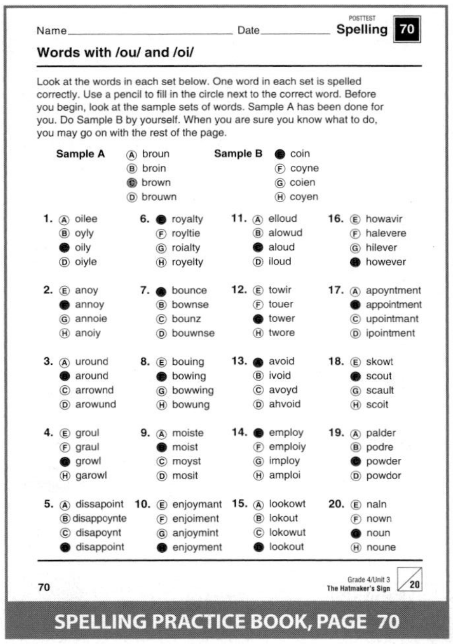

Name________________ Date__________ POSTTEST Spelling 70

Words with /ou/ and /oi/

Look at the words in each set below. One word in each set is spelled correctly. Use a pencil to fill in the circle next to the correct word. Before you begin, look at the sample sets of words. Sample A has been done for you. Do Sample B by yourself. When you are sure you know what to do, you may go on with the rest of the page.

Sample A: (A) broun (B) broin ● brown (D) brouwn
Sample B: ● coin (F) coyne (G) coien (H) coyen

1. (A) oilee (B) oyly ● oily (D) oiyle
2. (E) anoy ● annoy (G) annoie (H) anoiy
3. (A) uround ● around (C) arrownd (D) arownd
4. (E) groul (F) graul ● growl (H) garowl
5. (A) dissapoint (B) disappoynte (C) disapoynt ● disappoint
6. ● royalty (F) roytlie (G) roialty (H) royelty
7. ● bounce (B) bownse (C) bounz (D) bouwnse
8. (E) bouing ● bowing (G) bowwing (H) bowung
9. (A) moiste ● moist (C) moyst (D) mosit
10. (E) enjoymant (F) enjoiment (G) anjoymint ● enjoyment
11. (A) elloud (B) alowud ● aloud (D) iloud
12. (E) towir (F) touer ● tower (H) twore
13. ● avoid (B) ivoid (C) avoyd (D) ahvoid
14. ● employ (F) emploiy (G) imploy (H) amploi
15. (A) lookowt (B) lokout (C) lokowut ● lookout
16. (E) howavir (F) halevere (G) hilever ● however
17. (A) apoyntment ● appointment (C) upointmant (D) ipointment
18. (E) skowt ● scout (G) scault (H) scoit
19. (A) palder (B) podre ● powder (D) powdor
20. (E) naln (F) nown ● noun (H) noune

70 Grade 4/Unit 3 The Hatmaker's Sign 20

SPELLING PRACTICE BOOK, PAGE 70

Reaching All Learners

Concept
- Children's Art

Comprehension
- Fact and Opinion

Vocabulary
- exist
- image
- inspire
- loft
- reference
- sketch

Anthology

Pat Cummings: My Story

Selection Summary **This autobiography explains how children's illustrator Pat Cummings first started drawing as a young girl. It also tells why she enjoys drawing pictures of people she knows as well as of things in her imagination.**

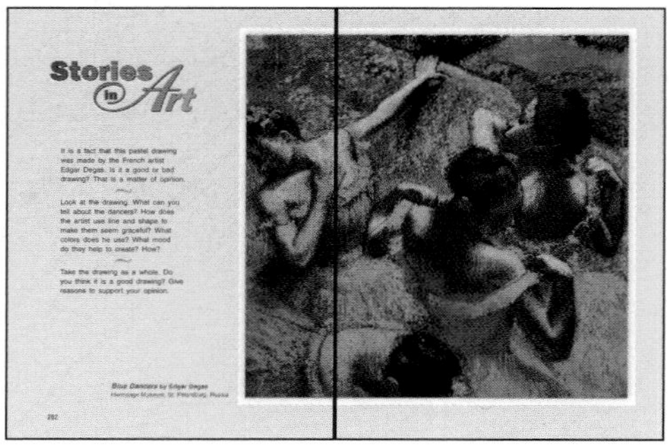

Stories in Art focuses on the **comprehension** skill

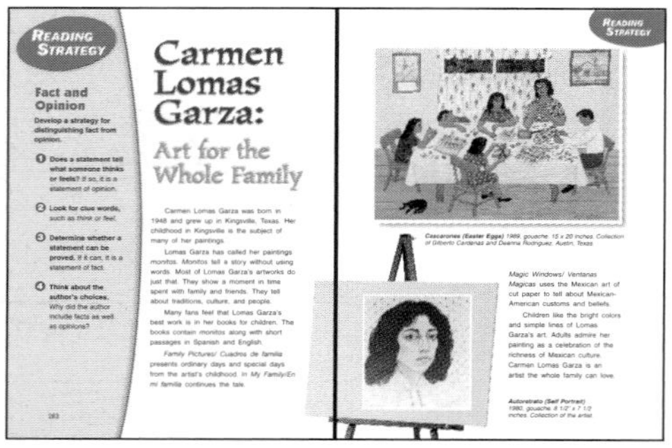

Reading Strategy applies the **comprehension** skill

Listening Library

INSTRUCTIONAL pages 284–297

About the Author/Illustrator Pat Cummings loves writing and illustrating children's books for a living. In *Pat Cummings: My Story,* she answers questions about her own books, but she also likes to interview other people to find out about their lives. She has written three volumes of *Talking with Artists* and one book titled *Talking with Adventurers.* Some books by Cummings that students may enjoy are *Willie's Not the Hugging Kind, Clean Your Room, Harvey Moon!,* and *I Need a Lunch Box.*

Same Concept, Skills and Vocabulary!

Leveled Books

EASY
Lesson on pages 297A and 297D

INDEPENDENT
Lesson on pages 297B and 297D

CHALLENGE
Lesson on pages 297C and 297D

Leveled Practice

EASY

Reteach, 82–88 blackline masters with reteaching opportunities for each assessed skill

INDEPENDENT/ON-LEVEL

Practice, 82–88 workbook with Take-Home stories and practice opportunities for each assessed skill and story comprehension

CHALLENGE

Extend, 82–88 blackline masters that offer challenge activities for each assessed skill

Quizzes Prepared by Accelerated Reader

WORKSTATION Activities

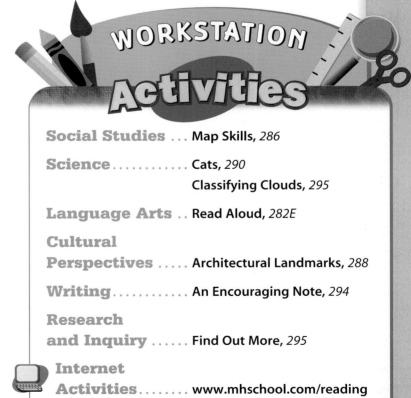

Social Studies ... Map Skills, *286*

Science ... Cats, *290*
Classifying Clouds, *295*

Language Arts .. Read Aloud, *282E*

Cultural Perspectives ..... Architectural Landmarks, *288*

Writing ... An Encouraging Note, *294*

Research and Inquiry ...... Find Out More, *295*

Internet Activities .... www.mhschool.com/reading

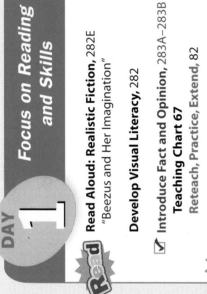

Suggested Lesson Planner

READING AND LANGUAGE ARTS	DAY 1 *Focus on Reading and Skills*	DAY 2 *Read the Literature*
Comprehension Vocabulary Phonics/Decoding Study Skills Listening, Speaking, Viewing, Representing	**Read Aloud: Realistic Fiction,** 282E "Beezus and Her Imagination" **Develop Visual Literacy,** 282 ☑ **Introduce Fact and Opinion,** 283A–283B **Teaching Chart 67** **Reteach, Practice, Extend,** 82 **Reading Strategy: Fact and Opinion,** 283 "Carmen Lomas Garza: Art for the Whole Family" Intervention Program	**Build Background,** 284A Develop Oral Language **Vocabulary,** 284B–284C *exist* *inspire* *reference* *image* *loft* *sketch* **Teaching Chart 68** Word Building Manipulative Cards **Reteach, Practice, Extend,** 83 **Read the Selection,** 284–293 ☑ **Fact and Opinion** ☑ **Summarize** **Genre: Autobiography,** 285 **Cultural Perspectives,** 288 Intervention Program
Curriculum Connections	Link **Works of Art,** 282	Link **Art,** 284A
Writing	**Writing Prompt:** Have you ever been to a dance performance? Describe the style of dance and what you enjoyed about the performance.	**Writing Prompt:** Think about Pat Cummings' unplanned trip to the ballet school. Write a paragraph about a time you went somewhere you didn't mean to go. **Journal Writing,** 293 Quick-Write
Grammar	**Introduce the Concept: Past and Future Tenses,** 297M Daily Language Activity 1. Last Friday I look at two books. looked 2. Yesterday I try to copy the art. tried 3. Last week I race home to paint. raced **Grammar Practice Book,** 71	**Teach the Concept: Past and Future Tenses,** 297M Daily Language Activity 1. Last Friday I order a book. ordered 2. Next Tuesday Joe mail the check. will mail 3. The box arrive tomorrow. will arrive **Grammar Practice Book,** 72
Spelling	**Pretest: Words with /ů/ and /yů/,** 297O **Spelling Practice Book,** 71, 72	**Explore the Pattern: Words with /ů/ and /yů/,** 297O **Spelling Practice Book,** 73

Intervention Program Available

Meeting Individual Needs

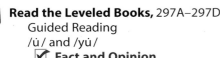

✔ = Skill Assessed in Unit Test

ⓘ Intervention Program Available

Read EVERY DAY

DAY 3 Read the Literature

Rereading for Fluency, 292

Story Questions and Activities, 294–295
- **Reteach, Practice, Extend,** 84

Study Skill, 296
- ✔ **Graphic Aids**
- **Teaching Chart 69**
- **Reteach, Practice, Extend,** 85

Test Power, 297

Read: **Read the Leveled Books,** 297A–297D
- Guided Reading
- /ù/ and /yù/
- ✔ **Fact and Opinion**
- ✔ **Instructional Vocabulary**

ⓘ Intervention Program

Activity: **Social Studies,** 286

Writing Prompt: Write about one picture you painted recently. Then write two sentences that tell about a picture you would like to paint.

Writing Process: Persuasive Writing, 297K
- Prewrite, Draft

Review and Practice: Past and Future Tenses, 297N

Daily Language Activity
1. Next week Pat visit us. will visit
2. Next Monday I ask her to sign my book. will ask
3. My dad paint the pictures a year ago. painted

Grammar Practice Book, 73

Practice and Extend: Words with /ù/ and /yù/, 297P
- **Spelling Practice Book,** 74

DAY 4 Build Skills

Read: **Read the Leveled Books and Self-Selected Books**

✔ **Review Fact and Opinion,** 297E–297F
- **Teaching Chart 70**
- **Reteach, Practice, Extend,** 86
- **Language Support,** 94

✔ **Review Summarize,** 297G–297H
- **Teaching Chart 71**
- **Reteach, Practice, Extend,** 87
- **Language Support,** 95

Minilessons, 287, 289, 291

ⓘ Intervention Program

Activity: **Science,** 290

Writing Prompt: Suppose that you wanted to illustrate a book. Write a letter to persuade the publisher to buy your illustrations.

Writing Process: Persuasive Writing, 297K, Revise

Meeting Individual Needs for Writing, 297L

Review and Practice: Past and Future Tenses, 297N

Daily Language Activity
1. Tomorrow Jean draw a picture. will draw
2. Yesterday I rub the crayon too hard. rubbed
3. Last week I study hard for my test. studied

Grammar Practice Book, 74

Proofread and Write: Words with /ù/ and /yù/, 297P
- **Spelling Practice Book,** 75

DAY 5 Build Skills

Read: **Read Self-Selected Books**

✔ **Review Suffixes,** 297I–297J
- **Teaching Chart 72**
- **Reteach, Practice, Extend,** 88
- **Language Support,** 96

Listening, Speaking, Viewing, Representing, 297L

Minilessons, 289, 291

Phonics Review, 287
- /ù/ and /yù/

Phonics/Phonemic Awareness Practice Book, 33–36

ⓘ Intervention Program

Activity: **Science,** 295

Writing Prompt: Write a letter to Pat Cummings explaining what you learned about her life and her work.

Writing Process: Persuasive Writing, 297K
- Edit/Proofread, Publish

Assess and Reteach: Past and Future Tenses, 297N

Daily Language Activity
1. Last time we trade pictures. traded
2. Yesterday Pat dab the paper with paint. dabbed
3. Next week we meet at the studio. will meet

Grammar Practice Book, 75, 76

Assess and Reteach: Words with /ù/ and /yù/, 297P
- **Spelling Practice Book,** 76

Link
Language Arts

Read Aloud

Beezus and Her Imagination

realistic fiction by Beverly Cleary

For Beezus Quimby, Miss Robbins's Friday afternoon art class at the recreation center is always something to look forward to. But Beezus becomes discouraged when she hears the day's assignment—to paint an imaginary animal. Her first try turns out to look like something real. But when Beezus decides to paint a second picture, she sees things in a much more imaginative way!

Beezus seized her brush and painted in another sky with bold, free strokes. Then she dipped her brush into green paint and started to outline a lizard on her paper. Let's see, what did a lizard look like? She could not remember. It didn't matter much, anyway—not for an imaginary animal. She had started the lizard with such brave, bold strokes that it took up most of the paper and looked more like a dragon.

Beezus promptly decided the animal was a dragon. Dragons breathed fire, but she did not have any orange paint, and she was so late in starting this picture that she didn't want to

Continued on page T3

Oral Comprehension

LISTENING AND SPEAKING Have students visualize Beezus painting as you read the story aloud. Ask:

- What problem did Beezus face as she began to paint?
- How did Beezus feel as she began to paint?

Now reread the story. Ask: How does Beezus describe the dragon? Why do Beezus's feelings about her painting change?

GENRE STUDY: REALISTIC FICTION Discuss realism and the use of details in the story.

- Point out that realistic fiction deals with characters, settings and events that could actually exist. Have students note the realistic elements in the story.
- Explain that Beezus's dragon comes from her imagination. Ask: Which aspects of the dragon are based in reality?
- Many of Beezus's ideas emerged as she worked. Ask: Which ideas emerged as solutions to artistic problems Beezus faced? Did her problem/solution seem realistic?

Activity Have students paint an imaginary animal with a partner and take turns adding details. Then have partners write a story using their imaginary animal as the main character. ▶ **Visual /Linguistic**

Develop Visual Literacy

Link
Works of Art

Stories in Art

It is a fact that this pastel drawing was made by the French artist Edgar Degas. Is it a good or bad drawing? That is a matter of opinion.

Look at the drawing. What can you tell about the dancers? How does the artist use line and shape to make them seem graceful? What colors does he use? What mood do they help to create? How?

Take the drawing as a whole. Do you think it is a good drawing? Give reasons to support your opinion.

Blue Dancers **by Edgar Degas**
Hermitage Museum, St. Petersburg, Russia

282

Objective: Distinguish Between Fact and Opinion

VIEWING This pastel drawing by Edgar Degas provides an intimate portrait of the world of ballet dancers. Give students a few moments to study the drawing. Afterward, ask: Why might the artist have chosen to show the dancers from an overhead perspective? Discuss the shapes and colors that they see. How does the blue create a mood in the drawing? How does it make them feel?

Read the page with students, encouraging individual interpretations of the drawing. Ask students to make distinctions between fact and opinion in the comments about the drawing.

For example:

- The dancers seem to be enjoying themselves. (opinion)
- The color blue is often used to create a quiet mood. (fact)
- The drawing is good because it makes the characters come alive. (opinion)

REPRESENTING Ask students to find a piece of music to which the dancers could be dancing. Have them consider music that is played at the ballet and will make the dancers seem poised and graceful.

Introduce Fact and Opinion

PREPARE

Make Statements of Fact and Opinion Have students tell what they know about a sport, such as soccer. Then ask them whether or not they like the sport.

TEACH

Define Fact and Opinion Tell students they have just made statements of fact and opinion. Statements of fact are those that can be verified, such as *Goalies use both their hands and feet*. Statements of opinion express feelings or ideas, such as *Soccer is the best game*. Explain that opinions often include words such as *I think, I feel,* and *probably*.

Choosing a Movie with Dad

A new movie theatre opened near my house. It had three screens and three new movies. I wanted to see a cartoon movie about pirates. I begged my dad to take me. I told him, "Everybody knows that cartoons make the best movies."

My dad said, "Bobby, what about the movie about a lost dog? That sounds more interesting to me."

I felt disappointed. Maybe the movie about the lost dog was good. But I thought a movie cartoon about pirates would be much better!

Teaching Chart 67

Read the Story and Model the Skill As you read **Teaching Chart 67** aloud, have students listen for sentences that are facts and those that are opinions. Model identifying a fact.

MODEL The first sentence presents a statement that could be a fact: *A new movie theatre opened near my house.* We can prove whether or not that is true.

Distinguish Between Fact and Opinion Have volunteers underline the sentences in the first paragraph that are facts. Then have them circle the sentence that is an opinion.

TESTED OBJECTIVES

Students will distinguish between statements of fact and opinion.

Skills Finder

Fact and Opinion

Introduce	283A-B
Review	297E-F, 333A-B, 359E-F
Test	Unit 3

LANGUAGE SUPPORT

ESL Have children take turns finishing opinion statements, such as *I think* _____ , *I feel* _____. Model examples for students and then have them make up their own. For example: *I think baseball is fun. I feel strongly that school lunches should be free. Perhaps the sun will shine today.*

TEACHING TIP

SUPPORTED INFERENCES
Discuss a *supported inference*, a type of statement that is like an opinion. Explain: Support statements based on firsthand experience or on the text make inferences more believable. Share an example.

The movie *Pirates* must be good because it won two Academy Awards. Besides, everyone I know who's seen *Pirates* has liked it a lot.

PRACTICE

Create a Fact and Opinion Chart

ONE

Have students reread the story and then use a Fact and Opinion chart like the one below to record the sentences that state facts and those that state opinions.

▶ **Linguistic/Logical**

FACTS	OPINIONS
A new movie theatre opened.	Cartoons make the best movies.
The theatre had three screens.	A movie about a lost dog is more interesting.
The theatre had three new movies.	A movie cartoon about pirates could be better.

ASSESS/CLOSE

Make Statements of Fact and Statements of Opinion

Ask students to make a statement of fact about cartoon movies they know about. Then have them make a statement of opinion by telling what they think about the movies.

ALTERNATE TEACHING STRATEGY

FACT AND OPINION

For a different approach to teaching this skill, see page T64.

Intervention Skills

Intervention Guide, for direct instruction and extra practice with fact and opinion

Meeting Individual Needs for Comprehension

EASY

Name________ Date______ **Reteach 82**

Fact and Opinion

A **fact** is a statement that can be proven in some way. An **opinion** is a statement of a person's belief that may not be able to be proven.

Read each story. Then write examples of facts or opinions from the story.

In the United States, there are three branches of government. The legislative branch is the Congress, which is made up of the Senate and the House of Representatives. The judicial branch is headed by the Supreme Court. The executive branch is headed by the President. This three-part system of government is the best in the world because no one branch has total power.

1. Write two facts. Possible response: In the United States, there are three branches of government. The executive branch is headed by the President.
2. Write one opinion. Possible response: This three-branch system of government is the best system in the world.

There are over 200 bones in the human body. The bones are joined together to make a skeleton. The bones help us stand and protect organs like the heart, lungs, and brain. Ben is convinced that his bones are unbreakable.

3. Write two facts. Possible response: There are over 200 bones in the human body. The bones are joined together to make a skeleton.
4. Write one opinion. Ben is convinced that his bones are unbreakable.

4 Book 4/Unit 3 **Pat Cummings: My Story**

At Home: Have students read an article in the newspaper and identify one fact and one opinion.

82

Reteach, 82

ON-LEVEL

Name________ Date______ **Practice 82**

Fact and Opinion

A **fact** is a statement that can be proven. An **opinion** is a statement that tells what a person thinks about something. Read the following passage. Then write whether you think each underlined statement is a fact or an opinion. Explain the reason for your decision.

Today, people use gas or electricity to cook food and heat their homes. Long ago, people built fires in their stoves to cook and to heat their homes. When the fire went out, the ashes were shoveled into an ashcan and carried outside. Ashcans were useful, but I can't imagine that anyone thought they were beautiful. Therefore, it surprised many people when in the early 1900s, a group of painters called themselves Ashcan school artists. They called themselves Ashcan artists because they painted realistic scenes of poor people, factories, and crowded streets. If you were to see this art, you would probably just love it.

Statement	Fact or Opinion	Explanation of Decision
1. Today people use gas or electricity to heat their stoves for cooking food.	Fact	This is a well-known fact that can be proven.
2. Ashcans were useful, but I can't imagine that anyone thought they were beautiful.	Opinion	It is one person's opinion and can't be proven true.
3. Therefore, it surprised many people when in the early 1900s, a group of painters called themselves Ashcan School artists.	Opinion	It is an opinion and can't be proven true.
4. They called themselves Ashcan artists because they painted realistic scenes of poor people, factories, and crowded streets.	Fact	It can be proven.

8 Book 4/Unit 3 **Pat Cummings: My Story**

At Home: Have students locate a fact and an opinion from a newspaper or magazine.

82

Practice, 82

CHALLENGE

Name________ Date______ **Extend 82**

Fact and Opinion

Some sentences are **facts**. That is, you can check to prove that they are true. Other sentences are **opinions**. They tell what a person feels or believes. You cannot prove that an opinion is true or false.

Read the four sentences below. Choose the sentence that is a fact. Explain your thinking.

1. Leonardo da Vinci is the greatest painter in history.
2. In addition to painting, Leonardo da Vinci drew plans for many inventions.
3. Leonardo da Vinci's most beautiful painting is *Mona Lisa*.
4. Some of Leonardo da Vinci's paintings have too many shadows.

Sentence 2 is a fact. You can check reference books and museums to find out if it is true.

Read the four sentences below. Choose the sentence that is an opinion. Explain your thinking.

5. Pottery is made by shaping and firing clay.
6. Pottery was first made in Egypt and the Near East.
7. The prettiest vases are made on a potter's wheel.
8. Applying glaze is one way to decorate a piece of pottery.

Sentence 7 is an opinion. Some people may believe this , but others may not. There is no way to prove that a potter's wheel makes the prettiest vases.

Book 4/Unit 3 **Pat Cummings: My Story**

At Home: Tell students to identify statements made during family conversations as facts or opinions.

82

Extend, 82

TESTED OBJECTIVES

Students will distinguish between statements of fact and opinion.

Apply Fact and Opinion

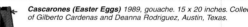

READING STRATEGY

Fact and Opinion

Develop a strategy for distinguishing fact from opinion.

1. **Does a statement tell what someone thinks or feels?** If so, it is a statement of opinion.
2. **Look for clue words,** such as *think* or *feel.*
3. **Determine whether a statement can be proved.** If it can, it is a statement of fact.
4. **Think about the author's choices.** Why did the author include facts as well as opinions?

283

READING STRATEGY

Carmen Lomas Garza: Art for the Whole Family

Carmen Lomas Garza was born in 1948 and grew up in Kingsville, Texas. Her childhood in Kingsville is the subject of many of her paintings.

Lomas Garza has called her paintings *monitos. Monitos* tell a story without using words. Most of Lomas Garza's artworks do just that. They show a moment in time spent with family and friends. They tell about traditions, culture, and people.

Many fans feel that Lomas Garza's best work is in her books for children. The books contain *monitos* along with short passages in Spanish and English.

Family Pictures/Cuadros de familia presents ordinary days and special days from the artist's childhood. *In My Family/En mi familia* continues the tale.

Cascarones (Easter Eggs) *1989, gouache. 15 x 20 inches. Collection of Gilberto Cardenas and Deanna Rodriguez, Austin, Texas.*

Magic Windows/Ventanas mágicas uses the Mexican art of cut paper to tell about Mexican-American customs and beliefs.

Children like the bright colors and simple lines of Lomas Garza's art. Adults admire her painting as a celebration of the richness of Mexican culture. Carmen Lomas Garza is an artist the whole family can love.

Autoretrato (Self Portrait) *1980, gouache. 8 1/2" x 7 1/2 inches. Collection of the artist.*

PREVIEW Have students preview "Carmen Lomas Garza: Art for the Whole Family." Point out that any discussion of art is likely to include the author's opinion as well as facts. Movie and book reviews are also examples of writing that include opinions as well as fact.

SET PURPOSES Ask students to apply what they have learned about fact and opinion as they read the passage.

APPLY THE STRATEGY Discuss the strategy for distinguishing fact from opinion in a selection and help students to apply it to this passage.

- Ask: Is this a statement of someone's belief or impression? The first sentence of the third paragraph is an example.
- Watch for clue words that indicate the author's opinion. For example, the word *love* in the last sentence may signal an opinion.
- Ask: Is this a statement that can be proved or checked? For example, the place where the artist lived as a child can be checked.
- Think: Why did the author use facts and opinions here?

Activity Have each student create a Fact and Opinion chart for the passage.

Build Background

Link
Art

Concept: Children's Art

Evaluate Prior Knowledge

CONCEPT: CHILDREN'S ART Getting children involved in art—either as makers of art or as consumers—is a theme uniting these selections. Have students brainstorm and discuss types of art they may have experienced. Ask them what they liked about those experiences.

ART WHEELS Have students think of four examples of art works from different media and place them in a concept wheel. Then have students fill in the center of the wheel by brainstorming what those art works might have in common. ▶ **Logical/Visual**

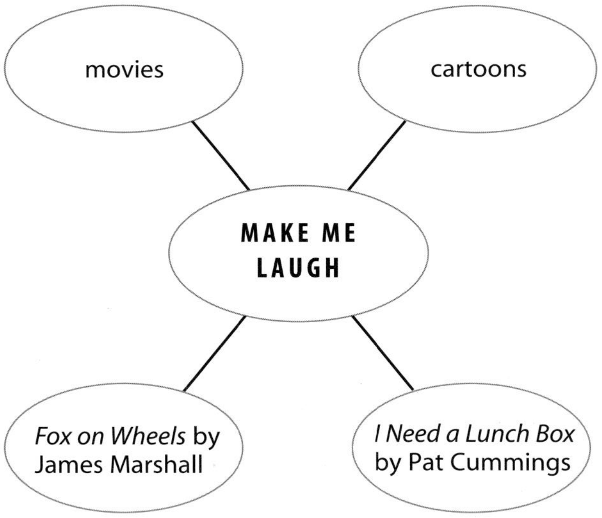

Graphic Organizer 29

WRITE CAPTIONS Have partners choose a picture book and write captions for several of the pictures. Invite partners to exchange captions with another pair. Have the new pair look through the book and try to match captions with pictures.

WRITING PARTNERS

Develop Oral Language

DISCUSS ART FOR CHILDREN Display examples of children's art, such as bright pictures, funny cartoons, pictures of favorite storybook characters, and so on. Place a number over each picture. Ask each student to write these phrases on a piece of paper: *Colorful pictures, Funny pictures,* and *Imaginary pictures*. Next, have students use the numbers to sort the pictures into these three categories.

ESL

Then ask students to share and compare their lists with a partner. Suggest that each person describe what it is in each picture that makes it colorful, funny, or imaginary. Then have each one choose a favorite picture and tell why they like it. Prompt them with a sentence starter such as, "I like this picture because…"

Anthology and Leveled Books

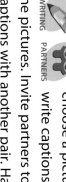

TEACHING TIP

MANAGEMENT Provide time for students to gather their favorite illustrated books of poetry, fiction, and nonfiction from home or from the school library. Use students' examples to complete the activity on this page.

Try to encourage students needing help developing Oral Language facility to note any relationships they see between art works they like.

LANGUAGE SUPPORT

See the **Language Support Book**, pages 89–92, for teaching suggestions for Build Background.

TESTED **OBJECTIVES**

Students will use context clues to determine the meanings of vocabulary words.

Definitions

exist (p. 291) to be found or to be real

image (p. 292) a picture or other likeness of a person or thing

reference (p. 291) a source of information, or aid

sketch (p. 288) to make a rough, quick drawing

loft (p. 289) the upper floor, room, or space in a building

inspire (p. 293) to stir the mind, feelings, or imagination

Story Words

These words from the selection may be unfamiliar. Before students read, have them check the meaning and pronunciation of each word in the Glossary, beginning on page 756, or in a dictionary.

- tutu, p. 285
- toeshoe, p. 285
- ballerina, p. 286
- editor, p. 288
- newsletter, p. 293
- portfolio, p. 293

exist
image
reference
sketch
loft
inspire

Vocabulary

Teach Vocabulary in Context

Identify Vocabulary Words Display **Teaching Chart 68** and read the passage with students. Volunteers can take turns circling the vocabulary words and underlining the other words that help them figure out the meanings.

Personal Computers and Art

1. Personal computers did not exist until about twenty-five years ago. **2.** Before their invention, a writer like Pat Cummings could not push a button and have a picture or an image come up on a computer screen. **3.** If she wanted to draw a tiger, she would have to look at a picture book or encyclopedia for reference. **4.** Or she would have to draw or sketch an object from memory. **5.** Today, from her loft apartment overlooking the Brooklyn Bridge, Pat can find about anything she wants. **6.** For Pat and millions like her, the personal computer offers a whole world of information to inform, excite, and inspire the imagination.

Teaching Chart 68

Discuss Meanings Ask questions like these to help clarify word meanings:

- Do koalas exist outside of Australia?
- Did you see your own image in the mirror this morning?
- What is a type of reference book?
- What materials can you use to sketch something?
- How would you describe a loft?
- What would most likely inspire you to draw a picture—a flower, a sunset, a monster, or a person you like?

Activities

Practice

Demonstrate Word Meaning (GROUP) Have volunteers choose a vocabulary card and draw a picture that gives clues to its meaning. Invite other students to study the picture clues and guess the word. ▶ **Visual/Linguistic**

sketch **image** **loft**

Word Building Manipulative Cards

Write Context Sentences (WRITING) Have students write sentences with one of the vocabulary words, cut the sentence into a few parts, exchange sentences with partners and look for context clues to help them reassemble the pieces.
▶ **Linguistic/Kinesthetic**

Assess Vocabulary

Use Words in Context (GROUP) Have students work in small groups to create a six-panel cartoon strip about the life of a famous person. Tell them to use the vocabulary words in speech balloons. Students can share their cartoon strips with the class.

SPELLING/VOCABULARY CONNECTIONS

See Spelling Challenge Words, pages 2970–297P.

LANGUAGE SUPPORT

See the Language Support Book, pages 89–92, for teaching suggestions for Vocabulary.

Vocabulary PuzzleMaker

Provides vocabulary activities

Meeting Individual Needs for Vocabulary

EASY

Name______ Date______ **Reteach 83**

Vocabulary

Complete each definition by writing the correct word on the line provided.

exist	image	inspire	loft	reference	sketch

1. A large room or open space on the upper floor of a building is a loft
2. A picture of something in the mind is an image
3. To make a quick drawing is to sketch
4. Something used for information is a reference
5. To stir the imagination is to inspire
6. To live is to exist

6

Reteach 84

Story Comprehension

Write the answers to these questions about "Pat Cummings: My Story." For help, you can look back at the story.

1. What was the first thing Pat Cummings drew that people could recognize? ballerinas
2. Where does Pat Cummings get her ideas? She gets ideas from things she sees, from traveling, and from dreams.
3. What does Pat Cummings like to draw? faces and things from her imagination
4. How does Pat Cummings go about drawing people? She uses old or new photographs or uses friends and family as models.
5. How did Tom Feelings inspire Cummings? He taught her many things about illustrating children's books. He taught her illustrators have to help each other. Looking at his work inspires Cummings.

At Home: Have students make a simple crossword puzzle using some of the vocabulary words. Book 4/Unit 3 Pat Cummings: My Story 5

83–84

Reteach, 83

ON-LEVEL

Name______ Date______ **Practice 83**

Vocabulary

Fill in the blank with the correct vocabulary word from the list.

exist	image	inspire	loft	reference	sketch

1. A painting or photograph might be the image of a person or animal.
2. One kind of reference book is an encyclopedia.
3. You can sketch a picture with a pencil and do a detailed drawing later.
4. A beautiful painting can inspire you to draw or paint.
5. Beautiful paintings by very young people do exist.
6. Some artists work in a big room called a loft.

83 At Home: Have students write sentences using each vocabulary word. Book 4/Unit 3 Pat Cummings: My Story 6

Practice, 83

ON-LEVEL

Making Art

Kamal's mom, a professional photographer, knows how to capture the *image* of a wild bird with her camera. Her photographs *inspire* Kamal to do the same thing. Looking up birds in a *reference* book, Kamal *sketches* the bird that he plans to photograph. Climbing into the hay *loft*, Kamal waits patiently until he sees a bird he has studied. It is stunning. Kamal captures the bird's image with his camera. People who will see his photograph will be amazed that this bird does *exist* locally.

1. What *image* does Kamal's mom know how to capture with her camera? The image of a wild bird
2. What *inspires* Kamal to take a picture of a local bird? He sees his mother taking a picture with her camera and he wants to try it too.
3. Why does Kamal use a *reference* book? He looks up birds and selects one; then he sketches it to help him recognize it.
4. Where does Kamal go to wait for the bird? Up in the hay loft.
5. What does Kamal find interesting about what his mother does for a living? Answers will vary, but may include that Kamal and his mother both like photography and photographing nature.

5 Book 4/Unit 3 Pat Cummings: My Story At Home: Have students describe their experience of using a camera. 83a

Practice, 83a
Take-Home Story

CHALLENGE

Name______ Date______ **Extend 83**

Vocabulary

exist	image	inspire
loft	reference	sketch

1. Which three vocabulary words are you most likely to find in a story about drawing? image; sketch; inspire
2. List four other words you might expect to find in a story about drawing. Answers will vary. Possible answers: pencil; easel; figure; line; shadow

Extend 84

Story Comprehension

Pat Cummings' interest in drawing began when she was a little girl. It eventually became her career. Turn Pat's story into a television interview. Write a list of questions a reporter might ask her. Find sentences from the story that answer the questions. Share your questions with the class. Take turns being the reporter and giving the answers.

83–84 At Home: Have students write about their interests and what they'd like to do for work as an adult. Book 4/Unit 3 Pat Cummings: My Story

Extend, 83

Comprehension

Prereading Strategies

PREVIEW AND PREDICT Have students preview the story, looking for clues about what Pat Cummings does for a living.

- Who is telling the story?
- What do you think you will learn about Pat Cummings?
- What kind of story is this? (It is an autobiography—a story about a person's life told by that person.) ***Genre***

Have students record their predictions about the story.

PREDICTIONS	WHAT HAPPENED
The story is about Pat Cummings's life.	
The story tells what she likes to draw and why.	

SET PURPOSES What do students want to find out about Pat Cummings from the story? For example:

- What inspires Pat Cummings to draw?
- What books has she written?

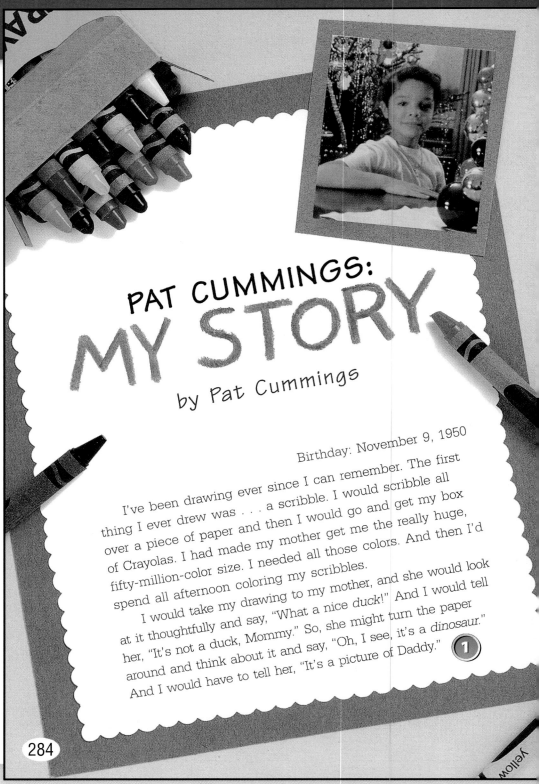

PAT CUMMINGS: MY STORY

by Pat Cummings

Birthday: November 9, 1950

I've been drawing ever since I can remember. The first thing I ever drew was . . . a scribble. I would scribble all over a piece of paper and then I would go and get my box of Crayolas. I had made my mother get me the really huge, fifty-million-color size. I needed all those colors. And then I'd spend all afternoon coloring my scribbles.

I would take my drawing to my mother, and she would look at it thoughtfully and say, "What a nice *duck*!" And I would tell her, "It's not a duck, Mommy." So, she might turn the paper around and think about it and say, "Oh, I see, it's a *dinosaur*." And I would have to tell her, "It's a picture of Daddy." 1

284

Meeting Individual Needs • Grouping Suggestions for Strategic Reading

EASY

Read Together Have students follow along as you read the story aloud or use the **Listening Library.** Pause as necessary and check students' comprehension. Have students use the Fact and Opinion chart to record statements of fact and opinion. Comprehension and Intervention prompts offer additional help.

ON-LEVEL

Guided Instruction Use the Comprehension questions to prompt students as they read the selection together or on their own. Have students use the Fact and Opinion chart to record statements made by Pat Cummings.

CHALLENGE

Read Independently Remind students that distinguishing between fact and opinion can help them better understand the story. Have them complete a Fact and Opinion chart as they read the selection on their own. After reading, students can highlight the more important statements and use them to summarize the selection.

It didn't take long to realize that nobody really knew what the pictures were supposed to be. But my mother would put them up on the refrigerator door, and that always made me feel good.

The first thing I remember drawing that people could recognize was the result of an adventure I had when I was about five years old.

My father was in the army and so my family moved every three years or so. At that time we lived in Kaiserslautern, Germany. My older sister, Linda, and I had decided to play outside and had taken lots of our toys and spread them out on the grass. After a while, she told me to watch all the toys while she went inside for a minute. She didn't come back.

I was getting very bored all by myself when a little bus came along and stopped at the corner. I got up, ran straight across the grass, and hopped on! I didn't know who the girls on the bus were or where they were headed and I certainly didn't speak any German, but the doors closed and we were off. After a while, we stopped at a small building and everyone got off the bus. So I got off the bus. They all ran into the building. So I ran in right behind them. Then they all got into tutus and toeshoes—it was a ballet school! (2)

The girls were dancing around and doing stretches, so I just danced around and tried to do whatever they did. The teacher looked at me like I had just landed from Mars. All the girls were older than I was. When class ended, the teacher pinned a note on my blouse that said, "Please don't send her back until she's at least eight."

285

Comprehension

☑ **Apply Fact and Opinion**

☑ **Apply Summarize**

STRATEGIC READING Before we begin reading, let's prepare our Fact and Opinion charts so we can organize what Pat Cummings says into story notes.

FACTS	OPINIONS

(1) **FACT AND OPINION** When was Pat Cummings born? (November 9, 1950) Is this a fact or opinion? (fact) When Mom says "Pat's drawing is a nice duck!" is this a fact or opinion? (opinion)

(2) Why did Pat get on the bus? (because she was left by herself and she was bored) Where did the bus take her? (to a ballet school) ***Cause and Effect***

LANGUAGE SUPPORT

A blackline master of the Fact and Opinion chart is available in the **Language Support Book.**

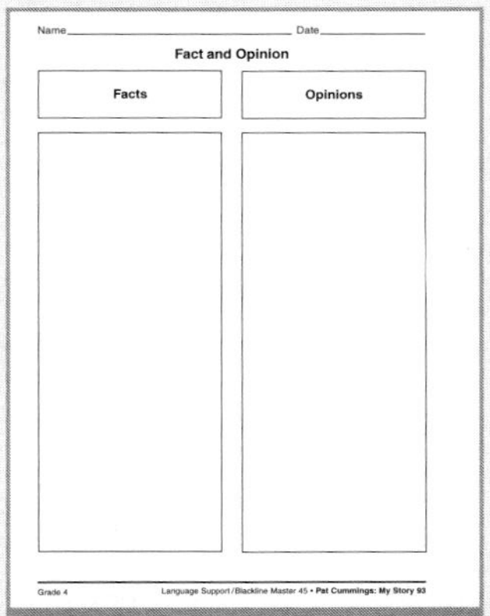

LANGUAGE SUPPORT, 93

Genre

Autobiography

Explain that an *autobiography* is a biography of a person told by himself or herself. The prefix *auto-* means "self" or "same." An autobiography:

- tells about the life of the person writing it.
- usually presents events in time order.
- focuses only on significant aspects of the writer's life.

Activity After students read Cummings's story, have them list ways she gets ideas for her drawings. Discuss why she may have used the interview format for this autobiographical piece.

Comprehension

(3) Act out what happened when Pat got bored and rode the bus. *Role-Play*

(4) **FACT AND OPINION** Reread the second paragraph on page 286. Which two statements are opinions? Explain.

MODEL Most of the statements in the second paragraph are facts. They can be proved. Pat Cummings drew ballerinas, got paid 5 cents or 10 cents for her drawings, and traded her drawings for things she wanted. But the statement, "That was as good as money" strikes me as opinion. Can the statement be proved? Could I buy my lunch with a candy bar? The statement that drawing "could be good business" sounds like an opinion, too. Everyone might not agree with that idea.

Let's add these statements to our chart.

FACTS	OPINIONS
Pat Cummings was born November 9, 1950.	Being paid with candy is as good as being paid with money.
	Drawing is a good business.

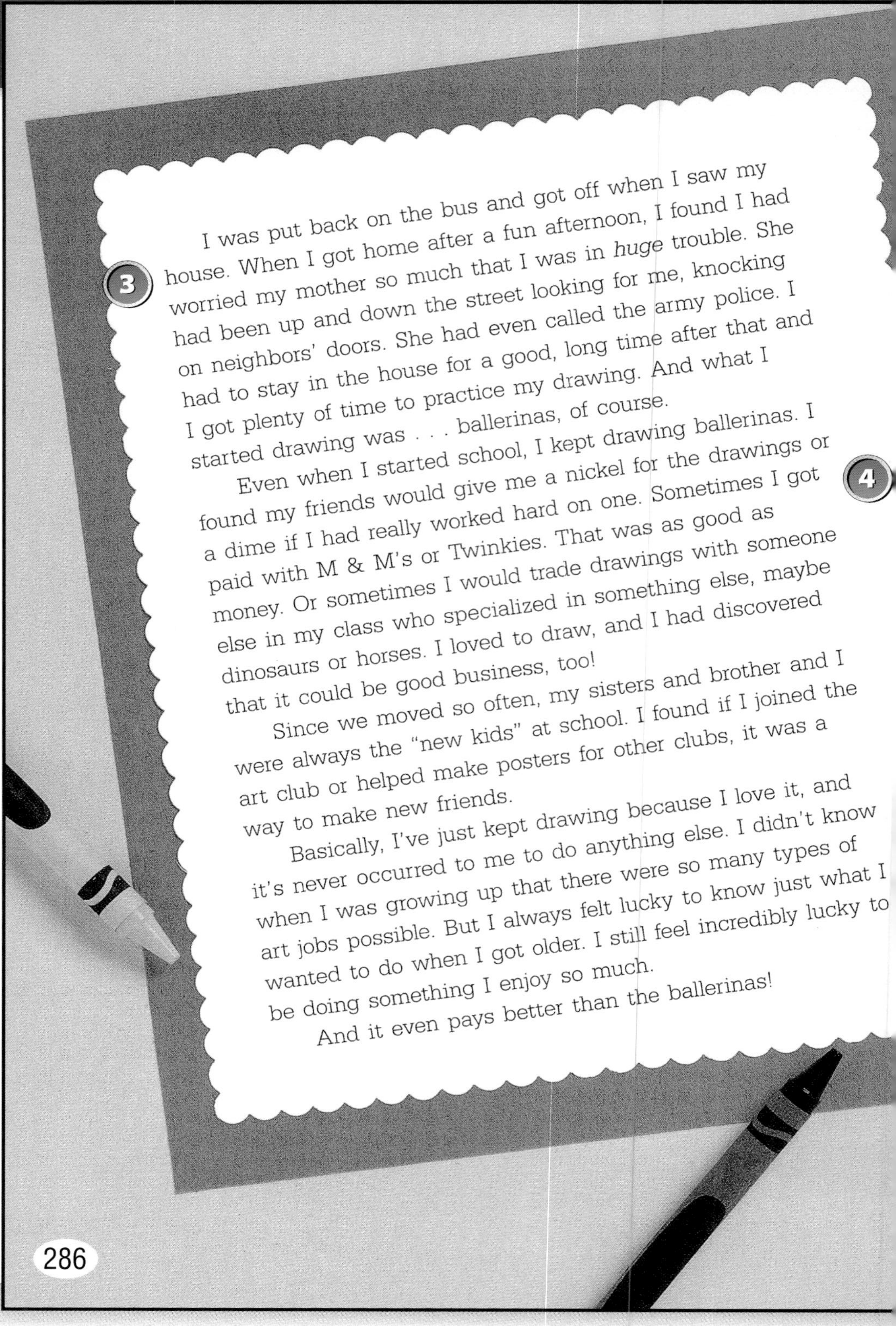

(3) I was put back on the bus and got off when I saw my house. When I got home after a fun afternoon, I found I had worried my mother so much that I was in *huge* trouble. She had been up and down the street looking for me, knocking on neighbors' doors. She had even called the army police. I had to stay in the house for a good, long time after that and I got plenty of time to practice my drawing. And what I started drawing was . . . ballerinas, of course.

Even when I started school, I kept drawing ballerinas. I found my friends would give me a nickel for the drawings or a dime if I had really worked hard on one. Sometimes I got paid with M & M's or Twinkies. That was as good as money. Or sometimes I would trade drawings with someone else in my class who specialized in something else, maybe dinosaurs or horses. I loved to draw, and I had discovered that it could be good business, too! (4)

Since we moved so often, my sisters and brother and I were always the "new kids" at school. I found if I joined the art club or helped make posters for other clubs, it was a way to make new friends.

Basically, I've just kept drawing because I love it, and it's never occurred to me to do anything else. I didn't know when I was growing up that there were so many types of art jobs possible. But I always felt lucky to know just what I wanted to do when I got older. I still feel incredibly lucky to be doing something I enjoy so much.

And it even pays better than the ballerinas!

286

Activity

Cross Curricular: Social Studies

MAP SKILLS Display a world map. Explain that when children's parents are in the army, like Pat's father, their families might travel the world.

RESEARCH AND INQUIRY: Have students use an atlas to:

- locate where they live in the U. S.
- locate Germany.
- locate the town of Kaiserslautern, where Pat Cummings was living.

▶ **Spatial**

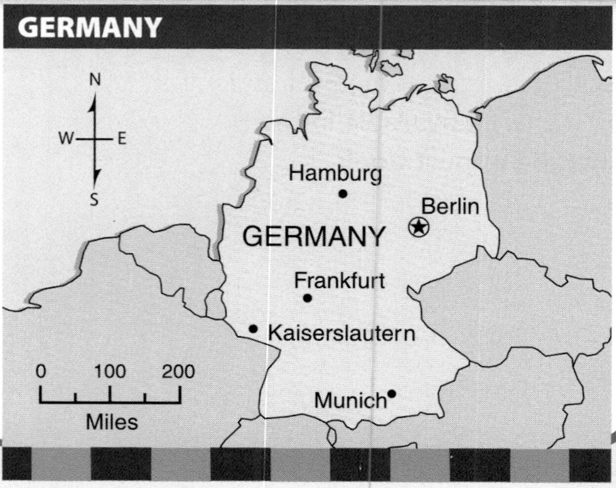

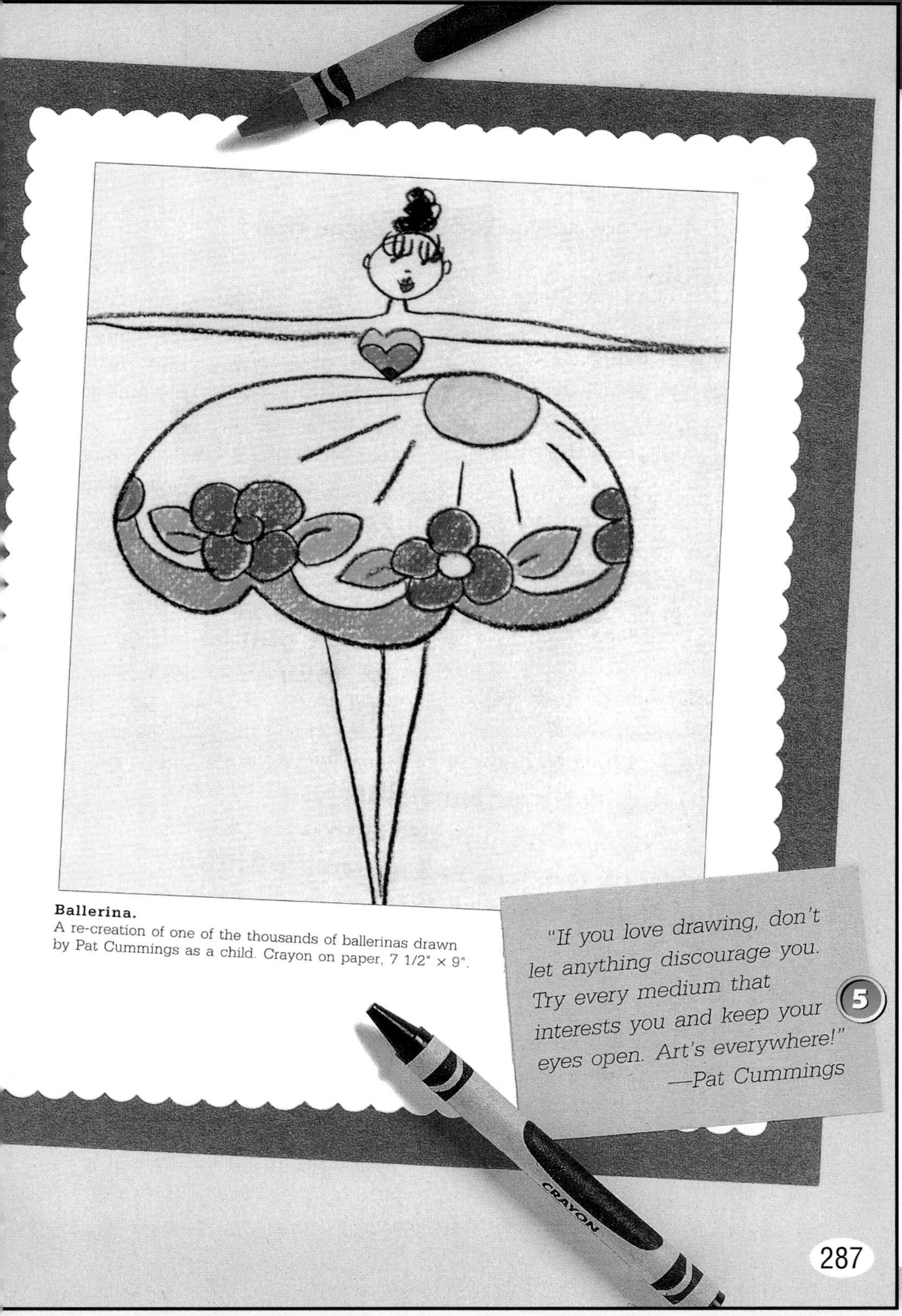

Ballerina.
A re-creation of one of the thousands of ballerinas drawn by Pat Cummings as a child. Crayon on paper, 7 1/2" × 9".

> "If you love drawing, don't let anything discourage you. Try every medium that interests you and keep your eyes open. Art's everywhere!"
> —Pat Cummings

5

287

Comprehension

5 **SUMMARIZE** To help us understand the story, let's summarize, or say in a few sentences, what we have learned about Pat Cummings so far.

MODEL: I know a summary should be brief and only have the most important information. So far, I have read that Pat Cummings has been drawing since she was a child. She started off drawing ballerinas, then moved on to other subjects. Now, as an adult, she makes a living from her illustrations.

 MULTIPLE-MEANING WORDS Read the paragraph on page 287. What is one meaning for the word *medium* on page 287? What do you think the word *medium* means in this sentence? *Semantic Cues*

Minilesson

REVIEW/MAINTAIN

/ü/ and /yü/

Have students find and say the words *put*, *good*, and *would* on page 286.

• Ask students what vowel sound these words have in common. (/ü/)

• Ask how the (/ü/) is spelled in each word. (u, oo, ou)

• Then say the words *fury* and *secure*. Have students identify the vowel sound these words have in common and the spellings of each. (/yü/ ; u, u-e)

Activity Have students brainstorm a list of words that contain /ü/ or /yü/. Have students check their responses in the dictionary.

PREVENTION/INTERVENTION

MULTIPLE-MEANING WORDS
Invite volunteers to use the word *medium* in a sentence. Students will most likely use the meaning "middle position or condition." Then have students read the quote on page 287. Point out that the word *medium* has a different meaning in this context.

Have students look for clues, such as *drawing* and *art*, to help them figure out the meaning of *medium*. (a material or technique used as a means of artistic expression) Then have them double check the meaning in the dictionary. *Semantic Cues*

Comprehension

6 **FACT AND OPINION** When Pat Cummings says "Your senses seem a little sharper," is she stating a fact or an opinion? (opinion) What word tells you the statement is something she thinks? *(seem)*

7 **SUMMARIZE** In one sentence, tell how Pat Cummings gets her ideas. (She gets ideas from places she goes, from her dreams, and when she's doing something else such as swimming or reading.)

SELF-MONITORING STRATEGY

SEARCH FOR CLUES Searching for clues in the text can help a reader understand the meaning of unfamiliar words.

MODEL When I see the word *aerial*, I'm not sure what it means. So I look for clues in the sentences before and after the word. I see the words *flying* and *views* being used in the same paragraph, so I can figure out that the word *aerial* means "high in the air."

1 Where do you get your ideas from?

Sometimes I get ideas from things I see around me, cloud formations or clothes people wear or things I've seen when I travel. One thing I really like about traveling to places where you don't speak or understand the language is that you usually look harder at things and see more. Your senses seem a little sharper. **6**

I also get ideas from my dreams, which are usually pretty entertaining. I have great flying dreams sometimes, and that is why I usually put aerial views in my books. I'm always so disappointed to wake up and find I can't really fly, but drawing a scene from that perspective gives me back a bit of the feeling I have in the dreams.

Sometimes, ideas hit me smack in the head when I'm doing something like swimming or reading, or when I'm halfway through a drawing. Then, if I'm smart, I'll stop and write them down or sketch what I saw in my imagination. I have even jumped out of bed to paint at three in the morning because an idea won't let me sleep. **7**

2 What is a normal day like for you?

I don't have any normal days because every job is different. Some days I meet with my editor, some days I get up early and work all day. Sometimes I work all night. Some days I teach a class at a local college. And sometimes I'm traveling to schools and libraries around the country. I work just about every day, and I work most of the time I'm home. If I have a deadline I am trying to meet, I might not leave the house for days at a

288

CULTURAL PERSPECTIVES

ARCHITECTURAL LANDMARKS
Discuss with students the significance of the Statue of Liberty, explaining that it was a gift from France in 1886. Explain that other countries also have historical landmarks—for instance, the Eiffel Tower in France and the pyramids in Egypt.

Activity Have pairs research famous statues and buildings in other countries and then create a chart to record their discoveries.
▶ **Interpersonal/Visual**

Country	Landmark
United States	Statue of Liberty
Egypt	Pyramids
Peru	Machu Picchu
France	Eiffel Tower

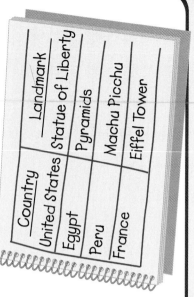

time. I'll work until I'm sleepy, sleep until I wake up, and start again. Usually, I do try to go to the gym, and I might go to the movies to reward myself for finishing a page. There are usually thirty-two pages in a book. That can get to be a lot of movies.

3 Where do you work?

I live and work in a big loft in beautiful downtown Brooklyn, New York. If I look out of my back windows, I see the Statue of Liberty. Looking out of the window near my desk, I see the Brooklyn Bridge. It's great on the Fourth of July! There are fifteen windows and five skylights, so there's plenty of sunlight and, sometimes, moonlight.

My drawing table, desk, shelves, and filing cabinets are on one side of the loft, and my husband's work area is right across from mine. The whole place is one big, open space that we are always working on. (8)

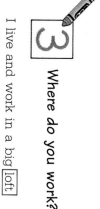

289

LANGUAGE SUPPORT

ESL Discuss the meanings of the words *loft, skylights,* and *drawing table*. Explain that a loft can be space just below the roof of a cabin or barn, or it can refer to the upper floor of a building or warehouse. Have students identify the two words in the compound word *skylight* to help identify its meaning. Lead students to conclude that a drawing table must be large so that an artist has plenty of room to draw illustrations. If possible, show pictures of these three objects. Then invite students to draw and label a picture of what they think Pat Cummings's loft looks like based on what they have read.

Comprehension

(8) **FACT AND OPINION** Read the answer Pat Cummings gives about where she works. What sentence gives an opinion? *(It's great on the Fourth of July!)*

TEACHING TIP

INTERVIEW **Point out that this selection has two sections. In the first half Pat Cummings gives a brief narrative account of how she became an artist. In the second half, she "interviews" herself. Point out that most interviews involve one person asking questions of another. Have students write out an "interview" with themselves designed to give a reader an idea of who they are.**

Minilesson

REVIEW/MAINTAIN

Root Words

Review with students that a root is a base word to which other word parts may be added. Understanding the meaning of a root word can help you figure out the meaning of an unfamiliar word.

- Ask students to find *formations* on page 288. Write it on the board, then ask a volunteer to circle the root word. *(form)*
- Discuss the meaning of *form* (*shape*; to give something shape), then try to figure out what *formation* means. (something that has been shaped)

Activity Have students look through the selection and make a list of long, difficult words that have root words. Volunteers may teach a word from their list to the class.

Comprehension

9 **FACT AND OPINION** Which two sentences in the second paragraph are facts about Pat's cat Cash? (She is on the cover of *Storm in the Night*. She comes when she's called, sits if you tell her to, and fetches if you throw her a toy.) Which statement is an opinion? (Cash is very smart.) Let's add these statements to our chart.

FACTS	OPINIONS
Pat Cummings was born November 9, 1950.	Being paid with candy is as good as being paid with money.
Cash is on the cover of *Storm in the Night.*	Drawing is a good business.
The cat comes when she's called, sits, and fetches.	Cash is very smart.

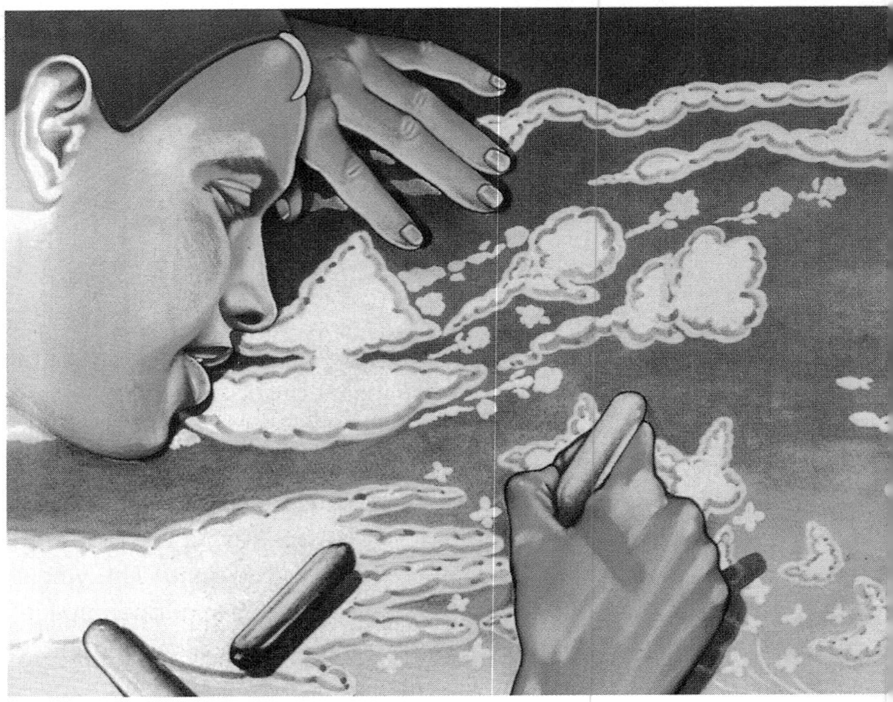

4 Do you have any children? Any pets?

We don't have any children, but we have talked about trying to find a twelve-year-old who likes to do dishes.

We have a cat named Cash who is very smart. She is on the cover of *Storm in the Night*. She comes when she's called, sits if you tell her to, and fetches if you throw her toy. I think she might be a dog. 9

290

Activity

Cross Curricular: Science

CATS Share the following cat facts:

- Cats communicate with over 60 sounds from a purr to a caterwaul.
- Because cats' eyes reflect light, cats see better than humans in dim light.

RESEARCH AND INQUIRY Have students research information about cats, and prepare a visual display. ▶ **Spatial**

interNET CONNECTION Students can learn more about cats by visiting ***www/mhschool.com/reading***

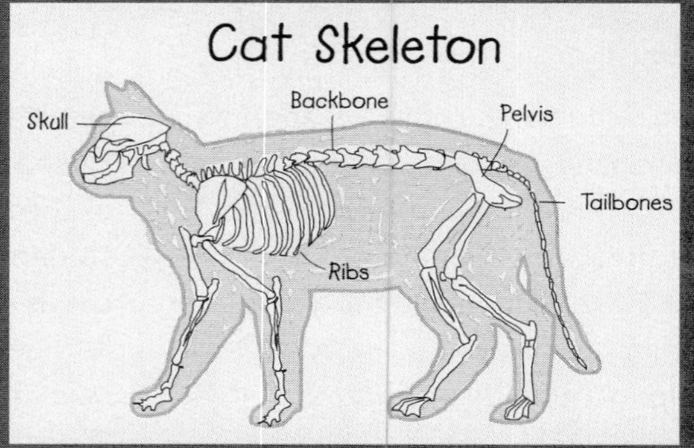

C.L.O.U.D.S. 1986.
Airbrush, watercolor, and pencil, 15 1/2" × 10".
Published by Lothrop, Lee & Shepard Books.

5 What do you enjoy drawing the most?

People I know and faces in general. There is so much going on in a person's face. I like fantasy, too . . . drawing things that only exist in the imagination. (10)

6 Do you ever put people you know in your pictures?

Definitely. Sometimes I do it to surprise the person. I might use old family photos or take new ones to use as reference. I draw my husband, Chuku, a lot. He's just about the only one who will pose for me

291

Comprehension

(10) Pat Cummings says people are what she enjoys drawing most. What do you think this says about her? What kind of person do you think she is? (Sample answer: I think Pat must be very friendly. She's an artist, so she's probably very observant. I'd say she likes people.) ***Character***

P/I **PHONICS/DECODING** Can you find two words on page 290 that end in *-hes*? Say these words. What do you notice about these two words? (The base words end in *-sh* and *-ch*; they both have two syllables.) ***Graphophonic Cues***

P/I PREVENTION/INTERVENTION

PHONICS/DECODING Write *dishes* and *fetches* on the board. Ask students how the two words are alike. (They both end in *es;* they both have two syllables.) Remind students that for base words ending in *sh, ch, x, s,* or *z,* they need to add *es* to make the words plural.

Brainstorm with students other words that end in *sh, ch, x, s,* or *z.* Then have them add *es* to each word and say the new word. ***Graphophonic Cues***

Minilesson

REVIEW/MAINTAIN

Main Idea

Remind students that when they read, they should think about the main idea of the paragraph, section, or story. The main idea is what the selection is mostly about. Sometimes the author states the main idea, and sometimes the reader must figure it out from story clues.

- Have students reread Pat Cummings's answer to question number 4 on page 290. Then have them state the main idea. (Pat Cummings does not have any children, but she has a cat that acts like a dog.)

Activity Have students work with a partner and write the main ideas for each question in the story. As a group, share and compare the main-idea statements that partners write.

Comprehension

(11) **FACT AND OPINION** Who has Pat used as models for the characters in her books? (her friends and relatives) What's her niece's opinion of *Just Us Women*? (Her picture is the only reason people read the book.) Let's complete our chart.

FACTS	OPINIONS
Pat Cummings was born November 9, 1950.	Being paid with candy is as good as being paid with money.
Cash is on the cover of *Storm in the Night.*	Drawing is a good business.
The cat comes when she's called, sits, and fetches.	Cash is very smart
Pat has used her friends and relatives in her books.	Her niece's picture is the only reason people read the book.

RETELL THE STORY Have partners work together to write a paragraph that summarizes how Pat Cummings came to work on her first book. *Summarize*

STUDENT SELF-ASSESSMENT

- How did using the strategy of distinguishing fact from opinion help me understand the story?

TRANSFERRING THE STRATEGY

- When might I try using this strategy again? In what other reading could the chart help me?

at two-thirty in the morning. I've drawn neighbors, neighbors' pets, and friends who might even ask me to change their hairstyles or make them look thinner. I will also find models to draw who fit the image I have in my mind of the characters in the book.

I used my sister Linda and my niece Keija on the cover of *Just Us Women.* Keija told me once that her picture was the only reason people read the book! That book is filled with family: my mother, Chuku, my brother-in-law Hassan, my grandfather, my sister Barbara, and a friend or two. It makes the book more personal for me.

7 **What do you use to make your pictures?**

(11) Everything. I like to use different materials. Sometimes it's big fun, but sometimes it's disastrous. I use watercolors and colored pencils most often; gouache, acrylics, pastels, airbrush, and pen and ink sometimes. I've experimented with collage and even rubber stamps, but I don't think I've tried half of the stuff I see in the art supply stores.

I also maintain a big picture file for reference. If I have to draw an armadillo, it helps a lot to have a picture to look at while I work.

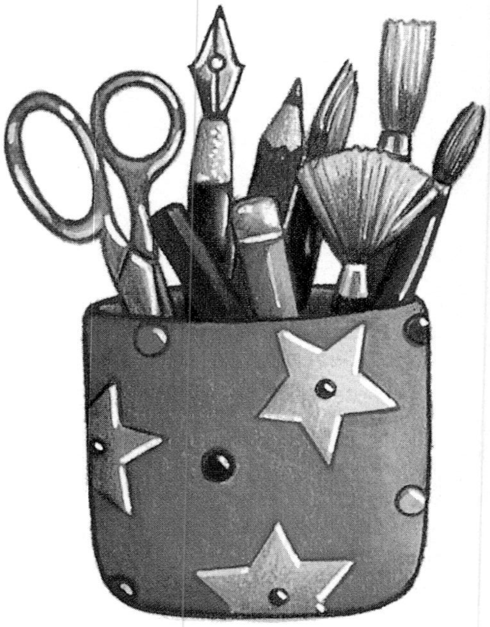

292

REREADING FOR *Fluency*

PARTNERS Have each partner choose his or her favorite page and read it aloud. Have them read as though they were Pat Cummings telling the story of her life.

READING RATE When you evaluate rate, have the student read aloud from the story for one minute. Place a stick-on note after the last word read. Count words read. To evaluate students' performance, see the Running Record in the **Fluency Assessment** book.

Intervention For leveled fluency lessons, passages, and norms charts, see **Skills Intervention Guide**, Part 4, Fluency.

8 How did you get to do your first book?

I put some illustrations from art school into a portfolio and went to see editors at publishing houses. They gave me good advice but no work. Then an editor saw my artwork in a newsletter and offered me a book to illustrate. I was so excited that when she asked if I knew what to do, I said, "Sure, no problem." I didn't have a clue how to start, but I didn't want to let her know.

I knew somebody, who knew somebody, who knew someone who used to know Tom Feelings, a children's book illustrator whose work I admired. So I looked in the phone book, called Tom up, and asked him if he would help me. He was wonderful. He gave me advice on how to pick which parts of the story to illustrate and how to decide where the pages should turn. He reminded me always to leave lots of room for the words to fit, to be sure that the character looks like the same person all the way through the book, and to try and keep important details away from the middle of the book, where the pages are sewn together. You don't want your reader pulling the book apart to see something important that's been hidden in the seam!

Tom taught me a lot that afternoon. He and many other illustrators still inspire me. I still learn from looking at their work. The most important thing I learned from Tom that day was that we have to help each other. He helped me get started, and I never forget that when someone who wants to illustrate calls me.

293

LITERARY RESPONSE

QUICK-WRITE Invite students to write their thoughts about the selection. Use questions like these to help them get started:

- What kind of person is Pat Cummings? How would you describe her personality?
- How has Pat Cummings inspired *you*? What have you learned about a career as an artist?

ORAL RESPONSE Students can share their journal writing and discuss the parts of the selection they enjoyed the most. Then have them choose their favorite illustrations by Pat Cummings and explain why they like the artwork.

Comprehension

Return to Predictions and Purposes

Review with students their story predictions and reasons for reading the selection. Ask students to compare their predictions to what actually happened in the story.

PREDICTIONS	WHAT HAPPENED
The story is about Pat Cummings's life.	Pat Cummings describes how she discovered a love of drawing.
The story tells what she likes to draw and why.	Pat Cummings explains how she gets ideas from her dreams.

INFORMAL ASSESSMENT

FACT AND OPINION

HOW TO ASSESS

- Have students explain how they can tell if a statement is a fact or an opinion.
- Ask students to give an opinion about Pat Cummings's artwork. Then have them state a fact.

Students should recognize factual statements as ones that can be proved. Their opinions should state their personal preference or what they think about her art.

FOLLOW UP If students have difficulty distinguishing between facts and opinions, choose an illustration from Pat Cummings's art. Then state a fact about the piece, and have students form an opinion about it.

Story Questions

Have students discuss or write answers to the questions on page 294.

Answers:

1. She drew ballerinas after she attended a ballet class. *Literal/Cause and Effect*
2. An opinion because it's a belief and can't be proved. *Inferential/Fact and Opinion*
3. Answers will vary. Sample answer: because she uses her imagination. *Inferential/Form Generalizations*
4. Pat Cummings is an artist who enjoys drawing illustrations for children's books. *Critical/Main Idea*
5. Pat has more confidence than John because she believes in her own abilities and learns how to achieve her goals. *Critical/Reading Across Texts*

Write an Encouraging Note For a full writing process lesson, see pages 297K–297L.

Story Questions & Activities

1. What event caused Pat Cummings to start drawing ballerinas?
2. Is the following statement a *fact* or an *opinion*? *I think Pat Cummings is the best artist today.* Explain why.
3. What makes Pat Cummings a good artist? Explain.
4. What is the main idea of this selection?
5. Compare Pat Cummings' attitude toward her work with John Thompson's feelings about his sign in "The Hatmaker's Sign." Who has more confidence in his or her work? How can you tell?

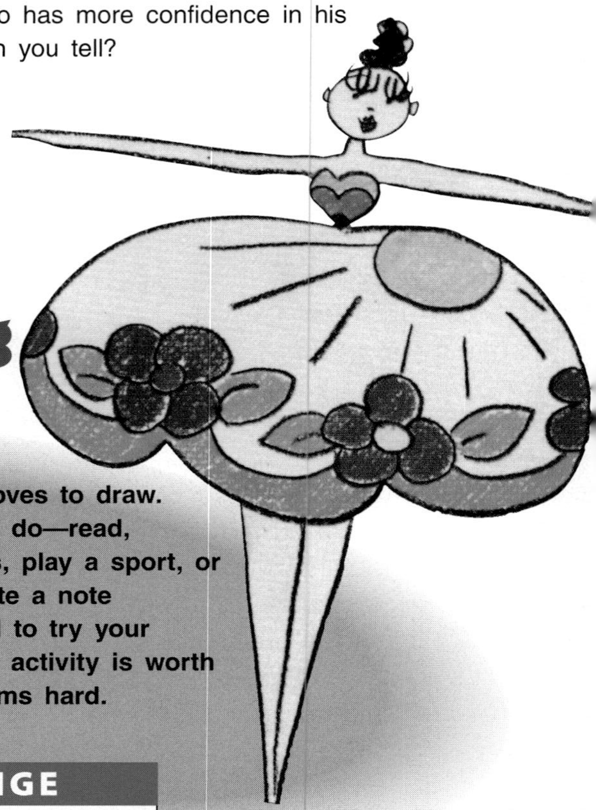

Write an Encouraging Note

Pat Cummings loves to draw. What do you love to do—read, dance, collect things, play a sport, or something else? Write a note encouraging a friend to try your activity. Tell why the activity is worth doing, even if it seems hard.

Meeting Individual Needs

EASY

Name______ Date______ **Reteach 83**

Vocabulary

Complete each definition by writing the correct word on the line provided.

exist image inspire loft reference sketch

1. A large room or open space on the upper floor of a building is a loft
2. A picture of something in the mind is an image
3. To make a quick drawing is to sketch
4. Something used for information is a reference
5. To stir the imagination is to inspire
6. To live is to exist

6

Reteach 84

Story Comprehension

Write the answers to these questions about "Pat Cummings: My Story." For help, you can look back at the story.

1. What was the first thing Pat Cummings drew that people could recognize? ballerinas
2. Where does Pat Cummings get her ideas? She gets ideas from things she sees, from traveling, and from dreams.
3. What does Pat Cummings like to draw? faces and things from her imagination
4. How does Pat Cummings go about drawing people? She uses old or new photographs or uses friends and family as models.
5. How did Tom Feelings inspire Cummings? He taught her many things about illustrating children's books. He taught her illustrators have to help each other. Looking at his work inspires Cummings.

83–84 At Home: Have students make a simple crossword puzzle using some of the vocabulary words. Book 4/Unit 3 Pat Cummings: My Story 5

Reteach, 84

ON-LEVEL

Name______ Date______ **Practice 84**

Story Comprehension

Read the statements below about "Pat Cummings: My Story." Write **T** if the statement is true. Write **F** if the statement is false. Refer to the story if necessary.

1. T Pat Cummings began her art by scribbling.
2. T Pat Cummings took a bus alone when she was very little.
3. F Pat Cummings never cared much for ballerinas.
4. T Pat Cummings loved to draw and discovered art could be a good business, too.
5. F Pat Cummings only gets her ideas from her friends.

Rewrite the following sentences to make them accurate. **Answers may vary.**

6. Pat Cummings began to draw when she was in high school. She began drawing when she was a small child.
7. Pat Cummings never puts people she knows in her pictures. She often draws faces from family photos.
8. Cummings draws everything from memory and never looks at other pictures. She often uses pictures from reference books, looking at them as she sketches.

84 At Home: Have students tell about Pat Cummings and her life as an artist. Book 4/Unit 3 Pat Cummings: My Story 8

Practice, 84

CHALLENGE

Name______ Date______ **Extend 83**

Vocabulary

exist	image	inspire
loft	reference	sketch

1. Which three vocabulary words are you most likely to find in a story about drawing? image; sketch; inspire
2. List four other words you might expect to find in a story about drawing. Answers will vary. Possible answers: pencil; easel; figure; line; shadow

Extend 84

Story Comprehension

Pat Cummings' interest in drawing began when she was a little girl. It eventually became her career. Turn Pat's story into a television interview. Write a list of questions a reporter might ask her. Find sentences from the story that answer the questions. Share your questions with the class. Take turns being the reporter and giving the answers.

83–84 At Home: Have students write about their interests and what they'd like to do for work as an adult. Book 4/Unit 3 Pat Cummings: My Story

Extend, 84

Do a Science Experiment

Pat Cummings gets ideas from clouds. To see how clouds form, put water in a jar. Cover it with plastic wrap. Hold it in place with a rubber band. Put ice cubes on the top. As the water warms inside the jar, it will turn into water vapor and rise to the top. The air cooled by the ice cubes turns the vapor back into water. You'll see the drops form inside the plastic wrap!

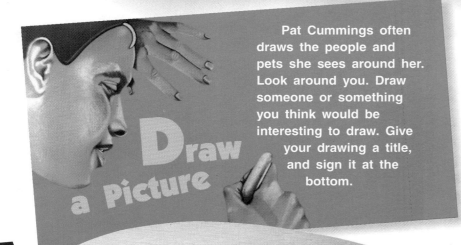

Draw a Picture

Pat Cummings often draws the people and pets she sees around her. Look around you. Draw someone or something you think would be interesting to draw. Give your drawing a title, and sign it at the bottom.

Find Out More

Pat Cummings' article is all about being an artist. How does someone become an artist? What is art school like? Start by interviewing an art teacher. Learn about some of the different jobs that artists have. Use what you learn to write an index card for each job you learn about. Then place the cards in your class's Job Box.

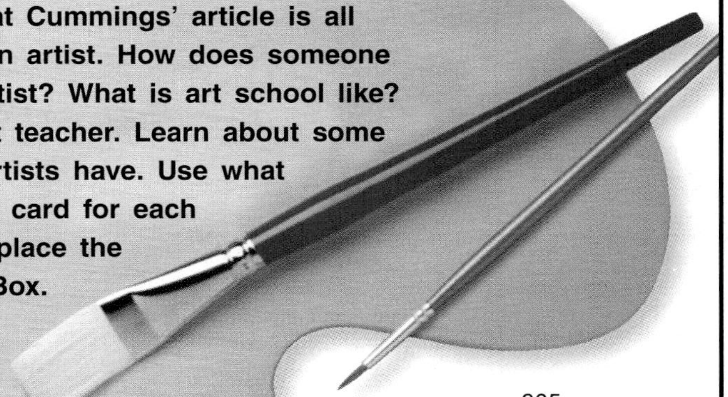

295

Activity

SCIENCE: CLASSIFYING CLOUDS Direct students to work in small groups and choose one type of cloud—*cirrus*, *stratus*, or *cumulus*—to research. Then have them create a poster that illustrates and describes how the cloud forms.

What to Look For Did the student:

- illustrate the clouds accurately?
- describe cloud formation clearly and accurately?

CHALLENGE

Story Activities

Do a Science Experiment

Materials: jar, plastic wrap, rubber band, ice cubes

GROUP Before performing the science experiment, ask students to explain how they think clouds form. After they place the rubber band on the jar, have them predict what they think will happen next. When finished, groups can discuss what they predicted and observed. Then have them record the results.

Draw a Picture

ONE Before students draw, have them look at their surroundings and brainstorm things they can draw, such as class plants, outside scenes, or each other. After they finish their drawings, invite volunteers to share their pictures.

Find Out More

RESEARCH AND INQUIRY Students can work with partners to interview an art teacher or community or family artist they know. Before the interview, have them write a list of questions they wish to ask. Tell students to jot down notes on what the person says during the interview. Then have them transfer the notes to an index card.

*inter***NET** CONNECTION To learn more about artists, have students visit ***www.mhschool.com/reading***

Formal Assessment

After page 295, see the Selection Assessment.

Study Skills

GRAPHIC AIDS

TESTED **OBJECTIVES** Students will use a chart or diagram to order steps in a process.

PREPARE Look at the flowchart with students and point out how one step leads to the next. Display **Teaching Chart 69.**

TEACH Ask students to explain how the chart makes it easier to read the steps.

PRACTICE Have students answer questions 1–5. **1.** The chart shows the steps of illustrating a book. **2.** The artist reads the book first. **3.** The artist gives the rough sketches to the editor. **4.** The editor tells the artist what to change. **5.** The artist does not have to make changes and can skip step five if the editor liked the rough sketches.

ASSESS/CLOSE Ask students to make a flowchart that lists the steps to complete a task, such as studying for a test, making a bed, or getting ready for school.

STUDY SKILLS

Read a Flowchart

Pat Cummings describes what it is like to draw pictures for children's books. In fact, she gives a step-by-step description. Look at the flowchart. A **flowchart** is a chart or a diagram that shows how to do something step-by-step. Read the steps that an artist takes to illustrate a book.

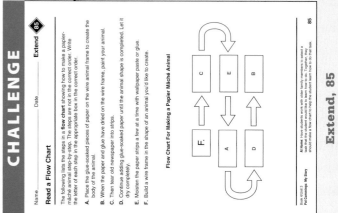

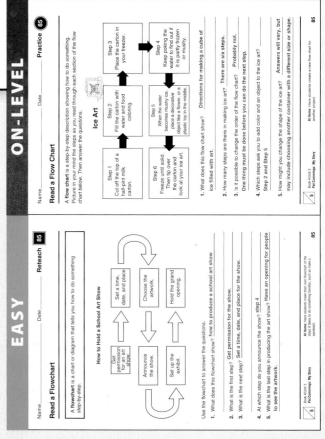

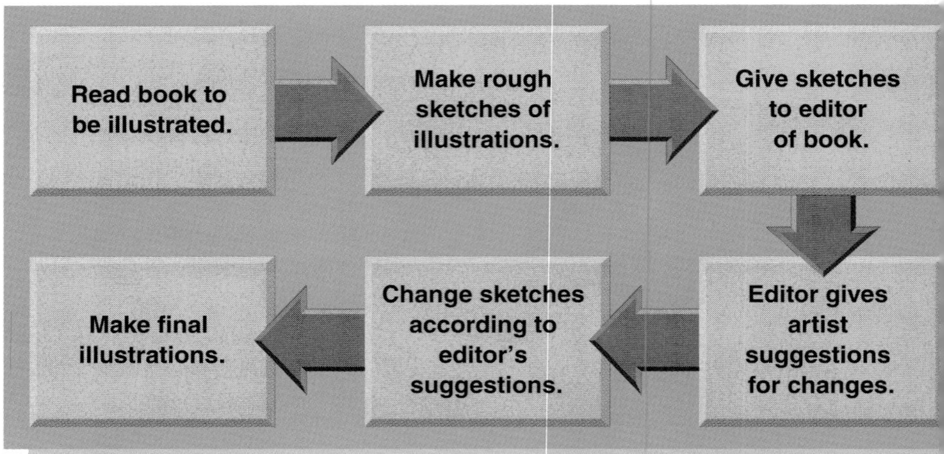
Read book to be illustrated.
Make rough sketches of illustrations.
Give sketches to editor of book.
Editor gives artist suggestions for changes.
Change sketches according to editor's suggestions.
Make final illustrations.

Use the flowchart to answer these questions.

1. What does this flowchart show?
2. What is the first thing an artist does to illustrate a book?
3. To whom does the artist give the rough sketches?
4. What does the editor tell the artist?
5. Which steps would an artist skip if the editor liked the rough sketches just as they were?

Meeting Individual Needs

EASY

Name______ Date______ Reteach 85

Read a Flowchart

A **flowchart** is a chart or diagram that tells you how to do something step-by-step.

How to Hold a School Art Show

Get permission for an art show. → Set a time, date, and place → Choose the artwork. → Announce the show. → Set up the exhibit. → Hold the grand opening.

Use the flowchart to answer the questions.

1. What does this flowchart show? how to produce a school art show
2. What is the first step? Get permission for the show.
3. What is the next step? Set a time, date, and place for the show.
4. At which step do you announce the show? step 4
5. What is the last step in producing the art show? Have an opening for people to see the artwork.

Book 4/Unit 3 Pat Cummings: My Story — At Home: Have students make their own flowchart of the steps it takes to do something familiar, such as make a sandwich. 85

Reteach, 85

ON-LEVEL

Name______ Date______ Practice 85

Read a Flow Chart

A **flow chart** is a step-by-step description showing how to do something. Picture in your mind the steps as you read through each section of the flow chart below. Then answer the questions.

Ice Art

Step 1 Cut off the top of a half-pint milk carton. → Step 2 Fill the carton with water and food coloring. → Step 3 Place the carton in your freezer. → Step 4 Keep poking the water to find out if it is partly frozen or mushy. → Step 5 When the water becomes mushy ice, place a decorative object like a flower, or a plastic toy in the middle. → Step 6 Freeze until solid. Then tip over the carton and look at your ice art.

1. What does this flow chart show? Directions for making a cube of ice filled with art.
2. How many steps are there in making ice art? There are six steps.
3. Is it possible to change the order of the flow chart? Probably not. One thing must be done before you can do the next step.
4. Which steps ask you to add color and an object to the ice art? Step 2 and Step 5
5. How might you change the shape of the ice art? Answers will vary, but may include choosing another container with a different size or shape.

Book 4/Unit 3 Pat Cummings: My Story — At Home: Have students create a new flow chart for another project. 85

Practice, 85

CHALLENGE

Name______ Date______ Extend 85

Read a Flow Chart

The following lists the steps in a **flow chart** showing how to make a papier-mâché animal step-by-step. The steps are not in the correct order. Write the letter of each step in the appropriate box in the correct order.

A. Place the glue-soaked pieces of paper on the wire animal frame to create the body of the animal.
B. When the paper and glue have dried on the wire frame, paint your animal.
C. Then tear old newspaper into strips.
D. Continue adding glue-soaked paper until the animal shape is completed. Let it dry completely.
E. Moisten the paper strips a few at a time with wallpaper paste or glue.
F. Build a wire frame in the shape of an animal you'd like to create.

Flow Chart For Making a Papier Mâché Animal

F. → C → E → A → D → B

Book 4/Unit 3 Pat Cummings: My Story — At Home: Have students work with older family members to select a task that the student would like to learn how to do. Together, they should make a flow chart to help the student learn how to do that task. 85

Extend, 85

TEST POWER

Test Tip
Ruling out wrong answers will make it easier to find the best answer.

DIRECTIONS
Read the sample story. Then read each question about the story.

SAMPLE

The Story of Soybeans

The soybean is part of our daily lives. It is used in a broad range of products like mayonnaise, noodles, and chocolate coatings.

Soybean seeds are round or oval-shaped and come in a variety of colors. Yellow seeds are ground into meal or used for their oil, while green seeds are used to grow soybeans for food products.

Two weeks after planting, the soybeans begin to sprout. Around the sixteenth week, the seeds are fully mature, and the plant itself begins to shrivel and die. The seeds must be harvested before the pods fall to the ground. If not, the seeds will spoil and rot.

1 In order for soybeans to be harvested, the seeds must be—

A oval
B spoiled
C shriveled
(D) mature

2 What is the main idea of the third paragraph?

(F) Soybeans sprout and then mature at about 16 weeks.
G Soybeans are round or oval-shaped and colored.
H The plants will grow green leaves.
J Soybean plants blossom and produce pods.

297

Test Power

THE PRINCETON REVIEW

Read the Page

Remind students that after reading the story they should summarize it in their own words. Instruct them to read *all* of the answer choices.

Discuss the Questions

Question 1: This question requires students to locate supporting facts in the passage. Instruct students to refer back to the passage to double-check *all* facts. They should *not* rely on their memories. Ask, "When can you harvest soybeans?" Answer: when they are fully mature. Eliminate wrong answers.

Question 2: This question asks students to determine the main idea of the third paragraph. Remind students to paraphrase what they have read in the third paragraph *before* looking at the answers. Point out that the correct answer must summarize the *third paragraph*, but not necessarily the whole story.

Leveled Books

EASY

Ping's Pictures

/ü/ and /yü/

- ☑ Fact and Opinion
- ☑ Instructional Vocabulary: ***exist, image, inspire, loft, reference, sketch***

Guided Reading

PREVIEW AND PREDICT Have students discuss the illustrations up to page 6 and write in their journals predictions about the story.

SET PURPOSES Have students set a purpose for reading and write a few questions they would like to have answered by the story.

READ THE BOOK Have students read the story independently. Then use the questions below to check their use of reading strategies.

Pages 2–3: Why is Ping so excited? (He wants to enter the drawing contest he saw advertised on the bus.) ***Cause and Effect***

Page 4: What is another word for *draw*? (sketch) ***Vocabulary***

Page 5: What opinion does Ping have about his drawings? (He thinks he cannot draw anything that looks real.) ***Fact and Opinion***

Page 6: Find the words *cartoons, zoo,* and *you* on page 6, and say the words aloud. Which vowel pair in each word makes the /ü/ sound? (oo, ou) ***Phonics***

Pages 9–12: What does Ping do to make his drawings look more realistic? (He studies real animals to see how they move and look.) ***Cause and Effect***

Page 13: Read the first sentence on page 13. Is this a fact or an opinion? Explain. (It is a fact; it can be proved true.) ***Fact and Opinion***

RETURN TO PREDICTIONS AND PURPOSES Review students' predictions and reasons for reading. Were their predictions about Ping accurate? Did they find out the answers to their questions?

LITERARY RESPONSE Discuss these questions:

- What do you think about Ping's drawings? Do you like them? Why or why not?
- If you could ask Ping to draw a picture of something, what would it be?

Also see the story questions and activity in *Ping's Pictures.*

Intervention Skills

Intervention Guide, for direct instruction and extra practice in vocabulary and comprehension

Answers to Story Questions

1. No, Ping thought his pictures looked like cartoons. He wanted to draw more realistic-looking animals.
2. Each time was a stated opinion, although after Ping finished his paintings the opinion was based on fact.
3. Answers will vary but could include that Ping had accomplished what he set out to do. With the help of his parents and a lot of practice on his part, Ping was able to paint the animals in a way that satisfied him.
4. It is about a boy who wants to enter an art contest. He learns a new style of art and improves his drawing skills as he gets an entry ready for the contest.
5. Answers will vary.

The *Story Questions and Activity* below appear in the *Easy Book.*

Story Questions and Activity

1. Was Ping happy with his pictures the first time he tried to draw?
2. Ping was called an artist several times in the story. When was it a fact and when was it an opinion?
3. Why do you think merely entering the contest made Ping so contented?
4. What is the story mostly about?
5. If Ping could ask Pat Cummings one question, what might it be?

Make Your Own Seal

1. With a pencil, etch your initial(s) as large as you can, on the face of the potato.
2. Cut bits of potato away from the letter(s) with a knife, so that each letter is raised. **Be very careful not to cut yourself.**
3. Dip the potato seal into the red paint, making sure the paint is not dripping and is only on the letter.
4. Carefully press the potato seal on the paper to sign your artwork.

from *Ping's Pictures*

Leveled Books

INDEPENDENT

How Do They Do That?

- ☑ **Fact and Opinion**
- ☑ **Instructional Vocabulary:** ***exist, image, inspire, loft, reference, sketch***

Guided Reading

PREVIEW AND PREDICT Have students read the table of contents. Then have them preview and describe what is happening in the illustrations up to page 8. Ask them to predict what the book is about, and record their predictions on chart paper.

SET PURPOSES Have students set a purpose for reading the story, such as learning about how a cartoon is made. Ask them to write down a few questions they have about animation.

READ THE BOOK Have students read independently. Use the questions below to check their use of reading strategies.

Pages 2–3: How many pictures does it take to make a 75-minute animated film? (108,000) If clay animation and computer animation take less time to make, why do you think most animation is still done the "old-fashioned" way? (Answers will vary.) ***Fact and Opinion***

Page 4: What words and phrases on page 4 help you figure out the meanings of the words *sketch, reference,* and *loft*? (Sample answers: *blueprint, consult, floors of old warehouses.*) ***Vocabulary***

Page 9: How is clay animation different from cel animation? (The filmmakers use three-dimensional clay characters, not flat drawings.) ***Compare and Contrast***

Page 16: Reread the second paragraph on page 16. Which sentence is an opinion? Which sentences are facts? (The first sentence is an opinion; the second two sentences are facts.) ***Fact and Opinion***

RETURN TO PREDICTIONS AND PURPOSES Talk with students about the predictions they made about the book. Did they find out the answers to the questions they wrote?

LITERARY RESPONSE Discuss these questions:

- What kind of animation is your favorite? Why?
- What is the most interesting fact you learned from this story?

Also see the story questions and activity in *How Do They Do That?*

Answers to Story Questions

1. Answers will vary.
2. Answers will vary, but may include that artists still get to use their creative skills to do the art, but do not have to do the tedious work of copying it over and over again to produce an animated feature.
3. Answers will vary. All answers will be opinions.
4. Animation can tell a story and bring characters to life.
5. Answers will vary.

The *Story Questions and Activity* below appear in the *Independent Book*.

Story Questions and Activity

1. List three facts that were given in this book.
2. Why do you think artists are turning to computers to do animation?
3. What is the best type of animation? Why? Is your answer a fact or an opinion?
4. What is the main idea of the book?
5. If the author of this book were to meet Pat Cummings, what do you think they would talk about?

Make a Storyboard

You will need: a pencil, a sheet of paper for the storyboard, a ruler.

- Use a ruler to draw six squares on your paper. Make each square 3"x 3".
- Create two characters, such as stick figures or animals.
- Think of a simple story for your characters. The story should have six parts.
- Draw each part of the story in one of the frames. Make sure to keep the parts in order.
- Share your storyboard with a partner.

from *How Do They Do That?*

Leveled Books

CHALLENGE

Wynton Marsalis: Music Man

- ☑ **Fact and Opinion**
- ☑ **Instructional Vocabulary:** ***exist, image, inspire, loft, reference, sketch***

Guided Reading

PREVIEW AND PREDICT Preview the photographs in the book. Have students chart their ideas about what the story will be about based on these photographs.

SET PURPOSES Students should decide what they want to learn about Wynton Marsalis before reading the story. Have them think of questions they would like to have answered. Encourage them to record their questions in their journals.

READ THE BOOK Use questions such as the following to guide students as they read or to check comprehension after they read independently.

Page 2: What clues does the author use to help you figure out the meaning of the word *reference?* (information, magazines, Internet) ***Vocabulary***

Page 3: What are some of the facts about Wynton's accomplishments? (He has recorded over 30 CDs, been nominated for 15 Grammy awards, and won eight.) ***Fact and Opinion***

Pages 4–5: Why didn't Wynton Marsalis become a musician at a young age? (He thought it was uncool to practice an instrument, and he wanted to be a regular kid.) ***Draw Conclusions***

Page 12: What does Wynton do to keep the American tradition of jazz alive? (He teaches at Lincoln Center and visits classrooms around the world to talk to children about music.) ***Problem and Solution***

RETURN TO PREDICTIONS AND PURPOSES Have students review their predictions and reasons for reading. Which predictions were accurate? Which were not? Did they find out what they wanted to know about Wynton Marsalis?

LITERARY RESPONSE Discuss these questions:

- Do you think it would be fun to be in a jazz band? Why or why not?
- If Wynton Marsalis gave a lecture at your school, what would you ask him?

Also, see the story questions and activity in *Wynton Marsalis: Music Man*

Answers to Story Questions

1. Wynton Marsalis plays both classical music and jazz, but he prefers jazz.
2. It is an opinion because the statement cannot be proved in a logical or scientific way.
3. Answers will vary but could include the idea that you can't be a good player if you don't practice and all the practice in the world won't make you a good player if you have no talent. He had talent and he put that talent to use.
4. Wynton Marsalis is a great trumpet player, composer, and educator.
5. Answers will vary.

The *Story Questions and Activity* below appear in the *Challenge Book*.

Story Questions and Activity

1. Which two main types of music does Wynton Marsalis play and which does he prefer?
2. On page 2, the author states that Wynton "is probably one of the greatest trumpet players in the world today." Is this a fact or an opinion? Explain.
3. When Wynton Marsalis learned to play the trumpet, do you think it was talent or practice that made him a good player?
4. What is the main idea of the book?
5. If Pat Cummings was going to illustrate a children's book about Wynton Marsalis, how would she go about it?

Listen to Wynton Marsalis

Find a jazz or classical recording featuring Wynton Marsalis. Your local public library or school library may have a recording you can listen to there or check out for listening at home. After listening, write a paragraph explaining how his music made you feel.

from *Wynton Marsalis: Music Man*

Activities

Bringing Groups Together

Anthology and Leveled Books

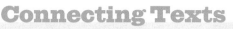

Connecting Texts

FACT CHARTS Write the story titles on a chart. Have students discuss in groups the most important facts they read in each story. Then call on volunteers from each group to list these facts. Record their suggestions on the chart.

Pat Cummings: My Story	Ping's Pictures	How Do They Do That?	Wynton Marsalis: Music Man
• Pat Cummings gets her ideas from things she sees and her imagination. • Pat Cummings enjoys drawing people she knows and faces in general. • Tom Feelings helped her with her first book.	• Ping and his father go to the zoo so Ping can practice drawing animals. • Ping learns to draw more realistic looking animals. • Ping wins the drawing contest.	• It takes 108,000 pictures to make a 75-minute animated feature. • In cel animation, each picture is hand-drawn. • In clay animation, clay figures are used instead of drawings. • Computer programs also are used to create animation.	• Wynton Marsalis is a trumpet player and conductor. • Wynton Marsalis has recorded over 30 CDs in the last 20 years. • Wynton Marsalis was born into a family of music lovers and musicians.

Viewing/Representing

GROUP PRESENTATIONS Divide the class into groups, one for each of the four books read in the lesson. (For *Pat Cummings: My Story*, combine students of different reading levels.) Have each group draw three to five pictures that tell about the main idea of the story. Then have them use the illustrations to retell the main idea to the rest of the class.

AUDIENCE RESPONSE Ask students to pay attention to each group's presentation. Have them look for informative details included in the illustrations. Allow time for questions and comments after each presentation.

Research and Inquiry

MORE ABOUT CHILDREN'S ART These four selections have focused on the time, skills, and effort involved in creating art. Have students research other children's artists and find out the following facts:

- names and facts about well-known children's artists
- different media used to create artwork
- the history of well-known cartoon characters and their creators, such as Snoopy and Charles Schulz

Students can make a Fact Wall of their facts about children's art and illustrators.

*inter*NET CONNECTION Have students visit ***www.mhschool.com/reading*** to find out more about children's art.

Review Fact and Opinion

PREPARE

Discuss Statements of Fact and Opinion

Review: To identify facts in a story, look for statements that can be proved to be true. To identify opinions, look for statements that express a person's feelings or ideas. Ask students to recall facts and opinions that were included in *Pat Cummings: My Story*.

TEACH

Read the Passage and Model the Skill

Ask students to listen for facts and opinions as you read **Teaching Chart 70** aloud.

The Art Contest

My art teacher decided to have a "Best Children's Artist" competition. He asked everyone to gather favorite examples of pictures and drawings from storybooks.

I brought in the book *I Need a Lunch Box*. Pat Cummings drew the pictures in the book. It makes me feel happy when I read it.

I held up the book for my classmates to see. I said, "This is the best illustrator I have ever seen." My classmates thought so, too. They voted Pat Cummings as the best artist.

Teaching Chart 70

Discuss clues in the passage that help readers tell the difference between statements of fact and opinion.

MODEL When the narrator says "This is the best illustrator I've ever seen," I know that the statement is an opinion. It is what the narrator thinks. But when the writer says "They voted Pat Cummings as the best artist," I can tell that the statement is a fact. It can be proved true.

TESTED OBJECTIVES

Students will distinguish between statements of fact and statements of opinion.

Skills Finder

Fact and Opinion

Introduce	283A-B
Review	297E-F, 333A-B, 359E-F
Test	Unit 3

TEACHING TIP

FACT/OPINION CARDS

To encourage all students to share their thoughts on whether a statement is a fact or an opinion, have students write *Fact* and *Opinion* on separate index cards and then hold up the appropriate card after each sentence of the passage is read aloud.

SELF-SELECTED Reading

Students may choose from the following titles.

ANTHOLOGY

- Pat Cummings: My Story

LEVELED BOOKS

- Ping's Pictures
- How Do They Do That?
- Wynton Marsalis: Music Man

Bibliography, pages T78–T79

PRACTICE

Recognize Statements of Fact and Opinion

GROUP

Have volunteers underline sentences in "The Art Contest" that contain facts and circle the sentences that contain opinions. Then ask students to write a sentence for each statement explaining whether it contains a fact or an opinion. ▶ **Linguistic/Logical**

ASSESS/CLOSE

Write About an Artist

PARTNERS

Have partners work together to choose a children's book illustrator they like. Have them write a paragraph about the artist's pictures. Then have them underline the factual statements that they wrote and circle the statements of opinion. ▶ **Linguistic/Logical**

ALTERNATE TEACHING STRATEGY

FACT AND OPINION

For a different approach to teaching this skill, see page T64.

Intervention ▶ Skills

Intervention Guide, for direct instruction and extra practice with fact and opinion

Meeting Individual Needs for Comprehension

EASY

Name________ Date________ Reteach 86

Fact and Opinion

As you read, it is important to be able to tell what are facts and what are opinions. **Facts** can be proven. **Opinions** cannot.

Read each paragraph. Then write whether each numbered statement is a fact or an opinion.

Art class is the best time of day. Mrs. James, the art teacher, is the nicest teacher in the school. Art class is on Friday mornings, and after a hard week of studying, it is fun to create something beautiful. For the past three weeks we have been painting in the styles of famous painters. Now we will be working with clay.

1. opinion Mrs. James is the nicest teacher in the school.
2. fact Art class is on Friday mornings.
3. fact Students have been painting in different styles.

Ben is a very good artist, but he does not work hard in art class. He hates to draw still lifes, and even tore up his last art class drawing. Michael sat next to Ben at lunch. When Ben opened his notebook, Michael saw that it was covered with cartoons and funny little drawings. Michael thinks that Ben's cartoons are pretty good.

4. fact Ben tore up his drawing.
5. fact Ben's notebook is covered with cartoons.
6. opinion Michael thinks that Ben's cartoons are pretty good.

86 At Home: Have students state two facts and two opinions about their favorite class at school. Book 4/Unit 3 Pat Cummings: My Story 6

Reteach, 86

ON-LEVEL

Name________ Date________ Practice 86

Fact and Opinion

When you read, look for information that is true and accurate. This helps you to tell the difference between a **fact** and an **opinion**.

"Pat Cummings: My Story" is a nonfiction story. It is a true story about an artist. Read each of the following statements about Pat Cummings.

Write fact or opinion to describe each statement.

1. The first things Pat Cummings ever drew were scribbles. Fact
2. Every person who sees her art would love Pat Cummings's work. Opinion
3. I think Pat Cummings likes to draw things that only exist in her imagination. Opinion
4. Pat Cummings believes it's important for people to help each other. Opinion
5. Before the age of eight, Pat Cummings went on a bus alone. Fact
6. Pat Cummings believes that traveling helps an artist grow. Opinion
7. Pat Cummings works in a loft in Brooklyn, New York. Fact
8. Pat Cummings uses watercolors, oil paints, and pencils. Fact

86 At Home: Have students list some facts and opinions about artists. Book 4/Unit 3 Pat Cummings: My Story 8

Practice, 86

CHALLENGE

Name________ Date________ Extend 86

Fact and Opinion

In "Pat Cummings: My Story," the author describes an event in her childhood and the work she does as an adult. She uses **facts** and **opinions**.

Write one or two paragraphs describing an event in your life or your favorite thing to do. Include at least two sentences that are facts and two sentences that are opinions. Underline each fact. Circle each opinion.

Answers will vary but should include two facts and two opinions.

86 At Home: Have students read a newspaper article. They should underline two facts and circle two opinions in the article. Book 4/Unit 3 Pat Cummings: My Story

Extend, 86

LANGUAGE SUPPORT

Name________ Date________

I Think I See...

1. Circle the correct word that goes in the "Fact" sentence. 2. Write a word to go in the "Opinion" blank.

Fact:
This is a ______. mountain (cloud)
Opinion:
I think this looks like a dog.

Fact:
This is a ______. (tree) river
Opinion:
I think this looks like a snake.

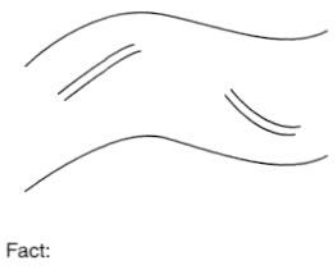

Fact:
This is a ______. house (river)
Opinion:
I think this looks like a sheet of glass.

Fact:
This is a ______. (rock) flower
Opinion:
I think this looks like a turtle.

94 Pat Cummings: My Story • Language Support/Blackline Master 46 Grade 4

Language Support, 94

Review Summarize

TESTED OBJECTIVES

Students will summarize a story.

Skills Finder

Summarize	
Introduce	281G-H
Review	297G-H, 359G-H
Test	Unit 3
Maintain	385, 415, 461, 507

TEACHING TIP

IMPORTANT INFORMATION To help students identify the important parts of the passage, have them cross out the unimportant parts. Read each sentence aloud, and have students decide whether or not it is needed to make the main idea clear. If you are using a transparency, invite volunteers to cross out unimportant information.

PREPARE

Define Summary

Review: When we summarize a selection, we tell about what we have read. A summary is brief and includes the main topic of the selection. A summary only includes the most important information in the story.

TEACH

Read the Passage and Model the Skill

As you read **Teaching Chart 71**, have students listen for its main idea and most important information.

Making New Friends

One day Sara was walking her dog Oscar along the river. Oscar saw a black dog named Morgan and swam and played with her. Soon they were friends. Sara began talking to Morgan's owner. They became friends, too.

Morgan's owner was named Leslie Evans. Leslie illustrated books for children. A few days later, Leslie took Sara to her studio.

Sara saw drawings of Morgan in many of Leslie's pictures, and also a girl from their neighborhood. When Sara looked at the illustrations, she felt as if she knew the characters.

Teaching Chart 71

Model summarizing the main idea of the story.

MODEL Sara and Leslie Evans, a children's book illustrator, become friends while walking their dogs.

Then have students think about how they would summarize the main events in their own words.

PRACTICE

Use a Summary Chart (GROUP)

Have volunteers take turns underlining the sentences with the most important information in the story. Then have students use a chart to help them summarize the events in the story. Complete the first box together to help them get started. ▶ **Linguistic/Visual**

SUMMARY CHART
Sara and her dog Oscar become friends with a dog named Morgan and her owner.

ASSESS/CLOSE

Use the Chart to Summarize (PARTNERS)

Have students summarize a favorite story, movie, or television show. Ask them to state the main idea in a sentence, construct a summary chart, and then write a short summary. Have partners exchange papers and help each other write more effective summaries if necessary. ▶ **Linguistic/Interpersonal**

ALTERNATE TEACHING STRATEGY

SUMMARIZE

For a different approach to teaching this skill, see page T62.

Intervention Skills

Intervention Guide, for direct instruction and extra practice in summarizing

Meeting Individual Needs for Comprehension

EASY

Name_______________ Date_________ Reteach 87

Summarize

When you **summarize**, you should include the main idea and the most important details from what you read.

Read the selection. Circle the letter beside the best response to each question.

Anna Mary Moses was an artist who never went to art school. She spent most of her life as a wife and mother of ten children. When she was 78 years of age, "Grandma" Moses took up painting. She sold her first painting for $3.

During the following years she painted over 1,500 pictures. They were mainly scenes of country life. Anna Mary Moses continued painting until just before her death at the age of 101. Today, Grandma Moses is thought of as an important American artist. Her paintings are in many museums.

1. Which is the main idea?
   - (a.) Grandma Moses became an artist at the age of 78.
   - b. Grandma Moses died at the age of 101.
2. Which detail is more important?
   - a. Grandma Moses had ten children.
   - (b.) Grandma Moses never went to art school.
3. Which detail is more important?
   - a. Grandma Moses once sold a painting for $3.
   - (b.) Grandma Moses painted scenes of country life.
4. Which is the better way to summarize the paragraph?
   - (a.) Grandma Moses, an important American artist, began to paint late in life. She had no art training but painted over 1,500 pictures of rural scenes.
   - b. Grandma Moses was a mother and a painter. She painted rural scenes. She once sold a painting for $3.

4 Book 4/Unit 3 Pat Cummings: My Story — **At Home:** Have students summarize their day at school, including the main idea and important details. 87

Reteach, 87

ON-LEVEL

Name_______________ Date_________ Practice 87

Summarize

In a **summary**, you tell a story's important events in your own words. Read the passages below about Pat Cummings. Then summarize each passage in one sentence. **Answers will vary.**

1. I have to laugh every time I think about a story Pat Cummings tells. She has such a great sense of humor. She says her mother would tell her she had drawn a nice duck. Then she would inform her mother that it was really a picture of her dad. **Summary:** The speaker thought the story of Pat Cummings's mother's response to her drawing of a duck was funny.
2. Pat Cummings and her older sister were playing outside when her sister left her alone. Before anyone could stop Pat, she hopped on the bus that had stopped at the corner. **Summary:** No one was watching Pat when a bus came along, so she got on it.
3. When the bus stopped in front of a building, everyone got off. Pat followed them into ballet class. Pat loved looking at the young ballerinas, but the teacher looked at Pat as if she had come from another planet. **Summary:** Pat followed the bus riders into ballet class, and the teacher was surprised to see her.
4. Pat Cummings and her family moved every three years. Pat made friends by joining an art club or by drawing posters. Everyone was impressed with her drawing talent, and she made many friends. **Summary:** Pat used her talent at drawing to make friends.
5. Sometimes ideas for art pieces just jump into Pat's head. Sometimes they happen even when she is sleeping. Jumping out of bed in the middle of the night, Pat will paint her idea. **Summary:** Pat gets ideas for her art whether she is awake or asleep.

5 Book 4/Unit 3 Pat Cummings: My Story — **At Home:** Have students write a summary of a favorite weekend activity. 87

Practice, 87

CHALLENGE

Name_______________ Date_________ Extend 87

Summarize

When you tell or write a summary of a person's life, you include important information about that person. You should include details that you think are important and interesting to your audience.

On a book jacket or book cover, you can often find a summary of the author's life. Sometimes there is also a summary of the life of the illustrator or photographer. These summaries include information that would be of interest to the person buying the book or borrowing the book from the library.

Write a summary of Pat Cummings' life that could be used on a book jacket. Try not to use more than four sentences.

Answers will vary. Possible summary: Pat Cummings has enjoyed drawing ever since she was old enough to scribble. The first drawings she sold were of ballerinas. Now her favorite things to draw are faces and fantasy things. Pat Cummings lives and works in Brooklyn, New York.

Book 4/Unit 3 Pat Cummings: My Story — **At Home:** Interview a family member about his or her life. Write a summary of that person's life. 87

Extend, 87

LANGUAGE SUPPORT

Name_______________ Date_________

That Reminds Me

1. Color the pictures that help you retell the story.

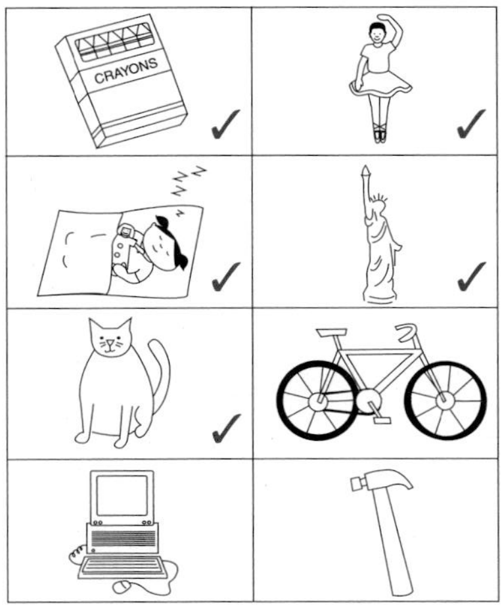

Grade 4 — Language Support/Blackline Master 47 • Pat Cummings: My Story 95

Language Support, 95

TESTED **OBJECTIVES**

Students will:

- add suffixes *-ful* and *-ous* to base words.
- understand new word meanings.

Skills Finder	
Suffixes	
Introduce	281I-J
Review	297I-J, 369I-J
Test	Unit 3
Maintain	433, 457, 553, 681

TEACHING TIP

SUFFIXES

- When you add the suffix *-ous*, you may need to drop the final *e* of the base word. (fame/famous)
- When a word ends in *y*, you may need to change the *y* to *i* before adding the suffix. (beauty/beautiful; fury/furious)

Review Suffixes

PREPARE

Discuss Meanings of the Suffixes *-ful* and *-ous*

Explain: We often categorize words with common characteristics into groups. This makes talking and learning about such words easier. For example, words with the same suffix can be grouped together. A suffix is a word part added to the end of a base word. By adding a suffix, we change the meaning of the base word. There are many different suffixes and each one has a different meaning. For example, the suffixes *–ful* and *–ous* mean "full of." The suffix *–ous* can also mean "characterized by" or "like."

TEACH

Read the Passage and Model the Skill

Display **Teaching Chart 72** and have students read it silently.

A Good Taste for Books

Yesterday, I bought a new copy of Pat Cummings's book, *Jimmy Lee Did It*. It has colorful pictures. I took the book home and read it from cover to cover. I was eating a jelly sandwich, so I was careful not to get my sticky fingers on the pages.

Later that day, my little baby sister came into the room. I had a feeling that something disastrous would happen. She picked up my wonderful book and took a bite out of one of the pages!

Most big brothers would have been furious. Not me. I think she has good taste in books.

Teaching Chart 72

MODEL The word *colorful* in the second sentence ends in *-ful*. The base word is *color*. If *-ful* means "full of," then *colorful* means "full of color." I'll read the sentence again and see if that meaning makes sense.

Identify Suffixes

Have students find the word *disastrous* in the second paragraph. Help them understand that the base word of *disastrous* is *disaster*. Then have them define *disastrous*. (like a disaster) Ask them if that meaning makes sense in the sentence.

PRACTICE

Identify Words with Suffixes

GROUP

Have volunteers underline each word in "A Good Taste for Books" that ends with the suffixes *-ful* or *-ous*. Then have them create a chart that lists each base word and its suffix. ▶ **Linguistic/Visual**

WORD WITH SUFFIX	BASE WORD	SUFFIX
colorful	color	-ful
wonderful	wonder	-ful

ASSESS/CLOSE

Form Words with Suffixes and Use Them in Sentences

PARTNERS

Write the following words on the chalkboard: *beauty, fame, glamour, plenty,* and *fear*. Have students copy each of the words and add the suffix *-ful* or *-ous* to each one. Then have students work with partners to write three or four sentences that include at least three of the words. Tell students that the sentences should be about Pat Cummings. ▶ **Linguistic**

ALTERNATE TEACHING STRATEGY

SUFFIXES

For a different approach to teaching this skill, see page T63.

Intervention **Skills**

Intervention Guide, for direct instruction and extra practice with suffixes

Meeting Individual Needs for Vocabulary

EASY

Name ______ Date ______ Reteach 88

Suffixes

A **suffix** is a word part that adds meaning to a word. The suffixes *-ful* and *-ous* add the meaning "full of" or "having."

Add the suffix *-ful* or *-ous* to each word.

1. danger + ous = dangerous
2. play + ful = playful
3. courage + ous = courageous
4. humor + ous = humorous
5. sorrow + ful = sorrowful
6. glamour + ous = glamorous

Now use one of the words above with *-ful* or *-ous* to complete each sentence.

7. The comic told Possible answer: humorous stories.
8. It is Possible answer: dangerous to play with matches.
9. Jena felt Possible answer: sorrowful when her friend moved.
10. Firefighters are Possible answer: courageous citizens.
11. Kittens and puppies are active and Possible answer: playful.
12. She looked Possible answer: glamorous in the gown.

At Home: Have students identify one more *-ful* and one more *-ous* suffixed word. — 88 — Book 4/Unit 3 Pat Cummings: My Story 12

Reteach, 88

ON-LEVEL

Name ______ Date ______ Practice 88

Suffixes

A **suffix** is a group of letters, such as *-ful* or *-ous*, added to the end of a base word. Read the words and their meanings, then complete the sentences. Remember that adding suffixes sometimes causes changes in spelling of the base, or root, word.

beauty — very pretty
beauti*ful* — full of beauty
wonder — feeling caused by something unusual or remarkable.
wonder*ful* — full of wonder
disaster — something that causes suffering
disastr*ous* — something bad
thought — what you think
thought*ful* — caring
thank — giving appreciation for something
thank*ful* — full of thanks

1. Getting an A on my report was wonderful.
2. Her singing was a wonder, she had the voice of an angel.
3. Jose shouted out an answer because he thought he knew it.
4. Celia was thoughtful when she asked about her friend's sick dog.
5. The diamond was considered a beauty.
6. Stephan created a beautiful sculpture made from wood.
7. He was so thankful to his mother for buying him the bike.
8. Sean remembered to thank his aunt for the gift.
9. The race was a disaster because of our poor running.
10. Walking home frome the football game was disastrous because we got caught in a snowstorm.

At Home: Have students identify words with suffixes as they read. — 88 — Book 4/Unit 3 Pat Cummings: My Story 10

Practice, 88

CHALLENGE

Name ______ Date ______ Extend 88

Suffixes

The **suffixes** *-ful* and *-ous* both mean "full of." Before you add *-ful* or *-ous* to some nouns, you must change the ending of the nouns. Change each base word as shown. The first one has been done for you. Then write sentences using the words you created. Sentences will vary.

1. Desire – e + ous = desirous
   In May I become desirous of summer vacation.
2. plenty – y + i + ful = plentiful
   Sample answer: In the fall we hope to celebrate a plentiful harvest.
3. disaster – e + ous = disastrous
   Sample answer: Because of the storm, the turnout for the play was disastrous.
4. color + ful = colorful
   Sample answer: Their uniforms were more colorful than ours.
5. space – e + i + ous = spacious
   Sample answer: Let's play in the gym where it's more spacious.
6. pity – y + i + ful = pitiful
   Sample answer: The wet puppy looked so small and pitiful.
7. danger + ous = dangerous
   Sample answer: Smoking is dangerous for your health.

At Home: List some other words that have the suffix *-ful* or *-ous*. Identify the words in which the base word's spelling was changed before the suffix was added. — 88 — Book 4/Unit 3 Pat Cummings: My Story

Extend, 88

LANGUAGE SUPPORT

Name ______ Date ______

Endings

1. Write each new word in the lines below. 2. Choose a picture to go with each new word. 3. Draw a line connecting the word to the picture it describes.

adventure – e + ous = adventurous

disaster – e + ous = disastrous

beauty – y + i + ful = beautiful

wonder + ful = wonderful

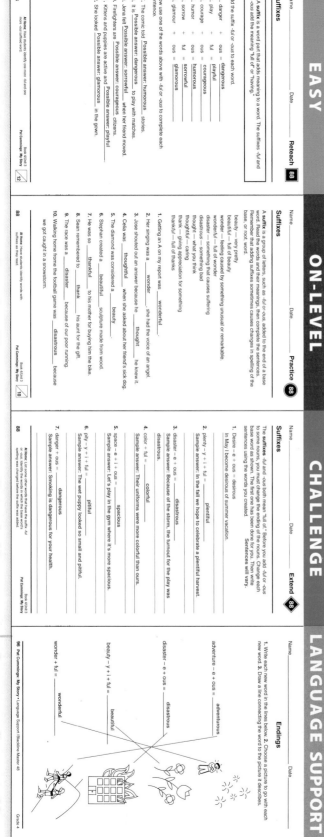

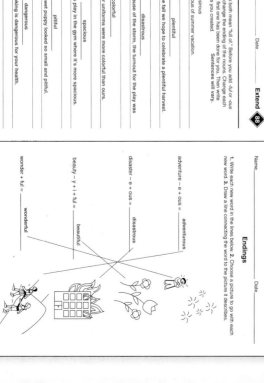

96 Pat Cummings: My Story • Language Support/Blackline Master 48 — Grade 4

Language Support, 96

GRAMMAR/SPELLING CONNECTIONS

See the 5-Day Grammar and Usage Plan on past and future tenses, pages 297M–297N.

See the 5-Day Spelling Plan on words with /ů/ and /yů/, pages 297O–297P.

TEACHING TIP

Technology Show students how to double-space a first draft. Explain that leaving room between lines will allow them to make corrections in the space above or below the line of type.

Handwriting Remind students to use cursive writing for drafts and revisions. All letters should have the same slant. For clarity, the ascenders and descenders should not overlap. Explain that it is important for the drafts to be legible, so students can read their own ideas.

Handwriting CD-ROM

Persuasive Writing

Prewrite

WRITE AN ENCOURAGING NOTE Present this writing assignment: Pat Cummings loves to draw. What do you love to do—read, dance, collect something, play a game or sport, or something else? Write a note encouraging a friend to try your activity. Say why your activity is worth doing, even if it seems hard.

BRAINSTORM IDEAS Have students brainstorm their favorite activities. List them on the board to spark other students.

Strategy: Word Webs Have students construct word webs around their favorite activity as they come up with reasons for engaging in it.

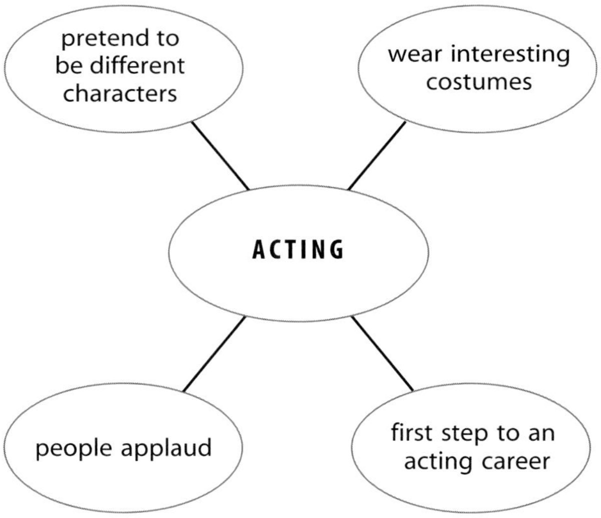

Draft

USE THE WORD WEB Have students use the reasons from their word webs to write their encouraging notes. Remind them to explain how the difficulties a newcomer might experience can be overcome.

Revise

SELF-QUESTIONING Ask students to assess their drafts.

- Did I include reasons to persuade others to try the activity?
- Did I include examples?
- Does my reasoning make sense?

PARTNERS Students can read their entries to a partner for feedback. Then have them add any more examples they thought of.

Edit/Proofread

CHECK FOR ERRORS Students can reread their entries for spelling, grammar, and punctuation. Have them also check for the inclusion of persuasive words.

Publish

SEND THE NOTE Have students draw names from a hat to choose a fellow student to send their note to. Recipients can tell which reasons they found most persuasive.

Dear Friend,

Have you ever considered acting? I think it's the most fun there is. Two days a week after school I go to an acting class. I love it because I get to pretend to be all sorts of different characters–this week an astronaut, next week a queen! Memorizing each part takes time, but it's no harder than memorizing the multiplication table.

Twice a year we put on a play. Then we get to dress up in wonderful costumes. It's a big thrill when the play is over and everyone applauds.

Someday I may want to make acting my career. This class is a good first step. But whether or not you want to be an actor when you grow up isn't important. I think you'll enjoy acting right now, just like me.

Your friend,
Jess

Presentation Ideas

DESIGN A BROCHURE Have students design and illustrate a brochure in question-and-answer format to promote their favorite activity. ▶ **Viewing/Representing**

HOLD A HOBBY FAIR Have students set up a booth for a hobby fair. They can use their brochures as props as they persuade interested visitors to try their activity.
▶ **Speaking/Listening**

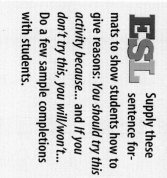

Consider students' creative efforts, possibly adding a plus (+) for originality, wit, and imagination.

Scoring Rubric

Excellent	Good	Fair	Unsatisfactory
4: The writer • describes an activity in some detail. • gives three solid reasons for engaging in the activity. • anticipates and responds to objections convincingly.	**3:** The writer • describes an activity. • gives reasons for engaging in the activity. • anticipates and responds to objections.	**2:** The writer • attempts to describe an activity. • gives at least one reason for engaging in the activity. • may not anticipate or respond to objections.	**1:** The writer • may not describe an activity. • gives no reasons for engaging in the activity. • does not anticipate or respond to objections.

Incomplete 0: The writer leaves the page blank or fails to respond to the writing task. The student does not address the topic or simply paraphrases the prompt. The response is illegible or incoherent.

For a 6-point or an 8-point scale, see pages T107–T108.

Meeting Individual Needs for Writing

EASY

Illustrate an Activity Have students draw a picture of an activity they like to engage in. Then have them label their picture or write a caption for it.

ON-LEVEL

A Future Career Ask students to draw a picture of themselves as an adult following a possible career. Have them interview their future selves, writing questions and answers about why they chose that career and why they like it.

CHALLENGE

How Did You Do It? Students can write a letter or E-mail to someone famous who is proficient in an activity they would enjoy. Have them ask that person how he or she achieved success.

Listening and Speaking

LISTENING STRATEGIES
As diary entries are read aloud, have students:
- face the speaker and listen attentively.
- jot down questions to ask later if any parts are unclear.

SPEAKING STRATEGIES
Have speakers:
- stand up straight and try not to be too nervous.
- vary tone of voice when expressing personal feelings.

LANGUAGE SUPPORT

ESL Supply these sentence formats to show students how to give reasons: *You should try this activity because...* and *If you don't try this, you will/won't...* Do a few sample completions with students.

PORTFOLIO Invite students to include their notes in their portfolios.

5 Day Grammar and Usage Plan

LANGUAGE SUPPORT

Write this sentence on the board: *He looks at the picture.* Then put the word *yesterday*, and then *tomorrow* in front of the sentence. Have students change the verb to past and future tenses. (looked, will look)

DAILY LANGUAGE ACTIVITIES

Write the Daily Language Activities on the chalkboard each day or use **Transparency 12.** Have students correct the sentences orally. For answers, see the transparency.

Day 1

1. Last Friday I look at two books.
2. Yesterday I try to copy the art.
3. Last week I race home to paint.

Day 2

1. Last Friday I order a book.
2. Next Tuesday Joe mail the check.
3. The box arrive tomorrow.

Day 3

1. Next week Pat visit us.
2. Next Monday I ask her to sign my book.
3. My dad paint the pictures a year ago.

Day 4

1. Tomorrow Jean draw a picture.
2. Yesterday I rub the crayon too hard.
3. Last week I study hard for my test.

Day 5

1. Last time we trade pictures.
2. Yesterday Pat dab the paper with paint.
3. Next week we meet at the studio.

Daily Language Transparency 12

DAY 1 Introduce the Concept

Oral Warm-Up Ask volunteers how to form present-tense verbs when the subject of a sentence is singular.

Introduce Past Tense Present and discuss the following:

Past Tense

- A verb in the **past tense** tells about an action that already happened. Add *-ed* to most verbs to show past tense.
- If a verb ends in *e*, drop *e* and add *-ed*.
- If a verb ends with a consonant and *y*, change *y* to *i* and add *-ed*.
- If a verb has only one vowel followed by one consonant, usually double the consonant and add *-ed*.

Present the Daily Language Activity. Then have students use the past tense of *look*, *try*, and *race* in sentences.

WRITING Assign the daily Writing Prompt on page 282C.

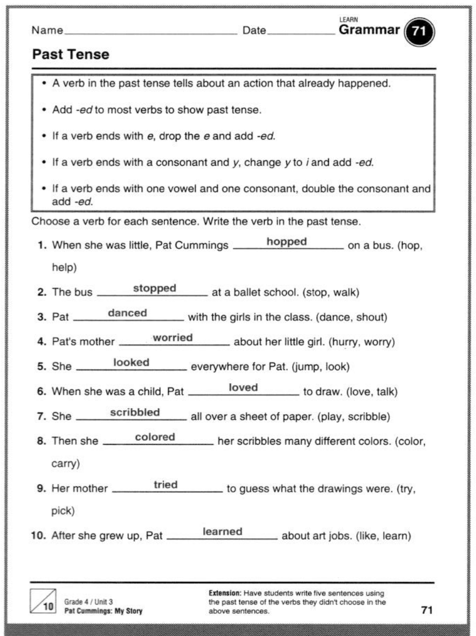
Name______ Date______ LEARN Grammar 71

Past Tense

- A verb in the past tense tells about an action that already happened.
- Add *-ed* to most verbs to show past tense.
- If a verb ends with *e*, drop the *e* and add *-ed*.
- If a verb ends with a consonant and *y*, change *y* to *i* and add *-ed*.
- If a verb ends with one vowel and one consonant, double the consonant and add *-ed*.

Choose a verb for each sentence. Write the verb in the past tense.

1. When she was little, Pat Cummings __hopped__ on a bus. (hop, help)
2. The bus __stopped__ at a ballet school. (stop, walk)
3. Pat __danced__ with the girls in the class. (dance, shout)
4. Pat's mother __worried__ about her little girl. (hurry, worry)
5. She __looked__ everywhere for Pat. (jump, look)
6. When she was a child, Pat __loved__ to draw. (love, talk)
7. She __scribbled__ all over a sheet of paper. (play, scribble)
8. Then she __colored__ her scribbles many different colors. (color, carry)
9. Her mother __tried__ to guess what the drawings were. (try, pick)
10. After she grew up, Pat __learned__ about art jobs. (like, learn)

10 Grade 4 / Unit 3 Pat Cummings: My Story

Extension: Have students write five sentences using the past tense of the verbs they didn't choose in the above sentences.

71

GRAMMAR PRACTICE BOOK, PAGE 71

DAY 2 Teach the Concept

Review Past Tense Have students explain how they can tell if a verb is in the past tense.

Introduce Future Tense To tell about an action that will happen in the future, you need a special helping verb. Present the following:

Future Tense

- A verb in the **future tense** tells about an action that is going to happen.
- To write about the future, use the special verb *will*.

Present the Daily Language Activity. Then invite students to write predictions on strips of paper. Collect the strips and invite volunteers to select and read them aloud. Then write all the future tense verbs used in the predictions on the chalkboard.

WRITING Assign the daily Writing Prompt on page 282C.

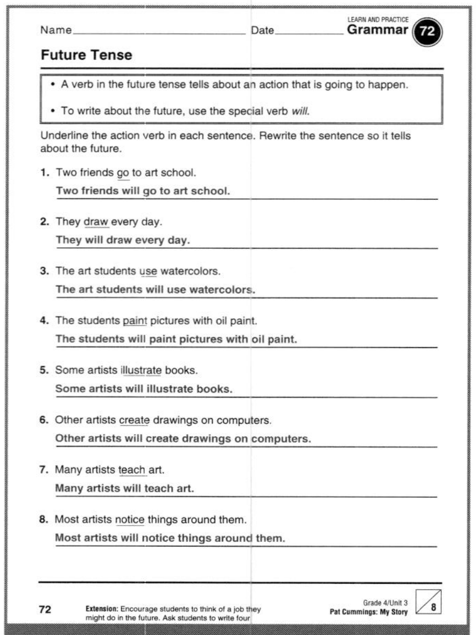
Name______ Date______ LEARN AND PRACTICE Grammar 72

Future Tense

- A verb in the future tense tells about an action that is going to happen.
- To write about the future, use the special verb *will*.

Underline the action verb in each sentence. Rewrite the sentence so it tells about the future.

1. Two friends go to art school.
   Two friends will go to art school.
2. They draw every day.
   They will draw every day.
3. The art students use watercolors.
   The art students will use watercolors.
4. The students paint pictures with oil paint.
   The students will paint pictures with oil paint.
5. Some artists illustrate books.
   Some artists will illustrate books.
6. Other artists create drawings on computers.
   Other artists will create drawings on computers.
7. Many artists teach art.
   Many artists will teach art.
8. Most artists notice things around them.
   Most artists will notice things around them.

72

Extension: Encourage students to think of a job they might do in the future. Ask students to write four

Grade 4/Unit 3 Pat Cummings: My Story 8

GRAMMAR PRACTICE BOOK, PAGE 72

Past and Future Tenses

DAY 3 Review and Practice

Learn from the Literature Review past-tense and future-tense verbs. Read the first sentence of the first complete paragraph on page 292 of *Pat Cummings: My Story:*

> **I used my sister Linda and my niece Keija on the cover of *Just Us Women*.**

Ask students what tense the sentence is in. (past tense) Then have them change the sentence to future tense.

Use Past- and Future-Tense Verbs Present the Daily Language Activity. Then have partners write present-tense verbs on separate index cards. Have students place the cards face down and then take turns selecting words, changing them to past tense or future tense, and using them in sentences.

WRITING Assign the daily Writing Prompt on page 282D.

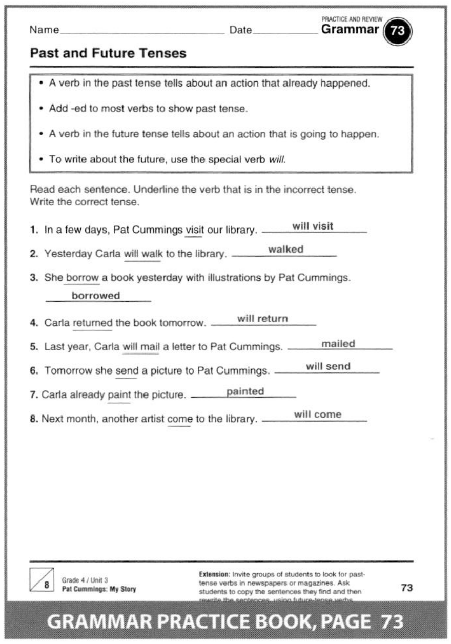
Name____________ Date________ PRACTICE AND REVIEW Grammar 73

Past and Future Tenses

- A verb in the past tense tells about an action that already happened.
- Add -ed to most verbs to show past tense.
- A verb in the future tense tells about an action that is going to happen.
- To write about the future, use the special verb *will*.

Read each sentence. Underline the verb that is in the incorrect tense. Write the correct tense.

1. In a few days, Pat Cummings visit our library. will visit
2. Yesterday Carla will walk to the library. walked
3. She borrow a book yesterday with illustrations by Pat Cummings. borrowed
4. Carla returned the book tomorrow. will return
5. Last year, Carla will mail a letter to Pat Cummings. mailed
6. Tomorrow she send a picture to Pat Cummings. will send
7. Carla already paint the picture. painted
8. Next month, another artist come to the library. will come

8 Grade 4 / Unit 3 Pat Cummings: My Story — Extension: Invite groups of students to look for past-tense verbs in newspapers or magazines. Ask students to copy the sentences they find and then rewrite the sentences, using future-tense verbs. 73

GRAMMAR PRACTICE BOOK, PAGE 73

DAY 4 Review and Practice

Review Past and Future Tense Have the class make a timeline of the week's events. Divide it into two sections labeled *Past* and *Future*. Invite volunteers to write sentences describing different events. Then present the Daily Language Activity.

Mechanics and Usage Before students begin the daily Writing Prompt on page 282D, review letter punctuation.

Letter Punctuation

- Begin the greeting and closing in a letter with a capital letter.
- Use a comma after the greeting and closing in a letter.
- Use a comma between the names of a city and a state.
- Use a comma between the day and year in a date.

WRITING Assign the daily Writing Prompt on page 282D.

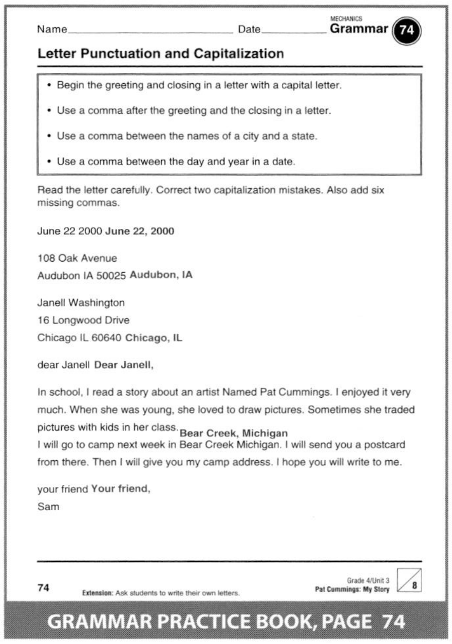
Name____________ Date________ MECHANICS Grammar 74

Letter Punctuation and Capitalization

- Begin the greeting and closing in a letter with a capital letter.
- Use a comma after the greeting and the closing in a letter.
- Use a comma between the names of a city and a state.
- Use a comma between the day and year in a date.

Read the letter carefully. Correct two capitalization mistakes. Also add six missing commas.

June 22 2000 **June 22, 2000**

108 Oak Avenue
Audubon IA 50025 **Audubon, IA**

Janell Washington
16 Longwood Drive
Chicago IL 60640 **Chicago, IL**

dear Janell **Dear Janell,**

In school, I read a story about an artist Named Pat Cummings. I enjoyed it very much. When she was young, she loved to draw pictures. Sometimes she traded pictures with kids in her class. **Bear Creek, Michigan**
I will go to camp next week in Bear Creek Michigan. I will send you a postcard from there. Then I will give you my camp address. I hope you will write to me.

your friend **Your friend,**
Sam

74 Extension: Ask students to write their own letters. Grade 4/Unit 3 Pat Cummings: My Story 8

GRAMMAR PRACTICE BOOK, PAGE 74

DAY 5 Assess and Reteach

Assess Use the Daily Language Activity and page 75 of the **Grammar Practice Book** for assessment.

Reteach Write these verbs on slips of paper: *scrub, paint, turn, work, cry, jump, watch, call, fetch*. Have volunteers choose a verb to pantomime. Before they perform the action, have them tell in a complete sentence what they will do. After they perform the action, have them tell what they did. Write both sentences on the board, and have students identify which one is in past tense and which is in future tense.

Have students create a word wall with lists of past-tense and future-tense verbs.

Use page 76 of the **Grammar Practice Book** for additional reteaching.

WRITING Assign the daily Writing Prompt on page 282D.

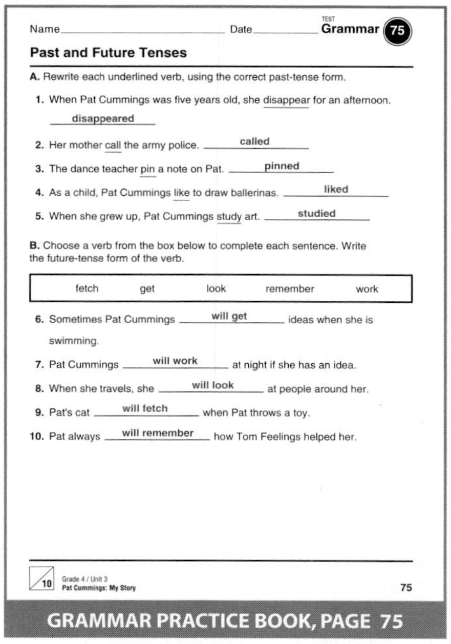
Name____________ Date________ TEST Grammar 75

Past and Future Tenses

A. Rewrite each underlined verb, using the correct past-tense form.

1. When Pat Cummings was five years old, she disappear for an afternoon. disappeared
2. Her mother call the army police. called
3. The dance teacher pin a note on Pat. pinned
4. As a child, Pat Cummings like to draw ballerinas. liked
5. When she grew up, Pat Cummings study art. studied

B. Choose a verb from the box below to complete each sentence. Write the future-tense form of the verb.

fetch	get	look	remember	work

6. Sometimes Pat Cummings will get ideas when she is swimming.
7. Pat Cummings will work at night if she has an idea.
8. When she travels, she will look at people around her.
9. Pat's cat will fetch when Pat throws a toy.
10. Pat always will remember how Tom Feelings helped her.

10 Grade 4 / Unit 3 Pat Cummings: My Story 75

GRAMMAR PRACTICE BOOK, PAGE 75

GRAMMAR PRACTICE BOOK, PAGE 76

5 Day Spelling Plan

LANGUAGE SUPPORT

Point out the Spelling Words with *r*-controlled vowels. Have students listen for the /yů/ and /ů/ sounds as you slowly say the following words: *curious, furious, pure, cure, sure, tour.*

DICTATION SENTENCES

Spelling Words

1. Many cats are curious.
2. The water tastes pure.
3. Are you fully dressed?
4. I am sure I will win.
5. They played with wooden dolls.
6. What should we do now?
7. A furious storm crashed into the coast.
8. There is no cure for a cold.
9. We have a handful of coins.
10. A crooked road has many turns.
11. I would like to take a trip.
12. The bulldozer is moving rocks.
13. The fire left black soot on everything.
14. We went on a tour of the city.
15. A butcher sells meat.
16. Put on woolen mittens.
17. This pudding tastes sweet.
18. His goodness shows in his kind acts.
19. A pulley can lift a car.
20. Try not to overlook your mistakes.

Challenge Words

21. Giants ten feet tall do not exist.
22. What image is in your mind?
23. Books can inspire us to write.
24. She has a reference file of names.
25. He made a sketch with a crayon.

DAY 1 Pretest

Assess Prior Knowledge Use the Dictation Sentences at the left and **Spelling Practice Book** page 71 for the pretest. Allow students to correct their own papers. Students who require a modified list may be tested on the first 10 words.

Spelling Words		Challenge Words
1. curious	11. **would**	21. **exist**
2. pure	12. bulldozer	22. **image**
3. fully	13. soot	23. **inspire**
4. **sure**	14. tour	24. **reference**
5. wooden	15. butcher	25. **sketch**
6. **should**	16. woolen	
7. furious	17. pudding	
8. cure	18. goodness	
9. handful	19. pulley	
10. crooked	20. overlook	

*Note: Words in **dark type** are from the story.*

Word Study On page 72 of the **Spelling Practice Book** are word study steps and an at-home activity.

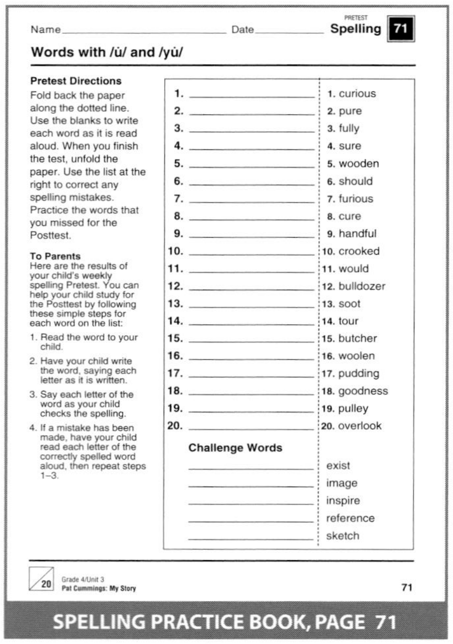
Name______ Date______ PRETEST Spelling 71

Words with /ů/ and /yů/

Pretest Directions
Fold back the paper along the dotted line. Use the blanks to write each word as it is read aloud. When you finish the test, unfold the paper. Use the list at the right to correct any spelling mistakes. Practice the words that you missed for the Posttest.

To Parents
Here are the results of your child's weekly Spelling Pretest. You can help your child study for the Posttest by following these simple steps for each word on the list:
1. Read the word to your child.
2. Have your child write the word, saying each letter as it is written.
3. Say each letter of the word as your child checks the spelling.
4. If a mistake has been made, have your child read each letter of the correctly spelled word aloud, then repeat steps 1–3.

1. curious, 2. pure, 3. fully, 4. sure, 5. wooden, 6. should, 7. furious, 8. cure, 9. handful, 10. crooked, 11. would, 12. bulldozer, 13. soot, 14. tour, 15. butcher, 16. woolen, 17. pudding, 18. goodness, 19. pulley, 20. overlook

Challenge Words: exist, image, inspire, reference, sketch

20 Grade 4/Unit 3 Pat Cummings: My Story 71

SPELLING PRACTICE BOOK, PAGE 71

WORD STUDY STEPS AND ACTIVITY, PAGE 72

DAY 2 Explore the Pattern

Sort and Spell Words Say the following words, and have students identify the vowel sound that they hear: *soot* /ů/, *pure* /yů/, *should* /ů/. Have students read the Spelling Words aloud and sort them as below.

Words with

/ů/ spelled *u*	/ů/ spelled *oo*
fully	wooden
handful	crooked
bulldozer	soot
butcher	woolen
pudding	goodness
pulley	overlook
/ů/ spelled *ou*	**/ů/ spelled *u-e***
should	sure
would	
tour	
/yů/ spelled *u*	**/yů/ spelled *u-e***
curious	pure
furious	cure

Word Wall Have students create a word wall based on the word sort and add more words from their reading.

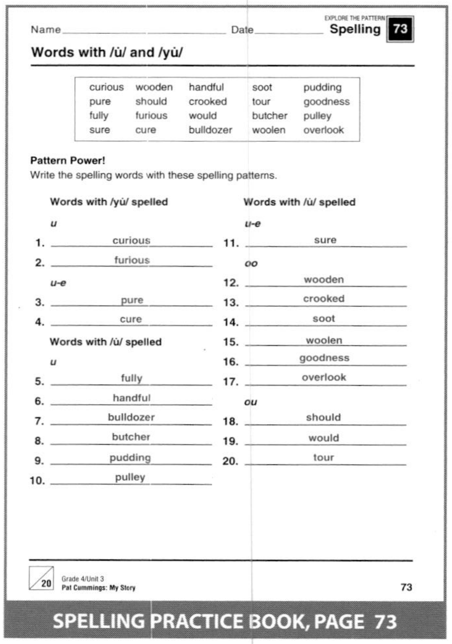
Name______ Date______ EXPLORE THE PATTERN Spelling 73

Words with /ů/ and /yů/

curious	wooden	handful	soot	pudding
pure	should	crooked	tour	goodness
fully	furious	would	butcher	pulley
sure	cure	bulldozer	woolen	overlook

Pattern Power!
Write the spelling words with these spelling patterns.

Words with /yů/ spelled
u
1. curious
2. furious
u-e
3. pure
4. cure

Words with /ů/ spelled
u
5. fully
6. handful
7. bulldozer
8. butcher
9. pudding
10. pulley

Words with /ů/ spelled
u-e
11. sure
oo
12. wooden
13. crooked
14. soot
15. woolen
16. goodness
17. overlook
ou
18. should
19. would
20. tour

20 Grade 4/Unit 3 Pat Cummings: My Story 73

SPELLING PRACTICE BOOK, PAGE 73

Words with /ů/ and /yů/

DAY 3 Practice and Extend

Word Meaning: Antonyms Remind students that words with opposite meanings are called *antonyms*. Have partners list antonyms for as many of the Spelling Words as they can. (Examples: *fully/partly, sure/unsure, furious/delighted, crooked/straight*) Then have partners share lists and sentences that include the words and their antonyms.

If students need extra practice, have partners give each other a midweek test.

Glossary Use the Language Note definition on page 728 of the Glossary to review the meaning of *synonym*. Then have partners:

- write each Challenge Word.
- look up each word to find any listed synonyms. (inspire has a synonym)
- write the words and their synonyms in sentences.

Name_______________ Date_______ PRACTICE AND EXTEND **Spelling 74**

Words with /ů/ and /yů/

curious	wooden	handful	soot	pudding
pure	should	crooked	tour	goodness
fully	furious	would	butcher	pulley
sure	cure	bulldozer	woolen	overlook

Definitions for You

Fill in the word from the spelling list that matches the definition.

1. made from the hair of sheep — woolen
2. interested in learning more — curious
3. to fail to notice — overlook
4. free of dirt or pollution — pure
5. made from trees — wooden
6. a word used to express duty — should
7. having bends or curves — crooked
8. the amount a hand can hold — handful
9. black particles left after wood or coal are burned — soot
10. completely or totally — fully
11. a word used to make a polite request — would
12. desirable qualities — goodness
13. a method that brings back health — cure
14. impossible to doubt — sure
15. to be very angry — furious
16. a creamy dessert — pudding

74 **Challenge Extension:** Pair up students. Have one partner use the dictionary to write short definitions for each Challenge Word. Then let the other partner use the definitions to make up one sentence for each. Grade 4/Unit 3 **Pat Cummings: My Story** 16

SPELLING PRACTICE BOOK, PAGE 74

DAY 4 Proofread and Write

Proofread Sentences Write these sentences on the chalkboard, including the misspelled words. Ask students to proofread, circling incorrect spellings and writing the correct spellings. There are two spelling errors in each sentence.

If you're courious, you shuld ask questions. (curious, should)

We took a toor of the wudden bridge. (tour, wooden)

Have students create additional sentences with errors for partners to correct.

WRITING Have students use as many spelling words as possible in the daily Writing Prompt on page 282D. Remind students to proofread their writing for errors in spelling, grammar, and punctuation.

Name_______________ Date_______ PROOFREAD AND WRITE **Spelling 75**

Words with /ů/ and /yů/

Proofreading Activity

There are six spelling mistakes in the paragraph. Circle the misspelled words. Write the words correctly on the lines below.

Last fall I went to the community crafts fair and saw lots of interesting things. One woman was making old-fashioned wudden toys from pieces of pine and maple. I bought a buledozer that really works for my little brother. A candlemaker was selling candles made from pur beeswax. A weaver was making beautiful wollen shawls and scarves. I bought a handfool of bright, shiny marbles. I got cyrious when I saw a crowd of people gathered in a circle. When I got closer I saw someone making blown glass animals. It was a fun day.

1. wooden 3. pure 5. handful
2. bulldozer 4. woolen 6. curious

Writing Activity

Using four spelling words, describe a crafts fair or other festival that you have attended.

10 Grade 4/Unit 3 **Pat Cummings: My Story** 75

SPELLING PRACTICE BOOK, PAGE 75

DAY 5 Assess and Reteach

Assess Students' Knowledge Use page 76 of the **Spelling Practice Book** or the Dictation Sentences on page 297O for the posttest.

JOURNAL **Personal Word List** Students can add any troublesome spelling words to their personal lists in their journals. Have students write a synonym or a definition after each word.

Students should refer to their word lists during later writing activities.

Name_______________ Date_______ POSTTEST **Spelling 76**

Words with /ů/ and /yů/

Look at the words in each set below. One word in each set is spelled correctly. Use a pencil to fill in the circle next to the correct word. Before you begin, look at the sample sets of words. Sample A has been done for you. Do Sample B by yourself. When you are sure you know what to do, you may go on with the rest of the page.

Sample A ● poor Ⓑ puer Ⓒ por Ⓓ puore
Sample B Ⓔ coulde ● could Ⓖ kould Ⓗ cuold

1. Ⓐ overloke Ⓑ ovirlook ● overlook Ⓓ ovarlouk
2. Ⓔ puley Ⓕ pullie Ⓖ pouley ● pulley
3. Ⓐ gudness ● goodness Ⓒ goodnis Ⓓ goudness
4. Ⓔ pulding Ⓕ pudden ● pudding Ⓗ pooding
5. ● woolen Ⓑ wulen Ⓒ woolin Ⓓ woulen
6. Ⓔ bucher ● butcher Ⓖ bootcher Ⓗ butsher
7. ● tour Ⓑ toor Ⓒ ture Ⓓ tuyre
8. ● soot Ⓕ sut Ⓖ soote Ⓗ soute
9. Ⓐ booldoxer Ⓑ bulldoxer Ⓒ buldozar ● bulldozer
10. Ⓔ wuld Ⓕ wolde ● would Ⓗ woold
11. Ⓐ krooked ● crooked Ⓒ crookad Ⓓ crucked
12. ● handful Ⓕ hanfull Ⓖ handfool Ⓗ hannful
13. Ⓐ cyure Ⓑ coure ● cure Ⓓ ciure
14. Ⓔ fureus Ⓕ furrius ● furious Ⓗ farious
15. ● should Ⓑ sould Ⓒ shuuld Ⓓ shold
16. ● wooden Ⓕ wuden Ⓖ woodan Ⓗ wouldin
17. Ⓐ soore ● sure Ⓒ suyre Ⓓ soure
18. Ⓔ fulie ● fully Ⓖ fooly Ⓗ fullyie
19. Ⓐ puyre Ⓑ poour ● pure Ⓓ puare
20. Ⓔ cureus Ⓕ kurious Ⓖ karius ● curious

76 Grade 4/Unit 3 **Pat Cummings: My Story** 20

SPELLING PRACTICE BOOK, PAGE 76

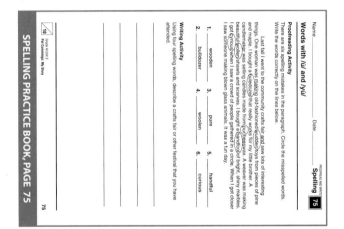

Lesson Overview

Reaching All Learners

Concept
- Poets and Poems

Comprehension
- Author's Purpose, Point of View

Vocabulary
- chanted
- nipped
- pouch
- restless
- scribbled
- stitching

Anthology

Grass Sandals

Selection Summary **Basho, a seventeenth century Japanese poet, travels through Japan describing the aspects of nature that touch his heart and mind.**

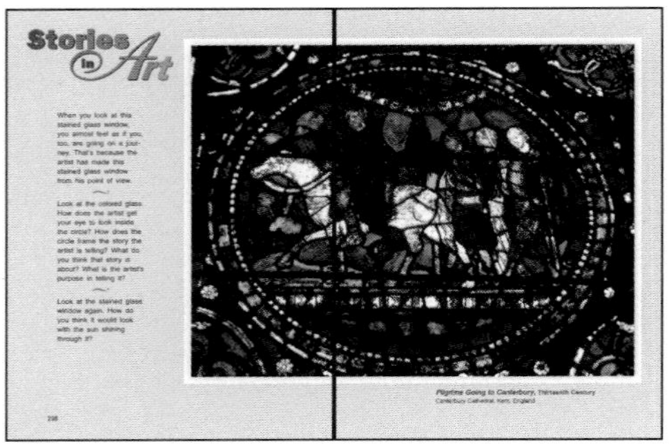

Stories in Art focuses on the **comprehension** skill

Reading Strategy applies the **comprehension** skill

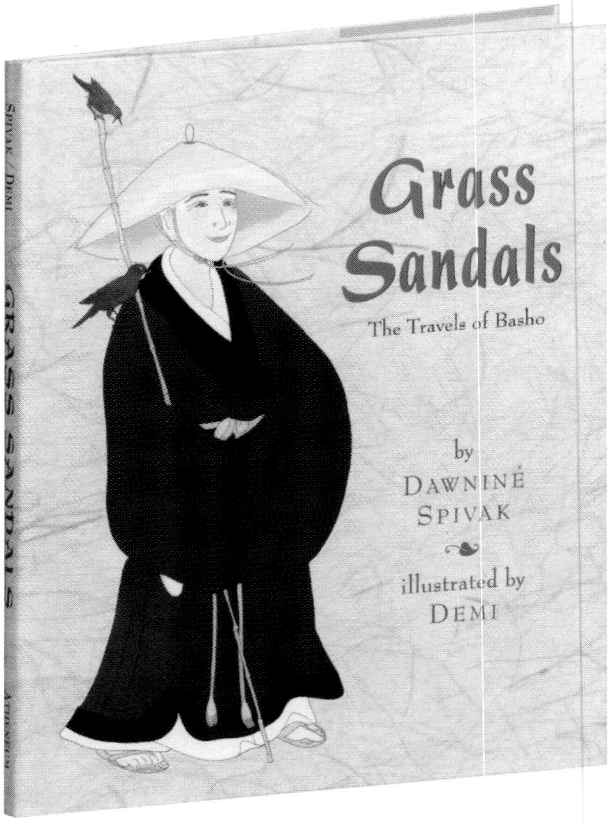

Listening Library

INSTRUCTIONAL pages 300-331

About the Author Dawnine Spivak lives in New England, enjoying the quiet and natural surroundings of the area. She finds that Japanese literature shares the same tranquillity. In the past, Spivak has taught college-level courses on Japanese literature and poetry.

About the Illustrator Demi Hitz has illustrated many children's books. Known by her first name in the art world, Demi enjoys creating larger works of art, such as murals and mosaics, in addition to her acclaimed book illustrations.

Same Concept, Skills and Vocabulary!

Leveled Books

EASY
Lesson on pages 331A and 331D

INDEPENDENT
Lesson on pages 331B and 331D
Take-Home version available

CHALLENGE
Lesson on pages 331C and 331D

Leveled Practice

EASY

Reteach, 89–95 blackline masters with reteaching opportunities for each assessed skill

INDEPENDENT/ON-LEVEL

Practice, 89–95 workbook with Take-Home stories and practice opportunities for each assessed skill and story comprehension

CHALLENGE

Extend, 89–95 blackline masters that offer challenge activities for each assessed skill

Quizzes Prepared by Accelerated Reader

WORKSTATION Activities

Social Studies	Map Skills, *324* Using an Elevation Map, *329*
Science	Natural Dyes, *320*
Math	Moon Watch, *318*
Art	Japanese Art, *302*
Language Arts	Read Aloud, *298E* Haiku, *322*
Cultural Perspectives	Compare Foods, 314
Writing	A Book Review, *328*
Research and Inquiry	Find Out More, *329*
Internet Activities	www.mhschool.com/reading

Suggested Lesson Planner

READING AND LANGUAGE ARTS	DAY 1 Focus on Reading and Skills	DAY 2 Read the Literature
Comprehension Vocabulary Phonics/Decoding Study Skills Listening, Speaking, Viewing, Representing	Read **Read Aloud: Poetry,** 298E "Four Haiku" **Develop Visual Literacy,** 298 ☑ **Introduce Author's Purpose, Point of View,** 299A–299B **Teaching Chart 73** **Reteach, Practice, Extend,** 89 Read **Reading Strategy: Author's Purpose and Point of View,** 299 "Shonto Begay" Intervention Program	**Build Background,** 300A Develop Oral Language **Vocabulary,** 300B, 300C *chanted* *pouch* *scribbled* *nipped* *restless* *stitching* **Teaching Chart 74** Word Building Manipulative Cards **Reteach, Practice, Extend,** 90 Read **Read the Selection,** 300–327 ☑ **Author's Purpose, Point of View** ☑ **Summarize** **Genre: Biographical Story,** 301 **Cultural Perspectives,** 314 Intervention Program
Curriculum Connections	Link **Work of Art,** 298	Link **Language Arts,** 300A
Writing	**Writing Prompt:** Write a letter to a friend telling about the places you have visited or things you have done in the last two days.	**Writing Prompt:** Page through the selection to find your four favorite illustrations. Describe what is happening in each. **Journal Writing,** 327 Quick-Write
Grammar	**Introduce the Concept: Main and Helping Verbs,** 331M Daily Language Activity 1. Look, Basho have planted a tree. has 2. His friends has waved good-bye. have 3. Yesterday, Basho have noticed a cricket in the pond. had **Grammar Practice Book,** 77	**Teach the Concept: Main and Helping Verbs,** 331M Daily Language Activity 1. Earlier, Basho were feeling tired. was 2. He go on a journey tomorrow. will 3. Right now, I are looking at the sky. am **Grammar Practice Book,** 78
Spelling	**Pretest: Words with Digraphs,** 331O **Spelling Practice Book,** 77, 78	**Explore the Pattern: Words with Digraphs,** 331O **Spelling Practice Book,** 79

Intervention Program Available

Meeting Individual Needs

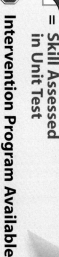

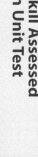

✓ = Skill Assessed in Unit Test

ⓘ Intervention Program Available

Read EVERY DAY

DAY 3 — Read the Literature

Rereading for Fluency, 326

Story Questions and Activities, 328–329
Reteach, Practice, Extend, 91

Study Skill, 330
✓ **Graphic Aids**
Teaching Chart 75
Reteach, Practice, Extend, 92

Test Power, 331

Read **Read the Leveled Books,** 331A–331D
Guided Reading
Digraphs
✓ **Author's Purpose, Point of View**
✓ **Instructional Vocabulary**

ⓘ Intervention Program

Activity Math, 318

Writing Prompt: Pretend you are a travel agent. A family has just booked a trip to the mountains. Write a paragraph telling the family where they will be going, how they will get there, and where they will be staying.

Writing Process: Persuasive Writing, 331K
Prewrite, Draft

Review and Practice: Main and Helping Verbs, 331N
Daily Language Activity
1. Basho have walked six miles today. has
2. He were surprised by the flowers. was
3. Crabs is climbing on his legs. are

Grammar Practice Book, 79

Practice and Extend: Words with Digraphs, 331P
Spelling Practice Book, 80

DAY 4 — Build Skills

Read **Read the Leveled Books and Self-Selected Books**

✓ **Review Author's Purpose, Point of View,** 331E–331F
Teaching Chart 76
Reteach, Practice, Extend, 93
Language Support, 102

✓ **Review Make Judgments and Decisions,** 331G–331H
Teaching Chart 77
Reteach, Practice, Extend, 94
Language Support, 103

Minilessons, 307, 309, 319, 323

Writer's Craft, 308

ⓘ Intervention Program

Activity Science, 320; Language Arts, 322

Writing Prompt: Write an ending to this story starter: Basho hadn't seen his friends in a long time. After he had climbed to the top of the mountain, he saw ....

Writing Process: Persuasive Writing, 331K
Revise

Meeting Individual Needs for Writing, 331L

Review and Practice: Main and Helping Verbs, 331N
Daily Language Activity
1. A woman have invited Basho for dinner today. has
2. She are cooking noodles. is
3. Next time they was eat and talk. will

Grammar Practice Book, 80

Proofread and Write: Words with Digraphs, 331P
Spelling Practice Book, 81

DAY 5 — Build Skills

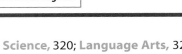

Read **Read Self-Selected Books**

✓ **Introduce Context Clues,** 331I–331J
Teaching Chart 78
Reteach, Practice, Extend, 95
Language Support, 104

Listening, Speaking, Viewing, Representing, 331L

Minilessons, 307, 309, 323

Phonics Review,
Digraphs, 319

Phonics/Phonemic Awareness Practice Book, 43–46

ⓘ Intervention Program

Activity Social Studies, 324, 329

Writing Prompt: Pretend you are sitting beside a pond. Write a paragraph telling what you see and hear as if it were happening.

Writing Process: Persuasive Writing, 331K
Edit/Proofread, Publish

Assess and Reteach: Main and Helping Verbs, 331N
Daily Language Activity
1. Last night, Basho and his friends was watching the moon. were
2. Tomorrow they write a poem. will write
3. Today, I has dyed my shoelaces. have

Grammar Practice Book, 81, 82

Assess and Reteach: Words with Digraphs, 331P
Spelling Practice Book, 82

Link
Language Arts

Read Aloud

Four Haiku
poetry by Myra Cohn Livingston

Spring

Shiny colored tents
pop up above people's heads
at the first raindrop

Summer

Not wishing to stop
his chirping the whole night long,
Cricket never does

Autumn

Searching for only
one clear puddle, I find my
rain-drenched reflection . . .

Winter

Snow sits on cold steps
leading to the front door, and
waits for my return

Oral Comprehension

LISTENING AND SPEAKING Ask students to ponder how the four poems are alike as you read and then reread each one aloud. Ask:

- How are the poems alike? Different?
- What image did you see as I read each haiku aloud?
- To which senses did each poem appeal?

GENRE STUDY: POETRY Discuss the haiku form.

- Explain: Haiku follow certain structural rules. Each poem has exactly three lines and 17 syllables (five syllables in line one, seven in line two, and five in line three). Write the first poem on the board. Have a volunteer count the syllables in each line.
- Read the poem "Summer" aloud, line by line. Ask: Does the poem follow the rules of haiku?
- Explain: Haiku also requires the poet to paint a single image in each poem. Ask: How does the imagery in the poem relate to the subject?

Activity Ask students to paint a picture (in water-colors, if possible) based on each haiku.

▶ **Visual/Kinesthetic**

Develop Visual Literacy

Link
Works of Art

Stories in Art

When you look at this stained glass window, you almost feel as if you, too, are going on a journey. That's because the artist has made this stained glass window from his point of view.

Look at the colored glass. How does the artist get your eye to look inside the circle? How does the circle frame the story the artist is telling? What do you think that story is about? What is the artist's purpose in telling it?

Look at the stained glass window again. How do you think it would look with the sun shining through it?

Pilgrims Going to Canterbury, **Thirteenth Century**
Canterbury Cathedral, Kent, England

298

Objective: Identify Author's Purpose and Point of View

VIEWING This beautiful stained glass window in Canterbury Cathedral in England depicts pilgrims on a religious journey. Have students describe the window, paying particular attention to the colors of the glass and to the facial expressions of the pilgrims. Ask them to suggest why the artist made this window and why the scene is framed by a circle.

Read the page with students, encouraging individual interpretations of the stained glass window.

Ask students to support inferences they make about the artist's purpose and point of view. For example:

- The artist chose to show a religious story because the window is meant for a church.
- The circle gets your eye to focus on the artist's picture in the center.

REPRESENTING Have students think of a journey they have taken. Then ask them to use crayons and the stained-glass technique of heavy black lines and color to draw a picture of themselves on that journey.

Introduce Author's Purpose, Point of View

TESTED OBJECTIVES

Students will identify an author's purpose and point of view.

Skills Finder

Author's Purpose, Point of View

Introduce	299A-B
Review	331E-F, 369E-F
Test	Unit 3

LANGUAGE SUPPORT

ESL Brainstorm a list of purposes authors might have for writing a story and write them on the board. You can give examples of stories students have already read and help them discover the different purposes the authors had.

PREPARE

Discuss Author's Purpose Display an almanac and a comic book. Have students discuss the differences between the books. Ask: Why was each book written? (to inform, to entertain)

TEACH

Define Author's Purpose and Point of View Tell students: An author has a reason for writing. This reason is called the author's purpose. For example, an author might write to inform, to entertain, to persuade, or to express a feeling. An author also shows his or her thoughts and attitudes. This is called the author's point of view.

Carla's Poetry

Carla stomped into the room. She frowned, grabbed a notebook, and flopped on her bed.

Carla had decided to write a poem because she was in a bad mood. Writing a poem always made Carla feel better. She usually wrote about her feelings. Today Carla wrote:

Black, angry clouds race across the sky.
They crash and crackle as they collide,
Sending blinding bolts of lightning to the ground.

Carla read over her words. "That sounds pretty good!" she thought. She smiled.

Carla was beginning to feel better already.

Teaching Chart 73

Read the Story and Model the Skill Display **Teaching Chart 73.** Afterward, have students circle clues to Carla's purpose for writing.

MODEL One way to find an author's purpose is by looking at the words he or she chooses. Words like *angry* and *collide* show a lot of emotion. I think Carla wrote to express her feelings.

PRACTICE

Create an Author's Purpose Chart

GROUP

Have students underline clues to the author's purpose for writing the story. Then have groups make an Author's Purpose chart.
▶ **Interpersonal/Visual**

CLUES		AUTHOR'S PURPOSE
• The author describes Carla's actions in colorful language. • The author shows how Carla solves a problem.	→	entertain and inform

ASSESS/CLOSE

Identify Author's Point of View

Have students reread Carla's poem in the Teaching Chart. Ask: How do you think she felt about the storm: angry, scared, pleased, or a mix?

ALTERNATE TEACHING STRATEGY

AUTHOR'S PURPOSE, POINT OF VIEW

For a different approach to teaching this skill, see page T66.

Intervention Skills

Intervention Guide, for direct instruction and extra practice with author's purpose and point of view

Meeting Individual Needs for Comprehension

EASY

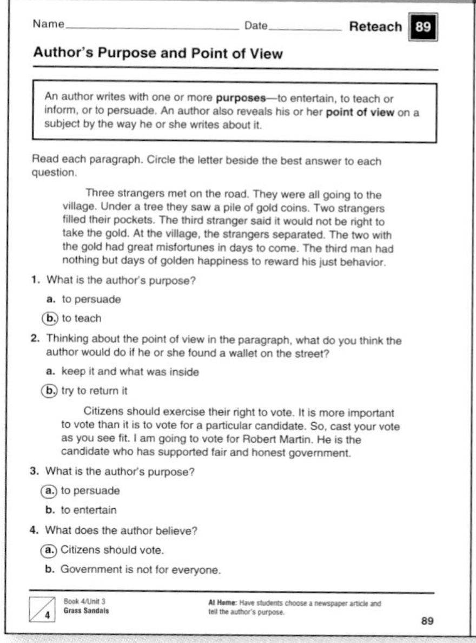
Name________ Date______ Reteach 89

Author's Purpose and Point of View

An author writes with one or more **purposes**—to entertain, to teach or inform, or to persuade. An author also reveals his or her **point of view** on a subject by the way he or she writes about it.

Read each paragraph. Circle the letter beside the best answer to each question.

Three strangers met on the road. They were all going to the village. Under a tree they saw a pile of gold coins. Two strangers filled their pockets. The third stranger said it would not be right to take the gold. At the village, the strangers separated. The two with the gold had great misfortunes in days to come. The third man had nothing but days of golden happiness to reward his just behavior.

1. What is the author's purpose?
   a. to persuade
   (b) to teach
2. Thinking about the point of view in the paragraph, what do you think the author would do if he or she found a wallet on the street?
   a. keep it and what was inside
   (b) try to return it

Citizens should exercise their right to vote. It is more important to vote than it is to vote for a particular candidate. So, cast your vote as you see fit. I am going to vote for Robert Martin. He is the candidate who has supported fair and honest government.

3. What is the author's purpose?
   (a) to persuade
   b. to entertain
4. What does the author believe?
   (a) Citizens should vote.
   b. Government is not for everyone.

4 Book 4/Unit 3 Grass Sandals — At Home: Have students choose a newspaper article and tell the author's purpose. 89

Reteach, 89

ON-LEVEL

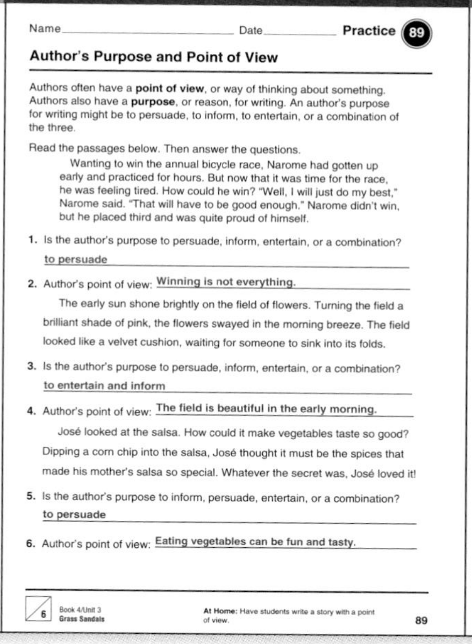
Name________ Date______ Practice 89

Author's Purpose and Point of View

Authors often have a **point of view**, or way of thinking about something. Authors also have a **purpose**, or reason, for writing. An author's purpose for writing might be to persuade, to inform, to entertain, or a combination of the three.

Read the passages below. Then answer the questions.

Wanting to win the annual bicycle race, Narome had gotten up early and practiced for hours. But now that it was time for the race, he was feeling tired. How could he win? "Well, I will just do my best," Narome said. "That will have to be good enough." Narome didn't win, but he placed third and was quite proud of himself.

1. Is the author's purpose to persuade, inform, entertain, or a combination? to persuade
2. Author's point of view: Winning is not everything.

The early sun shone brightly on the field of flowers. Turning the field a brilliant shade of pink, the flowers swayed in the morning breeze. The field looked like a velvet cushion, waiting for someone to sink into its folds.

3. Is the author's purpose to persuade, inform, entertain, or a combination? to entertain and inform
4. Author's point of view: The field is beautiful in the early morning.

José looked at the salsa. How could it make vegetables taste so good? Dipping a corn chip into the salsa, José thought it must be the spices that made his mother's salsa so special. Whatever the secret was, José loved it!

5. Is the author's purpose to inform, persuade, entertain, or a combination? to persuade
6. Author's point of view: Eating vegetables can be fun and tasty.

6 Book 4/Unit 3 Grass Sandals — At Home: Have students write a story with a point of view. 89

Practice, 89

CHALLENGE

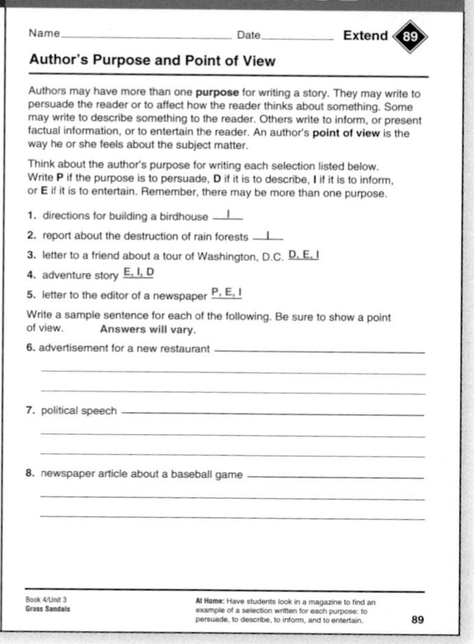
Name________ Date______ Extend 89

Author's Purpose and Point of View

Authors may have more than one **purpose** for writing a story. They may write to persuade the reader or to affect how the reader thinks about something. Some may write to describe something to the reader. Others write to inform, or present factual information, or to entertain the reader. An author's **point of view** is the way he or she feels about the subject matter.

Think about the author's purpose for writing each selection listed below. Write **P** if the purpose is to persuade, **D** if it is to describe, **I** if it is to inform, or **E** if it is to entertain. Remember, there may be more than one purpose.

1. directions for building a birdhouse I
2. report about the destruction of rain forests I
3. letter to a friend about a tour of Washington, D.C. D, E, I
4. adventure story E, I, D
5. letter to the editor of a newspaper P, E, I

Write a sample sentence for each of the following. Be sure to show a point of view. Answers will vary.

6. advertisement for a new restaurant
7. political speech
8. newspaper article about a baseball game

Book 4/Unit 3 Grass Sandals — At Home: Have students look in a magazine to find an example of a selection written for each purpose: to persuade, to describe, to inform, and to entertain. 89

Extend, 89

TESTED OBJECTIVES

Students will identify an author's purpose and point of view.

Apply Author's Purpose, Point of View

READING STRATEGY

Author's Purpose and Point of View

Develop a strategy for identifying purpose and point of view.

1. **Decide why the author wrote the selection.** How does the author feel about the topic?
2. **Look for clues to the author's purpose.** Is the author trying to persuade? to inform? to entertain?
3. **Look for clues to the author's point of view.** Are there words that tell how the author feels about the topic?
4. **Make up your own mind.** How do you feel about the topic?

READING STRATEGY

Shonto Begay

Shonto Begay was born in 1950 near Shonto, Arizona, the fifth of sixteen children. His father was a Navajo medicine man. His mother was a weaver. Reservation life was hard. The family had no running water or electricity.

Shonto Begay became an artist in spite of the hardships of his upbringing. He attended the Institute of American Indian Arts in Santa Fe, New Mexico. Then he moved to Oakland, California, to finish his college training in art.

Shonto Begay says that his art is "created from my heart and from the earth." All of his art connects back to Navajo customs and his Native American heritage.

Shonto Begay's paintings have been shown in galleries across the country. His work hangs in many public buildings. He has illustrated many children's books, such as *The Mud Pony*, as well as his own books of poetry. In 1996, the American Library Association awarded him a prize for his book *Navajo: Visions and Voices Across the Mesa.*

299

PREVIEW Have students preview "Shonto Begay." Explain that it is a biography. Discuss:

- What do you expect to learn from a biography? (facts about a person's life)
- How do authors choose people to be the subjects of biographies? (They select people who have done important or interesting things.)

SET PURPOSES Tell students that they will apply what they have learned about identifying author's purpose and point of view as they read "Shonto Begay."

APPLY THE STRATEGY Discuss the strategy for identifying author's purpose and point of view in a selection and help students apply it to the passage.

- Identify the author's main purpose for writing. Is it to inform, to entertain, or to persuade?
- Watch for clues. Describing words such as *great* and *horrible* may indicate writing meant to persuade. Dates and other facts usually signal writing meant to inform. Remember that authors may have secondary purposes.
- Watch for details that show the author's feelings about the subject. Do any details suggest how the author feels about Shonto Begay?
- Decide how *you* felt after reading. What did the author say to make you feel that way?

Activity Have each student create an Author's Purpose chart for the passage.

Build Background

Link
Language Arts

Concept: Poets and Poems

Evaluate Prior Knowledge

CONCEPT: POETS AND POEMS Explain: A poem is a form of writing that expresses thoughts or emotions. A poem is usually written in lines, not paragraphs, and often with a set rhythm and rhyming words. A person who writes poems is called a poet.

CREATE A SENSE STAR Have students visualize a lake. Ask: Which words would you use to describe the sounds you might hear? The things you might see or do? Have students list words and phrases to describe sights and sounds around a lake in a park.
▶ **Interpersonal/Linguistic**

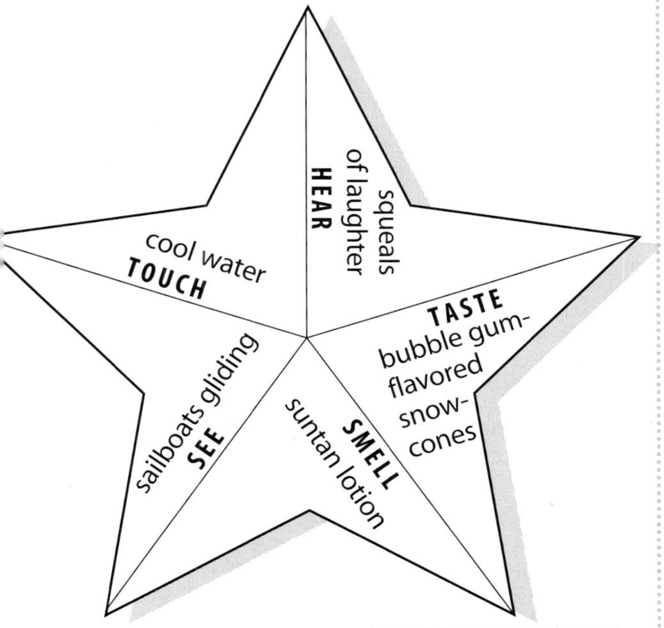

Graphic Organizer 35

BE A POET Invite students to be poets. They can use words and phrases from the sense star to write a poem about a day at a lake.

ONE WRITING

Develop Oral Language

DRAW A POETIC SCENE Review the five senses with students. Lead them in a discussion of how they would use their senses at a lake. Write key words on the board. Have students draw a picture of themselves at the lake. Suggest they use ideas from the words on the board. Help students label their pictures. Invite volunteers to share their pictures and read the words.

ESL

Also invite students to share knowledge they have about poems and poets. Discuss what poets and artists have in common.

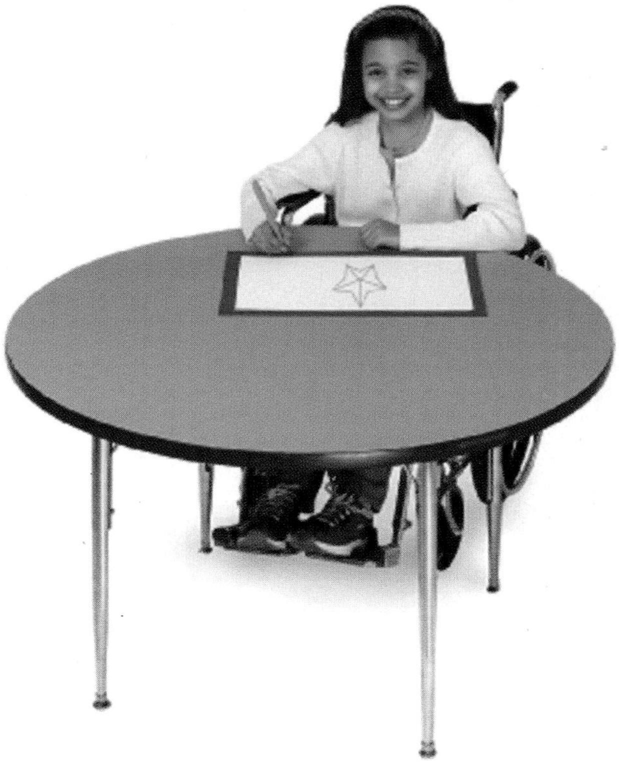

Anthology and Leveled Books

TEACHING TIP

MANAGEMENT Emphasize the importance of poetry in the story. Call on volunteers to take turns reading the main text aloud. Pause throughout the reading and invite the whole class to read the poems chorally.

LANGUAGE SUPPORT

See **Language Support Book, pages 97–100**, for teaching suggestions for Build Background.

TESTED OBJECTIVES

Students will use context and structural clues to determine the meanings of vocabulary words.

Definitions

stitching (p. 306) mending with a needle and thread; sewing

chanted (p. 311) sang or shouted words over and over

nipped (p. 312) bit or cut by pinching

pouch (p. 317) a bag or sack

scribbled (p. 307) wrote quickly

restless (p. 306) unable to rest; uneasy

Story Words

These words from the selection may be unfamiliar. Before students read, have them check the meaning and pronunciation of each word in the Glossary, beginning on page 756, or in a dictionary.

- ducked, p. 309
- orchard, p. 311
- clover, p. 316
- reflected, p. 318
- crisscrossing, p. 321

stitching
chanted
nipped
pouch
scribbled
restless

Vocabulary

Teach Vocabulary in Context

Identify Vocabulary Words Display **Teaching Chart 74**. Have volunteers circle each vocabulary word and underline words that provide clues to its meaning.

Preparing for a Trip

1. Basho sat under a tree, stitching a hole in his robe with a needle and thread. **2.** He chanted a song as he sewed. **3.** When the robe was fixed, Basho nipped the thread with his teeth. **4.** He put the needle back into his pouch and then put the bag over his shoulder. **5.** Basho then scribbled a note to remind himself to get tree bark to make a hat. **6.** Basho was feeling restless and would soon begin a long trip. He would need the hat to keep the sun and rain off his face.

Teaching Chart 74

Discuss Meanings Ask questions to help students determine word meanings:

- What do you need if you are stitching clothes?
- What is the base word in *chanted*? Give an example of what the base word means.
- If you are nipped by a dog, is it a hard or light bite?
- What are some other items you might put into a pouch?
- If you scribbled a note, would it be neat or sloppy?
- How would you feel if you were restless?

Activities

Practice

Illustrate Words (GROUP)
Have each student draw a picture that illustrates one vocabulary word. Play a game in which a student holds up his or her picture and the others guess the word. ▶ **Interpersonal/Visual**

pouch | restless | scribbled

Word Building Manipulative Cards

Round-Robin Story (WRITING)
Have students work in groups of six. Each student should use a vocabulary word to write one sentence, thereby beginning a story. Students should then trade papers, adding sentences until all the words have been used. ▶ **Interpersonal/Linguistic**

Assess Vocabulary

Use Words in Context (GROUP)
Have groups of students create a fill-in-the-blanks story, in which each blank stands for a vocabulary word. When finished, have students swap stories with another group and complete, filling in the blanks.

SPELLING/VOCABULARY CONNECTIONS

See Spelling Challenge Words, pages 331O–331P.

LANGUAGE SUPPORT

See the Language Support Book, pages 97–100, for teaching suggestions for Vocabulary.

Vocabulary PuzzleMaker

Provides vocabulary activities.

Meeting Individual Needs for Vocabulary

EASY

Name______ Date______ Reteach 90

Vocabulary

Choose a word from the list to complete each sentence.

chanted nipped pouch restless scribbled stitching

1. The child scribbled with a crayon.
2. The puppy nipped at the little girl's heels.
3. The choir chanted words as the music played.
4. The boy was restless and wanted to play outside.
5. My Mom is stitching the hole in my jeans.
6. The hiker carried supplies in a waterproof pouch.

6

Reteach 91

Story Comprehension

Write the answers to these questions about "Grass Sandals." You can refer to the story for help if you need to.

1. When and where did Basho live? He lived in Japan 300 years ago.
2. What did Basho promise his hat? He promised his hat that he would show it cherry blossoms.
3. Where did Basho begin his journey? He began his journey on a boat on a river near his village.
4. What did Basho write about? He wrote poetry about what he saw and felt on his journey.
5. Why is Basho known and loved in Japan? His writing tells of the simple, yet beautiful, experiences one can enjoy in Japan.

90–91 At Home: Have students recall their favorite part of Basho's journey. Book 4/Unit 3 Grass Sandals 5

Reteach, 90

ON-LEVEL

Name______ Date______ Practice 90

Vocabulary

Replace the underlined words with one of the vocabulary words.

chanted nipped pouch restless scribbled stitching

1. The small boy drew quickly and carelessly on the paper. scribbled
2. The mosquitoes made tiny bites at our arms. nipped
3. The class recited the same rhyme over and over again. chanted
4. Each boy had a small bag for carrying marbles or coins. pouch
5. The threads on the arms of her jacket were coming loose. stitching
6. The sisters were tired of waiting and couldn't sit still. restless

Write 2 sentences in which you use 2 of the vocabulary words in each sentence. **Answers will vary.**

7. ______
8. ______

90 At Home: Have students write a story about summertime using the vocabulary words. Book 4/Unit 3 Grass Sandals 8

Practice, 90

ON-LEVEL

Backyard Poet

One summer morning, Anna Tong sat in her backyard, waiting for something to happen. Little flies *nipped* at her arms. Anna felt bored and *restless*. She pulled at the yellow *stitching* on her dress. In the background, Anna could hear her little sister as she *chanted* a rhyme and jumped rope.

"Miss Mary Mack, Mack, Mack, all dressed in black, black, black. Had buttons, buttons, buttons, all down her back, back, back."

Anna remembered how much she had liked the rhyme. Then she had an idea. Quickly reaching into her small *pouch*, she pulled out a notebook and a pencil. Anna thought for a minute or two. Then she *scribbled* in her notebook. Smiling, she shared her new rhyme with her little sister.

"Little Sister Tong, Tong, Tong, sings the rhyming song, song, song. She is singing sweet, sweet, sweet, all morning long, long, long."

"It's sweet, sweet, sweet," *chanted* Anna's sister.

Answers will vary.

1. How can you tell that Anna is restless and uncomfortable? Flies were nipping at her and she picked at her stitching.
2. Where does Anna keep her notebook? in her pouch
3. How could you describe the way Anna wrote? She scribbled.
4. What was Anna's sister doing as she jumped rope? She chanted.
5. Why might writing rhymes make a morning fun? It can help you feel smart and clever. It's fun to rhyme words.

5 Book 4/Unit 3 Grass Sandals At Home: Have students write a chanting rhyme. 90a

Practice, 90a
Take-Home Story

CHALLENGE

Name______ Date______ Extend 90

Vocabulary

chanted restless nipped scribbled pouch stitching

Write a poem that includes at least three of the vocabulary words in the box.

Answers will vary, but each poem should contain at least three of the vocabulary words.

Extend 91

Story Comprehension

An author may write a selection to persuade, to describe, to inform, or to entertain.

Why do you think Dawnine Spivak wrote "Grass Sandals"? Explain your thinking.

Answers will vary. Possible answer: to inform; the author tells the reader about a journey Basho took and how it inspired his writing

What do you think Basho's purpose was for writing haiku? Explain your thinking.

Answers will vary. Possible answer: to describe; Basho wrote each poem to give the reader a mental picture of something.

90–91 At Home: Have students recall something beautiful they have seen. Discuss how they could convey an image of that thing to someone else. Book 4/Unit 3 Grass Sandals

Extend, 90

Comprehension

Prereading Strategies

PREVIEW AND PREDICT Have students preview the story, looking for clues to author's purpose and point of view.

- How do you think the author feels about the poet Basho? Why?
- This story includes poetry. How can you tell the difference between the poetry and the main story? (The poetry is written in italics.) ***Genre***
- What will the story most likely be about?
- Authors write stories to inform, to express, to persuade, or to entertain. Why do you think the author wrote this story?

Have students record predictions about what might happen in the story.

PREDICTIONS	WHAT HAPPENED
The main character will take a trip.	
The main character will write poetry.	

SET PURPOSES Have students set a purpose for reading. What do they want to find out? For example:

- Why does the character take a trip?
- How does the character write poems?

Meet Dawnine Spivak

Basho's poetry is a favorite of writer Dawnine Spivak. In fact, she has taught his poetry at several different universities in New England, where she lives. Spivak, who lives in a farmhouse, has also served as a member of the Vermont Anti-Hunger Corps. Her interest in the needs of others can be seen in her writing as well.

Meet Demi

Demi's full name is Demi Hitz. She has illustrated more than 130 children's books, including *The Empty Pot*, *Liang and the Magic Paint Brush*, and *The Nightingale*, a *New York Times* Best Book of the Year. Besides book illustrations, Demi likes to make larger works of art. She has painted murals in Mexico and gold-leaf mosaics in the dome of St. Peter and Paul's Church in Wilmington, California.

300

雨
火
友
馬
川
山
界
舟
月

Meeting Individual Needs • Grouping Suggestions for Strategic Reading

EASY

Read Together Read the story with students or invite them to use the **Listening Library**. Have students use the Author's Purpose chart to record examples of author's purpose. Comprehension and Intervention prompts offer additional help with decoding, vocabulary, and comprehension.

ON-LEVEL

Guided Instruction Invite students to read the story aloud. Pause during the read aloud to ask Comprehension questions. Have students use the Author's Purpose chart as they read to record clues to the author's purpose.

CHALLENGE

Read Independently Explain that authors give clues to their purposes for writing through the words they use. Have students read the story independently. Have them record specific examples that show the reasons the author wrote the story.

Comprehension

☑ Apply Author's Purpose, Point of View
☑ Apply Summarize

STRATEGIC READING Sometimes you can't really tell an author's purpose for writing until the end of a story. As we read, let's make a chart of clues. Then at the end we'll decide what the author's purpose was.

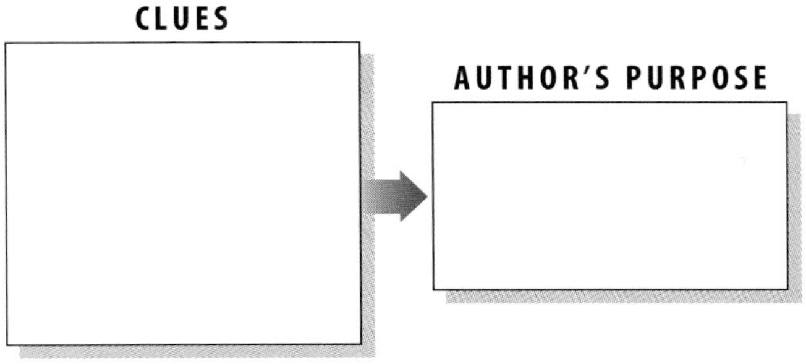

(1) **AUTHOR'S PURPOSE** What does the picture tell you about the main character? What might the author and illustrator want to tell you about this man? (Sample answer: The bird and the man are friends. The man is kind and likes animals.)

LANGUAGE SUPPORT

A blackline master of the Author's Purpose chart is available in the **Language Support Book.**

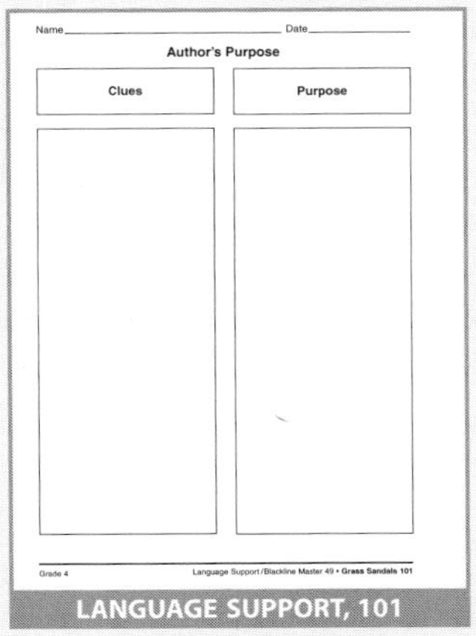
Name________ Date________

Author's Purpose

Clues	Purpose

Grade 4 Language Support/Blackline Master 49 • Grass Sandals 101

LANGUAGE SUPPORT, 101

Genre

Biographical Story

Explain that a biographical story:

- tells the story of a real person.
- may include some fictional elements, such as dialogue.
- focuses on only one or two events in the person's life.

Activity After students read *Grass Sandals: The Travels of Basho*, remind them that Basho was a real person and this story is basically true, but the author must have made up some parts, such as dialogue. Have students review the places Basho visited. Ask: Which sights along the way inspired the poet to write?

Comprehension

(2) **AUTHOR'S PURPOSE** In this passage, the writer Dawnine Spivak talks to her readers in a note. What can you infer from the note?

MODEL From the note, I learned some facts about haiku, a form of poetry, and about the Japanese language. From previewing the selection, I know there are Japanese words and poems included. Therefore, having this background information will probably help me to appreciate the story. I also inferred that one reason Spivak wrote the story is to educate the reader about the language and poetry of Japan.

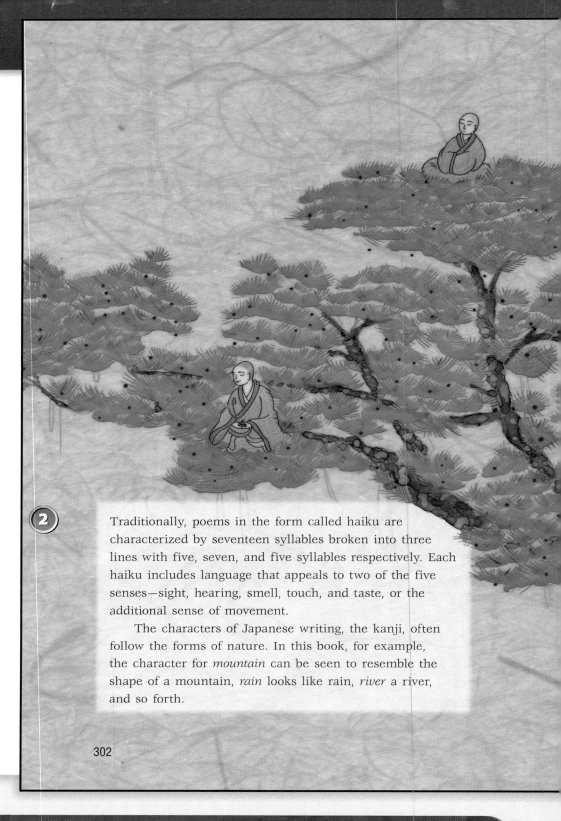

(2) Traditionally, poems in the form called haiku are characterized by seventeen syllables broken into three lines with five, seven, and five syllables respectively. Each haiku includes language that appeals to two of the five senses—sight, hearing, smell, touch, and taste, or the additional sense of movement.

The characters of Japanese writing, the kanji, often follow the forms of nature. In this book, for example, the character for *mountain* can be seen to resemble the shape of a mountain, *rain* looks like rain, *river* a river, and so forth.

302

Activity

Cross Curricular: Art

JAPANESE ART Explain that the illustrations in this selection are based on traditional Japanese styles of painting. Point out that Japanese artists often create scenes that tell stories, with characters reappearing in different places to suggest movement or time passsage, as on pages 308–309. The artist uses a minimum number of brush strokes to represent the subject, allowing the viewer to fill in the story. Display examples of Japanese art. Encourage students to paint pictures in a Japanese style.

▶ **Visual/Interpersonal**

There were old men of China who made themselves nests in trees and lived in the branches.

303

Comprehension

TEACHING TIP

POINT OF VIEW You may wish to challenge advanced students by making an important distinction. Explain that there is a difference between author's viewpoint and narrative point of view. The author's viewpoint refers to an author's thoughts and feelings about a subject. The narrative point of view refers to the person who tells the story. As students read the first sentence on page 305, tell students the word *me* tells the reader that this story is told from a first-person point of view. The narrator is either a character or the author—in this case, the author.

Comprehension

3 **AUTHOR'S PURPOSE** The symbol you see here is the Japanese character, or written symbol, for the word *mountain*. Why do you think the author has included it on the page? (Sample answer: She may want readers to learn about Japanese writing.)

4 **AUTHOR'S PURPOSE** These three lines of poetry are an example of a haiku—a kind of Japanese poem. Who do you think wrote the poem? Why do you think the author includes it? (Sample answer: Basho may have written it. The author may want to make readers familiar with his poems.) Let's add clues to the chart.

CLUES		AUTHOR'S PURPOSE
• includes Japanese writing • includes poetry	→	

Fluency

READ HAIKU POETRY Read the haiku aloud. Remind students to listen carefully. Point out that there is no noticeable rhythm or rhyme. Point out that there is little punctuation—only a dash, which suggests the reader pause at that spot. Have students practice reading the poem several times with a partner. Suggest they try emphasizing different words in each practice reading and also vary their oral reading rate.

3
山
YAMA
mountain
4
alone in my house—
only the morning glories
straggle to my door
304

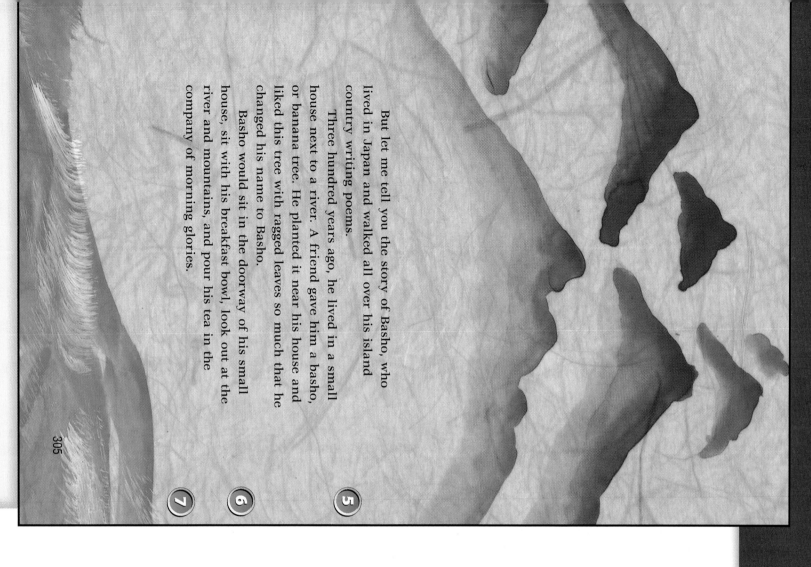

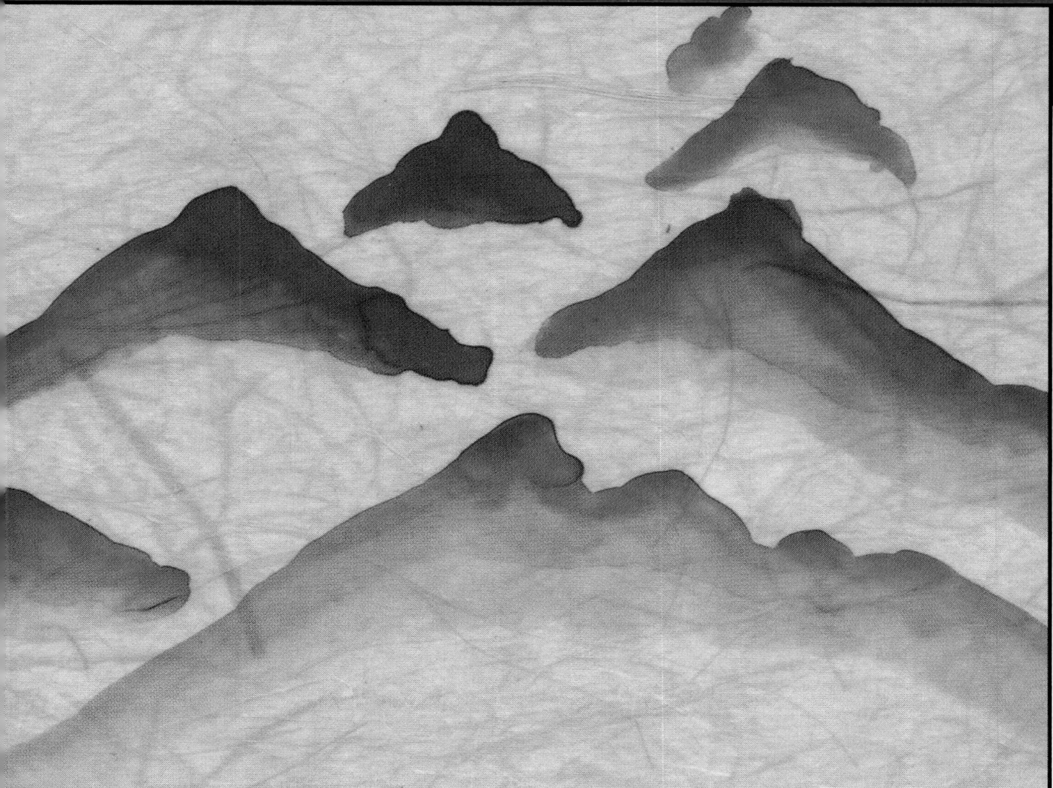

But let me tell you the story of Basho, who lived in Japan and walked all over his island country writing poems. 5

Three hundred years ago, he lived in a small house next to a river. A friend gave him a basho, or banana tree. He planted it near his house and liked this tree with ragged leaves so much that he changed his name to Basho. 6

Basho would sit in the doorway of his small house, sit with his breakfast bowl, look out at the river and mountains, and pour his tea in the company of morning glories. 7

Comprehension

5 **AUTHOR'S POINT OF VIEW** Basho, a real person who lived in the 1600's, was one of Japan's greatest poets. How do you think the author feels about him? (She probably likes his poetry and may think he led an interesting life).

6 In the passage on page 305 we learn that Basho named himself after a banana tree. This made me think about how people often name their children after family members or things that they value highly. What conclusion might I draw from this line of thought? (Basho loves the banana tree and almost thinks of it as his family.) ***Draw Conclusions***

7 In addition to liking the banana tree, Basho enjoys looking at the river and the mountains and drinking tea surrounded by flowers. What does this information tell you about the character? (Sample answer: Basho probably likes nature.) ***Character***

Comprehension

8 Basho is going to walk across the country, yet he doesn't take much with him. What does that tell you about him? (He doesn't care about possessions and has very simple needs.) ***Character***

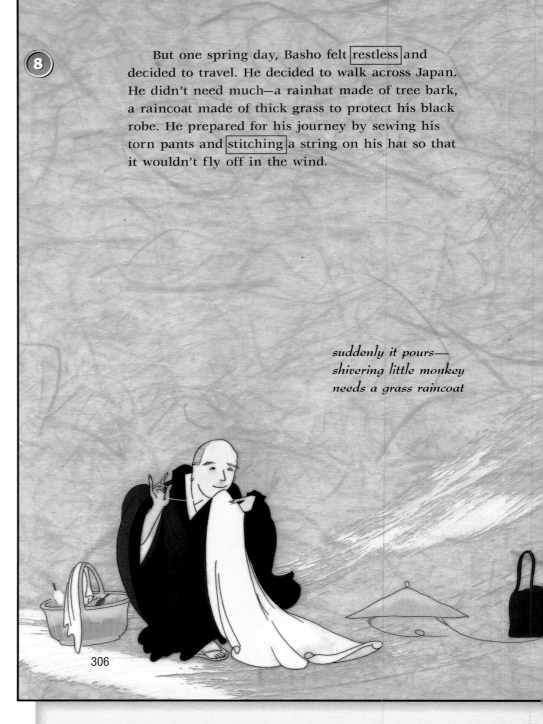

8 But one spring day, Basho felt restless and decided to travel. He decided to walk across Japan. He didn't need much—a rainhat made of tree bark, a raincoat made of thick grass to protect his black robe. He prepared for his journey by sewing his torn pants and stitching a string on his hat so that it wouldn't fly off in the wind.

suddenly it pours—
shivering little monkey
needs a grass raincoat

306

LANGUAGE SUPPORT

ESL Ask students to compare what they usually wear when it rains with what Basho wore. (They may wear a shirt and pants, a raincoat, and an umbrella. Basho wore mended pants, a black robe, a grass raincoat, and a hat made of tree bark.)

Read the first line of the poem and ask students what they think the words *it pours* mean. Lead them to understand that when it rains very hard, we say *It's pouring* as if the rain were milk being poured into a glass.

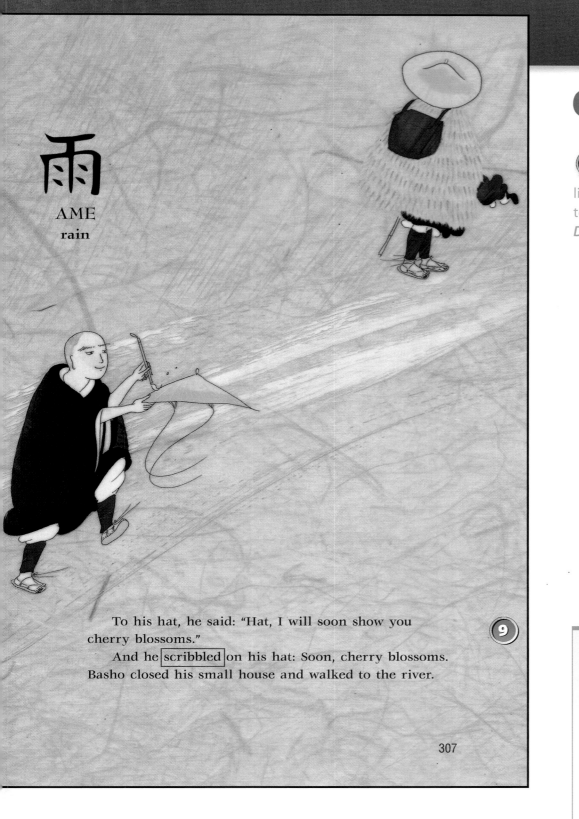

雨
AME
rain

To his hat, he said: "Hat, I will soon show you cherry blossoms."

(9)

And he scribbled on his hat: Soon, cherry blossoms. Basho closed his small house and walked to the river.

307

Comprehension

(9) Why do you think seeing cherry blossoms is important to Basho? (Basho likes nature, especially flowers. He sets a goal to see these flowers on his journey.)
Draw Conclusions

Minilesson

REVIEW/MAINTAIN

Main Idea

Explain that most of the time, the main idea of a paragraph or story is stated in the text. Sometimes, however, the reader needs to figure out the main idea by looking at important details that the author has written.

- Have students reread pages 306 and 307 to find out what Basho does to prepare for his journey. Ask students to tell how these details support the main idea.

Activity Have students write a paragraph describing the main thing they do to prepare for school. Have them exchange papers with a partner. Have partners read the paragraph and identify the main idea.

Comprehension

(10) The author tells us why Basho's friends give him a coat and a pair of sandals. Why do his friends also give him paper and an ink stone? (Sample answer: To keep a travel journal or to write about the things he sees.) ***Make Inferences***

(11) **SUMMARIZE** What have we learned about Basho so far? Answer in one sentence. (He is a poet who loves nature and lives very simply.)

SYNONYMS AND ANTONYMS What is a synonym for the word *began?* What is an antonym for the word *began?* ***Semantic Cues***

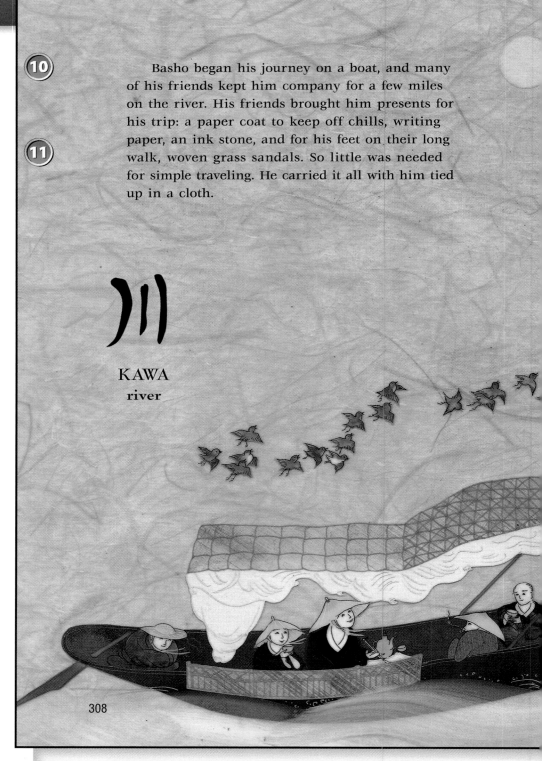

(10) (11) Basho began his journey on a boat, and many of his friends kept him company for a few miles on the river. His friends brought him presents for his trip: a paper coat to keep off chills, writing paper, an ink stone, and for his feet on their long walk, woven grass sandals. So little was needed for simple traveling. He carried it all with him tied up in a cloth.

川

KAWA
river

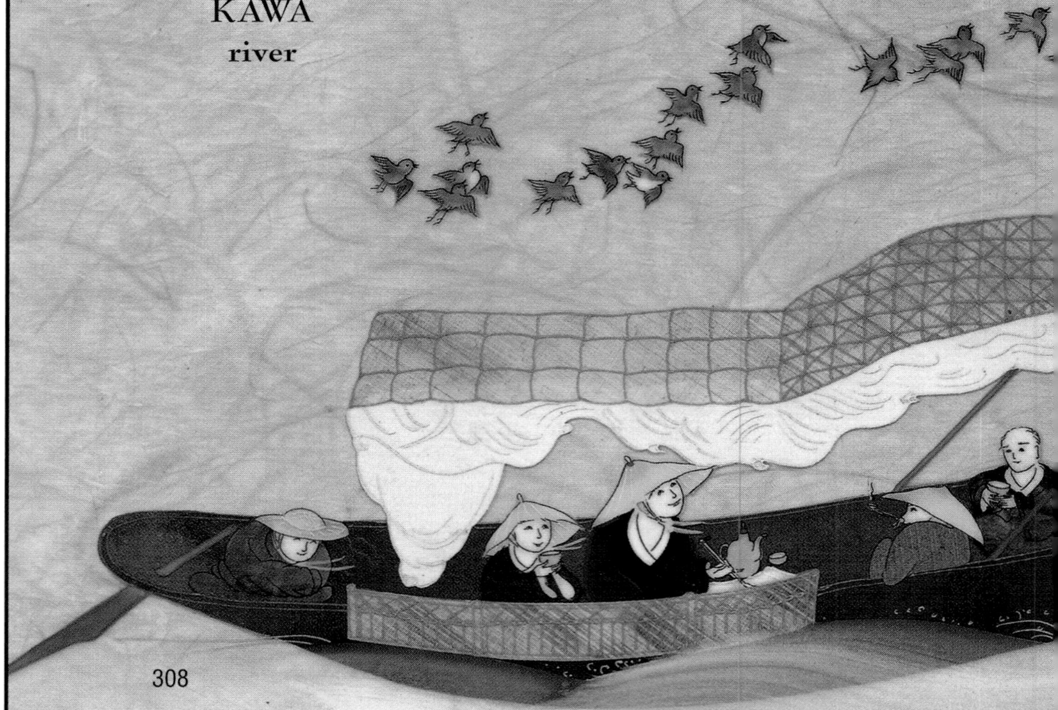

308

Writer's Craft

DESCRIPTIVE WRITING

Explain: Writers use descriptive language to evoke sensory images in the reader's mind.

Example: Discuss the last line on page 308, "He carried it all with him tied up in a cloth."

MODEL Hearing those words made me think of a bird soaring high in the sky. The idea of Basho traveling with so little made him seem as free as a bird. This is very different from my image of most travelers, who carry lots of heavy bags. A different image probably came into your mind as you heard those words.

GROUP Have students discuss descriptive language in the haiku featured in the story.

PREVENTION/INTERVENTION

SYNONYMS AND ANTONYMS Remind students that synonyms are words with the same or similar meanings and antonyms are words with opposite or nearly opposite meanings. Knowing many antonyms and synonyms allows writers more interesting word choices. Have students suggest synonyms for the words *began, friends,* and *simple.* (sample answers: started; pals; easy)

Ask them to substitute the words they suggested for the words *began, friends,* and *simple* on page 308 and determine if the sentences still make sense. Then have them name an antonym for each word. (sample answers: finished; enemies; difficult) ***Semantic Cues***

one morning at dawn
I wade in the wide river—
pants wet to my knees

(12)

When they had crossed the river, Basho climbed out of the boat and waved to his friends. On the shore was a waterfall. He ducked into a cave behind the streaming water and laughed as it sprinkled his face.

(13)

309

Comprehension

(12) Let's have two volunteers, one to read aloud this poem, the other to pantomime the action. Then tell us how you think Basho felt about wading in the river. *Role-Play/Pantomime*

(13) The author never says exactly what Basho is thinking or feeling. How can we tell how Basho feels about the waterfall? (We can tell Basho is happy because he laughs.) ***Make Inferences***

Minilesson

REVIEW/MAINTAIN

Context Clues

Remind students that the meaning of an unfamiliar word can often be figured out by looking for clues in the words and sentences around the word.

- Have students reread the poem on page 309. Discuss clues that help them determine the meaning of the word *wade*.

Activity Have students look back at the selection and choose two words they do not know. Ask them to find clues they can use to determine the meanings of the words.

LANGUAGE SUPPORT

ESL Pages 304–323 have an unusual format. Point out that each two-page spread incorporates three different types of text:

- the main story, written in paragraphs
- the poems, written in lines
- the Japanese characters, with pronunciations and English translations

The position of each type of text on the spread varies.

If students have difficulty with the format, have them focus on the main story first. Then have them go back to read the poetry and review the Japanese words.

Comprehension

(14) What makes this tree seem special? (Sample answer: The tree is much larger than any other object. There is no writing on the page. Basho is kneeling before the tree writing or drawing on paper.) ***Critical Thinking/Draw Conclusions***

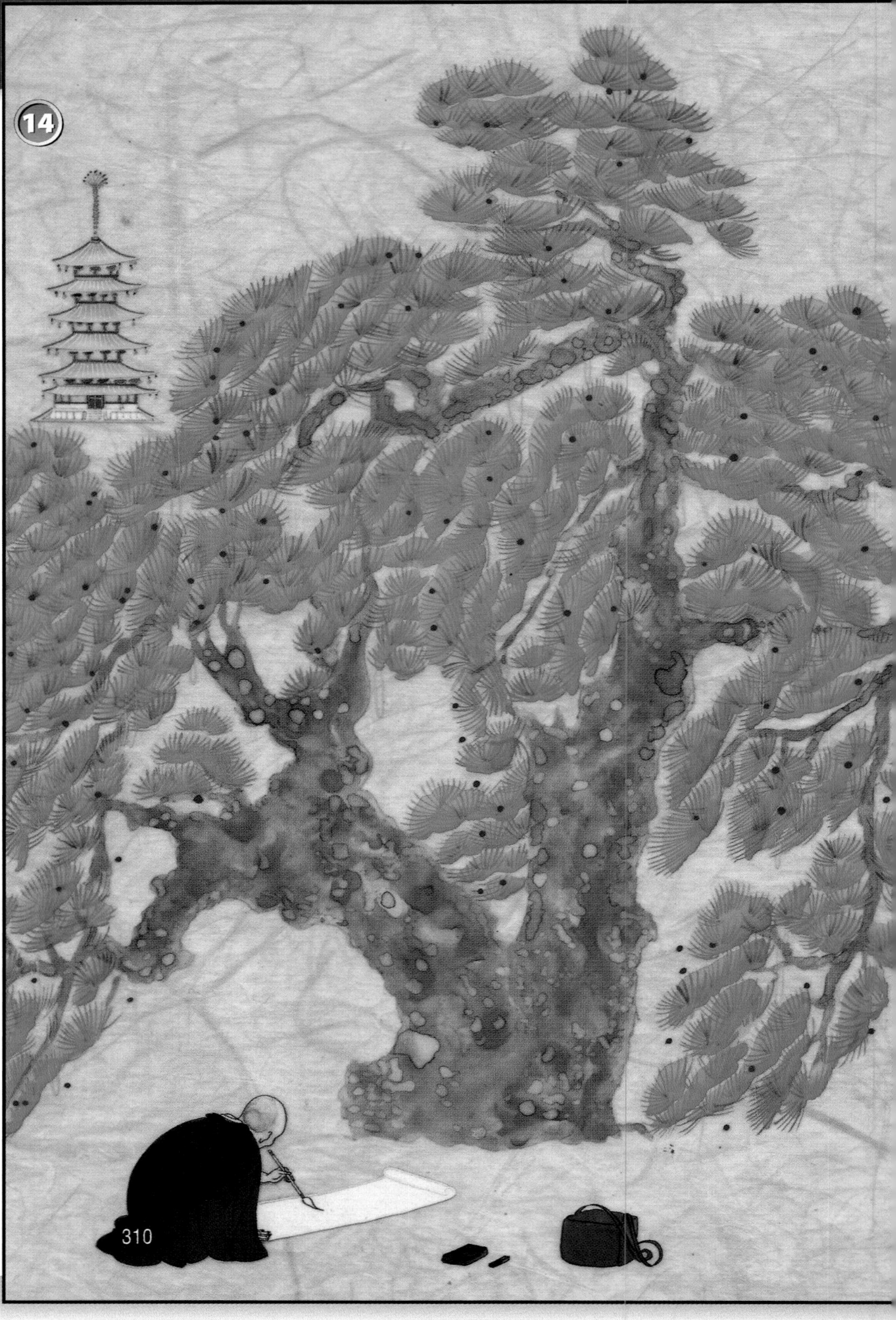

Visual Literacy

VIEWING AND REPRESENTING

Have students review pages 306, 310, and 312. Point out that Basho appears in the bottom corner of each of these left-hand pages. Lead students in a discussion of the direction Basho faces and where he appears on the right-hand pages.

Ask: Why do you think the illustrator shows Basho in the corners of the pages? (It shows that Basho is moving forward.) How do you think this visual device fits with the subtitle of the story, "The Travels of Basho"? (It helps readers have the sense that he is traveling a long way.)

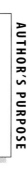

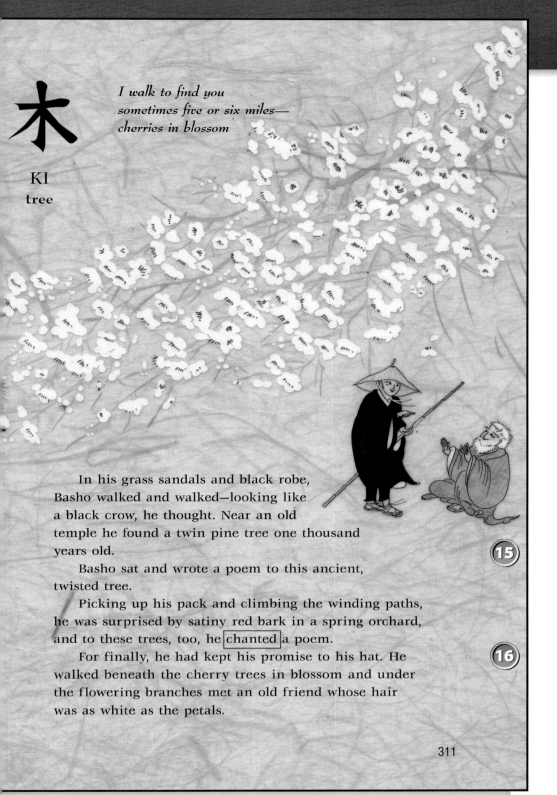

木

KI

tree

I walk to find you
sometimes five or six miles—
cherries in blossom

In his grass sandals and black robe, Basho walked and walked—looking like a black crow, he thought. Near an old temple he found a twin pine tree one thousand years old.

(15)

Basho sat and wrote a poem to this ancient, twisted tree.

Picking up his pack and climbing the winding paths, he was surprised by satiny red bark in a spring orchard, and to these trees, too, he chanted a poem.

(16)

For finally, he had kept his promise to his hat. He walked beneath the cherry trees in blossom and under the flowering branches met an old friend whose hair was as white as the petals.

311

PREVENTION/INTERVENTION

DECODING/WORD STRUCTURE
Write *cherries* on the board. Ask: What word ending do you see? Have students suggest other words that end in *-ies*, such as *babies*. Point out that *babies* is the plural of *baby*, and the *y* is changed to *-ies*.

Discuss how the ending *-ies* can signal the plural form of a noun that ends in the letter *y*. Have a volunteer erase the ending and write a *y*. Then have students read the word *cherry*.

Students may name verbs ending in *-ies* , such as *carries*. Point out that the base word changes the same way to form this present-tense verb. Discuss clues, including sentence position, that help in distinguishing nouns and verbs. ***Graphophonic Cues***

Comprehension

(15) **AUTHOR'S PURPOSE** What do all the poems have in common? (They are about nature.) Why do you think the author includes them so often? (Sample answers: They show what is important to Basho. They are fun to read.)

Many of the illustrations focus on nature, too. Why does that seem fitting? (Basho loved nature.) Let's add to our chart.

CLUES

- includes Japanese writing
- includes poetry
- writes about real poet
- shows illustrations of nature

→ **AUTHOR'S PURPOSE**

(16) A fact is something that can be proved. An opinion is a belief based on what a person thinks. Look at the first sentence on page 311. What opinion does it contain? (Basho thought he looked like a black crow.) ***Fact and Opinion***

DECODING/WORD STRUCTURE
Reread the last line in the haiku. What is the first word? (cherries) What do you think is the base word for *cherries?* (cherry) ***Graphophonic Cues***

Comprehension

17 The story tells about all the places Basho sleeps. Which place do you think Basho likes the least? Which word does the author use to let you know? (Basho probably liked sleeping in the bed least, because the fleas "nipped" him. The word *nipped* gives the reader the feeling that sleeping in the bed was uncomfortable.) ***Draw Conclusions***

TEACHING TIP

WRITING POETRY To ease students' apprehensions about writing poetry, point out that not all poems have rhythm or rhyming words. Encourage students to write poems choosing words that paint pictures or describe feelings.

Point out that the poems in this selection are all short and most use simple language. Stress that good writing does not always include unusual words or abundant detail. Sometimes strong, simple phrases communicate better.

17 At night he often rested his head on grass pillows. Sometimes he slept on flowers, in huts, or in paper rooms. Sometimes he rested in a horse stall or in a bed where fleas nipped him. He slept in fishing villages and smelled the fishy smells.

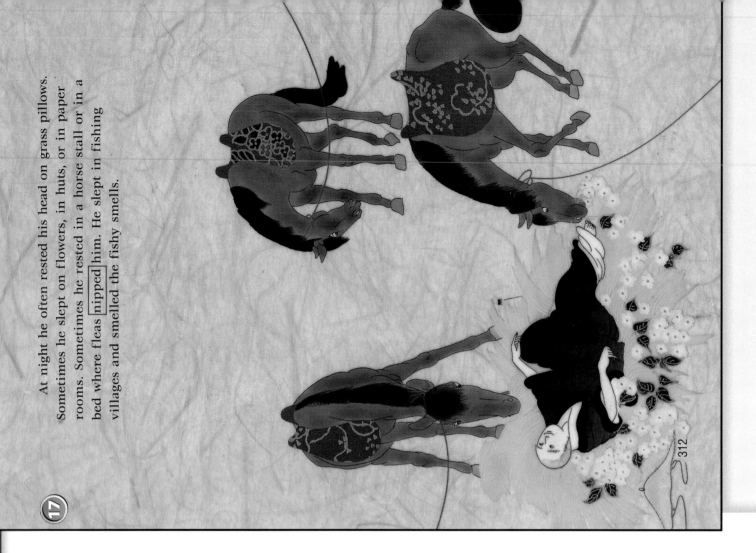

312

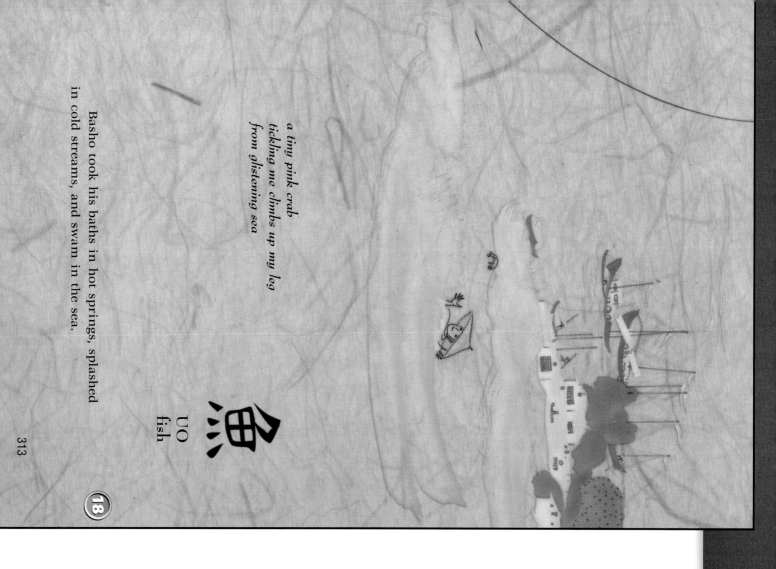

a tiny pink crab
tickling me climbs up my leg
from glistening sea

魚
UO
fish

18 Basho took his baths in hot springs, splashed in cold streams, and swam in the sea.

313

Comprehension

18 Do you think Basho likes bathing in the sea? Explain. (Yes, because Basho writes a poem about a crab that climbs up his leg while he is swimming.)
Make Inferences

SELF-MONITORING STRATEGY

ADJUST READING RATE Review: Adjusting the reading rate can help a reader understand an author's purpose.

MODEL Authors usually choose words with care. If I read too quickly, I may miss clues that show me what the author wants me to see. For example, the poem on page 313 tells about an experience Basho had with a crab. The author uses the words *tickling* and *glistening*—words that tell me the event was fun and beautiful. The main text at the bottom of the page only tells me where Basho takes his baths. To get the whole picture, I must take the time to read the poem carefully.

Comprehension

19 **AUTHOR'S PURPOSE** This page gives us detailed information about how Basho gets food and the kinds of food he eats. Why do you think the author wants us to know these details? (Sample answer: Because he eats leftovers and foods other people give him, we can tell Basho is not concerned about food as much as his enjoyment of nature.)

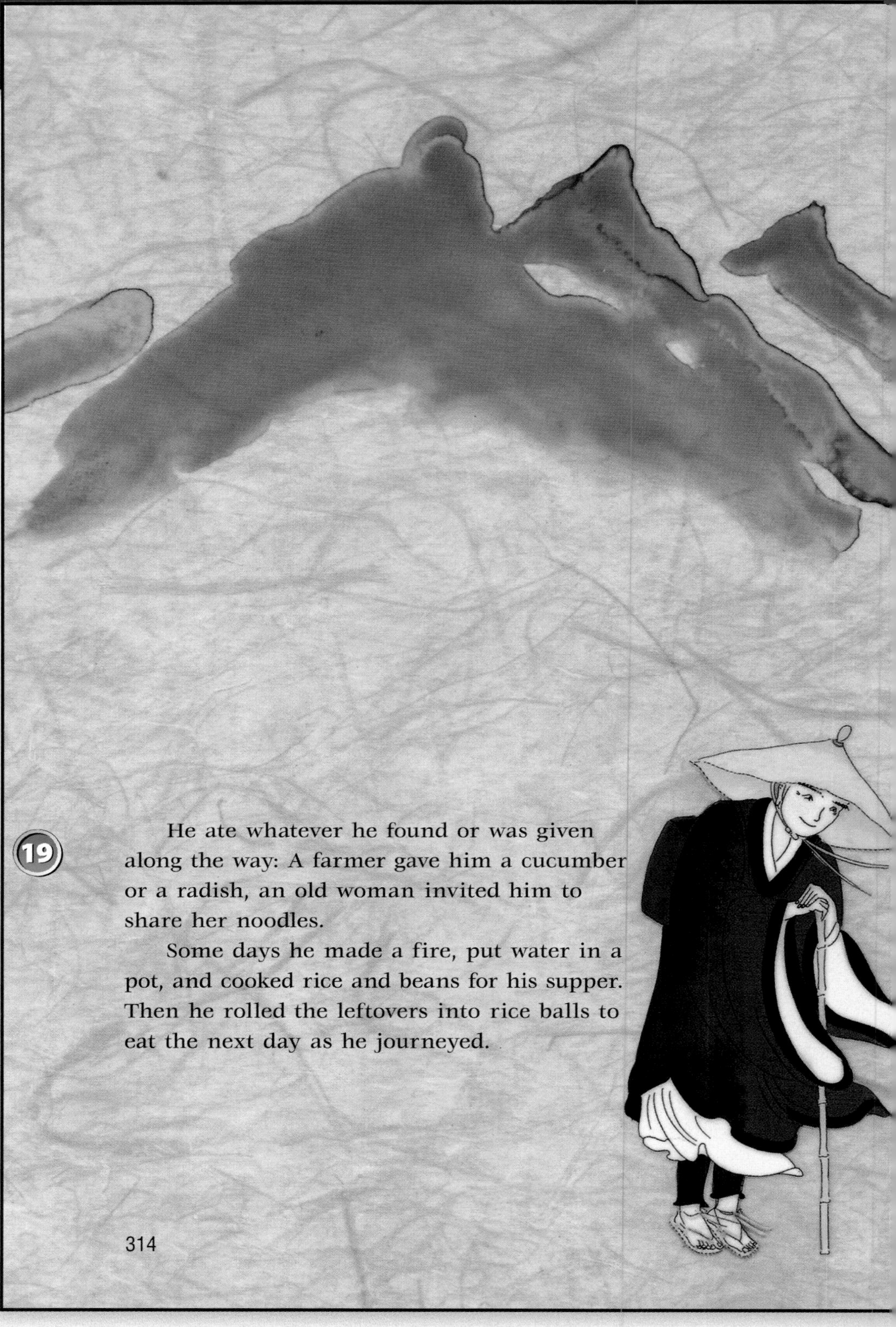

19 He ate whatever he found or was given along the way: A farmer gave him a cucumber or a radish, an old woman invited him to share her noodles.

Some days he made a fire, put water in a pot, and cooked rice and beans for his supper. Then he rolled the leftovers into rice balls to eat the next day as he journeyed.

314

CULTURAL PERSPECTIVES

COMPARE FOODS On his trip, Basho eats simple foods. Explain that traditional Japanese foods have changed little and people of this culture eat mainly rice and vegetables. Have students compare foods they eat with foods Basho eats.

- What vegetables do you eat?
- Do you eat rice or noodles?
- What kind of meat do you like?

Activity Have students create a diagram to compare what they eat with what Basho eats.

▶ **Interpersonal/Visual**

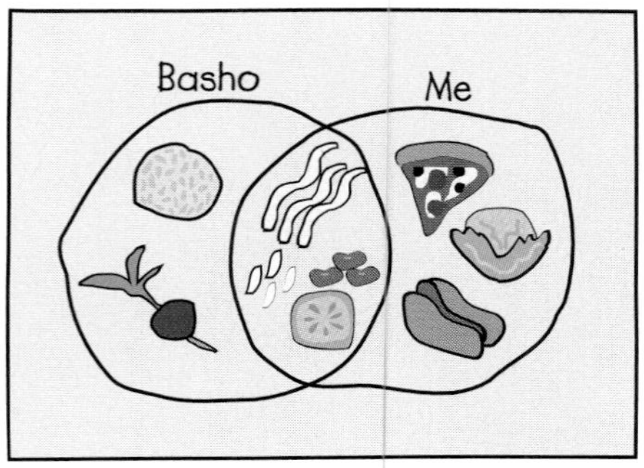

火
HI
fire
let's peel cucumbers
pick up fallen red apples
for our small supper
20
315

Comprehension

(20) Even though the food Basho eats is simple, Basho really enjoys it. How does the author let us know that? Explain. (Basho writes a poem about food. He only writes poems about things that are meaningful to him.) ***Critical Thinking***

Comprehension

21 **AUTHOR'S PURPOSE** Why do you think the author uses the word *suntanned* in the last sentence? (She wants to let the reader know that Basho has been traveling for a long time.)

馬

UMA
horse

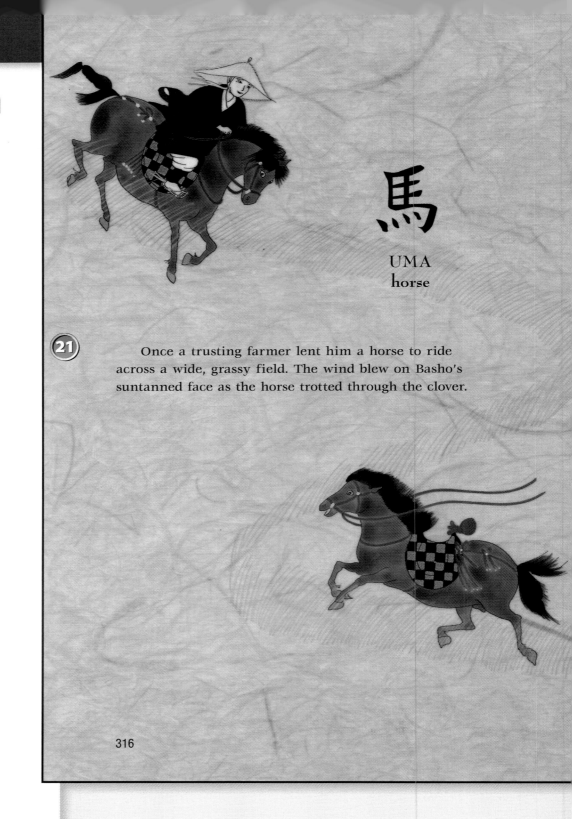

21 Once a trusting farmer lent him a horse to ride across a wide, grassy field. The wind blew on Basho's suntanned face as the horse trotted through the clover.

316

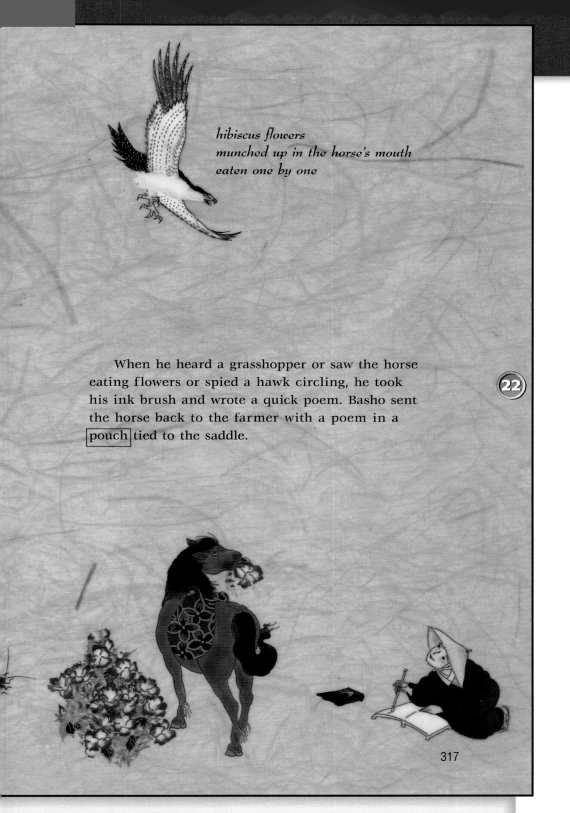

hibiscus flowers
munched up in the horse's mouth
eaten one by one

When he heard a grasshopper or saw the horse eating flowers or spied a hawk circling, he took his ink brush and wrote a quick poem. Basho sent the horse back to the farmer with a poem in a pouch tied to the saddle. (22)

317

Comprehension

(22) Why do you think Basho put a poem in the pouch? (It was his way of thanking the farmer.) ***Make Inferences***

PHONICS AND DECODING How do you say the third word in the first sentence? What vowel sound do you hear in it? (/ûr/) Does *heard* describe an action in present tense or past tense? (past tense) What word would you use to describe this same action in present tense? (hear) What vowel sound do you hear in the word *hear*? (/îr/) ***Graphophonic Cues***

PREVENTION/INTERVENTION

PHONICS AND DECODING Write the words *heard* and *hear* on the board. Circle the letters *ear* in each word. Invite students to use the words in sentences. Repeat their sentences, emphasizing the vowel sounds in the words *heard* and *hear*. Point out that the letters *ear* can stand for different sounds. Use the word *pear,* which has the /âr/ sound, as another example.

Write the words *fear* and *feared* on the board. Have students say the words, emphasizing the vowel sound in each word. Ask: Do these words have the same vowel sound? (yes) Do they have the same vowel sound as *heard* or *hear? (hear)* ***Graphophonic Cues***

Comprehension

23 ● **AUTHOR'S PURPOSE** What mood do you think the author wants to create? Why? (Sample answer: She wants to make me feel quiet and thoughtful. The illustrations encourage these feelings because the people are sitting still and all are looking up. The author talks about quiet things, like the moon and clouds.)

In a mountain village, Basho met friends and they had a party to watch the full moon. Drinking tea, each could find a small moon reflected in the bottom of his cup. While clouds and stars and shadows lifted, they created poems together, sitting under the night sky.

23

318

Activity

Cross Curricular: Math

MOON WATCH Basho and his friends have a party in honor of the full moon. Ask students what they know about the phases of the moon. Write their responses on the board.

RESEARCH AND INQUIRY Visit the school library. Have students look at a calendar that shows the moon's phases. Have them create a pictograph to show the number of days of each phase.

▶ **Visual/Mathematical**

*inter*NET CONNECTION Students can learn more about the moon by visiting **www.mhschool.com/reading**

November

Sun	Mon	Tues	Wed	Thur	Fri	Sat
	1	2	3	4	5	6
New 7 Moon 8	9	10	11	12	13	
14	15	16 1/4	17	18	19	20
21	22	23 Full	24	25	26	27
28	29 3/4	30

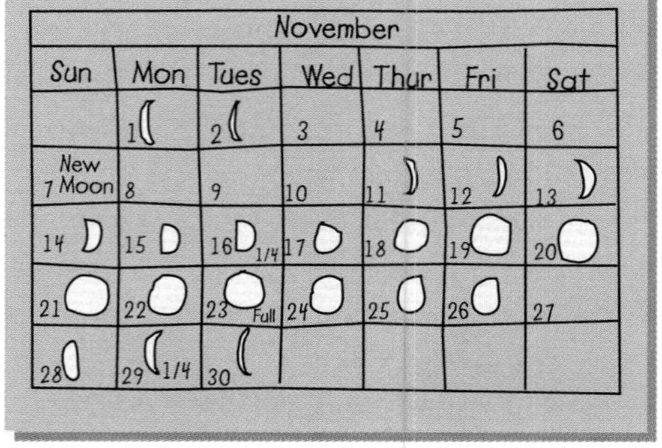

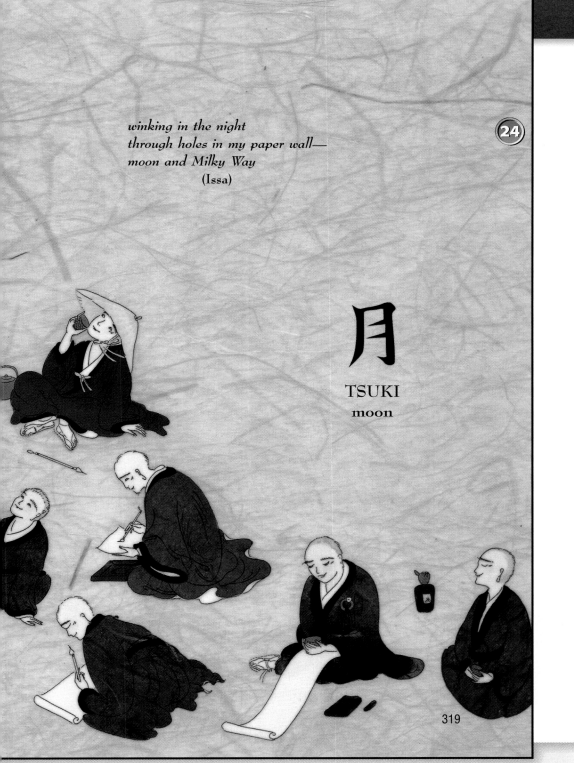

winking in the night
through holes in my paper wall—
moon and Milky Way
(Issa)

24

月

TSUKI
moon

319

Comprehension

24 **SUMMARIZE** What places has Basho visited?

MODEL Basho has been traveling for a long time. Trying to recall the places he visited will help me summarize the story. He went across the river, sat behind a waterfall, saw ancient pine trees near the temple, walked in a cherry orchard, slept in fishing villages, took baths in the hot springs, swam in the sea, rode horseback across a clover field, and met friends in a mountain village.

Minilesson

REVIEW/MAINTAIN

Digraphs

Read aloud the last sentence on page 318. Repeat the words *while* and *shadows*.

- Ask what sound students hear at the beginning of each word. (/hw/, /sh/)
- Point out *watch* and *each* on the same page. Ask what sound students hear at the end of these words. (/ch/)

Explain that two or more letters representing a single sound are called a *digraph*.

Activity Write the digraphs *th, tch, ch, wh,* and *sh* on the board. Assign each digraph to a group. Have groups brainstorm words that contain their digraphs. Ask groups to read their lists aloud.

Phonics Intervention Guide

Comprehension

(25) **AUTHOR'S PURPOSE** Why do you think the author includes the Japanese character for *friend* on this page? (because Basho has just spent time with his friends and received a gift from one)

TEACHING TIP

SIMILES Explain to students that simile is a literary technique in which two things are compared using the word *like* or *as*. A simile often helps the reader visualize or understand an image. Guide students to see that, by comparing the color blue to an iris, the author has helped us see the color of the sandal laces.

友

TOMO
friend

(25) The next morning as Basho was leaving, one friend gave him new grass sandals with laces dyed blue like the iris.

"Good-bye, my friend, and thank you, thank you."

320

Activity

Cross Curricular: Science

NATURAL DYES Point out that the sandal laces were dyed blue. Tell students that many years ago dyes were made from plants.

RESEARCH AND INQUIRY Working in groups, have students research plants and the dyes they produce.

Then have students create a chart that pairs dye colors with the plants that produce them. ▶ **Interpersonal/Spatial**

COLOR	PLANT
yellow	
brown	
purple	

Basho hugged his friend. Crisscrossing the blue ties of his sandals around his ankles, he set out again on his walk across his island country of Japan.

stems of new iris
blooming right on my own feet—
shoelaces dyed blue

321

Comprehension

26 What are Basho's three responses to the gift of the sandals? (words of thanks, a hug, a poem) Do you think the gift was special? Explain. (Yes. Usually, Basho only writes poetry, but in this case, he uses words, actions, and a poem to describe his feelings.) ***Draw Conclusions***

Comprehension

27 **SUMMARIZE** Which sentence in this paragraph sums up much of what happens in the story? (Basho stopped to write a poem when he found a creature, person, or plant that opened his eyes and his heart.)

28 **AUTHOR'S PURPOSE** Basho wrote many poems. How do you think the author chose which ones to include? (Sample answer: She chose poems about things that Basho saw on his journey and poems that reflected his feelings and inner thoughts.)

界
KAI
world

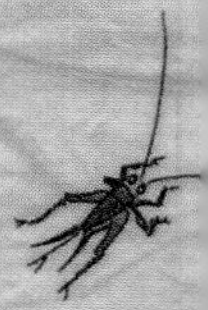

His blue-laced sandals carried him to distant beaches and fields and forests. Basho stopped to write a poem when he found a creature or person or plant that opened his eyes and his heart. He watched the fog curve over the hills. He noticed a cricket. Sleeping in a leaky hut, he smelled the rain. Each morning he tasted his tea. **27**

In the evening he heard a frog leap into a pond. And so, three hundred years ago he traveled, and the world was his home. **28**

322

Activity

Cross Curricular: Language Arts

HAIKU List the five senses on the board. Discuss how the senses help us learn about our world. Invite students to name ways they use their senses. Then have children reread the page to find out how Basho used each sense to learn about his world.

Explain the line and syllable structure for haiku poetry. Invite students to write their own haiku based on one of the senses. Encourage students to share their work so that others can identify the sense. ▶ **Interpersonal/Linguistic**

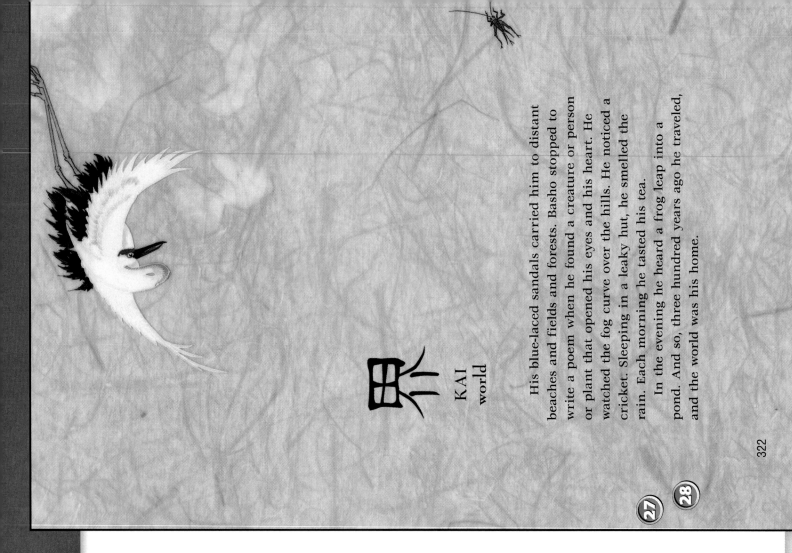

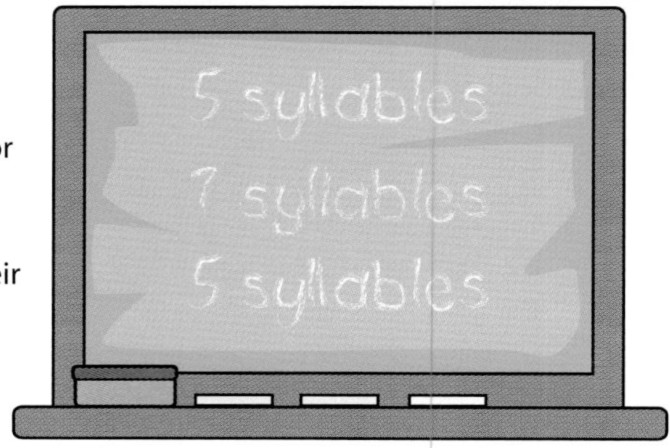

old and quiet pond
suddenly a frog plops in—
a deep water sound

29

323

Comprehension

29 Close your eyes. I am going to reread the poem on this page. Visualize the place you think Basho writes about. What other things do you think Basho could see, hear, and smell? *Visualize*

LANGUAGE SUPPORT

ESL Ask students to explain the meaning of the phrase *a creature or a person or a plant that opened his eyes and his heart*. Lead them to understand that he is talking about animals, people, and plants that give him a strong feeling or emotion.

Then ask them to suggest other things Basho probably wrote about based on the paragraphs on this page. (the fog, the smell of rain, the taste of his tea)

Minilesson

REVIEW/MAINTAIN

Character

Explain that authors often give hints about what a character is like by describing what the person does, thinks, or says.

- Have students reread the first paragraph on page 322. Ask them what they can learn about Basho from the author's description.

Activity Brainstorm a list of words that describe Basho, such as *kind*, *watchful*, and *quiet*. Ask students to imagine that Basho has come to their school playground or to a park nearby. Have each of them write a paragraph describing how Basho would act and what he would do.

Comprehension

(30) **SUMMARIZE** The map shows the places Basho visited on his journey. The information on page 325 tells the names of the places. Review the story. Choose four places from the list and name one thing Basho did in each place. (Sample answers: Edo, drank tea; Nikko, saw waterfall; Iwanuma, wrote poem; Mogami, met friends)

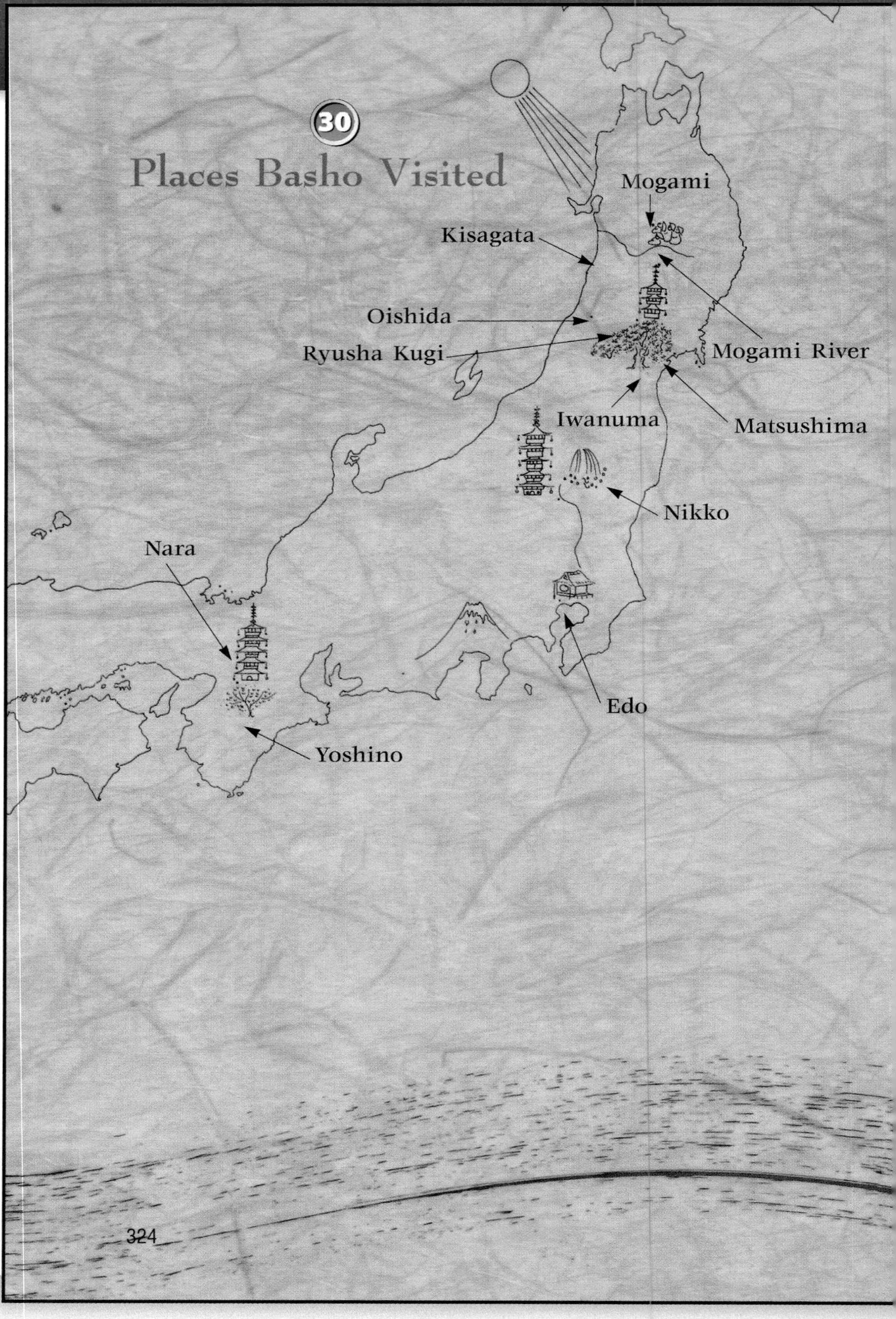

Activity

Cross Curricular: Social Studies

MAP SKILLS Display a world map and a physical map of Japan. Have students:

- locate the state in which they live.
- locate Japan and the ocean that surrounds it.
- use the legend to examine the variety of the topography in Japan.
- compare the map above on page 324 with a modern map of Japan to find the actual places Basho traveled and what these places are called today. (For example, Edo is now Tokyo.)

▶ **Spatial/Interpersonal**

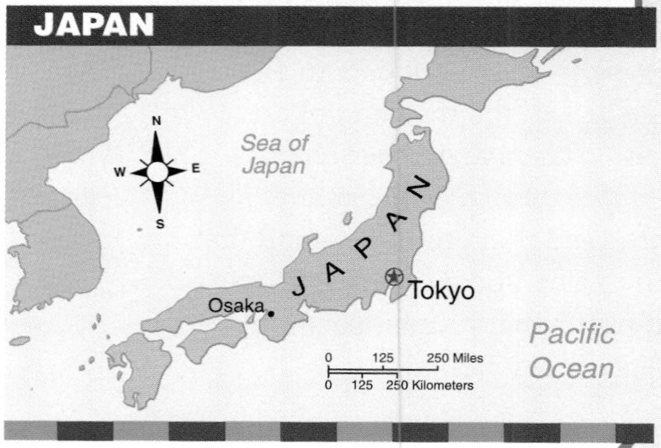

What Basho Saw

Edo	Basho's house
Nikko	Waterfall
Iwanuma	Twin pine tree and temple
Matsushima, Kisagata	Sea coast, fishing villages
Mogami, Mogami River, Oishida	Friends composing poetry while watching the moon
Ryusha Kugi	Mountain temple
Nara	Temple
Yoshino	Cherry orchards

31

325

Comprehension

31 **AUTHOR'S PURPOSE** Why do you think the author included the map on page 324 and the list of the places Basho visited? (Sample answer: They give information so the reader can better understand and enjoy the story.)

Comprehension

32 **AUTHOR'S POINT OF VIEW** How do you think the author feels about Basho? (She admires him greatly.)

33 **AUTHOR'S PURPOSE** Let's complete the chart of clues telling the author's purpose. What purpose or purposes did the author have for writing the selection?

CLUES		AUTHOR'S PURPOSE
• includes Japanese writing • includes poetry • writes about real poet • shows illustrations of nature • provides map and list of places Basho visits	→	to entertain and to inform readers about Basho

RETELL THE STORY Ask volunteers to tell the main events of the story. Then have partners refer to their charts and page back through the story to find specific examples of the author's purpose. *Summarize*

STUDENT SELF-ASSESSMENT

- How did using the strategy of determining an author's purpose help me understand the story?

TRANSFERRING THE STRATEGY

- When might I try using this strategy again? In what other reading could the chart help me?

Matsuo Basho, the haiku poet most loved and honored in his country, lived in seventeenth-century Japan (1644–1694).

He wrote journals of his travels in *haibun*, a diary of prose and poems. The places that he loved—the shrines and mountains and villages—can still be visited, and the poems remain as fresh as new leaves.

32 The journey of *Grass Sandals* compresses and combines events from several of Basho's travels.

33 At the age of fifty, Basho sold his small house in Edo and set out on his last journey.

The haiku on the page with the Japanese character Tsuki (moon) was created by Issa, another Japanese poet who lived a century after Basho.

326

REREADING FOR *Fluency*

PARTNERS Assign partners two pages. Have one person read the main text and the other read the poem.

READING RATE When you evaluate rate, have the student read aloud from the story for one minute. Place a stick-on note after the last word read. Count words read. To evaluate students' performance, see the Running Record in the **Fluency Assessment** book.

Intervention For leveled fluency lessons, passages, and norms charts, see **Skills Intervention Guide**, Part 4, Fluency.

Comprehension

Return to Predictions and Purposes

Review with students their story predictions and reasons for reading the story. Were their predictions correct? Did they find out what they wanted to know?

PREDICTIONS	WHAT HAPPENED
The main character will take a trip.	Basho travels to many locations in Japan.
The main character will write poetry.	Basho writes poetry about things that open his mind and heart.

INFORMAL ASSESSMENT

AUTHOR'S PURPOSE, POINT OF VIEW

HOW TO ASSESS

- Have students give specific examples that show the author is writing to entertain and to inform.
- Students should recognize that the author informs and entertains throughout the story in a variety of ways, including use of Japanese characters, poetry, and anecdotes.

FOLLOW UP If students are unable to identify the author's purpose, explain each category of author's purpose used in this story (inform, entertain), and help students find examples of each.

LITERARY RESPONSE

QUICK-WRITE Invite students to record thoughts about the story. These questions may get them started:

JOURNAL

- Of all the places Basho visited, which one would you most like to see? Why?
- What is your favorite place to visit? Write a haiku poem about it.

ORAL RESPONSE Have students share their journal writings and discuss the parts of the story they enjoyed the most.

Story Questions

Have students discuss or write answers to the questions on page 328.

Answers:

1. A friend gave him a basho, or banana tree. He liked it so much that he changed his name to Basho. *Literal/Character*
2. so Basho would be able to write as he traveled *Inferential/Character*
3. Sample answer: Basho was a famous writer. His story offers details about Japanese culture and history. *Inferential/Author's Purpose*
4. It is a biographical story about a Japanese poet who lived in the 17th century. *Critical/Summarize*
5. Sample answer: They both capture beauty around them, one in art, the other in poetry. *Critical/Reading Across Texts*

Write a Book Review For a related writing process lesson, see pages 331K–331L.

Story Questions & Activities

1. How did Basho get his name?
2. Why did Basho's friends give him writing paper and ink as he started on his journey?
3. Why do you think the author wrote about Basho? Explain.
4. What is this selection mostly about?
5. Both Pat Cummings and Basho enjoy the beauty around them. Compare what Pat Cummings does with the things she sees with what Basho does.

Write a Book Review

Write a book review of "Grass Sandals." Tell

- **who the main character is**
- **where and when the story takes place**
- **what happens in the story.**

Describe the pictures and the haiku poems used in the story. Then tell whether or not you would recommend the book to others to read. Give three good reasons.

Meeting Individual Needs

EASY

Name______ Date______ Reteach 90

Vocabulary

Choose a word from the list to complete each sentence.

chanted	nipped	pouch	restless	scribbled	stitching

1. The child scribbled with a crayon.
2. The puppy nipped at the little girl's heels.
3. The choir chanted words as the music played.
4. The boy was restless and wanted to play outside.
5. My Mom is stitching the hole in my jeans.
6. The hiker carried supplies in a waterproof pouch.

6

Reteach 91

Story Comprehension

Write the answers to these questions about "Grass Sandals." You can refer to the story for help if you need to.

1. When and where did Basho live? He lived in Japan 300 years ago.
2. What did Basho promise his hat? He promised his hat that he would show it cherry blossoms.
3. Where did Basho begin his journey? He began his journey on a boat on a river near his village.
4. What did Basho write about? He wrote poetry about what he saw and felt on his journey.
5. Why is Basho known and loved in Japan? His writing tells of the simple, yet beautiful, experiences one can enjoy in Japan.

At Home: Have students recall their favorite part of Basho's journey.
90–91 Book 4/Unit 3 Grass Sandals 5

Reteach, 91

ON-LEVEL

Name______ Date______ Practice 91

Story Comprehension

Answer the questions about "Grass Sandals: The Travels of Basho." Look back at the story to help you answer the questions.

1. Basho was one of the great Japanese poets. When and where did he live before he went on his journey? He lived 300 years ago in a small house near a river.
2. Where did Basho usually sit, and what did he do during breakfast? He sat in the doorway and looked at the mountains, river, and morning glories.
3. On the first page of the story, there is a haiku poem about morning glories. When do you think Basho may have written it? He may have written it right after he had breakfast.
4. How did Basho prepare for his first walking trip across Japan? He sewed his pants and stitched a string to his hat.
5. Why did Basho's friends give him grass sandals? He would need them for walking.
6. What did Basho do when he found a tree that was 1,000 years old? Basho wrote a poem to the ancient tree.
7. On his journey, Basho met a group of friends in the mountains. What did they do for entertainment? They looked at the moon and wrote poems.
8. Basho looked at everything very carefully as he traveled. How do you think this helped him write poetry. The more carefully he looked, the more he enjoyed the scene and the more he had to say in his poetry.

At Home: Have students write a haiku about something that they love to look at.
91 Book 4/Unit 3 Grass Sandals 8

Practice, 91

CHALLENGE

Name______ Date______ Extend 90

Vocabulary

chanted restless	nipped scribbled	pouch stitching

Write a poem that includes at least three of the vocabulary words in the box.
Answers will vary, but each poem should contain at least three of the vocabulary words.

Extend 91

Story Comprehension

An author may write a selection to persuade, to describe, to inform, or to entertain.

Why do you think Dawnine Spivak wrote "Grass Sandals"? Explain your thinking.
Answers will vary. Possible answer: to inform; the author tells the reader about a journey Basho took and how it inspired his writing

What do you think Basho's purpose was for writing haiku? Explain your thinking.
Answers will vary. Possible answer: to describe; Basho wrote each poem to give the reader a mental picture of something.

At Home: Have students recall something beautiful they have seen. Discuss how they could convey an image of that thing to someone else.
90–91 Book 4/Unit 3 Grass Sandals

Extend, 91

Paint Japanese Characters

火界友馬

In the story, the author uses some Japanese symbols, or characters, and tells what they mean. Now it's your turn. Use a paintbrush, thick art paper, and black paint to draw some of the Japanese characters in the story. Below each character, write the English word for it. Share your finished product with the class.

Write a Poem

Basho walked across his country to learn and write poems about it. Imagine that you are a poet. Look at a map of your state. Make a list of the interesting places you would like to see. Then write a poem about one of them.

Find Out More

Basho traveled through Japan in the 1600s and wrote poems about his experiences. What is Japan like today? Read about Japan in an encyclopedia or a travel guide. Use what you learn to write a travel brochure. Describe a few interesting places to visit. Include photographs or pictures of Japan.

329

Story Activities

Paint Japanese Characters

Materials: paintbrush, art paper, black paint

ONE Have students review the Japanese characters in the story before they paint characters of their own. When dry, display students' work on a bulletin board.

Write a Poem

ONE Look at a map of your state. Point out special features, such as mountains, deserts, and bodies of water. Have children brainstorm special places in the state they would like to visit. Write the structure for a haiku poem on the board:

Line 1: 5 syllables

Line 2: 7 syllables

Line 3: 5 syllables

Encourage students to share their poems.

Find Out More

RESEARCH AND INQUIRY Display a travel brochure. Have students examine it for the information included. Then allow students time to research interesting facts about Japan. When students complete their brochures, display them on a class bulletin board.

interNET CONNECTION To learn more about Japan, have students visit ***www.mhschool.com/reading***

FORMAL ASSESSMENT

After page 329, see Selection Assessment.

Activity

SOCIAL STUDIES: ELEVATION MAPS Have students research elevation maps and answer these questions in a short presentation.

- What does the word *elevation* mean?
- How does an elevation map show differences in elevation?
- How do we measure elevation?
- Why is it important to study elevation?

What to Look For Students should know these facts:

- *Elevation* means "height."
- Elevation maps use different colors to show differences in elevation.
- Sea level is the basis for measuring elevation.
- We study elevation to learn its effect on landforms, plants and animals.

CHALLENGE

Study Skills

GRAPHIC AIDS

TESTED OBJECTIVES Students will identify cities and countries on a map and use a compass rose.

PREPARE Read the passage with students. Display **Teaching Chart 75.**

TEACH Review how to use the compass rose and how to identify cities, countries, and geographical features. Have a student circle Tokyo and Osaka and tell whether Osaka is north, south, east, or west of Tokyo.

PRACTICE Have students answer questions 1–5. Review the answers. **1.** Tokyo; **2.** Yokohama, Osaka, Nagoya; **3.** southwest; from the compass rose **4.** Russia, North Korea, and South Korea; **5.** It is made up of islands.

ASSESS/CLOSE Have partners ask each other questions such as, "Where is the East China Sea?"

STUDY SKILLS

Read a Map

Basho began his journey on a boat. Then he walked across his island country of Japan. Japan lies in the North Pacific Ocean. Tall mountains and green hills cover most of the land. Like many countries today, Japan has several big cities. Edo, where Basho lived, is now called Tokyo. Tokyo is the capital and largest city in Japan.

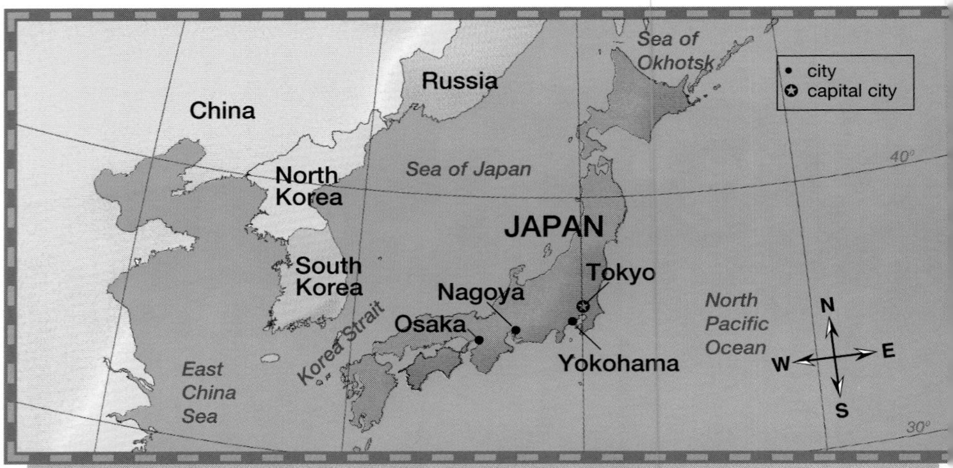

Use the map to answer these questions.

1. What is the capital of Japan?
2. Besides Tokyo, what are three other cities in Japan?
3. In which direction is Yokohama from Tokyo? How do you know?
4. Which three countries are nearest to Japan?
5. Why do you think Japan has the world's largest fishing industry?

Meeting Individual Needs

EASY

Name________ Date________ Reteach 92

Read a Map

Read the map to answer the questions.

1. What are three large cities on California's Pacific Ocean? Possible answers: San Diego, Los Angeles, San Francisco
2. Which city on the map is farthest from the Pacific Ocean? Sacramento
3. Which city is closest to the Mojave Desert? Los Angeles
4. If you traveled from San Francisco to Los Angeles, in what direction would you be heading? south
5. Which cities would you expect to trade with countries across the Pacific Ocean? Why? San Diego, Los Angeles, San Francisco. They are on or near the coast.

5 Book 4/Unit 3 Grass Sandals — At Home: Have students look at a map and name the capital and one other large city in their state. 92

Reteach, 92

ON-LEVEL

Name________ Date________ Practice 92

Read a Map

Study the map below. It shows some of the countries in East and Southeast Asia. Use the map to answer the questions below.

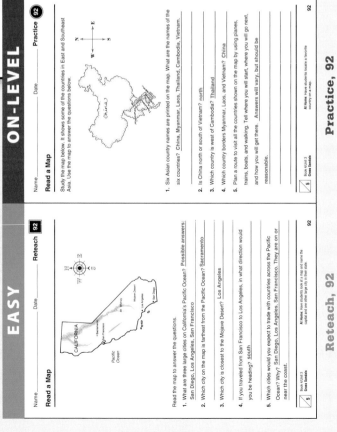

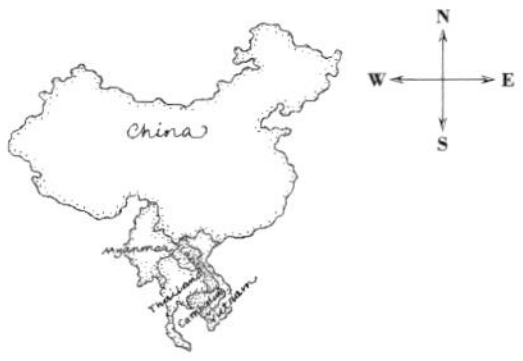

1. Six Asian country names are printed on the map. What are the names of the six countries? China, Myanmar, Laos, Thailand, Cambodia, Vietnam.
2. Is China north or south of Vietnam? north
3. Which country is west of Cambodia? Thailand
4. Which country borders Myanmar, Laos, and Vietnam? China
5. Plan a route to visit all the countries shown on the map by using planes, trains, boats, and walking. Tell where you will start, where you will go next, and how you will get there. Answers will vary, but should be reasonable.

5 Book 4/Unit 3 Grass Sandals — At Home: Have students locate a favorite country on a map. 92

Practice, 92

CHALLENGE

Name________ Date________ Extend 92

Use a Map

The map in "Grass Sandals" shows the names and locations of the places Basho visited. It also has pictures of some things Basho saw on his journey.

Think about how you would show your neighborhood on a map. Which streets you would show? Besides your home, what other places would you include? Would you show only street and place names, or would you include some pictures? How would you use color in your map? What kind of map key would you use?

Make a map of your neighborhood. Share your map with classmates.

Answers will vary.

Book 4/Unit 3 Grass Sandals — At Home: Look at a map of your state. Locate a place you would like to visit. Decide what route you would follow to get from your home to that place. 92

Extend, 92

TEST POWER

Test Tip

Keep your attention turned to your work.

DIRECTIONS

Read the sample story. Then read each question about the story.

SAMPLE

What goes in the corner?

Benoit's favorite plant, a fern with delicate, tender leaves, was sick. It had some kind of mold, and Benoit's parents said it was probably going to die.

He hurried home after school to see his fern. Benoit ran into the living room to the corner where his fern should have been. His mother came in and put a consoling arm around his shoulders.

"Your father is going to come home early today so we can go out together and buy a new plant for you. How does that sound?" she asked. Benoit looked up and said nothing. He couldn't picture anything replacing his fern.

1 Why was the fern probably going to die?

- **A** It took up too much space in the living room.
- **B** Benoit's parents didn't like it.
- **C** It was too big.
- **(D)** It had some kind of mold.

2 The word consoling in this story means—

- **F** too long
- **(G)** filled with caring
- **H** hard to understand
- **J** not very exciting

331

Test Power

THE PRINCETON REVIEW

Read the Page

Have students label paragraphs with one or two words. This way, they can locate information easily. Ask students to pay attention to the underlined word and to notice *when* events happen.

Discuss the Questions

Question 1: This question requires students to determine why the fern was probably going to die. Ask, "Where can you find that information? "Answer: paragraph 1. Have students recall that the fern "was sick" and that it "had some kind of mold." Remind students to choose the *best* answer.

Question 2: This question asks students to define a word in context. Have students look for context clues. In this passage, Benoit's feelings offer the best clue to the meaning of the underlined word. Remind students to eliminate answers that don't make sense.

Leveled Books

EASY

Bookworm's Band

Digraphs

☑ **Author's Purpose, Point of View**

☑ **Instructional Vocabulary:** ***chanted, nipped, pouch, restless, scribbled, stitching***

Guided Reading

PREVIEW AND PREDICT Have students look at the pictures through page 11 and ask them to infer how the boys seem to be getting along. Then have them predict how the boys' relationship will change. Students can record their ideas in their journals.

SET PURPOSES Have students write reasons for wanting to read the story. For example: *I want to find out how being a bookworm can help someone that wants to be in a band.*

READ THE BOOK Ask questions such as the following to guide a group reading or to check understanding after students have read the story independently.

Page 2: Find the word *nipped*. What letter in *nip* was doubled before adding the ending? (p) ***Vocabulary***

Pages 4–5: The band seems to be doing well, but there is one problem. What is it? (They need to find someone who can write lyrics.) ***Problem and Solution***

Page 7: Some consonants are used together to represent one sound. Find the words *leather, pouch, stitching*, and *where*. What consonants are used together in these words to represent one sound? (th, ch, tch, wh) ***Phonics and Decoders***

Pages 14–16: What message does the author send about making judgments without really knowing people? (We shouldn't be quick to judge others by appearances.) ***Author's Purpose and Point of View***

RETURN TO PREDICTIONS AND PURPOSES Have students review their predictions and purposes for reading. Which predictions were accurate? Did they find out what they wanted to know?

LITERARY RESPONSE Discuss these questions.

- Why did the band members think all Bookworm could do was read?
- Why does a band need members with many different talents?

Also see the story questions and activity in *Bookworm's Band*.

Intervention **Skills**

Intervention Guide, for direct instruction and extra practice with vocabulary and comprehension

Answers to Story Questions

1. The boys thought Ben was clumsy and nerdy until they discovered his talent with words.
2. Ben was always reading—on the playground, even at lunch.
3. Answers will vary but might include: poetry can play an important role in people's lives, especially in the field of music; the author appreciates music and values it.
4. This story is mainly about how Ben was befriended by Thunder and Lightning.
5. Answers will vary.

The *Story Questions and Activity* below appear in the *Easy Book*.

Story Questions and Activity

1. How did the boys feel about Ben in the beginning of the book? How and why did their opinion change?
2. Why did the boys call Ben "Bookworm"?
3. What do you think the author's point of view might be about poetry? What was her purpose in writing this book?
4. What was this story mainly about?
5. If the members of the band were to meet Basho from *Grass Sandals*, what do you think they might talk about?

Making Beautiful Music

If you played music with a group of musicians, what kind of group would you be? Would you be a string quartet, a jazz ensemble, a country western band, or a rock group? Write your own lyrics to the tune of your favorite song, or compose your own music and write lyrics for your work. Share your music with at least four other students. If possible, organize a talent show at your school.

from *Bookworm's Band*

Leveled Books

INDEPENDENT

Bad Day, Glad Day

- ☑ **Author's Purpose, Point of View**
- ☑ **Instructional Vocabulary: *chanted, nipped, pouch, restless, scribbled, stitching***

Guided Reading

PREVIEW AND PREDICT Read aloud the story title. Then invite students to preview the illustrations up to page 7. Have students record their predictions about the story in their journals.

SET PURPOSES Have students write in their journals several questions they hope will be answered by reading the story.

READ THE BOOK After students have read the story, ask questions such as those below to emphasize reading strategies.

Page 4: What caused the girls to roll their eyes and giggle during gym? (Naomi missed the ball and it went into the bleachers.) ***Cause and Effect***

Page 8: What notes might Naomi *scribble* about her bad day? (Possible answers: wore ugly plaid pants; stepped in mud; forgot to get bubbles out of clay) ***Vocabulary***

Pages 10–11: What was Naomi's purpose for writing the poem? (inform; entertain) ***Author's Purpose, Point of View***

Page 16: What was the author's purpose in writing *Bad Day, Glad Day?* Explain. (She informed readers by including poems written by famous poets. She expressed ideas by writing about the importance of working together. She entertained readers by writing a story mixed with poetry.) ***Author's Purpose, Point of View***

RETURN TO PREDICTIONS AND PURPOSES Have students reread their predictions and identify which ones were accurate and which were not. Encourage them to talk about whether their questions were answered or not.

LITERARY RESPONSE Discuss these questions:

- Why did writing about her day help Naomi feel better?
- What kinds of things do you do to make yourself feel better when you are sad or upset?

Also see the story questions and activity in *Bad Day, Glad Day.*

Answers to Story Questions

1. Naomi overslept, had to wear ugly pants to school, missed the bus, made her mom mad, stepped in a puddle, slipped in the classroom, forgot her math homework, missed the basket in gym class, and ruined her clay bear.
2. Naomi realized she was good at something—poetry. She had a talent that other kids admired.
3. The author wanted to include different types of poetry in the book and used Mr. Morgan to express the point of view that poetry offers us another way of expressing ourselves.
4. This story is about how self-expression can boost self-esteem. It's also about working together and sharing our areas of expertise.
5. Answers will vary.

The *Story Questions and Activity* below appear in the *Independent Book.*

Story Questions and Activity

1. Why was Naomi having a bad day?
2. What turned Naomi's bad day into a glad day?
3. Having read this story, describe the author's purpose and point of view.
4. What is the story mostly about?
5. If Naomi traveled awhile with Basho from *Grass Sandals*, what do you think they would talk about and what might they learn from each other?

Start Your Own Poetry Club

Find a convenient time to get together with your friends after school to read the work of famous poets aloud. Have a discussion about the poems you read. Which poet did you like the best? What was your favorite poem? Then choose a topic together and schedule another meeting at which time you can all share the poem you wrote about the topic selected.

from *Bad Day, Glad Day*

Leveled Books

CHALLENGE

Nonsense, Mr. Lear!

- ☑ **Author's Purpose, Point of View**
- ☑ **Instructional Vocabulary:** ***chanted, nipped, pouch, restless, scribbled, stitching***

Guided Reading

PREVIEW AND PREDICT Together, preview the Table of Contents. Then invite students to preview the illustrations up to page 11. Have them discuss the sketches and predict what the story will be about. Write students' responses on a chart.

SET PURPOSES Have students write in their journals several questions about what they would like to learn from the story.

READ THE BOOK After students have read the story independently, ask the following questions to encourage development of the targeted reading strategies.

Pages 2–3: What was Lear's purpose in writing limericks? Explain. (He wanted to entertain children.) ***Author's Purpose***

Pages 6–7: Why do you think the author includes Lear's cartoons in the book? (The cartoons are entertaining and informative.) ***Author's Purpose***

Page 11: Why do you think the author used the word *scribbled* instead of the word *wrote* to describe how Lear recorded his limericks? (It more clearly describes the manner in which Lear wrote: quickly, without much concern for neatness.) ***Vocabulary***

Page 15: How would the purpose of a travel book differ from a book of limericks? (A travel book would inform, whereas a limerick book would entertain.) ***Author's Purpose***

RETURN TO PREDICTIONS AND PURPOSES Have students review their predictions and questions. Which predictions were accurate? Which questions were answered?

LITERARY RESPONSE Discuss these questions:

- What kind of selection was this story?
- Why do you think Lear preferred to entertain children rather than adults?

Also see the story questions and activity in *Nonsense, Mr. Lear!*

Answers to Story Questions

1. No one knows for certain who invented the limerick, but the origins of these five-line humorous rhymes can be traced to Limerick, Ireland.
2. Lear earned his living by painting. He didn't take his poetry seriously. It was just for fun.
3. The author wanted to share information about Edward Lear's life and how he wrote amusing limericks that still entertain children and adults today.
4. This book is about the life and limericks of Edward Lear.
5. Answers will vary.

The *Story Questions and Activity* below appear in the *Challenge Book*.

Story Questions and Activity

1. Who invented the limerick?
2. Why didn't Lear give up painting to concentrate on writing limericks?
3. Why did the author write this book?
4. What is this book mainly about?
5. If Edward Lear had met Basho from *Grass Sandals* on his travels, how might each have influenced the other's poetry?

Rhyme Time

Write your own limerick about a fictitious person or pet. Fill in the line, "There once was a (person or animal) from (place)". Then write a second line that rhymes with the first. Rhyme the third and fourth lines. For the fifth line, repeat the first line with a slight variation. Share the limerick with your classmates.

from *Nonsense, Mr. Lear!*

Activities

Bringing Groups Together

Anthology and Leveled Books

Connecting Texts

AUTHOR'S PURPOSE CHARTS Write the story titles on a chart. Review how poetry was used in each story. Then have students identify why the characters wrote the poems.

Grass Sandals	Bookworm's Band	Bad Day, Glad Day	Nonsense, Mr. Lear!
• The poetry expressed a love of nature. • The poetry informed readers about the things the main character saw. • The poetry entertained the readers.	• The poetry was expressed through music to inform others. • The poetry was expressed through music to entertain others.	• The poetry expressed frustration. • The poetry entertained the readers and listeners.	• The poetry entertained children. • The poetry expressed ideas about how silly people could be.

Viewing/Representing

GROUP PRESENTATIONS Divide the class into four groups, one for each of the four books read in the lesson. (For *Grass Sandals*, combine students of different reading levels.) Ask groups to write summaries of their selections and explain why the poems are important to the plot. Invite each group to present their summary and read a poem from the selection.

AUDIENCE RESPONSE Ask students to listen to each presentation. Allow time for them to ask questions after each presentation.

Research and Inquiry

MORE ABOUT POETS AND POETRY The four stories are tied together through the use of poetry. *Grass Sandals* and *Nonsense, Mr. Lear!* are biographies about poets. Invite students to find a favorite contemporary poem and research information about the author. Ask them to copy the poem and write a biographical paragraph that includes the following:

- background information about the poet.
- what kinds of poems the poet writes.
- Post the work on a *Poet Tree* bulletin-board.

*inter*NET CONNECTION To find out more about poets, have students visit ***www.mhschool.com/reading***

Review Author's Purpose, Point of View

PREPARE

Discuss Author's Purpose and Point of View

Review: To determine the reason an author wrote a story, pay attention to clues throughout the story. The author's point of view is how he or she feels about the person or topic written about.

TEACH

Read "Basho" and Model the Skill

Direct students to pay close attention to the author's purpose and point of view as you read **Teaching Chart 76.**

Basho

Basho lived in Japan more than 300 years ago. He took a long journey. He took very little with him on his journey. He took some clothes, such as a hat and a paper coat, and writing paper, a brush, and an ink stone. On this journey, he wrote poems about the things he saw that were special. He wrote poems to animals, to people, and to the moon and stars. He even wrote a poem to blue shoelaces, because the color was so beautiful—like the blue of a flower. Basho's poetry became well known in Japan and throughout the world.

Teaching Chart 76

Discuss clues in the passage that help readers determine the author's purpose and point of view.

MODEL As I read the paragraph, I notice the author is telling me many facts about Basho. The paragraph tells me when Basho lived, what he took on his journey, and information about what he wrote in his poems. The author's main purpose seems to be to inform.

TESTED OBJECTIVES

Students will determine an author's purpose for writing and identify their point of view.

Skills Finder: Author's Purpose, Point of View	
Introduce	299A-B
Review	331E-F, 369E-F
Test	Unit 3

TEACHING TIP

AUTHOR'S PURPOSE
Encourage students to write to an author and ask him or her to explain how and why he/she came to write one of his/her books. Students should write to the author care of his/her publisher. The publisher's address often appears on a book's copyright page.

SELF-SELECTED Reading

Students may choose from the following titles.

ANTHOLOGY
- Grass Sandals

LEVELED BOOKS
- Bookworm's Band
- Bad Day, Glad Day
- Nonsense, Mr. Lear!

Bibliography, pages T78–T79

PRACTICE

Determine Author's Purpose and Point of View

GROUP

Have students underline clues in "Basho" that help them determine the author's purpose. Have groups discuss how they can identify the author's point of view. Ask: How does the author seem to feel about Basho?

Have students identify the reason the author wrote the passage and how the point of view helped determine the purpose.

▶ **Logical**

ASSESS/CLOSE

Write for a Purpose

GROUP

Display an empty box of cereal. Organize the class into four groups. Assign each group a purpose for writing—persuade, inform, express, or entertain. Have groups write and present the cereal in a way that represents the assigned purpose. For example, the group that has to persuade could write a television advertisement. The group that expresses could write a poem about how the cereal tastes.

ALTERNATE TEACHING STRATEGY

AUTHOR'S PURPOSE, POINT OF VIEW

For a different approach to teaching this skill, see page T66.

Intervention Skills

Intervention Guide, for direct instruction and extra practice with author's purpose and point of view

Meeting Individual Needs for Comprehension

EASY

Name______________ Date________ Reteach 93

Author's Purpose and Point of View

Authors often write to entertain or to persuade. These are their **purposes**. They often express **their point of view** about a subject through characters and story events.

Read each story. Then circle the letter beside the best response.

Julie and Andres enjoy hiking. They also enjoy biking along trails. In fact, it seems they take every opportunity to be outdoors. The mountain air and the woodsy smell of the forest make them feel happy and healthy. It makes them sad to see garbage left by people in natural areas. Together they have written letters to make stricter laws against littering.

1. Which would the author favor?
   a. indoor activities (b.) outdoor activities
2. How would he or she vote on stricter laws against littering?
   a. He or she would vote no. (b.) He or she would vote yes.

"Never!" shouted Sean. "I won't do it. Greasy fries, cold burgers, and little chicken parts are not real food. I prefer salads and fruit, and maybe some cheese. There are only empty calories in what they sell at this Snack Shack."

3. How does the author feel about fast food?
   a. The author probably likes it. (b.) He or she probably never eats it.
4. Which cause might the author support?
   (a.) Veggies in the schools b. National Corn Dog Day

At Home: Have students explain why they chose the responses they chose for the above paragraphs.

Book 4/Unit 3 Grass Sandals 4

93

Reteach, 93

ON-LEVEL

Name______________ Date________ Practice 93

Author's Purpose and Point of View

Authors often write with more than one **purpose**. They may want to tell an enjoyable story or to give readers ideas to think about. Sometimes, the main character shows the author's personal ideas and feelings. This is the author's **point of view**.

Read each statement below. Write **agree** or **disagree** to show how you think Dawnine Spivak, the author of "Grass Sandals," would feel about the idea. Then give an example from the story to support your answer. **Answers will vary.**

A. Looking out your door at the same scene every day could get boring.

1. Author's point of view: disagree
2. Example from the story: Basho enjoyed sitting in the doorway of his small house looking at the river and mountains every day. However, Basho felt restless and decided to travel.

B. The main purpose for walking across a country is to exercise and to be healthy.

3. Author's point of view: disagree
4. Example from the story: Basho wanted to see new things and visit new places. He wanted new experiences.

C. There are many beautiful and wonderful things to write about if we look at nature.

5. Author's point of view: agree
6. Example from the story: When he saw a horse eating flowers or a circling hawk, Basho wrote a poem about it.

At Home: Have students choose a purpose and write about what they see when they look out of their window at home.

Book 4/Unit 3 Grass Sandals 6

93

Practice, 93

CHALLENGE

Name______________ Date________ Extend 93

Author's Purpose and Point of View

The Japanese poet Basho wrote haiku. A haiku is a three-line poem having exactly 17 syllables. The first and third lines each have five syllables. The second line has seven syllables. The lines of a haiku do not rhyme. Look back at the story for examples.

Choose a topic, write a haiku, and then illustrate it. Share your haiku with classmates. Have them determine whether the **purpose** of your haiku is to persuade, to describe, to inform, to entertain, or whether you have several purposes.

Answers will vary but should be in haiku format.

At Home: Read several poems. Decide whether the purpose of each is to persuade, to describe, to inform, or to entertain.

Book 4/Unit 3 Grass Sandals

93

Extend, 93

LANGUAGE SUPPORT

Name______________ Date________

Why Read It?

1. Color the person below who should read "Grass Sandals".

"I want to read a good, entertaining story."
"I want to learn exactly how to make pottery."
"I want to show my friend why I like to listen to music."

102 Grass Sandals • Language Support/Blackline Master 50 Grade 4

Language Support, 102

Review Judgments and Decisions

PREPARE

Discuss Making Judgments and Decisions

Explain: A judgment is an opinion the reader forms about a character, action, or situation in the story. Readers bring their own experiences to the story, which helps them form opinions. A decision is the choice someone makes after thinking about a problem.

TEACH

Read the Story and Model the Skill

Direct students to think about how Basho prepares for his journey as you read **Teaching Chart 77.**

Packing for the Journey

Basho felt restless. It was time for a journey across Japan. There was so much he wanted to see. He made a tree bark hat and grass coat. Then he stitched up a hole in his pants and added a string to his hat. He was ready to go.

His friends gave him the last few things he needed—sandals, a paper coat, paper, and a writing stone. Now Basho was ready to walk across the country.

Teaching Chart 77

Have a volunteer underline the items Basho packs for his journey. Ask: Did Basho pack well? Why? Why not?

MODEL When I read about the things Basho packed for such a long journey, I wonder if he made good choices. True, he did live three hundred years ago, and life was much different back then. But I know that if I took a walking journey, I would want to pack food and water.

TESTED OBJECTIVES

Students will make judgments and decisions.

Skills Finder

Judgments and Decisions

Introduce	257A-B
Review	281E-F, 331G-H, 361A-B, 631G-H, 665A-B, 691E-F
Test	Unit 3, Unit 6

LANGUAGE SUPPORT

ESL Write the terms *decision* and *judgment* on the board. Give students an example of each and then ask them to add some examples of their own. For example, a decision might be *I decided to stay home from school yesterday*. A judgment might be *It was a good decision because I was too sick to learn anything.*

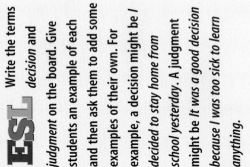

PRACTICE

Make a Venn Diagram

Have students draw a Venn diagram to show the items Basho packed and the items they would pack to take a walking journey.

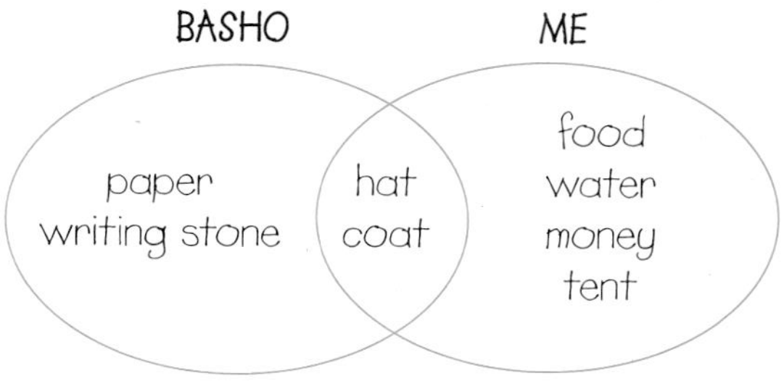

Then have them explain their judgments about how Basho prepared for his trip. Did he decide to take everything he needed?

ASSESS/CLOSE

Tell About a Decision

Ask students to think about a situation in which they had to make a decision. Have them write a brief paragraph telling about the situation. Then ask them to judge whether or not it was a good decision.

ALTERNATE TEACHING STRATEGY

JUDGMENTS AND DECISIONS

For a different approach to teaching this skill, see page T60.

Intervention Skills

Intervention Guide, for direct instruction and extra practice with judgments and decisions

Meeting Individual Needs for Comprehension

EASY

Name ______ Date ______ Reteach 94

Make Judgments and Decisions

Characters in a story often face difficult situations in which they must decide what to do. Readers often think about what they might do if they were in similar situations. This is called **making judgments and decisions**.

Read the story. Then answer the questions.

Jesse was excited about visiting his young cousin Sherry. Despite their age differences and the fact that Sherry was a girl, they had many things in common. Like Jesse, Sherry loved chess, reading, and action movies. So when Jesse saw one of his favorite videos on sale, he bought it as a gift for Sherry. His mom, whom he met at the Food Court, did not approve. "That is not a good gift for someone who already sits in front of the television too much," she said sternly.

Jesse's big sister came over and whispered in his ear, "What a nice thing to do. Sherry will love it."

1. Why did Jesse decide to get the video? **He knew Sherry liked action movies.**
2. Why do you think Jesse's mom is against the gift? **She thinks videos are another form of television, and Sherry already watches it too much. Sherry should spend her time better.**
3. If you were Jesse, what would you do—return the gift and choose something else or give it to Sherry anyway? Why? **Answers may vary but should show an awareness that the mother's advice is good.**
4. If Jesse asked you for advice, what would you tell him? **Possible answer: Give the gift to Sherry, but tell his mom he will choose better next time.**

4 Book 4/Unit 3 Grass Sandals — **At Home:** Have students think about a decision they made during the day and explain why they decided what they did. — 94

Reteach, 94

ON-LEVEL

Name ______ Date ______ Practice 94

Make Judgments and Decisions

When we read a story we **make judgments** and form opinions about the characters **decisions**. Read each passage below. Answer the questions about the characters. **Answers will vary.**

Deborah was new to Smithtown Elementary. On her first day, Kenny and Hasan showed her things she needed to know, such as where to put her coat and where to find notebook paper. Kenny and Hasan knew how it felt to be new to a school since they had entered Smithtown last year. Jennifer, who sat next to Deborah in health class wanted to help her too, but she was feeling tired. Tomorrow she hoped to give Deborah any help she needed.

1. Why do you think Kenny and Hasan decided to help Deborah? **They know how hard it is to be new to a school.**
2. Why didn't Jennifer help Deborah? **She was feeling tired.**
3. How would you feel about being in school with these students? **They were kind and helpful and it would be nice to know them.**

"Are we there yet?" whined Benjie. That's all the fourth graders heard from Benjie as they hiked to the picnic grounds.

"Benjie," shouted Mario. "Stop it. You're acting like a baby."

"You can do it," said Connor. "Maybe your pack is too heavy. Take something out. I'll carry it for you."

"Thanks," Benjie said. "I'm starting to feel better. I think I'm getting my second wind."

4. Would you like to go on a hike with Benjie? Why or why not? **Students may say that Benjie's complaints would be hard to listen to.**
5. Of all those who spoke to Benjie, who was most helpful? Explain. **Students may say Connor because he offered a solution.**
6. How do you think Benjie will react if it begins to rain? How might the others react? **He may complain and the others may ignore him.**

6 Book 4/Unit 3 Grass Sandals — **At Home:** Have students write a continuation of one of these stories based on the judgments they have made about the characters. — 94

Practice, 94

CHALLENGE

Name ______ Date ______ Extend 94

Make Judgments and Decisions

Think about "Grass Sandals." Read each of the given **judgments** or **decisions** that Basho may have made. Then fill in the blanks with the missing judgments or decisions. **Answers will vary, but should relate to facts of the story.**

1. **Judgment:** This banana tree is the most interesting plant near my house.
   Decision: **Possible answer: I'll change my name to Basho, which means banana tree.**
2. **Judgment:** **Possible answer: There must be more beautiful things to see in the world than my village.**
   Decision: I'm going to walk across Japan.
3. **Judgment:** I imagine the ocean will feel different than hot springs and streams.
   Decision: **Possible answer: I'll go for a swim in the ocean.**
4. **Judgment:** **Possible answer: The most beautiful thing in the night sky is a full moon.**
   Decision: We will have a party and watch the moon.
5. **Judgment:** The smell of rain is wonderful.
   Decision: **Possible answer: I'll stop and write a poem about the rain.**

Book 4/Unit 3 Grass Sandals — **At Home:** Have students think about a time they felt the need to do something interesting or different. Discuss what they did, how effective it was, and what else they could do. — 94

Extend, 94

LANGUAGE SUPPORT

Name ______ Date ______

Bedtime for Basho

1. Basho is tired and ready for bed. 2. Look at each bed shown below. 3. Tell why Basho does or does not like each bed. 4. Which bed would you choose to sleep in?

Answers will vary.

Grade 4 — Language Support / Blackline Master 51 • Grass Sandals 103

Language Support, 103

TESTED OBJECTIVES

Students will use context clues to determine the meanings of unfamiliar words.

Skills Finder

Context Clues	
Introduce	157I-J
Review	215I-J, 251I-J, 331I-J, 359I-J, 369G-H, 515I-J
Test	Units 2, 3, 5, 6
Maintain	309, 389, 523, 643

TEACHING TIP

CONTEXT CLUES Share steps for figuring out what an unfamiliar word means.

- When you come to a word you do not know, read to the end of the sentence.
- Use the words around the unfamiliar word to get clues about its meaning.
- Check a dictionary if you need more help.
- Reread the sentence once you know the word.

Review Context Clues

PREPARE

Discuss Context Clues

Explain: Sometimes while reading a story you will find a word you do not know. Often you can use the words around it to give you clues about what the word means. If there is a picture, sometimes it can help, too. These kinds of clues are called context clues.

TEACH

Read the Passage and Model the Skill

Read aloud the passage on **Teaching Chart 78.**

Visiting a Farm

Carla took a trip to Japan. She enjoyed visiting a little village in the country. It had big basho trees full of green and yellow bananas. The trees in the apple orchard were full of sweet-smelling flowers. One field near the village was covered with morning glories. When the morning sun flooded the field, the flowers opened, and the field looked like a purple carpet. Carla even met a woman who taught her how to write a haiku, a kind of Japanese poem. Of course, Carla wrote about the morning glories!

Teaching Chart 78

Reread the third sentence, and circle the word *basho.*

MODEL I've never seen this word. I don't know its meaning. There isn't a picture to help me either. But the word looks like it's important, so I am going to try to figure out the meaning using the words before and after it. The paragraph says that Carla visited a village in the country, so this is something you could see in the country. The sentence also tells me that this is a tree with bananas. So, a *basho* must be a banana tree.

PRACTICE

Use Context Clues

GROUP

Circle the words *orchard, morning glories,* and *haiku.* Have volunteers underline context clues that help show what the words mean. Have groups write definitions for each word based on context clues and then check them against dictionary definitions. ▶ **Linguistic**

ASSESS/CLOSE

Write Sentences with Context Clues

Write the words below on the board. Tell students they are to write a one-paragraph story using each word so a beginning reader would know what the words mean. Have students illustrate their paragraphs.

freckles **shiny** **empty** **curious**

ALTERNATE TEACHING STRATEGY

CONTEXT CLUES

For a different approach to teaching this skill, see page T65.

Intervention **Skills**

Intervention Guide, for direct instruction and extra practice with context clues

Meeting Individual Needs for Vocabulary

EASY

Name________ Date______ **Reteach 95**

Context Clues

When you come across words you don't know, many times you can figure out their meaning from the **context**. The words in the sentence, or the sentences before and after the word, can give you clues as to what the word means.

Read the paragraph. Circle the letter beside the meaning of each of the numbered words. Then write the clues in the paragraph that helped you figure out the meaning.

America was settled by pioneers. These courageous, early settlers traveled west despite danger and obstacles such as waterfalls, rivers, and mountains. They had to transport their canoes around waterfalls, lifting boats over steep rocks. They had to ford wide rivers in wagons pulled by oxen and guide horses along steep mountain cliffs and dry, rocky ground.

1. pioneers
   (a.) early explorers b. last to arrive
   Clues: courageous early settlers
2. obstacles
   a. easy passageways (b.) things in the way
   Clues: waterfalls, rivers, and mountains
3. transport
   (a.) carry from place to place b. hold in place
   Clues: lifting boats over steep rocks
4. ford
   a. to bypass (b.) to cross
   Clues: wide rivers in wagons pulled by oxen

At Home: Have students use two words from the exercise in sentences.

95 Book 4/Unit 3 Grass Sandals 4

Reteach, 95

ON-LEVEL

Name________ Date______ **Practice 95**

Context Clues

You may find words you don't know when you are reading a story. Sometimes the other words in the sentence can help you figure out what the difficult word means. Those other words in the sentence are called **context clues.**

Use the context clues to help you choose a word to complete each sentence.

orchard	**adventurers**	**Basho**	**reflected**
haiku	**temple**	**cricket**	**morning glories**

1. A great Japanese poet's name was __Basho__, whose name means banana tree.
2. The tourists walked to the beautiful, old __temple__ and went inside.
3. We went to the __orchard__ to pick apples.
4. The __morning glories__ in the garden were purple and became more beautiful as they grew.
5. The full moon was __reflected__ in the water of the lake.
6. The hopping insect that makes sounds at night is the __cricket__.
7. A __haiku__ poem is one with certain numbers of syllables in its three lines.
8. For centuries, many __adventurers__ have explored Japan.

At Home: Have students define words in context as they read.

95 Book 4/Unit 3 Grass Sandals 8

Practice, 95

CHALLENGE

Name________ Date______ **Extend 95**

Context Clues

Context clues can help you figure out the meaning of unfamiliar words. Context clues can be words or phrases in the same sentence or in nearby sentences. Read the context clues in the sentences. Then choose a word from the box to complete each sentence. Then use each word in a sentence of your own. Sentences will vary but each word should be used correctly.

clover	**ducked**	**crisscrossing**	**orchard**	**reflected**

1. Basho rode across a field of __clover__.
2. He tied his sandals on with strings that were __crisscrossing__ his ankles.
3. Basho __ducked__ his body low to enter the cave behind the water.
4. Basho walked through a group of fruit trees. It was a cherry __orchard__.
5. The mirror image of the moon was __reflected__ in their cups.

At Home: Have students read a story and identify any unfamiliar words. Then, use words in the same or nearby sentences to figure out the meaning of the words.

95 Book 4/Unit 3 Grass Sandals

Extend, 95

LANGUAGE SUPPORT

Name________ Date______

Find the Picture

1. Read each word in dark print in the text below. 2. Write the word in dark print on the line next to the picture it describes.

This is the story of a Haiku poet named Basho. He walked all over his country writing poetry. A friend once gave him a banana tree or **basho** which he planted near his **bamboo hut**. He liked the tree so much he decided to call himself Basho. Every morning he would have tea in his hut and look at the sea, mountains, and the **morning glories** right outside his door.

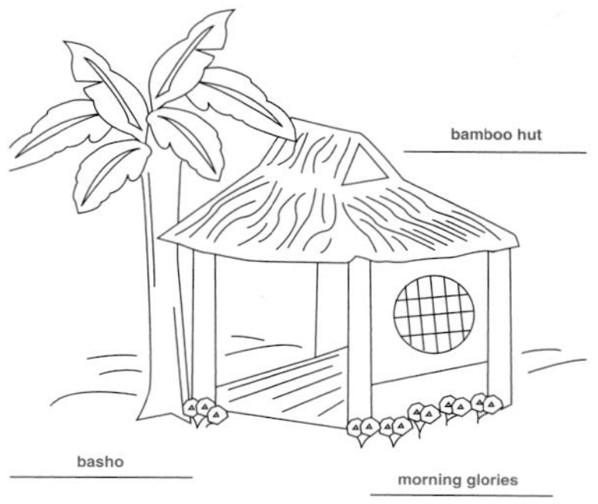

104 Grass Sandals • Language Support/Blackline Master 52 Grade 4

Language Support, 104

GRAMMAR/SPELLING CONNECTIONS

See the 5-Day Grammar and Usage Plan on main and helping verbs, pages 331M–331N.

See the 5-Day Spelling Plan on words with digraphs, pages 331O–331P.

TEACHING TIP

Technology
Remind students that they can use computer tools to enhance their book reports visually. For example, they can underline or boldface the title of the report—and italicize the name of the book.

Supporting Details
Have students review their drafts to make sure they have provided specific details to support their reasons for recommending or not recommending the book.

Handwriting CD-ROM

Persuasive Writing

Prewrite

WRITE A BOOK REVIEW Present the following writing assignment: Write a book review of *Grass Sandals*. Tell:

- who the main character is,
- where and when the story takes place, and
- what happens in the story.

Describe the pictures and the haiku poems used in the story. Then tell whether or not you would recommend the book to others to read. Give three good reasons.

BRAINSTORM IDEAS Have students brainstorm specific reasons why they liked *Grass Sandals*. The reasons should include information about art and poetry. List their ideas on the board.

Strategy: Focusing Questions Have students answer questions to highlight the basic story elements, such as:

- Who is the main character?
- What does the character do?
- Where does the character live?
- When does the story take place?
- Why is the character special?

Draft

USE THE QUESTIONS Have students write the book review using the answers to the focusing questions to explain the story plot. They should conclude the review with reasons someone should read the book. Students can refer to the list on the board for ending ideas. Remind students to write a brief but specific book review.

Revise

SELF-QUESTIONING Ask students to assess their drafts.

- Did I explain the basic story events in a concise way?
- Did I give specific reasons for reading the book?
- Were all my details important?

PARTNERS Have each student trade book reviews with a peer to get another point of view.

Edit/Proofread

CHECK FOR ERRORS Students should reread their book reviews for spelling, grammar, punctuation, and paragraph format.

Publish

SHARE THE REPORTS Have students write final drafts of their book reviews. Encourage them to exchange reports and compare the reasons for recommending or not recommending the book.

Book Review of Grass Sandals

Basho lived in Japan many years ago. He decided to take a long trip. He packed only clothes, paper, and pen, and then he began his walk. Basho wrote poems about things in nature that were special to him.

I suggest that everyone read this book. The illustrations are the kind of art people paint in Japan. The author also shows Japanese writing. The best part of Grass Sandals is the short poems. They describe different animals and things that I like to watch in nature.

Presentation Ideas

ILLUSTRATE THE BOOK REPORT Have students draw a picture to go with their favorite haiku and copy the poem on the page. Then display the picture and book review together. ▶ **Viewing/Representing**

BOOK CLUB Have students pretend they are members of a book club. Students can share their book reviews and then read their favorite haiku aloud. ▶ **Speaking/Listening**

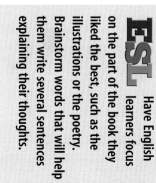

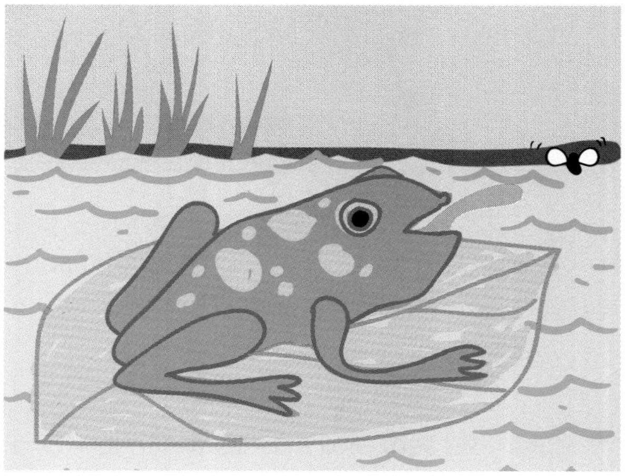

Consider students' creative efforts, possibly adding a plus (+) for originality, wit, and imagination.

Scoring Rubric

Excellent	Good	Fair	Unsatisfactory
4: The writer • clearly summarizes the story without telling the ending. • provides specific details from the book as to why someone would or would not like it. • gives concise information in an organized manner.	**3:** The writer • summarizes the story with some important information. • provides specific details, as to why someone should read the book. • attempts to organize the information.	**2:** The writer • relates the entire story rather than summarizing the key points. • gives subjective reasons for why someone should read the book. • provides more detail than required.	**1:** The writer • has provided incomplete or unclear details. • presents no reasons for reading the book. • provides no specific details.

Incomplete 0: The writer leaves the page blank or fails to respond to the writing task. The student does not address the topic or simply paraphrases the prompt. The response is illegible or incoherent.

For a 6-point or an 8-point scale, see pages T107–T108.

Meeting Individual Needs for Writing

EASY

Pack for a Trip Ask students to think about a place they would like to visit. Have them draw and label the items they would need to pack for their trip.

ON-LEVEL

Tour Guide Have students research interesting places to visit in their area. Then have them plan a day trip in which they would be tour guides. They should include a time schedule of events. Students can then create a brochure advertising their tour.

CHALLENGE

Write a Dialogue Have students create a dialogue between Basho and one of his friends as the two characters view the moon. What comments would they make? Would they only talk about the moon?

Listening and Speaking

LISTENING STRATEGIES
As book reviews are read aloud, have students:

- sit in an erect but relaxed position, facing the speaker.
- jot down questions to ask afterward.

SPEAKING STRATEGIES
Encourage speakers to:

- stand in an erect, relaxed position with feet planted firmly on the ground.
- avoid distracting movements, such as shifting weight from one foot to another.

LANGUAGE SUPPORT

ESL Have English learners focus on the part of the book they liked the best, such as the illustrations or the poetry. Brainstorm words that will help them write several sentences explaining their thoughts.

PORTFOLIO **Invite students to include their book reports or another writing project in their portfolios.**

5 Day Grammar and Usage Plan

LANGUAGE SUPPORT

ESL **Write several sentences with helping verbs on the board. Ask students to take turns circling the main verb and underlining the helping verb in each sentence.**

DAILY LANGUAGE ACTIVITIES

Write the Daily Language Activities on the chalkboard each day or use **Transparency 13.** Have students orally correct the sentences using the appropriate helping verb. For answers, see the transparency.

Day 1

1. Look, Basho have planted a tree.
2. His friends has waved good-bye.
3. Yesterday, Basho have noticed a cricket in the pond.

Day 2

1. Earlier, Basho were feeling tired.
2. He go on a journey tomorrow.
3. Right now, I are looking at the sky.

Day 3

1. Basho have walked six miles today.
2. He were surprised by the flowers.
3. Crabs is climbing on his legs.

Day 4

1. A woman have invited Basho for dinner today.
2. She are cooking noodles.
3. Next time, they was eat and talk.

Day 5

1. Last night, Basho and his friends was watching the moon.
2. Tomorrow, they write a poem.
3. Today, I has dyed my shoelaces.

Daily Language Transparency 13

DAY 1 Introduce the Concept

Oral Warm-Up Explain that some verbs have helpers that tell more about them.

Introduce Main and Helping Verbs Present and discuss the following:

Main and Helping Verbs

- The **main verb** in a sentence shows what the subject does or is.
- A **helping verb** helps the main verb show an action or make a statement.
- *Have*, *has*, and *had* are helping verbs.

Display sentences with *have*, *has*, and *had* plus a main verb ending with *-ed*. Explain that *has* is used with a singular subject and *have* with a plural subject, *I* or *you*. Point out the *-ed* ending.

Present the Daily Language Activity. Then have students write sentences using *have*, *has*, and *had*.

WRITING Assign the daily Writing Prompt on page 298C.

Name________ Date______ LEARN Grammar 77

Main and Helping Verbs

- The **main verb** in a sentence shows what the subject does or is.
- A **helping verb** helps the main verb show an action or make a statement.
- *Have, has,* and *had* are helping verbs.

Draw one line under each form of *has* that is a helping verb. Draw two lines under each main verb that it helps.

1. Basho got his name after he had planted a banana tree.
2. Basho has decided upon a trip across Japan.
3. When he had prepared for his trip, Basho left home.
4. Before leaving, Basho had stitched a string on his hat to keep it from blowing away.
5. The cherry blossoms have waited for Basho.
6. The poet has scribbled some words on his hat.
7. An old woman has invited Basho to share her noodles.
8. Basho's friends have joined him for part of the trip.
9. They have presented Basho with presents for his trip.
10. Basho left his friends after they had crossed the river.

10 Grade 4/Unit 3 Grass Sandals: The Travels of Basho — **Extension:** Ask students to write *has, have,* and *had* on separate index cards. Have them work in small groups, each choosing a card and constructing an oral sentence that uses the form chosen as a ... 77

GRAMMAR PRACTICE BOOK, PAGE 77

DAY 2 Teach the Concept

Review Helping Verbs Ask students what the main verb and helping verb do in a sentence.

Introduce Other Helping Verbs Present and discuss:

Helping Verbs

- *Is*, *are*, *am*, *was*, and *were* can be helping verbs.
- *Will* is a helping verb used to help show an action in the future.

Write a sentence for each form of *be*, using the *-ing* form of the main verb. Discuss agreement with a singular subject (is, was), plural subject or *you* (are, were), and *I* (am, was). Point out the main verb's *-ing* ending.

Present the Daily Language Activity. Then have students write sentences using *is*, *am*, *were*, and *will*.

WRITING Assign the daily Writing Prompt on page 298C.

Name________ Date______ LEARN AND PRACTICE Grammar 78

More Main and Helping Verbs

- *Is, are, am, was,* and *were* can be helping verbs.
- They are used with a main verb ending in *-ing*
- *Will* is a helping verb used to help show an action in the future.

Read each sentence. Study the helping verb. Circle the correct form of the main verb in parentheses.

1. Basho's friends were (wave, waving) as they left in the boat.
2. As he stands under a waterfall, Basho is (laugh, laughing).
3. Soon Basho's feet will (take, taking) him past an old temple.
4. The beautiful cherry trees are (bloom, blooming).
5. During his trip, Basho was (sleep, sleeping) in huts, houses, and stalls.
6. Most of the time, the poet ______ walking. (is, are).
7. Tomorrow Basho will (ride, riding) on a farmer's horse.
8. Along the way, people are (give, giving) Basho food.

78 **Extension:** Ask students to write three sentences that begin with "I am" and tell what they are doing right now. — Grade 4/Unit 3 Grass Sandals: The Travels of Basho 8

GRAMMAR PRACTICE BOOK, PAGE 78

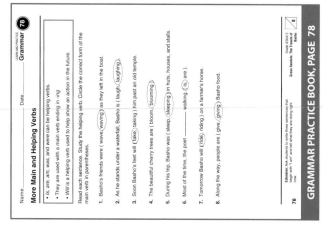

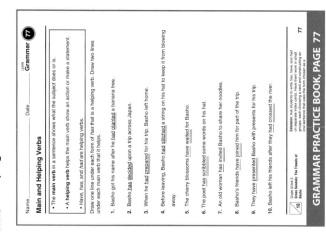

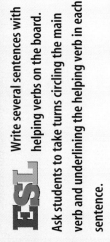

Main and Helping Verbs

DAY 3 Review and Practice

Learn from the Literature Review the helping verbs associated with main verbs ending with *-ed* and *-ing*. Then read aloud the first sentence on page 309 of *Grass Sandals*:

> **When they had crossed the river, Basho climbed out of the boat and waved to his friends.**

Ask students to identify the verb phrase that includes a main verb and a helping verb. Have students explain the role of the word *had*. (It is a helping verb that helps explain the order of past events.)

Identify Helping Verbs Present the Daily Language Activity. Then have students write five sentences that include the *have* and *be* forms of helping verbs.

WRITING Assign the daily Writing Prompt on page 298D.

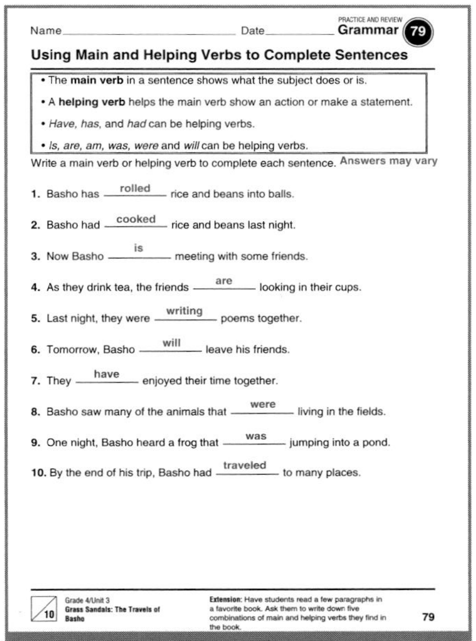

Name_______ Date_______ PRACTICE AND REVIEW Grammar 79

Using Main and Helping Verbs to Complete Sentences

- The **main verb** in a sentence shows what the subject does or is.
- A **helping verb** helps the main verb show an action or make a statement.
- *Have, has,* and *had* can be helping verbs.
- *Is, are, am, was, were* and *will* can be helping verbs.

Write a main verb or helping verb to complete each sentence. Answers may vary

1. Basho has ___rolled___ rice and beans into balls.
2. Basho had ___cooked___ rice and beans last night.
3. Now Basho ___is___ meeting with some friends.
4. As they drink tea, the friends ___are___ looking in their cups.
5. Last night, they were ___writing___ poems together.
6. Tomorrow, Basho ___will___ leave his friends.
7. They ___have___ enjoyed their time together.
8. Basho saw many of the animals that ___were___ living in the fields.
9. One night, Basho heard a frog that ___was___ jumping into a pond.
10. By the end of his trip, Basho had ___traveled___ to many places.

Grade 4/Unit 3 Grass Sandals: The Travels of Basho 10

Extension: Have students read a few paragraphs in a favorite book. Ask them to write down five combinations of main and helping verbs they find in the book. 79

GRAMMAR PRACTICE BOOK, PAGE 79

DAY 4 Review and Practice

Review Helping Verbs Write on a chart the corrected sentences from the Daily Language Activities for Days 1 and 2. Circle the verb phrases. Have students note main-verb endings and helping verbs. Then present the Daily Language Activity for Day 4.

Mechanics and Usage Discuss:

Contractions

- A **contraction** is a shortened form of two words.
- A contraction can be made by combining a verb with the word *not*.
- An apostrophe (') shows the letter *o* has been left out.

Have students brainstorm contractions, such as *isn't*, *aren't*, and *won't*. Note that *won't* changes spelling.

WRITING Assign the daily Writing Prompt on page 298D.

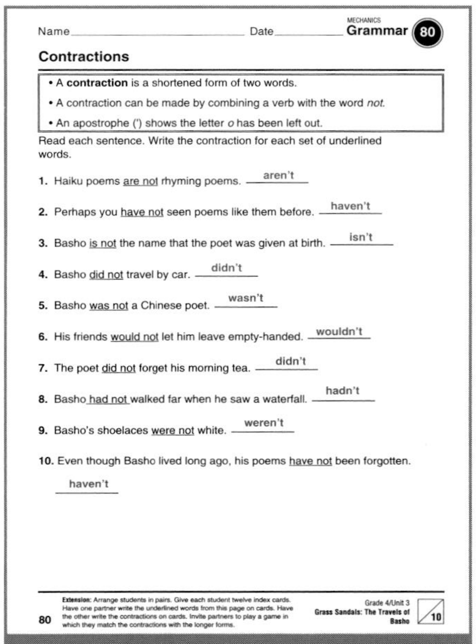

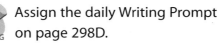

Name_______ Date_______ MECHANICS Grammar 80

Contractions

- A **contraction** is a shortened form of two words.
- A contraction can be made by combining a verb with the word *not*.
- An apostrophe (') shows the letter *o* has been left out.

Read each sentence. Write the contraction for each set of underlined words.

1. Haiku poems are not rhyming poems. ___aren't___
2. Perhaps you have not seen poems like them before. ___haven't___
3. Basho is not the name that the poet was given at birth. ___isn't___
4. Basho did not travel by car. ___didn't___
5. Basho was not a Chinese poet. ___wasn't___
6. His friends would not let him leave empty-handed. ___wouldn't___
7. The poet did not forget his morning tea. ___didn't___
8. Basho had not walked far when he saw a waterfall. ___hadn't___
9. Basho's shoelaces were not white. ___weren't___
10. Even though Basho lived long ago, his poems have not been forgotten. ___haven't___

Extension: Arrange students in pairs. Give each student twelve index cards. Have one partner write the underlined words from this page on cards. Have the other write the contractions on cards. Invite partners to play a game in which they match the contractions with the longer forms.

80 Grade 4/Unit 3 Grass Sandals: The Travels of Basho 10

GRAMMAR PRACTICE BOOK, PAGE 80

DAY 5 Assess and Reteach

Assess Use the Daily Language Activity and page 81 of the **Grammar Practice Book** for assessment.

Reteach Write various helping verbs on separate index cards, and write *looked* and *looking* as column heads on chart paper. Have students choose a helping verb and tape the card to the column of the main verb it would be paired with. Then have students say sentences that include one of the main verbs and a corresponding helping verb.

Have students create a word wall with pairs of main verbs and helping verbs.

Use page 82 of the **Grammar Practice Book** for additional reteaching.

WRITING Assign the daily Writing Prompt on page 298D.

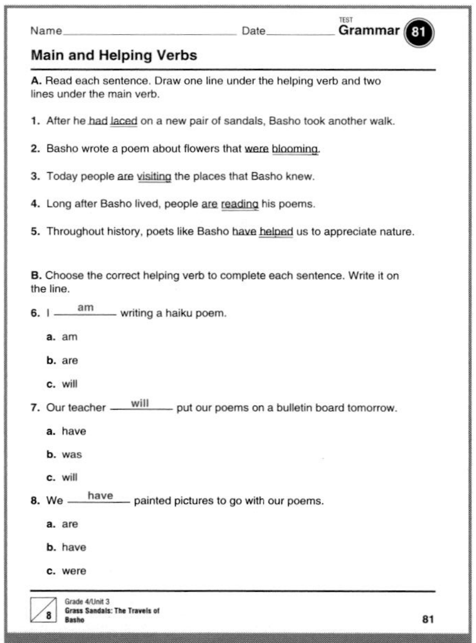

Name_______ Date_______ TEST Grammar 81

Main and Helping Verbs

A. Read each sentence. Draw one line under the helping verb and two lines under the main verb.

1. After he had laced on a new pair of sandals, Basho took another walk.
2. Basho wrote a poem about flowers that were blooming.
3. Today people are visiting the places that Basho knew.
4. Long after Basho lived, people are reading his poems.
5. Throughout history, poets like Basho have helped us to appreciate nature.

B. Choose the correct helping verb to complete each sentence. Write it on the line.

6. I ___am___ writing a haiku poem.
   a. am
   b. are
   c. will
7. Our teacher ___will___ put our poems on a bulletin board tomorrow.
   a. have
   b. was
   c. will
8. We ___have___ painted pictures to go with our poems.
   a. are
   b. have
   c. were

8 Grade 4/Unit 3 Grass Sandals: The Travels of Basho 81

GRAMMAR PRACTICE BOOK, PAGE 81

GRAMMAR PRACTICE BOOK, PAGE 82

5 Day Spelling Plan

LANGUAGE SUPPORT

Write the following words on the chalkboard, highlighting the digraphs with colored chalk: *watch, wheat, birch,* and *south*. Pronounce each word, stressing the digraph, and have students repeat it.

DICTATION SENTENCES

Spelling Words

1. He changed his shoes.
2. I like to watch baseball.
3. Are the beans fresh or frozen?
4. She hurt her shoulder.
5. In summer we do whatever we like.
6. The lake is south of the park.
7. Smoke came out of the chimney.
8. The boy started to scratch his head.
9. Don't shove the books on the shelf.
10. The bread is made from wheat.
11. Cut the cloth with care.
12. The basketball players read about themselves in the newspaper.
13. Does a carrot crunch when you chew it?
14. We ate the whole batch of cookies.
15. The weather is harsh in winter.
16. Her father likes to whittle.
17. The student looked thoughtful.
18. A birch is a white tree.
19. We can switch seats.
20. The new theater will open soon.

Challenge Words

21. The sisters chanted a slow song.
22. The coins are in a pouch.
23. You were acting restless.
24. She scribbled her address.
25. I am stitching the dress.

DAY 1 Pretest

Assess Prior Knowledge Use the Dictation Sentences at the left and **Spelling Practice Book** page 77 for the pretest. Allow students to correct their own papers. Students who require a modified list may be tested on the first ten words.

Spelling Words		Challenge Words
1. **changed**	12. **them-selves**	21. **chanted**
2. **watch**	13. crunch	22. **pouch**
3. fresh	14. batch	23. **restless**
4. shoulder	15. harsh	24. **scribbled**
5. **whatever**	16. whittle	25. **stitching**
6. south	17. thought-ful	
7. chimney	18. birch	
8. scratch	19. switch	
9. shove	20. theater	
10. wheat		
11. **cloth**		

*Note: Words in **dark type** are from the story.*

Word Study On page 78 of the **Spelling Practice Book** are word study steps and an at-home activity.

Name ________ Date ________ PRETEST Spelling 77

Words with Digraphs

Fold back the paper along the dotted line. Use the blanks to write each word as it is read aloud. When you finish the test, unfold the paper. Use the list at the right to correct any spelling mistakes. Practice the words you missed for the Posttest.

To Parents
Here are the results of your child's weekly Spelling Pretest. You can help your child study for the Posttest by following these simple steps for each word on the word list:
1. Read the word to your child.
2. Have your child write the word, saying each letter as it is written.
3. Say each letter of the word as your child checks the spelling.
4. If a mistake has been made, have your child read each letter of the correctly spelled word aloud, then repeat steps 1–3.

1. changed, 2. watch, 3. fresh, 4. shoulder, 5. whatever, 6. south, 7. chimney, 8. scratch, 9. shove, 10. wheat, 11. cloth, 12. themselves, 13. crunch, 14. batch, 15. harsh, 16. whittle, 17. thoughtful, 18. birch, 19. switch, 20. theater

Challenge Words: chanted, pouch, restless, scribbled, stitching

20 Grade 4/Unit 3 Grass Sandals 77

SPELLING PRACTICE BOOK, PAGE 77

WORD STUDY STEPS AND ACTIVITY, PAGE 78

DAY 2 Explore the Pattern

Sort and Spell Words Write *fresh, wheat,* and *south* on the chalkboard. Ask what digraph is at the end of *fresh (sh)*, at the beginning of *wheat (wh),* and at the end of *south (th)*. Have students read the Spelling Words and sort them as below.

Words with

ch	*sh*	*th*
changed	fresh	south
chimney	shoulder	cloth
crunch	shove	themselves
birch	harsh	thoughtful
		theater

tch	*wh*
watch	whatever
scratch	wheat
batch	whittle
switch	

Word Wall Have students create a word wall based on the word sort and add more words from their reading.

Name ________ Date ________ EXPLORE THE PATTERN Spelling 79

Words with Digraphs

changed whatever shove crunch thoughtful
watch south wheat batch birch
fresh chimney cloth harsh switch
shoulder scratch themselves whittle theater

Pattern Power
Write the words that have these spelling patterns.

ch: 1. changed 2. chimney 3. crunch 4. birch
tch: 5. watch 6. scratch 7. batch 8. switch
th: 9. south 10. cloth 11. themselves 12. thoughtful 13. theater
sh: 14. fresh 15. shoulder 16. shove 17. harsh
wh: 18. whatever 19. wheat 20. whittle

20 Grade 4/Unit 3 Grass Sandals 79

SPELLING PRACTICE BOOK, PAGE 79

Words with Digraphs

DAY 3 Practice and Extend

Word Meaning: Base Words Remind students that a verb with an *-ed* ending (such as *changed*) is in the past tense. Have students find at least four Spelling Words that are verbs. Then have them add *-ed* to each and use it in a sentence.

If students need extra practice, have partners give each other a midweek test.

Glossary Review several of the word histories in the Glossary. Have students:

- look up *chant* in the Glossary.
- find the word history for *chant*.
- identify the Middle English word on which *chant* is based. *(chaunten)*
- identify the Latin word which is the original basis of the word *chant*, and its meaning. (*cantare*, "to sing")

Name________________ Date________________ PRACTICE AND EXTEND **Spelling 80**

Words with Digraphs

changed	whatever	shove	crunch	thoughtful
watch	south	wheat	batch	birch
fresh	chimney	cloth	harsh	switch
shoulder	scratch	themselves	whittle	theater

What's the Word?
Complete each sentence with a spelling word.

1. Would you like to ___watch___ the parade with me?
2. My aunt likes to ___whittle___ small figures from tree branches.
3. Young children like to do things by ___themselves___.
4. During free time, we can do ___whatever___ we want.
5. He hurt his ___shoulder___ when he threw the ball too hard.
6. The ___birch___ tree has a pretty, white bark.
7. The smoke from the fireplace goes up the ___chimney___.
8. We may have to ___shove___ the stuck door to open it.
9. The midwestern states grow a lot of ___wheat___.
10. I'm going to the ___theater___ on Friday to see a play.

Just the Opposite
Write a word from the spelling list that has the opposite meaning from the word or phrase below.

11. stayed the same ___changed___
12. stale ___fresh___
13. north ___south___
14. mild ___harsh___
15. a single one ___batch___

Challenge Extension: Have students write a "fill-in-the-blank" sentence for each Challenge Word and then exchange papers with a partner to complete each other's sentences.

80 Grade 4/Unit 3 Grass Sandals 15

SPELLING PRACTICE BOOK, PAGE 80

DAY 4 Proofread and Write

Proofread Sentences Write these sentences on the chalkboard, including the misspelled words. Ask students to proofread, circling incorrect spellings and writing the correct spellings. There are two spelling errors in each sentence.

Jane made a bach of weat bread. (batch, wheat)

Be toughtful and cut some frech flowers. (thoughtful, fresh)

Have students create additional sentences with errors for partners to correct.

WRITING Have students use as many Spelling Words as possible in the daily Writing Prompt on page 298D. Remind students to proofread their writing for errors in spelling, grammar, and punctuation.

Name________________ Date________________ PROOFREAD AND WRITE **Spelling 81**

Words with Digraphs

Proofreading Activity
There are 6 spelling mistakes in the paragraph. Circle the misspelled words. Write the words correctly on the lines below.

My uncle has always enjoyed working with wood. He says it gives him time to be quiet and thotfull. I like to wach him while he works. He likes to witle small birds and forest animals from pieces of wood that he finds on his hikes. His favorite wood to use is bersh. He uses sandpaper to make the wood smooth, so it won't skracth him. Then he carefully uses a knife to make the shape of the animal. The first time I saw a piece of wood shanjed into a real-looking rabbit, I was amazed.

1. ___thoughtful___ 3. ___whittle___ 5. ___scratch___
2. ___watch___ 4. ___birch___ 6. ___changed___

Writing Activity
Write a paragraph about something you like to make. Use four words from your spelling list.

10 Grade 4/Unit 3 Grass Sandals 81

SPELLING PRACTICE BOOK, PAGE 81

DAY 5 Assess and Reteach

Assess Students' Knowledge Use page 82 of the **Spelling Practice Book** or the Dictation Sentences on page 331O for the posttest.

JOURNAL **Personal Word List** If students have trouble with any words in this lesson, have them add the words to their personal lists in their journals. Have students write illustrative sentences for these words in their journals.

Students should refer to their word lists during later writing activities.

Name________________ Date________________ POSTTEST **Spelling 82**

Words with Digraphs

Look at the words in each set below. One word in each set is spelled correctly. Use a pencil to fill in the circle next to the correct word. Before you begin, look at the sample sets of words. Sample A has been done for you. Do Sample B by yourself. When you are sure you know what to do, you may go on with the rest of the page.

Sample A: Ⓐ matsh Ⓑ macht ● match Ⓓ matsch
Sample B: ● ship Ⓕ sheip Ⓖ shyip Ⓗ shiip

1. Ⓐ wehat Ⓑ weet ● wheat Ⓓ hweat
2. Ⓔ kloth Ⓕ clotsh ● cloth Ⓗ cloath
3. Ⓐ thamselvs Ⓑ thimsilves Ⓒ temmselves ● themselves
4. ● changed Ⓕ shanged Ⓖ cahnged Ⓗ schanged
5. ● theater Ⓑ theeter Ⓒ tcheater Ⓓ tsheater
6. Ⓔ crounch ● crunch Ⓖ krunch Ⓗ cruntch
7. Ⓐ barsh ● birch Ⓒ birtch Ⓓ bersh
8. Ⓔ faresh Ⓕ fretch Ⓖ freetsh ● fresh
9. Ⓐ whutevir Ⓑ watevver Ⓒ wahtever ● whatever
10. Ⓔ chiminey ● chimney Ⓖ shimmney Ⓗ shemnie
11. Ⓐ shuv Ⓑ chove ● shove Ⓓ schuve
12. Ⓔ toutful Ⓕ tehoughtful ● thoughtful Ⓗ thougtfill
13. ● harsh Ⓑ hartch Ⓒ harrsh Ⓓ harss
14. Ⓔ skratch Ⓕ scrith Ⓖ scaracih ● scratch
15. Ⓐ chulder ● shoulder Ⓒ sahoulder Ⓓ thoulder
16. Ⓔ sawitch ● switch Ⓖ swithc Ⓗ siwatch
17. Ⓐ wathc ● watch Ⓒ wetch Ⓓ wahtc
18. ● south Ⓕ salth Ⓖ souhh Ⓗ sotch
19. ● whittle Ⓑ wuhitte Ⓒ hwittel Ⓓ whotel
20. Ⓔ batach Ⓕ basth Ⓖ bocht ● batch

82 Grade 4/Unit 3 Grass Sandals 20

SPELLING PRACTICE BOOK, PAGE 82

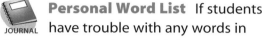

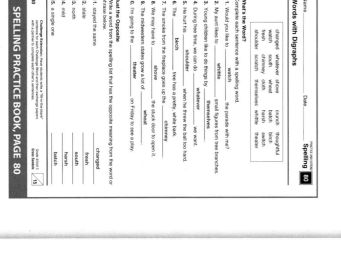

Reaching All Learners

Concept
- Slavery

Comprehension
- Fact and Opinion

Vocabulary
- fretted
- gourd
- plantation
- settlement
- sunrise
- weary

Anthology

A Place Called Freedom

Selection Summary **Students will read about a family of freed slaves who help set up a thriving community in Indiana in 1832.**

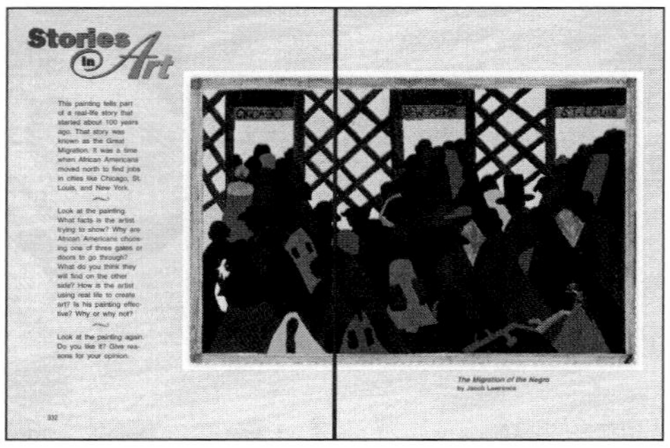

Stories in Art focuses on the **comprehension** skill

Reading Strategy applies the **comprehension** skill

Listening Library

INSTRUCTIONAL pages 334–359

About the Author Scott Russell Sanders is a native of Tennessee, where *A Place Called Freedom* begins. He now lives in Indiana, where much of the story takes place. Sanders is concerned with the ways that different ethnic groups interact with one another throughout the world.

About the Illustrator Thomas B. Allen is also a native of Tennessee. His art studies began when he was a child in a class for adults. Today, he lives in Kansas City and still draws and paints with a childlike wonder for his subject matter.

Same Concept, Skills and Vocabulary!

Leveled Books

EASY
Lesson on pages 359A and 359D

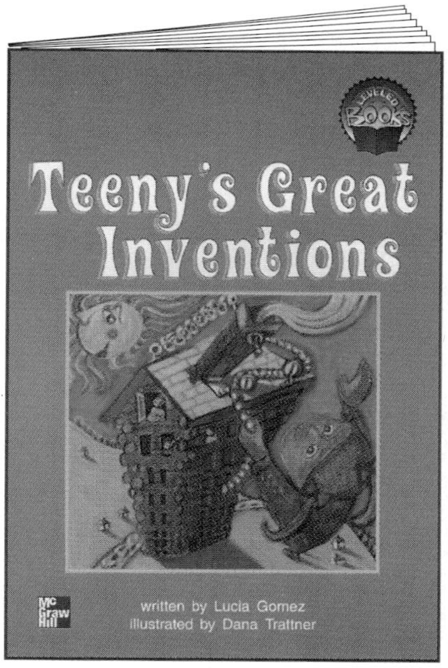

INDEPENDENT
Lesson on pages 359B and 359D

CHALLENGE
Lesson on pages 359C and 359D

Leveled Practice

EASY
Reteach, 96–102 blackline masters with reteaching opportunities for each assessed skill

INDEPENDENT/ON-LEVEL
Practice, 96–102 workbook with Take-Home stories and practice opportunities for each assessed skill and story comprehension

CHALLENGE
Extend, 96–102 blackline masters that offer challenge activities for each assessed skill

Quizzes Prepared by Accelerated Reader

WORKSTATION Activities

Social Studies	The Underground Railroad, *340*
Science	Constellations, *338*
Math	People and Mules, *344*
Music	Read Aloud, *332E* African American Spirituals, *357*
Cultural Perspectives	Buildings, *348*
Writing	An Editorial, *356*
Research and Inquiry	Find Out More, *357*
Internet Activities	www.mhschool.com/reading

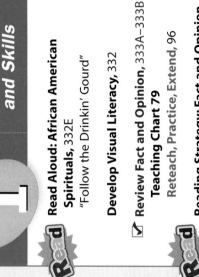

Suggested Lesson Planner

READING AND LANGUAGE ARTS	DAY 1 Focus on Reading and Skills	DAY 2 Read the Literature
• Comprehension • Vocabulary • Phonics/Decoding • Study Skills • Listening, Speaking, Viewing, Representing	**Read Aloud: African American Spirituals,** 332E "Follow the Drinkin' Gourd" **Develop Visual Literacy,** 332 ☑ **Review Fact and Opinion,** 333A–333B **Teaching Chart 79** **Reteach, Practice, Extend,** 96 **Reading Strategy: Fact and Opinion,** 333 "The Corncob Doll" Intervention Program	**Build Background,** 334A Develop Oral Language **Vocabulary,** 334B, 334C ***fretted*** ***plantation*** ***sunrise*** ***gourd*** ***settlement*** ***weary*** **Teaching Chart 80** Word Building Manipulative Cards **Reteach, Practice, Extend,** 97 **Read the Selection,** 334–355 ☑ **Fact and Opinion** ☑ **Judgments and Decisions** **Genre: Historical Fiction,** 335 **Cultural Perspectives,** 348 Intervention Program
• Curriculum Connections	Link **Works of Art,** 332	Link **Social Studies,** 334A
• Writing	**Writing Prompt:** Many former slaves, such as Frederick Douglass and Sojourner Truth, went on to do great things. Research one and write a short biography.	**Writing Prompt:** Pretend you're James Starman. Write a diary entry, telling how you felt on the day the town got its name. **Journal Writing,** 355 Quick-Write
• Grammar	**Introduce the Concept: Linking Verbs,** 359M Daily Language Activity 1. Mama am a good cook. is 2. We is free now. are 3. I were weary from walking. was **Grammar Practice Book,** 83	**Teach the Concept: Linking Verbs,** 359M Daily Language Activity 1. You is safe. are 2. Papa were a good storyteller. was 3. Lettie are my sister. is **Grammar Practice Book,** 84
• Spelling	**Pretest: Adding *-ed* and *-ing*,** 359O **Spelling Practice Book,** 83, 84	**Explore the Pattern: Adding *-ed* and *-ing*,** 359O **Spelling Practice Book,** 85

Intervention Program Available

Meeting Individual Needs

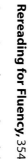

✓ = Skill Assessed in Unit Test

ⓘ Intervention Program Available

Read EVERY DAY

DAY 3 Read the Literature

Rereading for Fluency, 354

Story Questions and Activities, 356–357
Reteach, Practice, Extend, 98

Study Skill, 358
✓ **Graphic Aids**
Teaching Chart 81
Reteach, Practice, Extend, 99

Test Power, 359

Read **Read the Leveled Books,** 359A–359D
Guided Reading
Digraphs
✓ **Fact and Opinion**
✓ **Instructional Vocabulary**

ⓘ Intervention Program

Activity Science, 338

Writing Prompt: Imagine that you're a neighbor of the Starman family. Describe each of the Starmans.

Writing Process: Persuasive Writing, 359K
Prewrite, Draft

Review and Practice: Linking Verbs, 359N
Daily Language Activity
1. I are a farmer. am
2. "You is a good friend," the Old Man said. are
3. Our cousins was slaves. were

Grammar Practice Book, 85

Practice and Extend: Adding *-ed* and *-ing*, 359P
Spelling Practice Book, 86

DAY 4 Build Skills

Read **Read the Leveled Books and Self-Selected Books**

✓ **Review Fact and Opinion,** 359E–359F
Teaching Chart 82
Reteach, Practice, Extend, 100
Language Support, 110

✓ **Review Summarize,** 359G–359H
Teaching Chart 83
Reteach, Practice, Extend, 101
Language Support, 111

Minilessons, 337, 343, 345, 347, 353

Writer's Craft, 342

ⓘ Intervention Program

Activity Social Studies, 340

Writing Prompt: Pick a book, story, movie, or TV show about freedom. Describe your thoughts and feelings about it.

Writing Process: Persuasive Writing, 359K Revise

Meeting Individual Needs for Writing, 359L

Review and Practice: Linking Verbs, 359N
Daily Language Activity
1. The sailor were glad to take us on his boat. was
2. Night traveling were safer. was
3. The drinking gourd am the Big Dipper. is

Grammar Practice Book, 86

Proofread and Write: Adding *-ed* and *-ing*, 359P
Spelling Practice Book, 87

DAY 5 Build Skills

Read **Read Self-Selected Books**

✓ **Review Context Clues,** 359I–359J
Teaching Chart 84
Reteach, Practice, Extend, 102
Language Support, 112

Listening, Speaking, Viewing, Representing, 359L

Minilessons, 337, 343, 345, 347

Phonics Review,
Digraphs, 353

Phonics/Phonemic Awareness Practice Book, 43–46

ⓘ Intervention Program

Activity Math, 344; Music, 357

Writing Prompt: Are you glad the people named the town "Freedom"? Write a paragraph telling why.

Writing Process: Persuasive Writing, 359K
Edit/Proofread, Publish

Assess and Reteach: Linking Verbs, 359N
Daily Language Activity
1. I were big enough to walk. was
2. Our settlement am famous. is
3. The fisherman's face were wrinkled. was

Grammar Practice Book, 87, 88

Assess and Reteach: Adding *-ed* and *-ing*, 359P
Spelling Practice Book, 88

Link
Music

Read Aloud

Follow the Drinkin' Gourd
an African American spiritual
adapted by Paul Campbell

When the sun comes back and
  the first quail calls,
Follow the Drinkin' Gourd.
Then the Old Man is awaitin' for
  to carry you to freedom,
Follow the Drinkin' Gourd.

Follow the Drinkin' Gourd,
Follow the Drinkin' Gourd,
For the Old Man is awaitin' for to
  carry you to freedom,
Follow the Drinkin' Gourd.

Now the river bank'll make a
  mighty good road;
The dead trees'll show you
  the way.
And the left foot, pegfoot,
  travelin' on;
Just you follow the Drinkin'
  Gourd.

Now the river ends between
  two hills;
Follow the Drinkin' Gourd.
And there's another river on the
  other side,
Just you follow the Drinkin'
  Gourd.

Oral Comprehension

LISTENING AND SPEAKING Explain that during the time of slavery in the south, many enslaved Africans and African Americans ran away, traveling north to reach freedom. Have students try to imagine taking a journey as you say the song aloud. This song helped guide runaway slaves. Discuss: How can you tell the song is a guide? (It seems to be giving directions.)

GENRE STUDY: AFRICAN AMERICAN SPIRITUAL Explain: Some songs have hidden meanings. This song describes, in code, an escape route to freedom. Ask:

- Why was the song written in code?
- In the 1800s, many African Americans used the term "Drinking Gourd" to refer to the Big Dipper. Two stars in this constellation point to the North Star. What does the line "Follow the Drinkin' Gourd" mean? (Follow the North Star.)
- The Old Man in the song refers to the Mississippi River. In those days, the Mississippi was called Ol' Man River. What part did the river play in the escape route?

Activity Have volunteers pantomime walking along the riverbank at night as others recite the refrain and second verse. ▶ **Kinesthetic/Linguistic**

Develop Visual Literacy

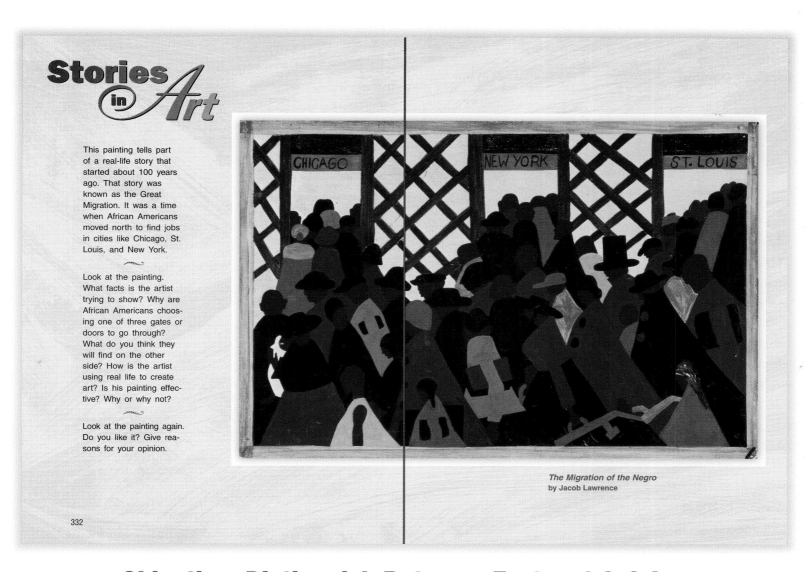

Link
Works of Art

Stories in Art

This painting tells part of a real-life story that started about 100 years ago. That story was known as the Great Migration. It was a time when African Americans moved north to find jobs in cities like Chicago, St. Louis, and New York.

Look at the painting. What facts is the artist trying to show? Why are African Americans choosing one of three gates or doors to go through? What do you think they will find on the other side? How is the artist using real life to create art? Is his painting effective? Why or why not?

Look at the painting again. Do you like it? Give reasons for your opinion.

The Migration of the Negro
by Jacob Lawrence

332

Objective: Distinguish Between Fact and Opinion

VIEWING In this painting Jacob Lawrence celebrates the events known as the Great Migration. Explain to students that beginning in the 1890s, thousands of African Americans in the South migrated to the cities of the North and Midwest in an attempt to escape poverty and discrimination. Discuss why the artist might have chosen to paint the figures in silhouette. Talk about how Lawrence has used a fact from history to express his opinion about it.

Read the page with students, encouraging individual interpretations of the painting.

Ask students to distinguish between fact and opinion by reading the text and thinking about the painting. For example:

- The artist makes his picture look like a series of railroad station gates leading to different cities. (fact)
- The people seem to be rushing through the doors of gates. (opinion)

REPRESENTING Encourage students to write a poem to show the scene in the painting. They can base their poem on facts in the painting and can also express their opinions.

Review Fact and Opinion

PREPARE

Discuss Fact and Opinion Ask a volunteer: "How many chairs are in our classroom?" Then ask a series of volunteers a question designed to evoke different responses, such as "What is the best book in the school library?"

TEACH

Define Fact and Opinion Tell students that they have just made statements of fact and opinion. Factual information, such as the number of chairs in the classroom, can be proved true. Opinions are statements of belief, thought, or feeling. Different people might have different opinions, for example, about what is the best book in the school library.

No More Slavery

I live in Indiana, the best state in the Union. Ten years ago, back in 1832, I was still living in Tennessee, where I was born. Tennessee is a slave state. Now despite what some people may think, slavery is a bad system. I know it firsthand, since I was born enslaved.

I was lucky. I made my way to freedom. It was risky and I was scared, but life without freedom is not worth living. We should stop slavery now, so we can all be free.

Teaching Chart 79

Read the Passage and Model the Skill Display and read **Teaching Chart 79** aloud. Model the skill.

MODEL I think the first sentence must contain both a fact and an opinion. There's no reason to doubt that the character lives in Indiana, so I'll consider that a fact. But saying Indiana is the best state is an opinion, since other characters might think other states are better.

TESTED OBJECTIVES

Students will distinguish between fact and opinion in a story.

Skills Finder

Fact and Opinion	
Introduce	283A-B
Review	297E-F, 333A-B, 359E-F
Test	Unit 3

TEACHING TIP

FACT AND OPINION
Explain that students should decide if a statement is fact or opinion *in the story*. If a statement could be verified by a *character,* then it should be considered a fact. If a statement tells a *character's* thoughts or feelings, it should be considered an opinion. Point out that even an opinion almost everyone agrees with, such as that slavery is wrong, is still an opinion, not a fact.

PRACTICE

Create a Fact and Opinion Chart

GROUP

Have volunteers underline statements that for the purposes of the story should be considered facts and circle statements that should be considered opinions.

Have students use a chart to record the facts and opinions in the passage. Help them begin filling in the chart. Encourage them to list items in their own words.

▶ **Linguistic/Logical**

FACT	OPINION
The narrator lives in Indiana.	Indiana is the best state.

ASSESS/CLOSE

Find More Facts and Opinions

PARTNERS

Have partners write a one paragraph story that contains facts and at least one opinion. Then have partners exchange papers and use a Fact and Opinion chart to record the facts and opinions they identify in their partners' paragraphs.

ALTERNATE TEACHING STRATEGY

FACT AND OPINION

For a different approach to teaching this skill, see page T64.

Intervention ▶ **Skills**

Intervention Guide, for direct instruction and extra practice with fact and opinion

Meeting Individual Needs for Comprehension

EASY

Name ________ Date ________ **Reteach 96**

Fact and Opinion

A **fact** is a statement that can be proven in some way. An **opinion** is a statement of someone's belief that cannot always be proven.

Read each paragraph. Write **F** if the statement is a fact. Write **O** if it is an opinion.

From the first days of their settlement, Europeans came to what is now the United States and moved inland from the coasts. I think moving is bad for children. My family has moved three times and I am only nine years old. But pioneer families used to move often. They would clear the land, stay a while, and then move on again when the area became crowded or the soil grew poor. I think the children in those families did not like moving. I hope we stay here for a long time.

1. I think moving is bad for kids. ___O___
2. People came to what is now the United States and moved inland from the coasts. ___F___
3. I hope we stay here for a long time. ___O___
4. My family has moved three times. ___F___
5. I think the children in those families did not like moving. ___O___

I like riding on trains. I really like the clickety-clack sound the train makes on the rails. My mom rides the train to work. She takes the same train every morning. I go to work with her sometimes. I love getting on the train early in the morning.

6. I like riding on trains. ___O___
7. The train makes a clickety-clack sound on the rails. ___F___
8. My mom rides the train to work. ___F___

8 Book 4/Unit 3 A Place Called Freedom — **At Home:** Have students find three facts and three opinions in a magazine article. 96

Reteach, 96

ON-LEVEL

Name ________ Date ________ **Practice 96**

Fact and Opinion

A **fact** is a statement that can be proven. An **opinion** is a statement that tells what a person thinks about something. Read the passage below. Then write **fact** or **opinion** after each statement.

By the year 1830, enslaved Africans had been working for many years without pay and freedom. People had been brought from Africa and sold in marketplaces. Many people in the United States believed that slavery was terrible. Slavery was especially strong in the South where there were big farms called plantations. Plantation owners earned enormous profits because they did not have to pay the slaves who worked for them. Everyone enjoyed living on plantations.

In the North, many people were against slavery. These people believed everyone in the United States should be free. They formed the American Anti-Slavery Society to abolish, or do away with, slavery. People, like Frederick Douglass, spoke about the evils of slavery. Everyone thought Frederick Douglass was right. Free blacks in the North belonged to the Society. White people who were against slavery did the same. Anti-Slavery Society members held the belief that people should refuse to buy crops from slave holders. Despite the hard work of the American Anti-Slavery Society, slavery continued until the end of the Civil War.

1. Enslaved people were never paid for their hard work. ___Fact___
2. Members of the American Anti-Slavery Society felt that all people should be free. ___Fact___
3. Plantation owners earned enormous profits because they did not have to pay workers. ___Fact___
4. Everyone thought Frederick Douglass was right. ___Opinion___
5. Slavery ended when the Civil War was over. ___Fact___

5 Book 4/Unit 3 A Place Called Freedom — **At Home:** Have students write two facts about slavery. 96

Practice, 96

CHALLENGE

Name ________ Date ________ **Extend 96**

Fact and Opinion

Have you ever tried to persuade someone to change his or her mind about something? If so, you probably began by stating your **opinion**. You may then have offered **facts** to support your opinion. Facts can be checked to prove that they are true.

Write a persuasive paragraph about your school. Start by stating your opinion. Your opinion may be about something you like about your school or something you think should be changed. Then support your opinion. Be sure to include facts. Share your paragraph with classmates.

Answers will vary but should be used in the correct context and use correct parts of speech.

Book 4/Unit 3 A Place Called Freedom — **At Home:** Talk with students about effective ways to be persuasive about matters that concern them. 96

Extend, 96

TESTED OBJECTIVES

Students will distinguish between fact and opinion in a story.

Apply Fact and Opinion

READING STRATEGY

Fact and Opinion

Develop a strategy for distinguishing fact from opinion.

1. **Look for clue words,** such as *I thought, beautiful,* or *wonderful.*
2. **Decide whether** a statement tells what someone thinks or believes. If so, it is a statement of opinion.
3. **Decide whether** a statement can be proved. If it can, it is a statement of fact.
4. **Identify one fact and one opinion** in "The Corncob Doll."

333

The Corncob Doll

One night in the spring of 1849, when I was ten years old, my mother made up her mind. "We've got to do something about the way people are being treated in this country," she said.

READING STRATEGY

The next day, she had a secret room built in the back of our barn. That's how our barn became a station on the Underground Railroad. In the months that followed, entire families found safety in that narrow room.

Mother gave me instructions. Every night, I carried a bucket of water to the barn. I hid the dipper in my shawl. Then I left the bucket and dipper beside the false wall of the secret room.

Most mornings, I would find the bucket empty, with the dipper placed neatly inside it.

One morning, I found a bundle in the bucket. I unwrapped it to find a little corncob doll. Its face was roughly painted, and its dress was made of burlap. I thought it was beautiful.

I worried that some runaway child had left the doll behind, but Mother said the doll was a gift for me. She said it was a wonderful thing that folks in need could still think of others. She said if I looked at that doll every day, I would learn something every day.

I still have the doll. It reminds me of a past I share with the families who passed through our barn on their way to freedom. And it reminds me of my mother, a quiet woman who did brave things.

PREVIEW Have students preview "The Corncob Doll." Explain that it is an example of historical fiction. Ask:

- What are two purposes an author might have for writing historical fiction? (to entertain and to inform)
- What kinds of facts do you expect to learn from historical fiction? (facts about how people lived long ago)

SET PURPOSES Have students apply what they have learned about fact and opinion as they read the passage.

APPLY THE STRATEGY Discuss the strategy for distinguishing fact from opinion in a selection. Help students apply the strategy to "The Corncob Doll."

- Look for words that indicate how the author or narrator feels about the subject. The word *brave* in the last sentence is an example.
- Remember: A statement that expresses someone's ideas or beliefs is an opinion.
- Remember: A statement that could be proved or checked is a fact.
- Find one fact and one opinion in the selection.

Activity Have each student create a Fact and Opinion chart for the passage.

Build Background

Link
Social Studies

Concept: Slavery

Evaluate Prior Knowledge

CONCEPT: SLAVERY Today the United States Constitution provides political equality for all citizens. Explain to students that this was not always the case. Point out that until the Civil War African Americans in the South were held as slaves and denied their most basic rights.

SLAVERY CHART Have students discuss what they think it means to have freedom. They can record their thoughts on a chart. Encourage them to do research to find out what conditions were like in the time of slavery and to add that information to their charts. ▶ **Logical/Visual**

FREEDOM	ENSLAVED
Participate in government	Cannot vote
Maintain family and cultural ties and identity	Lose your name, separated from family
Earn money in your chosen field of work	Forced to work without reward
Have possessions	Own nothing

Graphic Organizer 31

WRITE ABOUT SLAVERY WRITING GROUP Have students write a story about an enslaved person. Have them tell what the person would like to do, but can't. They should also tell what the person doesn't want to do, but must.

Develop Oral Language

DISCUSS SLAVERY ESL Bring in a picture book about the history of slavery in the United States. Share images of the way of life of people who lack freedom. Encourage students to ask questions about the pictures as a way of introducing new vocabulary words related to freedom. Possible words include:

- slave ship
- cotton
- plantation
- shackles
- slavery
- liberty

Write the list on the board. Discuss the meaning of each word, and have students use each in a sentence.

Anthology and Leveled Books

TEACHING TIP

MANAGEMENT As students fill out the chart, encourage them to think about the ways they use their freedoms in everyday life and what their lives would be like if those freedoms were denied them. While groups are working, present the Develop Oral Language activity to students needing help with oral language facility.

LANGUAGE SUPPORT

See the **Language Support Book**, pages 105–108, for teaching suggestions for Build Background.

Vocabulary

settlement
fretted
gourd
sunrise
weary

Teach Vocabulary in Context

Identify Vocabulary Words Display **Teaching Chart 80** and read the passage with students. Have volunteers circle each vocabulary word and underline other words and phrases that give clues to its meaning.

Escape to Freedom

1. We were scared the night we escaped the large farm where we had worked and finally put the plantation behind us. **2.** We were heading for a small community of friends who lived in a settlement in Indiana. **3.** We fretted and worried about whether we were really walking North. **4.** Papa said we could follow the Big Dipper, only he called it "the drinking gourd," because it is shaped like the shell of the dried fruit we drink from. **5.** As a new day began, we watched the sunrise. **6.** We were tired and weary from our long trip, but we knew we would soon be free.

Teaching Chart 80

Discuss Meanings Ask questions like these to help clarify word meanings:

- What kind of work did enslaved people on a plantation mainly do?
- Which is bigger—a settlement or a village?
- Have you ever fretted over a hard homework assignment?
- Does a gourd grow on a vine or on a tree?
- Have you ever seen a sunrise?
- When you carry all your schoolbooks home, does it make you weary?

Tested Objectives

Students will use context clues to determine the meaning of vocabulary words.

Definitions

plantation (p. 336) a large estate or farm worked by laborers who live there

settlement (p. 347) a small village or group of houses

fretted (p. 344) suffered emotional distress or irritation

gourd (p. 339) a rounded fruit related to the pumpkin or squash

sunrise (p. 340) the rising of the sun

weary (p. 339) very tired

Story Words

These words from the selection may be unfamiliar. Before students read, have them check the meaning and pronunciation of each word in the Glossary, beginning on page 756, or in a dictionary.

- wriggly, p. 336
- loaned, p. 340
- runaways, p. 347

Activities

Practice

Guess the Word (PARTNERS)

Have partners act out vocabulary words for each other to guess. Continue with other vocabulary cards. ▶**Kinesthetic/Linguistic**

Word Building Manipulative Cards

Write Context Sentences (WRITING)

Have one partner choose a card and write a sentence using the word on the card. Have the other partner read the sentence aloud and tell what the word means. Repeat with all six words.
▶ **Linguistic/Oral**

Assess Vocabulary

Use Words in Context (PARTNERS)

Have pairs of students write riddles, the answers to which are vocabulary words. When finished, have pairs swap riddles and solve.

SPELLING/VOCABULARY CONNECTIONS

See Spelling Challenge Words, pages 359O–359P.

LANGUAGE SUPPORT

See the **Language Support Book**, pages 105–108, for teaching suggestions for Vocabulary.

Vocabulary PuzzleMaker

Provides vocabulary activities.

Meeting Individual Needs for Vocabulary

EASY

Name______ Date______ Reteach 97

Vocabulary

Write a word from the list to complete each sentence.

fretted | gourd | plantation | settlement | sunrise | weary

1. A large farm or estate that grows a single crop was called a plantation.
2. If you stayed up all night and saw the sky grow light, you would see the sunrise.
3. Another word for *worried* is fretted.
4. A dried fruit shell sometimes used for drinking is a gourd.
5. Another word for *tired* is weary.
6. A small village or group of houses is called a settlement.

6

Story Comprehension Reteach 98

Write a ✔ next to every sentence that tells about "A Place Called Freedom." For help you may look back at the story.

1. ✔ The author and his family left Tennessee for Indiana.
2. ___ Starman had been the plantation owner's name.
3. ✔ The Starman family bought land near the Wabash River.
4. ___ Papa was not able to bring any relatives to Indiana.
5. ✔ Other people who had escaped from slavery came to the settlement to live.
6. ___ Papa and Mama wanted to name the village Starman.
7. ✔ The new town was named Freedom.
8. ✔ The narrator became a farmer like his father and a teacher like his mother.

8

97–98 **At Home:** Have students write a paragraph retelling the events in "A Place Called Freedom" in their own words. Book 4/Unit 3 **A Place Called Freedom**

Reteach, 97

ON-LEVEL

Name______ Date______ Practice 97

Vocabulary

Complete the sentences with the correct vocabulary word.

sunrise | gourd | weary | fretted | plantation | settlement

1. Reiko worried and fretted because she had left her backpack with all of her books at the library.
2. In early times, people sometimes scraped the fruit out of a gourd to make drinking cups or other containers.
3. The vacationers were so weary from hiking up the mountain that they fell asleep right away when they arrived back at the camp.
4. A plantation is a large farm where crops such as cotton and tobacco are grown for sale.
5. Before sunrise the farmer gets out of bed and starts to work on the first of many chores.
6. A new colony, or place away from the country that governs it, is called a settlement.

97 **At Home:** Have students write a sentence using each vocabulary word. Book 4/Unit 3 **A Place Called Freedom** 6

Practice, 97

ON-LEVEL

Travelers

The Graham family left the Georgia *plantation* house on horseback at *sunrise*. They rode for a long time past fields of cotton. The family was heading for their new home in a New Jersey *settlement*. Many families were already at the settlement. Both white and black people had come there to live together and start a new way of life. The Graham family rode until late at night. They slept near a river. The next morning they filled drinking *gourds* with water from the river and then they rode off. By the fifth day, they *fretted* that they were lost. Then all of a sudden, the Grahams were there. Friends and relatives ran out to meet them. The Grahams were *weary* but happy to have arrived.

1. What kind of home did the Grahams come from? a plantation
2. Where were the Grahams going? to a settlement in New Jersey
3. How is a settlement different from a plantation? A settlement is a town or village. A plantation is a large farm.
4. Why were the Grahams so weary? They had traveled by horse, starting at sunrise for many days.
5. Why do you think the Graham family wanted to start a new life? Possible answers: They wanted to live in a community with all kinds of people; They wanted to live in a place where all people are free.

5 Book 4/Unit 3 **A Place Called Freedom** **At Home:** Have students write a story about traveling using the vocabulary words and describing one event the travelers fretted over. 97a

Practice, 97a
Take-Home Story

CHALLENGE

Name______ Date______ Extend 97

Vocabulary

fretted | gourd | plantation | settlement | sunrise | weary

Suppose you and your family lived during the 1800s. You have just moved from a town to an area where no one else has settled. Write a letter to your best friend in the town, using as many of the vocabulary words as you can.
Answers will vary.

Story Comprehension Extend 98

Put yourself in Joshua Starman's place. You have settled your wife and children in Indiana and returned to Tennessee to bring more family members to Indiana. Think about what you would tell your family in Tennessee about the journey or about life in Indiana.
Answers will vary. Possible answer: There's nothing like the feeling of being able to work your own land.

97–98 **At Home:** Make a list of facts and opinions about your town. Book 4/Unit 3 **A Place Called Freedom**

Extend, 97

Comprehension

Prereading Strategies

PREVIEW AND PREDICT Have students read the title and preview the illustrations, noting how the pictures give clues to what the selection will be about.

- What does the title tell us about the story?
- Will the story be mostly fact, mostly opinion, or a combination?
- What will the story most likely be about?
- Could the story be considered historical fiction? What are the clues? (The clothes and houses are old-fashioned.) ***Genre***

Have students record their predictions.

PREDICTIONS	WHAT HAPPENED
An African American family moves to a new place.	
Other African Americans come to live and work in the new place.	

SET PURPOSES What do students want to find out by reading the story? For example:

- Why does the family move?
- Why is the place called Freedom?

Meet Scott Russell Sanders

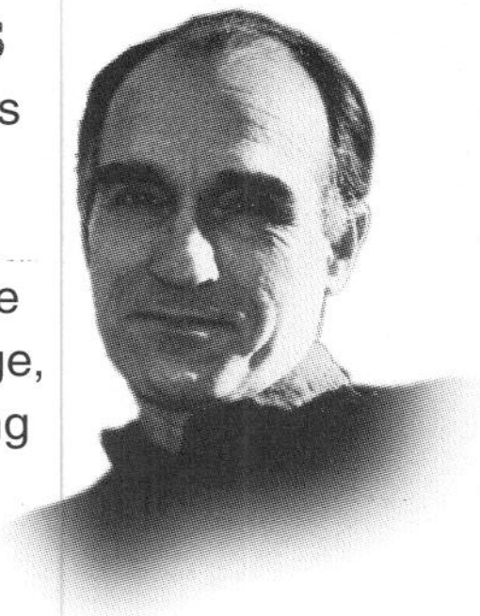

Scott Russell Sanders's three favorite things are small town life, the outdoors, and writing. He is able to put all three of these together in his work as an author. "I believe the writer should be the servant of language, community, and nature," he says. His writing is always about how many different kinds of people can get along together on our small planet.

Sanders was born in Memphis, Tennessee, and went to college in the United States and in England. Besides his work as an author, he is also a professor at a university. Sanders currently lives in Indiana with his wife and two children.

Meet Thomas B. Allen

Thomas B. Allen loved to draw when he was young. He grew up outside Nashville, Tennessee, and had to take a streetcar into town to attend art class. At the time, the only class was for adults. Yet he attended it, even though he was only nine years old!

Allen still loves to draw and paint. He says that his work studio is wherever he happens to be. Ideas for his work come "in my kitchen or while I am walking in the woods . . . in my den or the library, in a museum or out in the countryside."

Allen has taught at several art schools and universities. He is the father of three children and has two grandchildren. Currently, he lives in Kansas City.

334

Meeting Individual Needs • Grouping Suggestions for Strategic Reading

EASY

Read Together Read the story together or invite students to use the **Listening Library.** Have students use the Fact and Opinion chart from page 335. Comprehension and Intervention prompts offer additional help with decoding, vocabulary, and comprehension.

ON-LEVEL

Guided Instruction Have students read the story on their own first. Then choose from the Comprehension questions as you read the story with students—or after listening to the **Listening Library**. Have students record facts and opinions on the chart as they read.

CHALLENGE

Read Independently Set up a chart with students, as on page 335, and have them fill it in as they read. Have students read the story on their own. Remind them to distinguish between fact and opinion as they use their charts. After reading, they can use their charts to summarize the story.

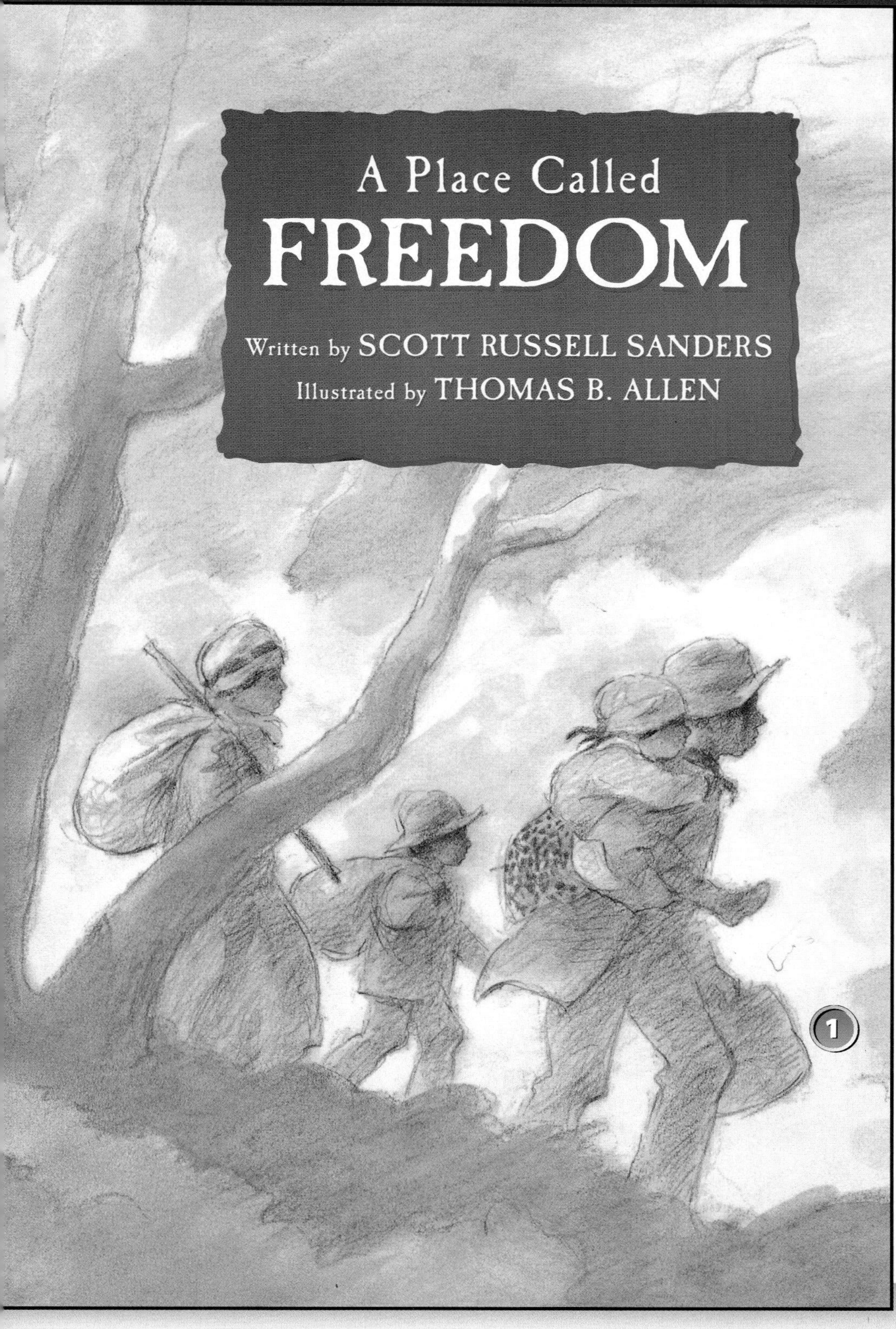

Comprehension

- ☑ **Apply Fact and Opinion**
- ☑ **Apply Judgments and Decisions**

STRATEGIC READING Before we begin reading, let's prepare a Fact and Opinion chart so we can write story notes to help us remember what we learn.

FACT	OPINION

(1) **FACT AND OPINION** The author of this story, Scott Russell Sanders, says he believes the writer should be the servant of language, community, and nature. Is that a fact or an opinion? (an opinion) Whose opinion is it? (Scott Russell Sanders') How do we know it's an opinion? (He says, "I believe ...")

LANGUAGE SUPPORT

A blackline master of the Fact and Opinion chart is available in the **Language Support Book.**

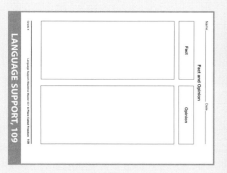

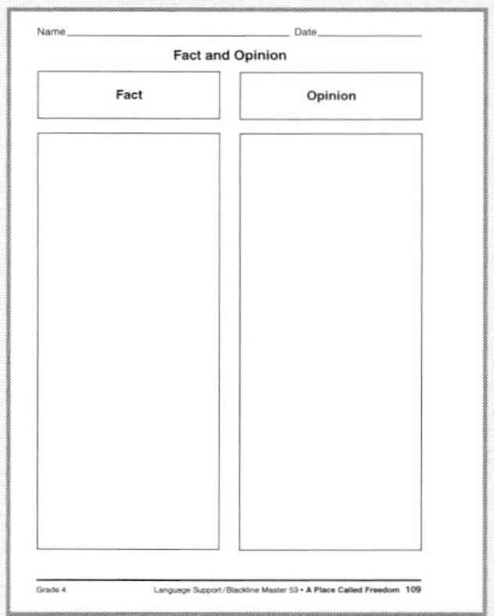

LANGUAGE SUPPORT, 109

Genre

Historical Fiction

Remind students that historical fiction:

- features believable characters who live in a historical time and place.
- uses real-world settings from the past.
- may portray people who actually lived as well as fictional people.

Activity After students read *A Place Called Freedom*, have them list details from the story that make Papa, Mama, Lettie, and James seem real. Ask: Why did the family name the new town Freedom?

Comprehension

2 **FACT AND OPINION** The first paragraph gives us some information about the character who is telling the story. Where was the character born? (Tennessee) What was the character's age in 1832? (seven) For the purposes of the story, should we consider these statements facts or opinions?

MODEL I know this is a fictional story, even though it is based on true events. So for the purposes of the story I have to see that certain statements are considered facts. Statements like where someone was born and how old they were at a certain time must, therefore, be facts for the purposes of the story.

Let's write these facts on our charts.

FACT	OPINION
The boy was born in Tennessee.	
In 1832 the boy was seven years old.	

3 **JUDGMENTS AND DECISIONS** Why do you think Papa thought it might be safer to travel at night? (Sample answer: Many people at that time didn't want African Americans to be free. They might have tried to stop the family.) Do you think this was a good decision? (Yes, it is best to be safe.)

2

Down in Tennessee, on the plantation where I was born, Mama worked in the big house and Papa worked in the fields. The master of that big house set us free in the spring of 1832, when I was seven years old and my sister, Lettie, was five.

Papa called Lettie a short drink of water, because she was little and wriggly, and he called me a long gulp of air, because I was tall and full of talk.

As soon as we could pack some food and clothes, we left the plantation, heading north for Indiana. Our aunts and uncles and cousins who were still slaves hugged us hard and waved until we were out of sight.

3

Papa said it would be safer to travel at night.

"How're we going to find our way in the dark?" I asked him.

337

Comprehension

4 The story is set in 1832, more than 150 years ago. What details in the illustration tell you the family lived a long time ago? (the way the people are dressed) *Use Illustrations*

LANGUAGE SUPPORT

Help students understand the word *wriggly*. Have volunteers show what they look like when they wriggle. Tell students that *wriggly* is an adjective that describes a person who is always moving back and forth, always squirming, a person who can't sit still, a person who *wriggles*.

Minilesson

REVIEW/MAINTAIN

Analyze Setting

Remind students that knowing something about the history of African Americans will allow a fuller understanding of the story, which is set before the Civil War.

- Have students reread page 336. Encourage them to question and discuss the text.
- Now ask: What might happen to the family while traveling north? (Law enforcement officials might stop them, thinking they are runaways.)

Activity Have students scan various sources, including their social studies books, to learn how African Americans were treated during the early 1800's.

Comprehension

5 Why does Papa choose a new name? (He gave up his old slave name.) What do you think giving up his old name and giving himself a new one meant to Papa? (Sample answer: Enslaved people weren't allowed even to have their own name. So when Papa chose a new name, it probably was a way of saying that he was now free.) *Make Inferences*

338

Activity

Cross Curricular: Science

CONSTELLATIONS Astronomers divide the night sky into 88 groups of stars called constellations. Ancient astronomers also named groups of stars, often after animals. The Big and Little Dippers are not constellations, but smaller groups called asterisms. ▶ **Mathematical/Spatial**

RESEARCH AND INQUIRY Ask students to look up asterisms and constellations, then draw and label one.

*inter***NET** **CONNECTION** To learn more about constellations, have students visit ***www.mhschool.com/reading***

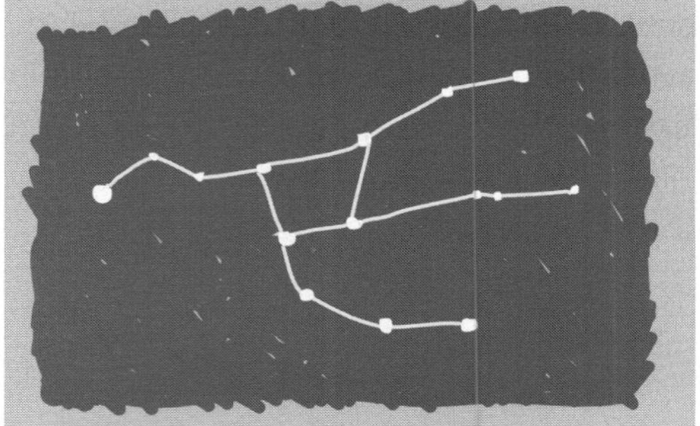

- Ursa Major means "Big Bear."
- Ursa Major contains the Big Dipper.

"We'll follow the drinking gourd," Papa answered. He pointed to the glittery sky, and I saw he meant the Big Dipper. He showed me how to find the North Star by drawing an arrow from the dipper's lip. Papa loved stars. That's why, when he gave up his old slave's name and chose a new one, he called himself Joshua Starman. And that's why my name is James Starman. 5

It was a weary, long way. Night after night as we traveled, the buttery bowl of the moon filled up, then emptied again. When Lettie got tired, she rode on Papa's shoulders for a while, or on Mama's hip. But I walked the whole way on my own feet. 6

339

Comprehension

6 The character who has been telling the story is named James Starman. James says the journey to Indiana was "a weary, long way," but he also says he walked the whole way. What do you think this says about James? (Sample answer: James is proud that he was able to walk all that way even though it was difficult.) ***Character***

P/I **WORD STRUCTURE** Papa chose a new last name that he made from two English words. What were those two words? (star, man)

P/I PREVENTION/INTERVENTION

WORD STRUCTURE Explain that sometimes big words are made from putting two smaller words together. When the Papa in this story was deciding on a name, he remembered his love of stars. So he called himself Starman. Ask students to pick a new last name for themselves by combining two words. Have them share their new names, and ask volunteers to write the new names on the chalkboard.

Comprehension

7 **FACT AND OPINION** A Quaker is a member of a Christian religious group. James says a Quaker family helped his family get established in Indiana because they believed "slavery was a sin." For the purposes of the story, do you think that this belief is a fact or an opinion?

MODEL People today believe slavery is wrong. But during the time in which the story is set, I know some people believed slavery was not wrong. So for the purposes of the story, I'd say the Quaker family's belief was an opinion.

Let's add this to our chart.

FACT	OPINION
The boy was born in Tennessee.	The Quaker family believed slavery was wrong.
In 1832 the boy was seven years old.	

8 Can someone summarize in a sentence what happened on this page? (Sample answer: the family arrived in Indiana and worked and planted on a Quaker farm.) ***Summarize***

At last one morning, just after sunrise, we came to the Ohio River. A fisherman with a face as wrinkled as an old boot carried us over the water in his boat. On the far shore we set our feet on the free soil of Indiana. White flowers covered the hills that day like feathers on a goose.

7 By and by we met a Quaker family who took us into their house, gave us seed, and loaned us a mule and a plow, all because they believed that slavery was a sin. We helped on their farm, working shoulder to shoulder, and we planted our own crops.

8 That first year Papa raised enough corn and wheat for us to buy some land beside the Wabash River, where the dirt was as black as my skin. Papa could grow anything, he could handle horses, and he could build a barn or a bed.

9

340

Activity

Cross Curricular: Social Studies

THE UNDERGROUND RAILROAD The Underground Railroad was not an actual railroad but an informal way of giving help to escapees from slave states. It helped as many as one hundred thousand people escape between 1830 and 1865.

RESEARCH AND INQUIRY Have partners research the Underground Railroad and draw a map showing some typical routes.

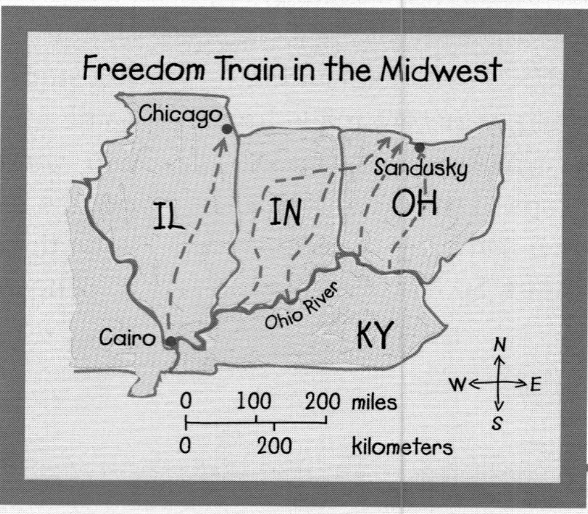

341

Comprehension

9 Let's look at the sketch on page 340. Do you think the fisherman has carried few or many people over the water in his boat? Has he been a fisherman for few or many years? (Sample answer: the man's wrinkled face and hands suggest that he has been a fisherman for many years. He may have carried many people across the water.) ***Make Inferences***

MULTIPLE-MEANING WORDS
Homographs are words with the same spelling but different meanings. Can anyone find a homograph on page 340? (raised) ***Semantic/Syntactic Cues***

PREVENTION/INTERVENTION

MULTIPLE-MEANING WORDS
Have students look in a dictionary and read aloud the different definitions of *raised*. Then have them write a sentence for each definition. Write volunteers' example sentences on the board.

Explain that homographs, or multiple-meaning words, can often be understood by looking at the way the word is used in the sentence and using context clues. Ask a volunteer to identify some context clues that helped to identify the meaning of *raised* in the passage as "grew." ***Semantic/Syntactic Cues***

Comprehension

10 JUDGMENTS AND DECISIONS
Where did Papa decide to buy land for farming and a new home? (beside the Wabash River) Why do you think Papa chose to buy land along the river?

MODEL Papa had to find a place that would provide his family with the best opportunities available to them. Since he was a good farmer, a place with rich soil would be best. I think this is why Papa settled along the river.

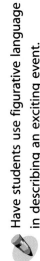

342

Writer's Craft

FIGURATIVE LANGUAGE

Explain: A writer uses figurative language to create vivid images. This strategy enlivens and adds interest to writing.

Example: Discuss the line on page 343, "... Papa told stories that made the shadows dance." What if the writer had written, "Papa told us good stories"? This sentence would be correct but not as precise or interesting as the original. Ask: What kind of story might make a shadow dance?

Discuss other figurative language on page 343: "...clothes that fit you like the wind"; "her cooking made your tongue glad."

Have students use figurative language in describing an exciting event.

Before winter, Papa and Mama built us a sturdy cabin. Every night we sat by the fire and Papa told stories that made the shadows dance. Every morning Mama held school for Lettie and me. Mama knew how to read and write from helping with lessons for the master's children. She could sew clothes that fit you like the wind, and her cooking made your tongue glad.

10

11

343

Comprehension

11 This page tells of the many things Mama and Papa are able to do. What do you think this says about their characters? (Sample answer: Mama and Papa must be very talented and skilled people.) ***Character***

Minilesson

REVIEW/MAINTAIN

Main Idea

Remind students that identifying the main idea can help them better understand a story.

- Have students reread page 343. Encourage them to talk about the many things they learned on this page.
- Then ask students to think about what this page is mostly about. (Mama and Papa know how to do many things for the family.)

Activity Ask students to choose one of the previous pages, reread the text, and then identify the main idea.

LANGUAGE SUPPORT

ESL Help students understand the figurative language on this page by asking these questions:

- How can a shadow dance?
- A little breeze always feels nice and comfortable, doesn't it? What kind of clothes fit you like the wind?
- How can food make your tongue glad?

Have volunteers pick one of the images and act it out. Can students show what a shadow looks like when it dances? How can clothes fit them like the wind? Can they show what it is like when a tongue is glad?

Comprehension

(12) Read the first paragraph on this page. In what season does it probably happen? (winter) How do you know? (The ground was still frozen. The nights were cold.) Why would Papa make his trips to Tennessee in the winter? (Sample answer: Papa is a farmer. During the winter months it isn't as important for him to be around the farm as it is in other seasons.) ***Make Inferences***

SELF-MONITORING STRATEGY

SEARCH FOR CLUES If a reader doesn't understand something in a story, searching for clues can sometimes help.

MODEL I am not certain why the family fretted until Papa showed up again. If I can find clues, they will help me understand. It says the ground was frozen, and the people had to travel on cold nights. I wouldn't want to do that, because it would be uncomfortable and dangerous. The family probably fretted, or worried, because Papa's trip was risky and unpleasant.

(12) While the ground was still frozen, Papa rode south through the cold nights, down to the plantation in Tennessee. We fretted until he showed up again at our door, leading two of my aunts, two uncles, and five cousins. They stayed with us until they could buy land near ours and build their own cabins.

Again and again Papa went back to Tennessee, and each time he came home with more of the folks we loved.

344

Activity

Cross Curricular: Math

PEOPLE AND MULES Have students work with "people and mules" math. Papa came back to Tennessee with 2 uncles, 2 aunts, and 5 cousins. Presume that the aunts and uncles were adults and the cousins were children.

- Counting father, how many people were on this trip? (10) How many adults? (5) How many children? (5)
- 1 adult and 2 children can fit on each mule. If father had 2 mules, how many adults would have to walk? (3) How many children have to walk? (1)
- Students may illustrate one of these equations or one of their own.

How many children equal the weight of one adult?
Answer=2
=

(13)

345

Comprehension

(13) The relatives that joined James' family followed a process much like the one James' family had followed. Can you describe it? (They left slavery in Tennessee, crossed the Ohio River and, just as James' family had lived with the Quaker family, the new family moved in with James' family until they could buy land and build a cabin.) ***Steps in a Process***

Minilesson

REVIEW/MAINTAIN

Character

Remind students that getting to know a character can help them better understand the story.

- Ask students to reread page 344.
- Invite students to talk about Papa's actions.
- Encourage students to think about how they might describe Papa to someone who doesn't know him.

Activity Ask partners to create a list of adjectives and phrases that might be used to describe other characters in the story. Have pairs share their lists.

Comprehension

14 Why do you think African Americans from all over the South came to the settlement when they heard about it? (The settlement was a place where African Americans could lead free lives together, which made it very attractive.) ***Cause and Effect***

346

Visual Literacy

VIEWING AND REPRESENTING

Sometimes, illustrations have to be combined to tell a story. Discuss the illustration on page 346. What is the man doing? (making something out of wood) From that picture *alone*, can the reader tell what he's making? (no) Look at page 347. What is shown in the illustration? (barrels and parts of barrels) Think about both pictures together. What is the man making? (barrels)

Hearing about our settlement, black people arrived from all over the South, some of them freed like us, some of them runaways. There were carpenters and blacksmiths, basket weavers and barrel makers. (14) (15)

347

Comprehension

(15) **FACT AND OPINION** James reports that carpenters, blacksmiths, basket weavers, and barrel makers joined the settlement. For the purposes of the story, do you think this is a fact or an opinion? Why or why not? (For the purposes of the story, this statement is a fact. It is something that other characters in the story could prove true.)

Let's add this to our charts.

FACT	OPINION
The boy was born in Tennessee.	The Quaker family believed slavery was wrong.
In 1832, the boy was seven years old.	
Carpenters, basket weavers, blacksmiths, and barrel makers moved to the settlement.	

Minilesson
REVIEW/MAINTAIN

Suffixes

Remind students that adding *-er* to the end of an action word creates a noun meaning "a person who does something."

- Have students look at the very last line on page 347. What are the two words that were formed by adding the suffix *-er* to a verb? (*weavers* and *makers*)
- What verbs were used to form these words? (*weave* and *make*)

Activity Have students create other nouns, using the following verbs and the suffix *-er*: *bake, ride, dance, read.* Ask them to use each new word in a sentence.

Comprehension

16 The first sentence lists the buildings in the settlement. What were they? (a church, a store, a stable, a mill) Two of these buildings would not be as important in a typical town today. Which buildings help show that the selection is set in the past? (the stable and the mill) ***Setting***

16 Soon we had a church, then a store, then a stable, then a mill to grind our grain. For the first time in our lives, we had money, just enough to get by, and we watched every penny.

348

CULTURAL PERSPECTIVES

BUILDINGS Other old-fashioned buildings are *blacksmith* and *seamstress* shops. In the 1800s people relied on horses. So, *blacksmiths* made shoes to protect the busy horses' feet while *seamstresses* were hired to sew people's clothes.

RESEARCH AND INQUIRY Have students research *blacksmith* and *seamstress* shops of the 1800s. Then, they can draw a picture of a shop and label all of the tools. ▶ **Spatial/Logical**

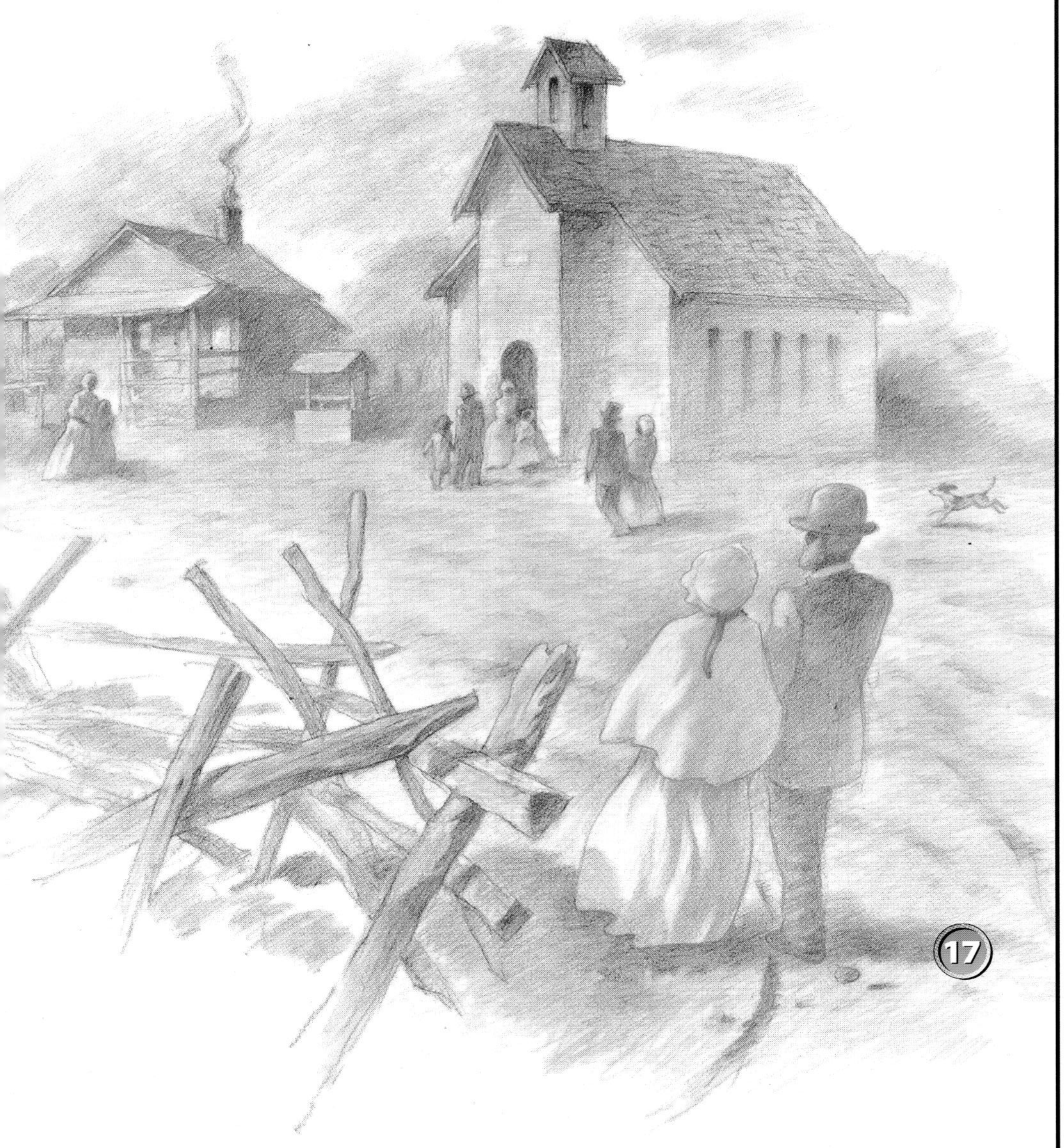

Comprehension

17 Look at the illustration on page 349. The small settlement has begun to grow into a town. The residents must be proud. Can I have two volunteers role-play a conversation that might be taking place among the people in the picture? *Role-Play*

TEACHING TIP

MAKING PREDICTIONS Before reading the text on each page, guide students to focus on the illustrations. Ask questions such as:

- Who is in this picture?
- What is each character doing?
- How would you describe this place?

Students can practice making predictions from the pictures, then confirm or revise their predictions as they read the text.

Comprehension

18 **FACT AND OPINION** What did the people name their settlement? (Freedom) Is that a fact or an opinion? (Fact) Why did they need to name their town? (The railroad was building a station there.) Let's add this new fact to our chart.

FACT	OPINION
The boy was born in Tennessee.	The Quaker family believed slavery was wrong.
In 1832, the boy was seven years old.	
Carpenters, basket weavers, blacksmiths, and barrel makers moved to the settlement.	
The settlement was named Freedom.	

Fluency

READ WITH EXPRESSION Page 350 describes how the town acquired its name and refers directly to the title. Ask students how they think this passage should be read aloud. There are a variety of options. The tone could be solemn to convey the importance of the moment, energetic to relay the author's excitement, or joyful due to the coming together of the community. Have students read the passage aloud, each using a different tone. Evaluate each student's reading rate and expression. If you wish, you can tape record the students, and then play it back to give them helpful pointers.

After a few years, the railroad decided to run tracks through our village, because so many people had gathered here. If our place was going to be on the map, it needed a name. At a meeting, folks said we should call it Starman, in honor of Mama and Papa. But Mama and Papa said, "No, let's name it Freedom."

18 And that's how we came to live in a place called Freedom.

Comprehension

19 **JUDGMENTS AND DECISIONS** Why do you think the railroad company decided to run tracks through the village? (The village was growing; townspeople might want to travel. The train could bring in supplies, which would mean more business for the railroad company.)

20 Why do you think Papa wanted to call the village Freedom? (Sample answer: Papa had worked hard to get freedom for his family.) ***Make Inferences***

Comprehension

21 How would you describe Mama?
(Sample answer: She was an intelligent, educated woman, who was an inspiration to those who wished to learn.)
Character

21

352

LANGUAGE SUPPORT

ESL Read the first sentence and ask students to say in their own words how the word *celebrate* is used here. (Here *celebrate* means to show happiness and pride. The people were excited about their town and the name they had chosen for it so they built a school to show their happiness and pride.)

Ask students what they think *to do sums* means. Lead them to understand that it means adding and subtracting numbers.

We all celebrated the new name by building a school, where Mama could teach everyone, young and old, to read and write and do sums. She made me want to learn everything there was to know.

When Mama first told me about the alphabet, I wondered how I could ever remember twenty-six different letters. But I learned them all in a flash. It was like magic to me, the way those letters joined up to make words. 22

353

Comprehension

22 **FACT AND OPINION** James Starman thought that he would have trouble learning the alphabet. Could you describe that statement as either a thought or an idea? (yes) So, is it a fact or an opinion? (opinion) Was James correct in that opinion? (no) Explain. (James' opinion was not correct, because he was able to learn the alphabet quickly.) Let's add this opinion to our charts.

FACT	OPINION
In 1832, the boy was seven years old.	James thought he would have trouble learning the alphabet.

P/I **MULTIPLE-MEANING WORDS** Read the first sentence in the second paragraph. What is the meaning of the word *letters* in this sentence? (marks that stand for spoken sounds) ***Semantic Cues***

Minilesson

REVIEW/MAINTAIN

Digraphs

Have students find and say the words *teach, those, when,* and *flash* on page 353.

- Ask students what sounds they hear at the beginning of *those* and *when.* (/th/ and /wh/) Have students identify the letters that represent these sounds. (*th, wh*)
- Ask students what sounds they hear at the end of *teach* and *flash.* (/ch/ and /sh/) Have students identify the letters that represent these sounds. (*ch, sh*)

Activity Have students brainstorm and list other words that contain the digraphs *th, wh, ch,* and *sh.*

Phonics Intervention Guide

P/I PREVENTION/INTERVENTION

MULTIPLE-MEANING WORDS Read the opening sentence in the second paragraph. Tell students that some words have more than one meanings. Ask: What are some meanings of the word *letters?* (marks that stand for spoken sounds; written messages; the initial of a school or college that is given to a student as a reward) Invite a volunteer to point out words that are clues to the meaning of the word *letters* in this sentence. (alphabet, twenty-six, joined up to make words) ***Semantic Cues***

Comprehension

(23) **FACT AND OPINION** What does Papa plant on his farm? (melons, corn, apples, and nuts) Is that a fact or an opinion? (fact) Let's add this last fact to our chart. How did the chart help you distinguish between fact and opinion?

FACT	OPINION
The boy was born in Tennessee.	The Quaker family believed slavery was wrong.
In 1832, the boy was seven years old.	James thought he would have trouble learning the alphabet.
Carpenters, basket weavers, blacksmiths, and barrel makers moved to the settlement.	
The settlement was named Freedom.	
Papa plants melons, corn, apples, and nuts on his farm.	

RETELL THE STORY Ask volunteers to tell the major events of the story. Students may refer to their charts. Then have partners write one or two sentences that summarize the story. *Summarize*

(23) Papa's farming was also like magic. He would put seeds in the ground, and before you knew it, here came melon vines or cornstalks. He planted trees, and here came apples or nuts or shade.

For a long while, I couldn't decide whether I wanted to grow up and become a farmer like Papa or a teacher like Mama.

"I don't see why a teacher can't farm," Mama said.

"I don't see why a farmer can't teach," said Papa.

354

STUDENT SELF-ASSESSMENT

- How did the strategy of thinking about fact and opinion help me understand and enjoy the story?
- How did the Fact and Opinion chart help me?

TRANSFERRING THE STRATEGY

- When might I try using this strategy again? In what other reading could the chart help me?

REREADING FOR *Fluency*

PARTNERS Have students choose a favorite section of the story to read to a partner. Encourage students to imagine how the main character feels.

READING RATE When you evaluate rate, have the student read aloud from the story for one minute. Place a stick-on note after the last word read. Count words read. To evaluate students' performance, see the Running Record in the **Fluency Assessment** book.

Intervention For leveled fluency lessons, passages, and norms charts, see **Skills Intervention Guide**, Part 4, Fluency.

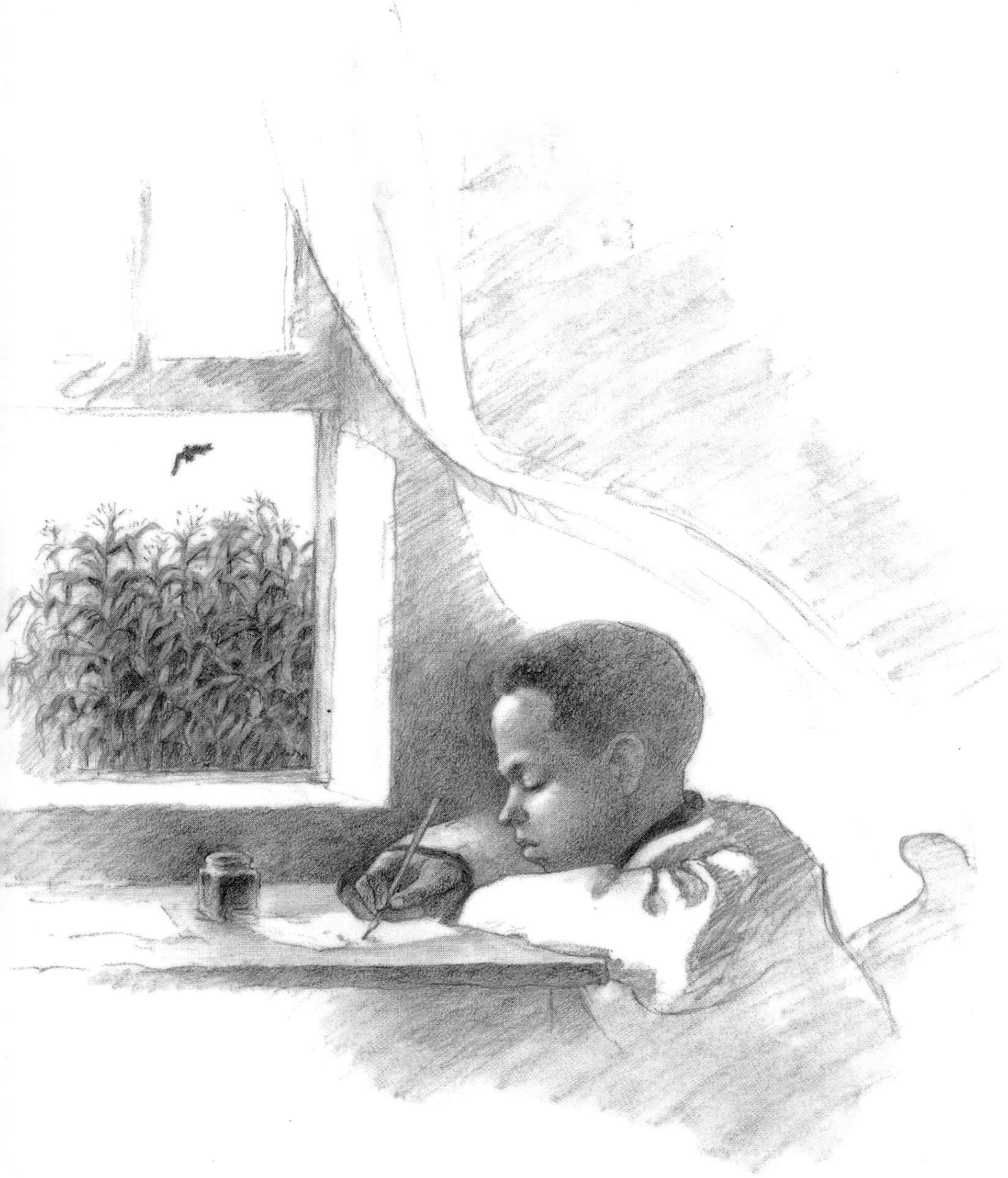

They were right, you know, because I raised the beans and potatoes for supper, and I wrote these words with my own hand.

LITERARY RESPONSE

QUICK-WRITE Invite students to record their opinions about the story. These questions may help get them started:

- Do you like the boy who told the story? Why or why not?
- Would you like to have lived in 1832? Why or why not?

ORAL RESPONSE Have students share their journal writings and discuss which part of the story they enjoyed most. Urge them to use opinion phrases such as *I think, I feel,* and *it seems to me.*

Comprehension

Return to Predictions and Purposes

Review with students their story predictions and reasons for reading the story. Were their predictions correct? Did they find out what they wanted to know?

PREDICTIONS	WHAT HAPPENED
An African American family moves to a new place.	An African American family travels by night from Tennessee to Indiana.
Other African Americans come to live and work in the new place.	African Americans live and work in a settlement called *Freedom*.

INFORMAL ASSESSMENT

FACT AND OPINION

HOW TO ASSESS

- Have students discuss the facts and opinions in the story.

Students should recognize that in fictional stories facts are statements that can be verified by other characters. Opinions tell a character's beliefs, thoughts, or feelings.

FOLLOW UP If students have trouble distinguishing between fact and opinion, ask them what happened in the story, then ask which statements are facts and which are opinions.

Story Questions

Have students discuss or write answers to the questions on page 356.

Answers:

1. James Starman. *Literal/Fact*
2. The "drinking gourd" was the Big Dipper, which steered them north. *Inferential/Fact*
3. The facts tell us who, what, where, and when. *Inferential/Facts*
4. Possible answer: An African American family is freed from slavery, moves to Indiana, and starts a settlement. *Critical/Summarize*
5. Possible answer: Yes. They had their own land and decided for themselves how to spend their time and money. *Critical/Reading Across Texts*

Write an Editorial For a full writing process lesson see pages 359K–359L.

Story Questions & Activities

1. Who is telling the story?
2. Why did people follow the "drinking gourd"?
3. How are facts important to this story?
4. What would you say to sum up this selection?
5. Thomas Jefferson's Declaration of Independence says that "All men are created equal." Do you think these words came true for the Starman family in a place called Freedom? Support your opinion with facts from the story.

Write an Editorial

What was life like for the family before they were given their freedom? Imagine that you are a newspaper editor right before the Civil War. Write an editorial for your paper. Explain why you think slavery is wrong. Support your opinions with facts. Try to persuade your readers to agree with you.

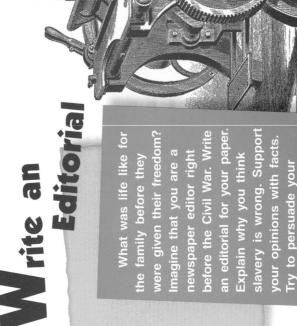

Meeting Individual Needs

EASY

Name______ Date______ **Reteach 97**

Vocabulary

Write a word from the list to complete each sentence.

fretted gourd plantation settlement sunrise weary

1. A large farm or estate that grows a single crop was called a plantation.
2. If you stayed up all night and saw the sky grow light, you would see the sunrise.
3. Another word for *worried* is fretted.
4. A dried fruit shell sometimes used for drinking is a gourd.
5. Another word for *tired* is weary.
6. A small village or group of houses is called a settlement.

6

Reteach 98

Story Comprehension

Write a ✓ next to every sentence that tells about "A Place Called Freedom." For help you may look back at the story.

1. ✓ The author and his family left Tennessee for Indiana.
2. ___ Starman had been the plantation owner's name.
3. ✓ The Starman family bought land near the Wabash River.
4. ___ Papa was not able to bring any relatives to Indiana.
5. ✓ Other people who had escaped from slavery came to the settlement to live.
6. ___ Papa and Mama wanted to name the village Starman.
7. ✓ The new town was named Freedom.
8. ✓ The narrator became a farmer like his father and a teacher like his mother.

97–98 **At Home:** Have students write a paragraph retelling the events in "A Place Called Freedom" in their own words. Book 4/Unit 3 A Place Called Freedom 8

Reteach, 98

ON-LEVEL

Name______ Date______ **Practice 98**

Story Comprehension

Answer the questions about "A Place Called Freedom." You may need to refer to the story to answer the questions.

1. In what state was the plantation where Mama and Papa worked? Tennessee
2. Why was the family able to leave the plantation? The master of the big house set the family free.
3. How did the family travel and when? They went on foot and moved only in the dark at night.
4. What did Papa call the pattern of stars that makes up the Little Dipper? the drinking gourd
5. Who helped the Starman family when they got to Indiana and why? A Quaker family helped them because they believed slavery was wrong.
6. How did the Starmans make a living? They raised crops, built houses and barns, and taught school.
7. How did Mr. Starman help those left behind at the plantation? He returned to Tennessee to bring relatives to Indiana.
8. Why are all the Starmans heroes? They put up with danger and hardship to make a better life for themselves and then helped others to make a better life.

98 **At Home:** Have students think of another hero and write down three reasons why that person is a hero to them. Book 4/Unit 3 A Place Called Freedom 8

Practice, 98

CHALLENGE

Name______ Date______ **Extend 97**

Vocabulary

fretted gourd plantation settlement sunrise weary

Suppose you and your family lived during the 1800s. You have just moved from a town to an area where no one else has settled. Write a letter to your best friend in the town, using as many of the vocabulary words as you can.
Answers will vary.

Extend 98

Story Comprehension

Put yourself in Joshua Starman's place. You have settled your wife and children in Indiana and returned to Tennessee to bring more family members to Indiana. Think about what you would tell your family in Tennessee about the journey or about life in Indiana.
Answers will vary. Possible answer: There's nothing like the feeling of being able to work your own land.

97–98 **At Home:** Make a list of facts and opinions about your town. Book 4/Unit 3 A Place Called Freedom

Extend, 98

Do a Science Experiment

James Starman explains that his father could grow anything in the dark soil. Find out which soil is better for certain plants. Get two cups. Put potting soil in one cup. Put sand in the other. Then place two or three radish seeds in each cup. Give the seeds some water and put them on a sunny windowsill. Radish seeds sprout quickly. Which soil—the light-colored sand or the dark potting soil—is better for growing seeds?

Name a Town

Many of James Starman's relatives came to live near him. So many arrived that they formed their own town and gave it a name. If you formed a new town, what would you call it? Choose a name. Then draw a welcome sign for your town.

Find Out More

James Starman's father helped his relatives escape to freedom. Find out about others who helped enslaved people escape. Start by reading about Harriet Tubman and the Underground Railroad. Check for information in a social studies textbook, an encyclopedia, or another book. Compare the experiences of Harriet Tubman with the experiences of the Starman family.

357

Activity

MUSIC: AFRICAN AMERICAN SPIRITUALS Explain: Folk songs are anonymous compositions passed on orally, often in many versions, which reflect different regions and cultures. One well-known type of folk song is the African American spiritual. Have students make a presentation about these deeply emotional songs. Encourage them to play recordings borrowed from the library, if possible, or to read the lyrics from a few spirituals.

What to Look For Did the student:

- point out that African American spirituals originated during slavery?
- find appropriate recordings or lyrics?

CHALLENGE

Story Activities

Do a Science Experiment

Materials: cups, potting soil, sand, radish seeds

PARTNERS Remind students to check their plants every day. As the seeds start to sprout, have partners discuss the differences between the growth in the two cups.

Name a Town

Materials: poster board or large paper, crayons, colored pencils, markers

GROUP Have children brainstorm ideas about what they'd like to put on their signs. What types of words and pictures should be included? What is special about their town, and how can they show that?

Find Out More

RESEARCH AND INQUIRY Students may have seen an educational television program or read about Harriet Tubman. Ask them to share what they know with the class.

*inter***NET CONNECTION** Students can learn more about the Underground Railroad by visiting ***www.mhschool.com/reading***

FORMAL ASSESSMENT

After page 357, see the Selection Assessment.

Study Skills

GRAPHIC AIDS

TESTED **OBJECTIVES** Students will find and apply information on a graph.

Prepare Read the passage with students. **Display Teaching Chart 81.**

Teach Review how information appears on a line graph. Show students how to find specific information by finding the point where the horizontal axis meets the vertical axis. Point out that the numbers on the left stand for millions of enslaved workers.

Practice Have students answer questions 1–5. Review the answers with them. **1.** About 750,000 **2.** Yes, because the line goes up from 1810 to 1820. **3.** Over 3 million **4.** 4 million **5.** More and more workers were needed as the years passed.

Assess/Close Have students figure out the difference between the enslaved population in 1800 and in 1860. (about 3,250,000 more enslaved people in 1860)

STUDY SKILLS

Read a Line Graph

James Starman says he was born on a plantation in the South. His mother worked in the big plantation house, and his father worked in the fields. At the time of the story, most people in the North and the South were farmers. Both areas had slaves. Yet the South had large plantations. It needed more workers to care for its cotton crop. Look at the graph to see the number of enslaved workers in the South in the 1800s.

Enslaved Population, 1800–1860

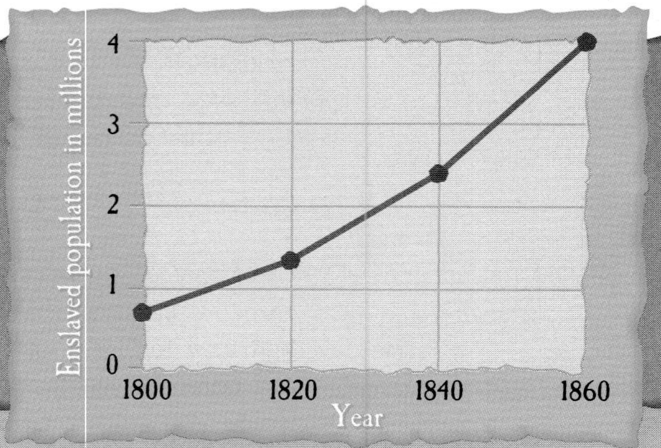

Use the line graph to answer these questions.

1. How many enslaved workers were in the South in 1800?
2. Were there more slaves in the South in 1820 than in 1810? How do you know?
3. How many enslaved workers did the South have in 1850?
4. By 1860, how many slaves were working on Southern plantations?
5. What does the graph tell you about the number of workers needed to grow and harvest cotton?

Meeting Individual Needs

EASY

Name________ Date________ Reteach 99

Read a Line Graph

Graphs of all kinds give information in a shorthand way. A **line graph** shows how a piece of information changes with time. It would take many words to describe the same changes you might "read" about in a graph.

Population of Libertyville

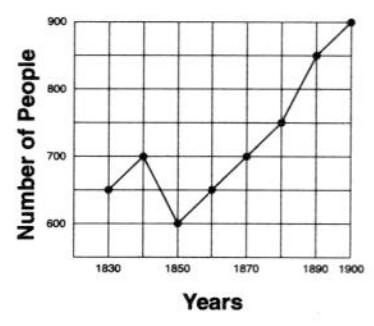

Use the line graph to answer the questions.

1. What was the population of Libertyville in 1850? 600
2. Compare the population of the year 1830 to 1860. Was the population in 1860 higher, lower, or the same as in 1830? the same
3. Which year had the lowest population? 1850
4. Which years had the greatest population growth? 1880–1900
5. Which years had the greatest loss in population? 1840–1850

Book 4/Unit 3 A Place Called Freedom — **At Home:** Have students make a line graph to record personal information, such as how much they save or spend month by month for a year or half year. 99

Reteach, 99

ON-LEVEL

Name________ Date________ Practice 99

Read a Line Graph

A **line graph** can give you information at a glance. Look at each section of the graph to see how you should read it. Ask yourself what the numbers and lines mean. Then answer the questions below the line graph.

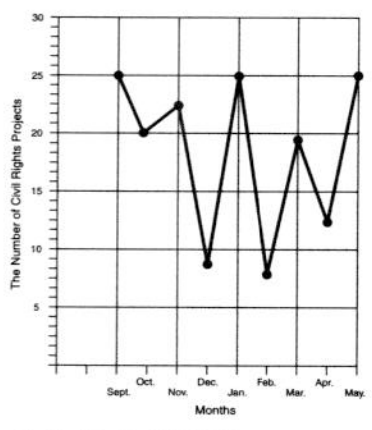

To learn about Civil Rights, fourth graders decided to do Civil Rights projects every month. This included reading books on civil rights leaders and events and also writing and drawing posters, stories, and poetry.

1. How many Civil Rights projects were completed in September? 25
2. How many Civil Rights projects were completed in December? 8
3. In what months were 20 or more projects completed? September, October, November, January, May
4. In what month were the fewest projects completed? February
5. How many more projects were completed in January compared to December? Students completed 17 more projects in January than December.

Book 4/Unit 3 A Place Called Freedom — **At Home:** Have students sketch a line graph showing something their class does often. 99

Practice, 99

CHALLENGE

Name________ Date________ Extend 99

Read a Line Graph

A **line graph** shows change over a period of time. The line graph below shows the number of states in the United States from 1780 to 2000.

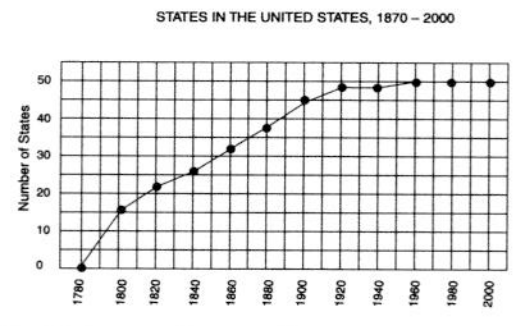

Use the line graph to answer these questions.

1. How many states were in the United States in 1900? 45
2. During which 20-year period were the most states added to the United States? 1780–1800
3. How did the number of states in the United States change from 1960 to 1980? How do you know? The number stayed the same; the line does not go up or down from the point for 1960 to the point for 1980.

Write two questions that can be answered using the line graph. Exchange questions with a classmate and answer the questions.

Question 1 Answers will vary, but should make appropriate use of the graph.

Question 2 ________

Book 4/Unit 3 A Place Called Freedom — **At Home:** Make a line graph of high temperatures. Use an outdoor thermometer or the weather report in the newspaper. 99

Extend, 99

TEST POWER

Test Tip
Make sure you read each question slowly and carefully.

DIRECTIONS
Read the sample story. Then read each question about the story.

SAMPLE

Jerome's First Sail

Jerome leaned back against the side of the boat and smiled. He had always loved visiting his Uncle Henry.

Henry kept a tiny two-person sailboat ready at all times. He had been taking Jerome out on the boat as long as Jerome could remember. Jerome had learned how to trim and set the sail, steer the rudder, and tack against the wind. Jerome had become a gifted sailor, and he knew that Uncle Henry was proud of him.

His uncle looked up from a rope he was coiling and grinned. "I think you're ready for your first solo sail."

Jerome was thrilled.

1 This story mostly takes place—

- **A** at Uncle Henry's house
- **B** at the marina
- **(C)** on the boat
- **D** at school

2 This story is mainly about

- **F** why Jerome was sick
- **G** how boats can be different
- **H** what Uncle Henry thinks about sailing
- **(J)** how Jerome learned to sail

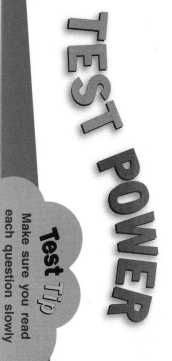

Did you reread the story to find the best answer? Tell why.

Test Power

THE PRINCETON REVIEW

Read the Page

As students read the story, remind them to summarize the story in their own words.

Discuss the Questions

Question 1: This question requires students to determine where the story mostly takes place. Remind students to refer back to the passage for clues. They should *not* rely on their memories. The passage says, "Jerome leaned back against the side of the boat."

Question 2: This question asks students to determine what the story is mainly about. This type of question requires students to summarize the story in a few words. As students read each answer choice, have them be ready to discuss why an *incorrect* choice is incorrect *even when* it contains a fact that is directly stated in the story.

Leveled Books

EASY

Walking in Beauty

Digraphs
☑ Fact and Opinion
☑ Instructional Vocabulary: ***fretted, gourd, plantation, settlement, sunrise, weary***

Guided Reading

PREVIEW AND PREDICT Preview the book to page 7. Have students discuss the illustrations and predict what the story will be about.

SET PURPOSES Have students write in their journals questions they would like to have answered by the story. For example, they may wish to know what it means to "walk in beauty."

READ THE BOOK Have students read the story independently, then use questions like the following to check students' reading.

Page 3: A law made by the government said that Native American children had to attend special schools. Is that statement fact or opinion? (fact) How do you know? (It can be verified. You can look up the law.) ***Fact and Opinion***

Page 4: Grandmother *fretted* that they would not get enough to eat at school. What's another way to say Grandmother *fretted*? (Grandmother worried.) ***Vocabulary***

Page 7: This page begins by calling the little girl *Alice* instead of *Always-Running*. What has happened so far that made the author change her name? (The little girl has left her home and is now attending a boarding school.) ***Summarize***

Page 13: What word on this page ends with a /sh/ sound? (English) What word on this page has a /ch/ sound in the middle of it? (teacher) ***Phonics and Decoding***

RETURN TO PREDICTIONS AND PURPOSES Have students review their predictions and questions. Which of their predictions were accurate and which were not? Did they find out what they wanted as they read the story? Were there any questions left unanswered?

LITERARY RESPONSE Discuss these questions with students.

- If you were Always-Running or Looks-Behind-Him, what would you say to your family when you came home?
- Do you think it was a good idea to send Navajo children to the school? Why or why not?

Also see the story questions and activity in *Walking in Beauty*.

Intervention **Skills**

Intervention Guide, for direct instruction and extra practice in vocabulary and comprehension

Answers to Story Questions

1. Always-Running and her brother had to go away to boarding school because it was the law.
2. Answers will vary but may include: she missed her home and her family; she did not like life at the school; she wanted to live like the Diné.
3. Accept all reasonable responses, which may include: at the school they learned useful things.
4. The story is mostly about having the freedom to live the way you want to live.
5. Answers will vary.

The *Story Questions and Activity* below appear in the *Easy Book*.

Story Questions and Activity

1. Why did Always-Running and her brother have to go away to boarding school?
2. Why did Always-Running think about going home?
3. What opinion might another person have had of the school?
4. What is this story mostly about?
5. In what ways were the children in this story similar to the family in *A Place Called Freedom*? How were they different?

To Stay or to Go?

Write a play in which Always-Running and the girls in her dormitory discuss her plan to leave the school late at night so no one else hears. What arguments might the girls have made for or against her going home? Working in a group, you can perform your play for the class.

from *Walking in Beauty*

Leveled Books

INDEPENDENT

Teeny's Great Inventions

- ☑ Fact and Opinion
- ☑ Instructional Vocabulary: ***fretted, gourd, plantation, settlement, sunrise, weary***

Guided Reading

PREVIEW AND PREDICT Preview the book through page 4. Have students describe the invention on page 4 and then write predictions about other things Teeny will invent.

SET PURPOSES Ask students to write a purpose for reading. For example: *I want to have fun reading a tall tale about Paul Bunyan and his daughter.*

READ THE BOOK Use questions like the following to lead a group reading or as a follow-up discussion after students read the book independently.

Pages 2–5: Paul's opinion seems to be that "free country" means that people can do whatever they want. Do you agree? (Sample answer: Freedom does not including causing harm to the country or to other people.) ***Fact and Opinion***

Page 6: What context clues help you understand the meaning of *weary?* (Teeny's hard work probably made her tired.) ***Vocabulary***

Page 9: Summarize the tall tale about how the Great Plains got its name. (After the trees were gone, Paul thought the area looked great. Teeny thought it looked plain. To avoid a fight, people used both words to name the area.) ***Summarize***

Page 10: What was Teeny's opinion about the way her father logged? (She thought what he did was wrong.) ***Fact and Opinion***

Pages 11–12: What fact about Minnesota did the author use in her story? (Minnesota has many pine trees.) ***Fact and Opinion***

RETURN TO PREDICTIONS AND PURPOSES Review students' predictions and purposes for reading. Were their predictions accurate? Were their purposes met?

LITERARY RESPONSE Discuss these questions:

- Do you think relogging was a good invention or not? Why?
- If Teeny were around today, what would you ask her to invent?

Also see the story questions and activity in *Teeny's Great Inventions.*

Answers to Story Questions

1. Teeny invents a hinge for the bunkhouse chimney, the chainsaw, and relogging.
2. Accept all reasonable responses.
3. At first, Paul believes that a man is free to cut down as many trees as he wants. Later, when all the forests are gone, Paul changes his opinion and decides that planting trees is important, too.
4. The story tells how Paul Bunyan's daughter Teeny found a way to replant the forests that her father had cut down.
5. Answers will vary, but the resolution should involve Teeny's great size or strength in some way.

The *Story Questions and Activity* below appear in the *Independent Book*.

Story Questions and Activity

1. What three things does Teeny invent in the story?
2. What events in the story did you think were funny? Tell why.
3. What is Paul's opinion about freedom when the story begins? How does his opinion change?
4. What is this story mostly about?
5. If Teeny Bunyan had decided to help the family in *A Place Called Freedom*, how might she have gone about it?

Tall Tale Comic Strip

What other problems in the environment might Teeny Bunyan be able to solve? How do you think she might do it? Draw a comic strip that shows the larger-than-life Teeny at work. If you like, you can have her team up with her famous father.

from *Teeny's Great Inventions*

Leveled Books

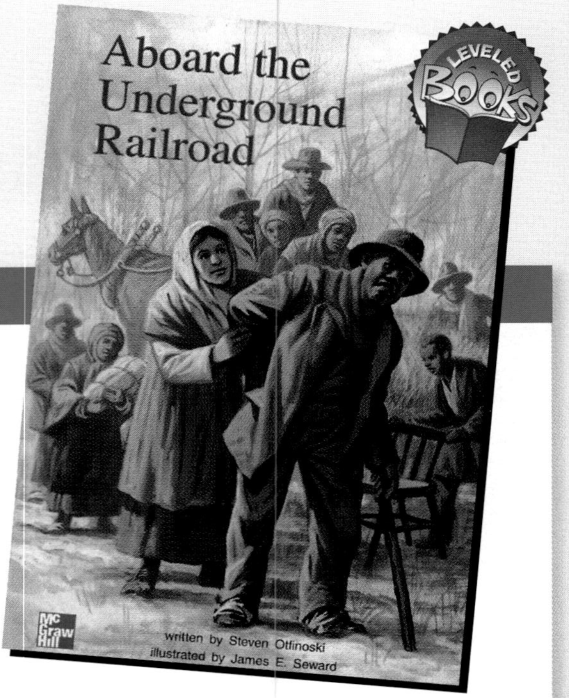

CHALLENGE

Aboard the Underground Railroad

- ☑ **Fact and Opinion**
- ☑ **Instructional Vocabulary:** ***fretted, gourd, plantation, settlement, sunrise, weary***

Guided Reading

PREVIEW AND PREDICT Preview the selection to page 8. Have students look closely at the illustrations and predict what they will learn.

SET PURPOSES Have students write questions that they hope to have answered by reading the story. For example, they might want to know the meaning of the word *railroad* in this context.

READ THE BOOK After students have read the story independently, return to the text and apply the strategies, using questions like the following.

Page 2: The people in the wagon looked cold and *weary*. Can you describe how people look when they're *weary?* (Sample answers: yawning, red eyes, bags under eyes, head drooping, and so on.) ***Vocabulary***

Page 3: Levi Coffin was a shopkeeper in a Quaker settlement. Is that fact or opinion? (fact) How do you know? (It can be verified.) ***Fact and Opinion***

Pages 8–11: Retell the steps runaway slaves might take from the time they leave the plantation until they get to the north. (Answers will vary.) ***Summarize***

Page 13: In Canada, the Fugitive Slave Law had no power. Is that fact or opinion? (It's fact; it can be verified.) ***Fact and Opinion***

RETURN TO PREDICTIONS AND PURPOSES Have students review their predictions. Did they learn what they expected to? Were they surprised by anything they learned?

LITERARY RESPONSE Discuss these questions with students:

- Pretend you're a runaway slave. Describe how you feel as you travel north.
- Imagine that your house was on the Underground Railroad. Where would you hide slaves?

Also see the story questions and activity in *Aboard the Underground Railroad.*

Answers to Story Questions

1. The Underground Railroad was a network of people helping African Americans to escape from slavery.
2. The Drinking Gourd, or Big Dipper, pointed to the North Star, which would guide them north to freedom.
3. Answers may include: the Underground Railroad further angered Southern whites who supported slavery, and contributed to the friction between North and South; opinion.
4. The Underground Railroad was important in helping slaves escape to freedom before the Civil War.
5. The family would probably be included with those who helped to free other slaves.

The *Story Questions and Activity* below appear in the *Challenge Book*.

Story Questions and Activity

1. What was the Underground Railroad?
2. Why did fugitive slaves "follow the Drinking Gourd"?
3. Do you think the Underground Railroad helped start the Civil War? Is your answer fact or opinion?
4. What is the main idea of the book?
5. If the family from *A Place Called Freedom* were included in this book, what would it say?

Joining the Underground

Suppose you are living in the Northern state of Ohio in the 1850s. Write a speech to persuade your parents and other family members that you should open your home to fugitive slaves. Base your argument on information from the book.

from *Aboard the Underground Railroad*

Activities

Bringing Groups Together

Anthology and Leveled Books

Connecting Texts

FREEDOM CHART Tell students that all the selections are about freedom and choices. Have students use information from the selections they read to complete the chart about the characters and the choices they had to make. Use the chart to start a discussion about what freedom means. Ask students what responsibilities go with freedom.

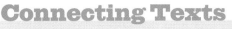

A Place Called Freedom	Walking in Beauty	Teeny's Great Inventions	Aboard the Underground Railroad
• The Starman family • To stay in the South where things were familiar or to make a new life in the North	• Always-Running (Finds-Her-Way-Home) and Looks-Behind-Him (Sees-Two-Ways) • To go to the city to work or to go back home	• Paul Bunyan and his daughter Teeny • To cut down trees or to restore them	• Slaves • To live out their lives as slaves or to make the dangerous journey on the Underground Railroad

Viewing/Representing

DEBATES Group students according to the Leveled Book they read. (For *A Place Called Freedom* combine students of different reading levels.) Have each group organize into two teams to debate about which choice from the chart the characters should have made. Remind students that debaters sometimes have to argue against their own opinions and that their goal is to make a good case for the choice they are assigned.

VOTE FOR THE WINNER After each presentation, have audience members vote for the side they think did the best job of presenting their case.

Research and Inquiry

MORE ABOUT FREEDOM Ask students to choose one of the selections and find out more about the selection topic by:

- researching settlements like the town of Freedom, reforestation, Indian boarding schools, or the Underground Railroad.
- drawing charts, maps, or illustrations to record their findings.
- presenting their information in an oral report.

*inter***NET** **CONNECTION** To find more information on the town of Freedom, Indiana, have students visit ***www.mhschool.com/reading***

TESTED OBJECTIVES

Students will distinguish between fact and opinion.

Skills Finder	
Fact and Opinion	
Introduce	283A-B
Review	297E-F, 333A-B, 359E-F
Test	Unit 3

TEACHING TIP

MANAGEMENT Have students write *Fact* and *Opinion* on separate index cards. Then, reread the passage on **Teaching Chart 82** to the class. Ask students to hold up the appropriate card after each sentence.

SELF-SELECTED Reading

Students may choose from the following titles:

ANTHOLOGY

- A Place Called Freedom

LEVELED BOOKS

- Walking in Beauty
- Teeny's Great Inventions
- Aboard the Underground Railroad

Bibliography, pages T78–T79

Review Fact and Opinion

PREPARE

Discuss Fact and Opinion

Review: To distinguish between fact and opinion, consider these questions: (1) In the story, can the statement be proved true or false by two or more characters? Then, for the purposes of the story it should be considered a fact. (2) Is the statement what a character thinks, imagines or believes? Then it's opinion.

TEACH

Read the Passage and Model the Skill

Ask students to pay close attention to fact and opinion as you read the passage on **Teaching Chart 82** aloud.

Our Journey North

Papa and Mama led the way as we left the plantation. I thought my sister Lettie was a little scared because we had to travel at night. Papa carried her most of the way. I bet she got heavier and heavier as the night went on.

As we looked up in the sky, Papa pointed to a bunch of stars. Some people believe that the stars look like a drinking gourd. They're actually called the Big Dipper. They can point the way north. When we reach the North, I hope we have no more worries.

Teaching Chart 82

Discuss statements in the passage and look for clues that help determine which sentences contain facts and which contain opinions.

MODEL The first sentence says that Mama and Papa led the way. For the purposes of the story, that must be a fact. The second sentence, however, expresses something that the author thinks but doesn't really know. So that's an opinion.

PRACTICE

Find Facts and Opinions

ONE

Have volunteers circle the sentences in "Our Journey North" that contain facts and underline those that contain opinions.

Ask a volunteer to retell the story reading only the statements of fact. Ask students if they think the story is more or less interesting than when the opinions are included as well. What do the opinions tell us about the character who expresses them?

ASSESS/CLOSE

Rewrite a Familiar Tale Using Fact and Opinion

GROUP

Have students pick a favorite tale, such as "Cinderella" or "Jack and the Beanstalk." Ask them to suppose they are characters in the story. What facts and opinions would they like to tell? Have them work in groups to write a scene. Have groups present their scenes to the class. Have the class use a Fact and Opinion chart to record the facts and opinions they identify as the scenes are being presented.

ALTERNATE TEACHING STRATEGY

FACT AND OPINION

For a different approach to teaching this skill, see page T64.

Intervention **Skills**

Intervention Guide, for direct instruction and extra practice in fact and opinion

Meeting Individual Needs for Comprehension

EASY

Name________ Date________ **Reteach 100**

Fact and Opinion

Knowing that a **fact** is a statement that can be proven to be true and that an **opinion** is someone's personal belief can help you understand what you read.

Read the paragraph. Write **F** if the statement is a fact. Write **O** if the statement is an opinion.

The big dipper is my favorite group of stars. If you follow the tip of the dipper, you can find the North Star. Enslaved African Americans escaping to freedom used the North Star to guide their way north. On a scout camping trip, we did a nighttime exercise finding stars in the sky. We all found the North Star easily in the beautiful sky.

1. F The big dipper is a group of stars.
2. F You can follow the tip of the dipper to find the North Star.
3. F Enslaved African Americans escaping to freedom used the North Star to guide their way north.
4. O The night sky is beautiful.

Now you try. Write two facts and then write two opinions about pies.

5. Fact: Possible response: Most pies are desserts.
6. Fact: Possible response: Many pies are made with fruit in them.
7. Opinion: Possible response: Apple Pie is the best.
8. Opinion: Possible response: Pie should be served warm.

At Home: Have students express their opinions about news events.

Book 4/Unit 3 A Place Called Freedom 8

100

Reteach, 100

ON-LEVEL

Name________ Date________ **Practice 100**

Fact and Opinion

Read each of the following statements that describe what happened in "A Place Called Freedom." Write **Fact** or **Opinion** to describe each statement. Look back at the story to help you.

1. At the beginning of the story, James Starman's parents were enslaved. Fact
2. All people in Indiana believed that slavery was bad. Opinion
3. All Quakers thought that all people should be free to work and live where they wanted. Opinion
4. A Quaker family helped the Starmans start their new life. Fact
5. After one year, Papa earned enough money to buy his own land. Fact
6. I believe reading is an important skill. Opinion
7. Relatives from the old Tennessee plantation stayed with the Starmans until they had money to buy their own land and build their own cabins. Fact
8. I think Papa was very brave to rescue his family. Opinion
9. Many of the people freed from slavery became carpenters and blacksmiths. Fact
10. The people in the settlement wanted to name their town Starman, but Papa wanted to call it Freedom. Fact

At Home: Have students write three opinions about slavery.

Book 4/Unit 3 A Place Called Freedom 10

100

Practice, 100

CHALLENGE

Name________ Date________ **Extend 100**

Fact and Opinion

When news reporters interview people, they ask two kinds of questions. One kind of question can be answered by giving **facts**. Another kind of question can be answered by giving **opinions**.

Work with a partner to conduct an interview of a character in "A Place Called Freedom." Choose a character. Have one person take the role of a news reporter and the other person take the role of the character. Together, write two fact questions and two opinion questions. Plan how the character will answer the questions. Then present your interview to the class.

Character Answers will vary.

Fact Question 1 ________

Answer ________

Fact Question 2 ________

Answer ________

Opinion Question 1 ________

Answer ________

Opinion Question 2 ________

Answer ________

At Home: Interview a family member or a neighbor to find out how they came to live in the town in which you now live.

Book 4/Unit 3 A Place Called Freedom

100

Extend, 100

LANGUAGE SUPPORT

Name________ Date________

Fact or Opinion?

1. Write "Fact" under each fact, something that is true. 2. Write "Opinion" next to each opinion, something that someone thinks or believes.

The stars are far away.
fact
I think it looks like a big spoon.
opinion
Sometimes the moon is full.
fact
The moon looks like a buttery bowl.
opinion
I think apples are the best fruit.
opinion
Apples grow on trees.
fact
Scott Russell Sanders wrote this story.
fact
I feel this is the best story in the world.
opinion

110 A Place Called Freedom • Language Support / Blackline Master 54 Grade 4

Language Support, 110

TESTED OBJECTIVES

Students will summarize a story.

Skills Finder	
Summarize	
Introduce	281G-H
Review	297G-H, 359G-H
Test	Unit 3
Maintain	415, 461, 507, 551

TEACHING TIP

TOPIC SENTENCE Tell students that a strong topic sentence will help them begin their summaries.

Review Summarize

PREPARE

Discuss Summarizing

Review: Summarizing requires thinking about what you've read. What were the *most important* points? How can you organize them to retell the story briefly in your own words? Remember that a good summary is short and simple.

TEACH

Read the Passage

Display **Teaching Chart 83.** Remind students to consider which points are most important as you read the passage with them.

Our Settlement

Dozens and dozens of wonderful people live, work, and play in our settlement. There are carpenters, blacksmiths, farmers, storekeepers, and teachers.

Whenever we pass anyone on the street, we stop and say, "Hello." We tell each other a joke, or talk about the weather, or ask how the family is. Everybody gets along with everybody else.

I guess that's because we all have something in common. We love our town called Freedom.

Teaching Chart 83

Model the Skill

Ask a volunteer to identify the important point in the first paragraph and underline it. Then ask students to put the important point into their own words.

MODEL How can I make this short and simple? Instead of saying, "dozens and dozens of wonderful people, "I'll just say "many people." Instead of "live, work, and play," I think I'll just say "live in our settlement." It's important to keep my summary down to just a few words.

PRACTICE

Identify Important Points

ONE

Have volunteers underline other sentences that contain information to include in a summary. Ask students to paraphrase those sentences in the simplest way they can on a piece of paper.
When volunteers have finished underlining the main points, have students summarize the entire passage in their own words.
▶ **Logical/Linguistic**

ASSESS/CLOSE

Summarize a Familiar Story

PARTNERS

Ask pairs of students to pick a favorite story or show. Have them write a summary of no more than three sentences, reminding them to keep it short and simple. ▶ **Linguistic**

ALTERNATE TEACHING STRATEGY

SUMMARIZE

For a different approach to teaching this skill, see page T62.

Intervention **Skills**

Intervention Guide, for direct instruction and extra practice with summarizing

Meeting Individual Needs for Comprehension

EASY

Name________ Date______ **Reteach 101**

Summarize

If you can **summarize** a story well, you can be sure that you have understood the most important parts of the story.

Read the paragraph and then answer the questions.

Mr. LeTour's house was flooded when the creek spilled over its banks. He needed help cleaning his collection of old baseball cards. My Dad says it is very valuable. Mr. LeTour had wrapped each card in a clear plastic envelope. The envelopes had kept the cards dry during the flood, but now the envelopes were covered with mud. He hired Carrie McCourt and me to clean them. All weekend long, we worked with rags dipped in a special cleaner. Mr. LeTour was a lot happier on Sunday when he saw his sparkling clean envelopes.

1. What is the main idea of the story? Possible answer: Mr. LeTour's valuable baseball card collection was saved after a flood but their envelopes needed to be cleaned.
2. Who are the characters in the story? Possible answer: Mr. LeTour, the speaker, his dad, and Carrie McCourt
3. What is the story problem and its solution? Mr. LeTour needed help cleaning the plastic envelopes protecting his baseball cards in order to save the cards from more damage. He hired the speaker and Carrie to do the cleaning.
4. Use your answers above to summarize the story. Possible answer: Mr. LeTour's house was flooded. He asked the speaker and a friend to help save his valuable card collection by cleaning the envelopes of the mud left by a flood.

4 Book 4/Unit 3 A Place Called Freedom — **At Home:** Have students summarize a familiar story. 101

Reteach, 101

ON-LEVEL

Name________ Date______ **Practice 101**

Summarize

Suppose you are James Starman from the story "A Place Called Freedom." Complete the letter to your cousin who is still enslaved on the Tennessee plantation. Describe James' experiences, thoughts, and feelings. Look back at the story to help you **summarize** it.
Answers will vary but should accurately tell what happened in the story.

Dear Cousin:
It was hard saying goodbye to you. I was worried that I would never see you again. Now I know Papa is on his way to get you. You will be here soon. I want to tell you how it will be. Then you will not be afraid or feel strange.
It was dark when we left the plantation that night. I was worried about finding our way.________

We were ready to cross over to Indiana, but the Ohio River was in the way.________

A kind Quaker family took us into their house because ________

My Mama and Papa worked hard to ________

Folks wanted to name our town Starman because ________

Love,
Your cousin James

5 Book 4/Unit 3 A Place Called Freedom — **At Home:** Have students write a note to James Starman summarizing what they think of his trip. 101

Practice, 101

CHALLENGE

Name________ Date______ **Extend 101**

Summarize

When you **summarize** a story, you retell the story in a few words. Newspapers use headlines to catch the reader's attention and to summarize the content of articles in a few words.

Suppose you are a reporter writing a series of newspaper articles about the Starman family's travels and the settlement of Freedom. Write headlines you could use for articles about the events from "A Place Called Freedom" described below.

1. James and his family pack up for their journey. James' father says they will find their way to Indiana by "following the drinking gourd."
Possible answer: Family Follows Stars to Indiana
2. The family was helped across the Ohio River by a fisherman they didn't know. Strangers eventually helped them settle on a farm.
Possible answer: The Kindness of Strangers
3. The family settled into a cabin before winter. The children attended classes taught by their mother, and enjoyed the food and clothing made by her.
Preparing for Winter
4. During the winter Mr. Starman made several nighttime trips back to Tennessee to pick up relatives and lead their way north.
Possible answer: Many Join the Starmans
5. Soon there were many people living in the area with many different trades. Then a railroad was built to pass through their settlement.
Possible answer: Settlement Becomes a Town
6. James learns from both his mother and father and tries to decide who he wants to be like when he grows up. Eventually he realizes he can be like them both.
Possible answer: Growing Up in Freedom

Book 4/Unit 3 A Place Called Freedom — **At Home:** Read the headlines of several newspaper articles. Think about what information the articles may contain. Then read the articles to check your thinking. 101

Extend, 101

LANGUAGE SUPPORT

Name________ Date______

Photos for the Album

1. The boy on the left is showing us pictures of how Freedom became a town.
2. Describe what happens in each picture.
Answers will vary.

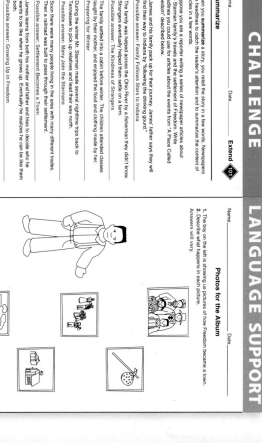

Grade 4 — Language Support/Blackline Master 55 • A Place Called Freedom 111

Language Support, 111

Review Context Clues

TESTED OBJECTIVES

Students will identify and use context clues to understand unfamiliar words.

Skills Finder

Context Clues	
Introduce	157I-J
Review	215I-J, 251I-J, 331I-J, 359I-J, 369G-H, 515I-J
Test	Units 2, 3, 5, 6
Maintain	309, 389, 523, 643

TEACHING TIP

CONTEXT CLUES As students create sentences for their unfamiliar words, have them ask: *Would I be able to figure out the meaning of this word if I were reading this sentence?*

PREPARE

Discuss Context Clues

Review: Sometimes a reader comes to an unfamiliar word. By reading carefully, the reader may find clues to the meaning of the word. Nearby words, inflectional endings, suffixes and prefixes, root words, and the parts of compound words can all give clues to meaning. So can the way the word is used in a sentence.

TEACH

Read the Passage and Model the Skill

Have students read "Escape" on **Teaching Chart 84.** Remind them to look for clues to unfamiliar words.

Escape

When we left for Indiana, my Uncle George's family stayed behind on the plantation. Each day the family would rise at dawn to toil in the big farm's fields. They worked hard, planting and picking cotton. They never got any wages or other pay for all their hard work.

But all the while they were planning to flee. One night, they made their escape. They were wary, and kept an eye out for the master, afraid he would follow. They walked all night until they arrived at their destination and found Papa there, waiting to lead them to their new home.

Teaching Chart 84

MODEL I don't understand the word *toil*. I'll check for clues to help me figure it out. The next sentence says that the slaves worked hard picking cotton. So *toiling* must mean working hard.

Ask a volunteer to circle the unfamiliar word and to underline the words in the sentence that give clues to what it means.

PRACTICE

Identify Context Clues

GROUP

Have students try the same strategy to figure out the meanings of *wages, flee, wary,* and *destination.*

ASSESS/CLOSE

Play a Context Clue Game

PARTNERS

Divide the students into pairs. Write unfamiliar words on index cards, one to a card, and include the definition on the back. Give two cards to each pair. Have each partner write two sentences that contain one of the unfamiliar words and context clues to its definition. Challenge the other partner to give the meaning.

ALTERNATE TEACHING STRATEGY

CONTEXT CLUES

For a different approach to teaching this skill, see page T65.

Intervention Skills

Intervention Guide, for direct instruction and extra practice with context clues

Meeting Individual Needs for Vocabulary

EASY

Name________________ Date________ Reteach 102

Context Clues

Use **context clues,** or other words and sentences in the text, to help you figure out an unfamiliar word.

Read the paragraph. Then circle the letter beside the meaning of each of the words listed below. Next tell which clues in the paragraph helped you figure out the meanings.

My grandfather loved to recount our family stories. He told again and again about his great-grandmother and other ancestors who escaped from slavery. I liked the part about how they had to improvise when the slave catchers came upon them suddenly. That's where we get the ability to solve things quickly, my grandfather told me. Grandpa always said that enslaved people who were fugitives from the law and made it to freedom had to be smart.

1. recount
   (a.) repeat   b. keep secret
   Clues: **told again and again**
2. ancestors
   (a.) family member who lived before you   b. family friends
   Clues: **great-grandmother and other**
3. improvise
   a. practice ahead of time   (b.) do something without planning
   Clues: **ability to make things up quickly; had to be smart**
4. fugitives
   (a.) runaways   b. officers
   Clues: **enslaved people; from the law; made it to freedom**

At Home: Have students find a word they don't know in a story and give its meaning from context clues.

Book 4/Unit 3 A Place Called Freedom 4

102

Reteach, 102

ON-LEVEL

Name________________ Date________ Practice 102

Context Clues

When you read, you may find words you don't know. The other words in the sentence often are **context clues** and can help you figure out the meaning of the word.

melon	enslaved	runaways	launched	blacksmith
carpenter	barrels	tongue	unpack	stable

Complete each sentence with a word from the list.

1. When people are captured and have their freedom taken away, we say they are **enslaved**.
2. Enslaved people who escaped were called **runaways**.
3. If you open your mouth and look in the mirror, you can see your **tongue**.
4. The scientists built the rocket, then they **launched** it.
5. The horses and the cows are fed in the **stable**.
6. A **blacksmith** uses hot fire to melt and twist iron into horse shoes.
7. Long ago people stored water and food in big wooden **barrels**.
8. After we returned from our vacation, the first thing my sister and I did was **unpack**.
9. One kind of fruit that grows on a vine is a **melon**.
10. The wooden table and chairs were built by a **carpenter**.

At Home: Have students circle the context clues in the sentences above.

Book 4/Unit 3 A Place Called Freedom 10

102

Practice, 102

CHALLENGE

Name________________ Date________ Extend 102

Context Clues

Context clues are words in a sentence or in nearby sentences that you use to figure out the meaning of unfamiliar words. Use context clues to fill in the blank in each sentence with one of these words from "A Place Called Freedom."

celebrated	glittery	gulp	loaned
runaways	sturdy	wriggly	

1. Look at how **glittery** the diamonds are when light shines on them.
2. My friend **loaned** me a pencil until I had a chance to go to the bookstore to buy my own.
3. We **celebrated** my birthday by having a slumber party.
4. It was hard to hold the worm still enough to get it on the fishhook because it was **wriggly**.
5. Those children are **runaways** because they did not have permission to be away from home.
6. I swallowed the rest of my sandwich in one big **gulp**.
7. Our **sturdy** house remained standing even though a tornado passed through our town.
8. Write a sentence using at least two of the unfamiliar words.
   Answers will vary.

At Home: Have students write their own "fill in the blank" sentences. Have family members use context clues to guess the correct word to fill in the blank.

Book 4/Unit 3 A Place Called Freedom

102

Extend, 102

LANGUAGE SUPPORT

Name________________ Date________

Find the Meaning

1. Read each word. 2. Read each clue to understand its meaning. 3. Circle the picture that goes with the word.

Word	Clue	Meaning
gourd		
plantation		
sunrise		

112 A Place Called Freedom • Language Support / Blackline Master 56 Grade 4

Language Support, 112

Persuasive Writing

Prewrite

WRITE AN EDITORIAL Present this writing assignment: What was life like for the family before they were given their freedom? Imagine that you are a newspaper editor right before the Civil War. Write an editorial for your paper. Explain why you think slavery is wrong. Support your opinions with facts. Try to persuade your readers to agree with you.

BRAINSTORM IDEAS Have students brainstorm facts and opinions on slavery. Urge them to think about what life must have been like for the slaves and why that was wrong. Remind them that they will be trying to persuade their readers, so they should make their editorials convincing.

Strategy: Make a List Have students list some facts they know about slavery and some opinions that they have. Prompt students with the following questions:

- What were slaves told to do by their owners?
- What do you think would happen to slaves if they didn't do what they were told?
- Why wouldn't you like to be a slave?

Draft

USE THE LIST In their editorials, students should include facts and opinions from their lists and make the strongest argument they can against slavery. Tell them that in an editorial, it's not necessary for a writer to include the words *I think* and *I feel*, because an editorial is always a statement of opinion.

Revise

SELF-QUESTIONING Ask students to assess their drafts.

- Did I include as many facts as I can?
- Have I elaborated on my opinions and made them really convincing?
- What would make my editorial more effective?

PARTNERS Have partners read each other's editorials aloud and discuss whether or not they are persuaded.

Edit/Proofread

CHECK FOR ERRORS Students should reread their editorials for spelling, grammar, and punctuation.

Publish

SHARE THE EDITORIALS Students can read their editorials to the class as if they were giving a speech. Encourage the class to discuss which facts and opinions persuaded them.

Slavery Must End!

Slavery is a terrible thing for our country. We claim that we are free, but some of us have no freedom at all. As long as slavery lasts, the ideas of our Founding Fathers sound like lies.

There are almost 4 million people living in slavery in the country today. Most of them are in the South, working on big plantations. They work so that others will get rich. This is not the American way.

GRAMMAR/SPELLING CONNECTIONS

See the 5-Day Grammar and Usage Plan on linking verbs, pages 359M–359N.

See the 5-Day Spelling Plan on adding *-ed* and *-ing*, pages 359O–359P.

TEACHING TIP

Technology
Remind students inputting work to frequently stop and save. Taking this precaution will prevent loss of the file in case of accident or power loss.

Editorial Format
Bring samples of newspaper editorials to class and discuss the format with students. Point out that newspaper editorials have titles that convey their message in just a few words. Encourage students to give their editorials titles that express their opinion.

Handwriting CD-ROM

Presentation Ideas

MAKE A POSTER Have students create a poster for an anti-slavery rally. Encourage them to include all the important information including time and place.
▶ **Viewing/Representing**

HAVE A RALLY Students can pretend to speak at the anti-slavery rally. Afterward, have audience members analyze the speaker's persuasive techniques.
▶ **Speaking/Listening**

SLAVERY NO!
Giant Rally. May 21
Town Meeting Hall
Speakers: Harriet Tubman
Levi Coffin

Consider students' creative efforts, possibly adding a plus (+) for originality, wit, and imagination.

Scoring Rubric

Excellent	Good	Fair	Unsatisfactory
4: The writer • clearly persuades the reader. • provides organized and well supported facts and opinions. • writes convincingly and with feeling.	**3:** The writer • attempts to persuade the reader. • provides adequate facts and opinions, and organizes them. • writes with some feeling.	**2:** The writer • tries to persuade the reader, but doesn't always succeed. • provides only some facts and opinions, and doesn't organize them well. • writes with little feeling.	**1:** The writer • doesn't persuade the reader at all. • provides few facts and opinions, and doesn't organize them. • writes poorly and with no feeling.

Incomplete 0: The writer leaves the page blank or fails to respond to the writing task. The student does not address the topic or simply paraphrases the prompt. The response is illegible or incoherent.

For a 6-point or an 8-point scale, see pages T107–T108.

Meeting Individual Needs for Writing

EASY

Map Have students draw a map of Freedom. Remind them to include buildings mentioned in the story and other buildings that may have gone up after the story was over. Ask them to write a few sentences about what's on their map.

ON-LEVEL

Diary Have students imagine that they are James Starman and are keeping a diary. Have them write an entry about a day in Freedom. Remind them to include facts and opinions.

CHALLENGE

New Story Have students imagine that they are a runaway slave child who arrives in Freedom. Have them write a story about their experiences fleeing and what they found when they arrived in the settlement.

Listening and Speaking

LISTENING STRATEGIES
As students read aloud their editorials, have listeners:
- jot down ideas for how to make the editorial more persuasive.
- summarize the editorial in their own words.

SPEAKING STRATEGIES
Encourage speakers to:
- practice saying any unfamiliar words before the presentation.
- speak loudly and enunciate clearly.

LANGUAGE SUPPORT

ESL Some English learners may need extra support putting their thoughts into persuasive words. Have them work with a fluent English-speaking partner who can help them come up with words and phrases that effectively express their thoughts.

PORTFOLIO **Invite students to include their editorials or another writing project in their portfolios.**

5 Day Grammar and Usage Plan

LANGUAGE SUPPORT

ESL Ask second-language learners to translate some sentences with linking verbs into their first language. Ask what the linking verbs are in that language. (Note: Some languages have sentences with only a subject and an object, without a linking verb.)

DAILY LANGUAGE ACTIVITIES

Write the Daily Language Activities on the chalkboard each day or use **Transparency 14.** Have students orally fix the form of *to be* for subject-verb agreement. For answers, see the transparency.

Day 1

1. Mama am a good cook.
2. We is free now.
3. I were weary from walking.

Day 2

1. You is safe.
2. Papa were a good storyteller.
3. Lettie are my sister.

Day 3

1. I are a farmer.
2. "You is a good friend," the Old Man said.
3. Our cousins was slaves.

Day 4

1. The sailor were glad to take us on his boat.
2. Night traveling were safer.
3. The drinking gourd am the Big Dipper.

Day 5

1. I were big enough to walk.
2. Our settlement am famous.
3. The fisherman's face were wrinkled.

Daily Language Transparency 14

DAY 1 Introduce the Concept

Oral Warm-Up Ask students to name forms of the verb *to be*.

Introduce Linking Verbs Explain that verbs usually show action. But not all verbs do that. Present the following:

Linking Verbs

- A **linking verb** does not show action. It connects the subject to the rest of the sentence.
- *Is*, *are*, *am*, *was*, and *were* are often used as linking verbs.

Write on the chalkboard: *I am*, *you are*, *he is*, *she is*, *it is*, *we are*, *they are*, *the dog is*, *the cats are*. Have students try the same subjects with *was* and *were*.

Present the Daily Language Activity. Then have students rewrite the three sentences, using, respectively, *you*, *they*, and *Papa* as the subject.

WRITING Assign the daily Writing Prompt on page 332C.

Name______ Date______ LEARN Grammar 83

Linking Verbs

- A **linking verb** does not show action. It connects the subject to the rest of the sentence.
- *Is, are, am, was,* and *were* are often used as linking verbs.

Read each sentence. Study the linking verbs in parentheses. Write the form of the linking verb that correctly completes each sentence.

1. The Big Dipper __is__ a group of stars. (is, are)
2. The children's names __were__ James and Lettie. (was, were)
3. Papa's new name __was__ Starman. (was, were)
4. Indiana __is__ the state where the family made their home. (is, are)
5. Barns and beds __are__ things that Papa can build. (is, are)
6. James thought Mama's cooking __was__ just wonderful. (was, were)
7. Mama and the children __were__ worried when Papa was away. (was, were)
8. The children certainly __are__ happy when Papa returns. (is, are)
9. Papa's relatives __were__ eager to leave the plantation. (was, were)
10. You __are__ older than James and Lettie. (am, are)

10 Grade 4/Unit 3 A Place Called Freedom — Extension: Ask students to write a paragraph describing the town of Freedom. Urge them to use linking verbs in their description. Invite students to share their descriptions. 83

GRAMMAR PRACTICE BOOK, PAGE 83

DAY 2 Teach the Concept

Review Linking Verbs Ask students what kind of verb does *not* show action.

More About Linking Verbs Remind students that a linking verb connects the subject to the rest of the sentence. Present the following:

Linking Verbs

- Some linking verbs link the subject to a noun in the predicate.
- Some linking verbs link the subject to an adjective in the predicate.

Present the Daily Language Activity. Then ask students to list some adjectives and some nouns. Write them on the chalkboard. Have students pick three adjectives and three nouns from the list and say sentences using their choices along with linking verbs.

WRITING Assign the daily Writing Prompt on page 332C.

Name______ Date______ LEARN AND PRACTICE Grammar 84

Linking Verbs

- Some linking verbs link the subject to a noun in the predicate.
- Some linking verbs link the subject to an adjective in the predicate.

Read each sentence. Circle the linking verb that links the subject to a noun or adjective in the predicate. Underline the noun or adjective.

1. Lettie (was) wriggly as a child.
2. Lettie's older brother, James, (was) tall.
3. Some people leaving Tennessee (were) runaways from plantations.
4. The travelers (were) weary from their long walk.
5. The face of the old fisherman (is) wrinkled.
6. How many of the new settlers (are) farmers?
7. Mama (was) the teacher in the village school.
8. A few people in the village (were) carpenters.
9. The vegetables that the boy raises (are) beans.
10. The name of the village (is) Freedom.

84 Extension: Have students identify whether each linking verb that they underlined in these sentences is in the present tense or the past tense. Grade 4/Unit 3 A Place Called Freedom 10

GRAMMAR PRACTICE BOOK, PAGE 84

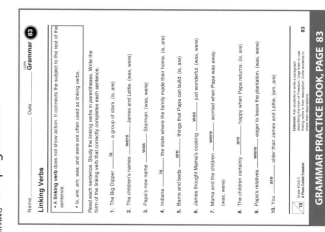

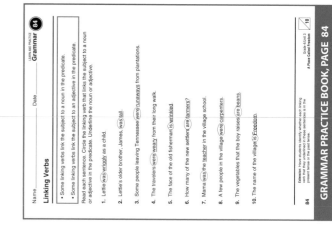

Linking Verbs

DAY 3 Review and Practice

Learn from the Literature Review linking verbs. Ask students to read the second paragraph on page 336 of *A Place Called Freedom*:

> **Papa called Lettie a short drink of water, because she was little and wriggly, and he called me a long gulp of air, because I was tall and full of talk.**

Ask students to find the linking verbs. Then have them identify the parts of the sentence that are linked by each verb.

Use Linking Verbs Present the Daily Language Activity. Then have students describe themselves by using linking verbs and nouns or adjectives in sentences.

WRITING Assign the daily Writing Prompt on page 332D.

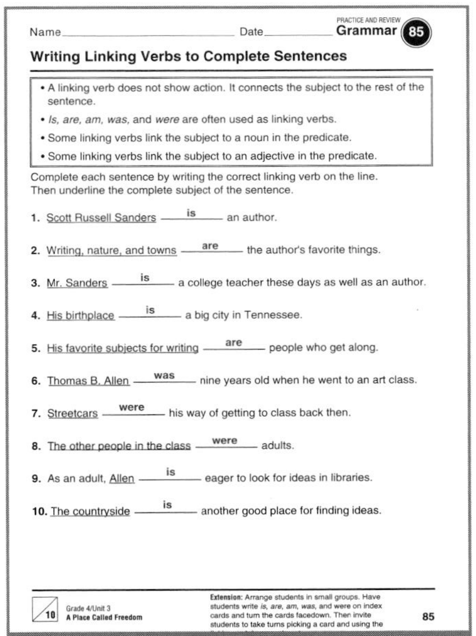
Name ______ Date ______ PRACTICE AND REVIEW Grammar 85

Writing Linking Verbs to Complete Sentences

- A linking verb does not show action. It connects the subject to the rest of the sentence.
- *Is, are, am, was,* and *were* are often used as linking verbs.
- Some linking verbs link the subject to a noun in the predicate.
- Some linking verbs link the subject to an adjective in the predicate.

Complete each sentence by writing the correct linking verb on the line. Then underline the complete subject of the sentence.

1. Scott Russell Sanders __is__ an author.
2. Writing, nature, and towns __are__ the author's favorite things.
3. Mr. Sanders __is__ a college teacher these days as well as an author.
4. His birthplace __is__ a big city in Tennessee.
5. His favorite subjects for writing __are__ people who get along.
6. Thomas B. Allen __was__ nine years old when he went to an art class.
7. Streetcars __were__ his way of getting to class back then.
8. The other people in the class __were__ adults.
9. As an adult, Allen __is__ eager to look for ideas in libraries.
10. The countryside __is__ another good place for finding ideas.

10 Grade 4/Unit 3 A Place Called Freedom

Extension: Arrange students in small groups. Have students write *is, are, am, was,* and *were* on index cards and turn the cards facedown. Then invite students to take turns picking a card and using the

85

GRAMMAR PRACTICE BOOK, PAGE 85

DAY 4 Review and Practice

Review Linking Verbs Have students look at the Daily Language Activities for Days 1–3. For each sentence, ask them if the linking verb links the subject with a noun or an adjective. Then present the Daily Language Activity.

Mechanics and Usage Before students begin the daily Writing Prompt on page 332D, introduce the following:

Titles

- Capitalize the first and last words and all important words in the titles of books and newspapers.
- Underline titles of books, newspapers, magazines, and television series.
- Put quotation marks around the titles of short stories, articles, songs, poems, and book chapters.

WRITING Assign the daily Writing Prompt on page 332D.

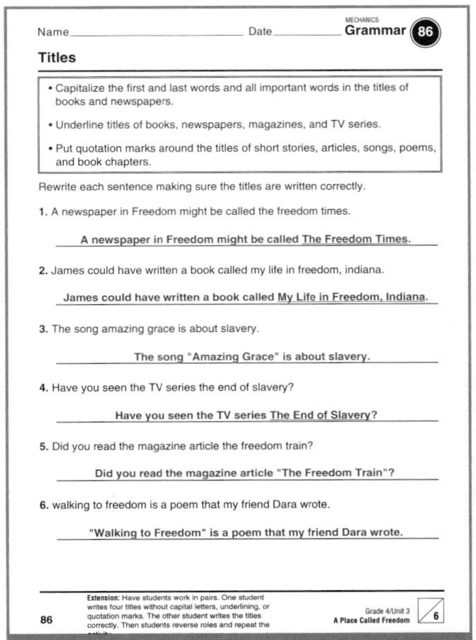
Name ______ Date ______ MECHANICS Grammar 86

Titles

- Capitalize the first and last words and all important words in the titles of books and newspapers.
- Underline titles of books, newspapers, magazines, and TV series.
- Put quotation marks around the titles of short stories, articles, songs, poems, and book chapters.

Rewrite each sentence making sure the titles are written correctly.

1. A newspaper in Freedom might be called the freedom times.
   A newspaper in Freedom might be called The Freedom Times.
2. James could have written a book called my life in freedom, indiana.
   James could have written a book called My Life in Freedom, Indiana.
3. The song amazing grace is about slavery.
   The song "Amazing Grace" is about slavery.
4. Have you seen the TV series the end of slavery?
   Have you seen the TV series The End of Slavery?
5. Did you read the magazine article the freedom train?
   Did you read the magazine article "The Freedom Train"?
6. walking to freedom is a poem that my friend Dara wrote.
   "Walking to Freedom" is a poem that my friend Dara wrote.

86

Extension: Have students work in pairs. One student writes four titles without capital letters, underlining, or quotation marks. The other student writes the titles correctly. Then students reverse roles and repeat the

Grade 4/Unit 3 A Place Called Freedom 6

GRAMMAR PRACTICE BOOK, PAGE 86

DAY 5 Assess and Reteach

Assess Use the Daily Language Activity and page 87 of the **Grammar Practice Book** for assessment.

Reteach Invite students to play "Fix It" in pairs. Player A uses an incorrect linking verb to link a subject and an adjective or noun. Then player B corrects the sentence. Have students switch roles and continue.

Have students use each form of *to be* to form a sentence about someone they know, such as a relative, friend, or neighbor.

Have students add linking verbs and a sentence for each to their classroom word wall.

Use page 88 of the **Grammar Practice Book** for additional reteaching.

WRITING Assign the daily Writing Prompt on page 332D.

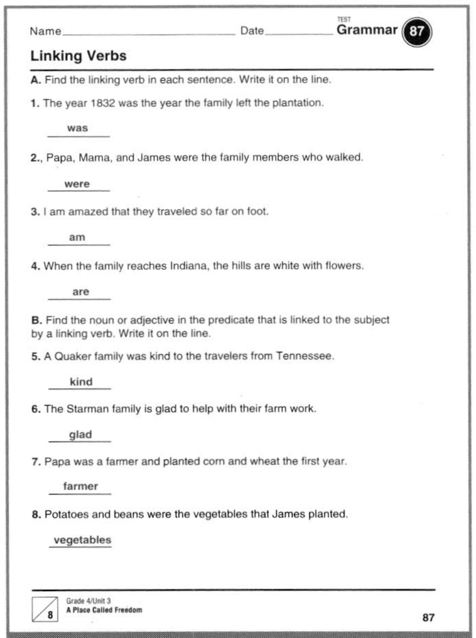
Name ______ Date ______ TEST Grammar 87

Linking Verbs

A. Find the linking verb in each sentence. Write it on the line.

1. The year 1832 was the year the family left the plantation.
   was
2. Papa, Mama, and James were the family members who walked.
   were
3. I am amazed that they traveled so far on foot.
   am
4. When the family reaches Indiana, the hills are white with flowers.
   are

B. Find the noun or adjective in the predicate that is linked to the subject by a linking verb. Write it on the line.

5. A Quaker family was kind to the travelers from Tennessee.
   kind
6. The Starman family is glad to help with their farm work.
   glad
7. Papa was a farmer and planted corn and wheat the first year.
   farmer
8. Potatoes and beans were the vegetables that James planted.
   vegetables

8 Grade 4/Unit 3 A Place Called Freedom

87

GRAMMAR PRACTICE BOOK, PAGE 87

GRAMMAR PRACTICE BOOK, PAGE 88

5 Day Spelling Plan

LANGUAGE SUPPORT

Remind students that many verbs undergo spelling changes when the endings *-ed* and *-ing* are added. Review the spelling rules that will help students spell such verb forms correctly. (examples: drop final *e*, double consonants, change *y* to *i*)

DICTATION SENTENCES

Spelling Words

1. We freed the mice from the trap.
2. My mom hugged me.
3. He emptied the tray.
4. We figured you were sleeping.
5. The trees are all budding.
6. He carried the ladder.
7. We believed his story.
8. The lights were dimmed in the theater.
9. They studied for hours.
10. Who is providing the money?
11. The animals are shedding their fur.
12. They are sledding down the hill.
13. The insects are magnified.
14. The window is wedged open.
15. The fish is rotting.
16. The fruit varied in shape.
17. Who just arrived at the house?
18. What is plugging the hole?
19. The sun is rising over the hill.
20. We celebrated the first day of summer.

Challenge Words

21. I fretted about the mistakes.
22. The gourd is big and green.
23. They used to grow rice on the plantation.
24. There was a settlement here.
25. We were up before sunrise.

DAY 1 Pretest

Assess Prior Knowledge Use the Dictation Sentences at the left and **Spelling Practice Book** page 83 for the pretest. Allow students to correct their own papers. Students who require a modified list may be tested on the first ten words.

Spelling Words		Challenge Words
1. **freed**	11. shedding	21. **fretted**
2. **hugged**	12. sledding	22. **gourd**
3. **emptied**	13. magnified	23. **plantation**
4. figured	14. wedged	24. **settlement**
5. budding	15. rotting	25. **sunrise**
6. **carried**	16. varied	
7. **believed**	17. **arrived**	
8. dimmed	18. plugging	
9. studied	19. rising	
10. providing	20. **celebrated**	

*Note: Words in **dark type** are from the story.*

Word Study On page 84 of the **Spelling Practice Book** are word study steps and an at-home activity.

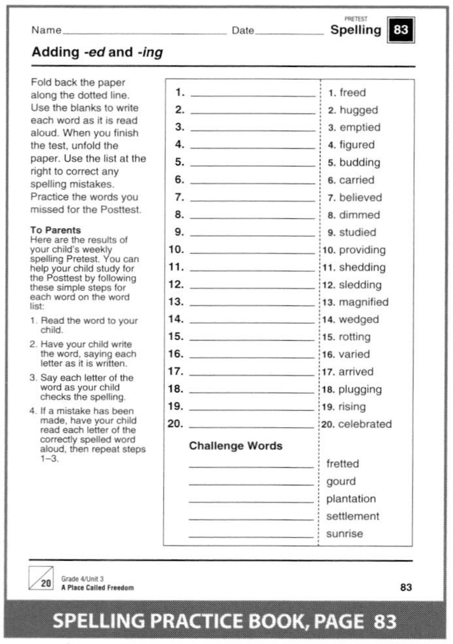
Name______ Date______ PRETEST Spelling 83

Adding *-ed* and *-ing*

Fold back the paper along the dotted line. Use the blanks to write each word as it is read aloud. When you finish the test, unfold the paper. Use the list at the right to correct any spelling mistakes. Practice the words you missed for the Posttest.

To Parents
Here are the results of your child's weekly spelling Pretest. You can help your child study for the Posttest by following these simple steps for each word on the word list:
1. Read the word to your child.
2. Have your child write the word, saying each letter as it is written.
3. Say each letter of the word as your child checks the spelling.
4. If a mistake has been made, have your child read each letter of the correctly spelled word aloud, then repeat steps 1–3.

1. freed 2. hugged 3. emptied 4. figured 5. budding 6. carried 7. believed 8. dimmed 9. studied 10. providing 11. shedding 12. sledding 13. magnified 14. wedged 15. rotting 16. varied 17. arrived 18. plugging 19. rising 20. celebrated

Challenge Words: fretted, gourd, plantation, settlement, sunrise

Grade 4/Unit 3 A Place Called Freedom 20 83

SPELLING PRACTICE BOOK, PAGE 83

WORD STUDY STEPS AND ACTIVITY, PAGE 84

DAY 2 Explore the Pattern

Sort and Spell Words Write *rise* and *rising.* Ask what spelling change occurred when *-ing* was added. (The final *e* was dropped.) Ask students to list other spelling changes when adding *-ed* and *-ing* to verbs. Have students read and sort words as below.

Drop final *e*

freed	arrived	providing
believed	rising	wedged
figured	celebrated	

Double consonants

hugged	shedding	rotting
budding	sledding	plugging
dimmed		

Change *y* to *i*

emptied	studied	magnified
carried	varied	

Syllable Patterns Have students locate the words with double consonants and divide them into syllables. The two-syllable words divide between the consonants; the one-syllable words cannot be divided.

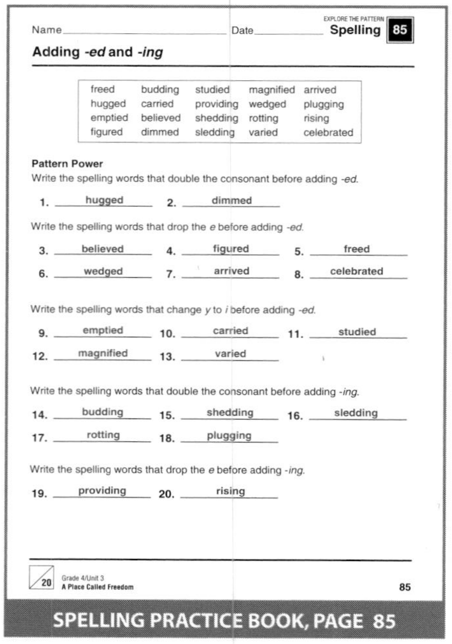
Name______ Date______ EXPLORE THE PATTERN Spelling 85

Adding *-ed* and *-ing*

freed, hugged, emptied, figured, budding, carried, believed, dimmed, studied, providing, shedding, sledding, magnified, wedged, rotting, varied, arrived, plugging, rising, celebrated

Pattern Power
Write the spelling words that double the consonant before adding *-ed.*
1. hugged 2. dimmed
Write the spelling words that drop the *e* before adding *-ed.*
3. believed 4. figured 5. freed 6. wedged 7. arrived 8. celebrated
Write the spelling words that change *y* to *i* before adding *-ed.*
9. emptied 10. carried 11. studied 12. magnified 13. varied
Write the spelling words that double the consonant before adding *-ing.*
14. budding 15. shedding 16. sledding 17. rotting 18. plugging
Write the spelling words that drop the *e* before adding *-ing.*
19. providing 20. rising

Grade 4/Unit 3 A Place Called Freedom 20 85

SPELLING PRACTICE BOOK, PAGE 85

Adding *-ed* and *-ing*

DAY 3 Practice and Extend

Word Meaning: Base Words Point out that all of the Spelling Words have an *-ed* or *-ing* ending. Have students write the base (root) word of each Spelling Word and identify how its spelling changes. (example: *rising/rise:* drop *-ing* and add *e*)

If students need extra practice, have partners give each other a midweek test.

Glossary Remind students that the Glossary shows how to divide each entry word into syllables. Have partners:

- write each Challenge Word.
- look up each word in the Glossary.
- find the place in the entry where the word is broken into syllables.
- copy each word, showing the breaks between syllables.

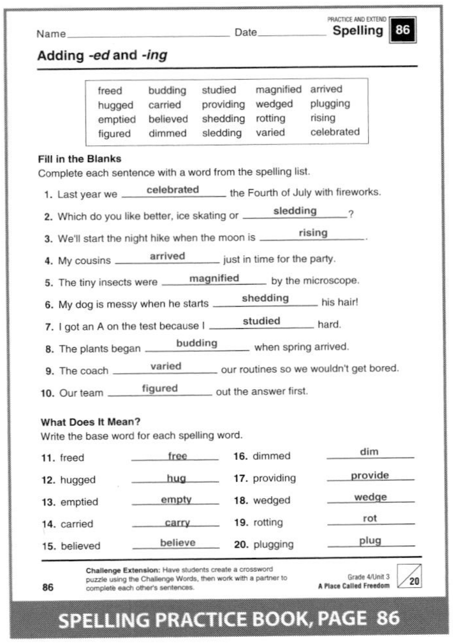

Name______ Date______ PRACTICE AND EXTEND Spelling 86

Adding *-ed* and *-ing*

freed	budding	studied	magnified	arrived
hugged	carried	providing	wedged	plugging
emptied	believed	shedding	rotting	rising
figured	dimmed	sledding	varied	celebrated

Fill in the Blanks
Complete each sentence with a word from the spelling list.

1. Last year we ___celebrated___ the Fourth of July with fireworks.
2. Which do you like better, ice skating or ___sledding___?
3. We'll start the night hike when the moon is ___rising___.
4. My cousins ___arrived___ just in time for the party.
5. The tiny insects were ___magnified___ by the microscope.
6. My dog is messy when he starts ___shedding___ his hair!
7. I got an A on the test because I ___studied___ hard.
8. The plants began ___budding___ when spring arrived.
9. The coach ___varied___ our routines so we wouldn't get bored.
10. Our team ___figured___ out the answer first.

What Does It Mean?
Write the base word for each spelling word.

11. freed	free	16. dimmed	dim
12. hugged	hug	17. providing	provide
13. emptied	empty	18. wedged	wedge
14. carried	carry	19. rotting	rot
15. believed	believe	20. plugging	plug

86 **Challenge Extension:** Have students create a crossword puzzle using the Challenge Words, then work with a partner to complete each other's sentences. Grade 4/Unit 3 A Place Called Freedom 20

SPELLING PRACTICE BOOK, PAGE 86

DAY 4 Proofread and Write

Proofread Sentences Write these sentences on the chalkboard, including the misspelled words. Ask students to proofread, circling incorrect spellings and writing the correct spellings. There are two spelling errors in each sentence.

The moon was rissing as I studyed. (rising, studied)

Mom huged me after I caried the bags to the car. (hugged, carried)

Have students create additional sentences with errors for partners to correct.

WRITING Have students use as many Spelling Words as possible in the daily Writing Prompt on page 332D. Remind students to proofread their writing for errors in spelling, grammar, and punctuation.

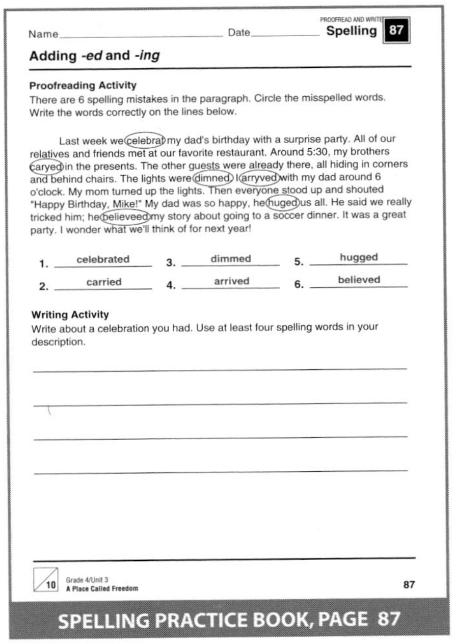

Name______ Date______ PROOFREAD AND WRITE Spelling 87

Adding *-ed* and *-ing*

Proofreading Activity
There are 6 spelling mistakes in the paragraph. Circle the misspelled words. Write the words correctly on the lines below.

Last week we celebrat my dad's birthday with a surprise party. All of our relatives and friends met at our favorite restaurant. Around 5:30, my brothers caryed in the presents. The other guests were already there, all hiding in corners and behind chairs. The lights were dimmed. I arryved with my dad around 6 o'clock. My mom turned up the lights. Then everyone stood up and shouted "Happy Birthday, Mike!" My dad was so happy, he huged us all. He said we really tricked him; he believeed my story about going to a soccer dinner. It was a great party. I wonder what we'll think of for next year!

1. celebrated 3. dimmed 5. hugged
2. carried 4. arrived 6. believed

Writing Activity
Write about a celebration you had. Use at least four spelling words in your description.

10 Grade 4/Unit 3 A Place Called Freedom 87

SPELLING PRACTICE BOOK, PAGE 87

DAY 5 Assess and Reteach

Assess Students' Knowledge Use page 88 of the **Spelling Practice Book** or the Dictation Sentences on page 359O for the posttest.

JOURNAL **Personal Word List** If students have trouble with any words in this lesson, have them add the words to their personal word lists in their journals. Have students write the spelling rule that applies to each word. (Example: drop final *e*)

Students should refer to their word lists during later writing activities.

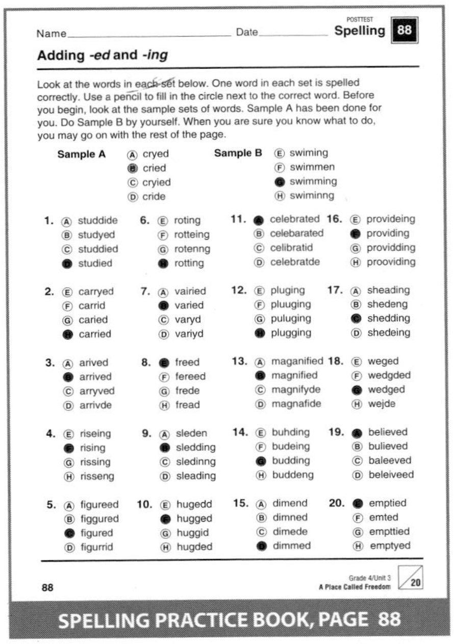

Name______ Date______ POSTTEST Spelling 88

Adding *-ed* and *-ing*

Look at the words in each set below. One word in each set is spelled correctly. Use a pencil to fill in the circle next to the correct word. Before you begin, look at the sample sets of words. Sample A has been done for you. Do Sample B by yourself. When you are sure you know what to do, you may go on with the rest of the page.

Sample A: (A) cryed ● cried (C) cryied (D) cride
Sample B: (E) swiming (F) swimmen ● swimming (H) swiminng

1. (A) studdide (B) studyed (C) studdied ● studied
2. (E) carryed (F) carrid (G) caried ● carried
3. (A) arived ● arrived (C) arryved (D) arrivde
4. (E) riseing ● rising (G) rissing (H) risseng
5. (A) figureed (B) figgured ● figured (D) figurrid
6. (E) roting (F) rotteing (G) rotenng ● rotting
7. (A) vairied ● varied (C) varyd (D) variyd
8. ● freed (F) fereed (G) frede (H) fread
9. (A) sleden ● sledding (C) sledinng (D) sleading
10. (E) hugedd ● hugged (G) huggid (H) hugded
11. ● celebrated (B) celebarated (C) celibratid (D) celebratde
12. (E) pluging (F) pluuging (G) puluging ● plugging
13. (A) maganified ● magnified (C) magnifyde (D) magnafide
14. (E) buhding (F) budeing ● budding (H) buddeng
15. (A) dimend (B) dimmed (C) dimede ● dimmed
16. (E) provideing ● providing (G) providding (H) prooviding
17. (A) sheading (B) shedeng ● shedding (D) shedeing
18. (E) weged (F) wedgded ● wedged (H) wejde
19. ● believed (B) bulieved (C) baleeved (D) beleiveed
20. ● emptied (F) emted (G) empttied (H) emptyed

88 Grade 4/Unit 3 A Place Called Freedom 20

SPELLING PRACTICE BOOK, PAGE 88

Lesson Overview

Cumulative Review with Expository Text

Time to Review

Anthology

Twisted Trails

Selection Summary **Adrian Fisher designs walk-through mazes for a living. He has found a way to combine math and science, his favorite subjects, in a way he can share with other people.**

Stories in Art focuses on the **comprehension** skill

Reading Strategy applies the **comprehension** skill

Listening Library

INSTRUCTIONAL pages 362–369

Time to Reread

Reread Leveled Books

EASY
Lesson on pages 369A and 369D

INDEPENDENT
Lesson on pages 369B and 369D

Take-Home version available

CHALLENGE
Lesson on pages 369C and 369D

Leveled Practice

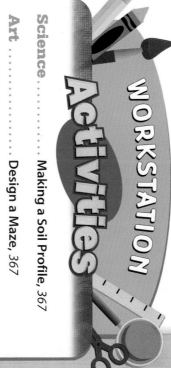

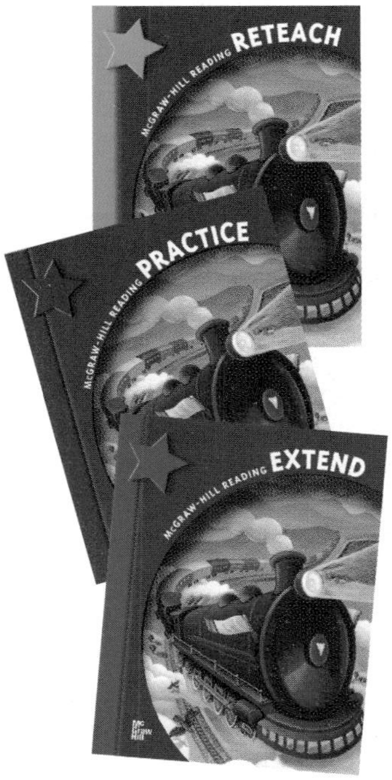

EASY

Reteach, 103–109 blackline masters with reteaching opportunities for each assessed skill

INDEPENDENT/ON-LEVEL

Practice, 103–109 workbook with Take-Home stories and practice opportunities for each assessed skill and story comprehension

CHALLENGE

Extend, 103–109 blackline masters that offer challenge activities for each assessed skill

Quizzes Prepared by Accelerated Reader®

WORKSTATION Activities

Science	Making a Soil Profile, *367*
Art	Design a Maze, *367*
Language Arts	Read Aloud, *360E*
	Make a List, *367*
Writing	A Letter, *366*
Research and Inquiry	Find Out More, *367*
Internet Activities	www.mhschool.com/reading

Suggested Lesson Planner

READING AND LANGUAGE ARTS	DAY 1 Focus on Reading and Skills	DAY 2 Read the Literature
• Comprehension • Vocabulary • Phonics/Decoding • Study Skills • Listening, Speaking, Viewing, Representing	Read **Read Aloud: Fairy Tale,** 360E "The Needle in the Haystack" **Develop Visual Literacy,** 360 ☑ **Review Judgments and Decisions,** 361A–361B **Teaching Chart 85** **Reteach, Practice, Extend,** 103 Read **Reading Strategy: Judgments and Decisions,** 361 "An Amazing Garden" Intervention Program	**Build Background,** 362A Develop Oral Language **Vocabulary,** 362B–362C ***challenge contained mazes combine entertaining requires*** **Teaching Chart 86** Word Building Manipulative Cards **Reteach, Practice, Extend,** 104 Read **Read the Selection,** 362–365 ☑ **Judgments and Decisions** ☑ **Summarize** **Genre: Social Studies Article,** 363 Intervention Program
• Curriculum Connections	Link **Works of Art,** 360	Link **Social Studies,** 362A
• Writing	**Writing Prompt:** Write a paragraph about the last picture you drew for a class assignment.	**Writing Prompt:** Imagine that you grew wings and were able to see the world from a bird's view. Write about what you saw as you flew over your town. **Journal Writing,** 365 Quick-Write
• Grammar	**Introduce the Concept: Irregular Verbs,** 369M Daily Language Activity 1. Yesterday, Mr. Fisher drawed a maze. drew 2. Last night we writed an article. wrote 3. The corn growed in a design. grew **Grammar Practice Book,** 89	**Teach the Concept: Irregular Verbs,** 369M Daily Language Activity 1. We flyed over the design. flew 2. He has maked many mazes. made 3. It has taked us an hour to finish. taken **Grammar Practice Book,** 90
• Spelling	**Pretest: Words from Art,** 369O **Spelling Practice Book,** 89, 90	**Explore the Pattern: Words from Art,** 369O **Spelling Practice Book,** 91

Intervention Program Available

Meeting Individual Needs

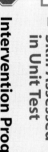

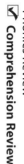

✓ = Skill Assessed in Unit Test

Intervention Program Available

Read EVERY DAY

DAY 3 — Read the Literature

Rereading for Fluency, 364

Story Questions and Activities, 366–367
Reteach, Practice, Extend, 105

Study Skill, 368
✓ **Graphic Aids**
Teaching Chart 87
Reteach, Practice, Extend, 106

Test Power, 369

Read the Leveled Books, 369A–369D
Guided Reading
Phonics Review
✓ **Comprehension Review**

Intervention Program

Activity: Art, 367

Writing Prompt: Write a paragraph about the last trip you took with your family.

Writing Process: Persuasive Writing, 369K
Prewrite, Draft

Review and Practice: Irregular Verbs, 369N
Daily Language Activity
1. My dad drived us to the maze. drove
2. We rided for three hours. rode
3. It had beginned to rain that day. begun

Grammar Practice Book, 91

Practice and Extend: Words from Art, 369P
Spelling Practice Book, 92

DAY 4 — Build and Review Skills

Read the Leveled Books and Self-Selected Books

✓ **Review Author's Purpose and Point of View,** 369E–369F
Teaching Chart 88
Reteach, Practice, Extend, 107
Language Support, 118

✓ **Review Context Clues,** 369G–369H
Teaching Chart 89
Reteach, Practice, Extend, 108
Language Support, 119

Intervention Program

Activity: Science, 367

Writing Prompt: Write a letter to Mr. Fisher asking what it was like to break the world's record with his largest maze.

Writing Process: Persuasive Writing, 369K
Revise

Meeting Individual Needs for Writing, 369L

Review and Practice: Irregular Verbs, 369N
Daily Language Activity
1. Yesterday, I swimmed in the lake. swam
2. Mr. Fisher has breaked the record for the largest mazes. broken
3. He telled us about his work. told

Grammar Practice Book, 92

Proofread and Write: Words from Art, 369P
Spelling Practice Book, 93

DAY 5 — Build and Review Skills

Read Self-Selected Books

✓ **Review Suffixes,** 369I–369J
Teaching Chart 90
Reteach, Practice, Extend, 109
Language Support, 120

Listening, Speaking, Viewing, Representing, 369L

Intervention Program

Writing Prompt: Write a paragraph about a tough problem that you recently solved. How did you find the right way?

Writing Process: Persuasive Writing 369K
Edit/Proofread, Publish

Assess and Reteach: Irregular Verbs, 369N
Daily Language Activity
1. Jill has drawed a maze for school. drawn
2. I have writed a plan for it. written
3. Yesterday we throwed a baseball around. threw

Grammar Practice Book, 93, 94

Assess and Reteach: Words from Art, 369P
Spelling Practice Book, 94

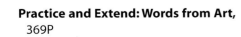

Link Language Arts

Read Aloud

The Needle in the Haystack

a fairy tale by John Hamma

Once in another time, there lived a King and Queen who had no children. The King worried about who would take his place when he grew too old to rule, so he asked his chief counselor what to do.

"Why not adopt a son, Your Majesty, and teach him the laws of the land?" his counselor suggested.

"But how will I find the right boy?" the King asked.

"Look for one who shows honesty, patience, and perseverance," the counselor told him. "It will be like looking for a needle in a haystack, but if you search wisely and well, you will find someone who is worthy."

"That's it!" the King exclaimed. "A needle in a haystack! Who would be more patient and persevering than a young man who could find a needle in a haystack? I will order my goldsmith to make a golden needle. Then I will hide it in one of the royal haystacks. The man who finds it will become Crown Prince. And to ensure honesty, I shall have the

Continued on pages T4–T5

Oral Comprehension

LISTENING AND SPEAKING Read the fairy tale aloud. Afterward, ask:

- Why did the King think the contest was a good way to choose the next king?
- Do you think the King made a good or a bad decision by choosing Franz as his heir? What makes you think so?

GENRE STUDY: FAIRY TALE Discuss some literary elements in this fairy tale. Explain: Characters in a fairy tale may be realistic or fantastical. The characters may have good or evil motives. Ask:

- Do you think the characters in this tale are basically realistic or fantastical? Why?
- What did Joseph try to do? What was the motive behind his actions?
- What did the King realize about Franz when he saw the second needle?

Activity Write the names King, Joseph I, Joseph II, and Franz, each on a different slip of paper. Then have each student choose a slip of paper and, in the role of the character he or she drew, name one decision the character made, the reasons for making it, and whether or not the decision was wise. ▶ **Logical/Linguistic**

Develop Visual Literacy

Stories in Art

Some pictures surprise us. Others keep us guessing. Some even make us wonder what is going on.

Look at the drawing. What can you tell about the people on the stairs? Are they all moving up or down on their own staircase? Will they ever get to where they are going? Explain your reason.

Imagine that you are the person sitting down near the staircases in the picture. Can you see everything from your seat? Are the people really moving up or down—or are they going nowhere? What would you tell them? Why?

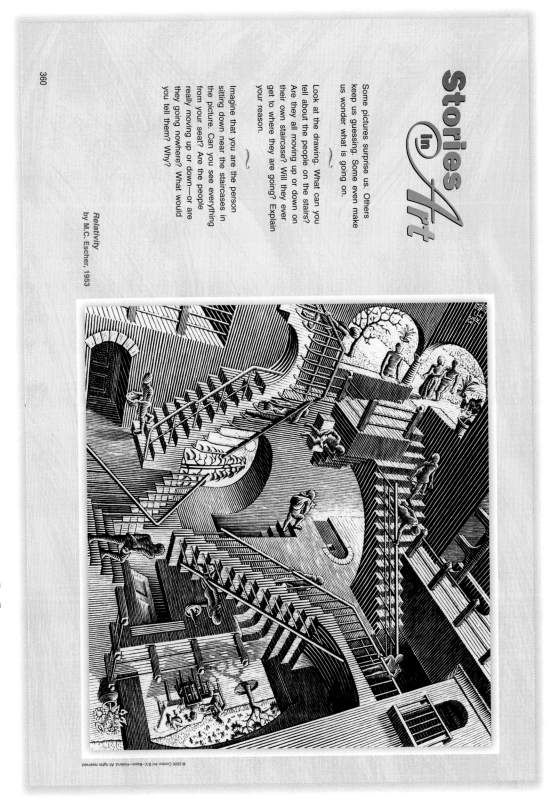

Relativity
by M.C. Escher, 1953

360

Objective: Make Judgments and Decisions

VIEWING In this complex lithograph, M.C. Escher plays with the viewer's sense of perspective and direction using only the simplest means of alternating black and white lines. Ask: "Do these lines create an up-and-down movement? How do they mirror the people on the stairs?" Have students describe specific details in the painting. Ask: "How would you judge the mood of the people shown? Is it happy, sad, confused, or calm? Do they seem aware of their surroundings?"

Read the page with students, encouraging individual interpretations of the etching.

Ask students to make judgments and decisions about the etching. For example:

- The space the figures are moving in has no real floor. This suggests that the figures are going nowhere.
- The seated figure seems to defy gravity.

REPRESENTING Invite students to write an art review of this etching. Have them consider the artist's technique and "message." Encourage them to include their thoughts about the drawing.

Review Judgments and Decisions

PREPARE

Discuss Judgments and Decisions Have students think of a movie they decided to go to and made a judgment about. Ask: What was the movie? How did you decide to go to that movie? What was your judgment of it?

TEACH

Define Judgments and Decisions Tell students: Making judgments and decisions means thinking about people, ideas, situations or issues and then choosing what to do. Skillful readers use what they have read and their own experience to make judgments. They also think about whether they agree with the author's views or a character's decisions.

The Best Career

The best career to have is that of a roller coaster designer. When you design roller coasters, you get to combine math and engineering with amusement park rides. Who wouldn't want to do that?

A roller coaster designer gets to spend a lot of time traveling to fun places. And best of all, he or she gets to ride the roller coasters for free!

I've decided to become a roller coaster designer when I grow up. I really like math and am good at it, and I love roller coasters.

Teaching Chart 85

Read the Article and Model the Skill Display **Teaching Chart 85.** Ask students to analyze the author's judgments and decision as they read.

MODEL The word *best* in the title tells me that the author is probably going to try to convince me of something. Let me think carefully about what he or she is saying. Is roller coaster designer really the best career? Not necessarily. I think the best career is whatever a person chooses, as long as it makes him or her happy.

TESTED OBJECTIVES

Students will identify and analyze judgments and decisions.

Skills Finder

Judgments and Decisions

Introduce	257A-B
Review	281E-F, 331G-H, 361A-B, 631G-H, 665A-B, 691E-F
Test	Unit 3, Unit 6

LANGUAGE SUPPORT

ESL Have students make and then walk through a maze of classroom desks. Explain that what they just made is a maze, and that they will now read an article about a person who designs and makes them. Have students turn to the article and discuss the photographs. Help students read all photo captions and discuss these before they read on.

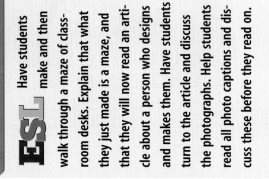

PRACTICE

Make and Explain Judgments and Decisions

ONE

Have students underline phrases that they could make judgments about and circle the decision the author has made.

Then, using a Judgments and Decisions chart like the one shown, have students decide whether a career as a roller coaster designer is a good occupation for the author. Have them explain their decision.

▶ **Linguistic/Intrapersonal**

JUDGMENTS	DECISIONS
A roller coaster designer needs to know math. A roller coaster designer gets to ride for free.	The author would like to be a roller coaster designer because the author likes math, is good at it, and loves roller coasters.

ASSESS/CLOSE

Make Judgments and Decisions

Ask students to think of a career that might be good for them. Have them make another Judgments and Decisions chart to explain and support their judgment.

ALTERNATE TEACHING STRATEGY

JUDGMENTS AND DECISIONS

For a different approach to teaching this skill, see page T60.

Intervention Skills

Intervention Guide, for direct instruction and extra practice with judgments and decisions

Meeting Individual Needs for Comprehension

EASY

Name______________ Date__________ Reteach 103

Make Judgments and Decisions

Making judgments and decisions is a natural part of storytelling and story reading. Characters must think about what they will do in difficult situations. Readers must think about what they might do in similar situations.

Read the story. Then write an answer to each question.

Mickey got off the bus. He stood still and stared straight ahead. He could see the building where the department store was. It was only about a half block away. This was the first time his dad had let him come downtown by himself to buy his own clothes. Now he almost wished his dad had come along. Mickey pictured the big store, the crowds, and the many choices he would have. Suddenly he didn't feel very well. He saw the bus that was headed back to his home, and he got a wild idea.

1. What decision does Mickey have to make? He has to decide whether to go to the department store or go back home.
2. Why did his dad decide to let him go downtown alone? He felt Mickey was old enough to travel alone and take responsibility.
3. Why does Mickey wish his dad had come along? There would be someone to help him feel less nervous about choosing his own clothes, and paying for them by himself.
4. If you were Mickey, what would you do? Even if I didn't want to go to the store, I would go anyway.

4 Book 4/Unit 3 Twisted Trails — **At Home:** Have students tell what they would say to Mickey if he had skipped his trip to the store. — 103

Reteach, 103

ON-LEVEL

Name______________ Date__________ Practice 103

Make Judgments and Decisions

Characters have reasons for the **judgments and decisions** they make. Think about this as you read the story below. Then answer each question.

The After-School Club was planning a Saturday trip to the Seaside Amusement Park. "We have to get the maximum amount of fun for our money," said Paulo. "We can each get a $21 ticket which gives us seven rides."

The club then decided to go on two rides together. They all went on the rollercoaster. Everyone likes the rollercoaster because it is scary. The club also chose to ride the free-fall parachute together.

"Wait a minute," said Lucia. "The rollercoaster and the parachute are our favorite rides. That means they will be the favorite rides of other kids, too. We'll spend most of the afternoon standing in line."

The others saw that Lucia was right. They decided to go on the rollercoaster first. Then they would try the parachute. After that, the group would break up in pairs and go on other rides that had shorter lines. Their good planning worked and everyone had a fun day at the amusement park.

1. Where did the After-School Club decide to go on Saturday? the Seaside Amusement Park
2. What type of ticket did they think was the best deal? the $21 dollar ticket
3. What rides did they decide would be good group rides? the rollercoaster and the parachute rides
4. Who showed good judgment in predicting a problem and what was that problem? Lucia because she predicted the lines for the rollercoaster and the parachute would be long because the rides were very popular.
5. What decision would you have made about rides if you were in the After-School Club? Answers will vary, but should reflect good judgment and the goal of getting the maximum enjoyment.

5 Book 4/Unit 3 Twisted Trails — **At Home:** Have students write about two decisions they have made and whether those decisions showed good judgment or not. — 103

Practice, 103

CHALLENGE

Name______________ Date__________ Extend 103

Make Judgments and Decisions

When you read a story, you make **judgments and decisions** about the story's characters.

Suppose you had to make a decision about how you would earn a living as an adult. What facts would you consider? Would you think about the kinds of jobs people in your town have? Would you think about the kind of training you would need? What opinions would you consider? Would you think about what you enjoy doing most or what others think you do best?

Write a paragraph stating your decision. Explain why you made that decision. Tell the facts and opinions you considered.

Answers will vary. Sentences should be written in the correct context and use the proper parts of speech.

Book 4/Unit 3 Twisted Trails — **At Home:** Talk with an adult family member about how he or she decided what to do to earn a living. — 103

Extend, 103

TESTED OBJECTIVES

Students will identify and analyze judgments and decisions.

Apply Judgments and Decisions

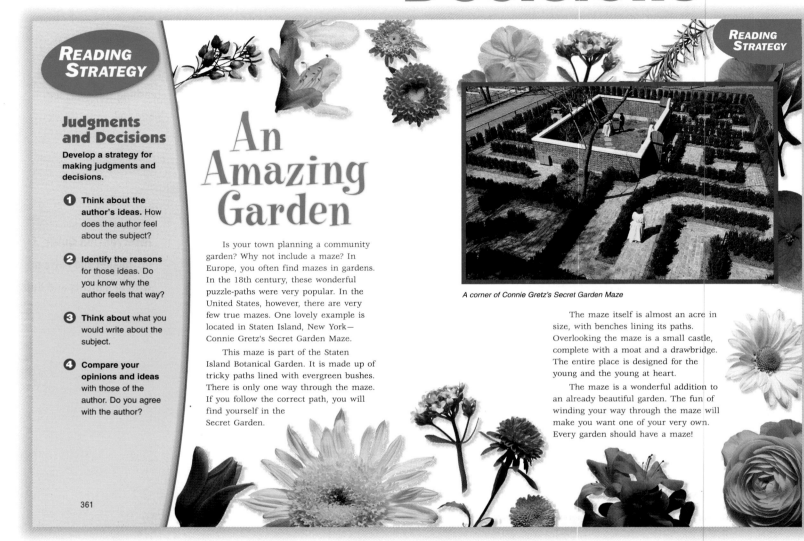

READING STRATEGY

Judgments and Decisions

Develop a strategy for making judgments and decisions.

1. **Think about the author's ideas.** How does the author feel about the subject?
2. **Identify the reasons** for those ideas. Do you know why the author feels that way?
3. **Think about** what you would write about the subject.
4. **Compare your opinions and ideas** with those of the author. Do you agree with the author?

361

An Amazing Garden

Is your town planning a community garden? Why not include a maze? In Europe, you often find mazes in gardens. In the 18th century, these wonderful puzzle-paths were very popular. In the United States, however, there are very few true mazes. One lovely example is located in Staten Island, New York—Connie Gretz's Secret Garden Maze.

This maze is part of the Staten Island Botanical Garden. It is made up of tricky paths lined with evergreen bushes. There is only one way through the maze. If you follow the correct path, you will find yourself in the Secret Garden.

A corner of Connie Gretz's Secret Garden Maze

The maze itself is almost an acre in size, with benches lining its paths. Overlooking the maze is a small castle, complete with a moat and a drawbridge. The entire place is designed for the young and the young at heart.

The maze is a wonderful addition to an already beautiful garden. The fun of winding your way through the maze will make you want one of your very own. Every garden should have a maze!

READING STRATEGY

PREVIEW Have students preview "An Amazing Garden." Explain that it is a nonfiction article about a garden on Staten Island. Ask: Based on the title, how would you say the author feels about the garden? (impressed)

SET PURPOSES Ask students to apply what they have learned about identifying and analyzing judgments and decisions as they read "An Amazing Garden."

APPLY THE STRATEGY Discuss the strategy for identifying and analyzing judgments and decisions in a selection. Help students apply the strategy to the passage.

- Determine what the author is trying to say about the topic.
- Think about why the author feels that way.
- Decide how you feel about the topic. Did you have an opinion about mazes before reading? Do you have one now?
- See if your opinions match those of the author.

Activity Have each student create a Judgments and Decisions chart for the passage.

Build Background

Link
cial Studies

Concept: Careers

Evaluate Prior Knowledge

CONCEPT: CAREERS A career is more than a job. It could be called a life's work. People often prepare for a career through study or gain hands-on experience by volunteering. Have students share their experiences with or knowledge of different careers.

COMPARE CAREERS Have students compare and contrast the career of a maze designer to that of a homebuilder. Help them create a Venn diagram.

▶ **Logical/Visual**

MAZE BUILDER Different	Alike	HOMEBUILDER Different
builds mazes	uses construction materials	builds homes
builds places for people to play in	makes and uses plans	builds places for people to live in
may or may not charge for admission	uses gardening for landscaping	sells home to owner

Graphic Organizer 14

DESCRIBE A CAREER Have partners describe a career they both might like to have and write a list of at least five reasons why.

WRITING PARTNERS

Develop Oral Language

DISCUSS CAREERS Write the names of the careers on the board and add some of the facts the students mention under each one.

Next, brainstorm with students additional information about each career. You might ask them where a person with this career might work, what they would do on a typical day, and how hard or easy they think the job is. Write these notes in the appropriate place on the board.

Then ask groups to choose a career and discuss it among themselves. Have them choose a leader to tell the class what they talked about and whether any of them would consider choosing that career as their life's work.

TEACHING TIP

MANAGEMENT You may need to provide information about maze-building for the Compare Careers task. After you explain it, pair students to complete Venn diagrams together. Maintain the pairings for Describe a Career. Urge partners to take turns focusing on each topic in the Venn diagram.

Wait until all pairs have completed both activities before setting up groups for the Develop Oral Language activity.

LANGUAGE SUPPORT

See the **Language Support Book**, pages 113–116, for teaching suggestions for Build Background.

TESTED **OBJECTIVES**

Students will use context clues to determine the meanings of vocabulary words.

Definitions

challenge (p. 365) something calling for effort and the use of one's talents

entertaining (p. 364) interesting; amusing

mazes (p. 363) confusing series of pathways or passageways

combine (p. 363) to join together

requires (p. 363) has a need of

contained (p. 363) included as a part of

Story Words

These words from the selection may be unfamiliar. Before students read, have them check the meanings and pronunciations of the words in the Glossary, beginning on page 756, or in a dictionary.

- cornfield, p. 363
- pathways, p. 363
- roadblocks, p. 364

challenge
entertaining
mazes
combine
requires
contained

Vocabulary

Teach Vocabulary in Context

Identify Vocabulary Words Display **Teaching Chart 86** and read it with students. Have volunteers circle each vocabulary word and underline words that are clues to its meaning.

Jamie's Career Plans

1. Jamie enjoys a tough challenge. **2.** She is entertaining to others because she enjoys jokes and riddles. **3.** Jamie plans to design some difficult, twisting, turning mazes for people to walk through. **4.** Her idea is to combine each maze together with an obstacle course. **5.** Jamie's idea requires lots of thinking, and experimenting will also be necessary. **6.** Could a maze work if it contained an obstacle course, or was that too much to include?

Teaching Chart 86

Discuss Meanings Ask questions like these to help clarify word meanings.

- What can you do easily? What is a challenge for you to do?
- What is the most entertaining television show you watch?
- Do you like walking in mazes?
- What happens when you combine blue and yellow paint?
- Which requires more of your time, homework or household chores?
- What kind of information is contained in a math textbook?

Activities

Practice

Demonstrate Word Meaning (GROUP)

Have groups choose a vocabulary card. Ask each group to make up a "rap" that uses the word they chose and perform it for the class.
▶ **Auditory/Linguistic**

Word Building Manipulative Cards

Write Context Sentences (WRITING)

Challenge students to use all vocabulary words in three or fewer sentences. Students can read their sentences aloud and compare word combinations.
▶ **Linguistic/Oral**

Assess Vocabulary

Use Words in Context (GROUP)

Have groups create a card for each vocabulary word. In addition, tell groups to make cards with the beginning and ends of sentences, so that the vocabulary cards fit in the middle. Then have groups exchange cards, match the sentence beginnings and endings, and insert the correct vocabulary cards to make complete sentences.

SPELLING/VOCABULARY CONNECTIONS

See Spelling Challenge Words, pages 369O–369P.

LANGUAGE SUPPORT

See the **Language Support Book**, pages 113–116, for teaching suggestions for Vocabulary.

Vocabulary PuzzleMaker

Provides vocabulary activities.

Meeting Individual Needs for Vocabulary

EASY

Name________ Date________ Reteach 104

Vocabulary

Use the correct word from the list.

challenge contained combine entertaining mazes requires

1. The ___mazes___ were like life-size puzzles.
2. It is a real ___challenge___ to try to find your way through a maze.
3. To find your way through a maze, you need to ___combine___ a sense of direction and a good memory.
4. Finding your way through a maze also ___requires___ paying attention to details.
5. My favorite maze ___contained___ many twisting paths.
6. It is ___entertaining___ to walk through a maze.

/6

Story Comprehension Reteach 105

Write an answer to each question about "Twisted Trails."

1. Who is Adrian Fisher? Adrian Fisher is a man who designs walk-through mazes for a living.
2. What kinds of skills does he need to design mazes? He needs science skills and artistic skills.
3. Why do people like corn mazes? Corn mazes are outdoors in the air and sunshine.
4. In what state is there a museum that has shown Fisher's mazes? Florida

104–105 At Home: Have students tell about the article "Twisted Trails." Book 4/Unit 3 Twisted Trails /4

Reteach, 104

ON-LEVEL

Name________ Date________ Practice 104

Vocabulary

Fill in the correct vocabulary word on each line. Then answer each question, using the vocabulary word in your response. Answers will vary.

combine challenge contained mazes entertaining requires

1. Why is it a ___challenge___ to play a new sport?
It is a challenge because you have never played it before, and it may take a lot of practice to learn to play well.
2. What would you do if a new sport ___contained___ more rules than any you had ever played? If a sport contained a lot of rules, you could ask a lot of questions to try to understand it.
3. If you could ___combine___ your two favorite activities in one day, what would you put together? I might combine swimming and camping.
4. What is the most ___entertaining___ thing you do on Saturday?
The most entertaining thing I do is to play with my best friend.
5. Why are ___mazes___ sometimes scary?
Mazes are sometimes scary because you may get lost in them.
6. Playing a sport well ___requires___ what from athletes?
Being a good athlete requires lots of discipline and practice.

104 At Home: Have students write a new sentence for each vocabulary word. Book 4/Unit 3 Twisted Trails /6

Practice, 104

ON-LEVEL

First Mazes

My sister and I are experts at going through *mazes*. Being good at mazes *requires* a lot of practice. We started out *entertaining* ourselves by completing the mazes that we found in magazines. Then when we were a little older, our parents gave us the *challenge* of going through a real maze in a botanical garden. This garden was in a big place where they grow different kinds of plants and trees. The maze *contained* paths, little bridges, flowers, and bushes cut into animal shapes. What made the maze really entertaining was that it would *combine* two challenges. The first one was to keep from getting wet. If you stepped in certain spots along the path, water would shoot up at you from the ground. The second challenge was to find your way out of the maze. When we returned home, my mother put up a sign on the refrigerator: James and Camilla Win the Maze Challenge!

1. Where did James and Camilla first discover mazes? They discovered mazes in magazines.
2. Why do James and Camilla like mazes? Mazes are entertaining.
3. How many challenges did the ground maze combine? two
4. Being good at mazes requires what? a lot of practice
5. What do you think should be contained in a maze to make it challenging?
Answers will vary, but might include lots of turns and twists, hidden traps, or statues.

/5 Book 4/Unit 3 Twisted Trails At Home: Have students draw a cartoon with character speech bubbles using as many vocabulary words as they can. 104a

Practice, 104a
Take-Home Story

CHALLENGE

Name________ Date________ Extend 104

Vocabulary

challenge entertaining contained mazes combine requires

Suppose a walk-through maze has been built in your town. Use as many vocabulary words as you can to write a commercial advertising the maze. Then present your commercial to your class. Use a separate sheet of paper if you need more space.

Story Comprehension Extend 105

"Twisted Trails" describes two mazes Adrian Fisher built in the shape of objects—a car and a submarine. He chose objects that would be of particular interest to the people living near the mazes.

Write a letter to Fisher suggesting a shape of maze he should create for your community. Tell him what you would like him to include in the maze based on what you know about his other mazes.
Answers will vary.

104–105 At Home: Find out what the mascot is for a local sports team. Think about why that mascot may have been chosen and whether it was a good choice. Book 4/Unit 3 Twisted Trails

Extend, 104

Comprehension

Prereading Strategies

PREVIEW AND PREDICT Have students preview the article, reading the title and looking at the photographs and captions for clues regarding the article's contents.

- What are the "twisted trails" referred to in the title?
- What or whom do you think this article might be about?
- What do you want to find out about the mazes?
- What is your reaction to mazes? Do you find them interesting? Confusing?
- How can you tell this is a nonfiction selection? (The article is about a real person. There are photographs of the mazes he has made.) ***Genre***

Have students record their predictions about what or whom the story is about.

SET PURPOSES Why are students reading this article? For example:

- Why might the author have written this article?
- Who made those mazes?

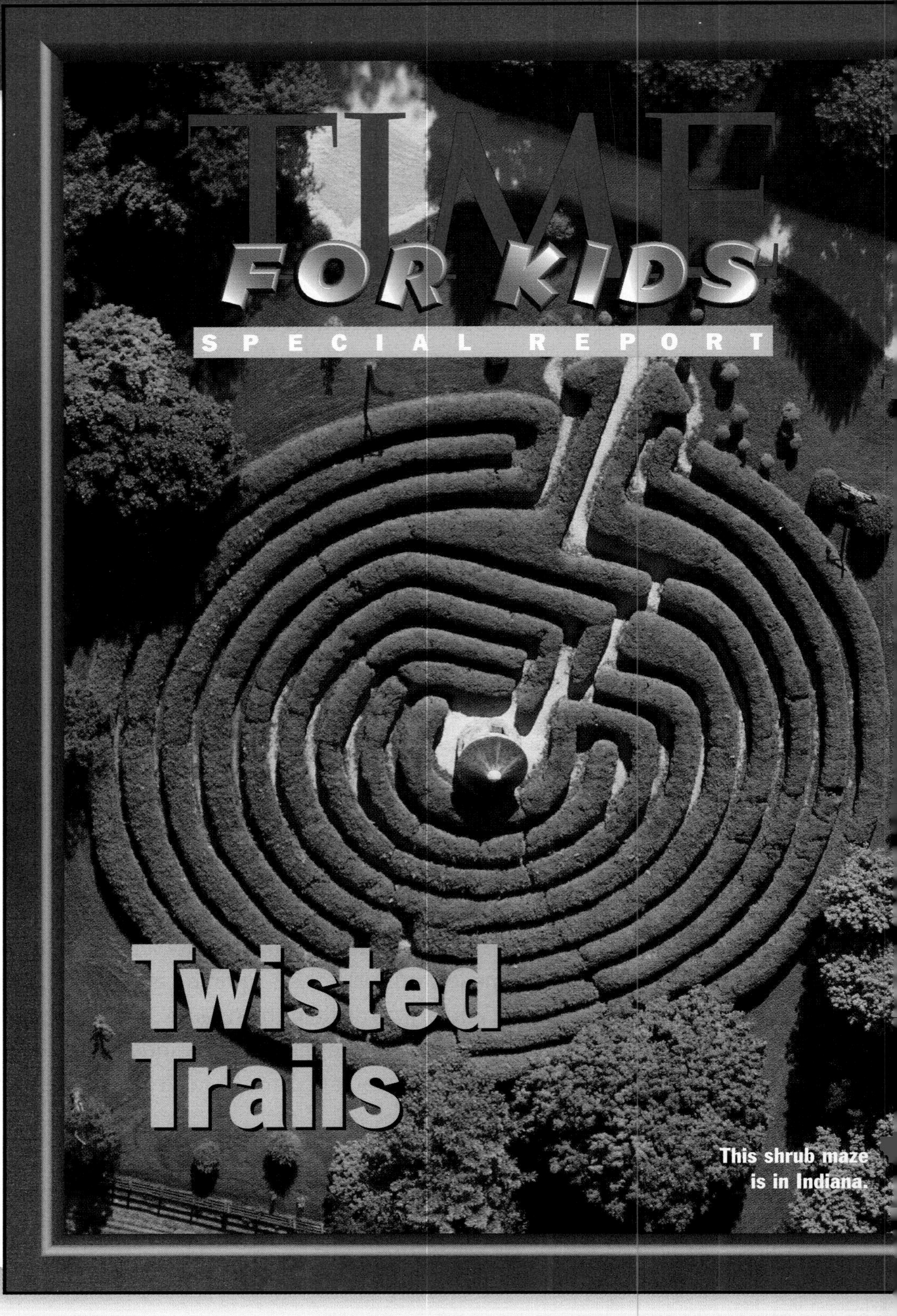

This shrub maze is in Indiana.

Meeting Individual Needs • Grouping Suggestions for Strategic Reading

EASY

Read Together Read the article with students or have them read along with the **Listening Library.** Have students use the Judgments and Decisions chart to record their thoughts about Adrian Fisher's career. Comprehension and Intervention prompts offer additional help with vocabulary and comprehension.

ON-LEVEL

Guided Instruction Have students read the article together first, or if you choose, have them read independently. Use the Comprehension questions to aid students. Have students use the Judgments and Decisions chart to record meaningful information while reading.

CHALLENGE

Read Independently Have students read the article independently. Remind them that a good reader makes judgments and decisions about what he or she reads. Have students create a Judgments and Decisions chart as on page 361B.

Meet a Maker of Mazes

From start to finish, no one knows mazes like Adrian Fisher

Adrian Fisher is A-MAZE-ING! Mr. Fisher, who lives in England, designs mazes for a living. He makes walk-through mazes that people must solve by finding a clear path from entrance to exit.

A good maze requires careful planning and a real understanding of math. Adrian Fisher's job requires him to be part scientist and part artist. "I studied math in school, and I always loved gardening," he says. "Building mazes is a way to combine these two loves." (1)

In 1996, Fisher broke a record by making the largest maze up to that time. This Michigan corn maze was in the shape of a car. It contained more than three miles of pathways between rows of corn plants. At least 2,000 people could try to find their way through it at once. (2)

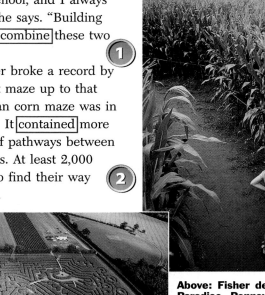

Above: Fisher designed this Paradise, Pennsylvania, cornfield maze. Left: An outdoor maze in England.

363

Comprehension

Apply Judgments and Decisions

Apply Summarize

STRATEGIC READING Before we begin, let's create a chart to help us make judgments and decisions about the main idea in this article: the career of Adrian Fisher, maze designer.

(1) **JUDGMENTS AND DECISIONS** Do you think designing mazes would be fun? Why or why not? (Sample answer: Yes. It would be fun because I would get to garden in a creative way.)

(2) **SUMMARIZE** How could you summarize in one sentence what Adrian Fisher does for a living? (He designs mazes for people to walk through.)

LANGUAGE SUPPORT

A blackline master of the Judgments and Decisions chart is available in the **Language Support Book.**

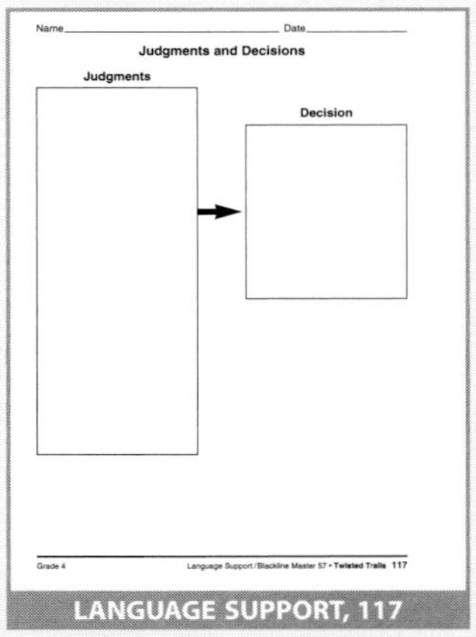
Name________ Date________

Judgments and Decisions

Judgments

Decision

Grade 4 Language Support/Blackline Master 57 • Twisted Trails 117

LANGUAGE SUPPORT, 117

Genre

Social Studies Article

Explain that a social studies article in or from a magazine:

- reports on events, discoveries, or new ideas.
- often includes sidebars or other features designed to increase reader interest.
- may include additional facts in features such as maps, photographs, captions, diagrams, and charts.

Activity After students read *Twisted Trails*, have them design mazes of their own. Discuss whether or not the student-drawn mazes could be turned into walk-through mazes like Mr. Fisher's.

Comprehension

3 Do you think the suggestions presented in Path Finder on page 365 can be used when completing mazes on paper? Why or why not? (Sample answer: Yes. Mazes on paper are probably designed in the same way as walk-through ones.) ***Draw Conclusions***

4 **JUDGMENTS AND DECISIONS** Discuss Adrian Fisher's decision to become a maze designer. Do you think this was a good decision? Use the Judgments and Decisions chart to help you organize information about this decision.

JUDGMENTS	DECISION
A maze designer needs to know math. A maze designer needs to be artistic. A maze designer needs to enjoy watching people.	Adrian Fisher decided to design mazes for a living.

ORGANIZE INFORMATION Ask volunteers to describe at least two mazes designed by Adrian Fisher. Then have partners write one or two sentences to summarize the article. Have them focus on the career of Adrian Fisher. ***Summarize***

You'd have to swim to get through this maze at the Getty Museum in California.

"People like corn mazes," Fisher told *TIME FOR KIDS.* "They're entertaining, out in the sunshine and open air." He has been building mazes for more than 20 years, and has built more than 135 of them so far. His specialty is setting up tricky roadblocks, including fountains, mirrors, and even tanks of live crocodiles!

One of Fisher's favorites is a Beatles maze in England. The maze includes a 51-foot-long yellow submarine. The submarine honors one of the many songs the famous English singing group made popular. Fisher has also made some colorful mazes for school playgrounds.

ADULTS SOMETIMES ACT LIKE KIDS

Mr. Fisher takes pleasure in watching people walk through his mazes. "Eleven- and 12-year-old children are often better than their parents" at making their way through mazes, Fisher

364

REREADING FOR *Fluency*

PARTNERS Have students choose a favorite paragraph to read and reread to a partner. With each additional reading, encourage students to strive for natural speech.

READING RATE When you evaluate reading rate, have the student read aloud from the story for one minute. Place a stick-on note after the last word read. Count words read.

To evaluate students' performance, see the Running Record in the **Fluency Assessment** book.

Intervention For leveled fluency lessons, passages, and norm charts, see **Skills Intervention Guide**, Part 4, Fluency.

says. "I especially like to watch adults go through them. They get lost right away, and it forces them to act like children for half an hour."

Do grown-ups take a professional puzzlemaker seriously? You bet. A museum in Florida has shown Fisher's mazes in a special show. That makes sense to Fisher. "Maze design is very much like art," says the maze master. "There's a story behind each one."

This maze in England keeps kids and adults busy.

FIND OUT MORE
Visit our website:
www.mhschool.com/reading

*inter*NET CONNECTION

Path Finder

How can you get through a life-size maze if you can't see your way to the end? In many older mazes, just follow the left-hand rule: When you've entered a maze and you come to a fork, always follow the left wall. If the fork is a dead end, turn around. The wall on your left will lead you back to the correct path. Sooner or later, you'll find your way through the maze.

Remember: A good maze-maker like Mr. Fisher knows the rule, too. And he can always find a way to break it. But after all, a maze with no challenge is no fun!

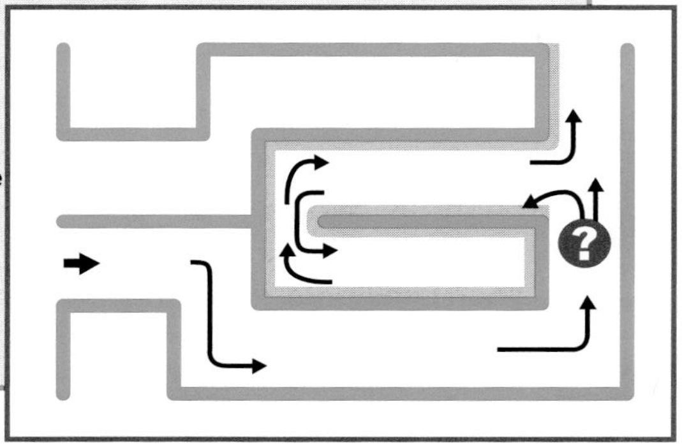

3

4

Based on an article in *TIME FOR KIDS.*

365

Comprehension

Return to Predictions and Purposes

Review with students their predictions about the article and reasons for reading it. Were their predictions correct? Did they learn what they wanted to know about maze designing?

INFORMAL ASSESSMENT

JUDGMENTS AND DECISIONS

HOW TO ASSESS

- Have students make judgments about the quality of Fisher's work.
- Have students decide if they think maze designing is a difficult job and give reasons for their decisions.

Students should be able to make judgments and decisions about Adrian Fisher's career based on the text.

FOLLOW UP If students have trouble making judgments about the quality of Fisher's work, have them revisit the photos to decide if the mazes look challenging, interesting, and fun to walk through. If students have trouble deciding if maze designing is a difficult job, have them list, in order, the steps they think it takes to create a life-size maze.

LITERARY RESPONSE

QUICK-WRITE Invite students to imagine going through one of Fisher's mazes. Have them record what they might be feeling as they go.

JOURNAL

ORAL RESPONSE Have students share their journal responses with partners to compare and contrast thoughts and ideas.

*inter*NET CONNECTION For more information or activities on life-size mazes, students can visit ***www.mhschool.com/reading***

Have students research to find out the approximate time it takes to complete a life-size maze.

Story Questions

Have students discuss or write answers to the questions on page 366.

Answers:

1. designs mazes *Literal/Details*
2. Maze design combines two things he loves—math and gardening. *Inferential/Judgments and Decisions*
3. their size and complexity, their landscaping and design *Inferential/Judgment and Decisions*
4. the career of Adrian Fisher, a maze designer *Critical/Summarize*
5. Sample answer: No. Mazes show a path with an entrance and an exit, but in the picture none of the paths connect. *Critical/Reading Across Texts*

Write a Letter For a full writing process lesson, see pages 369K–369L.

Story Questions & Activities

1. What does Adrian Fisher do for a living?
2. Why did Adrian Fisher decide to become a maze-maker?
3. What makes Adrian Fisher's mazes so interesting?
4. What is the main idea of this selection?
5. Imagine that you had a chance to show Adrian Fisher the picture on page 360. Do you think he could use it for one of his mazes? Why or why not?

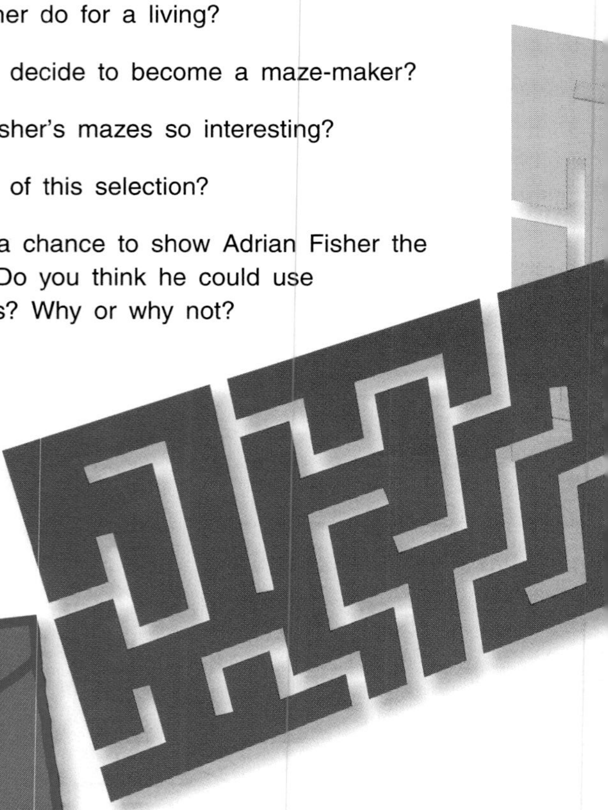

Write a Letter

Adrian Fisher likes to watch adults go through his mazes. The mazes make them "act like children," he says. Write a letter to an adult in your family. Persuade him or her to go with you to see one of Adrian Fisher's mazes. Give three good reasons why this grown-up should go.

Meeting Individual Needs

EASY

Name________ Date________ Reteach 104

Vocabulary

Use the correct word from the list.

challenge contained combine entertaining mazes requires

1. The mazes were like life-size puzzles.
2. It is a real challenge to try to find your way through a maze.
3. To find your way through a maze, you need to combine a sense of direction and a good memory.
4. Finding your way through a maze also requires paying attention to details.
5. My favorite maze contained many twisting paths.
6. It is entertaining to walk through a maze.

6

Reteach 105

Story Comprehension

Write an answer to each question about "Twisted Trails."

1. Who is Adrian Fisher? Adrian Fisher is a man who designs walk-through mazes for a living.
2. What kinds of skills does he need to design mazes? He needs science skills and artistic skills.
3. Why do people like corn mazes? Corn mazes are outdoors in the air and sunshine.
4. In what state is there a museum that has shown Fisher's mazes? Florida

At Home: Have students tell about the article "Twisted Trails."

104–105 Book 4/Unit 3 Twisted Trails 4

Reteach, 105

ON-LEVEL

Name________ Date________ Practice 105

Story Comprehension

Read the statements below. Write **True** if the statement describes "Twisted Trails." Write **False** if it does not. For the answers that are false, rewrite the sentence to make it a true statement.

1. Adrian Fisher lives in America.
   False. Adrian Fisher lives in England.
2. Designing mazes is Adrian Fisher's hobby and not his job.
   False. Fisher has made a career of maze design.
3. Fisher says he is part scientist and part artist.
   True
4. Being good at math helps in building mazes.
   True
5. Fisher has used live crocodiles in his mazes.
   True
6. Children are better at going through mazes than adults.
   True
7. If you keep getting lost in a maze, one good rule is to always turn right.
   False. The rule is to always turn left.
8. Building outdoor mazes is rather easy work.
   False. Building mazes takes a lot of skill, planning, and math.

At Home: Have students write a paragraph describing an area where Fisher might build a small maze in their town.

105 Book 4/Unit 3 Twisted Trails 8

Practice, 105

CHALLENGE

Name________ Date________ Extend 104

Vocabulary

challenge contained combine entertaining mazes requires

Suppose a walk-through maze has been built in your town. Use as many vocabulary words as you can to write a commercial advertising the maze. Then present your commercial to your class. Use a separate sheet of paper if you need more space.

Extend 105

Story Comprehension

"Twisted Trails" describes two mazes Adrian Fisher built in the shape of objects—a car and a submarine. He chose objects that would be of particular interest to the people living near the mazes.

Write a letter to Fisher suggesting a shape of maze he should create for your community. Tell him what you would like him to include in the maze based on what you know about his other mazes.

Answers will vary.

At Home: Find out what the mascot is for a local sports team. Think about why that mascot may have been chosen and whether it was a good choice.

104–105 Book 4/Unit 3 Twisted Trails

Extend, 105

Design a Maze

Adrian Fisher designs mazes for a living. Now it's your turn to design a maze. First, decide on the overall shape. Then draw the paths inside the maze. Remember to include roadblocks and dead ends. When you have finished, test your maze to make sure it can be solved in the way you had planned. Now see if a classmate can get through your maze.

Make a List

Do you remember reading about Adrian Fisher's corn maze? What happens when you make a *maze* of *maize*? Brainstorm with a partner to create a list of words that sound alike but have a different spelling and meaning. These words are called *homophones*. Use your list to write a silly sentence for each of your homophone pairs.

Find Out More

Adrian Fisher isn't the only person who designs mazes. One famous maze is in Colonial Williamsburg, in Virginia. Look for information about other famous mazes on the Internet or in activity books. Compare the mazes you learn about with the ones designed by Adrian Fisher.

367

Activity

SCIENCE: MAKING A SOIL PROFILE Explain that good soil is essential for any plant to grow. Have students research three different layers of soil: **topsoil, subsoil**, and **weathered rock**. Ask students to draw a soil profile that labels and describes each layer.

What to Look For Check to see that students have drawn and accurately labeled the three layers of soil.

CHALLENGE

Story Activities

Design a Maze

ONE Have students brainstorm interesting elements that could be included in their maze as well as ways to make it more difficult to get through. Invite each student to share how he or she might make improvements to the original design after a classmate tries to get through the maze.

Make a List

PARTNERS Have pairs read their sentences aloud and compare them to see which homophones were used by more than one group. Remind students that homophones may sound alike, but are often spelled differently. Write examples on the chalkboard, such as *see/sea* and *here/hear*.

Find Out More

RESEARCH AND INQUIRY Suggest books on mazes or reference source entries as research alternatives. If students cannot locate suitable information on life-size mazes, direct them to books of pen and paper mazes. Then ask students to record their comparisons by making two "pros and cons" charts—one for Adrian Fisher's mazes and one for the other mazes they learned about.

interNET CONNECTION For more information on mazes, have students go to ***www.mhschool.com/reading***

FORMAL ASSESSMENT

After page 369, see the Selection Assessment and Unit Assessment.

Study Skills

GRAPHIC AIDS

TESTED **OBJECTIVES** Students will:

- identify information on a diagram.
- use a diagram to answer questions.

PREPARE Read the passage with students. Display **Teaching Chart 87.**

TEACH Point out markings, pathways, and other labeled elements. Have a volunteer find the entrance and show the direction in which the "maze walker" would start.

PRACTICE Have students answer questions 1–5. Review the answers as a group. **1.** in the lower left corner **2.** along Path 1 where path 2 meets it **3.** a lake **4.** the statue **5.** two.

ASSESS/CLOSE Have each student write a list of three questions that can be answered by consulting the diagram of the maze. Have students read aloud their questions as the rest of the students try to answer them.

STUDY SKILLS

Read a Diagram

Did you know that a maze is a kind of diagram? A **diagram** is a plan or a drawing that shows the parts of a thing or how the parts go together. Look at this diagram. It shows a walk-through maze, seen from above. Notice how the maze is laid out. Then walk through the maze with your pencil.

Use the maze to answer these questions.

1. In which corner do you enter the maze?
2. Where is the first fork you would come to in the maze?
3. What blocks you at the end of Path 3?
4. What is the last obstacle you might come across?
5. How many different routes can you take to walk through this maze?

Meeting Individual Needs

EASY

Name_______ Date_______ Reteach 106

Read a Diagram

A **diagram** is a plan or a drawing. One kind of diagram shows the arrangement of things in a place.

Library / Floor 1

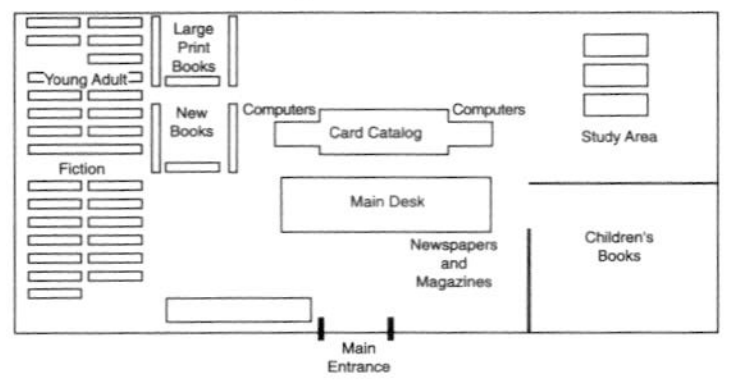

One place to find out more about mazes is in the library. Use the diagram of the library to answer the questions.

1. Where is the card catalog located? center of the floor
2. In the diagram, what is to the right of the newspapers and magazines? children's books
3. What is just in front of the card catalog? main desk
4. What is just behind the children's books? study area

4 Book 4/Unit 3 Twisted Trails — **At Home:** Have students draw a diagram of their classroom or school cafeteria. 106

Reteach, 106

ON-LEVEL

Name_______ Date_______ Practice 106

Read a Diagram

A **diagram** can be a picture of how something works or how something is made. A diagram can also be something like a map. It can show you paths to get from one place to another. One kind of diagram is a maze. Use a pencil to complete the following maze from start to finish. Remember what Adrian Fisher said: If you don't know where to go, keep turning left.

10 Book 4/Unit 3 Twisted Trails — **At Home:** Have students draw a diagram of their school. 106

Practice, 106

CHALLENGE

Name_______ Date_______ Extend 106

Read a Diagram

Suppose you are visiting a maze and have been given an old **diagram** of the maze to help you find your way. Write a story about what happened as you try to follow the diagram. Include an illustration of the diagram.

Answers will vary.

Book 4/Unit 3 Twisted Trails — **At Home:** Draw a diagram of a maze and have a family member trace his or her path through the maze with a pencil. 106

Extend, 106

TEST POWER

Test Tip

Read all answer choices for each question.

DIRECTIONS

Read the sample story. Then read each question about the story.

SAMPLE

Roger's Late Night

Today my mother dropped me off at soccer practice at the junior high school practice fields. As I was running off she said, "Your father will pick you up after practice, Roger."

By the end of practice, I was really tired. I waited for what seemed like hours, when my father pulled up, got out of the car and ran over to me. He could see that I was scared, so he gave me a big hug and apologized over and over again for being late. He had gone to the high school because he thought that my practice was there today.

We talked about it on the way home, and I said, "Dad, sometimes things just don't go the way we plan them."

1 The reader can tell from the story that when Roger was waiting, he was—

A happy

B lazy

(C) worried

D angry

2 Which of these happened last in the story?

F Roger was really tired.

(G) Roger and his father talked.

H Roger's father gave him a hug.

J Roger's mother dropped him off at soccer practice.

Test Power

THE PRINCETON REVIEW

Read the Page

Have students read the story. As a group, discuss what clues you can use to determine how Roger was feeling.

Discuss the Questions

Question 1: This question requires students to understand the feelings of a character. As you work through each of the answers, ask, "Do you think Roger was *happy*? Was he *lazy*? *worried*? *angry*?"

Question 2: This question asks students to arrange information sequentially and to determine which event happened *last* in the story. Explain that *all* of the answer choices will contain events that happened in this story. Have students look back at the story to find the choice that happened *last*. Students should eliminate choices that occurred earlier in the story.

Self-Selected Reading
Leveled Books

EASY

UNIT SKILLS REVIEW

Phonics

☑ **Comprehension**

Help students self-select an Easy Book to read and apply phonics and comprehension skills.

Guided Reading

PREVIEW AND PREDICT Discuss the book's illustrations with students. Then have them predict what the story will be about. Chart their ideas.

SET PURPOSES Have students record in their journals why they want to read the book. Have them share their purposes.

READ THE BOOK Use questions like the following to guide students' reading or to reinforce reading strategies after they have read the story independently.

- What are the main events of the story? *Summarize*
- Why do you think the author wrote this story? *Author's Purpose, Point of View*
- Do you agree with the decisions the main characters made in the story? Why or why not? *Judgments and Decisions*
- Find a sentence in the story that states an opinion. How do you know that this is an opinion? *Fact and Opinion*
- Look back through the story. Can you find any examples of words containing digraphs? *Phonics and Decoding*

RETURN TO PREDICTIONS AND PURPOSES Review students' predictions and purposes for reading. Were their predictions accurate? Did they find out what they wanted to know?

LITERARY RESPONSE Have students discuss questions like the following:

- Would you like to learn more about the people, places, or subjects in the story? What would you like to know?
- Do you think this story would make a good movie? Why or why not?
- How do you feel about what happens in the story?

Intervention **Skills**

Intervention Guide, for direct instruction and extra practice in vocabulary and comprehension

Phonics

- /oi/ and /ou/
- /ů/ and /yů/
- digraphs

☑ Comprehension

- make judgments and decisions
- fact and opinion
- author's purpose, point of view

Answers to Story Questions

Answers will vary and should include examples and details from the stories students have read.

EASY

Story Questions for Selected Reading

1. Who are the main characters in the story?
2. What judgment or decision did a character have to make that affected the ending to the story?
3. What parts of the story are facts?
4. What was the story mainly about?
5. Have you ever read a story similar to this one? How was it similar?

Draw a Picture

Draw a picture of one scene from the book.

Self-Selected Reading Leveled Books

INDEPENDENT

UNIT SKILLS REVIEW

Comprehension

Help students self-select an Independent Book to read and apply comprehension skills.

Guided Reading

PREVIEW AND PREDICT Discuss the illustrations in the beginning of the book and have students predict what the story will be about. Have them record their predictions in their journals. Ask students who are reading chapter books to use the headings to help them with their predictions.

SET PURPOSES Have students write a few questions about what they hope to learn by reading their selected book. Have them share their questions.

READ THE BOOK Use questions like the following to reinforce reading strategies after students have read the story independently.

- Where and when does this story take place? *Story Elements*
- What decisions mainly affected the outcome of the story? *Judgments and Decisions*
- What are the main ideas in the story? *Summarize*
- What point of view does the author have about the story's subject? *Author's Purpose, Point of View*
- What is an important fact in the story? *Fact and Opinion*

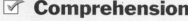

RETURN TO PREDICTIONS AND PURPOSES Have students review their predictions and questions. Encourage students to talk about whether their predictions were accurate, and whether they have any questions the story left unanswered. For students reading books with chapter headings, have them explain how the headings were useful.

LITERARY RESPONSE The following questions will help focus students' responses:

- What are the best and worst parts of this story?
- What did you learn from the story?
- What would you add to the story to make it better?

Comprehension

- **judgments and decisions**
- **fact and opinion**
- **author's purpose, point of view**

Answers to Story Questions

Answers will vary and should include examples and details from the stories students have read.

INDEPENDENT

Story Questions for Selected Reading

1. How does this story begin?
2. What do you think the author's purpose for the story is?
3. What are some of the facts in the story that teach something new?
4. Can you name the main events from beginning to end?
5. Think about other stories you have read recently. Is this story more or less interesting? Why?

Make a Chart

Make a chart outlining some of the most important facts in the book you read.

Self-Selected Reading
Leveled Books

CHALLENGE

UNIT SKILLS REVIEW

Comprehension

Help students self-select a Challenge Book to read and apply comprehension skills.

Guided Reading

PREVIEW AND PREDICT Discuss the illustrations in the beginning of the book. Have students predict what the story will be about. Ask them to record their predictions in their journals. If the book has chapter headings, ask students to use the headings to make their predictions.

SET PURPOSES Have students write why they want to read their selected book. Have them share their purposes.

READ THE BOOK Use questions like the following to reinforce reading strategies after students have read the story independently.

- Choose one decision the main character made in the story. Would you have made the same decision? Why or why not? ***Judgments and Decisions***
- What parts of the story are facts? How do you know? ***Fact and Opinion***
- Why do you think the author chose to tell this story? ***Author's Purpose, Point of View***
- If you were telling a friend about this book, what parts would you be sure to include? ***Summarize***

RETURN TO PREDICTIONS AND PURPOSES Have students review their predictions and purposes for reading. Encourage them to talk about the accuracy of their predictions and whether their purposes were met. For books with chapter headings, were the headings useful? How?

LITERARY RESPONSE Have students discuss questions like the following:

- Do you admire the main character in the story? Why or why not?
- What new information did you learn that you did not know before?
- If you could meet the author of this book, what would you like to ask her or him?

Comprehension

- judgments and decisions
- fact and opinion
- author's purpose, point of view

Answers to Story Questions

Answers will vary and should include examples and details from the stories students have read.

CHALLENGE

Story Questions for Selected Reading

1. Where does this story take place?
2. Is this story based on facts or opinions? Explain your answer.
3. What decisions do the characters face through the course of the story?
4. What was this story mainly about?
5. Have you read a book about this topic before? How does it compare to this story?

Write an Interview

Write an interview for yourself and the main character of the story.

Activities

Bringing Groups Together

Anthology and Leveled Books

Connecting Texts

CLASS DISCUSSION Have students discuss connections among the stories. For example, write these story titles horizontally across the top of a chart: *George Washington and the American Revolution; Bad Day, Glad Day; Aboard the Underground Railroad;* and *Nonsense, Mr. Lear!* Label the chart *Facts About Subject.* Talk with students about the story they read, and ask them to contribute facts from their reading. Write the facts under each book heading. When the chart is complete, ask students to explain why each statement is a fact.

Facts About Subject

George Washington and the American Revolution	Bad Day, Glad Day	Aboard the Underground Railroad	Nonsense, Mr. Lear!
• Washington was a leader of the Continental Army. • Washington defeated the Hessians at Trenton, New Jersey.	• Haiku and limericks are types of poetry. • Clay filled with air bubbles will explode when fired.	• Slaves that ran away on the Underground Railroad were known as "passengers." • Frederick Douglass was a famous abolitionist.	• Edward Lear suffered from epilepsy. • Mr. Lear drew Lord Stanley's collection of rare animals.

Viewing/Representing

CREATE SENTENCE STRIPS Organize students into groups, according to the book titles they have read. Ask each group to write several facts and opinions from the story they read on separate sentence strips. Have groups display their strips.

DISCUSSION Give students time to study the sentence strips. Encourage them to discuss which are facts and which are opinions. Group the strips on the board accordingly. Clarify and correct any errors.

Research and Inquiry

CHOOSE A TOPIC Have students choose a topic to research. Encourage them to choose a topic that relates to several of the books, such as women in history, children's art, poets, or the town of Freedom, Indiana. Then have them:

- list a few questions about their topics.
- think about ways to find information: encyclopedia, library books, magazines, organizations, or the Internet.
- make notes as they gather information.
- create a class encyclopedia with their findings.

interNET CONNECTION For links to Web pages on topics such as women in history, children's art, poets, or the town of Freedom, Indiana, have students log on to ***www.mhschool.com/reading***

Review Author's Purpose, Point of View

TESTED OBJECTIVES

Students will review an author's purpose and point of view.

Skills Finder
Author's Purpose, Point of View

Introduce	299A-B
Review	331E-F, 369E-F
Test	Unit 3

TEACHING TIP

AUTHOR'S PURPOSE
Present some clear examples of author's purposes and some types of writing geared to achieve those purposes.

- To persuade: advertisements, editorials, letters to the editor
- To inform: directions, research reports
- To entertain: stories, cartoons
- To describe: letters, journal entries

SELF-SELECTED Reading

Students may choose from the following titles.

ANTHOLOGY
- Twisted Trails

LEVELED BOOKS
- All titles for the unit

Bibliography, pages T78–T79

PREPARE

Discuss Author's Purpose and Point of View

Review: An author writes for one or more purposes, such as to inform, to entertain, to describe, or to persuade. The author's point of view reflects his or her opinions and ideas about the topic. Sometimes, as in an informative piece, that view may be indirectly conveyed. Ask students what they think the author's purpose was in writing *Twisted Trails* and how they know.

TEACH

Read the Passage and Model the Skill

Ask students to listen carefully to determine the author's purpose and point of view as you read **Teaching Chart 88.**

The Hall of Mirrors

The Riley County Fair opened this week with a variety of attractions. Among the most clever was The Hall of Mirrors, an outdoor maze in which fair-goers try to find their way from entrance to exit.

The maze consists of walls of individual mirrors, each angled in a different direction to fool travelers into going the wrong way. When asked how he liked the popular maze, one excited visitor commented, "It was hilarious. I can't tell you how many times I ran into a mirror!"

The fascinating Hall of Mirrors will be open until August 17, from 5:00 P.M. until 11:00 P.M.

Teaching Chart 88

Discuss clues in the passage that help readers determine purpose and point of view.

MODEL I can tell the author's purpose was to inform because the passage answers the questions *who?*, *what?*, *where?*, *when?*, and *how?* However, the author also conveys his or her point of view by focusing on the maze attraction and including a visitor's positive reaction.

PRACTICE

Determine Author's Purpose and Point of View

GROUP

Have students underline clues in "The Hall of Mirrors" that help them determine that the author's purpose was to inform. Ask students to circle words that show the author's point of view is favorable toward the maze attraction.

Ask groups to discuss how the passage might change if its purpose were solely to entertain. (Sample answer: The passage might be written in a humorous way.) ▶ **Linguistic**

ASSESS/CLOSE

Change Author's Purpose and Point of View

GROUP

Have groups rewrite "The Hall of Mirrors" so that its purpose is to persuade and it is written with the point of view that mazes are dangerous.

ALTERNATE TEACHING STRATEGY

AUTHOR'S PURPOSE, POINT OF VIEW

For a different approach to teaching this skill, see page T66.

Intervention Skills

Intervention Guide, for direct instruction and extra practice in author's purpose and point of view

Meeting Individual Needs for Comprehension

EASY

Name________ Date________ Reteach 107

Author's Purpose and Point of View

Authors often let readers know how they feel about a subject through the characters and situations they choose to write about. They express their **point of view** through their stories.

Read the story. Then answer the questions.

Some neighbors say that the prairie can be seen on Sara's face. Some admire her strength. Others feel sorry for her. In winter, Sara is pale, almost gray. She looks tired and cold like the snowy flat land around her. In summer, Sara is sunburned and seems always to be thirsty. No amount of water can take away the dryness of her hair or skin. To look at Sara is to know what life on the prairie is like.

1. What does the author use the character Sara to really talk about? What a prairie is like, and life on the prairie
2. Does the author think the prairie is an easy place to live? Tell how you know? It is a difficult place to live. The author's description of Sara shows the prairie has cold, gray times and hot, dry times.
3. Do you think the author has ever lived on the prairie? Why? Yes. The author describes it in detail.
4. Do you think the author admires Sara or feels sorry for her? Why? Possible answer: The author admires Sara for being able to live in the harsh environment, and feels sorry for the roughness of prairie life.

107 At Home: Have students reread a favorite story to see if they can tell how the author feels about a subject. Book 4/Unit 3 Twisted Trails 4

Reteach, 107

ON-LEVEL

Name________ Date________ Practice 107

Author's Purpose and Point of View

When an author writes an article, he or she may have more than one **purpose**. The purpose might be to entertain, inform, describe, or persuade. As we read the article, we also come to know what the author thinks. That is the author's **point of view**.

Think about the author's purpose and point of view in "Twisted Trails." Then answer each question below. **Answers will vary.**

What are three things about the article that entertained you?

1. Learning about the many different kinds of mazes.
2. Reading about mazes that are really unusual.
3. You never know what Adrian Fisher will use to make a maze.

What are three things you learned from reading this selection?

4. It is possible to have a maze that has three miles of pathways.
5. Being good at math helps in designing or going through mazes.
6. Some children are better than adults at mazes.
7. What is the author's point of view about having a job building mazes? It is interesting and provides fun for many people.
8. Do you agree with the author that building mazes is an interesting and exciting job? Or do you think it's a silly job? Explain your answer. Answers will vary.

107 At Home: Have students write a letter to the author saying whether he or she agrees or disagrees with the author's point of view. Book 4/Unit 3 Twisted Trails 8

Practice, 107

CHALLENGE

Name________ Date________ Extend 107

Author's Purpose and Point of View

An author may write a selection to persuade a reader, or to affect how the reader thinks about something. Author's may also write to describe, to inform, and to entertain the reader.

The author's main purpose in writing "Twisted Trails" is to inform the reader about Adrian Fisher and his mazes. Briefly describe a selection the author could have written about Adrian Fisher and mazes if the purpose had been to persuade, to describe, or to entertain.

1. If the purpose had been to persuade, the author could have written . . . Answers will vary. Possible answer: A selection explaining why Adrian Fisher has the most interesting job possible.
2. If the purpose had been to describe, the author could have written . . . Answers will vary. Possible answer: Detailed descriptions of some of Adrian Fisher's mazes.
3. If the purpose had been to entertain, the author could have written . . . Answers will vary. Possible answer: A story about someone lost in one of Adrian Fisher's mazes.

Suppose you were a writer assigned to do interviews with people as they exit one of Adrian Fisher's mazes. State what your point of view would be and list 2 questions you would ask in your interviews.

107 At Home: Choose an event that you or your family has been involved in recently. Plan four ways to tell about it: to inform, to persuade, to describe, and to entertain. Book 4/Unit 3 Twisted Trails

Extend, 107

LANGUAGE SUPPORT

Name________ Date________

How You Look At It

1. Write a sentence to answer the question. 2. Use one of the words shown on the right of the page in your answer.

Why do people build mazes? to entertain to teach

Answers may vary. Possible answer: People build mazes to entertain others.

The builders also like the challenge of making mazes.

118 Twisted Trails • Language Support/Blackline Master 58 Grade 4

Language Support, 118

Review Context Clues

TESTED OBJECTIVES

Students will use context clues to determine the meaning of unfamiliar words.

Skills Finder	
Context Clues	
Introduce	157I-J
Review	215I-J, 251I-J, 331I-J, 359I-J, 369G-H, 515I-J
Test	Units 2, 3, 5, 6
Maintain	309, 389, 523, 643, 703

TEACHING TIP

WORD WEBS Have students create word and picture webs for unfamiliar words. Ask students to write the unfamiliar word in a circle in the center of a sheet of paper. Show them how to add spokes to create a web. Then encourage them to look at the words and sentences that surround the unfamiliar word and fill in the web with any clues they find. They can fill in the web with words or pictures.

PREPARE

Discuss Use of Context Clues to Make Meaning

Review: If a reader comes across an unfamiliar word, he or she can study the words or sentences around the unknown word to help determine its meaning.

TEACH

Read the Passage and Model the Skill

Display and read the passage on **Teaching Chart 89.**

Ancient Mazes

Ancient mazes are sometimes called labyrinths. Labyrinths were designed so a person would have trouble finding the way out.

One famous labyrinth was a temple built by the Egyptian king Amenemhet II. It contained more than 3,000 different spaces. Another notable ancient maze may be only a well-known myth. The traditional story goes that Daedalus, a Greek craftsman, built a labyrinth as a prison for the Minotaur, a half-bull, half-human monster.

Teaching Chart 89

Point out the word *labyrinth* and model the skill of using context clues to determine the meanings of unfamiliar words. Underline the phrase that gives clues.

MODEL When I get to this word, *labyrinth*, and I don't know it, I can read the sentence before it, the sentence after it, and the words around it to help figure out what it means. From reading the first sentence, I can tell that *labyrinth* is a noun, or thing. From the third sentence in the second paragraph, I can tell a labyrinth must be another name for the word *maze*.

PRACTICE

Identify Context Clues to Determine Meaning

ONE

Have volunteers underline context clues and share how they would use them to determine the meaning of the words *notable* and *myth*. Remind them to consider how the word is used in the sentence.

▶ **Linguistic/Logical**

ASSESS/CLOSE

Use Context Clues to Determine Meaning

GROUP

Write the following sentence on the chalkboard and have students read it silently. Ask groups to determine what they think the underlined word means and how they came to that determination.

▶ **Linguistic/Logical**

The word *labyrinth* is sometimes used to describe maze-like patterns on the floors of medieval churches of the 12th through 16th centuries.

ALTERNATE TEACHING STRATEGY

CONTEXT CLUES

For a different approach to teaching this skill, see page T65.

Intervention Skills

Intervention Guide, for direct instruction and extra practice with context clues

Meeting Individual Needs for Comprehension

EASY

Name______________ Date________ **Reteach 108**

Context Clues

Good readers use **context clues** to help them figure out unfamiliar words.

Read the paragraph. Circle the letter giving the meaning of each of the words listed below. Then tell what clues in the paragraph helped you.

In the construction business there are lots of people who need to work together. Putting up big buildings is a complicated job. The architect draws the plans for the building. Architects need to consult with engineers who are the experts on how to build. Lawyers have to deal with legal matters. Someone has to set up the schedule to make sure things get done at the right time.

1. complicated
   a. simple to do (b.) hard to do
   Clues: Putting up big buildings
2. consult
   a. disagree with (b.) talk together about
   Clues: Architects need engineers who are the experts about how to build.
3. legal
   a. relating to money (b.) relating to the law
   Clues: lawyers have to deal with
4. schedule
   (a.) time plan b. list of workers
   Clues: to make sure things get done at the right time

Book 4/Unit 3 Twisted Trails — **At Home:** Have students use the numbered words in sentences of their own. — 108

Reteach, 108

ON-LEVEL

Name______________ Date________ **Practice 108**

Context Clues

Sometimes when you read, there will be words you don't know. You may be able to figure out what the word means by using the other words in the sentence. These words are called **context clues**.

Use context clues to choose a word from the list to complete each sentence.

maze	fountain	professional	fretted
combine	reflected	entertaining	twisted

1. A series of pathways is called a ___maze___.
2. Something that is not straight is ___twisted___.
3. A play, a movie, or a good game can be very ___entertaining___.
4. A person with a job that requires special education is a ___professional___.
5. A name for a place that spouts water is a ___fountain___.
6. The players worried and ___fretted___ until the game was over and they had won.
7. The moon was ___reflected___ in the pond.
8. When you put two things together, you ___combine___ them.

Book 4/Unit 3 Twisted Trails — **At Home:** Have students write a story using five words from the list above and context clues. — 108

Practice, 108

CHALLENGE

Name______________ Date________ **Extend 108**

Context Clues

Sometimes you can use **context clues**, words or phrases in the same or nearby sentences, to help you figure out the meaning of words. Write the group of words or sentence from "Twisted Trails" containing context clues that would help a reader figure out the meaning of each of these words.

designs	maze	pathways	pleasure	forces	professional

1. Answers will vary but should be written in the correct context and with correct parts of speech.
2. ______
3. ______
4. ______
5. ______
6. ______

Book 4/Unit 3 Twisted Trails — **At Home:** Write a sentence for a word containing context clues that could be used to teach the meaning of the word to a family member. — 108

Extend, 108

LANGUAGE SUPPORT

Name______________ Date________

Be Amazed!

1. Follow the path from Start to Finish. 2. Collect the letters at each dead-end, where you have to back up. 3. Write each dead-end letter in a box. 4. Unscramble the letters to make a word. 5. Write the word at the finish line.

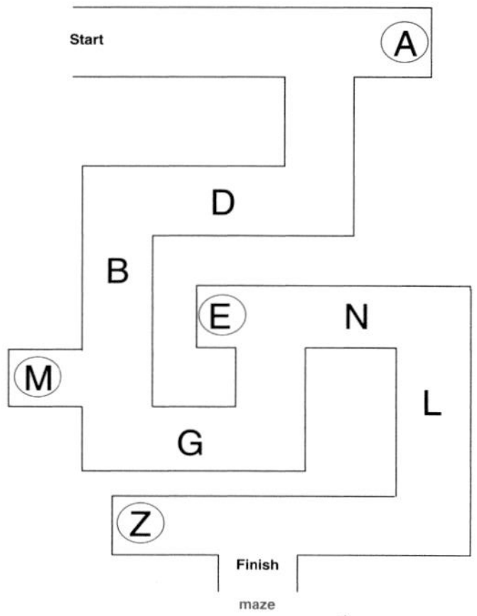

Grade 4 — Language Support/Blackline Master 59 • Twisted Trails 119

Language Support, 119

Review Suffixes

TESTED OBJECTIVES

Students will recognize how the suffixes *-ful* and *-ous* change word meaning.

Skills Finder

Suffixes	
Introduce	281I-J
Review	297I-J, 369I-J
Test	Unit 3
Maintain	433, 457, 553, 681

TEACHING TIP

SUFFIXES

- The letters *-ous* at the end of a word are not always a suffix. A word that ends in *ous* could be a word derived from the French language, such as *rendezvous.*
- Sometimes letters at the end of base words are dropped before adding *-ful* or *-ous*, such as when *awe* becomes *awful* or when *fame* becomes *famous.*

PREPARE

Discuss Meaning of the Suffixes *-ful* and *-ous*

Review: A suffix is a word part added to the end of a base word. Suffixes have their own meanings. The suffix *-ful* usually means "full of." The suffix *-ous* usually means "having" or "full of." When a suffix is added to a word, the meaning of the word changes. Sometimes, its part of speech also changes.

TEACH

Read the Passage and Model the Skill

Display and read **Teaching Chart 90.**

Be Careful!

It's important to be careful when you go through a famous walk-through maze. You need to be watchful—what looks like a passage may be a dangerous trick turn or dead end.

You need to be mindful of the way you came so you don't feel worried when you have to turn around. When you finally reach the end, you are sure to feel gleeful and joyous.

Teaching Chart 90

Model how to apply the knowledge of a suffix to determine a word's meaning using the word *careful.*

MODEL The word *careful* in the first sentence ends in *-ful.* The base word is *care.* If *-ful* means "full of," then *careful* means "full of care." I'll read this sentence again and see if that meaning makes sense.

Use Suffix to Determine Meaning

Have students define *famous* in the first sentence using the meaning of the suffix *-ous* ("having" or "full of"). Ask them whether that meaning makes sense in the sentence.

PRACTICE

Identify Words with Suffixes and Discuss Meaning

GROUP

Have volunteers underline each word that ends with the suffix *-ful* or *-ous* in "Be Careful!" Then have them circle the suffixes. Have students discuss the meanings of the words.

▶ **Linguistic/Interpersonal**

ASSESS/CLOSE

Use Words with Suffixes

PARTNERS

Have students write each of the words listed below. Then have them add the suffix *-ful* or *-ous* to each word. Ask them to work with partners to write poems using all the words. They may want to draw pictures to go with their poems.

joy **play** **prosper** **fame**

ALTERNATE TEACHING STRATEGY

SUFFIXES

For a different approach to teaching this skill, see page T63.

Intervention **Skills**

Intervention Guide, for direct instruction and extra practice with suffixes

Meeting Individual Needs for Vocabulary

EASY

Name_______________ Date_______ **Reteach 109**

Suffixes

Knowing the meaning a **suffix** adds to a word can help you read and understand unfamiliar words. The suffixes *-ful* and *ous* add the meaning "full of" or "having" to words.

Read the list of words with suffixes. Think about the meaning of each word. Then write a word to complete each sentence.

hazardous	restful	famous	pitiful
careful	healthful	disastrous	thoughtful

1. Fast food does not make a healthful meal.
2. We spent a restful afternoon lying on the beach.
3. The student looked thoughtful when questioned by his teacher.
4. Some bug sprays are hazardous to the environment.
5. The famous movie star signed my autograph book.
6. The shipwreck was a disastrous accident.
7. The sick parrot gave a pitiful cry.
8. It's important to be careful when you light the candles.

At Home: Have students explain the spelling changes needed to form famous, disastrous, and pitiful.

109 Book 4/Unit 3 Twisted Trails 8

Reteach, 109

ON-LEVEL

Name_______________ Date_______ **Practice 109**

Suffixes

A **suffix** is a group of letters added to the end of a base, or root, word. The suffix changes the meaning of the word slightly or changes the way it is used in a sentence. Choose a word to complete each sentence. Then circle the words with the suffixes.

care	careful	wonder	wonderful	famous
dangerous	colorful	fame	color	danger

1. The boy took care so that he would not bump into the baby.
2. The boy was careful when he held his baby brother.
3. The dog always barks when something is wrong and there is danger.
4. The father asks his children to stay away from dangerous places.
5. The students painted every color they could find on the scenery.
6. The students' costumes were bright and colorful.
7. One thing professional basketball players have is fame.
8. Kids who want to grow up to be baseball players often want to be famous.
9. The fireworks filled the little children with wonder.
10. The children called the fireworks wonderful.

At Home: Have students write sentences using pairs of words, one with a suffix, one without.

109 Book 4/Unit 3 Twisted Trails 10

Practice, 109

CHALLENGE

Name_______________ Date_______ **Extend 109**

Suffixes

The **suffixes** *-ful* and *-ous* mean "full of." Add the suffix *-ful* or *-ous* to each base word to create a related adjective. Remember that the base word's spelling may change when adding a suffix.

fame	famous	watch	watchful
care	careful	caution	cautious
color	colorful	wonder	wonderful
envy	envious	courtesy	courteous

Write an adventure story. Using as many of the adjectives above as possible.

Answers will vary but should make correct use of the words and use the correct parts of speech.

At Home: Identify words with suffixes in a newspaper or magazine article for a family member.

109 Book 4/Unit 3 Twisted Trails

Extend, 109

LANGUAGE SUPPORT

Name_______________ Date_______

Maze Mania

1. Read each word at the beginning of each maze. 2. Follow the maze. 3. Write the correct word you find at the end.

1. care
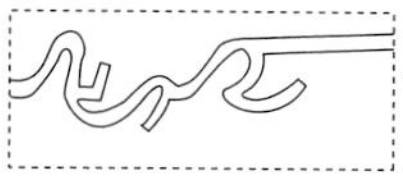
+ful
+ous
careful

2. fame

–e +ous
– +ful
famous

3. color
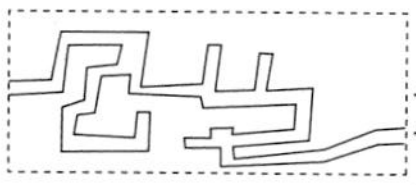
+ous
+ful
colorful

120 Twisted Trails • Language Support/Blackline Master 00 Grade 4

Language Support, 120

Persuasive Writing

Prewrite

WRITE A LETTER Present the following writing assignment: Adrian Fisher likes to watch adults go through his mazes. The mazes make them "act like children," he says. Write a letter to an adult in your family. Persuade him or her to go with you to see one of Adrian Fisher's mazes. Give three good reasons why this grown-up should go.

EXPLORE REASONS Have students brainstorm reasons why an adult should visit a maze. They will need to anticipate the concerns or questions the adult may have and address those in the letter.

Strategy: Outline Ideas Have students complete an outline that includes some of the following information:

- a clear opinion
- details of the maze
- reasons why the maze is worth visiting
- possible concerns and their solutions

Draft

USE THE OUTLINE In their letters, students should clearly state the action they want the addressee to take. Students should present reasons for the maze visit, along with responses to two or three key objections. The letters should include a heading with the writer's address and date, a greeting, and a closing signature.

Revise

SELF-QUESTIONING Ask students to assess their drafts.

- Did I give strong reasons?
- Have I answered questions this adult might have and provided details?
- What would make my letter more persuasive?

PARTNERS Have students trade letters with a peer to get another point of view.

Edit/Proofread

CHECK FOR ERRORS AND DETAILS Students should reread their letters for spelling, grammar, letter format, and punctuation. Have them revise once more for word use and elaboration.

Publish

SHARE THE LETTERS Students can take home their letters and ask a family member to read and respond. Encourage students to ask the recipients what was most convincing about their letters.

Claire Johnson
Anytown, USA
January 8, 20–

Dear Mom,

Remember you said you wanted to do something different for vacation this year? Well, I have an idea. Let's visit one of Adrian Fisher's mazes!

Mr. Fisher designs huge mazes that we can walk through. He says he designs them because he likes to see how much fun people have with them.

We could work together to figure out the maze. You are taller, so you could see further over the top. I could help figure out which way to go.

It may seem expensive to visit one of Mr. Fisher's mazes, but he has designed so many that one is sure to be nearby.

Please consider this, Mom. It would be a trip we would both remember for a long time.

Your daughter,
Claire

GRAMMAR/SPELLING CONNECTIONS

See the 5-Day Grammar and Usage Plan on irregular verbs, pages 369M–369N.

See the 5-Day Spelling Plan on words from art, pages 369O–369P.

TEACHING TIP

Technology Show students how to move across the page for typing headings, dates, and closings by using the tab key instead of the space bar. It's faster and lines items up evenly.

Formal Formats Make sure students can identify and name the five parts of a letter: heading, greeting, body, closing, and signature. Demonstrate the proper format for addressing an envelope. Then have students practice this format on their own.

Handwriting CD-ROM

Presentation Ideas

ADD A MAZE Have students design their own maze creations. Create a display of maze illustrations and letters.
▶ **Viewing/Representing**

READ ALOUD Have students listen carefully as classmates read their letters aloud. Ask listeners if they can repeat the persuasions used in each letter. ▶ **Speaking/Listening**

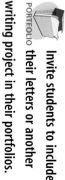

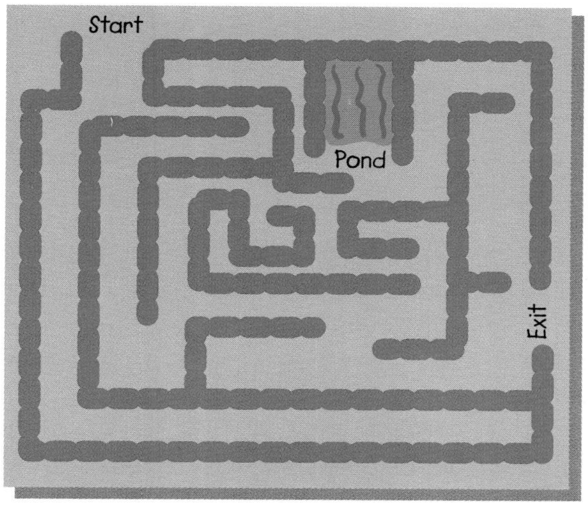

Consider students' creative efforts, possibly adding a plus (+) for originality, wit, and imagination.

Scoring Rubric

Excellent	Good	Fair	Unsatisfactory
4: The writer • clearly presents a vacation plan. • provides supporting reasons and examples. • presents potential concerns and answers them appropriately.	**3:** The writer • presents a vacation plan. • adequately organizes supporting details. • addresses potential concerns.	**2:** The writer • does not elaborate on ideas. • presents few supporting details • presents no potential concerns or presents them with unsatisfactory answers.	**1:** The writer • does not clearly present an opinion. • provides incomplete or unclear details. • presents no potential concerns.

Incomplete 0: The writer leaves the page blank or fails to respond to the writing task. The student does not address the topic or simply paraphrases the prompt. The response is illegible or incoherent.

For a 6-point or an 8-point scale, see pages T107–T108.

Meeting Individual Needs for Writing

EASY

Poster Have students think of an unusual type of maze that they will design and promote to the public. It can be created out of uncommon materials or be in an unexpected location. Students should illustrate their poster and use catchy titles to interest viewers in the maze.

ON-LEVEL

Newspaper Article Tell students to suppose a new Adrian Fisher maze is opening in their town. Have them write an article about it for the local newspaper. Remind students to use the 5 *Ws—who, what, where, when,* and *why.*

CHALLENGE

Interview Have students prepare for an interview with Adrian Fisher about his mazes. Tell them to write questions they think classmates might have. Then, using the selection article and their imaginations, have students write responses Mr. Fisher might make.

Viewing and Speaking

VIEWING STRATEGIES

After students have illustrated their letters, have them:

- **look for the main idea of the illustration.**
- **look for details supporting that main idea.**

SPEAKING STRATEGIES

As students read their letters aloud, have them:

- **speak loud enough for everyone to hear.**
- **share what they liked about each other's letters.**

LANGUAGE SUPPORT

ESL **Review the key elements in the format of a letter including the address at the top, the date, the salutation, the body, and the closing. Invite second-language learners to review their drafts with English-fluent students.**

PORTFOLIO **Invite students to include their letters or another writing project in their portfolios.**

5 Day Grammar and Usage Plan

LANGUAGE SUPPORT

ESL **To help English learners, write the following on cards: *eat*, *fly*, *write*, *throw*, and *swim*. As students act out each verb, have others take turns making up present tense and past tense sentences using that verb.**

DAILY LANGUAGE ACTIVITIES

Write the Daily Language Activities on the chalkboard each day or use **Transparency 15.** Have students correct the sentences orally. For answers, see the transparency.

Day 1

1. Yesterday Mr. Fisher drawed a maze.
2. Last night, we writed an article.
3. The corn growed in a design.

Day 2

1. We flyed over the design.
2. He has maked many mazes.
3. It has taked us an hour to finish.

Day 3

1. My dad drived us to the maze.
2. We rided for three hours.
3. It had beginned to rain that day.

Day 4

1. Yesterday, I swimmed in the lake.
2. Mr. Fisher has breaked the record for the largest mazes.
3. He telled us about his work.

Day 5

1. Jill has drawed a maze for school.
2. I have writed a plan for it.
3. Yesterday we throwed a baseball around.

Daily Language Transparency 15

DAY 1 Introduce the Concept

Oral Warm-Up Read this sentence aloud: *We ate our lunch.* Ask students to tell what *we* did. Did it happen now or in the past? *Ate* is past tense for what verb?

Introduce Irregular Verbs Some verbs take special forms when they tell about an action that has already happened.

Irregular Verbs

- An **irregular verb** is a verb that does not add *-ed* to form the past tense.

Present the Daily Language Activity. Then begin a two-column chart listing the *present* and *past tense* of the following verbs: *eat/ate*, *grow/grew*, *write/wrote*, *draw/drew*, *make/made*, *take/took*, *fly/flew*. Save the chart to continue on Day 2.

WRITING Assign the daily Writing Prompt on page 360C.

Name________ Date________ LEARN **Grammar 89**

Irregular Verbs

- An **irregular verb** is a verb that does not add *-ed* to form the past tense.

Write the correct past-tense form of the underlined verb on the line provided.

1. Adrian Fisher begin __began__ to make mazes more than 20 years ago.
2. Fisher make __made__ a huge maze in 1996.
3. This maze break __broke__ the record for the largest maze.
4. About 2,000 people find __found__ their way through it in one day.
5. Adults as well as children come __came__ to try the maze.
6. Children go __went__ through the maze faster than their parents.
7. Fisher do __did__ a special maze to honor a Beatles song.
8. A plane fly __flew__ over Adrian Fisher's mazes.
9. An artist draw __drew__ pictures of the mazes.
10. The drawings show what the pilot see __saw__.

10 Grade 4/Unit 3 **Twisted Trails**

Extension: Have students work with partners to find examples of irregular past-tense verbs in newspaper articles. Ask students to make and share a list of the verbs they find.

89

GRAMMAR PRACTICE BOOK, PAGE 89

DAY 2 Teach the Concept

Review Irregular Verbs Ask students to choose a past-tense verb from the chart and use it in a sentence.

More About Irregular Verbs Display and discuss:

Irregular Verbs with Helping Verbs

- Some irregular verbs have special spellings when used with the helping verb *have*, *has*, or *had*.

Present the Daily Language Activity. Then add a third column labeled *Past with Have, Has, or Had* to the chart begun on Day 1. List the past participle form of each verb: *eaten*, *grown*, *written*, *drawn*, *made*, *taken*, *flown*.

WRITING Assign the daily Writing Prompt on page 360C.

Name________ Date________ LEARN AND PRACTICE **Grammar 90**

Irregular Verbs

- Some irregular verbs have special spellings when used with the helping verb *have, has, or had.*

Read each sentence and the verb choices in parentheses. Underline the verb choice that correctly completes the sentence.

1. Adrian Fisher has (built, builded) more than 135 mazes.
2. He has (did, done) mazes in England and the United States.
3. Fisher had (make, made) the maze in Michigan in the shape of a car.
4. The cornstalks in his corn maze have (grew, grown) high.
5. He had (lay, laid) out the Beatles maze in the shape of a submarine.
6. This maze master has (put, putted) roadblocks in his mazes.
7. Sometimes there have (were, been) live crocodiles in his mazes, too.
8. Thousands of people have (seen, saw) Fisher's mazes.
9. He has (taken, took) a lot of care with his designs.
10. People have (begun, began) to take maze design seriously.

90

Extension: Ask students to rewrite the above sentences using past-tense verbs without using *have, has, or had.*

Grade 4/Unit 3 **Twisted Trails** 10

GRAMMAR PRACTICE BOOK, PAGE 90

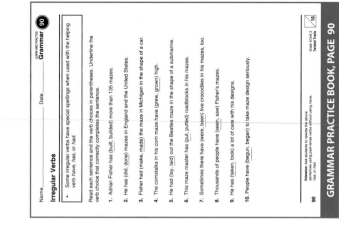

Irregular Verbs

DAY 3 Review and Practice

Learn from the Literature Review irregular verbs. Read the first sentence in the third paragraph on page 363 of *Twisted Trails*:

> **In 1996, Fisher broke a record by making the largest maze up to that time.**

Ask students to identify the past-tense verb. (broke) Have them state the present tense (break) and the past participle (broken) for this verb.

Form Irregular Verbs Present the Daily Language Activity and have students correct the sentences orally.

Ask students to review *Twisted Trails*, looking for verbs that have irregular past tense forms. Add these verbs to the correct column of the chart. (Examples: *know, build, find, keep*)

WRITING Assign the daily Writing Prompt on page 360D.

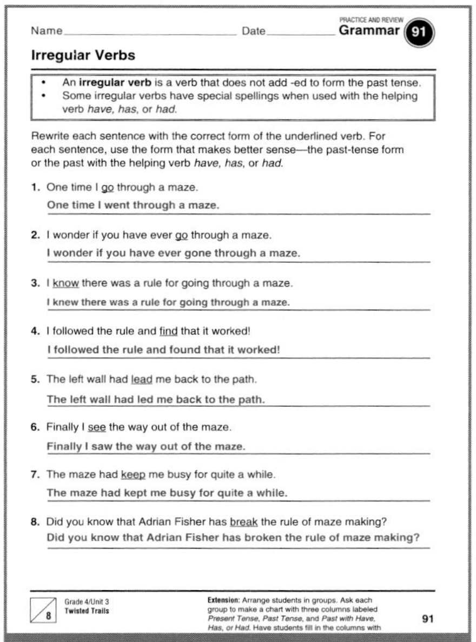

Name______ Date______ PRACTICE AND REVIEW Grammar 91

Irregular Verbs

- An **irregular verb** is a verb that does not add -ed to form the past tense.
- Some irregular verbs have special spellings when used with the helping verb *have, has,* or *had.*

Rewrite each sentence with the correct form of the underlined verb. For each sentence, use the form that makes better sense—the past-tense form or the past with the helping verb *have, has,* or *had.*

1. One time I go through a maze.
   One time I went through a maze.
2. I wonder if you have ever go through a maze.
   I wonder if you have ever gone through a maze.
3. I know there was a rule for going through a maze.
   I knew there was a rule for going through a maze.
4. I followed the rule and find that it worked!
   I followed the rule and found that it worked!
5. The left wall had lead me back to the path.
   The left wall had led me back to the path.
6. Finally I see the way out of the maze.
   Finally I saw the way out of the maze.
7. The maze had keep me busy for quite a while.
   The maze had kept me busy for quite a while.
8. Did you know that Adrian Fisher has break the rule of maze making?
   Did you know that Adrian Fisher has broken the rule of maze making?

8 Grade 4/Unit 3 Twisted Trails — **Extension:** Arrange students in groups. Ask each group to make a chart with three columns labeled *Present Tense, Past Tense,* and *Past with Have, Has, or Had.* Have students fill in the columns with — 91

GRAMMAR PRACTICE BOOK, PAGE 91

DAY 4 Review and Practice

Review Irregular Verbs Ask students to write sentences using each verb from column 3 of the class chart. Then present the Daily Language Activity.

Mechanics and Usage Before students begin the daily Writing Prompt on page 360D, review abbreviations.

Abbreviations

- An abbreviation is the shortened form of a word.
- Some abbreviations begin with a capital letter and end with a period.
- Abbreviate titles of people before names. You can abbreviate days of the week.
- You can also abbreviate most months.

Display the following examples: *Mrs., Mr., Dr., Mon., Tues., Jan., Dec.*

WRITING Assign the daily Writing Prompt on page 360D.

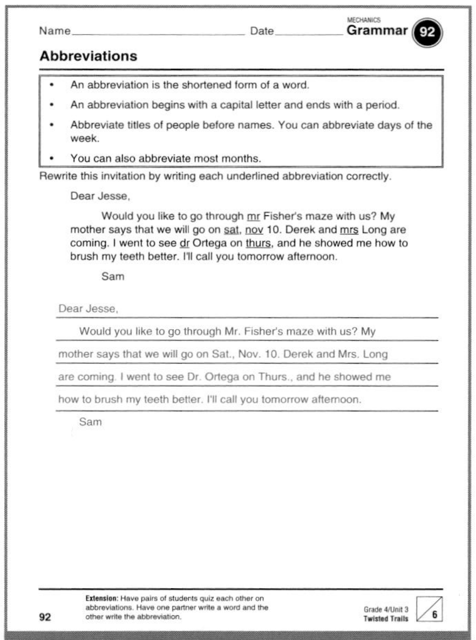

Name______ Date______ MECHANICS Grammar 92

Abbreviations

- An abbreviation is the shortened form of a word.
- An abbreviation begins with a capital letter and ends with a period.
- Abbreviate titles of people before names. You can abbreviate days of the week.
- You can also abbreviate most months.

Rewrite this invitation by writing each underlined abbreviation correctly.

Dear Jesse,

Would you like to go through mr Fisher's maze with us? My mother says that we will go on sat, nov 10. Derek and mrs Long are coming. I went to see dr Ortega on thurs, and he showed me how to brush my teeth better. I'll call you tomorrow afternoon.

Sam

Dear Jesse,

Would you like to go through Mr. Fisher's maze with us? My mother says that we will go on Sat., Nov. 10. Derek and Mrs. Long are coming. I went to see Dr. Ortega on Thurs., and he showed me how to brush my teeth better. I'll call you tomorrow afternoon.

Sam

92 — **Extension:** Have pairs of students quiz each other on abbreviations. Have one partner write a word and the other write the abbreviation. — Grade 4/Unit 3 Twisted Trails 6

GRAMMAR PRACTICE BOOK, PAGE 92

DAY 5 Assess and Reteach

Assess Use the Daily Language Activity and page 93 of the **Grammar Practice Book** for assessment.

Reteach Have students organize into two teams. Ask each team to write the verbs from the Daily Language Activities on pieces of construction paper. Teams should alternate displaying a verb while the other team calls out a sentence that correctly uses the past tense or past participle. Have them include additional irregular verbs, such as *drink*, *speak*, and *read*, that they come across in their reading.

Have students create a word wall of irregular verbs.

Use page 94 of the **Grammar Practice Book** for additional reteaching.

WRITING Assign the daily Writing Prompt on page 360D.

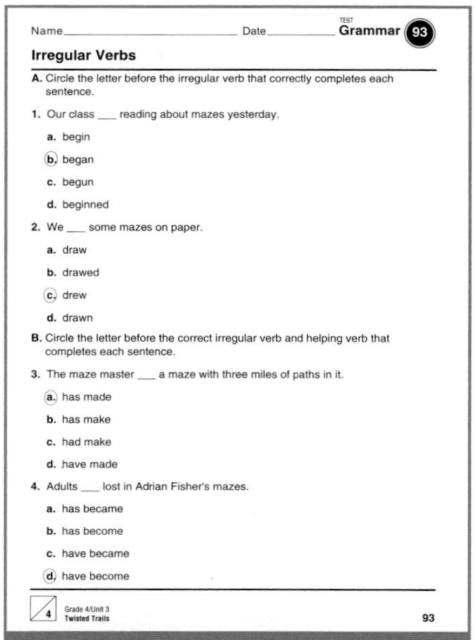

Name______ Date______ TEST Grammar 93

Irregular Verbs

A. Circle the letter before the irregular verb that correctly completes each sentence.

1. Our class ___ reading about mazes yesterday.
   a. begin
   (b.) began
   c. begun
   d. beginned
2. We ___ some mazes on paper.
   a. draw
   b. drawed
   (c.) drew
   d. drawn

B. Circle the letter before the correct irregular verb and helping verb that completes each sentence.

3. The maze master ___ a maze with three miles of paths in it.
   (a.) has made
   b. has make
   c. had make
   d. have made
4. Adults ___ lost in Adrian Fisher's mazes.
   a. has became
   b. has become
   c. have became
   (d.) have become

4 Grade 4/Unit 3 Twisted Trails — 93

GRAMMAR PRACTICE BOOK, PAGE 93

GRAMMAR PRACTICE BOOK, PAGE 94

5 Day Spelling Plan

LANGUAGE SUPPORT

To assist student understanding of the Spelling Words, write each word on a card and display it next to an object or picture that illustrates its meaning.

DICTATION SENTENCES

Spelling Words

1. She designs toys.
2. The artist is well known.
3. The building has many windows.
4. The activity was planned for today.
5. My mother works at a museum.
6. I made a work of art.
7. She will create a new tool.
8. He is a master painter.
9. She drew a new poster.
10. The statue is beautiful.
11. Assemble the bike with the directions.
12. I took a craft class.
13. Music can express beauty.
14. Arrange the brushes in the bottle.
15. She is a professional dancer.
16. The mold was opened.
17. Put the painting on the easel.
18. She shaped the plaster into a bird.
19. We saw the masterpiece.
20. The exhibit was at our school.

Challenge Words

21. The problem was a challenge to solve.
22. It contained many clues to help us.
23. We found it entertaining.
24. We walked through the mazes.
25. The work requires study.

DAY 1 Pretest

Assess Prior Knowledge Use the Dictation Sentences at the left and **Spelling Practice Book** page 89 for the pretest. Allow students to correct their own papers. Students who require a modified list may be tested on the first ten words.

Spelling Words		Challenge Words
1. **designs**	12. craft	21. **challenge**
2. **artist**	13. express	22. **contained**
3. **building**	14. arrange	23. **entertaining**
4. activity	15. **professional**	24. **mazes**
5. **museum**	16. mold	25. **requires**
6. art	17. easel	
7. create	18. plaster	
8. **master**	19. masterpiece	
9. poster	20. exhibit	
10. statue		
11. assemble		

*Note: Words in **dark type** are from the story.*

Word Study On page 90 of the **Spelling Practice Book** are word study steps and an at-home activity.

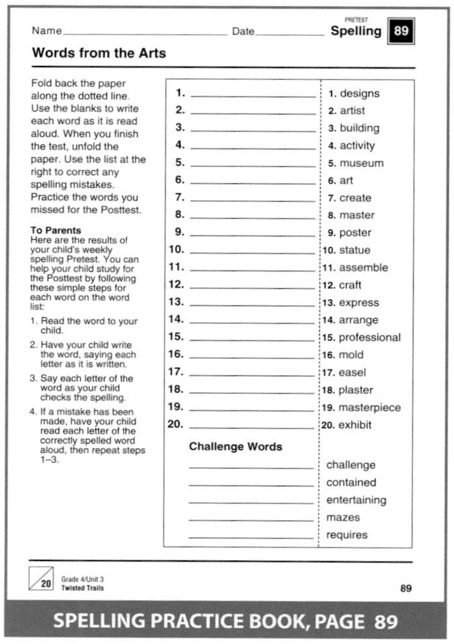
Name______ Date______ PRETEST Spelling 89

Words from the Arts

Fold back the paper along the dotted line. Use the blanks to write each word as it is read aloud. When you finish the test, unfold the paper. Use the list at the right to correct any spelling mistakes. Practice the words you missed for the Posttest.

To Parents
Here are the results of your child's weekly spelling Pretest. You can help your child study for the Posttest by following these simple steps for each word on the word list:
1. Read the word to your child.
2. Have your child write the word, saying each letter as it is written.
3. Say each letter of the word as your child checks the spelling.
4. If a mistake has been made, have your child read each letter of the correctly spelled word aloud, then repeat steps 1–3.

1. designs 2. artist 3. building 4. activity 5. museum 6. art 7. create 8. master 9. poster 10. statue 11. assemble 12. craft 13. express 14. arrange 15. professional 16. mold 17. easel 18. plaster 19. masterpiece 20. exhibit

Challenge Words: challenge, contained, entertaining, mazes, requires

20 Grade 4/Unit 3 Twisted Trails 89

SPELLING PRACTICE BOOK, PAGE 89

WORD STUDY STEPS AND ACTIVITY, PAGE 90

DAY 2 Explore the Pattern

Sort and Spell Words Write the words *arrange* and *activity* on the chalkboard. Ask students how they go about putting these two words in alphabetical order. (check each consecutive letter until one letter comes first) Have students read the Spelling Words and sort them as below.

Alphabetical Order

activity	create	mold
arrange	designs	museum
art	easel	plaster
artist	exhibit	poster
assemble	express	professional
building	master	statue
craft	masterpiece	

Word Wall Have students create a word wall based on the word sort and add more words from their reading.

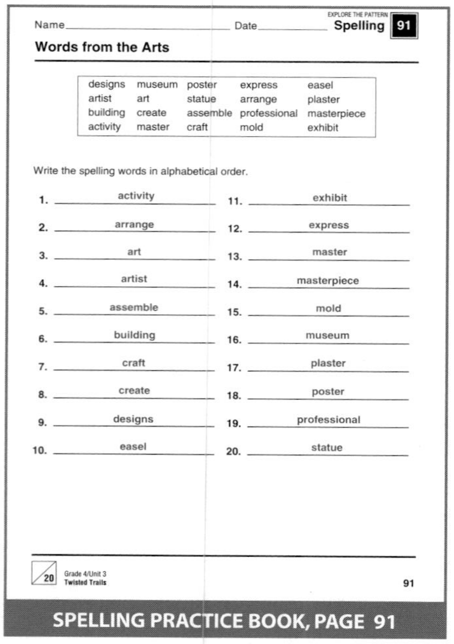
Name______ Date______ EXPLORE THE PATTERN Spelling 91

Words from the Arts

designs museum poster express easel artist art statue arrange plaster building create assemble professional masterpiece activity master craft mold exhibit

Write the spelling words in alphabetical order.

1. activity 2. arrange 3. art 4. artist 5. assemble 6. building 7. craft 8. create 9. designs 10. easel 11. exhibit 12. express 13. master 14. masterpiece 15. mold 16. museum 17. plaster 18. poster 19. professional 20. statue

20 Grade 4/Unit 3 Twisted Trails 91

SPELLING PRACTICE BOOK, PAGE 91

Words from Art

DAY 3 Practice and Extend

Word Meaning: Context Clues Remind students that context clues around an unfamiliar word can sometimes clarify the word's meaning in a sentence. Have students use Spelling Words to complete these sentences.

The _____ was displayed at the _____.
(poster, exhibit)

The _____ was carved by an _____.
(statue, artist)

Have students write a fill-in for a Spelling Word and exchange it with a partner.

If students need extra practice, have partners give each other a midweek test.

Glossary Remind students that the Glossary will give an example sentence showing correct usage. Have partners:

- write each Challenge Word.
- look up each Challenge Word.
- write a new example sentence for each Challenge Word.

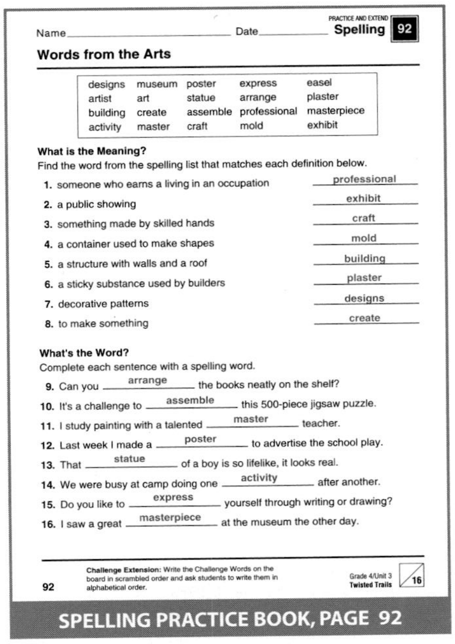
Name_____ Date_____ PRACTICE AND EXTEND Spelling 92

Words from the Arts

designs	museum	poster	express	easel
artist	art	statue	arrange	plaster
building	create	assemble	professional	masterpiece
activity	master	craft	mold	exhibit

What is the Meaning?
Find the word from the spelling list that matches each definition below.

1. someone who earns a living in an occupation professional
2. a public showing exhibit
3. something made by skilled hands craft
4. a container used to make shapes mold
5. a structure with walls and a roof building
6. a sticky substance used by builders plaster
7. decorative patterns designs
8. to make something create

What's the Word?
Complete each sentence with a spelling word.

9. Can you arrange the books neatly on the shelf?
10. It's a challenge to assemble this 500-piece jigsaw puzzle.
11. I study painting with a talented master teacher.
12. Last week I made a poster to advertise the school play.
13. That statue of a boy is so lifelike, it looks real.
14. We were busy at camp doing one activity after another.
15. Do you like to express yourself through writing or drawing?
16. I saw a great masterpiece at the museum the other day.

92 Challenge Extension: Write the Challenge Words on the board in scrambled order and ask students to write them in alphabetical order. Grade 4/Unit 3 Twisted Trails 16

SPELLING PRACTICE BOOK, PAGE 92

DAY 4 Proofread and Write

Proofread Sentences Write these sentences on the chalkboard, including the misspelled words. Ask students to proofread, circling incorrect spellings and writing the correct spellings. There are two spelling errors in each sentence.

The profeshunal artist showed us her dezines. (professional, designs)

The museeum is the new bilding on the corner. (museum, building)

Have students create additional sentences with errors for partners to correct.

WRITING Have students use as many Spelling Words as possible in the daily Writing Prompt on page 360D. Remind students to proofread their writing for errors in spelling, grammar, and punctuation.

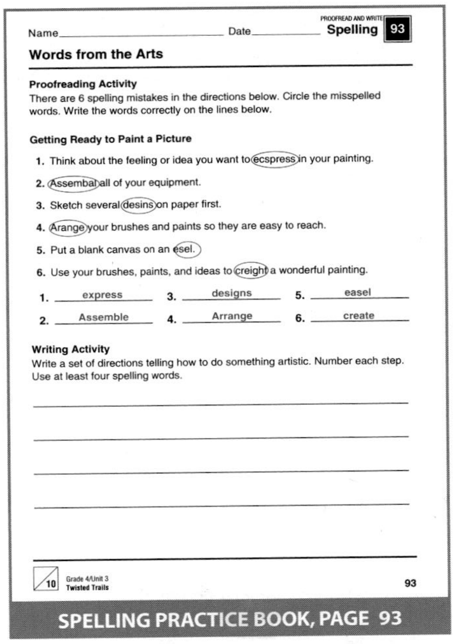
Name_____ Date_____ PROOFREAD AND WRITE Spelling 93

Words from the Arts

Proofreading Activity
There are 6 spelling mistakes in the directions below. Circle the misspelled words. Write the words correctly on the lines below.

Getting Ready to Paint a Picture

1. Think about the feeling or idea you want to ecspress in your painting.
2. Assembal all of your equipment.
3. Sketch several desins on paper first.
4. Arange your brushes and paints so they are easy to reach.
5. Put a blank canvas on an esel.
6. Use your brushes, paints, and ideas to creight a wonderful painting.

1. express 3. designs 5. easel
2. Assemble 4. Arrange 6. create

Writing Activity
Write a set of directions telling how to do something artistic. Number each step. Use at least four spelling words.

10 Grade 4/Unit 3 Twisted Trails 93

SPELLING PRACTICE BOOK, PAGE 93

DAY 5 Assess and Reteach

Assess Students' Knowledge Use page 94 of the **Spelling Practice Book** or the Dictation Sentences on page 369O for the posttest.

JOURNAL **Personal Word List** If students have trouble with any words in the lesson, have them add to their personal lists of troublesome words in their journals. Have students write example sentences for each word.

Students should refer to their word lists during later writing activities.

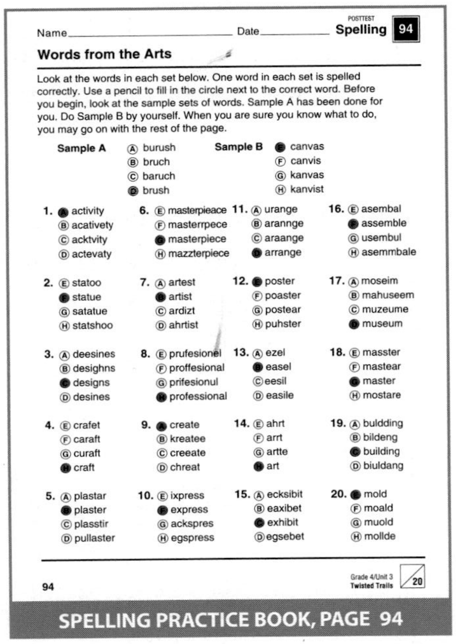
Name_____ Date_____ POSTTEST Spelling 94

Words from the Arts

Look at the words in each set below. One word in each set is spelled correctly. Use a pencil to fill in the circle next to the correct word. Before you begin, look at the sample sets of words. Sample A has been done for you. Do Sample B by yourself. When you are sure you know what to do, you may go on with the rest of the page.

Sample A (A) burush (B) bruch (C) baruch ● brush
Sample B ● canvas (F) canvis (G) kanvas (H) kanvist

1. ● activity (B) acativety (C) acktvity (D) actevaty
2. (E) statoo ● statue (G) satatue (H) statshoo
3. (A) deesines (B) desighns ● designs (D) desines
4. (E) crafet (F) caraft (G) curaft ● craft
5. (A) plastar ● plaster (C) plasstir (D) pullaster
6. (E) masterpieace (F) masterrpece ● masterpiece (H) mazzterpiece
7. (A) artest ● artist (C) ardizt (D) ahrtist
8. (E) prufesionel (F) proffesional (G) prifesionul ● professional
9. ● create (B) kreatee (C) creeate (D) chreat
10. (E) ixpress ● express (G) ackspres (H) egspress
11. (A) urange (B) arannge (C) araange ● arrange
12. ● poster (F) poaster (G) postear (H) puhster
13. (A) ezel ● easel (C) eesil (D) easile
14. (E) ahrt (F) arrt (G) artte ● art
15. (A) ecksibit (B) eaxibet ● exhibit (D) egsebet
16. (E) asembal ● assemble (G) usembul (H) asemmbale
17. (A) moseim (B) mahuseem (C) muzeume ● museum
18. (E) masster (F) mastear ● master (H) mostare
19. (A) buldding (B) bildeng ● building (D) biuldang
20. ● mold (F) moald (G) muold (H) mollde

94 Grade 4/Unit 3 Twisted Trails 20

SPELLING PRACTICE BOOK, PAGE 94

Wrap Up the Theme

Our Voices

We can each use our talents to communicate ideas.

REVIEW THE THEME Reread the theme statement. Then ask how the story selections supported the theme Our Voices. Invite students to share other examples of stories, art, or movies they have seen that reflected ways talent can communicate ideas.

READ THE POEM Read aloud "My Poems" by Alan Barlow. Ask students to tell how the poem relates to the theme. Then lead students in a discussion of how the author feels about writing poetry.

LISTENING LIBRARY The poem is available on **audiocassette** or on **compact disc.**

GROUP **MAKE CONNECTIONS** Have students work in small groups to brainstorm a list of ways that the stories, poems, and the *Time for Kids* magazine article relate to the theme Our Voices. Groups can then compare their lists as they share them with the class.

Have students tell which selections they liked best. Discuss the types of selections they most enjoy listening to or reading. Who are their favorite authors?

LOOKING AT GENRE

Have students review *Grass Sandals* and *A Place Called Freedom*. What makes *Grass Sandals* a biographical story? What makes *A Place Called Freedom* historical fiction? Using a genre chart, help students list characteristics of each genre. Ask students to name examples of other stories that have the same characteristics.

BIOGRAPHICAL STORY *Grass Sandals*	HISTORICAL FICTION *A Place Called Freedom*
• Characters are real people. • Events really happened. • Story told in third person.	• Characters are placed in a real historical settings. • Characters act out a fictional plot.

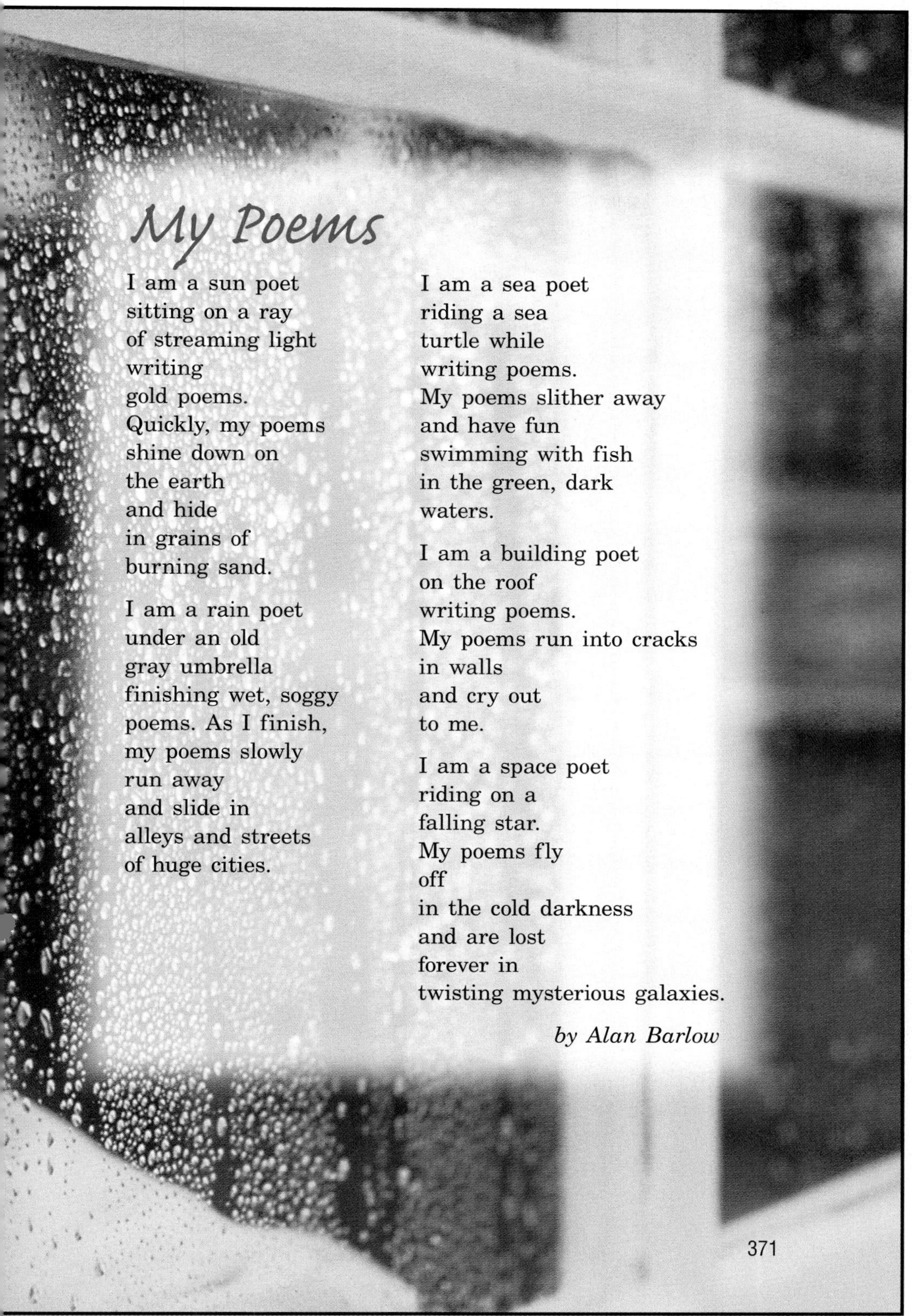

My Poems

I am a sun poet
sitting on a ray
of streaming light
writing
gold poems.
Quickly, my poems
shine down on
the earth
and hide
in grains of
burning sand.

I am a rain poet
under an old
gray umbrella
finishing wet, soggy
poems. As I finish,
my poems slowly
run away
and slide in
alleys and streets
of huge cities.

I am a sea poet
riding a sea
turtle while
writing poems.
My poems slither away
and have fun
swimming with fish
in the green, dark
waters.

I am a building poet
on the roof
writing poems.
My poems run into cracks
in walls
and cry out
to me.

I am a space poet
riding on a
falling star.
My poems fly
off
in the cold darkness
and are lost
forever in
twisting mysterious galaxies.

by Alan Barlow

371

LEARNING ABOUT POETRY

Literary Devices: Imagery Explain that some poets use unusual words to get the reader to think creatively about or imagine a particular topic. Reread the first stanza of the poem. Ask students to visualize a sunny beach. Then have them discuss why the poet might compare some of his poems to sandy land.

GROUP **Response Activity** Have students illustrate a stanza from the poem. When the pictures are complete, group together students who drew pictures of the same stanza. Ask them to discuss what they think the stanza means. Then have each group share their ideas when the class regroups.

Activity

Research and Inquiry

GROUP **Complete the Theme Project** Have students organize the project so that each individual will participate and use a talent. Remind students that a talent can be as simple as organizing chairs in a space or making someone feel happy. Next, help students gather props, equipment, and resources.

Present the Project Allow students to present their project. Encourage students after the presentation to share with the audience what they learned about talents and ways to communicate with them.

Draw Conclusions Help students draw conclusions about what they learned about talents and communication. Did they discover additional talents? Did they find unique ways to use their talents to communicate their ideas? Did they discover any useful Web sites?

Ask More Questions In a follow-up discussion, have students think about ways other people in the community use their talents to share ideas. Ask: How do these talents affect the community? What would happen if people didn't use their talents? Encourage students to ask relevant questions.

Reading Science

OBJECTIVES Students will:

- summarize the important information in a passage.
- use text features to monitor comprehension.

BUILD BACKGROUND

- Explain that the passages in this lesson come from an actual science textbook.
- Point out text features that often appear in science texts or other types of nonfiction writing, such as magazine articles. Text features might include headings, key words in color highlighting or bold type, photographs, and diagrams.

FEATURES OF SCIENCE TEXTS

- **scientific terms**
- **photographs**
- **activities**
- **experiments**
- **detailed instructions**
- **steps in a process**
- **diagrams and labels**
- **numerical data**

- Invite volunteers to look through their science books and note some of these features. Discuss how these features can help them understand what they read.
- Tell students that they will use the strategy of summarizing to help them read science texts. Explain that summarizing information in their own words will increase their understanding.

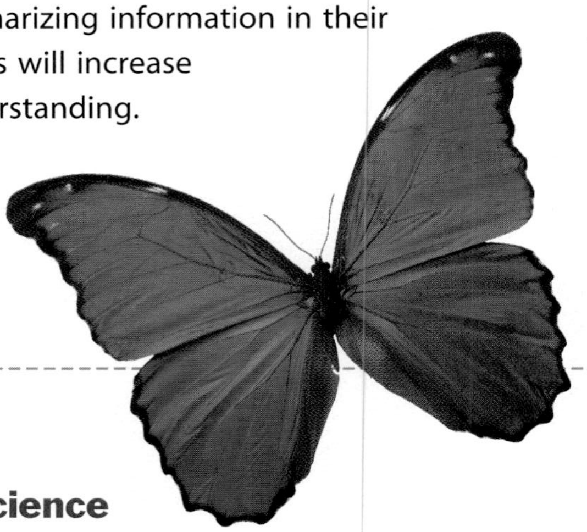

TEACHING TIP

Helping Students Read Science

BUILD PRIOR KNOWLEDGE Many students lack the background knowledge they need to read a science text successfully. In addition to providing prereading instruction on cells, encourage students to develop the prereading strategy of thinking about and writing down what they already know about this topic so they will be better equipped to comprehend new information.

UNDERSTAND NEW VOCABULARY Most science materials contain technical words, such as *oxygen* and *organism,* which students will need to master. In addition, there may be multiple-meaning words, such as *cell,* that have a specific meaning in a scientific context. Present or review strategies that will help students identify and learn scientific terms.

UNDERSTAND CONCEPTS AND ORGANIZATION Figuring out the organization of a science text often helps students comprehend the concepts. Focusing on the comparisons and contrasts between plant and animal cells, for example, will help students retain the main ideas in these passages. Students may also need to draw conclusions in order to grasp important ideas when reading and performing science experiments.

Reading Science

When you read a science book, you want to be sure that you understand what you have read. A good way to do this is to write down the most important information, and then rewrite or tell it in your own words.

In a **summary**, you *briefly* tell or write in your own words the main idea or ideas in a passage. Summarizing helps you to understand the information you read.

SUMMARY

Main Idea → 1. ______

Main Idea → 2. ______

Main Idea → 3. ______

Summarize

1. **Identify the topic** of the passage.
2. **Choose important information.** Read the passage and identify important information that you can use in a summary.
3. **Organize** the important information. Group related facts and ideas together.
4. **Summarize** by writing or telling the important information briefly in your own words.

1 **Identify the topic.** I'll look for titles, headings, and clue words.

2 **Choose important information.** As I read, I'll pick out the facts I think are the most important.

3 **Organize.** Words such as *covering, color,* and *shape* can help me identify other main ideas in the text.

4 **Summarize.** I'll write or give a short summary in my own words.

Can You Compare Plant and Animal Cells?

The basic differences between most plant and animal cells include their covering, color, and shape. Cells also differ depending on the types of jobs they do and the parts of the organism they make up.

How are plant cells and animal cells alike? Both are small. Both are filled with a jellylike substance. Both have outer coverings.

Plant cells and animal cells are also different in some ways, however:

- **Covering** A plant cell has a thick cell wall covering the cell membrane. An animal cell has only the thin cell membrane.
- **Color** Most plant cells have green coloring. An animal cell does not.
- **Shape** Most plant cells have a boxlike shape. Animal cells have many shapes.

Cell Shapes

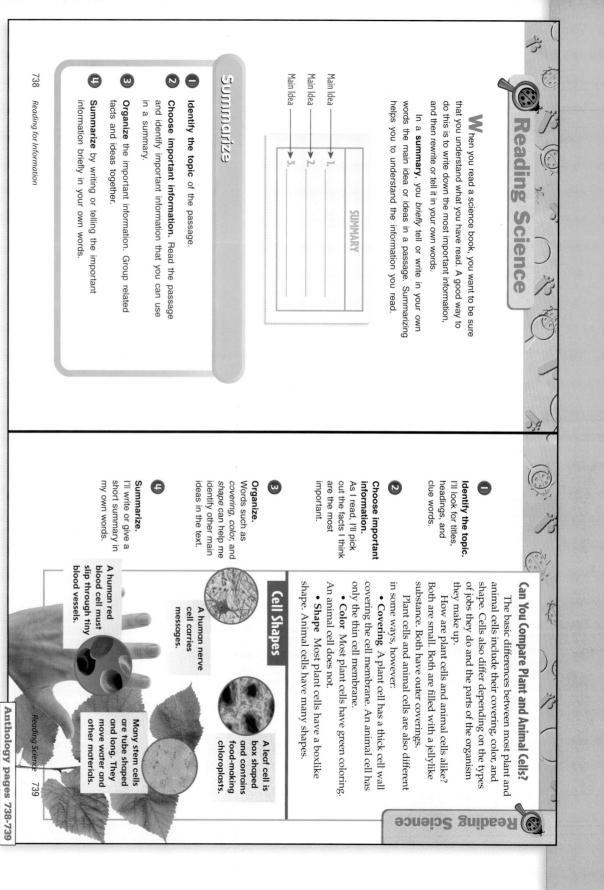

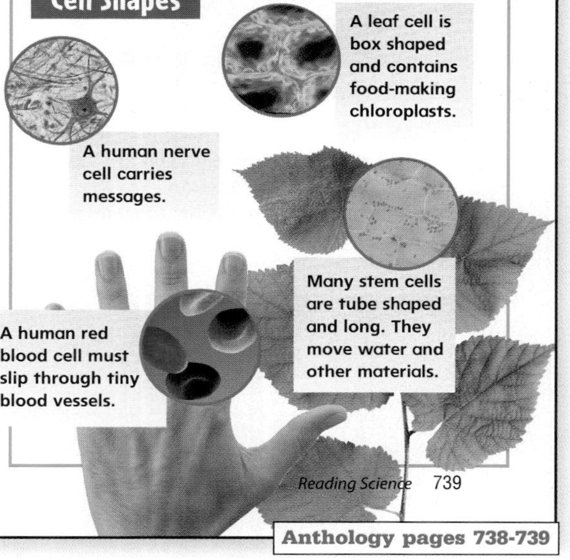

A leaf cell is box shaped and contains food-making chloroplasts.

A human nerve cell carries messages.

Many stem cells are tube shaped and long. They move water and other materials.

A human red blood cell must slip through tiny blood vessels.

Anthology pages 738-739

INTRODUCE Say: Summarizing is a useful strategy to help make sure you understand what you read in science. When you summarize, or sum up, a passage, you write or retell the most important information in your own words.

Have volunteers read the four steps of **Summarize** aloud. Explain that summarizing can become a regular part of reading science if they ask themselves:

- What is this passage all about?
- What facts are most important?
- How are the important facts and ideas related?
- How can I use my own words to retell this information briefly?

PRACTICE Say: Here is a short passage about plant and animal cells from a science book. The numbered items on the side show how you might use summarizing to better understand the passage.

Have students read "Can You Compare Plant and Animal Cells?" to practice summarizing. Then use the following questions to help them summarize it.

- What is the topic of this passage? (the differences between plant and animal cells)
- What are some key words? (covering, color, shape)
- What are some main ideas in this passage? (Plant and animal cells are both small and have an outer covering and jelly like substance within. They differ in their coverings, colors, and shapes.)
- Why is it important to use your own words in a summary? (You really have to understand a passage to sum it up in your own words.)

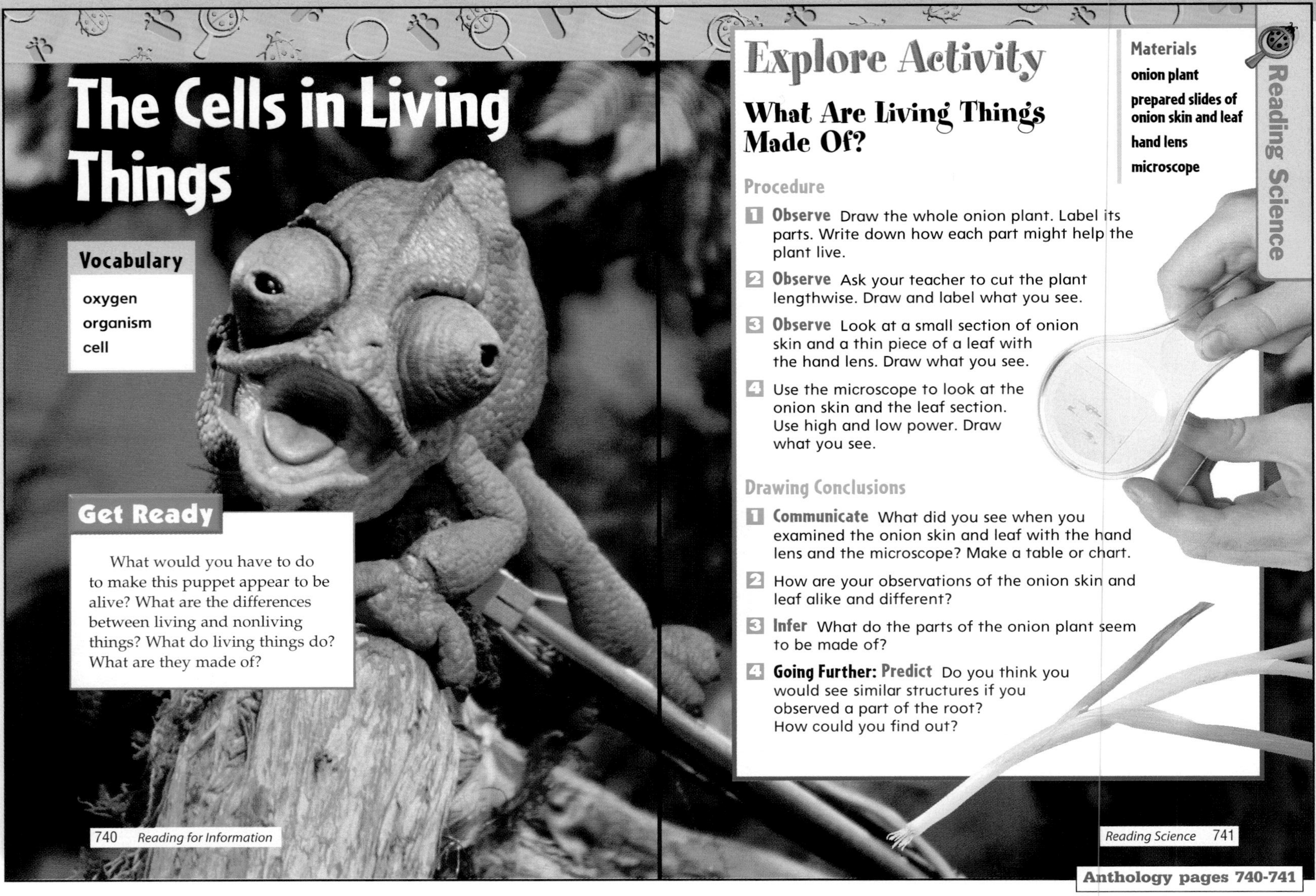

The Cells in Living Things

Vocabulary
oxygen
organism
cell

Get Ready

What would you have to do to make this puppet appear to be alive? What are the differences between living and nonliving things? What do living things do? What are they made of?

740 Reading for Information

Reading Science

Explore Activity

What Are Living Things Made Of?

Materials
onion plant
prepared slides of onion skin and leaf
hand lens
microscope

Procedure

1. **Observe** Draw the whole onion plant. Label its parts. Write down how each part might help the plant live.
2. **Observe** Ask your teacher to cut the plant lengthwise. Draw and label what you see.
3. **Observe** Look at a small section of onion skin and a thin piece of a leaf with the hand lens. Draw what you see.
4. Use the microscope to look at the onion skin and the leaf section. Use high and low power. Draw what you see.

Drawing Conclusions

1. **Communicate** What did you see when you examined the onion skin and leaf with the hand lens and the microscope? Make a table or chart.
2. How are your observations of the onion skin and leaf alike and different?
3. **Infer** What do the parts of the onion plant seem to be made of?
4. **Going Further: Predict** Do you think you would see similar structures if you observed a part of the root? How could you find out?

Reading Science 741

Anthology pages 740-741

APPLY Have students **preview** "The Cells in Living Things" on pages 740–743, noting the specialized features that they see in the selection. The **text features** include a list of key science terms, vocabulary words in color highlighting, the photographs, the step-by-step directions for an experiment, and the diagram. Also point out that the main idea of the text for pages 742–743 is stated in dark print at the beginning of page 742. Then have students read the selection and think about how they would summarize it in their own words. *(Set Purposes)*

MODEL When I begin to read this science text, I see a number of special features in the text that will help me summarize it. Most of the key words of the passage are listed at the beginning as vocabulary words, and I'll want to include these in my summary. The topic of the passage is clear from the heading—The Cells in Living Things. Also, the text gives me one of the main ideas in dark print on page 742. I should restate that idea in my own words in the summary.

As students read the passage, have them pay special attention to the diagram on page 742. When they are finished reading, point out the Review questions and elicit answers from volunteers. Then direct students to summarize the most important information on pages 740–743. Some students might want to make oral summaries to a partner. Others can write their summaries in a paragraph or two.

Read to Learn

Main Idea **All living things are made up of building blocks called cells.**

What Are Living Things?

Do you think you have anything in common with the onion plant?

The main thing you have in common is that you are both living things. Most living things share basic needs for food, water, a place to live, and **oxygen** (AHK·suh·juhn).

Most living things use oxygen to turn food into energy. Plants need oxygen to use the food they make. Another characteristic of living things is that they are made of parts. Each part has a specific job.

Plants, people, and other animals are all **organisms** (AWR·guh·niz·uhmz). An organism is a living thing that carries out five basic life functions on its own.

The Five Basic Life Functions

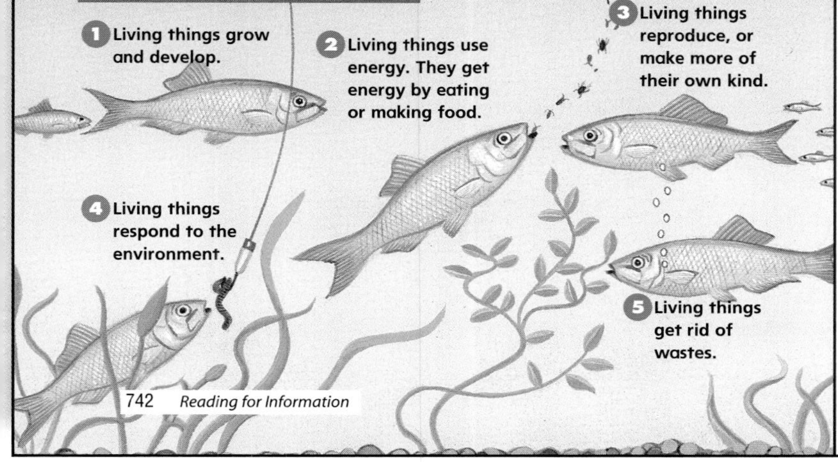

1 Living things grow and develop.
2 Living things use energy. They get energy by eating or making food.
3 Living things reproduce, or make more of their own kind.
4 Living things respond to the environment.
5 Living things get rid of wastes.

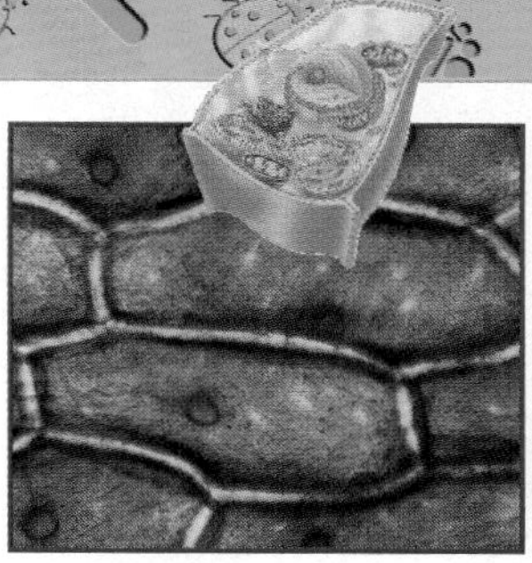

The cells of a plant have a boxlike shape. They contain chlorophyll, which gives them a green color.

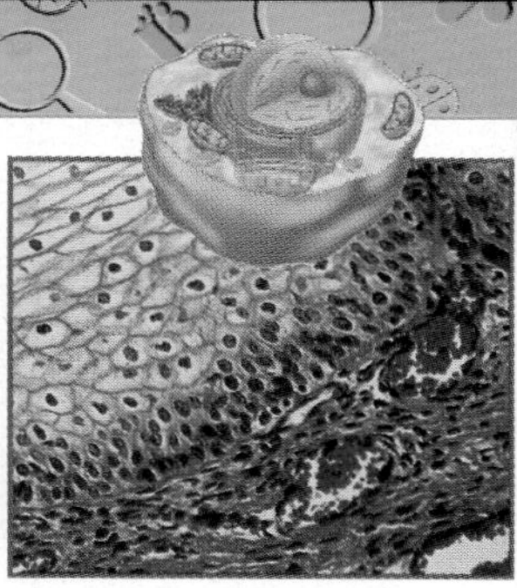

Animal cells are not shaped like small boxes. They do not contain chlorophyll.

Organisms come in all shapes and sizes. Tiny flies, onion plants, great blue whales—even you—are all organisms. It doesn't matter if an organism lives in the water, on the ground, or in the tops of the tallest trees. All organisms carry out five basic life functions.

The small, boxlike structures making up the onion plant are called **cells** (SELZ). A cell is the smallest unit of living matter. In other words, cells are the "building blocks" of living things. All living things are made of cells—even you.

Although all living things are made of cells, all cells are not the same. Plant cells have a boxlike shape. Some even contain a green material called *chlorophyll* (KLAWR·uh·fil). When sunlight strikes chlorophyll, the cell can make food for the plant. Animal cells don't contain chlorophyll and are not box shaped.

Review Questions

1. Name any two living things. How do you know they are living?
2. What is an organism?
3. How can summarizing information you have read help you to understand and remember it?

Anthology pages 742-743

ANSWERS TO REVIEW QUESTIONS

1. Examples of living things include onions and people. All living things need food, water, a place to live, and oxygen.
2. An organism is a living thing that carries out five life functions: Organisms grow and develop, use energy, reproduce, respond to the environment, and get rid of wastes.
3. Summarizing is a way to focus on the main ideas in a passage. Summarizing ideas in your own words helps you understand and remember them.

TRANSFER THE STRATEGY

Ask: How did summarizing help you understand this science lesson?

Discuss: Summarize the important information from a news story, magazine article, TV program or conversation.

Activity

How Do Human Cells Look?

Materials: microscope, slide and cover, toothpick or swab, iodine, pencil

What to do:

1. Place a drop of water on a microscope slide.
2. Very gently rub a toothpick on the inside of your cheek to collect skin cells.
3. Roll the end of the toothpick in the water on the slide. Add a drop of iodine. Place a cover slip over the slide.
4. Look at the cells through a microscope, first under the low power. Draw a few of the cells.
5. Look at the cells under high power and draw them again. Do the cells have a regular shape? (Skin cells are irregular in shape.)

Persuasive Writing

CONNECT TO LITERATURE In *The Hatmaker's Sign,* the author tells a story about Thomas Jefferson and the Declaration of Independence. In a discussion, have students give reasons why the hatmaker's story may have helped Jefferson to feel better about changes to his draft.

GROUP

Every day after lunch, our schoolyard is a mess. I think we should all get together to keep the yard clean. It not only looks dirty, but it can be dangerous, too. Last week, someone in my class slipped on a plastic bag and hurt their arm.

Let's make a student campaign to stop littering. I think we need some more trash bins outside, especially near the ball court. We can make signs telling everyone to pick up their own trash. We can also do clean-ups just before the end of recess. A clean schoolyard will be safer and nicer for every student in the school.

Prewrite

PURPOSE AND AUDIENCE Students will write editorials to persuade classmates to organize an activity that will benefit the whole school. Encourage them to consider their purpose and audience as they work.

STRATEGY: BRAINSTORM Have classmates name issues that they think have an impact on all students. Encourage them to consider a range of topics, within their school as well as locally or globally. Ask them to give specific reasons why their topics affect students' lives.

Use **Writing Process Transparency 3A** to model a Persuasive Writing Organizer.

FEATURES OF PERSUASIVE WRITING

- **clearly states a position on a specific topic**
- **offers convincing reasons and facts to persuade an audience**
- **may use appropriate personal anecdotes to elaborate the position**
- **draws a concrete, practical conclusion**

PREWRITE TRANSPARENCY

Smoking Campaign

Position Statement

There should be signs in our neighborhood stores that say kids can't buy cigarettes there.

Reason Too many kids are smoking at a young age.

Explanation
Some kids smoke before they get into high school.

Reason 20 stores in our neighborhood sell cigarettes to kids.

Explanation
The tribune did a survey.

Reason Smoking is dangerous.

Explanation
Smoking causes diseases such as emphysema and cancer.

Reason Selling cigarettes to kids is illegal.

Explanation
Stores have to pay a fine if they get caught selling cigarettes to kids.

Conclusion

We can help our friends stay away from cigarettes.

McGraw-Hill School Division

Grade 4/Unit 3: Persuasive Writing/Prewrite 3A

TEACHING TIP

ORGANIZATION Set up a research area with local and national periodicals. Have students gather facts that will support their persuasive articles. Give concrete examples of how to support personal opinion with detailed information. Guide them to begin with a forceful statement of purpose, and end with a strong, practical conclusion.

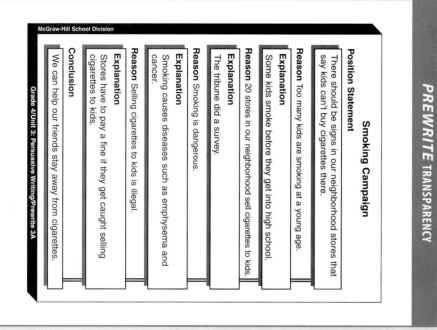

Persuasive Writing

Draft

STRATEGY: DEVELOP A MAIN IDEA Instruct students to begin with an opening sentence that states a firm position on their topic. From there, encourage them to freely write their opinions without self-editing. Urge them to consult their prewriting organizers and incorporate supporting facts into the text. Remind them that good persuasive writing includes a strongly stated practical plan of action.

WORD CHOICE Distribute copies of a few strong examples of student-opinion essays. Have students underline facts and details that they feel best support the author's position. Guide them to discuss the reasons for their choices and have them note persuasive words or phrases that they can use to enhance their own writing.

Use **Writing Process Transparency 3B** as a model.

LANGUAGE SUPPORT

Conference in small groups with students who need help expressing their ideas. Ask them to think of someone who is good at sharing opinions, such as a friend, family member, or public figure. Have them list words that tell why that person is convincing to others (e.g., *forceful, exciting, clear*). Help them find concrete ways to apply those traits in their own writing.

***DRAFT* TRANSPARENCY**

To many students are smoking at a young age. Some stores sell cigaretes to children who are not even in high school yet. In a Sunday tribune survey, they counted over 20 stores in our neighborhood that sell cigarettes to minors. even older students shouldn't be able to buy cigarettes before they turn eighteen.

Why don't we create anti-smoking posters from every grade. We can ask storekeepers to hang up behind his counters. They can also put them in their windows. Mr. Reed from the corner shop said he will display one, and will urged other storekeepers on your block to do the same thing. I think that there should be a sign in every store that says people under age can't buy cigarettes there.

I think it would also be fun to make a school art exhibit of all the posters. We could even vote on the best ones, and give out awards for the artist's work. If we all get together, we can help some students to keep away from smoking.

Grade 4/Unit 3: Persuasive Writing/Draft 3B

Revise

Have students work in small teams to note what they find convincing in each other's articles. Coach them in making constructive comments about how teammates might strengthen their arguments.

Use **Writing Process Transparency 3C** for classroom discussion on the revision process. Ask students to comment on how revisions may have improved this writing example.

STRATEGY: ELABORATION Have students examine their work for changes and additions that will enhance their arguments. Ask them to consider how the intended audience might react to their writing. Use the following questions to inspire the revision process:

- Does my writing clearly express my opinion?
- Did I back up my argument with facts that I can prove?
- Have I offered a real plan of action?
- Would an audience agree with me, and if so, why?

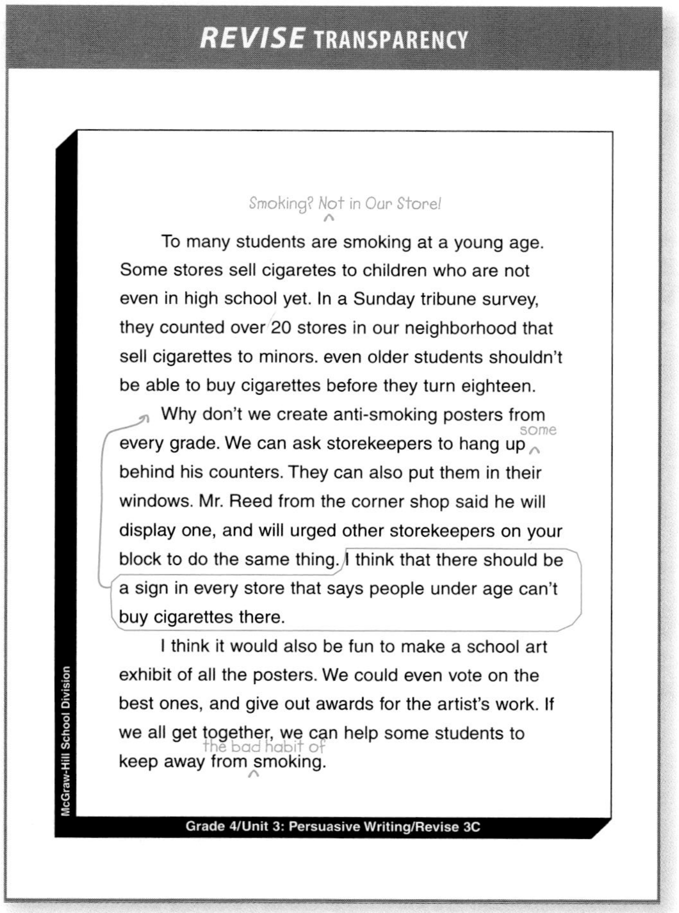
***REVISE* TRANSPARENCY**

Smoking? Not in Our Store!

To many students are smoking at a young age. Some stores sell cigaretes to children who are not even in high school yet. In a Sunday tribune survey, they counted over 20 stores in our neighborhood that sell cigarettes to minors. even older students shouldn't be able to buy cigarettes before they turn eighteen.

Why don't we create anti-smoking posters from every grade. We can ask storekeepers to hang up some behind his counters. They can also put them in their windows. Mr. Reed from the corner shop said he will display one, and will urged other storekeepers on your block to do the same thing. I think that there should be a sign in every store that says people under age can't buy cigarettes there.

I think it would also be fun to make a school art exhibit of all the posters. We could even vote on the best ones, and give out awards for the artist's work. If we all get together, we can help some students to keep away from the bad habit of smoking.

McGraw-Hill School Division

Grade 4/Unit 3: Persuasive Writing/Revise 3C

TEACHING TIP

TEACHER CONFERENCE

Reinforce the importance of balancing a strong personal feeling with solid facts and details. Ask students to consider these questions while revising:

- **Did you begin with a strong opening statement?**
- **What are the most convincing words and ideas in your piece?**
- **Is your argument logical? Will a reader understand it?**
- **Did you propose a detailed, practical plan of action? What is it?**

Persuasive Writing

Edit/Proofread

After students finish revising their texts, have them proofread for final corrections and additions.

GRAMMAR/SPELLING CONNECTIONS

See the 5-day Grammar and Usage Plans on verbs and tense, pp. 281M–281N, 297M–297N, 331M–331N, 359M–359N, and 369M–369N.

See the 5-day Spelling Plans, pp. 281O–281P, 297O–297P, 331O–331P, 359O–359P, and 369O–369P.

GRAMMAR, MECHANICS, USAGE

- correct use of singular and plural possessive nouns
- correct use of apostrophes in possessive nouns
- subject-verb agreement
- correct use of present, past, and future tenses

Publish

MAKE A MAGAZINE Combine students' articles in a class magazine called "Hear Us Out." Invite students to clip news photos or make drawings to illustrate their articles.

Use **Writing Process Transparency 3D** as a proofreading model, and **Writing Process Transparency 3E** to discuss presentation ideas for their writing.

***PROOFREAD* TRANSPARENCY**

Smoking? Not in Our Store!

To many students are smoking at a young age. Some stores sell cigaretes to children who are not even in high school yet. In a Sunday tribune survey, they counted over 20 stores in our neighborhood that sell cigarettes to minors. even older students shouldn't be able to buy cigarettes before they turn eighteen.

Why don't we create anti-smoking posters from every grade We can ask storekeepers to hang up behind his counters. They can also put them in their windows Mr. Reed from the corner shop said he will display one, and will urged other storekeepers on your block to do the same thing. I think that there should be a sign in every store that says people under age can't buy cigarettes there.

I think it would also be fun to make a school art exhibit of all the posters. We could even vote on the best ones, and give out awards for the artist's work. If we all get together, we can help some students to keep away from smoking.

McGraw-Hill School Division

Grade 4/Unit 3: Persuasive Writing/Proofread 3D

***PUBLISH* TRANSPARENCY**

Smoking? Not In Our Store!

Too many students are smoking at a young age. Some stores sell cigarettes to children who are not even in high school yet. In a Sunday Tribune survey, they counted over 20 stores in our neighborhood that sell cigarettes to minors. Even older students shouldn't be able to buy cigarettes before they turn eighteen.

I think that there should be a sign in every store that says people under age can't buy cigarettes there. Why don't we create anti-smoking posters from every grade? We can ask storekeepers to hang up some behind their counters. They can also put them in their windows. Mr. Reed from the corner shop said he will display one, and will urge other storekeepers on his block to do the same thing.

I think it would also be fun to make a school art exhibit of all the posters. We could even vote on the best ones, and give out awards for the artists' work. If we all get together, we can help some students to keep away from the bad habit of smoking.

McGraw-Hill School Division

Grade 4/Unit 3: Persuasive Writing/Publish 3E

Presentation Ideas

MAKE POSTERS Have students design photo-collage posters advertising the school projects they've described in their articles. Display the posters along with the class magazine in the library.
▶ **Representing/Viewing**

READ AND CHALLENGE Students can volunteer to read their writing aloud. Guide classmates to ask challenging questions, and to tell why they agree or disagree with the article's position. ▶ **Speaking/Listening**

Assessment

- Ask students to self-assess their writing. Present the persuasive writing features, page 371F, in question form on a chart.
- For a 6-point or an 8-point scale, see pages T107–T108.

Listening and Speaking

LISTENING STRATEGIES

- **Pay attention and be alert.**
- **Make eye contact with the speaker.**
- **Summarize main points and details.**

SPEAKING STRATEGIES

- **Use language appropriate to the audience.**
- **Give words the proper stress.**
- **Evaluate classroom presentations politely.**
- **Answer questions clearly and support opinions.**

Scoring Rubric: 6-Trait Writing

4 Excellent	3 Good	2 Fair	1 Unsatisfactory
• **Ideas & Content** crafts an unusually convincing argument, with extensive supporting details; shares fresh observations, and offers a workable plan.	• **Ideas & Content** crafts a solid, well-thought-out argument; details show knowledge of the topic; may make some fresh observations; offers a plan.	• **Ideas & Content** has some control of a persuasive argument, but may not offer clear or thorough details; may not hold the reader's attention.	• **Ideas & Content** does not successfully argue a position; it is hard to tell what the writer thinks or feels about the topic.
• **Organization** thoughtful strategy moves the reader logically and evenly through the text, from beginning to end; well-placed ideas and details strengthen the argument.	• **Organization** presents a capable, easy-to-follow strategy; reader can follow the argument logic from beginning to end; details fit and build on each other.	• **Organization** tries to structure an argument, but has trouble ordering facts and ideas; may lose control of topic after stating the main idea; reader may be confused by poorly-placed details.	• **Organization** extreme lack of organization makes the text hard to follow; ideas, facts, and details are not connected, and may not fit the purpose.
• **Voice** conveys a genuine personal message, with potential to influence a reader's opinion; deep involvement with the topic enlivens the content; reaches out to an audience.	• **Voice** clearly shows who is behind the words; personal style matches the topic; reaches out to convince the reader.	• **Voice** communicates a main idea, with some hint of who is behind the words; writer may seem personally uninvolved with the topic and an audience.	• **Voice** does not connect with the topic; is not involved in sharing ideas with a reader.
• **Word Choice** makes imaginative use of precise language; sophisticated word choices create a forceful, convincing tone.	• **Word Choice** uses a range of precise words to state opinions and facts; may experiment with new words, or use everyday words to share ideas in a fresh way.	• **Word Choice** gets the argument across, but experiments with few new words; may not use words intended to create a distinct picture for the reader.	• **Word Choice** does not use words that express an opinion or attempt to convince a reader; some words may detract from the meaning; words do not fit, or are overused.
• **Sentence Fluency** varied, effective sentences flow naturally; uses both simple and complex sentences creatively; varied beginnings, lengths, and patterns add appeal to the argument.	• **Sentence Fluency** crafts careful sentences that make sense, and are easy to read and understand; sentence lengths and patterns vary, and fit together well.	• **Sentence Fluency** sentences are understandable, but may be choppy, rambling, or awkward; some writing may be difficult to follow or read aloud, or may interfere with meaning.	• **Sentence Fluency** uses choppy, rambling, or confusing sentences; does not understand how words and sentences fit together; writing doesn't follow natural sentence patterns, and is hard to read aloud.
• **Conventions** has strong skills in most writing conventions; proper use of the rules of English enhances clarity, style, and cohesion of the argument; editing is largely unnecessary.	• **Conventions** uses most conventions correctly; some editing may be needed; errors are few and don't make the paper hard to understand.	• **Conventions** makes frequent noticeable mistakes which prevent a smooth reading of the text; extensive need for editing and revision.	• **Conventions** has repeated errors in spelling, word choice, punctuation and usage; some parts are impossible to read or understand.

0 Incomplete: This piece is either blank, or fails to respond to the writing task. The topic is not addressed, or the student simply paraphrases the prompt. The response may be illegible or incoherent.

UNIT 3 Unit Assessment

VOCABULARY

PARTNERS Have students choose a story and create a crossword puzzle with the vocabulary words. Then have students exchange papers and complete each other's puzzle.

Unit Review

The Hatmaker's Sign

admitted	displaying	strolling
brisk	elegantly	wharf

Pat Cummings: My Story

exist	inspire	reference
image	loft	sketch

Grass Sandals

chanted	pouch	scribbled
nipped	restless	stitching

A Place Called Freedom

fretted	plantation	sunrise
gourd	settlement	weary

Twisted Trails

challenge	contained	mazes
combine	entertaining	requires

Name__________ Date________ Practice 110

Unit 3 Vocabulary Review

A. Read each word in Column 1. Then find a word in Column 2 that means the opposite. Write the letter of the word on the line.

	column 1	column 2
e	1. displaying	a. drew
f	2. strolling	b. boring
c	3. sunrise	c. sunset
b	4. entertaining	d. denied
a	5. scribbled	e. hiding
d	6. admitted	f. running

B. Write the correct vocabulary word on the lines.

challenge inspire combine chanted plantation contained

1. Reading books can inspire you to write a good story.
2. The little children chanted the rhyming poem.
3. Climbing to the top was quite a challenge.
4. The box contained video games and board games.
5. A huge farm where crops such as cotton or sugar can be grown for sale is called a plantation.
6. They will combine flour and water to make the papier mâché.

12 Book 4/Unit 3 Unit 3 Vocabulary Review — At Home: Have students change or add suffixes to some vocabulary words in order to make new words. 110

PRACTICE BOOK, 110–111

GRAMMAR

GROUP Group students in threes and give each group a comic strip. Have students write a past, present, or future summarization of the action in the cartoon, then compare their writings to review verbs.

Unit Review

The Hatmaker's Sign
Present-Tense Verbs

Pat Cummings: My Story
Past-Tense and Future-Tense Verbs

Grass Sandals
Main and Helping Verbs

A Place Called Freedom
Linking Verbs

Twisted Trails
Irregular Verbs

Name__________ Date________ REVIEW Grammar 95

Verbs

Read each passage and look at the underlined parts. Is there a better way to write and say each part? If there is, which is the better way? Circle your answer.

The hatmaker sit write, and draws. (1) He creates a sign for his shop. He shows the sign to several people. They tells him to make changes. (2) The hatmaker rushes back to his shop and makes a new sign.

1. A The hatmaker sat, writes, and draws.
   B The hatmaker sits, wrote, and draws.
   (C) The hatmaker sits, writes, and draws.
   D No mistake
2. F Them told him to make changes.
   G They told he to make changes.
   (H) They tell him to make changes.
   J No mistake

December 1, 2000
777 Forest Street
Orange, MA 01364
Chris Little
129 Blueberry Circle
York, ME 03909

Dear Chris,
I looked at some books with drawings by Pat Cummings. She liked to draw when she was young. Then she study art and became an artist. (3) I think I will study art, too.
your's friend, (4)
Lucas

3. A Then her study art and became an artist.
   B Then she studyed art and become an artist.
   (C) Then she studied art and became an artist.
   D No mistake
4. (F) Your friend,
   G You're friend,
   H Your's friend,
   J No mistake

GRAMMAR PRACTICE BOOK, 95–96

SPELLING

GROUP Have groups of students write any ten words in scrambled order. After exchanging papers, have students unscramble the words and write sentences as a review.

Unit Review

/ou/ and /oi/
bounce
powder
oily
avoid
royalty

/ů/ and /yů/
curious
pure
pulley
soot
tour

Digraphs
crunch
whittle
batch
theater
harsh

-ed, -ing
freed
wedged
rotting
emptied
magnified

Art Words
exhibit
masterpiece
museum
professional
statue

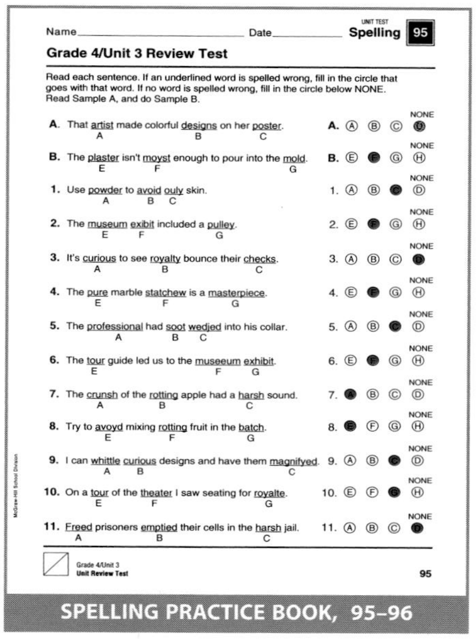

Name_______________ Date_________ UNIT TEST **Spelling** 95

Grade 4/Unit 3 Review Test

Read each sentence. If an underlined word is spelled wrong, fill in the circle that goes with that word. If no word is spelled wrong, fill in the circle below NONE. Read Sample A, and do Sample B.

A. That artist made colorful designs on her poster. A. Ⓐ Ⓑ Ⓒ ● (NONE)
B. The plaster isn't moyst enough to pour into the mold. B. Ⓔ ● Ⓖ Ⓗ
1. Use powder to avoid ouly skin. 1. Ⓐ Ⓑ ● Ⓓ
2. The museum exibit included a pulley. 2. Ⓔ ● Ⓖ Ⓗ
3. It's curious to see royalty bounce their checks. 3. Ⓐ Ⓑ Ⓒ ●
4. The pure marble statchew is a masterpiece. 4. Ⓔ ● Ⓖ Ⓗ
5. The professional had soot wedjed into his collar. 5. Ⓐ Ⓑ ● Ⓓ
6. The tour guide led us to the museeum exhibit. 6. Ⓔ ● Ⓖ Ⓗ
7. The crunsh of the rotting apple had a harsh sound. 7. ● Ⓑ Ⓒ Ⓓ
8. Try to avoyd mixing rotting fruit in the batch. 8. ● Ⓕ Ⓖ Ⓗ
9. I can whittle curious designs and have them magnifyed. 9. Ⓐ Ⓑ ● Ⓓ
10. On a tour of the theater I saw seating for royalte. 10. Ⓔ Ⓕ ● Ⓗ
11. Freed prisoners emptied their cells in the harsh jail. 11. Ⓐ Ⓑ Ⓒ ●

McGraw-Hill School Division

Grade 4/Unit 3 Unit Review Test 95

SPELLING PRACTICE BOOK, 95–96

SKILLS & STRATEGIES

Comprehension
- ☑ Judgments and Decisions
- ☑ Summarize
- ☑ Fact and Opinion
- ☑ Author's Purpose, Point of View

Vocabulary Strategies
- ☑ Suffixes
- ☑ Context Clues

Study Skills
- ☑ Graphic Aids

Writing
- ☑ Persuasive Writing

UNIT 3 TEST

Assessment Follow-Up

Use the results of the informal and formal assessment opportunities in the unit to help you make decisions about future instruction.

SKILLS AND STRATEGIES	Reteaching Blackline Masters	Alternate Teaching Strategies	Skills Intervention Guide
Comprehension			
Judgments and Decisions	75, 79, 94, 103	T60	✓
Summarize	80, 87, 101	T62	✓
Fact and Opinion	82, 86, 96, 100	T64	✓
Author's Purpose, Point of View	89, 93, 107	T66	✓
Vocabulary Strategy			
Suffixes	81, 88, 109	T63	✓
Context Clues	95, 102, 108	T65	✓
Study Skills			
Graphic Aids	78, 85, 92, 99, 106	T61	✓

Writing	Alternate Writing Project—Easy	Unit Writing Process Lesson
Persuasive Writing	281L, 297L, 331L, 359L, 369L	371E

McGraw-Hill School TECHNOLOGY

interNET CONNECTION Research and Inquiry Ideas. Visit ***www.mhschool.com/reading***

Glossary

Introduce students to the Glossary by reading through the introduction and looking over the pages with them. Encourage the class to talk about what they see.

Words in a glossary, like words in a dictionary, are listed in **alphabetical order.** Point out the **guide words** at the top of each page that tell the first and last words appearing on that page.

Point out examples of **entries** and **main entries.** Read through a simple entry with the class, identifying each part. Have students note the order in which information is given: entry word(s), definition(s), example sentence, syllable division, pronunciation respelling, part of speech, plural/verb/adjective forms.

Note that if more than one definition is given for a word, the definitions are numbered. Note also the format used for a word that is more than one part of speech.

Review the parts of speech by identifying each in a sentence:

inter.	***adj.***	***n.***	***conj.***	***adj.***	***n.***
Wow!	**A**	**dictionary**	**and**	**a**	**glossary**
v.	***adv.***	***pron.***	***prep.***	***n.***	
tell	**almost**	**everything**	**about**	**words!**	

Explain the use of the **pronunciation key** (either the **short key,** at the bottom of every other page, or the **long key,** at the beginning of the glossary). Demonstrate the difference between **primary** stress and **secondary** stress by pronouncing a word with both.

Point out an example of the small triangle signaling a homophone. **Homophones** are words with different spellings and meanings but with the same pronunciation. Explain that a pair of words with the superscripts **1** and **2** are **homographs**—words that have the same spelling, but different origins and meanings, and in some cases, different pronunciations.

The **Word History** feature tells what language a word comes from and what changes have occurred in its spelling and/or meaning. Many everyday words have interesting and surprising stories behind them. Note that word histories can help us remember the meanings of difficult words.

Allow time for students to further explore the Glossary and make their own discoveries.

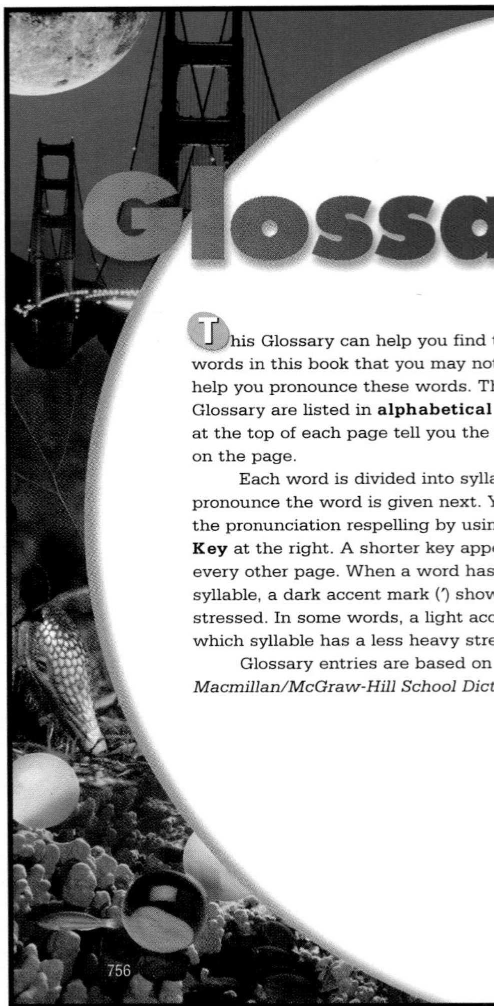

Glossary

This Glossary can help you find the **meanings** of words in this book that you may not know. It will also help you pronounce these words. The words in the Glossary are listed in **alphabetical order. Guide words** at the top of each page tell you the first and last words on the page.

Each word is divided into syllables. The way to pronounce the word is given next. You can understand the pronunciation respelling by using the **Pronunciation Key** at the right. A shorter key appears at the bottom of every other page. When a word has more than one syllable, a dark accent mark (′) shows which syllable is stressed. In some words, a light accent mark (′) shows which syllable has a less heavy stress.

Glossary entries are based on entries in *The Macmillan/McGraw-Hill School Dictionary 1.*

Guide Words

adobe/banner

First word on the page — Last word on the page

Sample Entry

Main entry — **adobe** A sandy kind of clay used to make bricks. Bits of straw are sometimes mixed with the clay, and the bricks are dried in the sun. — Definition

Example sentence — Many buildings in Mexico and the southwestern United States are made of *adobe.*

Syllable division — **a•do•be** (ə dō′ bē) *noun,* — Part of speech

plural **adobes.**

Plural form — Pronunciation

a	at, bad	d	dear, soda, bad
ā	ape, pain, day, break	f	five, defend, leaf, off, cough, elephant.
ä	father, car, heart	g	game, ago, fog, egg
âr	care, pair, bear, their, where	h	hat, ahead
e	end, pet, said, heaven, friend	hw	white, whether, which
ē	equal, me, feet, team, piece, key	j	joke, enjoy, gem, page, edge
i	it, big, English, hymn	k	kite, bakery, seek, tack, cat
ī	ice, fine, lie, my	l	lid, sailor, feel, ball, allow
îr	ear, deer, here, pierce	m	man, family, dream
o	odd, hot, watch	n	not, final, pan, knife
ō	old, oat, toe, low	ng	long, singer, pink
ô	coffee, all, taught, law, fought	p	pail, repair, soap, happy
ôr	order, fork, horse, story, pour	r	ride, parent, wear, more, marry
oi	oil, toy	s	sit, aside, pets, cent, pass
ou	out, now	sh	shoe, washer, fish, mission, nation
u	up, mud, love, double	t	tag, pretend, fat, button, dressed
ū	use, mule, cue, feud, few	th	thin, panther, both,
ü	rule, true, food	<u>th</u>	this, mother, smooth
ù	put, wood, should	v	very, favor, wave
ûr	burn, hurry, term, bird, word, courage	w	wet, weather, reward
ə	about, taken, pencil, lemon, circus	y	yes, onion
b	bat, above, job	z	zoo, lazy, jazz, rose, dogs, houses
ch	chin, such, match	zh	vision, treasure, seizure

Aa

abandon 1. To leave and not return; desert. The sailors *abandoned* the sinking ship. **2.** To give up completely. Because of heavy rain, we *abandoned* our picnic.
▲ **Synonym:** leave
a•ban•don (ə ban′ dən) *verb,* **abandoned, abandoning.**

Language Note
A **synonym** is a word with the same meaning as another word. A synonym for *abandon* is *desert.*

absorb 1. To soak up or take in. A towel *absorbed* the spilled water. **2.** To hold the interest of. The book about animals *absorbed* me.
ab•sorb (ab sôrb′ *or* ab zôrb′) *verb,* **absorbed, absorbing.**

accidental Not planned or expected; happening by chance. We did not know we would see each other; our meeting was *accidental.*
ac•ci•den•tal (ak′si den′təl) *adjective; adverb* **accidentally**.

admit 1. To make known that something is true; confess. They *admitted* that they had broken the lamp. **2.**To allow to enter; let in. We were *admitted* to the club last week.
ad•mit (ad mit′) *verb,* **admitted, admitting.**

affection A feeling of tenderness, fondness, or love. I have deep *affection* for my sister.
▲ **Synonym:** liking
af•fec•tion (ə fek′shən) *noun, plural* **affections.**

amazement Great surprise or wonder; astonishment. The people watching the whales swim by were filled with *amazement.*
a•maze•ment (ə māz′mənt) *noun.*

ancestor A person from whom one is descended. Your grandparents and great-grandparents are among your *ancestors.*
an•ces•tor (an′ses tər) *noun, plural* **ancestors.**

assure 1. To give confidence to. We *assured* the child that the dog was friendly. **2.** To state positively. I *assure* you that I won't be late.
as•sure (ə shùr′) *verb,* **assured, assuring.**

attendant A person who takes care of someone or provides service to other people. The *attendant* at the park showed us where we could rent a canoe.
at•ten•dant (ə ten′dənt) *noun, plural* **attendants.**

available 1. Possible to get. There are still a few seats available for the game. Strawberries become *available* in early summer. **2.** Ready for use or service. The telephone is now *available.*
a•vail•a•ble (ə vā′lə bəl) *adjective.*

awkward 1. Difficult or embarrassing. It was an *awkward* moment when the teacher found out that I hadn't done my homework. **2.** Lacking grace or poise in movement or behavior; clumsy or uncomfortable. The *awkward* colt had trouble standing up.
▲ **Synonym:** troublesome
awk•ward (ôk′wərd) *adjective; adverb,* **awkwardly.**

Bb

background 1. A person's experience or learning. Her *background* is in physics. **2.** The part of a picture that appears in the distance.
back•ground (bak′ground′) *noun, plural* **backgrounds**

ballerina A woman or girl who dances ballet.
bal•le•ri•na (bal′ə rē′ nə) *noun, plural* **ballerinas.**

barracks The building or buildings where soldiers live. The *barracks* are inspected every week. The word **barracks** may be used with a singular or a plural verb.
bar•racks (bar′əks) *plural noun.*

at; āpe; fär; câre; end; mē; it; īce; pîerce; hot; ōld; sông; fôrk; oil; out; up; ūse; rüle; pùll; tûrn; chin; sing; shop; thin; <u>th</u>is; **hw** in white; **zh** in treasure. The symbol **ə** stands for the unstressed vowel sound in about, taken, pencil, lemon, and circus.

beloved Loved very much. The dog was *beloved* by the whole neighborhood.
be•lov•ed (bi luv′id *or* bi luvd′) *adjective.*

bid To offer to pay. We *bid* thirty-five dollars for the old desk at the auction. *Verb.*— An offer to pay money. The rug was sold to the person who made the highest *bid. Noun.*
bid (bid) *verb,* **bid,** *or* **bidden, bidding;** *noun, plural* **bids.**

biscuit 1. A small cake of baked dough. For breakfast, he had eggs, bacon, juice, and a *biscuit.* **2.** A cracker. Every afternoon, she has tea and *biscuits.*
bis•cuit (bis′kit) *noun, plural* **biscuits.**

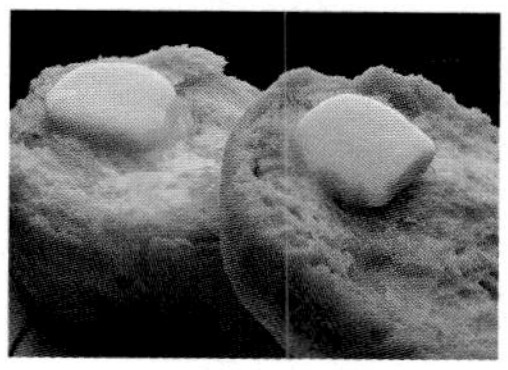

Word History
Cuit is the French word for "cooked." ***Biscuit*** comes from a 14th-century French word *bescuit,* meaning "twice-cooked bread."

brand-new Completely new. My aunt just bought a *brand-new* car.
brand-new (brand′nü *or* brand′nü) *adjective.*

brilliant 1. Very intelligent. That woman is a *brilliant* scientist. **2.** Very bright; sparkling. The North Star is a *brilliant* light in the sky.
bril•liant (bril′yənt) *adjective.*

brisk 1. Quick and lively. She walked at a *brisk* pace. **2.** Refreshing; keen; bracing. We walked in the *brisk* winter air.
brisk (brisk) *adjective,* **brisker, briskest.**

broad 1. Large from one side to the other side; wide. The side of the red barn is so *broad* that you can see it from a mile away. **2.** Wide in range; not limited. We have a *broad* knowledge of U.S. history.
broad (brôd) *adjective,* **broader, broadest.**

bulge To swell out. Because he put so many clothes in it, the suitcase *bulged. Verb.*— A rounded part that swells out. The rag made a *bulge* in the mechanic's back pocket. *Noun.*
bulge (bulj) *verb,* **bulged, bulging;** *noun, plural* **bulges;** *adjective,* **bulging.**

Cc

canoe To paddle or ride in a canoe. During the summer, they liked to go *canoeing* on the lake. *Verb.*— A light narrow boat, usually pointed at both ends and moved and steered with a paddle. The *canoe* tipped over when Eddie stood up. *Noun.*
ca•noe (kə nü′) *verb,* **canoed, canoeing;** *noun, plural* **canoes.**

captive A person or animal captured and held by force; prisoner. The police kept the *captive* in jail. *Noun.*—Held prisoner. The *captive* lion was kept in a cage. *Adjective.*
▲ **Synonym:** prisoner
cap•tive (kap′tiv) *noun, plural* **captives;** *adjective.*

captivity The state of being captive. Wolves live longer in *captivity* than in the wild.
cap•tiv•i•ty (kap ti′ və tē) *noun.*

celebration 1. The festivities carried on to observe or honor a special day or event. The wedding *celebration* is usually shared by friends and family. **2.** The act of celebrating. We went to the *celebration* of my cousin's graduation.
cel•e•bra•tion (sel′ ə brā′ shən) *noun, plural* **celebrations;** *adjective,* **celebratory.**

century A period of one hundred years. The time from 1651 to 1750 is one *century.*
century (sen′ chə rē) *noun, plural* **centuries**

challenge 1. Something calling for work, effort, and the use of one's talents. Chemistry is a real *challenge.* **2.** A call to take part in a contest or fight. In the days of duels, only a coward would refuse a *challenge. Noun.*—To question the truth or correctness of. They *challenged* my claim that bats are mammals. *Verb.*
chal•lenge (chal′ənj) *noun, plural* **challenges;** *verb,* **challenged, challenging.**

at; āpe; fär; câre; end; mē; it; īce; pîerce; hot; ōld; sông; fôrk; oil; out; up; ūse; rüle; pu̇ll; tûrn; chin; sing; shop; thin; t͟his; hw in white; zh in treasure. The symbol ə stands for the unstressed vowel sound in about, taken, pencil, lemon, and circus.

chant A singing or shouting of words over and over. *Chants* usually have a strong rhythm. *Noun.* — To sing or shout in a chant. At the election rally, the group *chanted* the name of their favorite candidate. *Verb.*
chant (chant) *noun, plural* **chants;** *verb,* **chanted, chanting.**

Word History
Chant, as it is spelled today, is based on the Middle English word *chaunten.* The Latin word *cantare,* which means "to sing," is the original basis of the word.

circulate 1. To pass from person to person. Bills and coins have *circulated* in the United States since Colonial times. **2.** To move around widely among different places. The window fan *circulates* air around the room.
cir•cu•late (sûr′kyə lāt′) *verb,* **circulated, circulating.**

climate The average weather conditions of a place or region through the year. Climate includes average temperature, rainfall, humidity, and wind conditions. Southern California has a warm, mild *climate.*
cli•mate (klī′mit) *noun, plural* **climates.**

cling To stick closely. The wet pants were *clinging* to her legs.
cling (kling) *verb,* **clung, clinging.**

clipper 1. A tool used for cutting. Use *clippers* to cut your fingernails. **2.** A fast sailing ship. American *clippers* sailed all over the world.
clip•per (klip′ər) *noun, plural* **clippers.**

clover A small plant with leaves of three leaflets and rounded, fragrant flowers of white, red, or purple.
clo•ver (klō′vər) *noun, plural* **clovers.**

cluster To grow or group in a cluster. We all *clustered* around the campfire. *Verb.*— A number of things of the same kind that grow or are grouped together. Grapes grow in *clusters. Noun.*
clus•ter (klus′tər) *verb,* **clustered, clustering;** *noun, plural* **clusters.**

combine To join together; unite. We *combined* eggs, flour, and milk to make the batter. *Verb.* — A farm machine that harvests and threshes grain. *Noun.*
com•bine (kəm bin′ *for verb;* kom′bin *for noun*) *verb,* **combined, combining;** *noun, plural* **combines.**

commercial An advertising message on radio or television. *Noun.*— Relating to business or trade. I plan to take *commercial* subjects in high school. *Adjective.*
com•mer•cial (kə mûr′shəl) *noun, plural* **commercials.**

communicate To exchange or pass along feelings, thoughts, or information. People *communicate* by speaking or writing.
com•mu•ni•cate (kə mū′ni kāt′) *verb,* **communicated, communicating.**

compare 1. To say or think that something is like something else. The writer *compared* the boom of big guns to the sound of thunder. **2.** To study in order to find out how persons or things are alike or different. We *compared* our watches and saw that your watch was five minutes ahead of mine.
com•pare (kəm pâr′) *verb,* **compared, comparing.**

compass 1. An instrument for showing directions; it has a magnetic needle that points to the north. Pilots, sailors, and many other people use compasses. The camper was able to get home because his *compass* showed him which way was west. **2.** An instrument for drawing circles or measuring distances, made up of two arms joined together at the top. One arm ends in a point and the other holds a pencil. Using a *compass,* the student was able to create a perfect circle on her drawing paper.
com•pass (kum′pəs) *noun, plural* **compasses.**

at; āpe; fär; câre; end; mē; it; īce; pîerce; hot; ōld; sông; fôrk; oil; out; up; ūse; rüle; pu̇ll; tûrn; chin; sing; shop; thin; t͟his; hw in white; zh in treasure. The symbol ə stands for the unstressed vowel sound in about, taken, pencil, lemon, and circus.

complicated Hard to understand or do. The directions for putting together the bicycle were too *complicated* for me to follow.
▲ **Synonym:** difficult
com•pli•ca•ted (kom′pli kā′tid) *adjective.*

confusion 1. The condition of being confused; disorder. In my *confusion,* I gave the wrong answer. **2.** A mistaking of one person or thing for another. Mistaking John for his twin brother Tom is a common *confusion.*
con•fu•sion (kən fū′zhən) *noun, plural* **confusions.**

connect 1. To fasten or join together. *Connect* the trailer to the car. **2.** To consider as related; associate. We *connect* robins with spring.
con•nect (kə nekt′) *verb,* **connected, connecting.**

contain 1. To include as a part of. Candy *contains* sugar. **2.** To hold. The jar *contains* candy.
con•tain (kən tān′) *verb,* **contained, containing.**

coral A hard substance like stone, found in tropical seas. Coral is made up of the skeletons of tiny sea animals. *Coral* is beautiful when growing underwater, and it is very pretty as a decoration out of the water, too. *Noun.*— Having the color coral; pinkish red. She decided to use a *coral* nail polish. *Adjective.*
cor•al (kôr′əl) *noun, plural* **corals;** *adjective.*

county 1. One of the sections into which a state or country is divided. The longest bridge in the whole state is in that *county.* **2.** The people living in a county. Most of the *county* came to the fair.
coun•ty (koun′tē) *noun, plural* **counties.**

crate A box made of slats of wood. We broke up the old apple *crates* to use in our bonfire. *Noun.* —To pack in a crate or crates. The farmer *crated* the lettuce. *Verb.*
crate (krāt) *noun, plural* **crates;** *verb,* **crated, crating.**

crate

crisscross To mark with crossing lines. The artist *crisscrossed* the paper with fine pencil marks.
criss•cross (kris′krôs) *verb,* **crisscrossed, crisscrossing.**

crumple 1. To press or crush into wrinkles or folds. He *crumpled* up the letter and threw it into the trash can. **2.** To fall down or collapse. The old shack *crumpled* when the bulldozer rammed it.
crum•ple (krum′pəl) *verb,* **crumpled, crumpling.**

cultured Having an appreciation of the arts, knowledge, and good taste and manners that are the result of education. The literature professor is a very *cultured* woman.
cul•tured (kul′chərd) *adjective.*

Dd

damage Harm that makes something less valuable or useful. The flood caused great *damage* to farms. *Noun.*— To harm or injure. Rain *damaged* the young plants. *Verb.*
dam•age (dam′ij) *noun, plural* **damages;** *verb,* **damaged, damaging.**

dart To move suddenly and quickly. The rabbit *darted* into the bushes. *Verb.*— A thin, pointed object that looks like a small arrow. He hit the target with each *dart* that he threw. *Noun.*
dart (därt) *verb,* **darted, darting;** *noun, plural* **darts.**

desire A longing; wish. I have always had a great *desire* to travel. *Noun.*—To wish for; long for. My sister *desires* a basketball more than anything. *Verb.*
de•sire (di zīr′) *noun, plural* **desires;** *verb,* **desired, desiring.**

at; āpe; fär; câre; end; mē; it; īce; pîerce; hot; ōld; sông; fôrk; oil; out; up; ūse; rüle; pu̇ll; tûrn; chin; sing; shop; thin; this; hw in white; zh in treasure. The symbol ə stands for the unstressed vowel sound in about, taken, pencil, lemon, and circus.

destroy To ruin completely; wreck. The earthquake *destroyed* the city.
▲ **Synonym:** ruin
de•stroy (di stroi′) *verb,* **destroyed, destroying.**

disaster 1. An event that causes much suffering or loss. The flood was a *disaster.* **2.** Something that does not go right. My birthday party was a *disaster* because it rained.
▲ **Synonym:** catastrophe
dis•as•ter (di zas′tər) *noun, plural* **disasters.**

display To show or exhibit. The art museum is now *displaying* some of Monet's paintings. *Verb.* —A show or exhibit. A hug is a *display* of affection. *Noun.*
dis•play (dis plā′) *verb,* **displayed, displaying;** *noun, plural* **displays.**

ditch A long, narrow hole dug in the ground. Ditches are used to drain off water. After the rain shower, the *ditch* was full. *Noun.*— To make an emergency landing in water. No pilot wants to have to *ditch* an airplane. *Verb.*
ditch (dich) *noun, plural* **ditches;** *verb,* **ditched, ditching.**

downstage Toward the front of a theatrical stage. The prop was supposed to land *downstage* left. *Adverb* or *adjective.*
down•stage (doun′stāj′) *adverb; adjective.*

Ee

editor 1. A person who edits. The *editor* made changes in the book after talking with its author. **2.** A person who writes editorials. The newspaper *editor* wrote an article in favor of raising city taxes.
ed•i•tor (ed′i tər) *noun, plural* **editors.**

eerie Strange in a scary way; making people frightened or nervous. Walking through that abandoned house was an *eerie* experience.
▲ **Synonym:** creepy
ee•rie (îr′ē) *adjective,* **eerier, eeriest.**

eldest Born first; oldest. I am the *eldest* of three children.
el•dest (el′dist) *adjective.*

elegant Rich and fine in quality. The museum has a major display of *elegant* costumes.
▲ **Synonym:** tasteful
el•e•gant (el′i gənt) *adjective; noun,* **elegance;** *adverb,* **elegantly.**

Word History
The word ***elegant*** first appeared in the English language in the 15th century. The word comes from the Latin *eligere,* which means "to select."

endanger 1. To threaten with becoming extinct. Pollution is *endangering* many different species of animals. **2.** To put in a dangerous situation. The flood *endangered* the lives of hundreds of people.
▲ **Synonym:** risk
en•dan•ger (en dān′jər) *verb,* **endangered, endangering.**

endless 1. Having no limit or end; going on forever. The drive across the desert seemed *endless.* **2.** Without ends. A circle is *endless.*
end•less (end′lis) *adjective.*

enterprise Something that a person plans or tries to do. An *enterprise* is often something difficult or important. The search for the treasure was an exciting *enterprise.*
en•ter•prise (en′tər prīz′) *noun, plural* **enterprises.**

entertain 1. To keep interested and amused. The clown *entertained* the children. **2.** To have as a guest. They often *entertain* people in their house in the country.
en•ter•tain (en′tər tān′) *verb,* **entertained, entertaining.**

at; āpe; fär; câre; end; mē; it; īce; pîerce; hot; ōld; sông; fôrk; oil; out; up; ūse; rüle; pu̇ll; tûrn; chin; sing; shop; thin; this; hw in white; zh in treasure. The symbol ə stands for the unstressed vowel sound in about, taken, pencil, lemon, and circus.

errand 1. A short trip to do something. I have to run several *errands* this morning. 2. Something a person is sent to do; the purpose of such a trip. Our *errand* was to buy the newspaper.
er•rand (er′ənd) *noun, plural* **errands.**

exist 1. To be found. Outside of zoos, polar bears *exist* only in arctic regions. 2. To be real. I do not believe that ghosts *exist.*
ex•ist (eg zist′) *verb,* **existed, existing.**

expensive Having a high price; very costly. The town bought an *expensive* new fire engine.
▲ **Synonym:** costly
ex•pen•sive (ek spen′siv) *adjective.*

extinct 1. No longer existing. The dodo became *extinct* because people hunted it for food. 2. No longer active. The village is built over an *extinct* volcano.
ex•tinct (ek stingkt′) *adjective; noun,* **extinction.**

extraordinary Very unusual; remarkable. The teacher said my friend had *extraordinary* talent.
ex•tra•or•di•nar•y (ek strôr′də ner′ē *or* ek′strə ôr′də ner′ē) *adjective.*

Ff

fang A long, pointed tooth. When trying to look threatening, a wolf shows its *fangs.*
fang (fang) *noun, plural* **fangs.**

feeble Not strong; weak. That is a *feeble* excuse.
fee•ble (fē′bəl) *adjective,* **feebler, feeblest;** *noun,* **feebleness;** *adverb,* **feebly.**

festival 1. A program of special activities or shows. We saw a foreign film at the film *festival.* 2. A celebration or holiday. There were plenty of delicious foods to try at the street *festival.*
fes•ti•val (fes′tə vəl) *noun, plural* **festivals.**

foggy 1. Full of or hidden by fog; misty. Driving is dangerous on *foggy* days and nights. 2. Confused or unclear. The ideas were *foggy* and the project needed more research to clear things up.
fog•gy (fôg′ē *or* fog′ē) *adjective,* **foggier, foggiest.**

footpath A trail or path for people to walk on. We walked on the *footpath* beside the road.
foot•path (fůt′path) *noun, plural* **footpaths.**

foul Very unpleasant or dirty. The water in the old well looked *foul. Adjective.* —A violation of the rules. The basketball player committed a *foul. Noun.*
▲ Another word that sounds like this is **fowl.**
foul (foul) *adjective,* **fouler, foulest;** *noun, plural* **fouls.**

fowl One of a number of birds used for food. Chicken, turkey, and duck are kinds of *fowl.* We always eat *fowl* for Thanksgiving dinner.
▲ Another word that sounds like this is **foul.**
fowl (foul) *noun, plural* **fowl** *or* **fowls.**

fowl

fragrance A sweet or pleasing smell. Roses have a beautiful *fragrance.*
▲ **Synonym:** smell
fra•grance (frā′grəns) *noun, plural* **fragrances.**

fray To separate into loose threads. Many years of wear had *frayed* the cuffs of the coat.
fray (frā) *verb,* **frayed, fraying.**

freeze 1. To harden because of the cold. When water *freezes,* it becomes ice. 2. To cover or block with ice. The cold weather *froze* the pipes.
freeze (frēz) *verb,* **froze, frozen, freezing.**

at; āpe; fär; câre; end; mē; it; īce; pîerce; hot; ōld; sông; fôrk; oil; out; up; ūse; rüle; půll; tûrn; chin; sing; shop; thin; this; hw in white; zh in treasure. The symbol ə stands for the unstressed vowel sound in about, taken, pencil, lemon, and circus.

fret To suffer emotional distress; irritation. My brother *frets* whenever he gets a low grade on a test. *Verb.* —One of the ridges fixed across the fingerboard of a stringed instrument such as a guitar. The notes get higher each time I move my finger up a *fret. Noun.*
fret (fret) *verb,* **fretted, fretting;** *noun, plural* **frets.**

Gg

gallon A unit of measure for liquids. A *gallon* equals four quarts, or about 3.8 liters.
gal•lon (gal′ən) *noun, plural* **gallons.**

garbage Things that are thrown out. All the spoiled food went into the *garbage.*
▲ **Synonym:** trash
gar•bage (gär′bij) *noun.*

generation 1. A group of persons born around the same time. My parents call us the younger *generation.* 2. One step in the line of descent from a common ancestor. A grandparent, parent, and child make up three *generations.*
gen•er•a•tion (jen′ə rāsh′ən) *noun, plural* **generations.**

gild To cover with a thin layer of gold. The artist *gilded* the picture frame.
▲ Another word that sounds like this is **guild.**
gild (gild) *verb,* **gilded** *or* **gilt, gilding.**

girth The measurement around an object. The *girth* of the old redwood tree was tremendous.
girth (gûrth) *noun, plural* **girths.**

glint To sparkle or flash. Her eyes *glinted* with merriment.
glint (glint) *verb,* **glinted, glinting.**

glisten To shine with reflected light. The snow *glistened* in the sun.
glis•ten (glis′ən) *verb,* **glistened, glistening.**

glum Very unhappy or disappointed. Every member of the losing team looked *glum* after the game.
glum (glum) *adjective,* **glummer, glummest.**

gourd A rounded fruit related to the pumpkin or squash. Gourds grow on vines and have a hard outer rind. The hollow *gourd* hung above the tub of water.
gourd (gôrd) *noun, plural* **gourds.**

governess A woman who supervises and cares for a child, especially in a private household. The *governess* made sure the children were ready for bed.
gov•ern•ess (guv′ər nis) *noun, plural* **governesses.**

graze 1. To feed on growing grass. The sheep *grazed* on the hillside. 2. To scrape or touch lightly in passing. The branch *grazed* the house when the wind blew.
graze (grāz) *verb,* **grazed, grazing.**

guilt 1. A feeling of having done something wrong; shame. I felt *guilt* because I got angry at a good friend. 2. The condition or fact of having done something wrong or having broken the law. The evidence proved the robber's *guilt.*
▲ Another word that sounds like this is **gilt.**
guilt (gilt) *noun; adjective,* **guilty.**

Hh

harbor A sheltered place along a coast. Ships and boats often anchor in a *harbor. Noun.*—To give protection or shelter to. It is against the law to *harbor* a criminal. *Verb.*
har•bor (här′bər) *noun, plural* **harbors;** *verb,* **harbored, harboring.**

haul To pull or move with force; drag. We *hauled* the trunk up the stairs. *Verb.*— The act of hauling. It was an easy *haul* by truck. *Noun.*
▲ Another word that sounds like this is **hall.**
haul (hôl) *verb,* **hauled, hauling;** *noun, plural* **hauls.**

at; āpe; fär; câre; end; mē; it; īce; pîerce; hot; ōld; sông; fôrk; oil; out; up; ūse; rüle; půll; tûrn; chin; sing; shop; thin; this; hw in white; zh in treasure. The symbol ə stands for the unstressed vowel sound in about, taken, pencil, lemon, and circus.

haze Mist, smoke, or dust in the air. The bridge was hidden in the *haze.*
haze (hāz) *noun, plural* **hazes.**

headlong 1. With the head first. The runner slid *headlong* into second base. **2.** In a reckless way; rashly. I rushed *headlong* into buying the bicycle.
head•long (hed′lông′) *adverb.*

healthy Having or showing good health. She has a *healthy* outlook on life.
health•y (hel′thē) *adjective,* **healthier, healthiest.**

heave 1. To lift, raise, pull, or throw using force or effort. I *heaved* a rock across the stream. **2.** To utter in an effortful way. I *heaved* a sigh of relief.
heave (hēv) *verb,* **heaved, heaving.**

hilltop The top of a hill. From the *hilltop,* the hikers could see the smoke from the campfire.
hill•top (hil′top′) *noun, plural* **hilltops.**

horizon 1. The line where the sky and the ground or the sea seem to meet. The fishing boat headed out to sea just as the sun rose above the *horizon.* **2.** The limit of a person's knowledge, interests, or experience. You can widen your *horizons* by reading books.
hor•i•zon (hə rī′zən) *noun, plural* **horizons.**

huddle To gather close together in a bunch. The scouts *huddled* around the campfire to keep warm. *Verb.*—A group of people or animals gathered close together. The football players formed a *huddle* to plan their next play. *Noun.*
hud•dle (hud′əl) *verb,* **huddled, huddling;** *noun, plural* **huddles.**

Ii

iceberg A very large piece of floating ice that has broken off from a glacier. Only the tip of the *iceberg* is visible above the surface of the water.
ice•berg (īs′bûrg′) *noun, plural* **icebergs.**

identify To find out or tell exactly who a person is or what a thing is; recognize. Can you *identify* this strange object?
▲ **Synonym:** recognize
i•den•ti•fy (ī den′tə fī′) *verb,* **identified, identifying.**

ignorant 1. Not informed or aware. I wasn't wearing my watch, so I was *ignorant* of the time. **2.** Showing a lack of knowledge. The young cowhands were *ignorant* at first of how to brand cattle, but they learned quickly.
ig•no•rant (ig′nər ənt) *adjective.*

image 1. A person who looks very similar to someone else. That girl is the *image* of her mother. **2.** A picture or other likeness of a person or thing. A penny has an *image* of Abraham Lincoln on one side of it.
im•age (im′ij) *noun, plural* **images.**

importance The state of being important; having great value or meaning. Rain is of great *importance* to farmers, since crops can't grow without water.
im•por•tance (im pôr′təns) *noun.*

ingredient Any one of the parts that go into a mixture. Flour, eggs, sugar, and butter are the main *ingredients* of this cake.
in•gre•di•ent (in grē′dē ənt) *noun, plural* **ingredients.**

injury Harm or damage done to a person or thing. The accident caused an *injury* to my leg.
in•ju•ry (in′jə rē) *noun, plural* **injuries.**

inning One of the parts into which a baseball or softball game is divided. Both teams bat during an inning until three players on each team are put out. Our team won the game by scoring five runs in the last *inning.*
in•ning (in′ing) *noun, plural* **innings.**

at; āpe; fär; câre; end; mē; it; īce; pîerce; hot; ōld; sông; fôrk; oil; out; up; ūse; rüle; pu̇ll; tûrn; chin; sing; shop; thin; this; hw in white; zh in treasure. The symbol ə stands for the unstressed vowel sound in about, taken, pencil, lemon, and circus.

inspect To look at closely and carefully. The official *inspected* our car and declared it safe to drive.
▲ **Synonym:** examine
in•spect (in spekt′) *verb,* **inspected, inspecting.**

inspire 1. To stir the mind, feelings, or imagination of. The senator's speech *inspired* the audience. **2.** To fill with a strong, encouraging feeling. Success in school *inspired* me with hope for the future.
▲ **Synonym:** encourage
in•spire (in spīr′) *verb,* **inspired, inspiring.**

instance An example; case. There are many *instances* of immigrants becoming famous Americans.
in•stance (in′stəns) *noun, plural* **instances.**

instinct A way of acting or behaving that a person or animal is born with and does not have to learn. Birds build nests by *instinct.*
in•stinct (in′stingkt′) *noun, plural* **instincts.**

Jj

jagged Having sharp points that stick out. Some eagles build nests on *jagged* cliffs.
jag•ged (jag′id) *adjective.*

Kk

keel To fall over suddenly; collapse. The heat in the crowded subway caused two people to *keel* over. *Verb.*— A wooden or metal piece that runs along the center of the bottom of many ships and boats. When we sailed through the shallow waters, the *keel* scraped along the bottom of the lake. *Noun.*
keel (kēl) *verb,* **keeled, keeling;** *noun, plural* **keels.**

knapsack A bag made of canvas, leather, nylon, or other material that is used for carrying clothes, books, equipment, or other supplies. A knapsack is strapped over the shoulders and carried on the back. Because she left her *knapsack* on the bus, she couldn't turn in her homework assignment.
▲ **Synonym:** backpack
knap•sack (nap′sak′) *noun, plural* **knapsacks.**

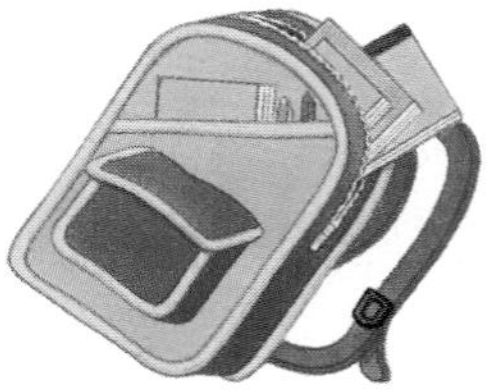

knowledge 1. An understanding that is gained through experience or study. I have enough *knowledge* of football to be able to follow a game. **2.** The fact of knowing. The *knowledge* that the car could slide on the icy road made the driver more careful.
knowl•edge (nol′ij) *noun.*

Ll

labor To do hard work. The two women *labored* over the quilt, hoping to finish it in time for the birthday party. *Verb.*—Hard work; toil. The farmers were tired after their *labor. Noun.*
la•bor (lā′bər) *verb,* **labored, laboring;** *noun, plural* **labors.**

launch To start something. The company *launched* its store with a big sale. *Verb.*—The act or process of launching. We watched the rocket *launch* on television. *Noun.*
launch (lônch) *verb,* **launched, launching;** *noun, plural* **launches.**

league 1. A number of people, groups, or countries joined together for a common purpose. Those two teams belong to the same *league.* **2.** A measure of distance used in the past, equal to about three miles. The army's camp was only two *leagues* from the city.
league (lēg) *noun, plural* **leagues.**

at; āpe; fär; câre; end; mē; it; īce; pîerce; hot; ōld; sông; fôrk; oil; out; up; ūse; rüle; pu̇ll; tûrn; chin; sing; shop; thin; this; hw in white; zh in treasure. The symbol ə stands for the unstressed vowel sound in about, taken, pencil, lemon, and circus.

linger To stay on as if not wanting to leave; move slowly. The fans *lingered* outside the stadium to see the team.
lin•ger (ling′gər) *verb,* **lingered, lingering.**

lodge A small house, cottage, or cabin. The hunters stayed at a *lodge* in the mountains. *Noun.*—To live in a place for a while. People *lodged* in the school during the flood. *Verb.*
lodge (loj) *noun, plural* **lodges;** *verb,* **lodged, lodging.**

loft 1. The upper floor, room, or space in a building. The artist cleaned his *loft.* **2.** An upper floor or balcony in a large hall or church. The choir sang in the choir *loft.*
loft (lôft) *noun, plural* **lofts.**

loosen 1. To make or become looser. *Loosen* your necktie. **2.** To set free or release. The dog had been *loosened* from its leash.
loosen (lü′sen) *verb,* **loosened, loosening.**

lurk 1. To lie hidden, especially in preparation for an attack. Snakes *lurk* under rocks. **2.** To move about quietly; sneak. Thieves *lurk* in the shadows.
lurk (lûrk) *verb,* **lurked, lurking.**

Mm

machine 1. A device that does a particular job, made up of a number of parts that work together. A lawn mower, a hair dryer, and a printing press are *machines.* **2.** A simple device that lessens the force needed to move an object. A lever and a pulley are simple *machines.*
ma•chine (mə shēn′) *noun, plural* **machines.**

malachite A green mineral that is used for making ornaments.
mal•a•chite (mal′ə kit′) *noun.*

mammal A kind of animal that is warm-blooded and has a backbone. Human beings are *mammals.*
mam•mal (mam′əl) *noun, plural* **mammals.**

marine Having to do with or living in the sea. Whales are *marine* animals. *Adjective.*—A member of the Marine Corps. She joined the *Marines* after she graduated. *Noun.*
ma•rine (mə rēn′) *adjective; noun, plural* **marines.**

marketplace A place where food and other products are bought and sold. In old towns the *marketplace* was often in a square.
mar•ket•place (mär′kit plās′) *noun, plural* **marketplaces.**

marvel To feel wonder and astonishment. We *marveled* at the acrobat's skill. *Verb.*—A wonderful or astonishing thing. Space travel is one of the *marvels* of modern science. *Noun.*
mar•vel (mär′vəl) *verb,* **marveled, marveling;** *noun, plural* **marvels.**

mature Having reached full growth or development; ripe. When a puppy becomes *mature* it is called a dog. *Adjective.*—To become fully grown or developed. The tomatoes are *maturing* fast. *Verb.*
ma•ture (mə chür′ *or* mə tür′) *adjective; verb,* **matured, maturing.**

maze A confusing series of paths or passageways through which people may have a hard time finding their way. I got lost in the *maze* of hallways in my new school.
maze (māz) *noun, plural* **mazes.**

at; āpe; fär; câre; end; mē; it; īce; pîerce; hot; ōld; sông; fôrk; oil; out; up; ūse; rüle; pu̇ll; tûrn; chin; sing; shop; thin; this; hw in white; zh in treasure. The symbol ə stands for the unstressed vowel sound in about, taken, pencil, lemon, and circus.

memorize To learn by heart; fix in the memory. You can *memorize* the poem by reciting it over and over.
mem•o•rize (mem′ə rīz′) *verb,* **memorized, memorizing.**

merely Nothing more than; only. Your explanations are *merely* excuses.
mere•ly (mîr′lē) *adverb.*

messenger A person who delivers messages or runs errands. The *messenger* was delayed by traffic.
mes•sen•ger (mes′ən jər) *noun, plural* **messengers.**

method 1. A way of doing something. Speaking on the telephone is a *method* of communicating. **2.** Order or system. I could not find what I wanted because the books had been shelved without *method.*
meth•od (meth′əd) *noun, plural* **methods.**

microscope A device for looking at things that are too small to be seen with the naked eye. It has one or more lenses that produce an enlarged image of anything viewed through it.
mi•cro•scope (mī′krə skōp′) *noun, plural* **microscopes.**

microscope

mingle 1. To put or come together; mix; join. This stream *mingles* with others to form a river. **2.** To move about freely; join; associate. We *mingled* with the other guests.
min•gle (ming′gəl) *verb,* **mingled, mingling.**

molar Any one of the large teeth at the back of the mouth. *Molars* have broad surfaces for grinding food.
mo•lar (mō′lər) *noun, plural* **molars.**

moonscape View of the surface of the moon.
moon•scape (mün′skāp′) *noun, plural* **moonscapes.**

mound A slightly raised area. The pitcher stands on the *mound* to pitch the ball. *Noun.*—To pile in a hill or heap. I like to *mound* ice cream on top of my pie. *Verb.*
mound (mound) *noun, plural* **mounds;** *verb,* **mounded, mounding.**

mug A large drinking cup with a handle, often made of pottery or metal. I drink tea out of my purple *mug. Noun.*—To attack and rob someone. A lady was *mugged* of all her belongings. *Verb.*
mug (mug) *noun, plural* **mugs;** *verb,* **mugged, mugging.**

mutter To speak in a low, unclear way with the mouth almost closed. I *muttered* to myself. *Verb.* —Oral sounds produced in a low, unclear way. There was a *mutter* of disapproval from the audience. *Noun.*
mut•ter (mut′ər) *verb,* **muttered, muttering;** *noun.*

Nn

native Originally living or growing in a region or country. Raccoons are *native* to America. *Adjective.* —A person who was born in a particular country or place. One of my classmates is a *native* of Germany. *Noun.*
na•tive (nā′tiv) *adjective; noun, plural* **natives.**

natural 1. Found in nature; not made by people; not artificial. *Natural* rock formations overlook the river. **2.** Existing from birth; not the result of teaching or training. Is your musical talent *natural,* or did you take lessons?
nat•u•ral (nach′ər əl) *adjective.*

neighbor A person, place, or thing that is next to or near another. Our *neighbor* took care of our dog while we were away.
neigh•bor (nā′bər) *noun, plural* **neighbors.**

newsletter A small publication containing news of interest to a special group of people. Our chess club publishes a monthly *newsletter.*
news•let•ter (nüz′let′ər) *noun, plural* **newsletters.**

at; āpe; fär; câre; end; mē; it; īce; pîerce; hot; ōld; sông; fôrk; oil; out; up; ūse; rüle; pu̇ll; tûrn; chin; sing; shop; thin; this; hw in white; zh in treasure. The symbol ə stands for the unstressed vowel sound in about, taken, pencil, lemon, and circus.

nip **1.** To bite or pinch quickly and not hard. The parrot *nipped* my finger. **2.** To cut off by pinching. The gardener *nipped* the dead leaves off the plants.
nip (nip) *verb,* **nipped, nipping.**

nursery **1.** A baby's bedroom. The baby's *nursery* was painted pink and blue. **2.** A place where young children are taken care of during the day.
nurs•er•y (nûr′sə rē) *noun, plural* **nurseries.**

Oo

occasion **1.** An important or special event. The baby's first birthday was an *occasion.* **2.** A time when something happens. I have met that person on several *occasions.*
oc•ca•sion (ə kā′zhən) *noun, plural* **occasions.**

opponent A person or group that is against another in a fight, contest, or discussion. The soccer team beat its *opponent.*
▲ **Synonym:** enemy
op•po•nent (ə pō′nənt) *noun, plural* **opponents.**

orchard An area of land where fruit trees are grown. We picked apples in the apple *orchard.*
or•chard (ôr′chərd) *noun, plural* **orchards.**

organization **1.** A group of people joined together for a particular purpose. The Red Cross is an international *organization.* **2.** The act of organizing. Who is responsible for the *organization* of the school dance?
or•gan•i•za•tion (ôr′gə nə zā′shən) *noun, plural* **organizations.**

original Relating to or belonging to the origin or beginning of something; first. The *original* owner of the house still lives there. *Adjective.* —Something that is original; not a copy, imitation, or translation. That painting is an *original* by Monet. *Noun.*
o•rig•i•nal (ə rij′ə nəl) *adjective; noun, plural* **originals.**

orphan A child whose parents are dead. The little *orphan* was raised by her grandparents. *Noun.* —To make an orphan of. The war *orphaned* many children. *Verb.*
or•phan (ôr′fən) *noun, plural* **orphans;** *verb,* **orphaned, orphaning.**

overalls Loose-fitting trousers with a piece that covers the chest and attached suspenders.
o•ver•alls (ō′vər ôlz′) *plural noun.*

overcome **1.** To get the better of; beat or conquer. The tired runner couldn't *overcome* the others in the race. **2.** To get over or deal with. I *overcame* my fear of small spaces.
▲ **Synonym:** defeat
o•ver•come (ō′vər kum′) *verb,* **overcame, overcome, overcoming.**

overflow To be so full that the contents spill over. The bathtub *overflowed. Verb.*— Something that flows over. We mopped up the *overflow. Noun.*
o•ver•flow (ō′vər flō′ *for verb;* ō′vər flō′ *for noun*) *verb,* **overflowed, overflowing;** *noun.*

oxygen A colorless, odorless gas that makes up about one fifth of our air.
ox•y•gen (ok′si jən) *noun.*

Pp

pathway A course or route taken to reach a particular place. This *pathway* leads to the rose garden.
path•way (path′wā′) *noun, plural* **pathways.**

patient A person under the care or treatment of a doctor. The pediatrician had many *patients* to see. *Noun.*—Having or showing an ability to put up with hardship, pain, trouble, or delay without getting angry or upset. I tried to be *patient* while I waited in the line at the post office. *Adjective.*
pa•tient (pā′shənt) *noun, plural* **patients;** *adjective.*

at; āpe; fär; câre; end; mē; it; īce; pîerce; hot; ōld; sông; fôrk; oil; out; up; ūse; rüle; pùll; tûrn; chin; sing; shop; thin; this; hw in white; zh in treasure. The symbol ə stands for the unstressed vowel sound in about, taken, pencil, lemon, and circus.

peddler One who carries goods from place to place and offers them for sale.
▲ **Synonym:** vendor
ped•dler (ped′lər) *noun, plural* **peddlers.**

percent The number of parts in every hundred. The symbol for *percent* when it is written with a number is %.
per•cent (pər sent′) *noun.*

permit To allow or let. My parents will not *permit* me to play outside after dark. *Verb.*—A written order giving permission to do something. You need a *permit* to fish here. *Noun.*
per•mit (pər mit′ *for verb;* pûr′mit *or* pər mit′ *for noun*) *verb,* **permitted, permitting;** *noun, plural* **permits.**

Word History
Permit comes from the Latin word *permittere,* "to let through."

pesky Troublesome or annoying. If that *pesky* fly does not stop buzzing in my ear, I'll swat it.
▲ **Synonym:** annoying
pes•ky (pes′kē) *adjective,* **peskier, peskiest.**

plantation A large estate or farm worked by laborers who live there. Cotton is grown on *plantations.*
plan•ta•tion (plan tā′shən) *noun, plural* **plantations.**

pod A part of a plant that holds a number of seeds as they grow. Beans and peas grow in *pods.*
pod (pod) *noun, plural* **pods.**

poisonous Containing a drug or other substance that harms or kills by chemical action. Many household chemicals are *poisonous.*
poi•son•ous (poi′zən əs) *adjective.*

poncho A cloak made of one piece of cloth or other material, with a hole in the middle for the head.
pon•cho (pon′chō) *noun, plural* **ponchos.**

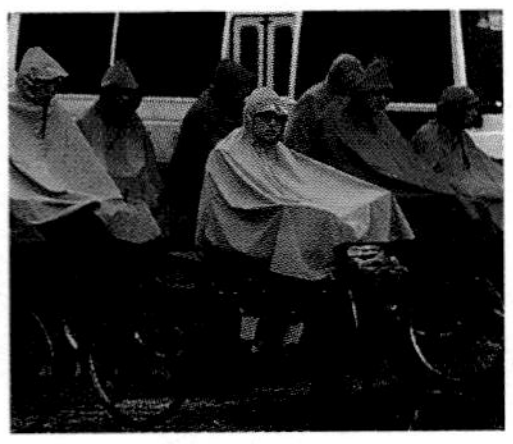

portable Easy to carry from place to place. *Portable* computers are very popular.
port•a•ble (pôr′tə bəl) *adjective.*

portfolio **1.** A case for carrying loose pictures, pamphlets, or papers. I placed all the pictures in my *portfolio.* **2.** A set of drawings or pictures bound in a book or a folder. I must get my *portfolio* ready for the meeting
port•fo•lio (pôrt fō′lē ō′) *noun, plural* **portfolios.**

pottery Pots, bowls, dishes, and other things made from clay. I made a bowl in *pottery* class.
pot•ter•y (pot′ə rē) *noun.*

pouch **1.** A bag; sack. The mail carrier took the letters out of her *pouch.* **2.** A pocket of skin in some animals. Kangaroos and opossums carry their young in *pouches.*
pouch (pouch) *noun, plural* **pouches.**

prairie Flat or rolling land covered with grass, and with few or no trees.
prai•rie (prâr′ē) *noun, plural* **prairies.**

prairie

praise An expression of high regard and approval. The teacher had nothing but *praise* for the student's drawing. *Noun.*—To worship. The minister *praised* God in her sermon. *Verb.*
praise (prāz) *noun, plural* **praises;** *verb,* **praised, praising.**

prance **1.** To spring forward on the hind legs. The colt *pranced* and leaped about the field. **2.** To move in a proud, happy way. The children *pranced* around the house in their fancy costumes.
prance (prans) *verb,* **pranced, prancing.**

at; āpe; fär; câre; end; mē; it; īce; pîerce; hot; ōld; sông; fôrk; oil; out; up; ūse; rüle; pùll; tûrn; chin; sing; shop; thin; this; hw in white; zh in treasure. The symbol ə stands for the unstressed vowel sound in about, taken, pencil, lemon, and circus.

prejudice Hatred or unfair treatment of a particular group, such as members of a race or religion. *Noun.*—To cause to have prejudice. Being hurt once by a dentist *prejudiced* me against all dentists. *Verb.*
  prej•u•dice (prej′ə dis) *noun, plural* **prejudices;** *verb,* **prejudiced, prejudicing.**

preserve To keep from being lost, damaged, or decayed; protect. It is important that we *preserve* our freedoms. *Verb.*—An area set aside for the protection of plants and animals. Rare birds and mammals breed in that nature *preserve. Noun.*
  pre•serve (pri zûrv′) *verb,* **preserved, preserving;** *noun, plural* **preserves.**

pressure The force exerted by one thing pushing against another. The *pressure* of his foot on the gas pedal caused the car to go faster. *Noun.*—To urge strongly. The salesperson tried to *pressure* me into buying something I didn't need. *Verb.*
  pres•sure (presh′ər) *noun, plural* **pressures;** *verb,* **pressured, pressuring.**

previously Before; at an earlier time. We had been introduced *previously.*
▲ **Synonym:** earlier
  pre•vi•ous•ly (prē′vē əs lē) *adverb.*

Qq

quibble A minor dispute or disagreement. It's foolish to have a *quibble* over nothing. *Noun.* To engage in petty arguing. The two sisters *quibbled* for half an hour about who would take out the garbage. *Verb.*
  quib•ble (kwi′bəl) *noun, plural* **quibbles;** *verb,* **quibbled, quibbling.**

Rr

racial Of or relating to a race of human beings. *Racial* prejudice is prejudice against people because of their race.
  ra•cial (rā′shəl) *adjective;* *adverb,* **racially.**

ramp A sloping platform or passageway connecting two different levels.
  ramp (ramp) *noun, plural* **ramps.**

reef A ridge of sand, rock, or coral at or near the surface of the ocean. We like to swim near the beautiful *reefs.*
  reef (rēf) *noun, plural* **reefs.**

reference 1. A person or thing referred to; source of information. The encyclopedia was the *reference* for my report. **2.** A statement that calls or directs attention to something. The authors made a *reference* to their book.
  ref•er•ence (ref′ər əns *or* ref′rəns) *noun, plural* **references.**

reflect 1. To give back an image of something. I saw myself *reflected* in the pond. **2.** To turn or throw back. Sand *reflects* light and heat from the sun.
  re•flect (ri flekt′) *verb,* **reflected, reflecting.**

rein One of two or more narrow straps attached to a bridle or bit, used to guide and control a horse. The jockey held tightly to the horse's *reins. Noun.*—To guide, control, or hold back. The rider tried to *rein* in the galloping horse. *Verb.*
  rein (rān) *noun, plural* **reins;** *verb,* **reined, reining.**

related 1. Belonging to the same family. You and your cousins are *related.* **2.** Having some connection. I have problems *related* to school.
  re•la•ted (ri lā′tid) *adjective.*

at; āpe; fär; câre; end; mē; it; īce; pîerce; hot; ōld; sông; fôrk; oil; out; up; ūse; rüle; pu̇ll; tûrn; chin; sing; shop; thin; t͟his; hw in white; zh in treasure. The symbol ə stands for the unstressed vowel sound in about, taken, pencil, lemon, and circus.

release To set free; let go. The hostage was *released* after being held prisoner for ten days. *Verb.* —The act of releasing or the state of being released. The criminal's *release* from prison made headlines. *Noun.*
  re•lease (ri lēs′) *verb,* **released, releasing;** *noun, plural* **releases.**

relieve 1. To free from discomfort or pain; comfort. The doctor gave me medicine to *relieve* my cough. **2.** To free from a job or duty. The lifeguards stayed on duty until they were *relieved.*
  re•lieve (ri lēv′) *verb,* **relieved, relieving.**

reptile One of a class of cold-blooded animals with a backbone and dry, scaly skin, which move by crawling on their stomachs or creeping on short legs.
  rep•tile (rep′təl *or* rep′tīl) *noun, plural* **reptiles.**

require 1. To have a need of. We all *require* food and sleep. **2.** To force, order, or demand. The law *requires* drivers to stop at a red light.
  re•quire (ri kwīr′) *verb,* **required, requiring.**

research A careful study to find and learn facts. I did *research* in the library for my report. *Noun.* —To do research on or for. I *researched* my speech by reading many books on the subject. *Verb.*
  re•search (ri sûrch′ *or* rē′sûrch′) *verb,* **researched, researching;** *noun, plural* **researches.**

resemble To be like or similar to. That hat *resembles* mine.
  re•sem•ble (ri zem′bəl) *verb,* **resembled, resembling.**

resound 1. To be filled with sound. The stadium *resounded* with cheers. **2.** To make a loud, long, or echoing sound. Thunder *resounded* in the air.
  re•sound (ri zound′) *verb,* **resounded, resounding.**

restless 1. Not able to rest. We got *restless* during the long speech. **2.** Not giving rest. The patient spent a *restless* night.
  rest•less (rest′lis) *adjective;* *adverb,* **restlessly;** *noun,* **restlessness.**

rhythm A regular or orderly repeating of sounds or movements. We marched to the *rhythm* of drums.
  rhythm (rith′əm) *noun, plural* **rhythms.**

roadblock A barrier or obstacle that prevents people or cars from passing through.
  road•block (rōd′blok′) *noun, plural* **roadblocks.**

robot A machine that can do some of the same things that a human being can do.
  ro•bot (rō′bət *or* rō′bot) *noun, plural* **robots.**

Ss

sacrifice The giving up of something for the sake of someone or something else. The parents made many *sacrifices* in order to send their children to college. *Noun.* —To offer as a sacrifice. Ancient peoples *sacrificed* animals to their gods. *Verb.*
  sac•ri•fice (sak′rə fīs′) *noun, plural* **sacrifices;** *verb,* **sacrificed, sacrificing;** *adjective,* **sacrificial.**

sage A very wise person, usually old and respected. *Noun.*— Having or showing great wisdom and sound judgment. My grandparents often give me *sage* advice. *Adjective.*
  sage (sāj) *noun, plural* **sages;** *adjective,* **sager, sagest.**

sagebrush A plant that grows on the dry plains of western North America.
  sage•brush (sāj′brush′) *noun.*

scamper To run or move quickly. The rabbit *scampered* into the woods.
  scam•per (skam′pər) *verb,* **scampered, scampering.**

at; āpe; fär; câre; end; mē; it; īce; pîerce; hot; ōld; sông; fôrk; oil; out; up; ūse; rüle; pu̇ll; tûrn; chin; sing; shop; thin; t͟his; hw in white; zh in treasure. The symbol ə stands for the unstressed vowel sound in about, taken, pencil, lemon, and circus.

scribble To write or draw quickly or carelessly. I *scribbled* a note to my friend. *Verb.*—Writing or drawing that is made by scribbling. The paper was covered with messy *scribbles. Noun.*
scrib•ble (skrib′əl) *verb,* **scribbled, scribbling;** *noun, plural* **scribbles;** *noun,* **scribbler.**

scuba (Self-Contained Underwater Breathing Apparatus) Equipment used for swimming underwater.
scu•ba (skü′bə) *noun.*

sediment 1. Rocks, dirt, or other solid matter carried and left by water, glaciers, or wind. **2.** Small pieces of matter that settle at the bottom of a liquid. There was *sediment* at the bottom of the bottle.
sed•i•ment (sed′ə mənt) *noun.*

segregation The practice of setting one group apart from another.
seg•re•ga•tion (seg′ri gā′shən) *noun.*

settlement 1. A small village or group of houses. During the 1800s, pioneers built many *settlements* in the American West. **2.** The act of settling or the condition of being settled. The *settlement* of Jamestown took place in 1607.
set•tle•ment (set′əl mənt) *noun, plural* **settlements.**

shanty A small, poorly built house; shack. During the Depression, many poor families lived in *shanties.*
▲ **Synonym:** shack
shan•ty (shan′tē) *noun, plural* **shanties.**

shoreline The line where a body of water and the land meet. My friend has a house near the *shoreline.*
shore•line (shôr′līn′) *noun.*

shortcut 1. A quicker way of reaching a place. I took a *shortcut* to school. **2.** A way of doing something faster. Don't use any *shortcuts* in your science experiment.
short•cut (shôrt′cut′) *noun, plural* **shortcuts.**

shriek A loud, sharp cry or sound. The child let out a *shriek* of laughter. *Noun.*—To utter a loud, sharp cry or sound. We all *shrieked* with laughter at her jokes. *Verb.*
shriek (shrēk) *noun, plural* **shrieks;** *verb,* **shrieked, shrieking.**

shutter 1. A movable cover for a window, usually attached to the frame by hinges. *Shutters* are used to shut out light **2.** The part of a camera that snaps open and shuts quickly to let light onto the film when a picture is taken.
shut•ter (shut′ər) *noun, plural* **shutters.**

siren A device that makes a loud, shrill sound, used as a signal or warning. Ambulances and police cars have *sirens.*
si•ren (sī′rən) *noun, plural* **sirens.**

sketch A rough, quick drawing. The artist made several *sketches* of the model before starting the painting. *Noun.*—To make a sketch of. I *sketched* an old barn for my art class. *Verb.*
sketch (skech) *verb,* **sketched, sketching;** *noun, plural* **sketches.**

Word History
Sketch comes from the Dutch word *schets* and the Italian word *schizzo,* meaning "splash." A sketch is often a rough drawing, a splash of an idea that will later become a detailed finished product.

skill The power or ability to do something. *Skill* comes with practice and experience.
skill (skil) *noun, plural* **skills.**

skillet A shallow pan with a handle. A *skillet* is used for frying.
skil•let (skil′it) *noun, plural* **skillets.**

skim 1. To remove from the surface of a liquid. The cook *skimmed* the fat from the soup. **2.** To read quickly. *Skim* the paper for the scores.
skim (skim) *verb,* **skimmed, skimming.**

at; āpe; fär; câre; end; mē; it; īce; pîerce; hot; ōld; sông; fôrk; oil; out; up; ūse; rüle; pu̇ll; tûrn; chin; sing; shop; thin; this; hw in white; zh in treasure. The symbol ə stands for the unstressed vowel sound in about, taken, pencil, lemon, and circus.

smog A combination of smoke and fog in the air. *Smog* is found especially over cities where there are factories and many cars.
smog (smog) *noun.*

Word History
The word ***smog*** was made using the first two letters of *smoke* and the last two letters of *fog.*

snout The front part of an animal's head, including nose, mouth, and jaws. My dog has a cute *snout.*
snout (snout) *noun, plural* **snouts.**

soapsuds Water that is bubbly with soap. I like my bath to be filled with *soapsuds.*
soap•suds (sōp′sudz′) *plural noun.*

soggy Very wet or damp; soaked. The soil was *soggy* after the rain.
sog•gy (sog′ē) *adjective,* **soggier, soggiest.**

soot A black, greasy powder that forms when such fuels as wood, coal, and oil are burned. The old chimney was caked with *soot.*
soot (su̇t *or* süt) *noun; adjective,* **sooty.**

spice The seeds or other parts of certain plants used to flavor food. Pepper, cloves, and cinnamon are spices. *Noun.*—To flavor with a spice or spices. I *spiced* the hamburgers. *Verb.*
spice (spīs) *noun, plural* **spices;** *verb,* **spiced, spicing;** *adjective,* **spicy.**

spike 1. Any sharp, pointed object or part that sticks out. Baseball shoes have *spikes* on the soles. **2.** A large, heavy nail used to hold rails to railroad ties. It was difficult to hammer in the railroad *spike.*
spike (spīk) *noun, plural* **spikes.**

sponge A simple water animal that has a body that is full of holes and absorbs water easily. The dried skeletons of some *sponge* colonies are used for cleaning and washing. *Noun.*—To clean with a sponge. We *sponged* and dried the dirty walls. *Verb.*
sponge (spunj) *noun, plural* **sponges;** *verb,* **sponged, sponging.**

squall A strong gust of wind that arises very suddenly. Squalls often bring rain, snow, or sleet. We were forced indoors by a *squall* of snow.
squall (skwôl) *noun, plural* **squalls.**

Word History
The word ***squall*** first appeared in the English language in 1699. It is probably based on the Swedish word *skval,* which means "rushing water."

squeal To make a loud, shrill cry or sound. The little pigs *squealed* with excitement. *Verb.* —A loud, shrill cry or sound. The *squeal* of the brakes hurt my ears. *Noun.*
squeal (skwēl) *verb,* **squealed, squealing;** *noun, plural* **squeals.**

stake A stick or post pointed at one end so that it can be driven into the ground. The campers drove in *stakes* and tied the corners of the tent to them. *Noun.* — To fasten or hold up with a stake. The gardener *staked* the beans. *Verb.*
▲ Another word that sounds like this is **steak.**
stake (stāk) *noun, plural* **stakes;** *verb,* **staked, staking.**

sterilize To make free of bacteria and microorganisms. The nurse *sterilized* the scalpels before the operation.
ster•il•ize (ster′ə līz′) *verb,* **sterilized, sterilizing.**

stitch To make, fasten, or mend with stitches; sew. I *stitched* up the tear in my shirt. *Verb.*—One complete movement made with a needle and thread. *Noun.*
stitch (stich) *verb,* **stitched, stitching;** *noun, plural* **stitches.**

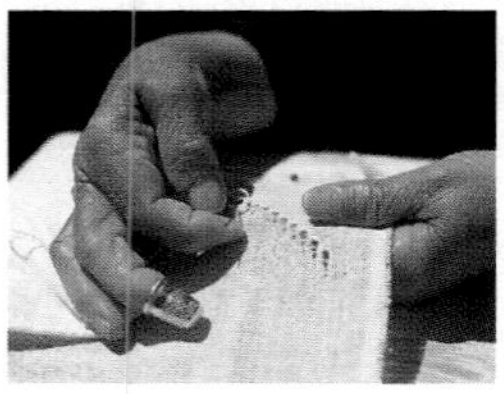

strew To spread by scattering. I have to clean my room because my clothes are *strewn* all over the place.
strew (strü) *verb,* **strewed, strewn, strewing.**

at; āpe; fär; câre; end; mē; it; īce; pîerce; hot; ōld; sông; fôrk; oil; out; up; ūse; rüle; pu̇ll; tûrn; chin; sing; shop; thin; this; hw in white; zh in treasure. The symbol ə stands for the unstressed vowel sound in about, taken, pencil, lemon, and circus.

stroll To walk in a slow, relaxed way. We *strolled* through the park. *Verb.* —A slow, relaxed walk. After dinner we took a *stroll. Noun.*
stroll (strōl) *verb,* **strolled, strolling;** *noun, plural* **strolls.**

sturdy Strong; hardy. Heavy trucks can drive on the *sturdy* bridge.
stur•dy (stûr′dē) *adjective,* **sturdier, sturdiest;** *adverb,* **sturdily;** *noun,* **sturdiness.**

success 1. A result hoped for; favorable end. The coach was pleased with the *success* of the game. **2.** A person or thing that does or goes well. The party was a big *success.*
suc•cess (sək ses′) *noun, plural* **successes;** *adjective,* **successful.**

sunrise The rising of the sun. We went to the beach to watch the *sunrise.*
sunrise (sun′rīz′) *noun, plural* **sunrises.**

swamp An area of wet land. The *swamp* looked scary and creepy. *Noun.* —To fill with water. High waves *swamped* the boat. *Verb.*
swamp (swomp) *noun, plural* **swamps;** *verb,* **swamped, swamping.**

swamp

Tt

talker One who exchanges spoken words in conversation. The two friends were great *talkers.*
talk•er (tôk′ ər) *noun, plural* **talkers**

teammate A person who is a member of the same team. We're basketball *teammates.*
team•mate (tēm′māt′) *noun, plural* **teammates.**

threat 1. A person or thing that might cause harm; danger. The outbreak of flu was a *threat* to the community. **2.** A statement of something that will be done to hurt or punish. The trespassers heeded our *threat.*
threat (thret) *noun, plural* **threats.**

ton A measure of weight equal to 2,000 pounds in the United States and Canada, and 2,240 pounds in Great Britain.
ton (tun) *noun, plural* **tons.**

tractor A vehicle with heavy tires or tracks. *Tractors* are used to pull heavy loads over rough ground.
trac•tor (trak′tər) *noun, plural* **tractors.**

tradition A custom or belief that is passed on from one generation to another.
tra•di•tion (trə dish′ən) *noun, plural* **traditions;** *adjective,* **traditional.**

travel To go from one place to another; to make a trip. We *traveled* through England. *Verb.* —The act of traveling. Camels are used for desert *travel. Noun.*
trav•el (trav′əl) *verb,* **traveled, traveling;** *noun, plural* **travels.**

tricorn A hat with the brim turned up on three sides.
tri•corn (trī′kôrn′) *noun, plural* **tricorns.**

tube A container of soft metal or plastic from which the contents are removed by squeezing. I need a new *tube* of toothpaste.
tube (tüb) *noun, plural* **tubes.**

tusk A long, pointed tooth that sticks out of each side of the mouth in certain animals. Elephants and walruses have *tusks.*
tusk (tusk) *noun, plural* **tusks.**

Ww

waddle To walk or move with short steps, swaying the body from side to side. The duck *waddled* across the yard. *Verb.*—A swaying or rocking walk. The audience laughed at the clown's *waddle. Noun.*
wad•dle (wod′əl) *verb,* **waddled, waddling;** *noun, plural* **waddles.**

at; āpe; fär; câre; end; mē; it; īce; pîerce; hot; ōld; sông; fôrk; oil; out; up; ūse; rüle; pu̇ll; tûrn; chin; sing; shop; thin; this; hw in white; zh in treasure. The symbol ə stands for the unstressed vowel sound in about, taken, pencil, lemon, and circus.

weary Very tired. The carpenter was *weary* after the day's hard work. *Adjective.*—To make or become weary; tire. The long walk *wearied* the children. *Verb.*
wea•ry (wîr′ē) *adjective,* **wearier, weariest;** *verb,* **wearied, wearying;** *adverb,* **wearily;** *noun,* **weariness.**

weird Strange or mysterious; odd. A *weird* sound came from the deserted old house.
▲ **Synonym:** peculiar
weird (wîrd) *adjective,* **weirder, weirdest;** *adverb,* **weirdly;** *noun,* **weirdness.**

wharf A structure built along a shore as a landing place for boats and ships; dock. We had to unload the boat once we reached the *wharf.*
wharf (hworf *or* wôrf) *noun, plural* **wharves** *or* **wharfs.**

whicker To neigh or whinny. The horse began *whickering* at the kids. *Verb.*—A neigh or whinny. The horse let out a *whicker. Noun.*
whick•er (hwi′kər) *verb,* **whickered, whickering;** *noun, plural* **whickers.**

whinny A soft neigh. We heard the *whinnies* of the horses. *Noun.* —To neigh in a low, gentle way. My horse *whinnied* when he saw me. *Verb.*
whin•ny (hwin′ē *or* win′ē) *verb,* **whinnied, whinnying;** *noun, plural* **whinnies.**

wildlife Wild animals that live naturally in an area. My favorite part of hiking is observing the *wildlife.*
wild•life (wīld′līf′) *noun.*

windowpane A framed sheet of glass in a window. I placed my candles by the *windowpane.*
win•dow•pane (win′dō pān′) *noun, plural* **windowpanes.**

wondrous Extraordinary; wonderful. The local theater put on a *wondrous* performance.
▲ **Synonym:** marvelous
won•drous (wun′drəs) *adjective;* *adverb,* **wondrously;** *noun,* **wondrousness.**

wrestle 1. To force by grasping. The champion *wrestled* his opponent to the mat. **2.** To struggle by grasping and trying to force and hold one's opponent to the ground, without punching. The children *wrestled* on the lawn.
wres•tle (res′əl) *verb,* **wrestled, wrestling.**

wriggle 1. To twist or turn from side to side with short, quick moves; squirm. The bored children *wriggled* in their seats. **2.** To get into or out of a position by tricky means. You always try to *wriggle* out of having to wash the dishes.
wrig•gle (rig′əl) *verb,* **wriggled, wriggling;** *adjective,* **wriggly.**

Word History

The word ***wriggle*** comes from the Old English word *wrigian,* which means "to turn."

at; āpe; fär; câre; end; mē; it; īce; pîerce; hot; ōld; sông; fôrk; oil; out; up; ūse; rüle; pu̇ll; tûrn; chin; sing; shop; thin; this; hw in white; zh in treasure. The symbol ə stands for the unstressed vowel sound in about, taken, pencil, lemon, and circus.

Cover Illustration: Terry Widener

The publisher gratefully acknowledges permission to reprint the following copyrighted material:

Autobiographical piece by Matt Christopher from PAUSES: AUTOBIOGRAPHICAL REFLECTIONS OF 101 CREATORS OF CHILDREN'S BOOKS by Lee Bennett Hopkins. Copyright © 1995 by Lee Bennett Hopkins. Used by permission of HarperCollins Children's Books, a division of HarperCollins Publishers.

Autobiographical piece by Robert Ballard from the book TALKING WITH ADVENTURERS by Pat and Linda Cummings. This excerpt copyright © 1998 by Robert Ballard. Used by permission of the National Geographic Society.

"The Bear and the Two Travelers" from MORE FABLES OF AESOP by Jack Kent. Copyright © 1974 by Jack Kent. Reprinted with the permission of Parents' Magazine Press.

"Beezus and Her Imagination" from BEEZUS AND RAMONA by Beverly Cleary (pp. 59–62). Copyright © 1955 by Beverly Cleary. Used by permission of Morrow Junior Books, a division of HarperCollins Publishers.

"The Biggest Problem (Is in Other People's Minds)" from FREE TO BE ... YOU AND ME AND FREE TO BE ... A FAMILY by Don Haynie. Copyright © 1987 by the Free to Be Foundation, Inc. Used by permission.

"Birdfoot's Grampa" from ENTERING ONANDAGA by Joseph Bruchac. Copyright © 1978 by Joseph Bruchac. Used by permission.

"Buffalo Dusk" by Carl Sandburg from THE COMPLETE POEMS OF CARL SANDBURG. Copyright © 1970, 1969 by Lilian Steichen Sandburg, Trustee. Reprinted by permission of Harcourt, Inc.

"Dakota Dugout" from DAKOTA DUGOUT by Ann Turner. Copyright © 1985 by Ann Turner. Reprinted with the permission of Simon & Schuster Books for Young Readers, an imprint of Simon & Schuster Children's Publishing Division.

"The Dentist" from ANOTHER FIRST POETRY BOOK by Judith Nicholls. Copyright © 1987 by Judith Nicholls. Reprinted by permission of the author.

"Don't Make a Bargain with a Fox" from THE KING OF THE MOUNTAINS: A TREASURY OF LATIN AMERICAN FOLK STORIES by M. A. Jagendorf and R. S. Boggs. Copyright © 1960 by M. A. Jagendorf and R. S. Boggs. Copyright renewed 1988 by Andre Jagendorf, Merna Alpert and R. S. Boggs. Used by permission of Random House Children's Books, a division of Random House, Inc.

"Earth Day Rap" by Doug Goodkin. Copyright © 1995. Used by permission of The McGraw-Hill Co., Inc.

"8,000 Stones" from 8,000 STONES: A CHINESE FOLKTALE by Diane Wolkstein. Text copyright © 1972 by Diane Wolkstein. Used by permission.

ACKNOWLEDGMENTS

The publisher gratefully acknowledges permission to reprint the following copyrighted material.

"Amelia's Road" by Linda Jacobs Altman, illustrated by Enrique O. Sanchez. Text copyright © 1993 by Linda Jacobs Altman. Illustrations copyright © 1993 by Enrique O. Sanchez. Permission granted by Lee & Low Books Inc., 95 Madison Avenue, New York, NY 10016.

"August 8" by Norman Jordan. From ABOVE MAYA, 1971, MAKE A JOYFUL SOUND, 1991, *Creative Classroom* magazine, 1995, *Connections* magazine, 1999.

"Baseball Saved Us" by Ken Mochizuki, illustrated by Dom Lee. Text copyright © 1993 by Ken Mochizuki. Illustrations copyright © 1993 by Dom Lee. Permission granted by Lee & Low Books Inc., 95 Madison Avenue, New York, NY 10016.

"Final Curve" from COLLECTED POEMS by Langston Hughes; Copyright © 1994 by the Estate of Langston Hughes. Reprinted by permission of Alfred A. Knopf, a Division of Random House, Inc.

"The Fox and the Guinea Pig"/"El zorro y el cuy" A Traditional Folk Tale translated by Mary Ann Newman, illustrated by Kevin Hawkes. Copyright © 1997 Macmillan/McGraw-Hill, a Division of the Educational and Professional Publishing Group of the McGraw-Hill Companies, Inc.

"The Garden We Planted Together" by Anuruddha Bose from A WORLD IN OUR HANDS. Reprinted with permission of A WORLD IN OUR HANDS by Peace Child Charitable Trust, illustrated by Sanjay Sinha ($15.95). Copyright © 1995 Tricycle Press (800-841-BOOK).

"Gluskabe and the Snow Bird" from FOUR ANCESTORS: STORIES, SONGS, AND POEMS FROM NATIVE NORTH AMERICA by Joseph Bruchac. Published by and reprinted with permission of Troll Communications, LLC.

"Grass Sandals/The Travels of Basho" by Dawnine Spivak, illustrated by Demi. Text copyright © 1997 by Dawnine Spivak, illustrations copyright © 1997 by Demi. Reprinted by permission of Atheneum Books for Young Readers, Simon and Schuster Children's Publishing Division. All rights reserved.

"The Hatmaker's Sign" by Candace Fleming, illustrated by Robert Andrew Parker. Text copyright © 1998 by Candace Fleming. Illustrations copyright © 1998 by Robert Andrew Parker. All rights reserved. Reprinted by permission by Orchard Books, New York.

"How to Tell the Top of a Hill" by John Ciardi from THE REASON FOR THE PELICAN. Copyright © 1959 by John Ciardi. Reprinted by permission of the Ciardi Family Trust, John L. Ciardi, Trustee.

"I Ask My Mother to Sing" by Li-Young Lee. Copyright © 1986 by Li-Young Lee. Reprinted from *Rose* with the permission of BOA Editions, Ltd., 260 East Ave., Rochester, NY 14604.

"Just a Dream" is from JUST A DREAM by Chris Van Allsburg. Copyright © 1990 by Chris Van Allsburg. Reprinted by permission of Houghton Mifflin Company.

"Justin and the Best Biscuits in the World" is from JUSTIN AND THE BEST BISCUITS IN THE WORLD by Mildred Pitts Walter. Copyright © 1986 by Mildred Pitts Walter. Used by permission of HarperCollins Publishers.

"Leah's Pony" by Elizabeth Friedrich, illustrated by Michael Garland. Text copyright © 1996 by Elizabeth Friedrich. Illustrations copyright © 1996 by Michael Garland. Used by permission of Boyds Mills Press.

"The Lost Lake" by Allen Say. Copyright © 1989 by Allen Say. Reprinted by permission of Houghton Mifflin Company. All rights reserved.

"The Malachite Palace" by Alma Flor Ada, translated by Rosa Zubizarreta, illustrated by Leonid Gore. Text copyright © 1998 by Alma Flor Ada, illustrations copyright © 1998 by Leonid Gore. Reprinted by permission of Atheneum Books for Young Readers, Simon and Schuster Children's Publishing Division. All rights reserved.

"Meet an Underwater Explorer" by Luise Woelflein. Reprinted from the June 1994 issue of RANGER RICK magazine, with the permission of the publisher, the National Wildlife Federation. Copyright © 1994 by the National Wildlife Federation.

"Mom's Best Friend" by Sally Hobart Alexander, photographs by George Ancona. Text copyright ©1992 by Sally Hobart Alexander. Photographs copyright © 1992 by George Ancona. Reprinted with permission of Simon & Schuster Books for Young Readers, Simon & Schuster Children's Publishing Division.

"My Poems" by Alan Barlow. From RISING VOICES: WRITINGS OF YOUNG NATIVE AMERICANS selected by Arlene B. Hirschfelder and Beverly R. Singer. Copyright © 1992. Published by Scribner's. Used by permission.

"On the Bus with Joanna Cole" excerpt from *On the Bus with Joanna Cole: A Creative Autobiography* by Joanna Cole with Wendy Saul. Copyright © 1996 by Joanna Cole. Published by Heinemann, a division of Reed Elsevier Inc. Reprinted by permission of the Publisher. Illustration on page 447 by Bruce Degen from THE MAGIC SCHOOL BUS INSIDE THE HUMAN BODY by Joanna Cole. Illustration copyright © 1989 by Bruce Degen. Reprinted with permission of Scholastic, Inc. THE MAGIC SCHOOL BUS is a registered trademark of Scholastic, Inc.

"Pat Cummings: My Story" reprinted with the permission of Simon & Schuster Books for Young Readers from TALKING WITH ARTISTS compiled and edited by Pat Cummings. Jacket illustration copyright © 1992 Pat Cummings. Copyright © 1992 Pat Cummings.

"A Place Called Freedom" by Scott Russell Sanders, illustrated by Thomas B. Allen. Text copyright © 1997 by Scott Russell Sanders, illustrations copyright © 1997 by Thomas B. Allen. Reprinted by permission of Atheneum Books for Young Readers, Simon and Schuster Children's Publishing Division. All rights reserved.

"The Poet Pencil" by Jesús Carlos Soto Morfín, translated by Judith Infante. From THE TREE IS OLDER THAN YOU ARE: A Bilingual Gathering of Poems and Stories from Mexico, selected by Naomi Shihab Nye. Copyright © 1995 Reprinted by permission of the author and María Guadalupe Morfín.

"The Rajah's Rice" from THE RAJAH'S RICE by David Barry, illustrated by Donna Perrone. Text Copyright © 1994 by David Barry. Art copyright © 1994 by Donna Perrone. Used with permission of W. H. Freeman and Company.

"Sarah, Plain and Tall" text excerpt from SARAH, PLAIN AND TALL by Patricia MacLachlan. Copyright © 1985 by Patricia MacLachlan. Reprinted by permission of HarperCollins Publishers. Cover permission for the Trophy Edition used by permission of HarperCollins Publishers.

"Scruffy: A Wolf Finds His Place in the Pack" by Jim Brandenburg. Copyright © 1996 by Jim Brandenburg. Published by arrangement with Walker Publishing Company, Inc.

"Seal Journey" From SEAL JOURNEY by Richard and Jonah Sobol. Copyright © 1993 Richard Sobol, text and photographs. Used by permission of Cobblehill Books, an affiliate of Dutton Children's Press, a division of Penguin USA, Inc.

"Teammates" from TEAMMATES by Peter Golenbock, text copyright © 1990 by Golenbock Communications, reprinted by permission of Harcourt, Inc.

"To" by Lee Bennett Hopkins from BEEN TO YESTERDAYS: Poems of a Life. Text copyright © 1995 by Lee Bennett Hopkins. Published by Wordsong/Boyds Mills Press. Reprinted by permission.

"The Toothpaste Millionaire" by Jean Merrill. Copyright © 1972 by Houghton Mifflin Company. Adapted and reprinted by permission of Houghton Mifflin Company. All rights reserved.

"Tortillas Like Africa" from CANTO FAMILIAR by Gary Soto. Copyright © 1995 Harcourt, Inc.

"Evergreen, Everblue" by Raffi. Copyright © 1990 Homeland Publishing, a division of Troubadour Records Ltd. Used by permission.

"Follow the Drinkin' Gourd," Words and Music by Ronnie Gilbert, Lee Hays, Fred Hellerman and Pete Seeger TRO- Copyright © 1951 (Renewed) Folkways Music Publishers, Inc., New York, New York. Used by permission.

"Fossils" from SOMETHING NEW BEGINS by Lilian Moore. Copyright © 1982 by Lilian Moore. Used by permission of Marian Reiner for the author.

Four haiku from CRICKET NEVER DOES: A COLLECTION OF HAIKU AND TANKA by Myra Cohn Livingston. Text copyright © 1977 by Myra Cohn Livingston. Used by permission of Margaret K. McElderry Books, an imprint of Simon & Schuster Children's Publishing Division.

"Whales" excerpt from WHALES by Seymour Simon. Copyright © 1989 by Seymour Simon. Reprinted by permission of HarperCollins Publishers.

"Yeh-Shen: A Cinderella Story from China" is from YEH-SHEN: A CINDERELLA STORY FROM CHINA by Ai-Ling Louie. Text copyright © 1982 by Ai-Ling Louie. Illustrations copyright © 1982 by Ed Young. Reprinted by permission of Philomel Books. Introductory comments by Ai-Ling Louie and used with her permission.

"Your World" by Georgia Douglas Johnson appeared originally in HOLD FAST TO DREAMS by Arna Bontemps. Originally published by Follett Publishing Company © 1969. Reprinted by permission of Pearson Learning.

Cover Illustration
Terry Widener

Illustration
Roberta Ludlow, 16-17; Jean and Mou-Sien Tseng, 128-129; David Ridley, 130-131; Elizabeth Rosen, 252-253; J. W. Stewart, 254-255; Bruno Paciulli, 372-373; Stefano Vitale, 408-419; Amy Vangsgard, 482-483; Susan Leopold, 484-485; Yoshi Miyake, 612-613; David Catrow, 666-687; B. J. Faulkner, 724-725; George Thompson, 758, 779; Rodica Prato, 762, 769; John Carrozza, 775, 789, 793.

Photography
5: m.r. Richard Sobol. 5: b.r. K. and K. Ammann/Bruce Coleman. 7: Lawrence Migdale/Photo Researchers, Inc. 9: Georg Gerster/Photo Researchers, Inc. 10: Jim Brandenburg/Minden Pictures. 11: t. Luise Woelflein. 12: George Ancona. 13: Marty Snyderman. 15: b. Galen Rowell/Corbis. 18–19: Owen Edgar Gallery, U.K./Fine Art Photographic Library, London/Art Resource, NY. 37: b.r. Courtesy, Allen Say. 42–43: © 2003 Artists Rights Society (ARS), New York/DACS, London/Bradford Art Galleries and Museums, West Yorkshire, U.K./The Bridgeman Art Library International. 44: t. Courtesy, Lee & Low Books. 44: b. Courtesy, Enrique O. Sanchez. 66: c. Superstock. 89: Courtesy, Patricia MacLachlan. 94: c. Shelburne Museum. 96: i. Courtesy, Richard Sobol. 111: t. Richard Sobol. 111: m. Richard Sobol. 111: b. Richard Sobol. 114: Richard Sobol. 115: Richard Sobol. 118: E.A. Barton Collection, The British Museum. 124: George Lepp/Corbis. 125: K. and K. Ammann/Bruce Coleman. 153: t. Courtesy, Mildred Pitts Walter. 153: b. Courtesy, Floyd Cooper. 158: © 1939 Turner Entertainment Company. All Rights Reserved./Photofest. 185: Courtesy, Chris Van Allsburg. 190: The Museum of Modern Art, New York/© Dorothea Lange Collection, Oakland Museum of California, City of Oakland. Gift of Paul S. Taylor. 192: t. Courtesy, Boyds Mills Press. 192: b. Courtesy, Boyds Mills Press. 216: Museo de Bellas Artes, Bilbao, Spain/Bridgeman Art Library International. 218: t. Courtesy, Lee & Low Books. 218: b. Courtesy, Lee & Low Books. 242: The British Museum, London/The Bridgeman Art Library International. 249: Lawrence Migdale/Photo Researchers. 250: Shelly Katz/TFK. 256: © Richard Estes/Licensed by VAGA, New York, NY/Marlborough Gallery, NY. 258: t. Courtesy, Orchard Books. 258: b. Courtesy, Orchard Books. 282: Hermitage Museum, St. Petersburg, Russia/Superstock. 294: Courtesy, Pat Cummings. 298: Canterbury Cathedral, Kent, UK/The Bridgeman Art Library International. 300: t. Courtesy, Dawnine Spivak. 300: b. Courtesy, Henry Holt and Company, Inc. 329: Susan Kuklin/Photo Researchers, Inc. 332: The Phillips Collection, Washington D.C. 334: t. Eva Sanders/Simon & Schuster Children's Division. 334: b. Alan Ferguson; courtesy, Ringling School of Art and Design, Sarasota, FL. 360: c. Cordon Art B. V. 367: Adrian Fisher. 370–71: Felicia Martinez/Photo Edit. 374: The Bridgeman Art Library International. 376: i. Anthony Brandenburg/Minden Pictures. 402: b.l. Jim Brandenburg/Minden Pictures. 403: E. Lemoine/Jacana Scientific Control/Photo Researchers, Inc. 406: The Heard Museum of Native Cultures and Art, Phoenix, AZ. 408: Courtesy, Fulcrum Publishing. 426–27: David Doubilet. 428: David Doubilet. 430–31: David Doubilet. 432: Doug Menuez. 433: b.r. Flip Schulke/Black Star. 434–45: b.l. Charles Nicklin/Al Giddings Images Inc. 435: i. Al Giddings Images Inc. 436: Al Giddings Images Inc. 438: b. Al Giddings Images Inc. 439: i. Courtesy, Luise Woelflein. 439: bkgd. Stuart Westmoreland/Stone. 440: b.l. Charles Nicklin/Al Giddings Images Inc. 444: Courtesy, Estate of Alexander Calder/Artists Rights Society. 446: Courtesy, Joanna Cole. 455: Myron/Tony Stone Images. 456: Index Stock Photography. 462: Michael Orton/Tony Stone Images. 472–73: Natural History Museum, London/The Bridgeman Art Library International. 486: c. Christies Images. 488: i. Karen P. Hawkes; courtesy, Penguin Putnam Books for Young Readers. 516: Cary Herz Photography. 531: t. George Ancona. 531: b. Courtesy, George Ancona. 532: George Ancona. 536: Hermitage Museum, St. Petersburg, Russia/Art Resource, NY. 565: r. Chris Johns/National Geographic Society Image Collection. 565: l. E Hanumantha Rao/Photo Researchers, Inc. 568: Phoebe Beasley/Omni-Photo Communications. 595: r. Courtesy, Ai-Ling Louie. 595: l. Courtesy, Ed Young. 597: Georg Gerster/Photo Researchers, Inc. 600: Maas Gallery, London/The Bridgeman Art Library International. 606: Nick Caloyianis/National Geographic Society Image Collection. 610: t. Robb Kendrick/Aurora. 610: m.i. The Picture Cube/Index Stock Imagery. 610: b.i. Bob Daemmrich/The Image Works. 610–11: Visual Horizons/FPG International. 614–15: Jonathan Green Studios, Inc. 627: i. Courtesy, Peter Golebock. 632–33: Reproduced by kind permission of the Trustees of the Chester Beatty Library, Dublin. 634: b. Courtesy, HK Portfolio, Inc. 634: t. Courtesy, Alma Flor Ada. 661: l. Photo Researchers, Inc. 664: c. Motion Picture and Television Archives. 666: t. Courtesy, Jean Merrill. 666: b. Courtesy, David Catrow. 692: c. Superstock. 694–95: Al Giddings/Images Unlimited. 696–97: t. Minden Pictures. 696–97: b. Minden Pictures. 699: t. Minden Pictures. 708: Minden Pictures. 714: c. The Bridgeman Art Library Ltd. 721: i. Galen Rowell/Corbis.

READING STRATEGY
Illustration
Mike DiGiorgio, pp. 95, 601A; Diane Blasius, pp. 133A, 665–665A ; Cedric Lucas, pp. 333–333A; Tom Leonard, pp. 425–425A; Debrah Wilson, p. 445A; Greg Harris, pp. 473–473A; John Wallner, pp. 487–487A; Fahimeh Amiri, pp. 537–537A; Oki Han, pp. 569–569A; Gail Piazza, pp. 633–633A;

Photography
Page 19 (inset), Bill Ivy/Stone; pages 19-19a, Dave G. Houser/Corbis; page 43, Hulton Getty; pages 43-43a, AP/Wide World Photos; pages 67-67a, Corbis/Bettmann; page 67a (top), George Eastman House/Lewis W. Hine/Archive Photos; pages 95-95a, Eric & David Hosking/Corbis; page 95a (inset), Hans Dieter Brandl/Frank Lane Picture Agency/Corbis; page 119, Mickey Pfleger/Photo 20-20/PictureQuest; page 119a, Courtesy Canine Companions for Independence; page 133-133a, John Loengard/Timepix; pages 159-159a (top), Erik Anderson/Stock Boston/PictureQuest; pages 159-159a (bottom), PhotoDisc; page 159a (inset), David Young-Wolf/PhotoEdit/PictureQuest; pages 191-191a, Charles Sleicher/Stone; page 217 (top), PhotoDisc; page 217 (bottom), Philip James Corwin/Corbis; pages 217-217a (top), Superstock; pages 217-217a (bottom), Duomo/Corbis; page 217a (top), Joe Patronite/The Image Bank; pages 243-243a, Peter Turnley/Corbis; pages 257-257a, Francis G. Mayer/Corbis; page 257a (bottom), Joe Viesti/Viesti Associates; page 283a, Courtesy Carmen Lomas Garza; pages 299-299a, John Warden/Stone; pages 361-361a, PhotoDisc; page 361a (top), Courtesy of the Staten Island Botanical Garden; page 375a (top), Ansel Adams Publishing Rights/Corbis; page 375a (bottom), Corbis; page 407, Araldo De Luca/Corbis; page 407a, Superstock; pages 517-517a, Hans Wolf/The Image Bank; page 517a (top), David Rubinger/Timepix; page 517a (bottom), S. Cordier/Photo Researchers; pages 601-601a, Jeff Hunter/The Image Bank; page 615 (inset), Corbis/Bettmann; pages 615-615a, Archive Photos/Timepix; page 615a (top), Flip Schulke/Corbis; pages 693-693a, Wolfgang Kaehler/Corbis; pages 715-715a (background), Larry Ulrich/Stone; pages 715-715a, James Carmichael/The Image Bank.

READING FOR INFORMATION, GLOSSARY
Table of Contents, pp. 726–727

Chess pieces	tl	Wides + Hall/FPG
Earth	mcl	M. Burns/Picture Perfect

"How It All Began" from THE STORY OF BASEBALL by Lawrence S. Ritter. Copyright © 1983, 1990 by Lawrence S. Ritter. Used by permission of Morrow Junior Books, a division of HarperCollins Publishers.

"Indians of the Plains" from WORLDS I KNOW AND OTHER POEMS by Myra Cohn Livingston. Text copyright © 1985 by Myra Cohn Livingston. Reprinted with the permission of Margaret K. McElderry Books, an imprint of Simon & Schuster Children's Publishing Division.

"Jackie Robinson" from FOLLOWERS OF THE NORTH STAR: RHYMES ABOUT AFRICAN AMERICAN HEROES, HEROINES, AND HISTORICAL TIMES by Susan Altman and Susan Lechner. Copyright © 1993 Childrens Press ®, Inc. Used by permission of Childrens Press.

"The Needle in the Haystack" from CRICKET MAGAZINE by John Hamma. Copyright © 1982 by John Hamma. Used by permission of Doris Hamma.

"Pack" text copyright © 1995 by Lee Bennett Hopkins from BEEN TO YESTERDAYS by Lee Bennett Hopkins. Reprinted by permission of Wordsong/Boyds Mills Press, Inc.

"The Paper Garden" from BREAKING THE SPELL: TALES OF ENCHANTMENT. Copyright © 1997, Kingfisher. Used by permission of the publisher, Larousse Kingfisher Chambers, Inc., New York.

"Rhodopis and Her Golden Sandals" from MULTICULTURAL FABLES AND FAIRY TALES by Tara McCarthy. Published by Scholastic Professional Books. Copyright © 1993 by Tara McCarthy. Reprinted by permission of Scholastic, Inc.

"Seal" from LAUGHING TIME by William Jay Smith. Copyright © 1990 by William Jay Smith. Used by permission of Farrar, Straus & Giroux, Inc.

"Spider in the Sky" by Anne Rose. Copyright © 1978 by Anne Rose. Used by permission of Harper Collins Publishers.

"Super-Goopy Glue" from THE NEW KID ON THE BLOCK by Jack Prelutsky. Text copyright © 1984 by Jack Prelutsky. Used by permission of Greenwillow Books, a division of HarperCollins Publishers.

"What's the Big Idea, Ben Franklin?" from WHAT'S THE BIG IDEA, BEN FRANKLIN? by Jean Fritz. Copyright © 1976 by Jean Fritz. Used by permission of Coward-McCann, a division of Penguin Putnam Inc.

"When Whales Exhale (Whale Watching)" from WHEN WHALES EXHALE AND OTHER POEMS by Constance Levy. Text copyright © 1996 by Constance King Levy. Used by permission of Margaret K. McElderry Books, an imprint of Simon & Schuster Children's Publishing Division.

"Windows of Gold" from WINDOWS OF GOLD AND OTHER GOLDEN TALES by Selma G. Lanes. Text copyright © 1989 by Selma G. Lanes. Reprinted with the permission of Simon and Schuster Books for Young Readers, an imprint of Simon and Schuster Children's Publishing Division.

"The Wolf" from THE RANDOM HOUSE BOOK OF POETRY FOR CHILDREN by Georgia Roberts Durston. Copyright © 1983. Used by permission of Random House.

ZB Font Method Copyright © 1996 Zaner-Bloser. Handwriting Models, Manuscript and Cursive. Used by permission.

Photography:
All photographs are by Macmillan/McGraw-Hill except as noted below.
page 129A left: Daniel Pangbourne Media/FPG.
page 129A right: M. Burns/Picture Perfect.
page 371A left: Jeff LePore/Natural Selection.
page 371A right: Stockbyte.

Pupil Edition (continued)

CD's	mcl	Michael Simpson/FPG
Newspapers	bl	Craig Orsini/Index Stock/PictureQuest
Clock	tc	Steve McAlister/The Image Bank
Kids circle	bc	Daniel Pangbourne Media/FPG
Pencils	tr	W. Cody/Corbis
Starfish	tc	Darryl Torckler/Stone
Keys	cr	Randy Faris/Corbis
Cells	br	Spike Walker/Stone
Stamps	tr	Michael W. Thomas/Focus Group/PictureQuest
Books	cr	Siede Preis/PhotoDisc
Sunflower	cr	Jeff LePore/Natural Selection
Mouse	br	Andrew Hall/Stone
Apples	tr	Siede Preis/PhotoDisc
Watermelons	br	Neil Beer/PhotoDisc
Butterfly	br	Stockbyte

All photographs are by Macmillan/McGraw-Hill (MMH); Stephen Ogilvy for MMH; and John Serafin for MMH, except as noted below:

p729 b.r.	United Sewerage Agency of Washington County
p732 t.r.	Anestis Diakopoulos/Stock Boston
p733 l.	Bob Daemmrich/Stock Boston
p737 m.i.r.	Cole Group/PhotoDisc
p737 m.i.l.	David Buffington/PhotoDisc
p737 bkgd.	PhotoLink/PhotoDisc (leaf bkgd.)
p739 t.c.	Biophoto Associates/Photo Researchers, Inc.
p739 t.l.	Biophoto Associates/Photo Researchers, Inc.
p739 b.l.	Photodisc
p739 m.l.	Ken Edwards/Photo Researchers, Inc
p739 m.r.	J.F. Gennaro/Photo Researchers, Inc.
p739 b.r.	PhotoDisc
p740	Jim Sugar Photography/Corbis
p743 t.l.	Biophoto Associates/Photo Researchers, Inc.
p743 m.l.	Biophoto Associates/Photo Researchers, Inc.
p743 t.r.	Barry Runk/Grant Heilman Photography, Inc.
p748 t.r.	PhotoDisc
p750 b.l.	CMCD/PhotoDisc
p756 l.	PhotoDisc
p759	Frank White/Liaison International
p760	Murray Photography/The Image Bank
p761	Guy Gillette/Photo Researchers
p763	Index Stock Photography, Inc.
p764	Jonathan Novrok/Photo Edit
p765	Farrell Grehan/Photo Researchers, Inc.
p767	Bokelberg/The Image Bank
p772 t.	Trehearne/Index Stock Photography, Inc.
p772 b.	Tony Freeman/Photo Edit
p776	Margo Taussig Pinkerton/Liaison International
p778	Charles D. Winters/Timeframe Photography, Inc./Photo Reseachers, Inc.
p780	Grant V. Faint/The Image Bank
p781	Harald Sund/The Image Bank
p782	Ron McMillan/Liaison International
p785 l.	Pete Seaward/Tony Stone Images
p785 r.	David R. Stoecklein/Tony Stone Images
p787	Michael Gallagher/Liaison International
p788	Charlie Ott/Photo Reseachers, Inc.
p790	Arvind Garg/Liaison International
p791	Cris Haigh/Tony Stone Images
p792	Peter Beney/The Image Bank
p794	Index Stock Photography, Inc.
p795	Ed Malitsky

Backmatter Contents

Read Aloud Selections T2

Annotated Workbooks T6

Alternate Teaching Strategies T60

Handwriting T68

Teachers' Resources

Awards, Authors and Illustrators T74
Theme Bibliography T78
Directory of Resources T80
Word List T82
Scope and Sequence T88
Index T96

Scoring Chart T106

What's the Big Idea, Ben Franklin?

biography by Jean Fritz

Benjamin Franklin lived on High Street, the busiest and noisiest street in Philadelphia. On one end of the street was the Delaware River to jump into when he felt like swimming. On the other end of the street was Debbie Read, whom he courted and married.

Benjamin and Debbie were married in 1730. Benjamin was 24 years old. He had his own printshop and owned his own newspaper.

Yet no matter how busy he was, Benjamin found time to try out new ideas.

Sometimes Benjamin's ideas were for the improvement of Philadelphia. He formed the first circulating library in America. He helped organize Philadelphia's fire department. He suggested ways to light the streets, deepen the rivers, dispose of garbage, and keep people from slipping on ice in winter.

Sometimes his ideas turned into inventions. At the head of his bed he hung a cord which was connected to an iron bolt on his door. When he wanted to lock his door at night, ▶ he didn't have to get out of bed. He just pulled the cord, rolled over, and shut his eyes.

He invented a stepladder stool with a seat that turned up. And a rocking chair with a fan over it. When he rocked, the fan would turn and keep the flies off his head. He fixed up a pole with movable fingers to use when he wanted to take books down from high shelves. He cut a hole in his kitchen wall and put in a windmill to turn his meat roaster. And he invented an iron stove with a pipe leading outside. The stove gave off more heat than an ordinary fireplace, cost less to operate, was less smoky, and became very popular.

Benjamin was 40 years old when he first became interested in electricity. His Big Idea was that electricity and lightning were the same. What was more, Franklin believed he could prove it. Let a box be built on the top of high tower, he wrote a scientist in Europe. Put a pointed rod in the tower and let a man stand in the box during a storm. Franklin knew that electricity was attracted to pointed iron rods. If the man in the box could find that lightning was also attracted to a rod, that would prove they were the same. The only reason Franklin didn't make the experiment himself was that Philadelphia didn't have a high enough tower.

Finally, Benjamin thought of a way that he could prove his Big Idea. One stormy day he raised a kite with a long pointed wire at the tip. Soon, he felt electric shocks come through a key that he had tied to the kite string near his hand.

A Big Idea, however, meant little to Benjamin Franklin unless he could put it to everyday use. So he invented the lightning rod, a pointed rod that could be raised from the roof of a house or barn to attract lightning and lead it harmlessly through a wire and into the ground. For his own lightning rod, he also fixed up a contraption that would ring a bell in the house whenever lightning hit. (Debbie hated that bell.)

Benjamin would have liked to do nothing but experiment with his ideas, but people had discovered that he was more than an inventor. Whatever needed doing, he seemed able and willing to do it.

When the time came to write the Declaration of Independence, he was one of those asked to do it. As it turned out, Thomas Jefferson did the writing, but Franklin made changes.

Beezus and Her Imagination

from *Beezus and Ramona*
by Beverly Cleary

For Beezus Quimby, Miss Robbins's Friday afternoon art class at the recreation center is always something to look forward to. But Beezus becomes discouraged when she hears the day's assignment—to paint an imaginary animal. Her first try turns out to look like something real. But when Beezus decides to paint a second picture, she sees things in a much more imaginative way!

Beezus seized her brush and painted in another sky with bold, free strokes. Then she dipped her brush into green paint and started to outline a lizard on her paper. Let's see, what did a lizard look like? She could not remember. It didn't matter much, anyway—not for an imaginary animal. She had started the lizard with such brave, bold strokes that it took up most of the paper and looked more like a dragon.

Beezus promptly decided the animal was a dragon. Dragons breathed fire, but she did not have any orange paint, and she was so late in starting this picture that she didn't want to take time to mix any. She dipped her brush into pink paint instead and made flames come out of the dragon's mouth. Only they didn't look like flames. They looked more like the spun-sugar candy Beezus had once eaten at the circus. And a dragon breathing clouds of pink candy was more fun than an ordinary flame-breathing dragon.

Forgetting everyone around her, Beezus made the pink clouds bigger and fluffier. Dragons had pointed things down their backs, so Beezus made a row of spines down the back. They did not look quite right—more like slanting sticks than spines. Lollipop sticks, of course!

At that Beezus laughed to herself. Naturally a dragon that breathed pink spun sugar would have lollipops down its back. Eagerly she dipped her brush into red paint and put a strawberry lollipop on one of the sticks. She painted a different flavor on each stick, finishing with a grape-flavored lollipop.

Then she held her drawing board at arm's length. She was pleased with her dragon. It was funny and colorful and really imaginary. Beezus wondered what she should do next. Then she remembered that Miss Robbins often said it was important for an artist to know when to stop painting. Maybe she'd spoil her picture if she added anything. No, just one more touch. She dipped her brush in yellow paint and gave the dragon an eye—a lemon-drop eye. There! Her imaginary animal was finished!

By that time it was four-thirty and most of the boys and girls had put away their drawing boards and washed their muffin tins. Several mothers who had come for their children were wandering around the room looking at the paintings.

"Those who have finished, wash your hands clean," said Miss Robbins. "And I mean clean." Then she came across the room to Beezus. "Why, Beezus!" she exclaimed. "This is a picture to be proud of!"

"I didn't know whether a dragon should have lollipops down his back or not, but they were fun to paint," said Beezus.

"Of course he can have lollipops down his back. It's a splendid idea. After all, no one has ever seen a dragon, so no one knows how one should look." Miss Robbins turned to several of the mothers and said, with admiration in her voice, "Here's a girl with real imagination."

Beezus smiled modestly at her toes while the mothers admired her picture.

"We'll tack this in the very center of the wall for next week's classes to see, " said Miss Robbins.

"It was fun to paint, " confided Beezus, her face flushed with pleasure.

Four Haiku
by Myra Cohn Livingston

Spring

Shiny colored tents
pop up above people's heads
at the first raindrop

Summer

Not wishing to stop
his chirping the whole night long,
Cricket never does

Autumn

Searching for only
one clear puddle, I find my
rain-drenched reflection…

Winter

Snow sits on cold steps
leading to the front door, and
waits for my return

Follow the Drinkin' Gourd
an African American spiritual
adapted by Paul Campbell

When the sun comes back and the first quail calls,
Follow the Drinkin' Gourd.
Then the Old Man is awaitin' for to carry you to freedom,
Follow the Drinkin' Gourd.

Follow the Drinkin' Gourd,
Follow the Drinkin' Gourd,
For the Old Man is awaitin' for to carry you to freedom,
Follow the Drinkin' Gourd.

Now the river bank'll make a mighty good road;
The dead trees'll show you the way.
And the left foot, pegfoot, travelin' on;
Just you follow the Drinkin' Gourd.

Now the river ends between two hills;
Follow the Drinkin' Gourd.
And there's another river on the other side,
Just you follow the Drinkin' Gourd.

The Needle in the Haystack
a fairy tale by John Hamma

Once in another time, there lived a King and Queen who had no children. The King worried about who would take his place when he grew too old to rule, so he asked his chief counselor what to do.

"Why not adopt a son, Your Majesty, and teach him the laws of the land?" his counselor suggested.

"But how will I find the right boy?" the King asked.

"Look for one who shows honesty, patience, and perseverance," the counselor told him. "It will be like looking for a needle in a haystack, but if you search wisely and well, you will find someone who is worthy."

"That's it!" the King exclaimed. "A needle in a haystack! Who would be more patient and persevering than a young man who could find a needle in a haystack? I will order my goldsmith to make a golden needle. Then I will hide it in one of the royal haystacks. The man who finds it will become ▶Crown Prince. And to ensure honesty, I shall have the needle inscribed with words only I know. That way no dishonest man will bring me a false needle."

Pleased with his decision, the King went to the goldsmith's shop that very afternoon. Franz, the son of the goldsmith, was the only one there. He explained that his father was sick with a fever.

"But perhaps I can help you, Your Majesty," Franz said. "My father has taught me all the secrets of his craft."

"Could you make a needle of gold?" the King asked.

"Yes," answered Franz.

"And could you write words on the needle?"

"Why I could write a whole song on the head of a pin," Franz said.

"And," asked the King sternly, "could you keep the secret of what is written on the needle?"

"Yes," Franz said simply.

"Very well," said the King, and told Franz how he wanted the needle made. As he turned to leave, the King warned, "Remember, *only* you and I are to know the words on the needle."

Two days later, Franz brought the needle to the castle. The King examined it closely with a magnifying glass and praised the young man. "You have done all you said you could, Franz. Your father must be proud of you. Here is your payment—and remember, not a word to anyone!" Franz bowed and accepted the bag holding twenty gold pieces.

That night the King set out secretly to hide the needle. The next afternoon he ordered Joseph, his first minister, to appear before him. After Joseph had bowed, the King said, "Last night I placed a golden needle in one of the royal haystacks. Today you will post a proclamation. All young men between the ages of eighteen and twenty-five have

▶ Continue reading here.

three days to search for this needle. The one who finds and brings the needle to me will become heir to the throne."

"Right away, Your Majesty," Joseph said, and after several more bows, he left the room. He rubbed his hands as he walked into the courtyard. What a good thing I saw young Franz hand the golden needle to the King yesterday, he thought. It has given me the chance I've been waiting for. I shall see to it that my son, Joseph II, presents a golden needle to the King and is pronounced heir. Through him I shall rule the kingdom.

First Joseph had to find out which haystack the King had visited. He asked the farmers who worked the fields surrounding the castle. Finally he found an old man who said he had seen a man put something in one of his haystacks and leave. Joseph noted that the haystack stood near a blue and white windmill. Then he went to visit the royal goldsmith's shop.

He found Franz making a silver bird and complimented his work. Franz thanked him and asked, "How may I help you, Your Excellency?"

"I am here on the King's business," Joseph said. "You are the one who made the golden needle for His Majesty, are you not?"

Franz said nothing. He was going to keep his promise to the King.

Joseph read his silence correctly. "I know that the King has sworn you to secrecy, so you need not answer. Just listen. The King has lost the needle. He was drinking from a well of fresh mountain water, and the needle fell in. He now asks that you make an exact copy."

Franz nodded, and Joseph placed twenty gold pieces on the counter. "Can you have it ready for me by tomorrow afternoon?"

Again, Franz nodded.

"I see I need not warn you about keeping my visit a secret. If word got out that the King had lost the needle, the kingdom would be in an uproar."

The next day, the first minister picked up the new needle from Franz. He hurried home to give it to his son, along with instructions about what he must do for his part of the plot.

The following morning, Joseph II joined the other young men from all over the country who were searching through the royal haystacks. At first, he deliberately looked in the wrong haystack. Then as evening neared, he rode to the haystack near the blue and white windmill. Some of the young men were standing near the field, with hay all over their clothing and in their hair. They shouted to Joseph II that he was wasting his time, for they had already flattened the haystack without finding the needle. He just smiled and started searching through the scattered mounds of hay. Suddenly he shouted in triumph and stood up, holding the golden needle in his hand.

Later that evening, Joseph II kneeled before the royal throne and proudly presented the needle to the King. The King took it from him, reached into the pocket of his royal robe, and brought out his magnifying glass. As he read the inscription, his face grew dark with anger. "Where did you get this needle?" he demanded.

"Why, in the h-h-haystack, Your Majesty," Joseph II stammered.

The King turned to his first minister. "Perhaps *you* have an explanation?"

"For what, Your Majesty?" the older Joseph said.

"Come here," the King commanded, "and read this."

The first minister read the writing on the needle: *Exact copy of first needle: Patience, Perseverance, Honesty*. Color left his face.

The next day, Franz heard that the first minister and his family had been banished from the kingdom and that the needle search had been called off. His heart sank. Surely this had something to do with the second needle he had made without asking the King!

He was ready for the worst when he heard a knock on the door and saw the King standing outside with his royal guard. But to his surprise, the King gave him a very friendly smile as he entered the shop.

"No doubt you have heard that I have called off the contest," the King said to Franz, "and that I have banished the first minister for trying to trick me with the second needle?"

"Yes, Your Majesty," Franz answered in a low voice.

"I have called off the contest for three reasons," the King continued. "The first reason is that everybody knows by now which haystack the needle is in. Secondly, the contest was not a good idea; the hay is ruined—thrown all over the field, and I will have to have my royal harvesters gather more. And finally, I have found my heir."

"You have?" Franz asked.

"Yes," said the King. "You."

"Me?" Franz looked at the King as if he had gone mad.

"Yes, you," repeated the King firmly. "It took patience and perseverance to craft the needle and honesty not to betray a confidence. And more importantly, you are intelligent. You knew that if I had truly lost the needle, the words 'exact copy' would not matter, and if I had not lost it, the words would reveal a trickster to me. I am proud to make you my royal heir and son."

So Franz, the goldsmith's son, came to be the King's heir. In time he ruled the kingdom with patience, perseverance, honesty—and intelligence.

The Hatmaker's Sign • PRACTICE

Name______________ Date__________ **Practice 75**

Make Judgments and Decisions

Read the story below about Keeshawn and the **judgments and decisions** he makes. Then answer each question.

Entering the soapbox derby, Keeshawn knew he had to build the soapbox car himself. It was the most important rule of the derby. He worked hard all day. Then he went to see his friend, Charles. Charles' older brother was helping Charles build his car. Keeshawn was angry because Charles was cheating. You weren't supposed to have help. Tomorrow he'd report Charles to the judges.

The next morning Keeshawn practiced racing his car. Later, he went to the library to research building cars. He found two ideas to make his car lighter, and therefore faster.

That night, Keeshawn thought again about Charles. Maybe other kids had help building their cars, too. Was Keeshawn going to report everyone? No. Instead he would compete against himself and try his best to win.

1. Who is the main character? Keeshawn
2. How did he feel when he saw Charles getting help? It made him angry.
3. What did Keeshawn decide to do when he saw Charles' brother helping him? He decided to report Charles.
4. What did Keeshawn do to make his car better? He practiced racing and by doing research, he figured out how to build a faster car.
5. What new decision did Keeshawn make about Charles, and why did he make it? Answers will vary, but should mention Keeshawn's decision not to report Charles because of the possibility that other racers had help also.

At Home: Have students write about a decision they have made to work at doing something better.

Name______________ Date__________ **Practice 76**

Vocabulary

Fill in each blank with the correct vocabulary word from the list.

admitted	**brisk**	**displaying**	**elegantly**	**strolling**	**wharf**

1. Many ships were docked at the wharf.
2. Some people were strolling slowly down the sidewalk.
3. The queen held her head high and walked elegantly.
4. My dad was in a rush, so he walked at a brisk pace.
5. She admitted that she was late.
6. We were displaying our art collections so that other classes could view them.

At Home: Have students use the vocabulary words in new sentences.

The Wharf Fundraiser

Karla and her mother were active with the community fundraiser to rebuild the *wharf* at the lake. Karla and her mother decided to make huge cardboard cutouts of pirates. The cutouts had no faces, so people could pose as pirates. One pirate was a captain with a hook and was dressed very *elegantly*. The other pirate had a parrot perched on his shoulder.

Business was *brisk*. Many of the people *strolling* on the wharf stopped to have their pictures taken. Laughing, most people *admitted* they looked silly, but they were having fun! *Displaying* their sense of humor and generosity, the people in the community raised enough money to rebuild the wharf.

1. Who was dressed *elegantly*? the captain with a hook
2. Where did Karla and her mother set up the cardboard cutouts? on the wharf
3. What word in the story describes Karla's business? brisk
4. What is another word for people walking slowly? strolling
5. Why did Karla and her mother do this project? To help the community raise money.

At Home: Have students use the vocabulary words to describe a pirate they have read about or have seen in the movies.

Name______________ Date__________ **Practice 77**

Story Comprehension

Answer the questions about "The Hatmaker's Sign." Look back at the story to help you answer the questions.

1. At the beginning of the story, Thomas Jefferson is reading what he wrote in The Declaration of Independence. What does he think of his writing? Answers will vary but should include: He thought it was perfect and that the Congress would love it.
2. What happened when Thomas Jefferson showed The Declaration of Independence to Congress? They wanted words and paragraphs changed. Congress made 87 changes to Jefferson's draft.
3. Who tells the story of the hatmaker's sign? Benjamin Franklin
4. How did the sign change from the beginning to the end of the story? At first, it had words and pictures, then few words, then it was blank, and finally it ended as it had begun.
5. What was Benjamin Franklin's point in telling Thomas Jefferson that story? No matter how good your writing is, people will have different opinions and will want to change it. Revision is part of writing.

At Home: Have students retell the story.

Name________________ Date__________ **Practice 78**

Read Signs

Signs communicate messages. Some signs give information while others advertise things. Signs may warn of danger, tell which way to go, or list rules.

Look at the signs below. Write what each one means.

1. telephone

2. no smoking

3. library

4. no cycling

5. disabled access

6. information

At Home: Have students draw two signs that they see on their way to school every morning. Have them label each sign with its meaning.

Name________________ Date__________ **Practice 79**

Make Judgments and Decisions

Making **judgments** about the actions of characters is a natural part of reading a story. That is how you make **decisions** about whether or not you like or respect a character. Read each statement, and then tell if the statement is **True** or **False.**

1. Thomas Jefferson believed the people in America should be free. True
2. Thomas Jefferson believed he was a fine writer. True
3. The other members of the Continental Congress thought The Declaration of Independence was written perfectly. False
4. Benjamin Franklin told a story to make Thomas Jefferson feel better. True
5. The story of the hatmaker and his sign proves that everyone has an opinion about hats. Explain your answer. False; they changed the sign and said nothing about hats.

Use your own ideas from "The Hatmaker's Sign" to write what you think of Thomas Jefferson and Benjamin Franklin. **Answers will vary.**

6. I think that Thomas Jefferson Answers will vary, but may include: believed in freedom, liked his writing, and was a smart man.
7. I believe that Benjamin Franklin Answers will vary, but may include: was a kind and smart man, cared for others, and was a good storyteller.
8. Telling stories such as "The Hatmaker's Sign" is a good way to get a point across. Choose to agree or disagree, then explain your answer.
Answers will vary.

At Home: Have students discuss which of Jefferson's or Franklin's actions helped them make a judgment about the two men.

Name________________ Date__________ **Practice 80**

Summarize

A **summary** is a short retelling of a story in your own words. In summarizing you should describe the setting, the main characters, and the most important events. Complete the summary of "The Hatmaker's Sign" below. **Answers will vary.**

When Thomas Jefferson's wonderful writing was read aloud to the Congress, a noisy **(1)** debate broke out. Some members of Congress didn't like one **(2)** word and others wanted to remove whole **(3)** paragraphs. Thomas Jefferson looked to **(4)** Benjamin Franklin for help. He told Thomas Jefferson a **(5)** story.

A hatmaker, John Thompson, wrote words on a piece of parchment and then drew a picture of a **(6)** hat. He decided to take this design to a **(7)** sign maker. John Thompson met many people on his way to the sign maker's shop. Each one said he should **(8)** take out something from his sign. By the time the hatmaker got to the sign maker's shop, his parchment was **(9)** blank When the sign maker saw the hatmaker's parchment, he suggested that the sign should **(10)** have the same words and picture that the hatmaker had had in the beginning.

At Home: Have students write a summary of the story and read it to someone at home.

Name________________ Date__________ **Practice 81**

Suffixes

A **suffix** is a group of letters, such as *-ful,* added to the end of a base word, or root word. Use the words below to complete the sentences.

wonderful	**unlawful**	**willful**	**thoughtful**
plentiful	**handful**	**bountiful**	**surprisingly**

1. The harvest was rich and bountiful.
2. The queen looked thoughtful as she read the new law.
3. The baker made a chocolate cake that was wonderful.
4. The number of apples picked was plentiful, so we shared them with our neighbors.
5. Dumping waste in the river is unlawful.
6. I could hold only a handful of those large marbles.
7. Marcus was very willful and stubborn.
8. The day looks cold, but it is surprisingly warm.

At Home: Have students write sentences using the words.

The Hatmaker's Sign • RETEACH

Name________________ Date__________ **Reteach 75**

Make Judgments and Decisions

> **Making judgments and decisions** is a natural part of storytelling and story reading. When you read a story you read about characters who think about what they will do in difficult situations. As a reader, you too, can think about what you may do in similar situations.

Read the story. Then answer the questions. **Answers may vary.**

Lucinda was excited as she finished writing her story. She thought she had a good chance to win the story contest. She had read the rules carefully, and had thought a lot about what her story was going to be about. Then she had written it, choosing her words carefully. When she finished writing the story she read it and thought it was great. Then she showed it to her best friend, Pam. Pam told her to change several things about the story to make it different. Lucinda liked Pam, but was confused by her advice.

1. What decision does Lucinda have to make?
   Possible answer: She has to decide whether or not to take Pam's advice and change a story she thinks is good as it is.
2. What things should Lucinda think about before she makes a decision?
   She should think about why Pam made her comments. She should think about which changes she agrees with and which changes she will not make.
3. Suppose you were Lucinda. What might you say to Pam?
   "How do you think these changes will help my story?"
4. Who else might help Lucinda decide what to do?
   a teacher, her parents, an adult friend

At Home: Have students discuss a decision they have made and how they came to it.

Name________________ Date__________ **Reteach 76**

Vocabulary

Read each clue. Then find the vocabulary word in the row of letters and circle it.

admitted	brisk	displaying	elegantly	strolling	wharf

1. quick — n (b r i s k) d a q t e c f
2. richly or beautifully — p r w s c (e l e g a n t l y) i
3. showing — t r v m (d i s p l a y i n g) f e
4. confessed — w u n (a d m i t t e d) k o l
5. landing place for boats — a l d p i r (w h a r f) k n d s
6. walking slowly and in a relaxed way — l e (s t r o l l i n g) r c b n k

6

Reteach 77

Story Comprehension

Write a complete sentence to answer each question about "The Hatmaker's Sign."

1. Who is the main character of the story?
   The main character is John Thompson.
2. How did the hatmaker feel about his sign before he talked to others?
   He liked the sign the way he had planned it.
3. How did everyone want him to change the sign?
   Each person wanted him to take something off of the sign.
4. What did the sign maker suggest about changing the sign?
   He suggested that John's sign read as he had planned it originally.
5. Why did Ben Franklin share this story with Jefferson?
   He wanted Jefferson to know he was not the only one who had to deal with people's suggestions.

At Home: Have students retell the main events of "The Hatmaker's Sign."

Name________________ Date__________ **Reteach 78**

Read Signs

> Signs are all around us. Many signs use symbols to tell us things in a short, quick way. These kinds of signs have simple drawings that stand for actions, objects, or directions.

Read the signs. Draw a line from each sign to the correct meaning.

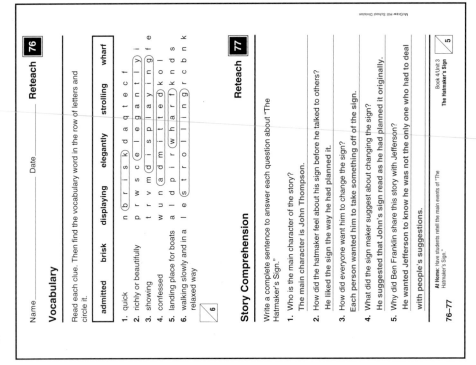

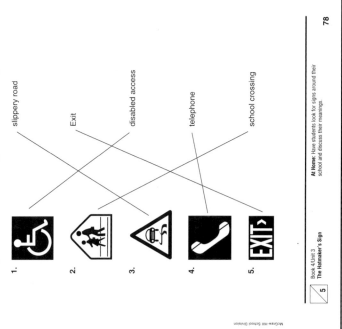

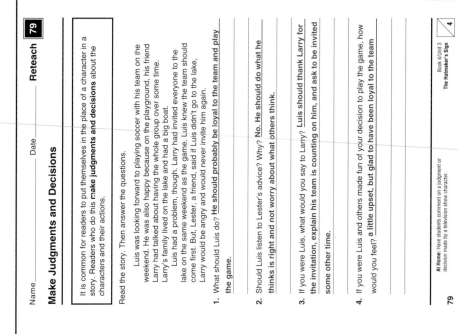

1. 2. 3. 4. 5.

slippery road

Exit

disabled access

telephone

school crossing

At Home: Have students look for signs around their school and discuss their meanings.

Name________________ Date__________ **Reteach 79**

Make Judgments and Decisions

> It is common for readers to put themselves in the place of a character in a story. Readers who do this **make judgments and decisions** about the characters and their actions.

Read the story. Then answer the questions.

Luis was looking forward to playing soccer with his team on the weekend. He was also happy because on the playground, his friend Larry had talked about having the whole group over some time. Larry's family lived on the lake and had a big boat.

Luis had a problem, though. Larry had invited everyone to the lake on the same weekend as the game. Luis knew the team should come first. But, Lester, a friend, said if Luis didn't go to the lake, Larry would be angry and would never invite him again.

1. What should Luis do? **He should probably be loyal to the team and play the game.**
2. Should Luis listen to Lester's advice? Why? **No. He should do what he thinks is right and not worry about what others think.**
3. If you were Luis, what would you say to Larry? **Luis should thank Larry for the invitation, explain his team is counting on him, and ask to be invited some other time.**
4. If you were Luis and others made fun of your decision to play the game, how would you feel? **a little upset, but glad to have been loyal to the team**

At Home: Have students comment on a judgment or decision made by a television show character.

Name________________ Date__________ **Reteach 80**

Summarize

When you **summarize**, you tell the most important parts of something you have read. Include the main idea and only important details.

Read the selection. Then answer the questions.

Thomas Jefferson was a talented and respected man. He is most famous for writing The Declaration of Independence, but he also served as the third President of the United States.

Jefferson was a shy man who preferred reading and studying to being with groups of people. He was a scientist, inventor, and builder. His home in Virginia is studied as an example of beautiful architecture. Jefferson also founded the University of Virginia in his home state. In his time, Jefferson was very important in the United States. People looked up to him and asked his advice on many matters of importance.

1. What is the main idea? **Thomas Jefferson was a talented and respected man.**
2. What is Jefferson most famous for? **writing The Declaration of Independence**
3. What else was Jefferson famous for? **being the third President; being a scientist, an inventor, a builder; and having founded the University of Virginia**
4. How would you summarize the selection? **Jefferson, our third President and the writer of The Declaration of Independence, did many different things. He was a scientist, inventor, and builder. People respected him and his talents.**

At Home: Have students summarize a favorite movie.

Name________________ Date__________ **Reteach 81**

Suffixes

Suffixes are word endings. They add to the meaning of a word. The suffix *-ful* adds the meaning "full of" to a word.

Add the suffix *-ful* to each word.

1. fear + ful = **fearful**
2. help + ful = **helpful**
3. hope + ful = **hopeful**
4. joy + ful = **joyful**
5. doubt + ful = **doubtful**
6. health + ful = **healthful**

Now use one of the words above with *-ful* to complete each sentence.

7. Carrot sticks are a **healthful** snack.
8. She was **doubtful** that she could finish on time.
9. My brother is **fearful** of dark places.
10. Birthdays are **joyful** occasions.
11. Can you be **helpful** and hand me the hammer?
12. Aaron is **hopeful** he will win the contest.

At Home: Have students use three words they formed in sentences of their own.

The Hatmaker's Sign • EXTEND

Name______________________ Date__________ **Extend 75**

Make Judgments and Decisions

A statement in a conversation may be a **judgment**, or the speaker's opinion about something. Another statement may be a **decision**, or what the speaker has decided to do. Read each statement below. Then write **J** if it is a judgment, **D** if it is a decision, or **N** if it is neither a judgment nor a decision.

1. The clothes in that store don't look good on me. J
2. I am going to go to another store. D
3. I think this is the best looking sweater in the whole world. J
4. I already have a blue sweater. N
5. This sweater would look great in red. J
6. I will buy this sweater for my cousin. D

Write a statement that is a judgment about a store in which you have shopped.

Answers will vary.

Write a statement that is a decision about shopping for something you want to buy.

Answers will vary.

At Home: Identify statements made during family conversations that are judgments or decisions.

Name______________________ Date__________ **Extend 76**

Vocabulary

admitted	**brisk**	**displaying**
elegantly	**strolling**	**wharf**

Write a paragraph about going shopping, using as many vocabulary words from the box as you can. Then erase those vocabulary words or cover them with tape. Exchange paragraphs with a partner and fill in the blanks.

Extend 77

Story Comprehension

Suppose you were the first person to whom John Thompson showed his idea for a sign. Make a judgment about how he could change his sign. Then write what you would have told him to change. Explain why he should make that change.

At Home: Find an ad in a newspaper or magazine. Discuss how it could be changed to be more effective.

Name______________________ Date__________ **Extend 78**

Read Signs

Signs are a quick way to communicate information. Signs often use symbols, simple drawings that stand for actions, objects, or directions.

Identify each sign and write its meaning on the line below

1. ______________

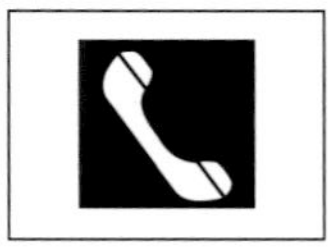

2. ______________

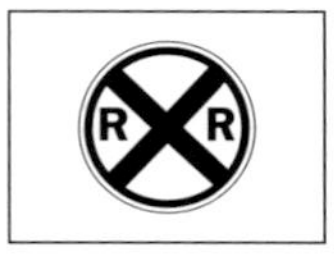

3. ______________

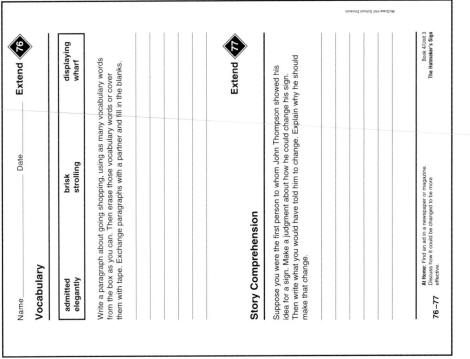

4. ______________

Create a sign that will tell people that no bears are allowed to cross the street.

At Home: Have students record unusual signs that they see in their neighborhoods.

Name______________________ Date__________ **Extend 79**

Make Judgments and Decisions

In "The Hatmaker's Sign," you read the **judgments** that several people made about John Thompson's sign. You also read about John's **decisions** to change the sign after hearing the judgments.

Design a sign to hang on the wall over your bed. It should say something about you. Include your first name, words or pictures that tell what you want to say, and any other important details.

Show your design to three friends. Ask them if you should make any changes to your sign. Have them explain. Record your friends' judgments below.

Friend 1 ______________

Friend 2 ______________

Friend 3 ______________

Now decide if you will change your sign and, if so, how. Explain your decision below. Then make any changes to your sign.

At Home: Tell students to share their signs with family members and discuss the various judgments.

Name________________ Date__________ **Extend 80**

Summarize

When you don't have the time to tell a whole story or have the space to write it all down, you can tell or write a summary of the story. To **summarize** a story, include the main idea of the story and the important characters.

Write a summary of the story Benjamin Franklin told to Thomas Jefferson in "The Hatmaker's Sign." Try not to use more than five sentences.

Answers will vary. Possible answer: John Thompson designed a sign for his hat store. Everyone to whom he showed the design suggested that he make changes in the sign. John made all the changes, and was left with a blank sign. When John showed the design to the sign maker, the sign maker suggested words and a picture for the sign. They were the same words John first had on the sign.

At Home: Ask students to summarize a book or story they have read recently to family members.

Name________________ Date__________ **Extend 81**

Suffixes

Word parts that are added to the end of words, such as *-ed* and *-ing*, are called **suffixes**. The suffix *-ful* means "full of." When you add *-ful* to a noun, it forms an adjective. For example, *wonderful* is an adjective that means "full of wonder." Add *-ful* to each noun to create adjectives. Then write sentences using the adjectives you created. Sentences will vary.

1. thought ___thoughtful___
Sample: It was thoughtful of her to remember my birthday.

2. use ___useful___
Sample: A shovel is useful when working in the garden.

3. sorrow ___sorrowful___
Sample: Saying goodbye can be sorrowful.

4. help ___helpful___
Sample: I try to be helpful by mowing the lawn.

5. care ___careful___
Sample: Be careful when you cross the street.

6. joy ___joyful___
Sample: Holidays can be a joyful time.

7. hope ___hopeful___
Sample: Shandra was hopeful that she did well on the test.

At Home: Direct students to create adjectives by adding *-ful* to nouns and use the adjectives in conversation.

The Hatmaker's Sign • GRAMMAR

Name__________ Date__________ LEARN **Grammar 65**

Action Verbs in the Present Tense

- An **action verb** tells what the subject does or did.
- A verb in the **present tense** tells what happens now.
- The present tense must have **subject-verb agreement**. Add *-s* to most verbs if the subject is singular. Do not add *-s* if the subject is plural or *I* or *you.*

Write the correct present tense of each underlined verb on the lines provided.

1. John Thompson <u>place</u> hats in the window of his shop. **places**
2. He <u>stack</u> hatboxes along a wall. **stacks**
3. John <u>write</u> some words on parchment. **writes**
4. He <u>draw</u> a picture of a hat under the words. **draws**
5. John <u>show</u> his idea for a sign to his wife. **shows**
6. His wife giggles when she <u>read</u> the words. **reads**
7. John <u>make</u> changes in his sign. **makes**
8. The hatmaker <u>walk</u> to the sign maker's shop. **walks**
9. The hatmaker <u>meet</u> many people on the way. **meets**
10. What does the sign maker <u>say</u> to the hat maker? **say**

10 | Grade 4/Unit 3 **The Hatmaker's Sign**

Extension: Have students write three sentences about the story, using the present tense of these verbs: *grab, rewrite, suggest.* Ask students to circle the verbs in their sentences.

65

Name__________ Date__________ LEARN & PRACTICE **Grammar 66**

Action Verbs

- Add *-es* to verbs that end in *s, ch, sh, x,* or *z* if the subject is singular.
- Change *y* to *i* and add *-es* to verbs that end with a consonant and *y.*
- Do not add *-es* to a present-tense verb when the subject is plural or *I* or *you.*

Read each sentence. Write the correct present tense of each underlined verb on the line provided.

1. Thomas Jefferson is angry, and his face <u>flush</u> red. **flushes**
2. Benjamin Franklin <u>try</u> to make Jefferson feel better. **tries**
3. The hatmaker <u>kiss</u> Lady Manderly's hand. **kisses**
4. The lady <u>snatch</u> the parchment away from the hatmaker. **snatches**
5. John Thompson <u>toss</u> coins to the boys. **tosses**
6. He <u>push</u> the parchment under a man's nose. **pushes**
7. John <u>hurry</u> home to his shop several times. **hurries**
8. The hatmaker <u>fix</u> the words on his sign. **fixes**
9. John <u>rush</u> to the sign maker's shop. **rushes**
10. Do you <u>realize</u> what happens to the hatmaker's sign? **realize**

66

Extension: Ask students to write five sentences, using these verbs: watch, watches; worry, worries.

Grade 4/Unit 3 **The Hatmaker's Sign** | 10

Name__________ Date__________ PRACTICE AND REVIEW **Grammar 67**

Write Subject-Verb Agreement

- The present tense must have **subject-verb agreement**. Add *-s* to most verbs if the subject is singular.
- Add *-es* to verbs that end in *s, ch, sh, x,* or *z* if the subject is singular.
- Change *y* to *i* and add *-es* to verbs that end with a consonant and *y.*
- Do not add *-s* or *-es* to a present-tense verb when the subject is plural or *I* or *you.*

Correct each sentence for subject-verb agreement or the correct spelling of a present tense verb. Write your answer on the line provided.

1. Jefferson write for hours. **writes**
2. Many men listens to Jefferson read. **listen**
3. They argues about Jefferson's words. **argue**
4. Jefferson wishs they would stop quibbling. **wishes**
5. He worrys about his writing. **worries**
6. Franklin pat Jefferson on the shoulder. **pats**
7. John carrys the parchment to the sign maker's shop. **carries**
8. Do you likes the story about the hatmaker? **like**

8 | Grade 4/Unit 3 **The Hatmaker's Sign**

Extension: Have students look in classroom books for sentences with present-tense verbs. Then have the students read the sentences aloud, identify the verbs, and tell whether the subject is singular or plural.

67

Name__________ Date__________ MECHANICS **Grammar 68**

Commas in a Series

- A **comma** tells the reader to pause between the words that it separates.
- Use commas to separate three or more words in a series.
- Do not use a comma after the last word in a series.

Rewrite the sentences below by adding commas where they belong.

1. A good writer thinks writes and rewrites.
   A good writer thinks, writes, and rewrites.
2. The delegates shouted quibbled and argued over sentences.
   The delegates shouted, quibbled, and argued over sentences.
3. Benjamin Franklin stood smiled and spoke to Jefferson.
   Benjamin Franklin stood, smiled, and spoke to Jefferson.
4. Then Benjamin Franklin Jefferson's friend told a story.
   Then Benjamin Franklin, Jefferson's friend, told a story.
5. John Thompson a hatmaker wanted a sign for his shop.
   John Thompson, a hatmaker, wanted a sign for his shop.
6. John's shop was in Boston Massachusetts.
   John's shop was in Boston, Massachusetts.
7. John's wife Hannah thought his sign was funny.
   John's wife, Hannah, thought his sign was funny.
8. Under the words on his sign John drew a hat.
   Under the words on his sign, John drew a hat.
9. John rewrote rewrote and rewrote his sign.
   John rewrote, rewrote, and rewrote his sign.
10. Surprised the sign maker gazed at the blank parchment.
    Surprised, the sign maker gazed at the blank parchment.

68

Extension: Ask students to write three sentences, using commas. Then tell students to rewrite the sentences without the commas. Have students exchange papers and put the missing commas in

Grade 4/Unit 3 **The Hatmaker's Sign** | 10

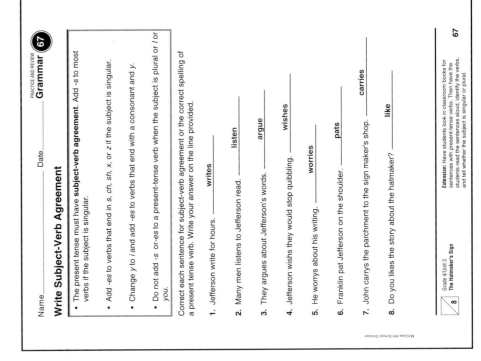

Name_________________________ Date___________ TEST **Grammar 69**

Action Verbs in the Present Tense

A. Read each sentence. Circle the letter of the sentence that has correct subject-verb agreement.

1. a. Jefferson sit down.

b. He listen carefully.

(c.) Franklin tells a story.

d. The delegates talks loudly.

2. a. The man draw a hat.

(b.) His wife giggles.

c. The lady wear gloves.

d. John bow to the magistrate.

B. Read each sentence. Circle the letter before the present-tense verb that belongs in the sentence. Make sure the spelling is correct.

3. Jefferson ____ the meaning of Franklin's story.

a. know

(b.) knows

c. knowes

d. knowies

4. The wind ____ the hatmaker's sign from his hand.

a. snatch

b. snatchs

(c.) snatches

d. snatchies

Name_________________________ Date___________ MORE PRACTICE **Grammar 70**

Present Tense

- The present tense must have subject-verb agreement.
- Add *-s* to most verbs if the subject is singular.
- Add *-es* to verbs that end in *s, ch, sh, x,* or *z* if the subject is singular.
- Change *y* to *i* and add *-es* to verbs that end with a consonant and *y.*

Mechanics

- A comma tells the reader to pause between words that it separates.
- Use commas to separate three or more words in a series.
- Do not use a comma after the last word in a series.

Rewrite each sentence correctly paying attention to the present tense verb and comma rules. Then use the information in the sentences to draw the missing parts of the picture.

1. A hatmaker James hang a sign on his shop's door.

A hatmaker, James, hangs a sign on his shop's door.

2. George a clerk polishs a round mirror.

George, a clerk, polishes a round mirror.

3. One man sit and try on a top hat.

One man sits and tries on a top hat.

4. Two ladies likes hats with bows ribbons and feathers.

Two ladies like hats with bows, ribbons, and feathers.

The Hatmaker's Sign • SPELLING

Name________________ Date________ PRETEST **Spelling 65**

Words with /ou/ and /oi/

Pretest Directions

Fold back the paper along the dotted line. Use the blanks to write each word as it is read aloud. When you finish the test, unfold the paper. Use the list at the right to correct any spelling mistakes. Practice the words you missed for the Posttest.

To Parents

Here are the results of your child's weekly spelling Pretest. You can help your child study for the Posttest by following these simple steps for each word on the word list:

1. Read the word to your child.
2. Have your child write the word, saying each letter as it is written.
3. Say each letter of the word as your child checks the spelling.
4. If a mistake has been made, have your child read each letter of the correctly spelled word aloud, and then repeat steps 1–3.

1. ______	1. oily
2. ______	2. annoy
3. ______	3. around
4. ______	4. growl
5. ______	5. disappoint
6. ______	6. royalty
7. ______	7. bounce
8. ______	8. bowing
9. ______	9. moist
10. ______	10. enjoyment
11. ______	11. aloud
12. ______	12. tower
13. ______	13. avoid
14. ______	14. employ
15. ______	15. lookout
16. ______	16. however
17. ______	17. appointment
18. ______	18. scout
19. ______	19. powder
20. ______	20. noun

Challenge Words

______	admitted
______	displaying
______	elegantly
______	strolling
______	wharf

Name________________ Date________ AT HOME WORD STUDY **Spelling 66**

Words with /ou/ and /oi/

Using the Word Study Steps

1. LOOK at the word.
2. SAY the word aloud.
3. STUDY the letters in the word.
4. WRITE the word.
5. CHECK the word.

Did you spell the word right? If not, go back to step 1.

Spelling Tips

Think of a word you know that has the same spelling pattern as the word you want to spell.

sc<u>ou</u>t b<u>ou</u>nce ar<u>ou</u>nd

Word Scramble

Unscramble each set of letters to make a spelling word.

1. loiy	oily	11. tylyora	royalty
2. idvoa	avoid	12. tsmoi	moist
3. kuoootl	lookout	13. ntiopapntem	appointment
4. olmepy	employ	14. necuob	bounce
5. verwohe	however	15. wniogb	bowing
6. tousc	scout	16. uonn	noun
7. drewop	powder	17. rlwog	growl
8. ppnotiasid	disappoint	18. mtneyojen	enjoyment
9. yonan	annoy	19. ludoa	aloud
10. nuodra	around	20. woter	tower

To Parents or Helpers

Using the Word Study Steps above as your child comes across any new words will help him or her learn to spell words effectively. Review the steps as you both go over this week's spelling words.

Go over each Spelling Tip with your child. Help your child look at some of the spelling words to see which ones have the same spelling pattern.

Help your child complete the word scramble.

Name________________ Date________ EXPLORE THE PATTERN **Spelling 67**

Words with /ou/ and /oi/

oily	disappoint	moist	avoid	appointment
annoy	royalty	enjoyment	employ	scout
around	bounce	aloud	lookout	powder
growl	bowing	tower	however	noun

Pattern Power!

Write the spelling words with these spelling patterns.

oi

1. oily
2. disappoint
3. moist
4. avoid
5. appointment

oy

6. annoy
7. royalty
8. enjoyment
9. employ

ou

10. around
11. bounce
12. aloud
13. lookout
14. scout
15. noun

ow

16. growl
17. bowing
18. tower
19. however
20. powder

Name________________ Date________ PRACTICE AND EXTEND **Spelling 68**

Words with /ou/ and /oi/

oily	disappoint	moist	avoid	appointment
annoy	royalty	enjoyment	employ	scout
around	bounce	aloud	lookout	powder
growl	bowing	tower	however	noun

What's the Word?

Complete each sentence with a word from the spelling list.

1. The baby likes to look **around** to see what is going on.
2. Keep the soil around the plant **moist** or the plant will die.
3. Did you make an **appointment** to see the dentist?
4. A king and a queen are **royalty**.
5. What a loud **growl** that dog made!
6. The wet road had a slick, **oily** coating from all of the traffic.
7. I really like that dress; **however**, I can't buy it now.
8. Do you like to read stories **aloud** to younger children?
9. In the old days, **bowing** was a polite form of greeting.
10. Mom gets a lot of **enjoyment** out of working in the garden.

What Do You Mean?

Read each dictionary definition below. Then write the spelling word that matches the definition.

11. To bother someone **annoy**
12. To rebound after hitting something **bounce**
13. To stay clear of **avoid**
14. A part of speech that names a person, place, or thing **noun**
15. To provide with paying work **employ**

Challenge Extension: Have students write dictionary definitions of the Challenge Words. Then exchange with a partner and write the Challenge Words that match each other's definitions.

The Hatmaker's Sign • SPELLING

Name______________________ Date____________ PROOFREAD AND WRITE **Spelling 69**

Words with /ou/ and /oi/

Proofreading Activity
There are 6 spelling mistakes in the paragraph below. Circle the misspelled words. Write the words correctly on the lines below.

Benjamin Franklin was an interesting man. He was comfortable with common men and roialty. He liked to take walks arownd Philadelphia, and was always on the lookouwt for ways to improve the city. He invented things for his own enjoiment. He was never known to avoyd a problem or task. Ben would not disappoynt a friend in need.

1.	royalty	3.	lookout	5.	avoid
2.	around	4.	enjoyment	6.	disappoint

Writing Activity
Do you have a favorite person from history? Write something you think that person might say if he or she were alive today, using four spelling words.

____

____

____

____

Name______________________ Date____________ POSTTEST **Spelling 70**

Words with /ou/ and /oi/

Look at the words in each set below. One word in each set is spelled correctly. Use a pencil to fill in the circle next to the correct word. Before you begin, look at the sample sets of words. Sample A has been done for you. Do Sample B by yourself. When you are sure you know what to do, you may go on with the rest of the page.

Sample A (A) broun (B) broin (C) brown (D) brouwn

Sample B (E) coin (F) coyne (G) coien (H) coyen

1. (A) oilee (B) oyly (C) oily (D) oiyle
2. (E) anoy (F) annoy (G) annoie (H) anoiy
3. (A) uround (B) around (C) arrownd (D) arowund
4. (E) groul (F) graul (G) growl (H) garowl
5. (A) dissapoint (B) disappoynte (C) disapoynt (D) disappoint
6. (E) royalty (F) royltie (G) roialty (H) royelty
7. (A) bounce (B) bownse (C) bounz (D) bouwnse
8. (E) bouing (F) bowing (G) bowwing (H) bowung
9. (A) moiste (B) moist (C) moyst (D) mosit
10. (E) enjoymant (F) enjoiment (G) anjoymint (H) enjoyment
11. (A) elloud (B) alowud (C) aloud (D) iloud
12. (E) towir (F) touer (G) tower (H) twore
13. (A) avoid (B) ivoid (C) avoyd (D) ahvoid
14. (E) employ (F) emploiy (G) imploy (H) amploi
15. (A) lookowt (B) lokout (C) lokowut (D) lookout
16. (E) howavir (F) halevere (G) hilever (H) however
17. (A) apoyntment (B) appointment (C) upointmant (D) ipointment
18. (E) skowt (F) scout (G) scault (H) scoit
19. (A) palder (B) podre (C) powder (D) powdor
20. (E) naln (F) nown (G) noun (H) noune

Pat Cummings: My Story • PRACTICE

Name________________ Date________ **Practice 82**

Fact and Opinion

A **fact** is a statement that can be proven. An **opinion** is a statement that tells what a person thinks about something. Read the following passage. Then write whether you think each underlined statement is a fact or an opinion. Explain the reason for your decision.

Today, people use gas or electricity to cook food and heat their homes. Long ago, people built fires in their stoves to cook and to heat their homes. When the fire went out, the ashes were shoveled into an ashcan and carried outside. Ashcans were useful, but I can't imagine that anyone thought they were beautiful. Therefore, it surprised many people when in the early 1900s, a group of painters called themselves Ashcan school artists. They called themselves Ashcan artists because they painted realistic scenes of poor people, factories, and crowded streets. If you were to see this art, you would probably just love it.

Statement	Fact or Opinion	Explanation of Decision
1. Today people use gas or electricity to heat their stoves for cooking food.	Fact	This is a well-known fact that can be proven.
2. Ashcans were useful, but I can't imagine that anyone thought they were beautiful.	Opinion	It is one person's opinion and can't be proven true.
3. Therefore, it surprised many people when in the early 1900s, a group of painters called themselves Ashcan School artists.	Opinion	It is an opinion and can't be proven true.
4. They called themselves Ashcan artists because they painted realistic scenes of poor people, factories, and crowded streets.	Fact	It can be proven.

At Home: Have students locate a fact and an opinion from a newspaper or magazine.

Name________________ Date________ **Practice 83**

Vocabulary

Fill in the blank with the correct vocabulary word from the list.

exist	image	inspire	loft	reference	sketch

1. A painting or photograph might be the **image** of a person or animal.
2. One kind of **reference** book is an encyclopedia.
3. You can **sketch** a picture with a pencil and do a detailed drawing later.
4. A beautiful painting can **inspire** you to draw or paint.
5. Beautiful paintings by very young people do **exist**.
6. Some artists work in a big room called a **loft**.

At Home: Have students write sentences using each vocabulary word.

Making Art

Kamal's mom, a professional photographer, knows how to capture the *image* of a wild bird with her camera. Her photographs *inspire* Kamal to do the same thing. Looking up birds in a *reference* book, Kamal *sketches* the bird that he plans to photograph. Climbing into the hay *loft*, Kamal waits patiently until he sees a bird he has studied. It is stunning. Kamal captures the bird's image with his camera. People who will see his photograph will be amazed that this bird does *exist* locally.

1. What *image* does Kamal's mom know how to capture with her camera? **The image of a wild bird**
2. What *inspires* Kamal to take a picture of a local bird? **He sees his mother taking a picture with her camera and he wants to try it too.**
3. Why does Kamal use a *reference* book? **He looks up birds and selects one; then he sketches it to help him recognize it.**
4. Where does Kamal go to wait for the bird? **Up in the hay loft.**
5. What does Kamal find interesting about what his mother does for a living? **Answers will vary, but may include that Kamal and his mother both like photography and photographing nature.**

At Home: Have students describe their experience of using a camera.

Name________________ Date________ **Practice 84**

Story Comprehension

Read the statements below about "Pat Cummings: My Story." Write **T** if the statement is true. Write **F** if the statement is false. Refer to the story if necessary.

1. **T** Pat Cummings began her art by scribbling.
2. **T** Pat Cummings took a bus alone when she was very little.
3. **F** Pat Cummings never cared much for ballerinas.
4. **T** Pat Cummings loved to draw and discovered art could be a good business, too.
5. **F** Pat Cummings only gets her ideas from her friends.

Rewrite the following sentences to make them accurate. **Answers may vary.**

6. Pat Cummings began to draw when she was in high school.
   She began drawing when she was a small child.
7. Pat Cummings never puts people she knows in her pictures.
   She often draws faces from family photos.
8. Cummings draws everything from memory and never looks at other pictures.
   She often uses pictures from reference books, looking at them as she sketches.

At Home: Have students tell about Pat Cummings and her life as an artist.

Pat Cummings: My Story • PRACTICE

Name________________________ Date____________ **Practice 85**

Read a Flow Chart

A **flow chart** is a step-by-step description showing how to do something. Picture in your mind the steps as you read through each section of the flow chart below. Then answer the questions.

Ice Art

Step 1
Cut off the top of a half-pint milk carton.

Step 2
Fill the carton with water and food coloring.

Step 3
Place the carton in your freezer.

Step 4
Keep poking the water to find out if it is partly frozen or mushy.

Step 5
When the water becomes mushy ice, place a decorative object like a flower, or a plastic toy in the middle.

Step 6
Freeze until solid. Then tip over the carton and look at your ice art.

1. What does this flow chart show? **Directions for making a cube of ice filled with art.**
2. How many steps are there in making ice art? **There are six steps.**
3. Is it possible to change the order of the flow chart? **Probably not. One thing must be done before you can do the next step.**
4. Which steps ask you to add color and an object to the ice art? **Step 2 and Step 5**
5. How might you change the shape of the ice art? **Answers will vary, but may include choosing another container with a different size or shape.**

At Home: Have students create a new flow chart for another project.

Name________________________ Date____________ **Practice 86**

Fact and Opinion

When you read, look for information that is true and accurate. This helps you to tell the difference between a **fact** and an **opinion**.

"Pat Cummings: My Story" is a nonfiction story. It is a true story about an artist. Read each of the following statements about Pat Cummings.

Write fact or opinion to describe each statement.

1. The first things Pat Cummings ever drew were scribbles. **Fact**
2. Every person who sees her art would love Pat Cummings's work. **Opinion**
3. I think Pat Cummings likes to draw things that only exist in her imagination. **Opinion**
4. Pat Cummings believes it's important for people to help each other. **Opinion**
5. Before the age of eight, Pat Cummings went on a bus alone. **Fact**
6. Pat Cummings believes that traveling helps an artist grow. **Opinion**
7. Pat Cummings works in a loft in Brooklyn, New York. **Fact**
8. Pat Cummings uses watercolors, oil paints, and pencils. **Fact**

At Home: Have students list some facts and opinions about artists.

Name________________________ Date____________ **Practice 87**

Summarize

In a **summary**, you tell a story's important events in your own words. Read the passages below about Pat Cummings. Then summarize each passage in one sentence. **Answers will vary.**

1. I have to laugh every time I think about a story Pat Cummings tells. She has such a great sense of humor. She says her mother would tell her she had drawn a nice duck. Then she would inform her mother that it was really a picture of her dad. **Summary: The speaker thought the story of Pat Cummings's mother's response to her drawing of a duck was funny.**
2. Pat Cummings and her older sister were playing outside when her sister left her alone. Before anyone could stop Pat, she hopped on the bus that had stopped at the corner. **Summary: No one was watching Pat when a bus came along, so she got on it.**
3. When the bus stopped in front of a building, everyone got off. Pat followed them into ballet class. Pat loved looking at the young ballerinas, but the teacher looked at Pat as if she had come from another planet. **Summary: Pat followed the bus riders into ballet class, and the teacher was surprised to see her.**
4. Pat Cummings and her family moved every three years. Pat made friends by joining an art club or by drawing posters. Everyone was impressed with her drawing talent, and she made many friends. **Summary: Pat used her talent at drawing to make friends.**
5. Sometimes ideas for art pieces just jump into Pat's head. Sometimes they happen even when she is sleeping. Jumping out of bed in the middle of the night, Pat will paint her idea. **Summary: Pat gets ideas for her art whether she is awake or asleep.**

At Home: Have students write a summary of a favorite weekend activity.

Name________________________ Date____________ **Practice 88**

Suffixes

A **suffix** is a group of letters, such as *-ful* or *-ous*, added to the end of a base word. Read the words and their meanings, then complete the sentences. Remember that adding suffixes sometimes causes changes in spelling of the base, or root, word.

beauty — very pretty
beauti*ful* — full of beauty
wonder — feeling caused by something unusual or remarkable.
wonder*ful* — full of wonder
disaster — something that causes suffering
disastr*ous* — something bad
thought — what you think
thought*ful* — caring
thank — giving appreciation for something
thank*ful* — full of thanks

1. Getting an A on my report was **wonderful**.
2. Her singing was a **wonder**, she had the voice of an angel.
3. Jose shouted out an answer because he **thought** he knew it.
4. Celia was **thoughtful** when she asked about her friend's sick dog.
5. The diamond was considered a **beauty**.
6. Stephan created a **beautiful** sculpture made from wood.
7. He was so **thankful** to his mother for buying him the bike.
8. Sean remembered to **thank** his aunt for the gift.
9. The race was a **disaster** because of our poor running.
10. Walking home frome the football game was **disastrous** because we got caught in a snowstorm.

At Home: Have students identify words with suffixes as they read.

Pat Cummings: My Story • RETEACH

Name__________ Date________ **Reteach 82**

Fact and Opinion

A **fact** is a statement that can be proven in some way. An **opinion** is a statement of a person's belief that may not be able to be proven.

Read each story. Then write examples of facts or opinions from the story.

In the United States, there are three branches of government. The legislative branch is the Congress, which is made up of the Senate and the House of Representatives. The judicial branch is headed by the Supreme Court. The executive branch is headed by the President. This three-part system of government is the best in the world because no one branch has total power.

1. Write two facts. **Possible response: In the United States, there are three branches of government. The executive branch is headed by the President.**
2. Write one opinion. **Possible response: This three-branch system of government is the best system in the world.**

There are over 200 bones in the human body. The bones are joined together to make a skeleton. The bones help us stand and protect organs like the heart, lungs, and brain. Ben is convinced that his bones are unbreakable.

3. Write two facts. **Possible response: There are over 200 bones in the human body. The bones are joined together to make a skeleton.**
4. Write one opinion. **Ben is convinced that his bones are unbreakable.**

At Home: Have students read an article in the newspaper and identify one fact and one opinion.

Name__________ Date________ **Reteach 83**

Vocabulary

Complete each definition by writing the correct word on the line provided.

exist	image	inspire	loft	reference	sketch

1. A large room or open space on the upper floor of a building is a **loft**.
2. A picture of something in the mind is an **image**.
3. To make a quick drawing is to **sketch**.
4. Something used for information is a **reference**.
5. To stir the imagination is to **inspire**.
6. To live is to **exist**.

6

Reteach 84

Story Comprehension

Write the answers to these questions about "Pat Cummings: My Story." For help, you can look back at the story.

1. What was the first thing Pat Cummings drew that people could recognize? **ballerinas**
2. Where does Pat Cummings get her ideas? **She gets ideas from things she sees, from traveling, and from dreams.**
3. What does Pat Cummings like to draw? **faces and things from her imagination**
4. How does Pat Cummings go about drawing people? **She uses old or new photographs or uses friends and family as models.**
5. How did Tom Feelings inspire Cummings? **He taught her many things about illustrating children's books. He taught her illustrators have to help each other. Looking at his work inspires Cummings.**

At Home: Have students make a simple crossword puzzle using some of the vocabulary words.

Name__________ Date________ **Reteach 85**

Read a Flowchart

A **flowchart** is a chart or diagram that tells you how to do something step-by-step.

How to Hold a School Art Show

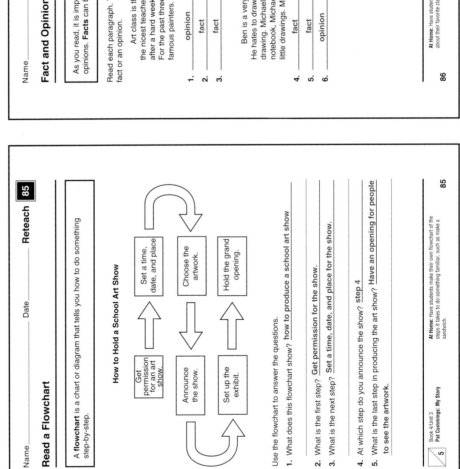

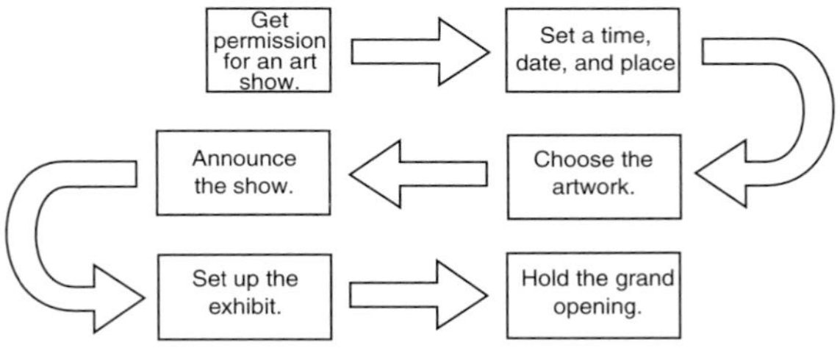
Get permission for an art show.
Set a time, date, and place
Choose the artwork.
Announce the show.
Set up the exhibit.
Hold the grand opening.

Use the flowchart to answer the questions.

1. What does this flowchart show? **how to produce a school art show**
2. What is the first step? **Get permission for the show.**
3. What is the next step? **Set a time, date, and place for the show.**
4. At which step do you announce the show? **step 4**
5. What is the last step in producing the art show? **Have an opening for people to see the artwork.**

At Home: Have students make their own flowchart of the steps it takes to do something familiar, such as make a sandwich.

Name__________ Date________ **Reteach 86**

Fact and Opinion

As you read, it is important to be able to tell what are facts and what are opinions. **Facts** can be proven. **Opinions** cannot.

Read each paragraph. Then write whether each numbered statement is a fact or an opinion.

Art class is the best time of day. Mrs. James, the art teacher, is the nicest teacher in the school. Art class is on Friday mornings, and after a hard week of studying, it is fun to create something beautiful. For the past three weeks we have been painting in the styles of famous painters. Now we will be working with clay.

1. **opinion** Mrs. James is the nicest teacher in the school.
2. **fact** Art class is on Friday mornings.
3. **fact** Students have been painting in different styles.

Ben is a very good artist, but he does not work hard in art class. He hates to draw still lifes, and even tore up his last art class drawing. Michael sat next to Ben at lunch. When Ben opened his notebook, Michael saw that it was covered with cartoons and funny little drawings. Michael thinks that Ben's cartoons are pretty good.

4. **fact** Ben tore up his drawing.
5. **fact** Ben's notebook is covered with cartoons.
6. **opinion** Michael thinks that Ben's cartoons are pretty good.

At Home: Have students state two facts and two opinions about their favorite class at school.

Pat Cummings: My Story • RETEACH

Name__________ Date__________ **Reteach 87**

Summarize

When you **summarize**, you should include the main idea and the most important details from what you read.

Read the selection. Circle the letter beside the best response to each question.

Anna Mary Moses was an artist who never went to art school. She spent most of her life as a wife and mother of ten children. When she was 78 years of age, "Grandma" Moses took up painting. She sold her first painting for $3.

During the following years she painted over 1,500 pictures. They were mainly scenes of country life. Anna Mary Moses continued painting until just before her death at the age of 101. Today, Grandma Moses is thought of as an important American artist. Her paintings are in many museums.

1. Which is the main idea?

(**a.**) Grandma Moses became an artist at the age of 78.

b. Grandma Moses died at the age of 101.

2. Which detail is more important?

a. Grandma Moses had ten children.

(**b.**) Grandma Moses never went to art school.

3. Which detail is more important?

a. Grandma Moses once sold a painting for $3.

(**b.**) Grandma Moses painted scenes of country life.

4. Which is the better way to summarize the paragraph?

(**a.**) Grandma Moses, an important American artist, began to paint late in life. She had no art training but painted over 1,500 pictures of rural scenes.

b. Grandma Moses was a mother and a painter. She painted rural scenes. She once sold a painting for $3.

At Home: Have students summarize their day at school, including the main idea and important details.

Name__________ Date__________ **Reteach 88**

Suffixes

A **suffix** is a word part that adds meaning to a word. The suffixes *-ful* and *-ous* add the meaning "full of" or "having."

Add the suffix *-ful* or *-ous* to each word.

1. danger	+	ous	=	**dangerous**
2. play	+	ful	=	**playful**
3. courage	+	ous	=	**courageous**
4. humor	+	ous	=	**humorous**
5. sorrow	+	ful	=	**sorrowful**
6. glamour	+	ous	=	**glamorous**

Now use one of the words above with *-ful* or *-ous* to complete each sentence.

7. The comic told **Possible answer: humorous** stories.

8. It is **Possible answer: dangerous** to play with matches.

9. Jena felt **Possible answer: sorrowful** when her friend moved.

10. Firefighters are **Possible answer: courageous** citizens.

11. Kittens and puppies are active and **Possible answer: playful**.

12. She looked **Possible answer: glamorous** in the gown.

At Home: Have students identify one more *-ful* and one more *-ous* suffixed word.

Pat Cummings: My Story • EXTEND

Name________________ Date________ **Extend 82**

Fact and Opinion

Some sentences are **facts**. That is, you can check to prove that they are true. Other sentences are **opinions**. They tell what a person feels or believes. You cannot prove that an opinion is true or false.

Read the four sentences below. Choose the sentence that is a fact. Explain your thinking.

1. Leonardo da Vinci is the greatest painter in history.
2. In addition to painting, Leonardo da Vinci drew plans for many inventions.
3. Leonardo da Vinci's most beautiful painting is *Mona Lisa.*
4. Some of Leonardo da Vinci's paintings have too many shadows.

Sentence 2 is a fact. You can check reference books and museums to find out if it is true.

Read the four sentences below. Choose the sentence that is an opinion. Explain your thinking.

5. Pottery is made by shaping and firing clay.
6. Pottery was first made in Egypt and the Near East.
7. The prettiest vases are made on a potter's wheel.
8. Applying glaze is one way to decorate a piece of pottery.

Sentence 7 is an opinion. Some people may believe this , but others may not. There is no way to prove that a potter's wheel makes the prettiest vases.

At Home: Tell students to identify statements made during family conversations as facts or opinions.

Name________________ Date________ **Extend 83**

Vocabulary

exist	image	inspire
loft	reference	sketch

1. Which three vocabulary words are you most likely to find in a story about drawing?
   image; sketch; inspire
2. List four other words you might expect to find in a story about drawing.
   Answers will vary. Possible answers: pencil; easel; figure; line; shadow

Extend 84

Story Comprehension

Pat Cummings' interest in drawing began when she was a little girl. It eventually became her career. Turn Pat's story into a television interview. Write a list of questions a reporter might ask her. Find sentences from the story that answer the questions. Share your questions with the class. Take turns being the reporter and giving the answers.

At Home: Have students write about their interests and what they'd like to do for work as an adult.

Name________________ Date________ **Extend 85**

Read a Flow Chart

The following lists the steps in a **flow chart** showing how to make a papier-mâché animal step-by-step. The steps are not in the correct order. Write the letter of each step in the appropriate box in the correct order.

A. Place the glue-soaked pieces of paper on the wire animal frame to create the body of the animal.
B. When the paper and glue have dried on the wire frame, paint your animal.
C. Then tear old newspaper into strips.
D. Continue adding glue-soaked paper until the animal shape is completed. Let it dry completely.
E. Moisten the paper strips a few at a time with wallpaper paste or glue.
F. Build a wire frame in the shape of an animal you'd like to create.

Flow Chart For Making a Papier Mâché Animal

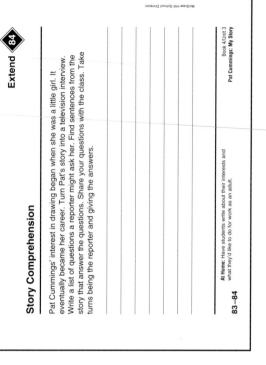

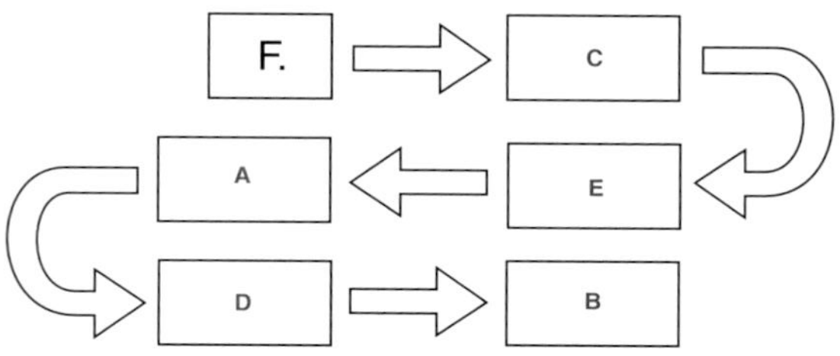

At Home: Have students work with older family members to select a task that the student would like to learn how to do. Together, they should make a flow chart to help the student learn how to do that task.

Name________________ Date________ **Extend 86**

Fact and Opinion

In "Pat Cummings: My Story," the author describes an event in her childhood and the work she does as an adult. She uses **facts** and **opinions**.

Write one or two paragraphs describing an event in your life or your favorite thing to do. Include at least two sentences that are facts and two sentences that are opinions. Underline each fact. Circle each opinion.

Answers will vary but should include two facts and two opinions.

At Home: Have students read a newspaper article. They should underline two facts and circle two opinions in the article.

Name______________________ Date____________ **Extend 87**

Summarize

When you tell or write a summary of a person's life, you include important information about that person. You should include details that you think are important and interesting to your audience.

On a book jacket or book cover, you can often find a summary of the author's life. Sometimes there is also a summary of the life of the illustrator or photographer. These summaries include information that would be of interest to the person buying the book or borrowing the book from the library.

Write a summary of Pat Cummings' life that could be used on a book jacket. Try not to use more than four sentences.

Answers will vary. Possible summary: Pat Cummings has enjoyed drawing ever since she was old enough to scribble. The first drawings she sold were of ballerinas. Now her favorite things to draw are faces and fantasy things. Pat Cummings lives and works in Brooklyn, New York.

At Home: Interview a family member about his or her life. Write a summary of that person's life.

Name______________________ Date____________ **Extend 88**

Suffixes

The **suffixes** *-ful* and *-ous* both mean "full of." Before you add *-ful* or *-ous* to some nouns, you must change the ending of the nouns. Change each base word as shown. The first one has been done for you. Then write sentences using the words you created. **Sentences will vary.**

1. Desire – e + ous = desirous
   In May I become desirous of summer vacation.
2. plenty – y + i + ful = **plentiful**
   Sample answer: In the fall we hope to celebrate a plentiful harvest.
3. disaster – e + ous = **disastrous**
   Sample answer: Because of the storm, the turnout for the play was disastrous.
4. color + ful = **colorful**
   Sample answer: Their uniforms were more colorful than ours.
5. space – e + i + ous = **spacious**
   Sample answer: Let's play in the gym where it's more spacious.
6. pity – y + i + ful = **pitiful**
   Sample answer: The wet puppy looked so small and pitiful.
7. danger + ous = **dangerous**
   Sample answer: Smoking is dangerous for your health.

At Home: List some other words that have the suffix *-ful* or *-ous*. Identify the words in which the base word's spelling was changed before the suffix was added.

Name________________ Date__________ LEARN Grammar 71

Past Tense

- A verb in the past tense tells about an action that already happened.
- Add *-ed* to most verbs to show past tense.
- If a verb ends with *e*, drop the *e* and add *-ed*.
- If a verb ends with a consonant and *y*, change *y* to *i* and add *-ed*.
- If a verb ends with one vowel and one consonant, double the consonant and add *-ed*.

Choose a verb for each sentence. Write the verb in the past tense.

1. When she was little, Pat Cummings **hopped** on a bus. (hop, help)
2. The bus **stopped** at a ballet school. (stop, walk)
3. Pat **danced** with the girls in the class. (dance, shout)
4. Pat's mother **worried** about her little girl. (hurry, worry)
5. She **looked** everywhere for Pat. (jump, look)
6. When she was a child, Pat **loved** to draw. (love, talk)
7. She **scribbled** all over a sheet of paper. (play, scribble)
8. Then she **colored** her scribbles many different colors. (color, carry)
9. Her mother **tried** to guess what the drawings were. (try, pick)
10. After she grew up, Pat **learned** about art jobs. (like, learn)

Extension: Have students write five sentences using the past tense of the verbs they didn't choose in the above sentences.

Name________________ Date__________ LEARN AND PRACTICE Grammar 72

Future Tense

- A verb in the future tense tells about an action that is going to happen.
- To write about the future, use the special verb *will.*

Underline the action verb in each sentence. Rewrite the sentence so it tells about the future.

1. Two friends go to art school.
   Two friends will go to art school.
2. They draw every day.
   They will draw every day.
3. The art students use watercolors.
   The art students will use watercolors.
4. The students paint pictures with oil paint.
   The students will paint pictures with oil paint.
5. Some artists illustrate books.
   Some artists will illustrate books.
6. Other artists create drawings on computers.
   Other artists will create drawings on computers.
7. Many artists teach art.
   Many artists will teach art.
8. Most artists notice things around them.
   Most artists will notice things around them.

Extension: Encourage students to think of a job they might do in the future. Ask students to write four sentences telling what they will do as part of their job.

Name________________ Date__________ PRACTICE AND REVIEW Grammar 73

Past and Future Tenses

- A verb in the past tense tells about an action that already happened.
- Add -ed to most verbs to show past tense.
- A verb in the future tense tells about an action that is going to happen.
- To write about the future, use the special verb *will.*

Read each sentence. Underline the verb that is in the incorrect tense. Write the correct tense.

1. In a few days, Pat Cummings visit our library. **will visit**
2. Yesterday Carla will walk to the library. **walked**
3. She borrow a book yesterday with illustrations by Pat Cummings. **borrowed**
4. Carla returned the book tomorrow. **will return**
5. Last year, Carla will mail a letter to Pat Cummings. **mailed**
6. Tomorrow she send a picture to Pat Cummings. **will send**
7. Carla already paint the picture. **painted**
8. Next month, another artist come to the library. **will come**

Extension: Invite groups of students to look for past-tense verbs in newspapers or magazines. Ask students to copy the sentences they find and then rewrite the sentences, using future-tense verbs.

Name________________ Date__________ MECHANICS Grammar 74

Letter Punctuation and Capitalization

- Begin the greeting and closing in a letter with a capital letter.
- Use a comma after the greeting and the closing in a letter.
- Use a comma between the names of a city and a state.
- Use a comma between the day and year in a date.

Read the letter carefully. Correct two capitalization mistakes. Also add six missing commas.

June 22 2000 **June 22, 2000**

108 Oak Avenue
Audubon IA 50025 **Audubon, IA**

Janell Washington
16 Longwood Drive
Chicago IL 60640 **Chicago, IL**

dear Janell **Dear Janell,**

In school, I read a story about an artist Named Pat Cummings. I enjoyed it very much. When she was young, she loved to draw pictures. Sometimes she traded pictures with kids in her class. **Bear Creek, Michigan**
I will go to camp next week in Bear Creek Michigan. I will send you a postcard from there. Then I will give you my camp address. I hope you will write to me.

your friend **Your friend,**
Sam

Extension: Ask students to write their own letters.

Name________________ Date__________ TEST Grammar 75

Past and Future Tenses

A. Rewrite each underlined verb, using the correct past-tense form.

1. When Pat Cummings was five years old, she disappear for an afternoon. **disappeared**

2. Her mother call the army police. **called**

3. The dance teacher pin a note on Pat. **pinned**

4. As a child, Pat Cummings like to draw ballerinas. **liked**

5. When she grew up, Pat Cummings study art. **studied**

B. Choose a verb from the box below to complete each sentence. Write the future-tense form of the verb.

fetch	get	look	remember	work

6. Sometimes Pat Cummings **will get** ideas when she is swimming.

7. Pat Cummings **will work** at night if she has an idea.

8. When she travels, she **will look** at people around her.

9. Pat's cat **will fetch** when Pat throws a toy.

10. Pat always **will remember** how Tom Feelings helped her.

Name________________ Date__________ MORE PRACTICE Grammar 76

Past and Future Tenses

- Add *-ed* to most verbs to show past tense.
- If a verb ends with *e*, drop the *e* and add *-ed*.
- If a verb ends with a consonant and *y*, change *y* to *i* and add *-ed*.
- If a verb ends with one vowel and one consonant, double the consonant and add *-ed*.
- To write about the future, use the special verb *will*.

Mechanics:

- Begin the greeting and closing in a letter with a capital letter.
- Use a comma after the greeting and the closing in a letter.
- Use a comma between the name of a city and a state.
- Use a comma between the day and year in a date.

Change each underlined verb to the correct past or future tense. Also add any missing commas and correct the capitalization mistakes.

February 5 2000 **February 5, 2000**

333 Coronado Court
Modesto CA 95350 **Modesto, CA**

Alberto Rivera
789 Prairie Street
Fort Wayne IN 46815 **Fort Wayne, IN**

hi Alberto **Hi Alberto,**
Yesterday, I try **tried** to draw a picture of my dog. At first, he move **moved** so much, I couldn't do it. Then I pet **petted** him a lot, and he sat still. When I grow up, I paint **will paint** beautiful paintings. Someday, I draw **will draw** pictures for children's books, too.
your cousin **Your cousin,**
Marco

Pat Cummings: My Story • SPELLING

Name________________ Date__________ PRETEST **Spelling** **71**

Words with /ù/ and /yù/

Pretest Directions

Fold back the paper along the dotted line. Use the blanks to write each word as it is read aloud. When you finish the test, unfold the paper. Use the list at the right to correct any spelling mistakes. Practice the words that you missed for the Posttest.

To Parents

Here are the results of your child's weekly spelling Pretest. You can help your child study for the Posttest by following these simple steps for each word on the list:

1. Read the word to your child.
2. Have your child write the word, saying each letter as it is written.
3. Say each letter of the word as your child checks the spelling.
4. If a mistake has been made, have your child read each letter of the correctly spelled word aloud, then repeat steps 1–3.

1. ________	1. curious
2. ________	2. pure
3. ________	3. fully
4. ________	4. sure
5. ________	5. wooden
6. ________	6. should
7. ________	7. furious
8. ________	8. cure
9. ________	9. handful
10. ________	10. crooked
11. ________	11. would
12. ________	12. bulldozer
13. ________	13. soot
14. ________	14. tour
15. ________	15. butcher
16. ________	16. woolen
17. ________	17. pudding
18. ________	18. goodness
19. ________	19. pulley
20. ________	20. overlook
Challenge Words	
________	exist
________	image
________	inspire
________	reference
________	sketch

Name________________ Date__________ AT HOME WORD STUDY **Spelling** **72**

Words with /ù/ and /yù/

Using the Word Study Steps

1. LOOK at the word.
2. SAY the word aloud.
3. STUDY the letters in the word.
4. WRITE the word.
5. CHECK the word.

   Did you spell the word right? If not, go back to step 1.

Spelling Tip

Words with a vowel sound as in the word *fully* are often spelled with *u*. (butcher, handful)

Words with a vowel sound as in the word *wooden* are often spelled with *oo*. (crooked, woolen)

Find and Circle

Where are the spelling words?

pfuriouszakbulldozervbdbntoherxxgoodness
uwfullyopckwoodenrlstovldrrsootuucurexxzz
rqvtoursuregspuremubutcherwwhandfulyyre
epulleyzacuriouseardlulrpuddinguucrooked
boverlookexdwouldbnewoolenuushouldaabb

To Parents or Helpers

Using the Word Study Steps above as your child comes across any new words will help him or her learn to spell words effectively. Review the steps as you both go over this week's spelling words.

Go over each Spelling Tip with your child. Ask your child to find other spelling words spelled with u and oo that sound like fully and wooden.

Help your child complete the spelling activity.

Name________________ Date__________ EXPLORE THE PATTERN **Spelling** **73**

Words with /ù/ and /yù/

curious	wooden	handful	soot	pudding
pure	should	crooked	tour	goodness
fully	furious	would	butcher	pulley
sure	cure	bulldozer	woolen	overlook

Pattern Power!

Write the spelling words with these spelling patterns.

Words with /yù/ spelled

u

1. curious
2. furious

u-e

3. pure
4. cure

Words with /ù/ spelled

u

5. fully
6. handful
7. bulldozer
8. butcher
9. pudding
10. pulley

Words with /ù/ spelled

u-e

11. sure

oo

12. wooden
13. crooked
14. soot
15. woolen
16. goodness
17. overlook

ou

18. should
19. would
20. tour

Name________________ Date__________ PRACTICE AND EXTEND **Spelling** **74**

Words with /ù/ and /yù/

curious	wooden	handful	soot	pudding
pure	should	crooked	tour	goodness
fully	furious	would	butcher	pulley
sure	cure	bulldozer	woolen	overlook

Definitions for You

Fill in the word from the spelling list that matches the definition.

1. made from the hair of sheep — woolen
2. interested in learning more — curious
3. to fail to notice — overlook
4. free of dirt or pollution — pure
5. made from trees — wooden
6. a word used to express duty — should
7. having bends or curves — crooked
8. the amount a hand can hold — handful
9. black particles left after wood or coal are burned — soot
10. completely or totally — fully
11. a word used to make a polite request — would
12. desirable qualities — goodness
13. a method that brings back health — cure
14. impossible to doubt — sure
15. to be very angry — furious
16. a creamy dessert — pudding

Challenge Extension: Pair up students. Have one partner use the dictionary to write short definitions for each Challenge Word. Then let the other partner use the definitions to make up one sentence for each

Name______________________ Date____________ PROOFREAD AND WRITE **Spelling 75**

Words with /u̇/ and /yu̇/

Proofreading Activity

There are six spelling mistakes in the paragraph. Circle the misspelled words. Write the words correctly on the lines below.

Last fall I went to the community crafts fair and saw lots of interesting things. One woman was making old-fashioned wudden toys from pieces of pine and maple. I bought a buledozer that really works for my little brother. A candlemaker was selling candles made from pur beeswax. A weaver was making beautiful wollen shawls and scarves. I bought a handfool of bright, shiny marbles. I got cyrious when I saw a crowd of people gathered in a circle. When I got closer I saw someone making blown glass animals. It was a fun day.

1. wooden
2. bulldozer
3. pure
4. woolen
5. handful
6. curious

Writing Activity

Using four spelling words, describe a crafts fair or other festival that you have attended.

____

____

____

____

Name______________________ Date____________ POSTTEST **Spelling 76**

Words with /u̇/ and /yu̇/

Look at the words in each set below. One word in each set is spelled correctly. Use a pencil to fill in the circle next to the correct word. Before you begin, look at the sample sets of words. Sample A has been done for you. Do Sample B by yourself. When you are sure you know what to do, you may go on with the rest of the page.

Sample A (A) poor (B) puer (C) por (D) puore

Sample B (E) coulde (F) could (G) kould (H) cuold

1. (A) overloke (B) ovirlook (C) overlook (D) ovarlouk
2. (E) puley (F) pullie (G) pouley (H) pulley
3. (A) gudness (B) goodness (C) goodnis (D) goudness
4. (E) pulding (F) pudden (G) pudding (H) pooding
5. (A) woolen (B) wulen (C) woolin (D) woulen
6. (E) bucher (F) butcher (G) bootcher (H) butsher
7. (A) tour (B) toor (C) ture (D) tuyre
8. (E) soot (F) sut (G) soote (H) soute
9. (A) booldoxer (B) bulldoxer (C) buldozar (D) bulldozer
10. (E) wuld (F) wolde (G) would (H) woold
11. (A) krooked (B) crooked (C) crookad (D) crucked
12. (E) handful (F) hanfull (G) handfool (H) hannful
13. (A) cyure (B) coure (C) cure (D) ciure
14. (E) fureus (F) furrius (G) furious (H) farious
15. (A) should (B) sould (C) shuuld (D) shold
16. (E) wooden (F) wuden (G) woodan (H) wouldin
17. (A) soore (B) sure (C) suyre (D) soure
18. (E) fulie (F) fully (G) fooly (H) fullyie
19. (A) puyre (B) poour (C) pure (D) puare
20. (E) cureus (F) kurious (G) karius (H) curious

Name__________ Date__________ **Practice 89**

Author's Purpose and Point of View

Authors often have a **point of view**, or way of thinking about something. Authors also have a **purpose**, or reason, for writing. An author's purpose for writing might be to persuade, to inform, to entertain, or a combination of the three.

Read the passages below. Then answer the questions.

Wanting to win the annual bicycle race, Narome had gotten up early and practiced for hours. But now that it was time for the race, he was feeling tired. How could he win? "Well, I will just do my best," Narome said. "That will have to be good enough." Narome didn't win, but he placed third and was quite proud of himself.

1. Is the author's purpose to persuade, inform, entertain, or a combination? **to persuade**
2. Author's point of view: **Winning is not everything.**

The early sun shone brightly on the field of flowers. Turning the field a brilliant shade of pink, the flowers swayed in the morning breeze. The field looked like a velvet cushion, waiting for someone to sink into its folds.

3. Is the author's purpose to persuade, inform, entertain, or a combination? **to entertain and inform**
4. Author's point of view: **The field is beautiful in the early morning.**

José looked at the salsa. How could it make vegetables taste so good? Dipping a corn chip into the salsa, José thought it must be the spices that made his mother's salsa so special. Whatever the secret was, José loved it!

5. Is the author's purpose to inform, persuade, entertain, or a combination? **to persuade**
6. Author's point of view: **Eating vegetables can be fun and tasty.**

 At Home: Have students write a story with a point of view.

Name__________ Date__________ **Practice 90**

Vocabulary

Replace the underlined words with one of the vocabulary words.

chanted	nipped	pouch	restless	scribbled	stitching

1. The small boy <u>drew quickly and carelessly</u> on the paper. **scribbled**
2. The mosquitoes <u>made tiny bites</u> at our arms. **nipped**
3. The class <u>recited</u> the same rhyme over and over again. **chanted**
4. Each boy had a <u>small bag</u> for carrying marbles or coins. **pouch**
5. The <u>threads</u> on the arms of her jacket were coming loose. **stitching**
6. The sisters were <u>tired of waiting</u> and couldn't sit still. **restless**

Write 2 sentences in which you use 2 of the vocabulary words in each sentence. **Answers will vary.**

7. __________
8. __________

 At Home: Have students write a story about summertime using the vocabulary words.

Backyard Poet

One summer morning, Anna Tong sat in her backyard, waiting for something to happen. Little flies *nipped* at her arms. Anna felt bored and *restless.* She pulled at the yellow *stitching* on her dress. In the background, Anna could hear her little sister as she *chanted* a rhyme and jumped rope.

"Miss Mary Mack, Mack, Mack, all dressed in black, black, black.
Had buttons, buttons, buttons, all down her back, back, back."

Anna remembered how much she had liked the rhyme. Then she had an idea. Quickly reaching into her small *pouch,* she pulled out a notebook and a pencil. Anna thought for a minute or two. Then she *scribbled* in her notebook. Smiling, she shared her new rhyme with her little sister.

"Little Sister Tong, Tong, Tong, sings the rhyming song, song, song. She is singing sweet, sweet, sweet, all morning long, long, long."

"It's sweet, sweet, sweet," *chanted* Anna's sister.

Answers will vary.

1. How can you tell that Anna is restless and uncomfortable? **Flies were nipping at her and she picked at her stitching.**
2. Where does Anna keep her notebook? **in her pouch**
3. How could you describe the way Anna wrote? **She scribbled.**
4. What was Anna's sister doing as she jumped rope? **She chanted.**
5. Why might writing rhymes make a morning fun? **It can help you feel smart and clever. It's fun to rhyme words.**

 At Home: Have students write a chanting rhyme.

Name__________ Date__________ **Practice 91**

Story Comprehension

Answer the questions about "Grass Sandals: The Travels of Basho." Look back at the story to help you answer the questions.

1. Basho was one of the great Japanese poets. When and where did he live before he went on his journey? **He lived 300 years ago in a small house near a river.**
2. Where did Basho usually sit, and what did he do during breakfast? **He sat in the doorway and looked at the mountains, river, and morning glories.**
3. On the first page of the story, there is a haiku poem about morning glories. When do you think Basho may have written it? **He may have written it right after he had breakfast.**
4. How did Basho prepare for his first walking trip across Japan? **He sewed his pants and stitched a string to his hat.**
5. Why did Basho's friends give him grass sandals? **He would need them for walking.**
6. What did Basho do when he found a tree that was 1,000 years old? **Basho wrote a poem to the ancient tree.**
7. On his journey, Basho met a group of friends in the mountains. What did they do for entertainment? **They looked at the moon and wrote poems.**
8. Basho looked at everything very carefully as he traveled. How do you think this helped him write poetry. **The more carefully he looked, the more he enjoyed the scene and the more he had to say in his poetry.**

 At Home: Have students write a haiku about something that they love to look at.

Grass Sandals: The Travels of Basho • PRACTICE

Name_______________ Date_________ **Practice 92**

Read a Map

Study the map below. It shows some of the countries in East and Southeast Asia. Use the map to answer the questions below.

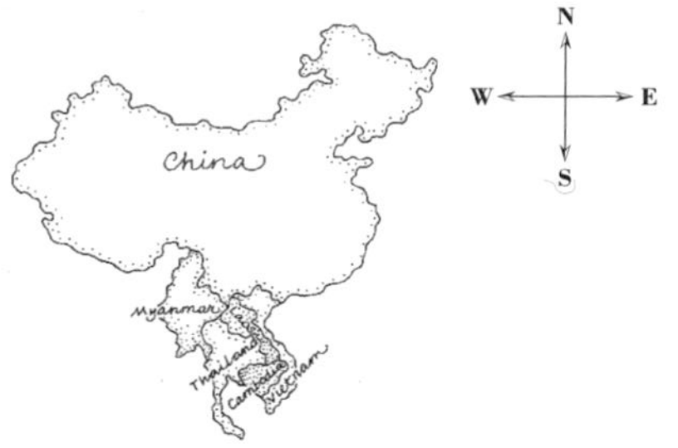

1. Six Asian country names are printed on the map. What are the names of the six countries? **China, Myanmar, Laos, Thailand, Cambodia, Vietnam.**
2. Is China north or south of Vietnam? **north**
3. Which country is west of Cambodia? **Thailand**
4. Which country borders Myanmar, Laos, and Vietnam? **China**
5. Plan a route to visit all the countries shown on the map by using planes, trains, boats, and walking. Tell where you will start, where you will go next, and how you will get there. **Answers will vary, but should be reasonable.**

At Home: Have students locate a favorite country on a map.

Name_______________ Date_________ **Practice 93**

Author's Purpose and Point of View

Authors often write with more than one **purpose**. They may want to tell an enjoyable story or to give readers ideas to think about. Sometimes, the main character shows the author's personal ideas and feelings. This is the author's **point of view**.

Read each statement below. Write **agree** or **disagree** to show how you think Dawnine Spivak, the author of "Grass Sandals," would feel about the idea. Then give an example from the story to support your answer. **Answers will vary.**

A. Looking out your door at the same scene every day could get boring.

1. Author's point of view: **disagree**
2. Example from the story: **Basho enjoyed sitting in the doorway of his small house looking at the river and mountains every day. However, Basho felt restless and decided to travel.**

B. The main purpose for walking across a country is to exercise and to be healthy.

3. Author's point of view: **disagree**
4. Example from the story: **Basho wanted to see new things and visit new places. He wanted new experiences.**

C. There are many beautiful and wonderful things to write about if we look at nature.

5. Author's point of view: **agree**
6. Example from the story: **When he saw a horse eating flowers or a circling hawk, Basho wrote a poem about it.**

At Home: Have students choose a purpose and write about what they see when they look out of their window at home.

Name_______________ Date_________ **Practice 94**

Make Judgments and Decisions

When we read a story we **make judgments** and form opinions about the characters **decisions**. Read each passage below. Answer the questions about the characters. **Answers will vary.**

Deborah was new to Smithtown Elementary. On her first day, Kenny and Hasan showed her things she needed to know, such as where to put her coat and where to find notebook paper. Kenny and Hasan knew how it felt to be new to a school since they had entered Smithtown last year. Jennifer, who sat next to Deborah in health class wanted to help her too, but she was feeling tired. Tomorrow she hoped to give Deborah any help she needed.

1. Why do you think Kenny and Hasan decided to help Deborah? **They know how hard it is to be new to a school.**
2. Why didn't Jennifer help Deborah? **She was feeling tired.**
3. How would you feel about being in school with these students? **They were kind and helpful and it would be nice to know them.**

"Are we there yet?" whined Benjie. That's all the fourth graders heard from Benjie as they hiked to the picnic grounds.
"Benjie," shouted Mario. "Stop it. You're acting like a baby."
"You can do it," said Connor. "Maybe your pack is too heavy. Take something out. I'll carry it for you."
"Thanks," Benjie said. "I'm starting to feel better. I think I'm getting my second wind."

4. Would you like to go on a hike with Benjie? Why or why not? **Students may say that Benjie's complaints would be hard to listen to.**
5. Of all those who spoke to Benjie, who was most helpful? Explain. **Students may say Connor because he offered a solution.**
6. How do you think Benjie will react if it begins to rain? How might the others react? **He may complain and the others may ignore him.**

At Home: Have students write a continuation of one of these stories based on the judgments they have made about the characters.

Name_______________ Date_________ **Practice 95**

Context Clues

You may find words you don't know when you are reading a story. Sometimes the other words in the sentence can help you figure out what the difficult word means. Those other words in the sentence are called **context clues.**

Use the context clues to help you choose a word to complete each sentence.

orchard	**adventurers**	**Basho**	**reflected**
haiku	**temple**	**cricket**	**morning glories**

1. A great Japanese poet's name was **Basho**, whose name means banana tree.
2. The tourists walked to the beautiful, old **temple** and went inside.
3. We went to the **orchard** to pick apples.
4. The **morning glories** in the garden were purple and became more beautiful as they grew.
5. The full moon was **reflected** in the water of the lake.
6. The hopping insect that makes sounds at night is the **cricket**.
7. A **haiku** poem is one with certain numbers of syllables in its three lines.
8. For centuries, many **adventurers** have explored Japan.

At Home: Have students define words in context as they read.

Name______________ Date________ **Reteach 89**

Author's Purpose and Point of View

An author writes with one or more **purposes**—to entertain, to teach or inform, or to persuade. An author also reveals his or her **point of view** on a subject by the way he or she writes about it.

Read each paragraph. Circle the letter beside the best answer to each question.

Three strangers met on the road. They were all going to the village. Under a tree they saw a pile of gold coins. Two strangers filled their pockets. The third stranger said it would not be right to take the gold. At the village, the strangers separated. The two with the gold had great misfortunes in days to come. The third man had nothing but days of golden happiness to reward his just behavior.

1. What is the author's purpose?
   a. to persuade
   (b.) to teach
2. Thinking about the point of view in the paragraph, what do you think the author would do if he or she found a wallet on the street?
   a. keep it and what was inside
   (b.) try to return it

Citizens should exercise their right to vote. It is more important to vote than it is to vote for a particular candidate. So, cast your vote as you see fit. I am going to vote for Robert Martin. He is the candidate who has supported fair and honest government.

3. What is the author's purpose?
   (a.) to persuade
   b. to entertain
4. What does the author believe?
   (a.) Citizens should vote.
   b. Government is not for everyone.

Name______________ Date________ **Reteach 90**

Vocabulary

Choose a word from the list to complete each sentence.

chanted	nipped	pouch	restless	scribbled	stitching

1. The child **scribbled** with a crayon.
2. The puppy **nipped** at the little girl's heels.
3. The choir **chanted** words as the music played.
4. The boy was **restless** and wanted to play outside.
5. My Mom is **stitching** the hole in my jeans.
6. The hiker carried supplies in a waterproof **pouch**.

6

Reteach 91

Story Comprehension

Write the answers to these questions about "Grass Sandals." You can refer to the story for help if you need to.

1. When and where did Basho live? **He lived in Japan 300 years ago.**
2. What did Basho promise his hat? **He promised his hat that he would show it cherry blossoms.**
3. Where did Basho begin his journey? **He began his journey on a boat on a river near his village.**
4. What did Basho write about? **He wrote poetry about what he saw and felt on his journey.**
5. Why is Basho known and loved in Japan? **His writing tells of the simple, yet beautiful, experiences one can enjoy in Japan.**

Name______________ Date________ **Reteach 92**

Read a Map

Read the map to answer the questions.

1. What are three large cities on California's Pacific Ocean? **Possible answers: San Diego, Los Angeles, San Francisco**
2. Which city on the map is farthest from the Pacific Ocean? **Sacramento**
3. Which city is closest to the Mojave Desert? **Los Angeles**
4. If you traveled from San Francisco to Los Angeles, in what direction would you be heading? **south**
5. Which cities would you expect to trade with countries across the Pacific Ocean? Why? **San Diego, Los Angeles, San Francisco. They are on or near the coast.**

Name______________ Date________ **Reteach 93**

Author's Purpose and Point of View

Authors often write to entertain or to persuade. These are their **purposes**. They often express **their point of view** about a subject through characters and story events.

Read each story. Then circle the letter beside the best response.

Julie and Andres enjoy hiking. They also enjoy biking along trails. In fact, it seems they take every opportunity to be outdoors. The mountain air and the woodsy smell of the forest make them feel happy and healthy. It makes them sad to see garbage left by people in natural areas. Together they have written letters to make stricter laws against littering.

1. Which would the author favor?
   a. indoor activities (b.) outdoor activities
2. How would he or she vote on stricter laws against littering?
   a. He or she would vote no. (b.) He or she would vote yes.

"Never!" shouted Sean. "I won't do it. Greasy fries, cold burgers, and little chicken parts are not real food. I prefer salads and fruit, and maybe some cheese. There are only empty calories in what they sell at this Snack Shack."

3. How does the author feel about fast food?
   a. The author probably likes it. (b.) He or she probably never eats it.
4. Which cause might the author support?
   (a.) Veggies in the schools b. National Corn Dog Day

Name________________ Date__________ **Reteach 94**

Make Judgments and Decisions

> Characters in a story often face difficult situations in which they must decide what to do. Readers often think about what they might do if they were in similar situations. This is called **making judgments and decisions**.

Read the story. Then answer the questions.

Jesse was excited about visiting his young cousin Sherry. Despite their age differences and the fact that Sherry was a girl, they had many things in common. Like Jesse, Sherry loved chess, reading, and action movies. So when Jesse saw one of his favorite videos on sale, he bought it as a gift for Sherry. His mom, whom he met at the Food Court, did not approve. "That is not a good gift for someone who already sits in front of the television too much," she said sternly.

Jesse's big sister came over and whispered in his ear, "What a nice thing to do. Sherry will love it."

1. Why did Jesse decide to get the video? **He knew Sherry liked action movies.**

2. Why do you think Jesse's mom is against the gift? **She thinks videos are another form of television, and Sherry already watches it too much. Sherry should spend her time better.**

3. If you were Jesse, what would you do—return the gift and choose something else or give it to Sherry anyway? Why? **Answers may vary but should show an awareness that the mother's advice is good.**

4. If Jesse asked you for advice, what would you tell him? **Possible answer: Give the gift to Sherry, but tell his mom he will choose better next time.**

At Home: Have students think about a decision they made during the day and explain why they decided what they did.

Name________________ Date__________ **Reteach 95**

Context Clues

> When you come across words you don't know, many times you can figure out their meaning from the **context**. The words in the sentence, or the sentences before and after the word, can give you clues as to what the word means.

Read the paragraph. Circle the letter beside the meaning of each of the numbered words. Then write the clues in the paragraph that helped you figure out the meaning.

America was settled by pioneers. These courageous, early settlers traveled west despite danger and obstacles such as waterfalls, rivers, and mountains. They had to transport their canoes around waterfalls, lifting boats over steep rocks. They had to ford wide rivers in wagons pulled by oxen and guide horses along steep mountain cliffs and dry, rocky ground.

1. pioneers

(**a.**) early explorers **b.** last to arrive

Clues: **courageous early settlers**

2. obstacles

a. easy passageways (**b.**) things in the way

Clues: **waterfalls, rivers, and mountains**

3. transport

(**a.**) carry from place to place **b.** hold in place

Clues: **lifting boats over steep rocks**

4. ford

a. to bypass (**b.**) to cross

Clues: **wide rivers in wagons pulled by oxen**

At Home: Have students use two words from the exercise in sentences.

Name__________ Date______ **Extend 89**

Author's Purpose and Point of View

Authors may have more than one **purpose** for writing a story. They may write to persuade the reader or to affect how the reader thinks about something. Some may write to describe something to the reader. Others write to inform, or present factual information, or to entertain the reader. An author's **point of view** is the way he or she feels about the subject matter.

Think about the author's purpose for writing each selection listed below. Write **P** if the purpose is to persuade, **D** if it is to describe, **I** if it is to inform, or **E** if it is to entertain. Remember, there may be more than one purpose.

1. directions for building a birdhouse I
2. report about the destruction of rain forests I
3. letter to a friend about a tour of Washington, D.C. D, E, I
4. adventure story E, I, D
5. letter to the editor of a newspaper P, E, I

Write a sample sentence for each of the following. Be sure to show a point of view. **Answers will vary.**

6. advertisement for a new restaurant __________
7. political speech __________
8. newspaper article about a baseball game __________

At Home: Have students look in a magazine to find an example of a selection written for each purpose: to persuade, to describe, to inform, and to entertain.

Name__________ Date______ **Extend 90**

Vocabulary

chanted	**nipped**	**pouch**
restless	**scribbled**	**stitching**

Write a poem that includes at least three of the vocabulary words in the box.

Answers will vary, but each poem should contain at least three of the vocabulary words.

Extend 91

Story Comprehension

An author may write a selection to persuade, to describe, to inform, or to entertain.

Why do you think Dawnine Spivak wrote "Grass Sandals"? Explain your thinking.

Answers will vary. Possible answer: to inform; the author tells the reader about a journey Basho took and how it inspired his writing

What do you think Basho's purpose was for writing haiku? Explain your thinking.

Answers will vary. Possible answer: to describe; Basho wrote each poem to give the reader a mental picture of something.

At Home: Have students recall something beautiful they have seen. Discuss how they could convey an image of that thing to someone else.

Name__________ Date______ **Extend 92**

Use a Map

The map in "Grass Sandals" shows the names and locations of the places Basho visited. It also has pictures of some things Basho saw on his journey.

Think about how you would show your neighborhood on a map. Which streets you would show? Besides your home, what other places would you include? Would you show only street and place names, or would you include some pictures? How would you use color in your map? What kind of map key would you use?

Make a map of your neighborhood. Share your map with classmates.

Answers will vary.

At Home: Look at a map of your state. Locate a place you would like to visit. Decide what route you would follow to get from your home to that place.

Name__________ Date______ **Extend 93**

Author's Purpose and Point of View

The Japanese poet Basho wrote haiku. A haiku is a three-line poem having exactly 17 syllables. The first and third lines each have five syllables. The second line has seven syllables. The lines of a haiku do not rhyme. Look back at the story for examples.

Choose a topic, write a haiku, and then illustrate it. Share your haiku with classmates. Have them determine whether the **purpose** of your haiku is to persuade, to describe, to inform, to entertain, or whether you have several purposes.

Answers will vary but should be in haiku format.

At Home: Read several poems. Decide whether the purpose of each is to persuade, to describe, to inform, or to entertain.

Grass Sandals: The Travels of Basho • EXTEND

Name____________________ Date__________ **Extend 94**

Make Judgments and Decisions

Think about "Grass Sandals." Read each of the given **judgments** or **decisions** that Basho may have made. Then fill in the blanks with the missing judgments or decisions. **Answers will vary, but should relate to facts of the story.**

1. **Judgment:** This banana tree is the most interesting plant near my house.
   Decision: **Possible answer: I'll change my name to Basho, which means banana tree.**
2. **Judgment:** **Possible answer: There must be more beautiful things to see in the world than my village.**
   Decision: I'm going to walk across Japan.
3. **Judgment:** I imagine the ocean will feel different than hot springs and streams.
   Decision: **Possible answer: I'll go for a swim in the ocean.**
4. **Judgment:** **Possible answer: The most beautiful thing in the night sky is a full moon.**
   Decision: We will have a party and watch the moon.
5. **Judgment:** The smell of rain is wonderful.
   Decision: **Possible answer: I'll stop and write a poem about the rain.**

At Home: Have students think about a time they felt the need to do something interesting or different. Discuss what they did, how effective it was, and what else they could do.

Name____________________ Date__________ **Extend 95**

Context Clues

Context clues can help you figure out the meaning of unfamiliar words. Context clues can be words or phrases in the same sentence or in nearby sentences. Read the context clues in the sentences. Then choose a word from the box to complete each sentence. Then use each word in a sentence of your own. **Sentences will vary but each word should be used correctly.**

clover	**ducked**	**crisscrossing**	**orchard**	**reflected**

1. Basho rode across a field of **clover**.
2. He tied his sandals on with strings that were **crisscrossing** his ankles.
3. Basho **ducked** his body low to enter the cave behind the water.
4. Basho walked through a group of fruit trees. It was a cherry **orchard**.
5. The mirror image of the moon was **reflected** in their cups.

At Home: Have students read a story and identify any unfamiliar words. Then, use words in the same or nearby sentences to figure out the meaning of the words.

Grass Sandals: The Travels of Basho • GRAMMAR

Name______________ Date________ LEARN **Grammar 77**

Main and Helping Verbs

- The **main verb** in a sentence shows what the subject does or is.
- A **helping verb** helps the main verb show an action or make a statement.
- *Have, has,* and *had* are helping verbs.

Draw one line under each form of *has* that is a helping verb. Draw two lines under each main verb that it helps.

1. Basho got his name after he had planted a banana tree.
2. Basho has decided upon a trip across Japan.
3. When he had prepared for his trip, Basho left home.
4. Before leaving, Basho had stitched a string on his hat to keep it from blowing away.
5. The cherry blossoms have waited for Basho.
6. The poet has scribbled some words on his hat.
7. An old woman has invited Basho to share her noodles.
8. Basho's friends have joined him for part of the trip.
9. They have presented Basho with presents for his trip.
10. Basho left his friends after they had crossed the river.

Extension: Ask students to write *has, have,* and *had* on separate index cards. Have them work in small groups, each choosing a card and constructing an oral sentence that uses the form chosen as a helping verb.

Name______________ Date________ LEARN AND PRACTICE **Grammar 78**

More Main and Helping Verbs

- *Is, are, am, was,* and *were* can be helping verbs.
- They are used with a main verb ending in *-ing*
- *Will* is a helping verb used to help show an action in the future.

Read each sentence. Study the helping verb. Circle the correct form of the main verb in parentheses.

1. Basho's friends were (wave, waving) as they left in the boat.
2. As he stands under a waterfall, Basho is (laugh, laughing).
3. Soon Basho's feet will (take, taking) him past an old temple.
4. The beautiful cherry trees are (bloom, blooming).
5. During his trip, Basho was (sleep, sleeping) in huts, houses, and stalls.
6. Most of the time, the poet ______ walking. (is, are).
7. Tomorrow Basho will (ride, riding) on a farmer's horse.
8. Along the way, people are (give, giving) Basho food.

Extension: Ask students to write three sentences that begin with "I am" and tell what they are doing right now.

Name______________ Date________ PRACTICE AND REVIEW **Grammar 79**

Using Main and Helping Verbs to Complete Sentences

- The **main verb** in a sentence shows what the subject does or is.
- A **helping verb** helps the main verb show an action or make a statement.
- *Have, has,* and *had* can be helping verbs.
- *Is, are, am, was, were* and *will* can be helping verbs.

Write a main verb or helping verb to complete each sentence. **Answers may vary**

1. Basho has __rolled__ rice and beans into balls.
2. Basho had __cooked__ rice and beans last night.
3. Now Basho __is__ meeting with some friends.
4. As they drink tea, the friends __are__ looking in their cups.
5. Last night, they were __writing__ poems together.
6. Tomorrow, Basho __will__ leave his friends.
7. They __have__ enjoyed their time together.
8. Basho saw many of the animals that __were__ living in the fields.
9. One night, Basho heard a frog that __was__ jumping into a pond.
10. By the end of his trip, Basho had __traveled__ to many places.

Extension: Have students read a few paragraphs in a favorite book. Ask them to write down five combinations of main and helping verbs they find in the book.

Name______________ Date________ MECHANICS **Grammar 80**

Contractions

- A **contraction** is a shortened form of two words.
- A contraction can be made by combining a verb with the word *not.*
- An apostrophe (') shows the letter *o* has been left out.

Read each sentence. Write the contraction for each set of underlined words.

1. Haiku poems are not rhyming poems. __aren't__
2. Perhaps you have not seen poems like them before. __haven't__
3. Basho is not the name that the poet was given at birth. __isn't__
4. Basho did not travel by car. __didn't__
5. Basho was not a Chinese poet. __wasn't__
6. His friends would not let him leave empty-handed. __wouldn't__
7. The poet did not forget his morning tea. __didn't__
8. Basho had not walked far when he saw a waterfall. __hadn't__
9. Basho's shoelaces were not white. __weren't__
10. Even though Basho lived long ago, his poems have not been forgotten. __haven't__

Extension: Arrange students in pairs. Give each student twelve index cards. Have one partner write the underlined words from this page on cards. Have the other write the contractions on cards. Invite partners to play a game in which they match the contractions with the longer forms.

Grass Sandals: The Travels of Basho • GRAMMAR

Name__________ Date______ TEST Grammar 81

Main and Helping Verbs

A. Read each sentence. Draw one line under the helping verb and two lines under the main verb.

1. After he had laced on a new pair of sandals, Basho took another walk.
2. Basho wrote a poem about flowers that were blooming.
3. Today people are visiting the places that Basho knew.
4. Long after Basho lived, people are reading his poems.
5. Throughout history, poets like Basho have helped us to appreciate nature.

B. Choose the correct helping verb to complete each sentence. Write it on the line.

6. I __am__ writing a haiku poem.
   a. am
   b. are
   c. will
7. Our teacher __will__ put our poems on a bulletin board tomorrow.
   a. have
   b. was
   c. will
8. We __have__ painted pictures to go with our poems.
   a. are
   b. have
   c. were

Name__________ Date______ MORE PRACTICE Grammar 82

Main and Helping Verbs

- The **main verb** in a sentence shows what the subject does or is.
- A **helping verb** helps the main verb show an action or make a statement.
- *Have, has,* and *had* can be helping verbs.
- *Is, are, am, was, were,* and *will* can be helping verbs.

Mechanics:

- A contraction is a shortened form of two words.
- A contraction can be made by combining a verb with the word *not.*
- An apostrophe (') shows the letter *o* has been left out.

Look at the picture. Proofread the paragraph. Correct mistakes in main verbs and helping verbs. Change the underlined words to contractions. Rewrite the paragraph on the lines.

In many poems, Basho was write about animals. In one of his poems, a crab are tickling his leg. In another poem, a horse have chewed a flower. Was not there a poem in this story about a frog? Basho is not alive today, but you can read his poems.

In many poems, Basho was writing about animals. In one of his poems, a crab is tickling his leg. In another poem, a horse has chewed a flower. Wasn't there a poem in this story about a frog? Basho isn't alive today, but you can read his poems.

Name________________ Date__________ PRETEST **Spelling 77**

Words with Digraphs

Fold back the paper along the dotted line. Use the blanks to write each word as it is read aloud. When you finish the test, unfold the paper. Use the list at the right to correct any spelling mistakes. Practice the words you missed for the Posttest.

To Parents
Here are the results of your child's weekly spelling Pretest. You can help your child study for the Posttest by following these simple steps for each word on the word list:

1. Read the word to your child.
2. Have your child write the word, saying each letter as it is written.
3. Say each letter of the word as your child checks the spelling.
4. If a mistake has been made, have your child read each letter of the correctly spelled word aloud, then repeat steps 1–3.

1. ________	1. changed
2. ________	2. watch
3. ________	3. fresh
4. ________	4. shoulder
5. ________	5. whatever
6. ________	6. south
7. ________	7. chimney
8. ________	8. scratch
9. ________	9. shove
10. ________	10. wheat
11. ________	11. cloth
12. ________	12. themselves
13. ________	13. crunch
14. ________	14. batch
15. ________	15. harsh
16. ________	16. whittle
17. ________	17. thoughtful
18. ________	18. birch
19. ________	19. switch
20. ________	20. theater
Challenge Words	
________	chanted
________	pouch
________	restless
________	scribbled
________	stitching

Name________________ Date__________ AT HOME WORD STUDY **Spelling 78**

Words with Digraphs

Using the Word Study Steps

1. LOOK at the word.
2. SAY the word aloud.
3. STUDY the letters in the word.
4. WRITE the word.
5. CHECK the word.

Did you spell the word right? If not, go back to step 1.

Spelling Tip
If the /ch/ immediately follows a short vowel in a one-syllable word, it is spelled *tch*: *watch, scratch*.
There are a few exceptions in English: *much, such, which,* and *rich*.

Word Scramble

1. hctarcs	scratch	11. hrcib	birch
2. veslesmeht	themselves	12. hcawt	watch
3. hruncc	crunch	13. hsrfe	fresh
4. htolc	cloth	14. lreduohs	shoulder
5. hhsra	harsh	15. eymnich	chimney
6. hctba	batch	16. voehs	shove
7. denaghc	changed	17. teltihw	whittle
8. veretahw	whatever	18. lutfhgouht	thoughtful
9. houts	south	19. thciws	switch
10. aethw	wheat	20. taehtre	theater

To Parents or Helpers
Using the Word Study Steps above as your child comes across any new words will help him or her learn to spell words effectively. Review the steps as you both go over this week's spelling words.
Go over each Spelling Tip with your child. Help your child find other spelling words spelled with *tch*.
Help your child complete the spelling activity.

Name________________ Date__________ EXPORE THE PATTERN **Spelling 79**

Words with Digraphs

changed	whatever	shove	crunch	thoughtful
watch	south	wheat	batch	birch
fresh	chimney	cloth	harsh	switch
shoulder	scratch	themselves	whittle	theater

Pattern Power
Write the words that have these spelling patterns.

ch
1. changed
2. chimney
3. crunch
4. birch

tch
5. watch
6. scratch
7. batch
8. switch

th
9. south
10. cloth
11. themselves
12. thoughtful
13. theater

sh
14. fresh
15. shoulder
16. shove
17. harsh

wh
18. whatever
19. wheat
20. whittle

Name________________ Date__________ PRACTICE AND EXTEND **Spelling 80**

Words with Digraphs

changed	whatever	shove	crunch	thoughtful
watch	south	wheat	batch	birch
fresh	chimney	cloth	harsh	switch
shoulder	scratch	themselves	whittle	theater

What's the Word?
Complete each sentence with a spelling word.

1. Would you like to watch the parade with me?
2. My aunt likes to whittle small figures from tree branches.
3. Young children like to do things by themselves.
4. During free time, we can do whatever we want.
5. He hurt his shoulder when he threw the ball too hard.
6. The birch tree has a pretty, white bark.
7. The smoke from the fireplace goes up the chimney.
8. We may have to shove the stuck door to open it.
9. The midwestern states grow a lot of wheat.
10. I'm going to the theater on Friday to see a play.

Just the Opposite
Write a word from the spelling list that has the opposite meaning from the word or phrase below.

11. stayed the same — changed
12. stale — fresh
13. north — south
14. mild — harsh
15. a single one — batch

Challenge Extension: Have students write a "fill-in-the-blank" sentence for each Challenge Word and then exchange papers with a partner to complete each other's sentences.

Name________________________ Date____________ PROOFREAD AND WRITE **Spelling 81**

Words with Digraphs

Proofreading Activity
There are 6 spelling mistakes in the paragraph. Circle the misspelled words. Write the words correctly on the lines below.

My uncle has always enjoyed working with wood. He says it gives him time to be quiet and thotfull. I like to wach him while he works. He likes to witle small birds and forest animals from pieces of wood that he finds on his hikes. His favorite wood to use is bersh. He uses sandpaper to make the wood smooth, so it won't skracth him. Then he carefully uses a knife to make the shape of the animal. The first time I saw a piece of wood shanjed into a real-looking rabbit, I was amazed.

1. thoughtful 3. whittle 5. scratch
2. watch 4. birch 6. changed

Writing Activity
Write a paragraph about something you like to make. Use four words from your spelling list.

____

____

____

____

Name________________________ Date____________ POSTTEST **Spelling 82**

Words with Digraphs

Look at the words in each set below. One word in each set is spelled correctly. Use a pencil to fill in the circle next to the correct word. Before you begin, look at the sample sets of words. Sample A has been done for you. Do Sample B by yourself. When you are sure you know what to do, you may go on with the rest of the page.

Sample A (A) matsh (B) macht ● (C) match (D) matsch

Sample B ● ship (F) sheip (G) shyip (H) shiip

1. (A) wehat (B) weet ● wheat (D) hweat
2. (E) kloth (F) clotsh ● cloth (H) cloath
3. (A) thamselvs (B) thimsilves (C) temmselves ● themselves
4. ● changed (F) shanged (G) cahnged (H) schanged
5. ● theater (B) theeter (C) tcheater (D) tsheater
6. (E) crounch ● crunch (G) krunch (H) cruntch
7. (A) barsh ● birch (C) birtch (D) bersh
8. (E) faresh (F) fretch (G) freetsh ● fresh
9. (A) whutevir (B) watevver (C) wahtever ● whatever
10. (E) chiminey ● chimney (G) shimmney (H) shemnie
11. (A) shuv (B) chove ● shove (D) schuve
12. (E) toutful (F) tehoughtful ● thoughtful (H) thougtfill
13. ● harsh (B) hartch (C) harrsh (D) harss
14. (E) skratch (F) scrith (G) scaracih ● scratch
15. (A) chulder ● shoulder (C) sahoulder (D) thoulder
16. (E) sawitch ● switch (G) swithc (H) siwatch
17. (A) wathc ● watch (C) wetch (D) wahtc
18. ● south (F) salth (G) souhh (H) sotch
19. ● whittle (B) wuhittle (C) hwittel (D) whotel
20. (E) batach (F) basth (G) bocht ● batch

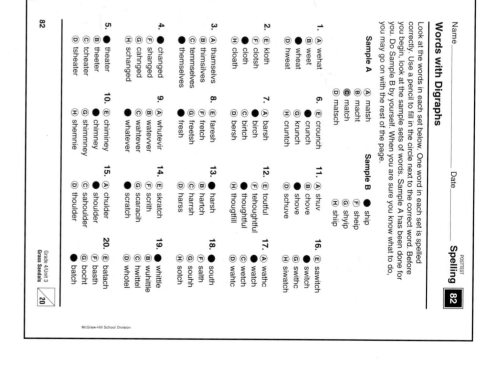

A Place Called Freedom • PRACTICE

Name_______________ Date_______ Practice 96

Fact and Opinion

A **fact** is a statement that can be proven. An **opinion** is a statement that tells what a person thinks about something. Read the passage below. Then write **fact** or **opinion** after each statement.

By the year 1830, enslaved Africans had been working for many years without pay and freedom. People had been brought from Africa and sold in marketplaces. Many people in the United States believed that slavery was terrible. Slavery was especially strong in the South where there were big farms called plantations. Plantation owners earned enormous profits because they did not have to pay the slaves who worked for them. Everyone enjoyed living on plantations.

In the North, many people were against slavery. These people believed everyone in the United States should be free. They formed the American Anti-Slavery Society to abolish, or do away with, slavery. People, like Frederick Douglass, spoke about the evils of slavery. Everyone thought Frederick Douglass was right. Free blacks in the North belonged to the Society. White people who were against slavery did the same. Anti-Slavery Society members held the belief that people should refuse to buy crops from slave holders. Despite the hard work of the American Anti-Slavery Society, slavery continued until the end of the Civil War.

1. Enslaved people were never paid for their hard work. __Fact__
2. Members of the American Anti-Slavery Society felt that all people should be free. __Fact__
3. Plantation owners earned enormous profits because they did not have to pay workers. __Fact__
4. Everyone thought Frederick Douglass was right. __Opinion__
5. Slavery ended when the Civil War was over. __Fact__

At Home: Have students write two facts about slavery.

Name_______________ Date_______ Practice 97

Vocabulary

Complete the sentences with the correct vocabulary word.

sunrise	gourd	weary	fretted	plantation	settlement

1. Reiko worried and __fretted__ because she had left her backpack with all of her books at the library.
2. In early times, people sometimes scraped the fruit out of a __gourd__ to make drinking cups or other containers.
3. The vacationers were so __weary__ from hiking up the mountain that they fell asleep right away when they arrived back at the camp.
4. A __plantation__ is a large farm where crops such as cotton and tobacco are grown for sale.
5. Before __sunrise__ the farmer gets out of bed and starts to work on the first of many chores.
6. A new colony, or place away from the country that governs it, is called a __settlement__.

At Home: Have students write a sentence using each vocabulary word.

Travelers

The Graham family left the Georgia *plantation* house on horseback at *sunrise.* They rode for a long time past fields of cotton. The family was heading for their new home in a New Jersey *settlement.* Many families were already at the settlement. Both white and black people had come there to live together and start a new way of life. The Graham family rode until late at night. They slept near a river. The next morning they filled drinking *gourds* with water from the river and then they rode off. By the fifth day, they *fretted* that they were lost. Then all of a sudden, the Grahams were there. Friends and relatives ran out to meet them. The Grahams were *weary* but happy to have arrived.

1. What kind of home did the Grahams come from? __a plantation__
2. Where were the Grahams going? __to a settlement in New Jersey__
3. How is a settlement different from a plantation? __A settlement is a town or village. A plantation is a large farm.__
4. Why were the Grahams so weary? __They had traveled by horse, starting at sunrise for many days.__
5. Why do you think the Graham family wanted to start a new life? __Possible answers: They wanted to live in a community with all kinds of people; They wanted to live in a place where all people are free.__

At Home: Have students write a story about traveling using the vocabulary words and describing one event the travelers fretted over.

Name_______________ Date_______ Practice 98

Story Comprehension

Answer the questions about "A Place Called Freedom." You may need to refer to the story to answer the questions.

1. In what state was the plantation where Mama and Papa worked? __Tennessee__
2. Why was the family able to leave the plantation? __The master of the big house set the family free.__
3. How did the family travel and when? __They went on foot and moved only in the dark at night.__
4. What did Papa call the pattern of stars that makes up the Little Dipper? __the drinking gourd__
5. Who helped the Starman family when they got to Indiana and why? __A Quaker family helped them because they believed slavery was wrong.__
6. How did the Starmans make a living? __They raised crops, built houses and barns, and taught school.__
7. How did Mr. Starman help those left behind at the plantation? __He returned to Tennessee to bring relatives to Indiana.__
8. Why are all the Starmans heroes? __They put up with danger and hardship to make a better life for themselves and then helped others to make a better life.__

At Home: Have students think of another hero and write down three reasons why that person is a hero to them.

Name______________________ Date____________ **Practice 99**

Read a Line Graph

A **line graph** can give you information at a glance. Look at each section of the graph to see how you should read it. Ask yourself what the numbers and lines mean. Then answer the questions below the line graph.

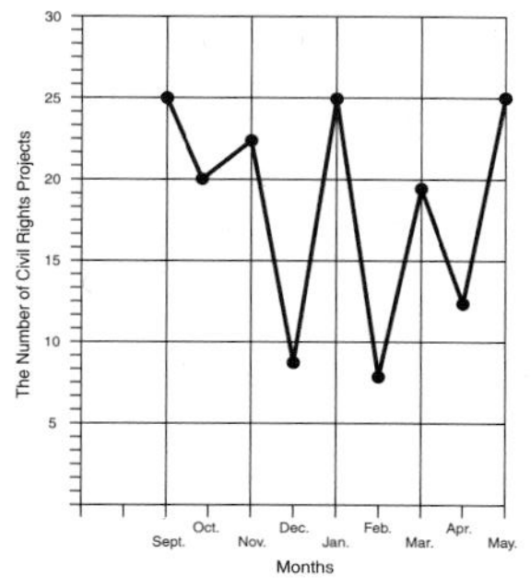

To learn about Civil Rights, fourth graders decided to do Civil Rights projects every month. This included reading books on civil rights leaders and events and also writing and drawing posters, stories, and poetry.

1. How many Civil Rights projects were completed in September? **25**
2. How many Civil Rights projects were completed in December? **8**
3. In what months were 20 or more projects completed? **September, October, November, January, May**
4. In what month were the fewest projects completed? **February**
5. How many more projects were completed in January compared to December? **Students completed 17 more projects in January than December.**

At Home: Have students sketch a line graph showing something their class does often.

Name______________________ Date____________ **Practice 100**

Fact and Opinion

Read each of the following statements that describe what happened in "A Place Called Freedom." Write **Fact** or **Opinion** to describe each statement. Look back at the story to help you.

1. At the beginning of the story, James Starman's parents were enslaved. **Fact**
2. All people in Indiana believed that slavery was bad. **Opinion**
3. All Quakers thought that all people should be free to work and live where they wanted. **Opinion**
4. A Quaker family helped the Starmans start their new life. **Fact**
5. After one year, Papa earned enough money to buy his own land. **Fact**
6. I believe reading is an important skill. **Opinion**
7. Relatives from the old Tennessee plantation stayed with the Starmans until they had money to buy their own land and build their own cabins. **Fact**
8. I think Papa was very brave to rescue his family. **Opinion**
9. Many of the people freed from slavery became carpenters and blacksmiths. **Fact**
10. The people in the settlement wanted to name their town Starman, but Papa wanted to call it Freedom. **Fact**

At Home: Have students write three opinions about slavery.

Name______________________ Date____________ **Practice 101**

Summarize

Suppose you are James Starman from the story "A Place Called Freedom." Complete the letter to your cousin who is still enslaved on the Tennessee plantation. Describe James' experiences, thoughts, and feelings. Look back at the story to help you **summarize** it.
Answers will vary but should accurately tell what happened in the story.

Dear Cousin:
It was hard saying goodbye to you. I was worried that I would never see you again. Now I know Papa is on his way to get you. You will be here soon. I want to tell you how it will be. Then you will not be afraid or feel strange.
It was dark when we left the plantation that night. I was worried about finding our way.______________________

We were ready to cross over to Indiana, but the Ohio River was in the way.______________________

A kind Quaker family took us into their house because ______________________

My Mama and Papa worked hard to ______________________

Folks wanted to name our town Starman because ______________________

Love,
Your cousin James

At Home: Have students write a note to James Starman summarizing what they think of his trip.

Name______________________ Date____________ **Practice 102**

Context Clues

When you read, you may find words you don't know. The other words in the sentence often are **context clues** and can help you figure out the meaning of the word.

melon	**enslaved**	**runaways**	**launched**	**blacksmith**
carpenter	**barrels**	**tongue**	**unpack**	**stable**

Complete each sentence with a word from the list.

1. When people are captured and have their freedom taken away, we say they are **enslaved**.
2. Enslaved people who escaped were called **runaways**.
3. If you open your mouth and look in the mirror, you can see your **tongue**.
4. The scientists built the rocket, then they **launched** it.
5. The horses and the cows are fed in the **stable**.
6. A **blacksmith** uses hot fire to melt and twist iron into horse shoes.
7. Long ago people stored water and food in big wooden **barrels**.
8. After we returned from our vacation, the first thing my sister and I did was **unpack**.
9. One kind of fruit that grows on a vine is a **melon**.
10. The wooden table and chairs were built by a **carpenter**.

At Home: Have students circle the context clues in the sentences above.

A Place Called Freedom • RETEACH

Name________________ Date__________ **Reteach 96**

Fact and Opinion

A **fact** is a statement that can be proven in some way. An **opinion** is a statement of someone's belief that cannot always be proven.

Read each paragraph. Write **F** if the statement is a fact. Write **O** if it is an opinion.

From the first days of their settlement, Europeans came to what is now the United States and moved inland from the coasts. I think moving is bad for children. My family has moved three times and I am only nine years old. But pioneer families used to move often. They would clear the land, stay a while, and then move on again when the area became crowded or the soil grew poor. I think the children in those families did not like moving. I hope we stay here for a long time.

1. I think moving is bad for kids. ___O___
2. People came to what is now the United States and moved inland from the coasts. ___F___
3. I hope we stay here for a long time. ___O___
4. My family has moved three times. ___F___
5. I think the children in those families did not like moving. ___O___

I like riding on trains. I really like the clickety-clack sound the train makes on the rails. My mom rides the train to work. She takes the same train every morning. I go to work with her sometimes. I love getting on the train early in the morning.

6. I like riding on trains. ___O___
7. The train makes a clickety-clack sound on the rails. ___F___
8. My mom rides the train to work. ___F___

At Home: Have students find three facts and three opinions in a magazine article.

Name________________ Date__________ **Reteach 97**

Vocabulary

Write a word from the list to complete each sentence.

fretted	gourd	plantation	settlement	sunrise	weary

1. A large farm or estate that grows a single crop was called a ___plantation___.
2. If you stayed up all night and saw the sky grow light, you would see the ___sunrise___.
3. Another word for *worried* is ___fretted___.
4. A dried fruit shell sometimes used for drinking is a ___gourd___.
5. Another word for *tired* is ___weary___.
6. A small village or group of houses is called a ___settlement___.

6

Reteach 98

Story Comprehension

Write a ✔ next to every sentence that tells about "A Place Called Freedom." For help you may look back at the story.

1. ___✔___ The author and his family left Tennessee for Indiana.
2. ______ Starman had been the plantation owner's name.
3. ___✔___ The Starman family bought land near the Wabash River.
4. ______ Papa was not able to bring any relatives to Indiana.
5. ___✔___ Other people who had escaped from slavery came to the settlement to live.
6. ______ Papa and Mama wanted to name the village Starman.
7. ___✔___ The new town was named Freedom.
8. ___✔___ The narrator became a farmer like his father and a teacher like his mother.

At Home: Have students write a paragraph retelling the events in "A Place Called Freedom" in their own words.

Name________________ Date__________ **Reteach 99**

Read a Line Graph

Graphs of all kinds give information in a shorthand way. A **line graph** shows how a piece of information changes with time. It would take many words to describe the same changes you might "read" about in a graph.

Population of Libertyville

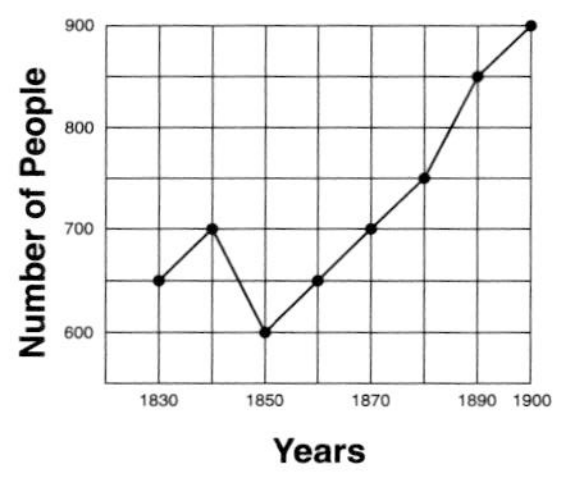

Use the line graph to answer the questions.

1. What was the population of Libertyville in 1850? ___600___
2. Compare the population of the year 1830 to 1860. Was the population in 1860 higher, lower, or the same as in 1830? ___the same___
3. Which year had the lowest population? ___1850___
4. Which years had the greatest population growth? ___1880–1900___
5. Which years had the greatest loss in population? ___1840–1850___

At Home: Have students make a line graph to record personal information, such as how much they save or spend month by month for a year or half year.

Name________________ Date__________ **Reteach 100**

Fact and Opinion

Knowing that a **fact** is a statement that can be proven to be true and that an **opinion** is someone's personal belief can help you understand what you read.

Read the paragraph. Write **F** if the statement is a fact. Write **O** if the statement is an opinion.

The big dipper is my favorite group of stars. If you follow the tip of the dipper, you can find the North Star. Enslaved African Americans escaping to freedom used the North Star to guide their way north. On a scout camping trip, we did a nighttime exercise finding stars in the sky. We all found the North Star easily in the beautiful sky.

1. ___F___ The big dipper is a group of stars.
2. ___F___ You can follow the tip of the dipper to find the North Star.
3. ___F___ Enslaved African Americans escaping to freedom used the North Star to guide their way north.
4. ___O___ The night sky is beautiful.

Now you try. Write two facts and then write two opinions about pies.

5. Fact: **Possible response: Most pies are desserts.**
6. Fact: **Possible response: Many pies are made with fruit in them.**
7. Opinion: **Possible response: Apple Pie is the best.**
8. Opinion: **Possible response: Pie should be served warm.**

At Home: Have students express their opinions about news events.

Name________________ Date________ Reteach 101

Summarize

If you can **summarize** a story well, you can be sure that you have understood the most important parts of the story.

Read the paragraph and then answer the questions.

Mr. LeTour's house was flooded when the creek spilled over its banks. He needed help cleaning his collection of old baseball cards. My Dad says it is very valuable. Mr. LeTour had wrapped each card in a clear plastic envelope. The envelopes had kept the cards dry during the flood, but now the envelopes were covered with mud. He hired Carrie McCourt and me to clean them. All weekend long, we worked with rags dipped in a special cleaner. Mr. LeTour was a lot happier on Sunday when he saw his sparkling clean envelopes.

1. What is the main idea of the story? **Possible answer: Mr. LeTour's valuable baseball card collection was saved after a flood but their envelopes needed to be cleaned.**
2. Who are the characters in the story? **Possible answer: Mr. LeTour, the speaker, his dad, and Carrie McCourt**
3. What is the story problem and its solution? **Mr. LeTour needed help cleaning the plastic envelopes protecting his baseball cards in order to save the cards from more damage. He hired the speaker and Carrie to do the cleaning.**
4. Use your answers above to summarize the story. **Possible answer: Mr. LeTour's house was flooded. He asked the speaker and a friend to help save his valuable card collection by cleaning the envelopes of the mud left by a flood.**

At Home: Have students summarize a familiar story.

Name________________ Date________ Reteach 102

Context Clues

Use **context clues,** or other words and sentences in the text, to help you figure out an unfamiliar word.

Read the paragraph. Then circle the letter beside the meaning of each of the words listed below. Next tell which clues in the paragraph helped you figure out the meanings.

My grandfather loved to recount our family stories. He told again and again about his great-grandmother and other ancestors who escaped from slavery. I liked the part about how they had to improvise when the slave catchers came upon them suddenly. That's where we get the ability to solve things quickly, my grandfather told me. Grandpa always said that enslaved people who were fugitives from the law and made it to freedom had to be smart.

1. recount
   (a.) repeat　　**b.** keep secret
   Clues: **told again and again**
2. ancestors
   (a.) family member who lived before you　　**b.** family friends
   Clues: **great-grandmother and other**
3. improvise
   a. practice ahead of time　　(b.) do something without planning
   Clues: **ability to make things up quickly; had to be smart**
4. fugitives
   (a.) runaways　　**b.** officers
   Clues: **enslaved people; from the law; made it to freedom**

At Home: Have students find a word they don't know in a story and give its meaning from context clues.

Name________________ Date________ **Extend 96**

Fact and Opinion

Have you ever tried to persuade someone to change his or her mind about something? If so, you probably began by stating your **opinion**. You may then have offered **facts** to support your opinion. Facts can be checked to prove that they are true.

Write a persuasive paragraph about your school. Start by stating your opinion. Your opinion may be about something you like about your school or something you think should be changed. Then support your opinion. Be sure to include facts. Share your paragraph with classmates.

Answers will vary but should be used in the correct context and use correct parts of speech.

At Home: Talk with students about effective ways to be persuasive about matters that concern them.

Name________________ Date________ **Extend 97**

Vocabulary

fretted	gourd	plantation	settlement	sunrise	weary

Suppose you and your family lived during the 1800s. You have just moved from a town to an area where no one else has settled. Write a letter to your best friend in the town, using as many of the vocabulary words as you can.

Answers will vary.

Extend 98

Story Comprehension

Put yourself in Joshua Starman's place. You have settled your wife and children in Indiana and returned to Tennessee to bring more family members to Indiana. Think about what you would tell your family in Tennessee about the journey or about life in Indiana.

Answers will vary. Possible answer: There's nothing like the feeling of being able to work your own land.

At Home: Make a list of facts and opinions about your town.

Name________________ Date________ **Extend 99**

Read a Line Graph

A **line graph** shows change over a period of time. The line graph below shows the number of states in the United States from 1780 to 2000.

STATES IN THE UNITED STATES, 1870 – 2000

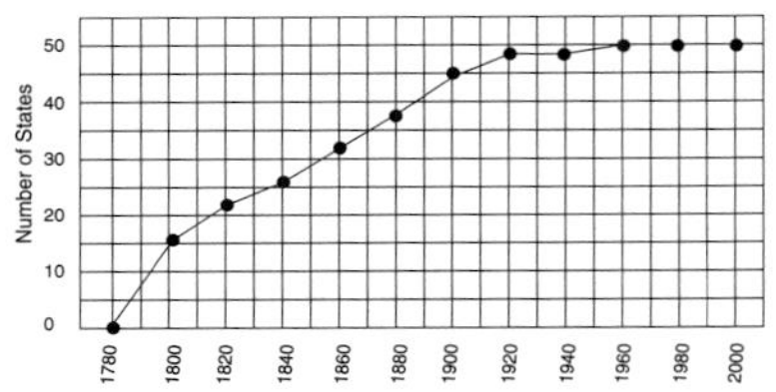

Use the line graph to answer these questions.

1. How many states were in the United States in 1900? **45**
2. During which 20-year period were the most states added to the United States? **1780–1800**
3. How did the number of states in the United States change from 1960 to 1980? How do you know? **The number stayed the same; the line does not go up or down from the point for 1960 to the point for 1980.**

Write two questions that can be answered using the line graph. Exchange questions with a classmate and answer the questions.

Question 1 **Answers will vary, but should make appropriate use of the graph.**

Question 2 ________________

At Home: Make a line graph of high temperatures. Use an outdoor thermometer or the weather report in the newspaper.

Name________________ Date________ **Extend 100**

Fact and Opinion

When news reporters interview people, they ask two kinds of questions. One kind of question can be answered by giving **facts**. Another kind of question can be answered by giving **opinions**.

Work with a partner to conduct an interview of a character in "A Place Called Freedom." Choose a character. Have one person take the role of a news reporter and the other person take the role of the character. Together, write two fact questions and two opinion questions. Plan how the character will answer the questions. Then present your interview to the class.

Character **Answers will vary.**

Fact Question 1 ________________

Answer ________________

Fact Question 2 ________________

Answer ________________

Opinion Question 1 ________________

Answer ________________

Opinion Question 2 ________________

Answer ________________

At Home: Interview a family member or a neighbor to find out how they came to live in the town in which you now live.

Name_______________ Date_______ Extend 101

Summarize

When you **summarize** a story, you retell the story in a few words. Newspapers use headlines to catch the reader's attention and to summarize the content of articles in a few words.

Suppose you are a reporter writing a series of newspaper articles about the Starman family's travels and the settlement of Freedom. Write headlines you could use for articles about the events from "A Place Called Freedom" described below.

1. James and his family pack up for their journey. James' father says they will find their way to Indiana by "following the drinking gourd."
   Possible answer: Family Follows Stars to Indiana
2. The family was helped across the Ohio River by a fisherman they didn't know. Strangers eventually helped them settle on a farm.
   Possible answer: The Kindness of Strangers
3. The family settled into a cabin before winter. The children attended classes taught by their mother, and enjoyed the food and clothing made by her.
   Preparing for Winter
4. During the winter Mr. Starman made several nighttime trips back to Tennessee to pick up relatives and lead their way north.
   Possible answer: Many Join the Starmans
5. Soon there were many people living in the area with many different trades. Then a railroad was built to pass through their settlement.
   Possible answer: Settlement Becomes a Town
6. James learns from both his mother and father and tries to decide who he wants to be like when he grows up. Eventually he realizes he can be like them both.
   Possible answer: Growing Up in Freedom

At Home: Read the headlines of several newspaper articles. Think about what information the articles may contain. Then read the articles to check your thinking.

Name_______________ Date_______ Extend 102

Context Clues

Context clues are words in a sentence or in nearby sentences that you use to figure out the meaning of unfamiliar words. Use context clues to fill in the blank in each sentence with one of these words from "A Place Called Freedom."

celebrated	**glittery**	**gulp**	**loaned**
runaways	**sturdy**	**wriggly**	

1. Look at how **glittery** the diamonds are when light shines on them.
2. My friend **loaned** me a pencil until I had a chance to go to the bookstore to buy my own.
3. We **celebrated** my birthday by having a slumber party.
4. It was hard to hold the worm still enough to get it on the fishhook because it was **wriggly**.
5. Those children are **runaways** because they did not have permission to be away from home.
6. I swallowed the rest of my sandwich in one big **gulp**.
7. Our **sturdy** house remained standing even though a tornado passed through our town.
8. Write a sentence using at least two of the unfamiliar words.
   Answers will vary.

At Home: Have students write their own "fill in the blank" sentences. Have family members use context clues to guess the correct word to fill in the blank.

A Place Called Freedom • GRAMMAR

Name__________ Date______ LEARN **Grammar** 83

Linking Verbs

- A **linking verb** does not show action. It connects the subject to the rest of the sentence.
- *Is, are, am, was,* and *were* are often used as linking verbs.

Read each sentence. Study the linking verbs in parentheses. Write the form of the linking verb that correctly completes each sentence.

1. The Big Dipper **is** a group of stars. (is, are)
2. The children's names **were** James and Lettie. (was, were)
3. Papa's new name **was** Starman. (was, were)
4. Indiana **is** the state where the family made their home. (is, are)
5. Barns and beds **are** things that Papa can build. (is, are)
6. James thought Mama's cooking **was** just wonderful. (was, were)
7. Mama and the children **were** worried when Papa was away. (was, were)
8. The children certainly **are** happy when Papa returns. (is, are)
9. Papa's relatives **were** eager to leave the plantation. (was, were)
10. You **are** older than James and Lettie. (am, are)

Extension: Ask students to write a paragraph describing the town of Freedom. Urge them to use linking verbs in their description. Invite students to share their descriptions.

Name__________ Date______ LEARN AND PRACTICE **Grammar** 84

Linking Verbs

- Some linking verbs link the subject to a noun in the predicate.
- Some linking verbs link the subject to an adjective in the predicate.

Read each sentence. Circle the linking verb that links the subject to a noun or adjective in the predicate. Underline the noun or adjective.

1. Lettie (was) wriggly as a child.
2. Lettie's older brother, James, (was) tall.
3. Some people leaving Tennessee (were) runaways from plantations.
4. The travelers (were) weary from their long walk.
5. The face of the old fisherman (is) wrinkled.
6. How many of the new settlers (are) farmers?
7. Mama (was) the teacher in the village school.
8. A few people in the village (were) carpenters.
9. The vegetables that the boy raises (are) beans.
10. The name of the village (is) Freedom.

Extension: Have students identify whether each linking verb that they underlined in these sentences is in the present tense or the past tense.

Name__________ Date______ PRACTICE AND REVIEW **Grammar** 85

Writing Linking Verbs to Complete Sentences

- A linking verb does not show action. It connects the subject to the rest of the sentence.
- *Is, are, am, was,* and *were* are often used as linking verbs.
- Some linking verbs link the subject to a noun in the predicate.
- Some linking verbs link the subject to an adjective in the predicate.

Complete each sentence by writing the correct linking verb on the line. Then underline the complete subject of the sentence.

1. Scott Russell Sanders **is** an author.
2. Writing, nature, and towns **are** the author's favorite things.
3. Mr. Sanders **is** a college teacher these days as well as an author.
4. His birthplace **is** a big city in Tennessee.
5. His favorite subjects for writing **are** people who get along.
6. Thomas B. Allen **was** nine years old when he went to an art class.
7. Streetcars **were** his way of getting to class back then.
8. The other people in the class **were** adults.
9. As an adult, Allen **is** eager to look for ideas in libraries.
10. The countryside **is** another good place for finding ideas.

Extension: Arrange students in small groups. Have students write *is, are, am, was,* and were on index cards and turn the cards facedown. Then invite students to take turns picking a card and using the linking verb in an oral sentence.

Name__________ Date______ MECHANICS **Grammar** 86

Titles

- Capitalize the first and last words and all important words in the titles of books and newspapers.
- Underline titles of books, newspapers, magazines, and TV series.
- Put quotation marks around the titles of short stories, articles, songs, poems, and book chapters.

Rewrite each sentence making sure the titles are written correctly.

1. A newspaper in Freedom might be called the freedom times.
   A newspaper in Freedom might be called The Freedom Times.
2. James could have written a book called my life in freedom, indiana.
   James could have written a book called My Life in Freedom, Indiana.
3. The song amazing grace is about slavery.
   The song "Amazing Grace" is about slavery.
4. Have you seen the TV series the end of slavery?
   Have you seen the TV series The End of Slavery?
5. Did you read the magazine article the freedom train?
   Did you read the magazine article "The Freedom Train"?
6. walking to freedom is a poem that my friend Dara wrote.
   "Walking to Freedom" is a poem that my friend Dara wrote.

Extension: Have students work in pairs. One student writes four titles without capital letters, underlining, or quotation marks. The other student writes the titles correctly. Then students reverse roles and repeat the activity.

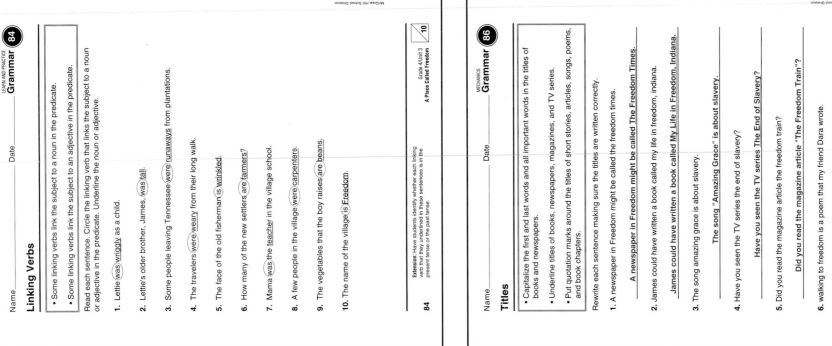

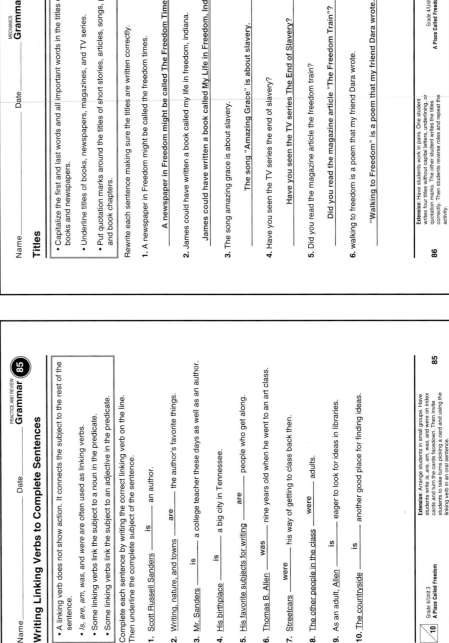

Name________________ Date________ TEST Grammar 87

Linking Verbs

A. Find the linking verb in each sentence. Write it on the line.

1. The year 1832 was the year the family left the plantation.

was

2., Papa, Mama, and James were the family members who walked.

were

3. I am amazed that they traveled so far on foot.

am

4. When the family reaches Indiana, the hills are white with flowers.

are

B. Find the noun or adjective in the predicate that is linked to the subject by a linking verb. Write it on the line.

5. A Quaker family was kind to the travelers from Tennessee.

kind

6. The Starman family is glad to help with their farm work.

glad

7. Papa was a farmer and planted corn and wheat the first year.

farmer

8. Potatoes and beans were the vegetables that James planted.

vegetables

Name________________ Date________ MORE PRACTICE Grammar 88

Linking Verbs

- A **linking verb** does not show action. It connects the subject to the rest of the sentence.
- *Is, are, am, was,* and *were* are often used as linking verbs.
- Some linking verbs link the subject to a noun in the predicate.
- Some linking verbs link the subject to an adjective in the predicate.

Mechanics:

- Capitalize the first and last words and all important words in the titles of books and newspapers.
- Underline titles of books, newspapers, magazines, and TV series.
- Put quotation marks around the titles of short stories, articles, songs, poems, and book chapters.

Work with a partner. Take turns reading the following paragraph aloud. Listen for mistakes in linking verbs. Think about which words are titles. Decide together what corrections need to be made and rewrite the paragraph correctly.

Our social studies book is social studies today. The books is new. The title of yesterday's chapter were slavery in the south. I are ready to give a report today. I wrote a poem about slavery that I call freedom.

Our social studies book is Social Studies Today. The books are new. The title of yesterday's chapter was "Slavery in the South." I am ready to give a report today. I wrote a poem about slavery that I call "Freedom."

A Place Called Freedom • SPELLING

Name__________ Date__________ PRETEST **Spelling 83**

Adding *-ed* and *-ing*

Fold back the paper along the dotted line. Use the blanks to write each word as it is read aloud. When you finish the test, unfold the paper. Use the list at the right to correct any spelling mistakes. Practice the words you missed for the Posttest.

To Parents
Here are the results of your child's weekly spelling Pretest. You can help your child study for the Posttest by following these simple steps for each word on the word list:

1. Read the word to your child.
2. Have your child write the word, saying each letter as it is written.
3. Say each letter of the word as your child checks the spelling.
4. If a mistake has been made, have your child read each letter of the correctly spelled word aloud, then repeat steps 1–3.

1. ______	1. freed
2. ______	2. hugged
3. ______	3. emptied
4. ______	4. figured
5. ______	5. budding
6. ______	6. carried
7. ______	7. believed
8. ______	8. dimmed
9. ______	9. studied
10. ______	10. providing
11. ______	11. shedding
12. ______	12. sledding
13. ______	13. magnified
14. ______	14. wedged
15. ______	15. rotting
16. ______	16. varied
17. ______	17. arrived
18. ______	18. plugging
19. ______	19. rising
20. ______	20. celebrated
Challenge Words	
______	fretted
______	gourd
______	plantation
______	settlement
______	sunrise

Name__________ Date__________ AT HOME WORD STUDY **Spelling 84**

Adding *-ed* and *-ing*

Using the Word Study Steps

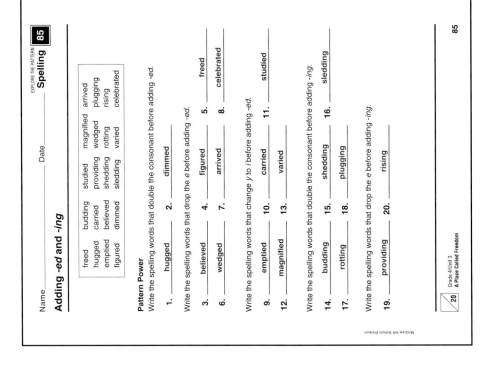

1. LOOK at the word.
2. SAY the word aloud.
3. STUDY the letters in the word.
4. WRITE the word.
5. CHECK the word.

Did you spell the word right? If not, go back to step 1.

Spelling Tip

When words end in silent *e*, drop the *e* when adding an ending that begins with a vowel.
believe - e + ing = believing

When a one syllable word ends in one vowel followed by one consonant, double the consonant before adding an ending that begins with a vowel.
hug + ed = hugged

When a word ends with a consonant followed by *y*, change the *y* to *i* when adding any ending except endings that begin with *i*.
empty + ed = emptied

Word Endings
Write the spelling word by crossing off the final -e and then adding *-ed* or *-ing*.

1. fre~~e~~ **ed**
2. believ~~e~~ **ed**
3. figur~~e~~ **ed**
4. arriv~~e~~ **ed**
5. ris~~e~~ **ing**
6. celebrat~~e~~ **ed**
7. provid~~e~~ **ing**
8. wedg~~e~~ **ed**

Write the spelling word by doubling the final consonant and adding *-ed* or *-ing*.

9. hug **ged**
10. bud **ding**
11. dim **med**
12. shed **ding**

Write the spelling word by changing *y* to *i* and then adding *-ed*.

13. empt~~y~~ **ied**
14. carr~~y~~ **ied**
15. stud~~y~~ **ied**
16. var~~y~~ **ied**

To Parents or Helpers
Using the Word Study Steps above as your child comes across any new words will help him or her learn to spell words effectively. Review the steps as you both go over this week's spelling words.
Go over each Spelling Tip with your child. Ask him or her to add -s or -es to form plurals. Ask if he or she knows other words that end with a consonant followed by y. Help your child to use the Spelling Tips to add endings to the words to make them plural.
Help your child complete the spelling activity.

Name__________ Date__________ EXPLORE THE PATTERN **Spelling 85**

Adding *-ed* and *-ing*

freed	budding	studied	magnified	arrived
hugged	carried	providing	wedged	plugging
emptied	believed	shedding	rotting	rising
figured	dimmed	sledding	varied	celebrated

Pattern Power
Write the spelling words that double the consonant before adding *-ed*.

1. **hugged** 2. **dimmed**

Write the spelling words that drop the *e* before adding *-ed*.

3. **believed** 4. **figured** 5. **freed**
6. **wedged** 7. **arrived** 8. **celebrated**

Write the spelling words that change *y* to *i* before adding *-ed*.

9. **emptied** 10. **carried** 11. **studied**
12. **magnified** 13. **varied**

Write the spelling words that double the consonant before adding *-ing*.

14. **budding** 15. **shedding** 16. **sledding**
17. **rotting** 18. **plugging**

Write the spelling words that drop the *e* before adding *-ing*.

19. **providing** 20. **rising**

Name__________ Date__________ PRACTICE AND EXTEND **Spelling 86**

Adding *-ed* and *-ing*

freed	budding	studied	magnified	arrived
hugged	carried	providing	wedged	plugging
emptied	believed	shedding	rotting	rising
figured	dimmed	sledding	varied	celebrated

Fill in the Blanks
Complete each sentence with a word from the spelling list.

1. Last year we **celebrated** the Fourth of July with fireworks.
2. Which do you like better, ice skating or **sledding**?
3. We'll start the night hike when the moon is **rising**.
4. My cousins **arrived** just in time for the party.
5. The tiny insects were **magnified** by the microscope.
6. My dog is messy when he starts **shedding** his hair!
7. I got an A on the test because I **studied** hard.
8. The plants began **budding** when spring arrived.
9. The coach **varied** our routines so we wouldn't get bored.
10. Our team **figured** out the answer first.

What Does It Mean?
Write the base word for each spelling word.

11. freed	**free**	16. dimmed	**dim**
12. hugged	**hug**	17. providing	**provide**
13. emptied	**empty**	18. wedged	**wedge**
14. carried	**carry**	19. rotting	**rot**
15. believed	**believe**	20. plugging	**plug**

Challenge Extension: Have students create a crossword puzzle using the Challenge Words, then work with a partner to complete each other's sentences.

Name______________________ Date__________ PROOFREAD AND WRITE **Spelling 87**

Adding *-ed* and *-ing*

Proofreading Activity
There are 6 spelling mistakes in the paragraph. Circle the misspelled words. Write the words correctly on the lines below.

Last week we celebrat my dad's birthday with a surprise party. All of our relatives and friends met at our favorite restaurant. Around 5:30, my brothers caryed in the presents. The other guests were already there, all hiding in corners and behind chairs. The lights were dimned. I arryved with my dad around 6 o'clock. My mom turned up the lights. Then everyone stood up and shouted "Happy Birthday, Mike!" My dad was so happy, he huged us all. He said we really tricked him; he believeed my story about going to a soccer dinner. It was a great party. I wonder what we'll think of for next year!

1. celebrated
2. carried
3. dimmed
4. arrived
5. hugged
6. believed

Writing Activity
Write about a celebration you had. Use at least four spelling words in your description.

____

____

____

____

Name______________________ Date__________ POSTTEST **Spelling 88**

Adding *-ed* and *-ing*

Look at the words in each set below. One word in each set is spelled correctly. Use a pencil to fill in the circle next to the correct word. Before you begin, look at the sample sets of words. Sample A has been done for you. Do Sample B by yourself. When you are sure you know what to do, you may go on with the rest of the page.

Sample A Ⓐ cryed ● cried Ⓒ cryied Ⓓ cride

Sample B Ⓔ swiming Ⓕ swimmen ● swimming Ⓗ swiminng

1. Ⓐ studdide Ⓑ studyed Ⓒ studdied ● studied
2. Ⓔ carryed Ⓕ carrid Ⓖ caried ● carried
3. Ⓐ arived ● arrived Ⓒ arryved Ⓓ arrivde
4. Ⓔ riseing ● rising Ⓖ rissing Ⓗ risseng
5. Ⓐ figureed Ⓑ figgured ● figured Ⓓ figurrid
6. Ⓔ roting Ⓕ rotteing Ⓖ rotenng ● rotting
7. Ⓐ vairied ● varied Ⓒ varyd Ⓓ variyd
8. ● freed Ⓕ fereed Ⓖ frede Ⓗ fread
9. Ⓐ sleden ● sledding Ⓒ sledinng Ⓓ sleading
10. Ⓔ hugedd ● hugged Ⓖ huggid Ⓗ hugded
11. ● celebrated Ⓑ celebarated Ⓒ celibratid Ⓓ celebratde
12. Ⓔ pluging Ⓕ pluuging Ⓖ puluging ● plugging
13. Ⓐ maganified ● magnified Ⓒ magnifyde Ⓓ magnafide
14. Ⓔ buhding Ⓕ budeing ● budding Ⓗ buddeng
15. Ⓐ dimend Ⓑ dimned Ⓒ dimede ● dimmed
16. Ⓔ provideing ● providing Ⓖ providding Ⓗ prooviding
17. Ⓐ sheading Ⓑ shedeng ● shedding Ⓓ shedeing
18. Ⓔ weged Ⓕ wedgded ● wedged Ⓗ wejde
19. ● believed Ⓑ bulieved Ⓒ baleeved Ⓓ beleiveed
20. ● emptied Ⓕ emted Ⓖ empttied Ⓗ emptyed

Twisted Trails • PRACTICE

Name______________________ Date__________ **Practice 103**

Make Judgments and Decisions

Characters have reasons for the **judgments and decisions** they make. Think about this as you read the story below. Then answer each question.

The After-School Club was planning a Saturday trip to the Seaside Amusement Park. "We have to get the maximum amount of fun for our money," said Paulo. "We can each get a $21 ticket which gives us seven rides."

The club then decided to go on two rides together. They all went on the rollercoaster. Everyone likes the rollercoaster because it is scary. The club also chose to ride the free-fall parachute together.

"Wait a minute," said Lucia. "The rollercoaster and the parachute are our favorite rides. That means they will be the favorite rides of other kids, too. We'll spend most of the afternoon standing in line."

The others saw that Lucia was right. They decided to go on the rollercoaster first. Then they would try the parachute. After that, the group would break up in pairs and go on other rides that had shorter lines. Their good planning worked and everyone had a fun day at the amusement park.

1. Where did the After-School Club decide to go on Saturday?
   the Seaside Amusement Park
2. What type of ticket did they think was the best deal?
   the $21 dollar ticket
3. What rides did they decide would be good group rides?
   the rollercoaster and the parachute rides
4. Who showed good judgment in predicting a problem and what was that problem? **Lucia because she predicted the lines for the rollercoaster and the parachute would be long because the rides were very popular.**
5. What decision would you have made about rides if you were in the After-School Club? **Answers will vary, but should reflect good judgment and the goal of getting the maximum enjoyment.**

At Home: Have students write about two decisions they have made and whether those decisions showed good judgment or not.

Name______________________ Date__________ **Practice 104**

Vocabulary

Fill in the correct vocabulary word on each line. Then answer each question, using the vocabulary word in your response.
Answers will vary.

combine	**challenge**	**contained**	**mazes**	**entertaining**	**requires**

1. Why is it a **challenge** to play a new sport?
   It is a challenge because you have never played it before, and it may take a lot of practice to learn to play well.
2. What would you do if a new sport **contained** more rules than any you had ever played? **If a sport contained a lot of rules, you could ask a lot of questions to try to understand it.**
3. If you could **combine** your two favorite activities in one day, what would you put together? **I might combine swimming and camping.**
4. What is the most **entertaining** thing you do on Saturday?
   The most entertaining thing I do is to play with my best friend.
5. Why are **mazes** sometimes scary?
   Mazes are sometimes scary because you may get lost in them.
6. Playing a sport well **requires** what from athletes?
   Being a good athlete requires lots of discipline and practice.

At Home: Have students write a new sentence for each vocabulary word.

First Mazes

My sister and I are experts at going through *mazes*. Being good at mazes *requires* a lot of practice. We started out *entertaining* ourselves by completing the mazes that we found in magazines. Then when we were a little older, our parents gave us the *challenge* of going through a real maze in a botanical garden. This garden was in a big place where they grow different kinds of plants and trees. The maze *contained* paths, little bridges, flowers, and bushes cut into animal shapes. What made the maze really entertaining was that it would *combine* two challenges. The first one was to keep from getting wet. If you stepped in certain spots along the path, water would shoot up at you from the ground. The second challenge was to find your way out of the maze. When we returned home, my mother put up a sign on the refrigerator: James and Camilla Win the Maze Challenge!

1. Where did James and Camilla first discover mazes? **They discovered mazes in magazines.**
2. Why do James and Camilla like mazes? **Mazes are entertaining.**
3. How many challenges did the ground maze combine? **two**
4. Being good at mazes requires what? **a lot of practice**
5. What do you think should be contained in a maze to make it challenging?
   Answers will vary, but might include lots of turns and twists, hidden traps, or statues.

At Home: Have students draw a cartoon with character speech bubbles using as many vocabulary words as they can.

Name______________________ Date__________ **Practice 105**

Story Comprehension

Read the statements below. Write **True** if the statement describes "Twisted Trails." Write **False** if it does not. For the answers that are false, rewrite the sentence to make it a true statement.

1. Adrian Fisher lives in America.
   False. Adrian Fisher lives in England.
2. Designing mazes is Adrian Fisher's hobby and not his job.
   False. Fisher has made a career of maze design.
3. Fisher says he is part scientist and part artist.
   True
4. Being good at math helps in building mazes.
   True
5. Fisher has used live crocodiles in his mazes.
   True
6. Children are better at going through mazes than adults.
   True
7. If you keep getting lost in a maze, one good rule is to always turn right.
   False. The rule is to always turn left.
8. Building outdoor mazes is rather easy work.
   False. Building mazes takes a lot of skill, planning, and math.

At Home: Have students write a paragraph describing an area where Fisher might build a small maze in their town.

Name__________ Date__________ Practice 106

Read a Diagram

A **diagram** can be a picture of how something works or how something is made. A diagram can also be something like a map. It can show you paths to get from one place to another. One kind of diagram is a maze. Use a pencil to complete the following maze from start to finish. Remember what Adrian Fisher said: If you don't know where to go, keep turning left.

At Home: Have students draw a diagram of their school.

Name__________ Date__________ Practice 107

Author's Purpose and Point of View

When an author writes an article, he or she may have more than one **purpose.** The purpose might be to entertain, inform, describe, or persuade. As we read the article, we also come to know what the author thinks. That is the author's **point of view**.

Think about the author's purpose and point of view in "Twisted Trails." Then answer each question below. **Answers will vary.**

What are three things about the article that entertained you?

1. **Learning about the many different kinds of mazes.**
2. **Reading about mazes that are really unusual.**
3. **You never know what Adrian Fisher will use to make a maze.**

What are three things you learned from reading this selection?

4. **It is possible to have a maze that has three miles of pathways.**
5. **Being good at math helps in designing or going through mazes.**
6. **Some children are better than adults at mazes.**

7. What is the author's point of view about having a job building mazes?
   It is interesting and provides fun for many people.

8. Do you agree with the author that building mazes is an interesting and exciting job? Or do you think it's a silly job? Explain your answer.
   Answers will vary.

At Home: Have students write a letter to the author saying whether he or she agrees or disagrees with the author's point of view.

Name__________ Date__________ Practice 108

Context Clues

Sometimes when you read, there will be words you don't know. You may be able to figure out what the word means by using the other words in the sentence. These words are called **context clues**.

Use context clues to choose a word from the list to complete each sentence.

maze	**fountain**	**professional**	**fretted**
combine	**reflected**	**entertaining**	**twisted**

1. A series of pathways is called a **maze**.
2. Something that is not straight is **twisted**.
3. A play, a movie, or a good game can be very **entertaining**.
4. A person with a job that requires special education is a **professional**.
5. A name for a place that spouts water is a **fountain**.
6. The players worried and **fretted** until the game was over and they had won.
7. The moon was **reflected** in the pond.
8. When you put two things together, you **combine** them.

At Home: Have students write a story using five words from the list above and context clues.

Name__________ Date__________ Practice 109

Suffixes

A **suffix** is a group of letters added to the end of a base, or root, word. The suffix changes the meaning of the word slightly or changes the way it is used in a sentence. Choose a word to complete each sentence. Then circle the words with the suffixes.

care	**careful**	**wonder**	**wonderful**	**famous**
dangerous	**colorful**	**fame**	**color**	**danger**

1. The boy took **care** so that he would not bump into the baby.
2. The boy was **careful** (circled) when he held his baby brother.
3. The dog always barks when something is wrong and there is **danger**.
4. The father asks his children to stay away from **dangerous** (circled) places.
5. The students painted every **color** they could find on the scenery.
6. The students' costumes were bright and **colorful** (circled).
7. One thing professional basketball players have is **fame**.
8. Kids who want to grow up to be baseball players often want to be **famous** (circled).
9. The fireworks filled the little children with **wonder**.
10. The children called the fireworks **wonderful** (circled).

At Home: Have students write sentences using pairs of words, one with a suffix, one without.

Twisted Trails • RETEACH

Name________________ Date__________ **Reteach 103**

Make Judgments and Decisions

Making judgments and decisions is a natural part of storytelling and story reading. Characters must think about what they will do in difficult situations. Readers must think about what they might do in similar situations.

Read the story. Then write an answer to each question.

Mickey got off the bus. He stood still and stared straight ahead. He could see the building where the department store was. It was only about a half block away. This was the first time his dad had let him come downtown by himself to buy his own clothes. Now he almost wished his dad had come along. Mickey pictured the big store, the crowds, and the many choices he would have. Suddenly he didn't feel very well. He saw the bus that was headed back to his home, and he got a wild idea.

1. What decision does Mickey have to make? **He has to decide whether to go to the department store or go back home.**
2. Why did his dad decide to let him go downtown alone? **He felt Mickey was old enough to travel alone and take responsibility.**
3. Why does Mickey wish his dad had come along? **There would be someone to help him feel less nervous about choosing his own clothes, and paying for them by himself.**
4. If you were Mickey, what would you do? **Even if I didn't want to go to the store, I would go anyway.**

At Home: Have students tell what they would say to Mickey if he had skipped his trip to the store.

Name________________ Date__________ **Reteach 104**

Vocabulary

Use the correct word from the list.

challenge	contained	combine	entertaining	mazes	requires

1. The **mazes** were like life-size puzzles.
2. It is a real **challenge** to try to find your way through a maze.
3. To find your way through a maze, you need to **combine** a sense of direction and a good memory.
4. Finding your way through a maze also **requires** paying attention to details.
5. My favorite maze **contained** many twisting paths.
6. It is **entertaining** to walk through a maze.

6

Reteach 105

Story Comprehension

Write an answer to each question about "Twisted Trails."

1. Who is Adrian Fisher? **Adrian Fisher is a man who designs walk-through mazes for a living.**
2. What kinds of skills does he need to design mazes? **He needs science skills and artistic skills.**
3. Why do people like corn mazes? **Corn mazes are outdoors in the air and sunshine.**
4. In what state is there a museum that has shown Fisher's mazes? **Florida**

At Home: Have students tell about the article "Twisted Trails"

Name________________ Date__________ **Reteach 106**

Read a Diagram

A **diagram** is a plan or a drawing. One kind of diagram shows the arrangement of things in a place.

Library / Floor 1

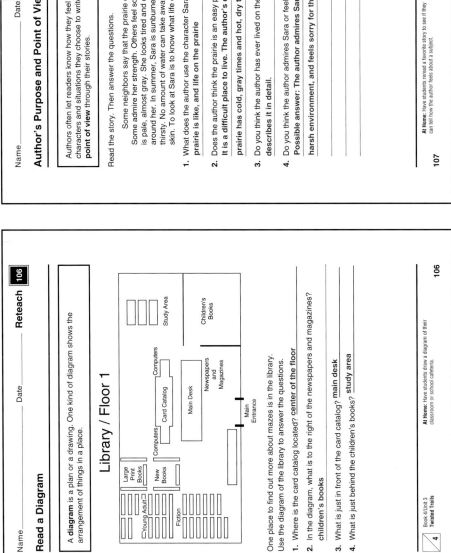

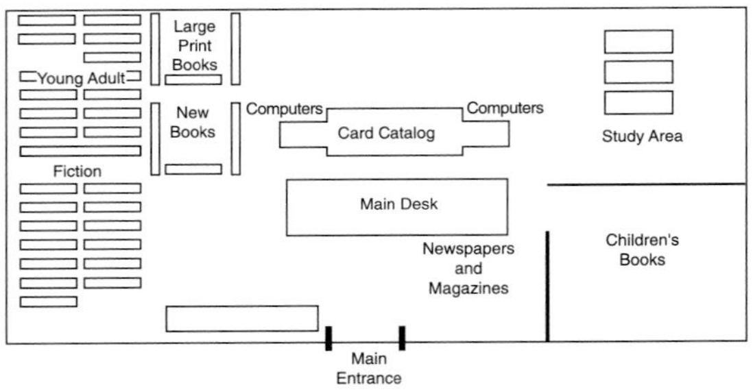

One place to find out more about mazes is in the library. Use the diagram of the library to answer the questions.

1. Where is the card catalog located? **center of the floor**
2. In the diagram, what is to the right of the newspapers and magazines? **children's books**
3. What is just in front of the card catalog? **main desk**
4. What is just behind the children's books? **study area**

At Home: Have students draw a diagram of their classroom or school cafeteria.

Name________________ Date__________ **Reteach 107**

Author's Purpose and Point of View

Authors often let readers know how they feel about a subject through the characters and situations they choose to write about. They express their **point of view** through their stories.

Read the story. Then answer the questions.

Some neighbors say that the prairie can be seen on Sara's face. Some admire her strength. Others feel sorry for her. In winter, Sara is pale, almost gray. She looks tired and cold like the snowy flat land around her. In summer, Sara is sunburned and seems always to be thirsty. No amount of water can take away the dryness of her hair or skin. To look at Sara is to know what life on the prairie is like.

1. What does the author use the character Sara to really talk about? **What a prairie is like, and life on the prairie**
2. Does the author think the prairie is an easy place to live? Tell how you know? **It is a difficult place to live. The author's description of Sara shows the prairie has cold, gray times and hot, dry times.**
3. Do you think the author has ever lived on the prairie? Why? **Yes. The author describes it in detail.**
4. Do you think the author admires Sara or feels sorry for her? Why? **Possible answer: The author admires Sara for being able to live in the harsh environment, and feels sorry for the roughness of prairie life.**

At Home: Have students reread a favorite story to see if they can tell how the author feels about a subject.

Name______________________ Date__________ **Reteach 108**

Context Clues

Good readers use **context clues** to help them figure out unfamiliar words.

Read the paragraph. Circle the letter giving the meaning of each of the words listed below. Then tell what clues in the paragraph helped you.

In the construction business there are lots of people who need to work together. Putting up big buildings is a complicated job. The architect draws the plans for the building. Architects need to consult with engineers who are the experts on how to build. Lawyers have to deal with legal matters. Someone has to set up the schedule to make sure things get done at the right time.

1. complicated

a. simple to do (**b.**) hard to do

Clues: **Putting up big buildings**

2. consult

a. disagree with (**b.**) talk together about

Clues: **Architects need engineers who are the experts about how to build.**

3. legal

a. relating to money (**b.**) relating to the law

Clues: **lawyers have to deal with**

4. schedule

(**a.**) time plan **b.** list of workers

Clues: **to make sure things get done at the right time**

At Home: Have students use the numbered words in sentences of their own.

Name______________________ Date__________ **Reteach 109**

Suffixes

Knowing the meaning a **suffix** adds to a word can help you read and understand unfamiliar words. The suffixes *-ful* and *ous* add the meaning "full of" or "having" to words.

Read the list of words with suffixes. Think about the meaning of each word. Then write a word to complete each sentence.

hazardous	**restful**	**famous**	**pitiful**
careful	**healthful**	**disastrous**	**thoughtful**

1. Fast food does not make a **healthful** meal.

2. We spent a **restful** afternoon lying on the beach.

3. The student looked **thoughtful** when questioned by his teacher.

4. Some bug sprays are **hazardous** to the environment.

5. The **famous** movie star signed my autograph book.

6. The shipwreck was a **disastrous** accident.

7. The sick parrot gave a **pitiful** cry.

8. It's important to be **careful** when you light the candles.

At Home: Have students explain the spelling changes needed to form famous disastrous, and pitiful.

Twisted Trails • EXTEND

Name______________________ Date__________ **Extend 103**

Make Judgments and Decisions

When you read a story, you make **judgments and decisions** about the story's characters.

Suppose you had to make a decision about how you would earn a living as an adult. What facts would you consider? Would you think about the kinds of jobs people in your town have? Would you think about the kind of training you would need? What opinions would you consider? Would you think about what you enjoy doing most or what others think you do best?

Write a paragraph stating your decision. Explain why you made that decision. Tell the facts and opinions you considered.

Answers will vary. Sentences should be written in the correct context and use the proper parts of speech.

At Home: Talk with an adult family member about how he or she decided what to do to earn a living.

Name______________________ Date__________ **Extend 104**

Vocabulary

challenge	**contained**	**combine**
entertaining	**mazes**	**requires**

Suppose a walk-through maze has been built in your town. Use as many vocabulary words as you can to write a commercial advertising the maze. Then present your commercial to your class. Use a separate sheet of paper if you need more space.

Extend 105

Story Comprehension

"Twisted Trails" describes two mazes Adrian Fisher built in the shape of objects—a car and a submarine. He chose objects that would be of particular interest to the people living near the mazes.

Write a letter to Fisher suggesting a shape of maze he should create for your community. Tell him what you would like him to include in the maze based on what you know about his other mazes.

Answers will vary.

At Home: Find out what the mascot is for a local sports team. Think about why that mascot may have been chosen and whether it was a good choice.

Name______________________ Date__________ **Extend 106**

Read a Diagram

Suppose you are visiting a maze and have been given an old **diagram** of the maze to help you find your way. Write a story about what happened as you try to follow the diagram. Include an illustration of the diagram.

Answers will vary.

At Home: Draw a diagram of a maze and have a family member trace his or her path through the maze with a pencil.

Name______________________ Date__________ **Extend 107**

Author's Purpose and Point of View

An author may write a selection to persuade a reader, or to affect how the reader thinks about something. Author's may also write to describe, to inform, and to entertain the reader.

The author's main purpose in writing "Twisted Trails" is to inform the reader about Adrian Fisher and his mazes. Briefly describe a selection the author could have written about Adrian Fisher and mazes if the purpose had been to persuade, to describe, or to entertain.

1. If the purpose had been to persuade, the author could have written . . .
   Answers will vary. Possible answer: A selection explaining why Adrian Fisher has the most interesting job possible.
2. If the purpose had been to describe, the author could have written . . .
   Answers will vary. Possible answer: Detailed descriptions of some of Adrian Fisher's mazes.
3. If the purpose had been to entertain, the author could have written . . .
   Answers will vary. Possible answer: A story about someone lost in one of Adrian Fisher's mazes.

Suppose you were a writer assigned to do interviews with people as they exit one of Adrian Fisher's mazes. State what your point of view would be and list 2 questions you would ask in your interviews.

At Home: Choose an event that you or your family has been involved in recently. Plan four ways to tell about it: to inform, to persuade, to describe, and to entertain.

Name________________ Date__________ Extend 108

Context Clues

Sometimes you can use **context clues**, words or phrases in the same or nearby sentences, to help you figure out the meaning of words. Write the group of words or sentence from "Twisted Trails" containing context clues that would help a reader figure out the meaning of each of these words.

designs maze pathways pleasure forces professional

1. Answers will vary but should be written in the correct context and with correct parts of speech.
2. ________________
3. ________________
4. ________________
5. ________________
6. ________________

At Home: Write a sentence for a word containing context clues that could be used to teach the meaning of the word to a family member.

Name________________ Date__________ Extend 109

Suffixes

The **suffixes** *-ful* and *-ous* mean "full of." Add the suffix *-ful* or *-ous* to each base word to create a related adjective. Remember that the base word's spelling may change when adding a suffix.

fame	famous	watch	watchful
care	careful	caution	cautious
color	colorful	wonder	wonderful
envy	envious	courtesy	courteous

Write an adventure story. Using as many of the adjectives above as possible.

Answers will vary but should make correct use of the words and use the correct parts of speech.

At Home: Identify words with suffixes in a newspaper or magazine article for a family member.

Twisted Trails • GRAMMAR

Name________________ Date__________ LEARN Grammar 89

Irregular Verbs

- An **irregular verb** is a verb that does not add *-ed* to form the past tense.

Write the correct past-tense form of the underlined verb on the line provided.

1. Adrian Fisher begin __began__ to make mazes more than 20 years ago.
2. Fisher make __made__ a huge maze in 1996.
3. This maze break __broke__ the record for the largest maze.
4. About 2,000 people find __found__ their way through it in one day.
5. Adults as well as children come __came__ to try the maze.
6. Children go __went__ through the maze faster than their parents.
7. Fisher do __did__ a special maze to honor a Beatles song.
8. A plane fly __flew__ over Adrian Fisher's mazes.
9. An artist draw __drew__ pictures of the mazes.
10. The drawings show what the pilot see __saw__.

Extension: Have students work with partners to find examples of irregular past-tense verbs in newspaper articles. Ask students to make and share a list of the verbs they find.

Name________________ Date__________ LEARN AND PRACTICE Grammar 90

Irregular Verbs

- Some irregular verbs have special spellings when used with the helping verb *have, has,* or *had.*

Read each sentence and the verb choices in parentheses. Underline the verb choice that correctly completes the sentence.

1. Adrian Fisher has (built, builded) more than 135 mazes.
2. He has (did, done) mazes in England and the United States.
3. Fisher had (make, made) the maze in Michigan in the shape of a car.
4. The cornstalks in his corn maze have (grew, grown) high.
5. He had (lay, laid) out the Beatles maze in the shape of a submarine.
6. This maze master has (put, putted) roadblocks in his mazes.
7. Sometimes there have (were, been) live crocodiles in his mazes, too.
8. Thousands of people have (seen, saw) Fisher's mazes.
9. He has (taken, took) a lot of care with his designs.
10. People have (begun, began) to take maze design seriously.

Extension: Ask students to rewrite the above sentences using past-tense verbs without using *have, has,* or *had.*

Name________________ Date__________ PRACTICE AND REVIEW Grammar 91

Irregular Verbs

- An **irregular verb** is a verb that does not add -ed to form the past tense.
- Some irregular verbs have special spellings when used with the helping verb *have, has,* or *had.*

Rewrite each sentence with the correct form of the underlined verb. For each sentence, use the form that makes better sense—the past-tense form or the past with the helping verb *have, has,* or *had.*

1. One time I go through a maze.
   One time I went through a maze.
2. I wonder if you have ever go through a maze.
   I wonder if you have ever gone through a maze.
3. I know there was a rule for going through a maze.
   I knew there was a rule for going through a maze.
4. I followed the rule and find that it worked!
   I followed the rule and found that it worked!
5. The left wall had lead me back to the path.
   The left wall had led me back to the path.
6. Finally I see the way out of the maze.
   Finally I saw the way out of the maze.
7. The maze had keep me busy for quite a while.
   The maze had kept me busy for quite a while.
8. Did you know that Adrian Fisher has break the rule of maze making?
   Did you know that Adrian Fisher has broken the rule of maze making?

Extension: Arrange students in groups. Ask each group to make a chart with three columns labeled *Present Tense, Past Tense,* and *Past with Have, Has, or Had.* Have students fill in the columns with forms for the verbs in parentheses.

Name________________ Date__________ MECHANICS Grammar 92

Abbreviations

- An abbreviation is the shortened form of a word.
- An abbreviation begins with a capital letter and ends with a period.
- Abbreviate titles of people before names. You can abbreviate days of the week.
- You can also abbreviate most months.

Rewrite this invitation by writing each underlined abbreviation correctly.

Dear Jesse,

Would you like to go through mr Fisher's maze with us? My mother says that we will go on sat, nov 10. Derek and mrs Long are coming. I went to see dr Ortega on thurs, and he showed me how to brush my teeth better. I'll call you tomorrow afternoon.

Sam

Dear Jesse,

Would you like to go through Mr. Fisher's maze with us? My mother says that we will go on Sat., Nov. 10. Derek and Mrs. Long are coming. I went to see Dr. Ortega on Thurs., and he showed me how to brush my teeth better. I'll call you tomorrow afternoon.

Sam

Extension: Have pairs of students quiz each other on abbreviations. Have one partner write a word and the other write the abbreviation.

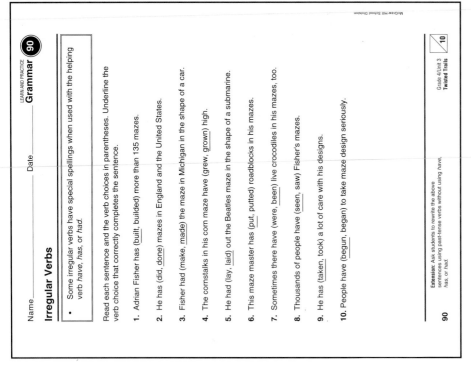

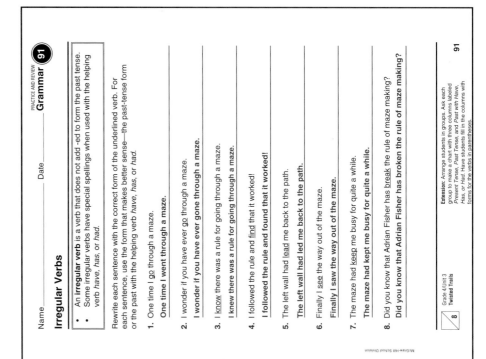

Name__________ Date__________ TEST **Grammar 93**

Irregular Verbs

A. Circle the letter before the irregular verb that correctly completes each sentence.

1. Our class ___ reading about mazes yesterday.

a. begin

(**b.**) began

c. begun

d. beginned

2. We ___ some mazes on paper.

a. draw

b. drawed

(**c.**) drew

d. drawn

B. Circle the letter before the correct irregular verb and helping verb that completes each sentence.

3. The maze master ___ a maze with three miles of paths in it.

(**a.**) has made

b. has make

c. had make

d. have made

4. Adults ___ lost in Adrian Fisher's mazes.

a. has became

b. has become

c. have became

(**d.**) have become

Name__________ Date__________ MORE PRACTICE **Grammar 94**

Irregular Verbs

- An **irregular verb** is a verb that does not add *-ed* to form the past tense.
- Some irregular verbs have special spellings when used with the helping verb *have, has,* or *had.*

Mechanics

- An abbreviation is the shortened form of a word. An abbreviation begins with a capital letter and ends with a period.
- Abbreviate titles of people before names. You can abbreviate days of the week and most months.

Read the sentences about the picture below. Change the verbs that are not written correctly. Put capital letters and periods where they belong in the abbreviations. Rewrite the sentences on the lines below.

1. The students in ms Ming's class have drew a circular maze.
The students in Ms. Ming's class have drawn a circular maze.

2. Last week they taked their maze to mr Johnson's class.
Last week they took their maze to Mr. Johnson's class.

3. This morning mrs Green's class come to see the maze.
This morning Mrs. Green's class came to see the maze.

4. Later they gived the maze to the principal, dr Miller.
Later they gave the maze to the principal, Dr. Miller.

5. Now everyone in the school has see the maze.
Now everyone in the school has seen the maze.

Twisted Trails • SPELLING

PRETEST **Spelling 89**

Name______________ Date__________

Words from the Arts

Fold back the paper along the dotted line. Use the blanks to write each word as it is read aloud. When you finish the test, unfold the paper. Use the list at the right to correct any spelling mistakes. Practice the words you missed for the Posttest.

To Parents
Here are the results of your child's weekly spelling Pretest. You can help your child study for the Posttest by following these simple steps for each word on the word list:

1. Read the word to your child.
2. Have your child write the word, saying each letter as it is written.
3. Say each letter of the word as your child checks the spelling.
4. If a mistake has been made, have your child read each letter of the correctly spelled word aloud, then repeat steps 1–3.

1. ______	1. designs
2. ______	2. artist
3. ______	3. building
4. ______	4. activity
5. ______	5. museum
6. ______	6. art
7. ______	7. create
8. ______	8. master
9. ______	9. poster
10. ______	10. statue
11. ______	11. assemble
12. ______	12. craft
13. ______	13. express
14. ______	14. arrange
15. ______	15. professional
16. ______	16. mold
17. ______	17. easel
18. ______	18. plaster
19. ______	19. masterpiece
20. ______	20. exhibit
Challenge Words	
______	challenge
______	contained
______	entertaining
______	mazes
______	requires

AT HOME WORD STUDY **Spelling 90**

Name______________ Date__________

Words from the Arts

Using the Word Study Steps

1. LOOK at the word.
2. SAY the word aloud.
3. STUDY the letters in the word.
4. WRITE the word.
5. CHECK the word.

Did you spell the word right?
If not, go back to step 1.

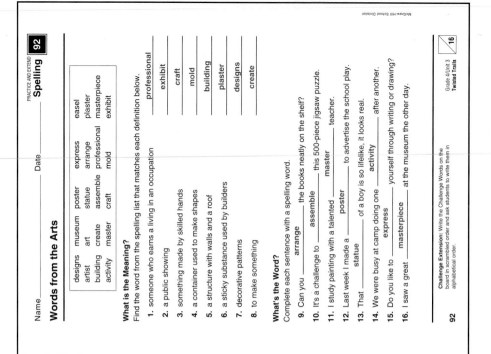

Spelling Tip
Look for word chunks or smaller words that help you remember the spelling of a word.
assemble = as sem ble
professional = pro fes sion al
masterpiece = mas ter piece

Word Scramble
Unscramble each set of letters to make a spelling word.

1. tyiavcit ____activity____
2. srofeasipnlo ____professional____
3. ateemriscep ____masterpiece____
4. starti ____artist____
5. beamsles ____assemble____
6. srespex ____express____
7. frtca ____craft____
8. rateec ____create____
9. sotepr ____poster____
10. alsee ____easel____
11. sigends ____designs____
12. gudilibn ____building____
13. smarte ____master____
14. geararn ____arrange____
15. doml ____mold____
16. xeitbih ____exhibit____
17. parstel ____plaster____
18. rat ____art____
19. umusme ____museum____
20. usteat ____statue____

To Parents or Helpers
Using the Word Study Steps above as your child comes across any new words will help him or her learn to spell words effectively. Review the steps as you both go over this week's spelling words.
Go over the Spelling Tip with your child. Help your child find the smaller words within the spelling words.
Help your child complete the spelling activity.

EXPLORE THE PATTERN **Spelling 91**

Name______________ Date__________

Words from the Arts

designs	museum	poster	express	easel
artist	art	statue	arrange	plaster
building	create	assemble	professional	masterpiece
activity	master	craft	mold	exhibit

Write the spelling words in alphabetical order.

1. ____activity____
2. ____arrange____
3. ____art____
4. ____artist____
5. ____assemble____
6. ____building____
7. ____craft____
8. ____create____
9. ____designs____
10. ____easel____
11. ____exhibit____
12. ____express____
13. ____master____
14. ____masterpiece____
15. ____mold____
16. ____museum____
17. ____plaster____
18. ____poster____
19. ____professional____
20. ____statue____

PRACTICE AND EXTEND **Spelling 92**

Name______________ Date__________

Words from the Arts

designs	museum	poster	express	easel
artist	art	statue	arrange	plaster
building	create	assemble	professional	masterpiece
activity	master	craft	mold	exhibit

What is the Meaning?
Find the word from the spelling list that matches each definition below.

1. someone who earns a living in an occupation ____professional____
2. a public showing ____exhibit____
3. something made by skilled hands ____craft____
4. a container used to make shapes ____mold____
5. a structure with walls and a roof ____building____
6. a sticky substance used by builders ____plaster____
7. decorative patterns ____designs____
8. to make something ____create____

What's the Word?
Complete each sentence with a spelling word.

9. Can you ____arrange____ the books neatly on the shelf?
10. It's a challenge to ____assemble____ this 500-piece jigsaw puzzle.
11. I study painting with a talented ____master____ teacher.
12. Last week I made a ____poster____ to advertise the school play.
13. That ____statue____ of a boy is so lifelike, it looks real.
14. We were busy at camp doing one ____activity____ after another.
15. Do you like to ____express____ yourself through writing or drawing?
16. I saw a great ____masterpiece____ at the museum the other day.

Challenge Extension: Write the Challenge Words on the board in scrambled order and ask students to write them in alphabetical order.

Name________________________ Date__________ PROOFREAD AND WRITE **Spelling 93**

Words from the Arts

Proofreading Activity
There are 6 spelling mistakes in the directions below. Circle the misspelled words. Write the words correctly on the lines below.

Getting Ready to Paint a Picture

1. Think about the feeling or idea you want to (ecspress) in your painting.
2. (Assembal) all of your equipment.
3. Sketch several (desins) on paper first.
4. (Arange) your brushes and paints so they are easy to reach.
5. Put a blank canvas on an (esel.)
6. Use your brushes, paints, and ideas to (creight) a wonderful painting.

1. express
2. Assemble
3. designs
4. Arrange
5. easel
6. create

Writing Activity
Write a set of directions telling how to do something artistic. Number each step. Use at least four spelling words.

____

____

____

____

Name________________________ Date__________ POSTTEST **Spelling 94**

Words from the Arts

Look at the words in each set below. One word in each set is spelled correctly. Use a pencil to fill in the circle next to the correct word. Before you begin, look at the sample sets of words. Sample A has been done for you. Do Sample B by yourself. When you are sure you know what to do, you may go on with the rest of the page.

Sample A Ⓐ burush Ⓑ bruch Ⓒ baruch ● brush

Sample B ● canvas Ⓕ canvis Ⓖ kanvas Ⓗ kanvist

1. ● activity Ⓑ acativety Ⓒ acktvity Ⓓ actevaty
2. Ⓔ statoo ● statue Ⓖ satatue Ⓗ statshoo
3. Ⓐ deesines Ⓑ deseighns ● designs Ⓓ desines
4. Ⓔ crafet Ⓕ caraft Ⓖ curaft ● craft
5. Ⓐ plastar ● plaster Ⓒ plasstir Ⓓ pullaster
6. Ⓔ masterpieace Ⓕ masterrpece ● masterpiece Ⓗ mazzterpiece
7. Ⓐ artest ● artist Ⓒ ardizt Ⓓ ahrtist
8. Ⓔ prufesionel Ⓕ proffesional Ⓖ prifesionul ● professional
9. ● create Ⓑ kreatee Ⓒ creeate Ⓓ chreat
10. Ⓔ ixpress ● express Ⓖ ackspres Ⓗ egspress
11. Ⓐ urange Ⓑ arannge Ⓒ araange ● arrange
12. ● poster Ⓕ poaster Ⓖ postear Ⓗ puhster
13. Ⓐ ezel ● easel Ⓒ eesil Ⓓ easile
14. Ⓔ ahrt Ⓕ arrt Ⓖ artte ● art
15. Ⓐ ecksibit Ⓑ eaxibet ● exhibit Ⓓ egsebet
16. Ⓔ asembal ● assemble Ⓖ usembul Ⓗ asemmbale
17. Ⓐ moseim Ⓑ mahuseem Ⓒ muzeume ● museum
18. Ⓔ masster Ⓕ mastear ● master Ⓗ mostare
19. Ⓐ buldding Ⓑ bildeng ● building Ⓓ biuldang
20. ● mold Ⓕ moald Ⓖ muold Ⓗ mollde

Unit 3 Review • PRACTICE and RETEACH

Name__________ Date______ **Practice 110**

Unit 3 Vocabulary Review

A. Read each word in Column 1. Then find a word in Column 2 that means the opposite. Write the letter of the word on the line.

	column 1	column 2
e	1. displaying	a. drew
f	2. strolling	b. boring
c	3. sunrise	c. sunset
b	4. entertaining	d. denied
a	5. scribbled	e. hiding
d	6. admitted	f. running

B. Write the correct vocabulary word on the lines.

challenge inspire combine chanted plantation contained

1. Reading books can __inspire__ you to write a good story.
2. The little children __chanted__ the rhyming poem.
3. Climbing to the top was quite a __challenge__.
4. The box __contained__ video games and board games.
5. A huge farm where crops such as cotton or sugar can be grown for sale is called a __plantation__.
6. They will __combine__ flour and water to make the papier mâché.

At Home: Have students change or add suffixes to some vocabulary words in order to make new words.

Name__________ Date______ **Practice 111**

Unit 3 Vocabulary Review

Answer each question using the underlined vocabulary word in the answer.
Answers will vary.

1. What do you think would cause hikers to be so tired and weary?
   The hikers were weary from walking five miles.
2. What is the most entertaining type of movie to you?
   I think the most entertaining type of movie is a comedy.
3. Why is everyone in the class so restless?
   The class is restless because they've been sitting still too long.
4. What is it the teacher requires from us when we leave in the afternoon?
   The teacher requires that we bring home our homework.
5. What can we combine to make a really good sandwich?
   We can combine cheese and lettuce.
6. Is a storybook or an encyclopedia a reference book?
   An encyclopedia is a reference book.
7. What did you use to make that sketch of your little sister?
   I used a pencil to draw the sketch.
8. How can you make an exact image of your friend?
   Taking a photograph with a camera will give me an exact image.
9. How do you move when you go for a brisk walk?
   You move quickly when you go for a brisk walk.
10. What is your greatest challenge in school?
    My greatest challenge is writing reports.

At Home: Have students write a story using as many vocabulary words as they can.

Name__________ Date______ **Reteach 110**

Unit 3 Vocabulary Review

A. Write a word from the list to complete each sentence.

sunrise brisk entertaining weary strolling mazes

1. Louie went for a __brisk__ walk.
2. He came across Denise __strolling__ through the park.
3. We got up before __sunrise__.
4. It is no surprise that we were __weary__ by afternoon.
5. We walked through the __mazes__.
6. It was an __entertaining__ afternoon.

B. Read each clue. Then find the vocabulary word from the list in the row of letters and circle it.

displaying wharf fretted exist

1. worried m a (f r e t t e d) y u d a w
2. showing l k a s n (d i s p l a y i n g) a f
3. to live o j f (e x i s t) r g v s q a
4. boat landing m r o j (w h a r f) n c v

At Home: Have students use three vocabulary words in sentences of their own.

Name__________ Date______ **Reteach 111**

Unit 3 Vocabulary Review

A. Read each question. Then write a word from the list to answer each question.

chanted sketch loft plantation pouch

1. If you were to draw quickly, what would you do? __sketch__
2. What was a large farm that usually grew one crop called? __plantation__
3. What is a small bag or sack called? __pouch__
4. What might the choir have done as the organ played? __chanted__
5. What is a large room or open space on the upper floor of a building called? __loft__

B. Write a word from the list to complete each sentence.

reference inspire restless challenge image

1. I was so excited I couldn't sit still. After a while, Mom asked why I was so __restless__.
2. Older kids help me learn. They __inspire__ me.
3. She often uses her state almanac as a __reference__.
4. Aunt Bertha stared at little Carrie. She was the __image__ of her mother.
5. The book was 300 pages long. It was a __challenge__, but I read it all.

At Home: Encourage students to use the vocabulary words in their personal writing.

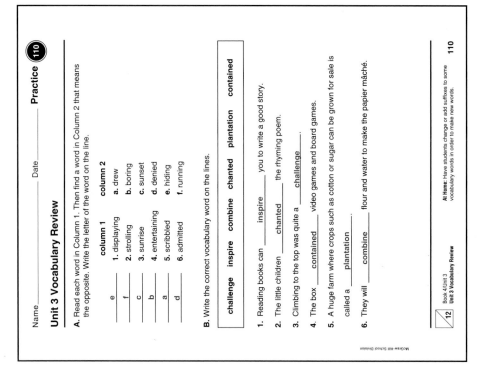

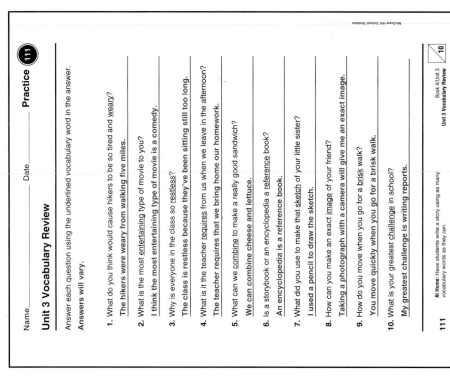

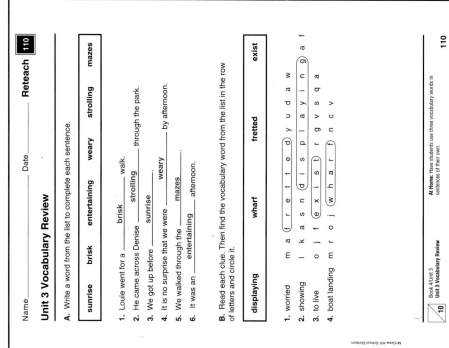

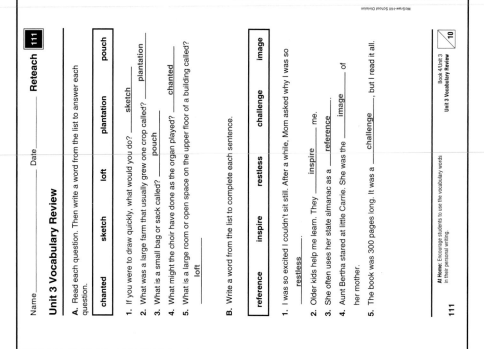

Unit 3 Review • EXTEND and GRAMMAR

Name__________ Date______ **Extend 110**

Unit 3 Vocabulary Review

Write a story using the vocabulary words below. Continue your story on a separate piece of paper if necessary.

admitted	**brisk**	**combine**	**contained**	**exist**
fretted	**gourd**	**loft**	**mazes**	**nipped**
pouch	**reference**	**restless**	**sunrise**	**wharf**

Stories should make correct use of the vocablary and use the correct parts of speech.

At Home: Design a word search using six different words that have something in common. Have a family member try to solve the word search.

Name__________ Date______ **Extend 111**

Unit 3 Vocabulary Review

Chose six of the words from the list below to make your own crossword puzzle. Write brief definitions of the words you choose to fill in the **Across** and **Down** columns. Remember to number the definitions appropriately. Then use a separate sheet of paper to draw and number the boxes of the puzzle to match your definitions. Exchange your puzzle with a partner's and try to solve it.

challenge	**chanted**	**displaying**	**elegantly**	**entertaining**
image	**inspire**	**plantation**	**requires**	**scribbled**
settlement	**sketch**	**stitching**	**strolling**	**weary**

Across

Down

At Home: Choose several words from the list above. For each, provide clues to family members until they are able to figure out the word.

Name__________ Date______ REVIEW **Grammar 95**

Verbs

Read each passage and look at the underlined parts. Is there a better way to write and say each part? If there is, which is the better way? Circle your answer.

The hatmaker sit write, and draws. (1) He creates a sign for his shop. He shows the sign to several people. They tells him to make changes. (2) The hatmaker rushes back to his shop and makes a new sign.

1. A The hatmaker sat, writes, and draws.
   B The hatmaker sits, wrote, and draws.
   (C) The hatmaker sits, writes, and draws.
   D No mistake

2. F Them told him to make changes.
   G They told he to make changes.
   (H) They tell him to make changes.
   J No mistake

December 1, 2000
777 Forest Street
Orange, MA 01364
Chris Little
129 Blueberry Circle
York, ME 03909

Dear Chris,
I looked at some books with drawings by Pat Cummings. She liked to draw when she was young. Then she study art and became an artist. (3) I think I will study art, too.
your's friend, (4)
Lucas

3. A Then her study art and became an artist.
   B Then she studyed art and become an artist.
   (C) Then she studied art and became an artist.
   D No mistake

4. (F) Your friend,
   G You're friend,
   H Your's friend,
   J No mistake

Name__________ Date______ REVIEW **Grammar 96**

Verbs

Basho is preparing to walk across Japan. He isnt taken much with him. (5) Basho is a poet, and he will write poems during his journey. His friends has given him a pair of sandals paper, and ink. (6)

5. A He isnt taking much with him.
   B He isn't taken much with he.
   (C) He isn't taking much with him.
   D No mistake

6. F His friend's have gave him a pair of sandals, paper, and ink.
   (G) His friends have given him a pair of sandals, paper, and ink.
   H His friend have given him a pair of sandals, paper, and ink.
   J No mistake

Each group in my class wrote a song about the town of Freedom. My group's song is called "A Place to Be Free." (7) All the groups sang their songs to the class. Ms. Brady said our songs was wonderful. (8)

7. A my group's song is called "a place to be free."
   B My group song is called A Place to Be Free.
   C My groups song is called "A Place to Be Free."
   (D) No mistake

8. F Ms Brady said our song's is wonderful.
   G Ms. brady says our songs was wonderful.
   (H) Ms. Brady said our songs were wonderful.
   J No mistake

Dee write a list of things to do for the week. (9) heres her list: (10) 1. Mon.—Read article about mazes. 2. Tues.—Visit magazine's Web site. 3. Wed.—Get book of mazes from library. 4. Thurs.—Draw my own maze. 5. Fri.—Show my maze to Cathy.

9. A Dee has wrote a list of things to do for the week.
   B dee has written a list of things to do for the week
   (C) Dee has written a list of things to do for the week.
   D No mistake

10. (F) Here's her list:
    G Hear's her list:
    H Heres her list:
    J No mistake

Unit 3 Review • SPELLING

Name____________________ Date__________

Grade 4/Unit 3 Review Test

Read each sentence. If an underlined word is spelled wrong, fill in the circle that goes with that word. If no word is spelled wrong, fill in the circle below NONE. Read Sample A, and do Sample B.

A. That artist (A) made colorful designs (B) on her poster (C).
A. Ⓐ Ⓑ Ⓒ ● (NONE)

B. The plaster (E) isn't moyst (F) enough to pour into the mold (G).
B. Ⓔ ● Ⓖ Ⓗ (NONE)

1. Use powder (A) to avoid (B) ouly (C) skin.
1. Ⓐ Ⓑ ● Ⓓ (NONE)

2. The museum (E) exibit (F) included a pulley (G).
2. Ⓔ ● Ⓖ Ⓗ (NONE)

3. It's curious (A) to see royalty (B) bounce their checks (C).
3. Ⓐ Ⓑ Ⓒ ● (NONE)

4. The pure (E) marble statchew (F) is a masterpiece (G).
4. Ⓔ ● Ⓖ Ⓗ (NONE)

5. The professional (A) had soot (B) wedjed (C) into his collar.
5. Ⓐ Ⓑ ● Ⓓ (NONE)

6. The tour (E) guide led us to the museeum (F) exhibit (G).
6. Ⓔ ● Ⓖ Ⓗ (NONE)

7. The crunsh (A) of the rotting (B) apple had a harsh (C) sound.
7. ● Ⓑ Ⓒ Ⓓ (NONE)

8. Try to avoyd (E) mixing rotting (F) fruit in the batch (G).
8. ● Ⓕ Ⓖ Ⓗ (NONE)

9. I can whittle (A) curious (B) designs and have them magnifyed (C).
9. Ⓐ Ⓑ ● Ⓓ (NONE)

10. On a tour (E) of the theater (F) I saw seating for royalte (G).
10. Ⓔ Ⓕ ● Ⓗ (NONE)

11. Freed (A) prisoners emptied (B) their cells in the harsh (C) jail.
11. Ⓐ Ⓑ Ⓒ ● (NONE)

Name____________________ Date__________

Grade 4/Unit 3 Review Test

12. He emptyed (E) an account to avoid (F) having a check bounce (G).
12. ● Ⓕ Ⓖ Ⓗ (NONE)

13. We will powdir (A) the batch (B) of cookies with pure (C) sugar.
13. ● Ⓑ Ⓒ Ⓓ (NONE)

14. During the theatir (E) tour (F), they will use a pulley (G).
14. ● Ⓕ Ⓖ Ⓗ (NONE)

15. He will wittle (A) a wood statue (B) and give it to royalty (C).
15. ● Ⓑ Ⓒ Ⓓ (NONE)

16. The soot (E) looks like powder (F) when magnified (G).
16. Ⓔ Ⓕ Ⓖ ● (NONE)

17. The professional (A) freed (B) up his time for a masterpeice (C).
17. Ⓐ Ⓑ ● Ⓓ (NONE)

18. He wedged (E) the roting (F) oily (G) board in the corner.
18. Ⓔ ● Ⓖ Ⓗ (NONE)

19. The crunch (A) became magnified (B) with each dropped bache (C).
19. Ⓐ Ⓑ ● Ⓓ (NONE)

20. A profesional (E) will set up the museum (F) exhibit (G).
20. ● Ⓕ Ⓖ Ⓗ (NONE)

21. The statue (A) in the theater (B) is a masterpiece (C).
21. Ⓐ Ⓑ Ⓒ ● (NONE)

22. He would whittle (E) the wedged (F) stick until he was freeed (G).
22. Ⓔ Ⓕ ● Ⓗ (NONE)

23. She heard a harsh (A) crunch (B) and a cureous (C) bang.
23. Ⓐ Ⓑ ● Ⓓ (NONE)

24. He emptied (E) the box and saw a pulley (F) bounce (G) out.
24. Ⓔ Ⓕ Ⓖ ● (NONE)

25. We saw soot (A) and oily (B) spots on the pur (C) white floor.
25. Ⓐ Ⓑ ● Ⓓ (NONE)

Judgments and Decisions

TESTED OBJECTIVES **Students will list criteria in making judgments and decisions. They will participate in a debate to support a position on an assigned topic.**

Alternate Activities

Visual

REPORT CARDS

ONE **Materials:** construction paper, markers

Students will make a report card to record judgments about a literary character.

- Have students select a character from a story they have recently read. Ask them to design a report card to evaluate the character's traits or actions in the story. For example, students might want to rate the character's honesty, cooperation, kindness, and self-control, as well as decisions the character made.
- Have students develop a rating scale for the report card. Instruct them to back up their comments with story quotes and examples that support the assigned rating.

▶ **Linguistic**

Kinesthetic

THINK-ABOUT-IT SKIT

GROUP Students will create and perform skits that focus on criteria used to make a decision.

- Lead students in a discussion about decisions made by literary characters they have recently read about. Encourage students to talk about broad questions people can ask when making a decision about something, such as *How will this affect me? How will this affect others?*
- Organize students into small groups. Have them work together to present a skit, a rap, or another kind of musical presentation to help students as they make judgments and decisions. Suggest that they focus on the kinds of questions they can ask as they prepare to make decisions.

▶ **Bodily/Kinesthetic**

Auditory

DEBATE

GROUP Students will participate in debate teams on current issues.

- Organize students into teams. Have two teams debate topics of current interest to students, such as year-round school, the protection of rain forests, or students wearing uniforms. Assign each team a position to defend.
- Allow students time to work together to prepare for the debate. Then have each side present its position.
- Ask audience members whether the debates changed their thinking on an issue.

▶ **Interpersonal**

See Reteach 75, 79, 94, 103

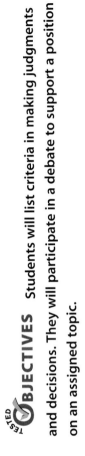

Graphic Aids

TESTED OBJECTIVES **Students will use, create, and explain the following graphic aids: diagrams, flow charts, and maps.**

Alternate Activities

Visual

RELIEF MAP

GROUP **Materials:** modeling dough or clay, cardboard, paints, markers.

Students will use modeling dough to make a relief map.

- Organize students into small groups. Have each group select an area to create a map of. You may wish to suggest that students map a part of the city, state, or geographic region in which you live. Or they might choose a fictional land from literature, or from their own imagination.
- Provide students with modeling dough or clay.
- Have students create their maps. When the maps have dried, encourage students to add details by painting or drawing.

▶ **Spatial**

Kinesthetic

HOOP DIAGRAMS

PARTNERS **Materials:** two large plastic play hoops

Have students use hoops to create a Venn diagram they can stand in.

- Show students how to overlap the hoops to create a Venn diagram on the floor. Have students use the diagram to make comparisons. Suggest that they arrange word cards, objects, pictures, or even people to make their comparisons.
- Have pairs present their comparisons to the group.

▶ **Bodily/Kinesthetic**

Auditory

TALK IT THROUGH

ONE **Materials:** magazines, reference materials

Students will explain how to use and create specific types of graphic aids.

- Have each student look through printed materials to select a graphic aid, such as a diagram, a flow chart, or a map, to share with classmates.
- Encourage students to take turns presenting their graphic aids to a small group. Suggest that they explain how to use the graphic aid, and to tell how to create a similar one.

▶ **Linguistic**

See Reteach 78, 85, 92, 99, 106

Summarize

TESTED OBJECTIVES **Students will create story summaries through art, movement, and games.**

Alternate Activities

Visual

SUMMARY ARTWORKS

ONE **Materials:** art materials, such as paper, paints, markers, scissors, glue

Students will create a written summary in a format that relates to the story.

- Remind students that a summary tells the main points of a story.

WRITING Have students select a story and write a brief summary of it. Encourage them to incorporate their summaries into artwork that relates in some way to the content of the story. For example, the summary could be written on a menu, a headband, or a drawing of a T-shirt.

▶ **Intrapersonal**

Auditory

JEOPARDY SUMMARIES

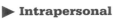

PARTNERS **Materials:** index cards, marker, poster board, masking tape

Students will write summaries of familiar stories and compile them into a simulation of a television game show.

- Organize students into pairs. Assign pairs several familiar stories, such as classic literature, to summarize. Have them write their summaries in several sentences on index cards.
- Compile partners' cards. Attach them face down to the poster board to create a game board.
- Have students play a game similar to *Jeopardy*. Have them choose a card. Read the summary. Have students respond with *What is* (story title)?

▶ **Logical/Mathematical**

Kinesthetic

SUMMARY COMMERCIALS

PARTNERS Students will act out an advertisement for a book by creating a summary of the story.

- Organize students into pairs. Have partners select a book to summarize and discuss.
- Ask partners to dramatize their summary to create a commercial for the book.

▶ **Bodily/Kinesthetic**

See Reteach 80, 87, 101

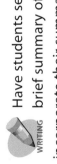

Suffixes *-ful, -ous*

OBJECTIVES **Students will use words with suffixes *-ful* and *-ous* in activities and games.**

Alternate Activities

Kinesthetic

SUFFIX CARD GAME

PARTNERS **Materials:** index cards, markers

Students will play a card game to form words with the suffixes *-ful*, *-ous*

- Prepare word cards for the base words *care, mind, play, poison, joy, nerve,* and for the suffixes *-ful* and *-ous*.
- Organize students into pairs. Have pairs place the base-word cards face down in one area and the suffix cards face down in another area. Have them take turns turning over a card from each area to see if they can make a word with a suffix. Remind students that base words can undergo spelling changes when *-ous* is added.

  ▶ **Linguistic**

Auditory

SUFFIX BINGO

GROUP **Materials:** blank Bingo grids

Students will play Bingo using words with the suffixes *-ful* and *-ous*.

- On the board or word wall, display words that have the suffixes *-ful* and *-ous*.
- Give students blank Bingo grids. Ask them to fill in the grids with words from the board or word wall.
- Invite students to play Bingo. Instead of calling out the word, call out the word's meaning. For example, say *full of joy* or *in a boasting way*.

  ▶ **Interpersonal**

Visual

CROSSWORD PUZZLERS

ONE **Materials:** paper, pencils

Students will create a crossword puzzle for a classmate to solve, featuring words with suffixes *-ful*, *-ous*.

- Refer students to a list of words with the suffixes *-ful* and *-ous*. Have each student create, using words from the list, a crossword puzzle that contains at least three words going down and three across. Instruct them to write clues for the puzzle.
- Have students switch puzzles and solve them.

  ▶ **Logical/Mathematical**

See Reteach 81, 88, 109

Fact and Opinion

TESTED OBJECTIVES **Students will practice making statements that are either fact or opinion. They will listen to classmates to distinguish whether statements are fact or opinion.**

Alternate Activities

Kinesthetic

FACT/OPINION RACE

GROUP

Students will move along a path as they listen to facts. They will stop when they hear opinions.

- Remind students about the differences between facts and opinions. Have students list several words or phrases that serve as signals for opinions, such as *I think, my favorite*, and so on.
- Organize students into small groups and take them outdoors. Have students take turns being the speaker and the racers. Racers move along a designated path when the speaker tells facts. Racers stop when the speaker states an opinion.

▶ **Bodily/Kinesthetic**

Visual

TELEGRAMS TO TELL

ONE

Materials: paper, colored pens

Students will write telegrams that include facts and opinions.

- Have students brainstorm occasions to send a telegram. Ask them to pretend to write a telegram. Instruct them to include in the telegram several facts and several opinions, using different colors of ink to distinguish the two.
- Invite partners to read one another's telegrams.

▶ **Linguistic**

Auditory

SPINNER GAME

GROUP

Materials: paper plates, construction paper, scissors, paper fasteners

Students will use spinners to guide them to give facts or opinions about a topic.

- Organize students into small groups. Have each group create two spinners: a fact/opinion indicator and a topic selector. On the fact/opinion indicator, have students divide the plate in two, label each section *fact* or *opinion*, and attach an arrow. On the topic selector, have students divide the plate into eight sections; label each with a general topic, such as *food*, *sports*, *hobbies*, *books*; and attach an arrow.
- Have group members take turns spinning each spinner and making a statement that meets both criteria.

▶ **Interpersonal**

See Reteach 82, 86, 100

Context Clues

TESTED OBJECTIVES **Students will use context clues to figure out the meaning of unfamiliar words. They will assign meaning to nonsense words by using context.**

Alternate Activities

Auditory

NONSENSE IN CONTEXT

GROUP Read aloud the following example to students: *You can check out books at the pleal. You can read magazines and newspapers at a pleal. Sometimes you can see puppet shows or movies at a pleal. What is a pleal?*

- After students answer the question, focus on how they knew.
- Organize students into small groups. Have students take turns providing similar examples of a nonsense word in context to help group members figure it out.

▶ **Logical/Mathematical**

Kinesthetic

DIRECTIONS GAME

PARTNERS **Materials:** index cards, marker

Have students use context clues to follow directions containing unfamiliar words.

- Prepare a set of task cards for students that contain unfamiliar words supported by context clues. For example, you might ask students to hang up any *apparel* on the closet floor.
- Organize students into pairs and have them use the context clues to read the cards and perform the tasks.

▶ **Bodily/Kinesthetic**

Visual

MASK NOUNS

GROUP **Materials:** chart paper, marker, self-stick notes

Students will use context to figure out missing nouns in a paragraph.

- On chart paper, write a paragraph about a topic of interest to students. Cover all the nouns with self-stick notes.
- Organize students into small groups. Have each group take a turn reading the paragraph silently, then using the context to predict each missing word. Have a volunteer remove the self-stick notes and read the missing words.
- Encourage students to explain how they were able to figure out the missing words.

▶ **Linguistic**

See Reteach 95, 102, 108

Author's Purpose and Point of View

TESTED **OBJECTIVES** **Students will identify author's purpose and the point of view that various stories are told from.**

Alternate Activities

Kinesthetic

POINT-OF-VIEW PEEK BOX

PARTNERS **Materials:** one shoe box per pair of students, construction paper, scissors, markers, glue

- Organize students into pairs. Have pairs select a story they have recently read. Encourage them to think about the point of view from which the story is told.
- Have students create a diorama of the story in a shoe box. Have students cut a hole in the lid to allow viewers to peek into the box.

WRITING Ask students to write a paragraph about the story, noting the point of view from which it is told. Have them glue the paragraph to the lid under the peek hole.

▶ **Bodily/Kinesthetic**

Visual

AUTHOR'S-PURPOSE BOOKMARKS

ONE **Materials:** construction paper, crayons or markers

Students will create a bookmark that details an author's purpose.

- Lead students in a discussion about a book or article in which the author's purpose is clear.
- Have students cut a piece of construction paper in half lengthwise. Have them fold it to create a bookmark.

WRITING Ask students to write on the bookmark a brief description of the author's purpose. Encourage them to include illustrations to enhance their bookmarks.

▶ **Spatial**

Auditory

POINT-OF-VIEW ID

GROUP Have students take turns telling brief stories and identifying the point of view.

- Organize students into small groups. Have students take turns telling brief stories or parts of stories.
- Ask listeners to identify the point of view from which the story was told and to give reasons for their choice.

▶ **Linguistic**

See Reteach 89, 93, 107

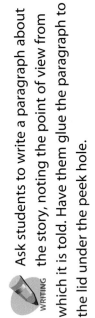

A Communication Tool

Although typewriters and computers are readily available, many situations continue to require handwriting. Tasks such as keeping journals, completing forms, taking notes, making shopping or organizational lists, and the ability to read handwritten manuscript or cursive writing are a few examples of practical application of this skill.

BEFORE YOU BEGIN

Before children begin to write, certain fine motor skills need to be developed. Examples of activities that can be used as warm-up activities are:

- **Simon Says** Play a game of Simon Says using just finger positions.
- **Finger Plays and Songs** Sing songs that use Signed English, American Sign Language or finger spelling.
- **Mazes** Mazes are available in a wide range of difficulty. You can also create mazes that allow children to move their writing instruments from left to right.

Determining Handedness

Keys to determining handedness in a child:

- Which hand does the child eat with? This is the hand that is likely to become the dominant hand.
- Does the child start coloring with one hand and then switch to the other? This may be due to fatigue rather than lack of hand preference.
- Does the child cross midline to pick things up or use the closest hand? Place items directly in front of the child to see if one hand is preferred.
- Does the child do better with one hand or the other?

The Mechanics of Writing

DESK AND CHAIR

- Chair height should allow for the feet to rest flat on the floor.
- Desk height should be two inches above the level of the elbows when the child is sitting.
- The chair should be pulled in allowing for an inch of space between the child's abdomen and the desk.
- Children sit erect with the elbows resting on the desk.
- Children should have models of letters on the desk or at eye level, not above their heads.

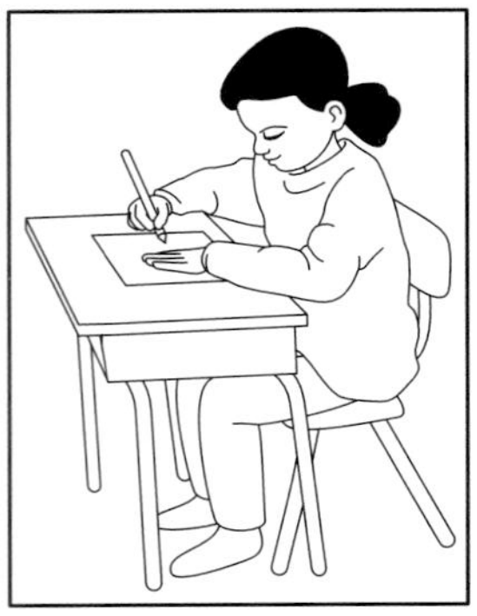

PAPER POSITION

- **Right-handed children** should turn the paper so that the lower left-hand corner of the paper points to the abdomen.

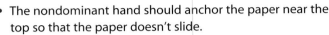

- **Left-handed children** should turn the paper so that the lower right-hand corner of the paper points to the abdomen.

- The nondominant hand should anchor the paper near the top so that the paper doesn't slide.
- The paper should be moved up as the child nears the bottom of the paper. Many children won't think of this and may let their arms hang off the desk when they reach the bottom of a page.

The Writing Instrument Grasp

For handwriting to be functional, the writing instrument must be held in a way that allows for fluid dynamic movement.

FUNCTIONAL GRASP PATTERNS

- **Tripod Grasp** With open web space, the writing instrument is held with the tip of the thumb and the index finger and rests against the side of the third finger. The thumb and index finger form a circle.

- **Quadrupod Grasp** With open web space, the writing instrument is held with the tip of the thumb and index finger and rests against the fourth finger. The thumb and index finger form a circle.

INCORRECT GRASP PATTERNS

- **Fisted Grasp** The writing instrument is held in a fisted hand.

- **Pronated Grasp** The writing instrument is held diagonally within the hand with the tips of the thumb and index finger on the writing instrument but with no support from other fingers.

- **Five-Finger Grasp** The writing instrument is held with the tips of all five fingers.

TO CORRECT WRITING INSTRUMENT GRASPS

- Have children play counting games with an eye dropper and water.
- Have children pick up small objects with a tweezer.
- Do counting games with children picking up small coins using just the thumb and index finger.

FLEXED OR HOOKED WRIST

- The writing instrument can be held in a variety of grasps with the wrist flexed or bent. This is typically seen with left-handed writers but is also present in some right-handed writers. To correct wrist position, have children check their writing posture and paper placement.

Evaluation Checklist

Functional writing is made up of two elements, legibility and functional speed.

LEGIBILITY

MANUSCRIPT

Formation and Strokes

- ☑ Does the child begin letters at the top?
- ☑ Do circles close?
- ☑ Are the horizontal lines straight?
- ☑ Do circular shapes and extender and descender lines touch?
- ☑ Are the heights of all upper-case letters equal?
- ☑ Are the heights of all lower-case letters equal?
- ☑ Are the lengths of the extenders and descenders the same for all letters?

Directionality

- ☑ Are letters and words formed from left to right?
- ☑ Are letters and words formed from top to bottom?

Spacing

- ☑ Are the spaces between letters equidistant?
- ☑ Are the spaces between words equidistant?
- ☑ Do the letters rest on the line?
- ☑ Are the top, bottom and side margins even?

CURSIVE

Formation and Strokes

- ☑ Do circular shapes close?
- ☑ Are the downstrokes parallel?
- ☑ Do circular shapes and downstroke lines touch?
- ☑ Are the heights of all upper-case letters equal?
- ☑ Are the heights of all lower-case letters equal?
- ☑ Are the lengths of the extenders and descenders the same for all letters?
- ☑ Do the letters which finish at the top join the next letter? (*b, o, v, w*)
- ☑ Do the letters which finish at the bottom join the next letter? (*a, c, d, h, i, k, l, m, n, r, s, t, u, x*)
- ☑ Do letters with descenders join the next letter? (*f, g, j, p, q, y, z*)
- ☑ Do all letters touch the line?
- ☑ Is the vertical slant of all letters consistent?

Directionality

- ☑ Are letters and words formed from left to right?
- ☑ Are letters and words formed from top to bottom?

Spacing

- ☑ Are the spaces between letters equidistant?
- ☑ Are the spaces between words equidistant?
- ☑ Do the letters rest on the line?
- ☑ Are the top, bottom and side margins even?

SPEED

The prettiest handwriting is not functional for classroom work if it takes the child three times longer than the rest of the class to complete work assignments. After the children have been introduced to writing individual letters, begin to add time limitations to the completion of copying or writing assignments. Then check the child's work for legibility.

Handwriting Models—Manuscript

A B C D E F G H

I J K L M N O P

Q R S T U V W

X Y Z

a b c d e f g h

i j k l m n o p

q r s t u v w

x y z

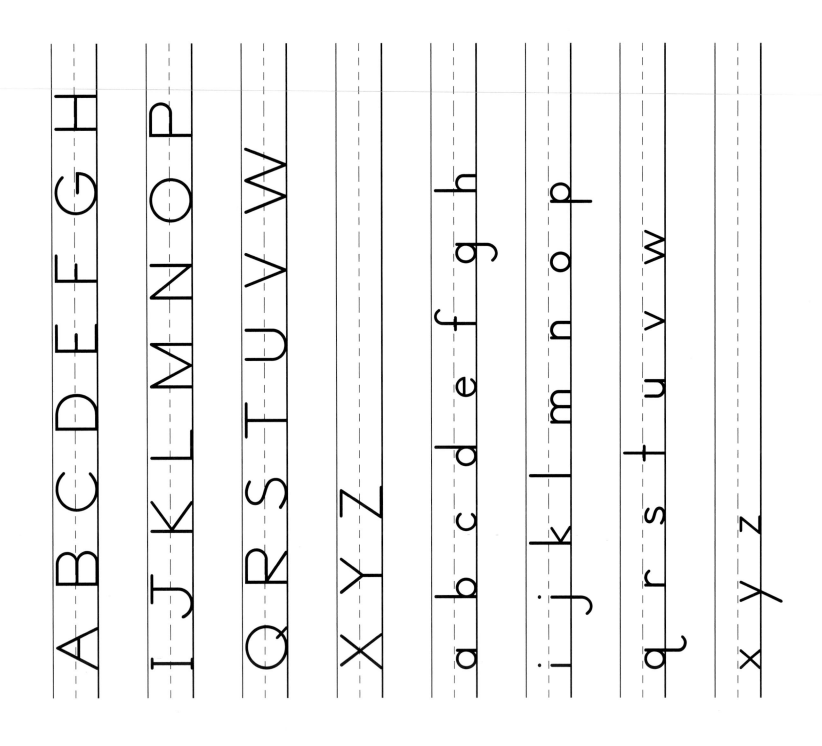

Handwriting Models—Cursive

A B C D E F G H I

J K L M N O P Q R

S T U V W X Y Z

a b c d e f g h i j

k l m n o p q r s

t u v w x y z

Handwriting Models—Slant

A B C D E F G H

I J K L M N O P

Q R S T U V W

X Y Z

a b c d e f g h

i j k l m n o p

q r s t u v w

x y z

Handwriting Practice

Selection Titles	Honors, Prizes, and Awards
TO Unit 1, p. 16 by ***Lee Bennett Hopkins***	**Poet: Lee Bennett Hopkins,** winner of Golden Kite Honor Book Award (1995), Christopher Award (1996) for *Been to Yesterday: Poems of a Life*
THE LOST LAKE Unit 1, p. 20 by ***Allen Say***	**Author/Illustrator: Allen Say,** winner of Christopher Award (1985) for *How My Parents Learned to Eat*; Boston Globe-Horn Book Award (1988), Caldecott Honor, ALA Notable (1989) for *The Boy of the Three-Year Nap*; Caldecott Medal, Boston Globe-Horn Book Award, ALA Notable, New York Times Best Illustrated (1994) for *Grandfather's Journey*
AMELIA'S ROAD Unit 1, p. 44 by ***Linda Jacobs Altman*** Illustrated by ***Enrique O. Sanchez***	**Illustrator: Enrique O. Sanchez,** winner of Parent's Choice Award (1993) for *Abuela's Weave*
SARAH, PLAIN AND TALL Unit 1, p. 68 by ***Patricia MacLachlan*** Illustrated by ***Burton Silverman***	**Golden Kite Award for Fiction, IRA-CBC Children's Choice, School Library Best of the Best (1985), Newbery Medal, Christopher Award, Scott O'Dell Historical Fiction Award (1986)**
SEAL JOURNEY Unit 1, p. 96 by ***Richard and Jonah Sobol*** Photographs by ***Richard Sobol***	**Outstanding Science Trade Book for Children (1994)**
JUSTIN AND THE BEST BISCUITS IN THE WORLD Unit 2, p. 134 by ***Mildred Pitts Walter*** Illustrated by ***Floyd Cooper***	**Coretta Scott King Award (1987)** **Illustrator: Floyd Cooper,** winner of Coretta Scott King Honor (1995) for *Meet Danitra Brown*
JUST A DREAM Unit 2, p. 160 by ***Chris Van Allsburg***	**Author/Illustrator: Chris Van Allsburg,** winner of ALA Notable, Caldecott Medal (1982) for *Jumanji*; ALA Notable (1984) for *The Wreck of the* Zephyr; ALA Notable, Boston Globe-Horn Book Honor, Caldecott Medal (1986) for *The Polar Express*; NSTA Outstanding Science Trade Book for Children (1988), IRA-CBC Children's Choice (1989) for *Two Bad Ants*; ALA Notable (1994) for *The Sweetest Fig*

Selection Titles	Honors, Prizes, and Awards
LEAH'S PONY Unit 2, p. 192 by ***Elizabeth Friedrich*** Illustrated by ***Michael Garland***	**National Council of Trade Books Award, Golden Kite Award, Parent's Magazine Best Book of the Year, IRA Teacher's Choice Award (1997), Texas Bluebonnet Award (1997-98)**
BASEBALL SAVED US Unit 2, p. 218 by ***Ken Mochizuki*** Illustrated by ***Dom Lee***	**Parent's Choice Award (1993)**
THE HATMAKER'S SIGN Unit 3, p. 258 by ***Candace Fleming*** Illustrated by ***Robert Andrew Parker***	**Illustrator: Robert Andrew Parker,** winner of Caldecott Honor (1970) for *Pop Corn and Ma Goodness*
PAT CUMMINGS: MY STORY Unit 3, p. 284 by ***Pat Cummings***	**Boston Globe-Horn Book Award (1992), ALA Notable (1993)**
GRASS SANDALS: THE TRAVELS OF BASHO Unit 3, p. 300 by ***Dawnine Spivak*** Illustrated by ***Demi***	**National Council of Trade Books Award (1998)** **Illustrator: Demi,** winner of the New York Times Best Illustrated Children's Books of the Year (1985) for *The Nightingale*
A PLACE CALLED FREEDOM Unit 3, p. 334 by ***Scott Russell Sanders*** Illustrated by ***Thomas B. Allen***	**Notable Children's Book in the Field of Social Studies (1998)**
FINAL CURVE Unit 4, p. 372 by ***Langston Hughes***	**Poet: Langston Hughes,** winner of Witter Bynner Prize (1926); Harmon Foundation Literature Award (1931); Guggenheim Fellowship (1935); American Academy of Arts and Letters Grant (1946); Spingarn Medal (1960)

Selection Titles	Honors, Prizes, and Awards
SCRUFFY Unit 4, p. 376 by ***Jim Brandenburg***	**Author/Photographer: Jim Brandenburg,** winner ALA Best Book for Young Adults Award, Orbis Picture Award for Outstanding Non-fiction Honor Book, Minnesota Book Award (1994) for *To the Top of the World: Adventures with Arctic Wolves*; Parent's Choice Award, Outstanding Science Trade Book for Children, John Burroughs List of Outstanding Nature Books for Children (1995) for *Sand and Fog: Adventures in South Africa*; ALA Best Book for Young Adults (1996) for *An American Safari: Adventures on the North American Prairie*
GLUSKABE AND THE SNOW BIRD Unit 4, p. 408 by ***Joseph Bruchac*** Illustrated by ***Stefano Vitale***	**Author: Joseph Bruchac,** winner of the Skipping Stones Honor Award for Multicultural Children's Literature (1997) for *Four Ancestors*
ON THE BUS WITH JOANNA COLE Unit 4, p. 446 by ***Joanna Cole with Wendy Saul***	**Author: Joanna Cole,** winner of Washington Children's Choice Picture Book Award, Colorado Children's Book Award (1989) for *The Magic School Bus at the Waterworks*; Parenting's Reading Magic Awards (1989) for *The Magic School Bus Inside the Human Body*
TORTILLAS LIKE AFRICA Unit 4, p. 482 by ***Gary Soto***	**Poet: Gary Soto,** winner of Academy of American Poets Award (1975); American Book Award (1984) for *Living Up the Street*; California Library Association's John And Patricia Beatty Award, Best Books for Young Adults Awards (1991) for *Baseball in April and Other Stories*; Americás Book Award, Honorable Mention (1995) for *Chato's Kitchen*; Americás Book Award, Commended List (1995) for *Canto Familiar*; (1996) for *The Old Man and His Door*; (1997) for *Buried Onions*
HOW TO TELL THE TOP OF A HILL Unit 5, p. 484 by ***John Ciardi***	**Poet: John Ciardi,** winner of New York Times Best Illustrated Children's Books of the Year (1959) for *The Reason for the Pelican*; (1960) for *Scruffy The Pup*; (1966) for *The Monster Den: Or, Look What Happened at My House—and to It*; ALA Best Book Award (1961) for *I Met a Man*; (1963) for *John Plenty and Fiddler Dan: A New Fable of the Grasshopper and the Ant*; National Council of Teachers of English Award for Excellence in Poetry for Children (1982)

Selection Titles	Honors, Prizes, and Awards
MOM'S BEST FRIEND Unit 5, p. 518 by ***Sally Hobart Alexander*** Photographs by ***George Ancona***	**Author: Sally Hobart Alexander**, winner of Christopher Award (1995) for *Taking Hold: My Journey Into Blindness*
YEH-SHEN Unit 5, p. 570 retold by **Ai-Ling Louie** Illustrated by **Ed Young**	**ALA Notable, School Library Journal Best Books of the Year (1982), Boston Globe-Horn Book Honor (1983)** **Illustrator: Ed Young,** winner of Caldecott Honor (1968) for *The Emperor and the Kite*; Boston Globe-Horn Book Honor (1984) for *The Double Life of Pocahontas*; NCSS Notable Children's Book Award (1989), Caldecott Medal, Boston Globe-Horn Book Award, ALA Notable (1990) for *Lon Po Po*; ALA Notable (1991) for *Mice Are Nice*; ALA Notable (1992) for *All Of You Was Singing*; ALA Notable, Boston Globe-Horn Book Award, Caldecott Honor (1993) for *Seven Blind Mice;* ALA Notable (1994) for *Sadako*; National Council for Social Studies Notable Children's Book Awards (1998) for *Genesis* and *Voices of the Heart*
TEAMMATES Unit 6, p. 616 by ***Peter Golenbock*** Illustrated by **Paul Bacon**	**Author: Peter Golenbock,** winner of National Council of Trade Books in Social Studies Award; Redbook Children's Picture Book Award (1990)
THE MALACHITE PALACE Unit 6, p. 634 by ***Alma Flor Ada*** Illustrated by ***Leonid Gore***	**Author: Alma Flor Ada,** winner of Christopher Award (1992) for *The Gold Coin*
WHALES Unit 6, p. 694 by ***Seymour Simon***	**Author: Seymour Simon,** winner of ALA Notable (1985) for *Moon*; (1986) for *Saturn*; (1987) for *Mars*; (1993) for *Our Solar System* and *Snakes*; Texas Blue Bonnet Master List (1996–97) for *Sharks*; NSTA Outstanding Science Tradebook for Children (1997) for *The Heart*
DECISIONS Unit 6, p. 724 by ***Angela Shelf Medearis***	**Poet: Angela Shelf Medearis,** winner IRA-Teacher's Choice Award, Primary Grades (1995) for *Our People*

Trade Books

Additional fiction and nonfiction trade books related to each selection can be shared with students throughout the unit.

The Hatmaker's Sign

Sybil Ludington's Midnight Ride
Marsha Amstel, illustrated by Ellen Beier (First Avenue Editions, 2000)

The story of a how a heroine of the American Revolution embarks on a perilous mission to save a town from the onslaught of British troops. *Historical Fiction*

Yours Truly, Goldilocks
Alma Flor Ada, illustrated by Leslie Tryon (Atheneum, 1998)

Familiar fairy-tale characters come to life through their exchange of letters. *Fiction*

Coming Home: From the Life of Langston Hughes
Floyd Cooper (Philomel Books, 1994)

The poignant story of how a poet was born from the loneliness of childhood and how Langston Hughes discovered "home" inside himself. *Biography*

Pat Cummings: My Story

If You Were a Writer
Joan Lowery Nixon, illustrated by Bruce Degen (Simon & Schuster, 1995)

The various aspects of writing are explored when Melia decides she wants to be a writer like her mother. *Poetry*

What Do Illustrators Do?
Eileen Christelow (Houghton Mifflin, 1999)

A humorous behind-the-scenes look at two illustrators working on two different picture-book editions of the same story. *Informational Story*

Talking With Artists – Volume 2
Pat Cummings (Simon & Schuster, 1997)

Thirteen well-known illustrators of children's books introduce themselves, their art, and their workplaces. *Biography*

Technology

Multimedia resources can be used to enhance students' understanding of the selections.

The Hatmaker's Sign

Declaration of Independence (Phoenix/BFA) Video, 9 min. A depiction of the debate that took place over changes in the wording of the Declaration of Independence.

The Declaration of Independence: A Foundation of Ideas for a New Age (SVE/Churchill) Video, 24 min. A look at the principles, words, and ideas of the writers of the Declaration of Independence.

Jean Fritz: Six Revolutionary War Figures (AIMS) Video, 13 min. An introduction to the ideas of, and impact made by, six famous Americans.

Pat Cummings: My Story

Ultimate Writing & Creativity Center (SVE/Churchill) CD-ROM. Guides students through the writing process.

Let's Write a Story! (Second Edition) (SVE/Churchill) Video, 11 min. Inspires young writers by having them write vivid phrases, sentences, and then a complete story.

Creative Writing: What's Riding Hood Without the Wolf? (SVE/Churchill) Video, 13 min. Learn why obstacles are necessary for a good plot.

TIME FOR KIDS

Grass Sandals

Gabriella's Song
Candace Fleming, illustrated by Giselle Potter (Atheneum, 1997)

A great symphony begins when the tune young Gabriella hums passes through many people and finally reaches a composer. *Fiction*

Life Around the Lake: Embroideries by the Women of Lake Patzcuaro
Maricel E. Presilla (Henry Holt, 1996)

A unique method of cultural preservation practiced by the Tarascan people of Central Mexico. *Nonfiction*

Cool Melons—Turn to Frogs! The Life and Poems of Issa
Matthew Gollub, illustrated by Kazuko G. Stone and Keiko Smith (Lee & Low, 1998)

The life of Japanese poet Issa is honored in this illustrated biography featuring thirty-three of his haiku poems. *Biography*

Poetry in a Nutshell (SVE/Churchill) CD-ROM. This CD-ROM introduces the work of leading American, Canadian, and British poets and offers lessons about poetry.

Haiku (AIMS/Pied Piper) Video or filmstrip, 12 min. An introduction to the poetry of Issa, Shiki, and Basho.

T Shapes a Poem Can Take: Different Types of Poetry (SVE/Churchill) Video, 17 min. Covers various poetic forms and shows how a change in form affects meaning.

A Place Called Freedom

Appalachia: The Voices of Sleeping Birds
Cynthia Rylant, illustrated by Barry Moser (Harcourt Brace, 1991)

A poetic recollection of the author's homeland, with full-color portraits of the people living there. *Poetry*

Abraham's Battle
Sara Harrell Banks (Atheneum, 1999)

Abraham, an ex-slave living in Gettysburg, meets a young Confederate soldier during the Civil War. The two have a conversation about war and slavery, and Abraham tries to save the injured soldier's life. *Historical Fiction*

Dear Dr. King: Today's Children Write to Dr. Martin Luther King, Jr.
Jan Colbert and Ann McMillan Harms (Disney Pr., Juvenile Trade, 1998)

Thought-provoking letters to Dr. King by contemporary children, with photographs that illustrate the civil rights movement then and now. *Nonfiction*

African American History: Heroism, Struggle and Hope (ESI) CD-ROM, Macintosh, Windows. An introduction to African American history from pre-slavery to the present.

Fighters for Freedom, Black Heroes Series (SVE/Churchill) Filmstrip, 7 min., Video, 20 min. The story of black freedom fighters, cowboys, settlers, and other African American heroes.

Heritage of the Black West (National Geographic Society) Video, 25 min. This award-winning film describes how African Americans shaped the expansion of the American West.

Twisted Trails

Citymaze! A Collection of City Mazes
Wendy Madgwick, illustrated by Don Courtney (Millbrook Press, 1995)

A tour of some of the most beautiful mazes in the world, with solutions to the mazes at the back of the book. *Nonfiction*

Junior Garden Book
Felder Rushing (Meredith Books, 1999)

This guide features an easy-to-follow, step-by-step approach to more than forty garden projects for kids, with fun, zany illustrations. *Nonfiction*

Now You See It, Now You Don't
Seymour Simon, illustrated by Constance Ftera (Morrow Junior Books, 1998)

Students will enjoy reading about and viewing the amazing world of optical illusions. *Nonfiction*

Picture Puzzle (National Geographic Society) CD-ROM, Macintosh, Windows. An interactive exploration of puzzles and pictures.

Refraction and Reflection (SVE/Churchill) Video, 24 min. Decribes the properties of light and explains some optical illusions.

Asking the Right Questions (SVE/Churchill) Video, 15 min. Explains how to narrow questions for research and inquiry.

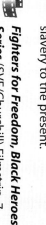

Publishers Directory

Aladdin Paperbacks
(Imprint of Simon & Schuster Children's Publishing)

Annick Press
(Imprint of Firefly, Ltd.)

Atheneum
(Imprint of Simon & Schuster Children's Publishing)

Avon Books
(Division of Hearst Corp.)
1350 Ave. of the Americas
New York, NY 10019
(212) 261-6800 • (800) 238-0658
Fax (800) 223-0239
www.avonbooks.com

Bantam Doubleday Dell Books for Young Readers
(Imprint of Random House)

Beech Tree Books
(Imprint of William Morrow & Co.)

Blackbirch Press
260 Amity Road
Woodbridge, CT 06525
(203) 387-7525 • (800) 831-9183
www.blackbirch.com

Blue Sky Press
(Imprint of Scholastic)

Bradbury Press
(Imprint of Simon & Schuster Children's Publishing)

BridgeWater Books
(Distributed by Penguin Putnam Inc.)

Candlewick Press
2067 Massachusetts Avenue
Cambridge, MA 02140
(617) 661-3330 • Fax (617) 661-0565
www.candlewick.com

Carolrhoda Books
(Division of Lerner Publications Co.)

Cartwheel Books
(Imprint of Scholastic)

Charlesbridge Publishing Inc.
85 Main Street
Watertown, MA 02472
(617) 926-0329 • (800) 225-3214
Fax (617) 926-5720
www.charlesbridge.com

Children's Book Press
246 First St., Suite 101
San Francisco, CA 94105
(415) 995-2200 • Fax (415) 995-2222

Children's Press (Division of Grolier, Inc.)
P.O. Box 1795
Danbury, CT 06816-1333
(800) 621-1115 • www.grolier.com

Chronicle Books
85 Second Street, Sixth Floor
San Francisco, CA 94105
(415) 537-3730 • Fax (415) 537-4460
(800) 722-6657
www.chroniclebooks.com

Clarion Books
(Imprint of Houghton Mifflin, Inc.)
215 Park Avenue South
New York, NY 10003
(212) 420-5800 • (800) 225-3362
www.houghtonmifflinbooks.com/clarion

Crabtree Publishing Co.
350 Fifth Ave., Suite 3308
New York, NY 10118
(212) 496-5040 • (800) 387-7650
Fax (800) 355-7166
www.crabtree-pub.com

Crowell (Imprint of HarperCollins)

Crown Publishing Group
(Imprint of Random House)

Delacorte
(Imprint of Random House)

Dial Books
(Imprint of Penguin Putnam Inc.)

Discovery Enterprises, Ltd.
31 Laurelwood Dr.
Carlisle, MA 01741
(978) 287-5401 • (800) 729-1720
Fax (978) 287-5402

Disney Press
(Division of Disney Book Publishing, Inc., A Walt Disney Co.)
114 Fifth Ave.
New York, NY 10011
(212) 633-4400 • Fax (212) 633-4833
www.disneybooks.com

Dorling Kindersley (DK Publishing)
95 Madison Avenue
New York, NY 10016
(212) 213-4800 • Fax (212) 213-5290
(888) 342-5357 • www.dk.com

Doubleday (Imprint of Random House)

E. P. Dutton Children's Books
(Imprint of Penguin Putnam Inc.)

Farrar, Straus and Giroux
19 Union Square West
New York, NY 10003
(212) 741-6900 • Fax (212) 741-6973
(888) 330-8477

Firefly Books, Ltd.
PO Box 1338
Endicott Station
Buffalo, NY 14205
(416) 499-8412 • Fax (800) 565-6034
(800) 387-5085
www.firefly.com

First Avenue Editions
(Imprint of Lerner Publishing Group)

Four Winds Press
(Imprint of Macmillan, see Simon & Schuster Children's Publishing)

Franklin Watts, Inc.
Affiliate of Grolier Company
90 Sherman Turnpike
Danbury, CT 06816
(203) 797-3500 • Fax (203) 797-6986
www.publishing.grolier.com

Greenwillow Books
(Imprint of William Morrow & Co, Inc.)

Gulliver Green Books
(Imprint of Harcourt Brace & Co.)

Harcourt Brace & Co.
6277 Sea Harbor Drive
Orlando, FL 32887
(407) 345-2000 • (800) 225-5425

Harper & Row (Imprint of HarperCollins)

HarperCollins Children's Books
1350 Avenue of the Americas
New York, NY 10019
(212) 261-6500 • Fax (212) 261-6689
(800) 242-7737
www.harperchildrens.com

Harper Trophy
(Imprint of HarperCollins)

Holiday House
425 Madison Avenue
New York, NY 10017
(212) 688-0085 • Fax (212) 421-6134

Henry Holt and Company
115 West 18th Street
New York, NY 10011
(212) 886-9200 • (212) 633-0748
(888) 330-8477 • www.henryholt.com/byr/

Houghton Mifflin
222 Berkeley Street
Boston, MA 02116
(617) 351-5000 • Fax (617) 351-1125
(800) 225-3362
www.houghtonmifflinbooks.com

Hyperion Books
(Division of ABC, Inc.)
77 W. 66th Street, Eleventh Floor
New York, NY 10023
(212) 456-0100 • (800) 343-9204
www.disney.com

Just Us Books
356 Glenwood Avenue
E. Orange, NJ 07017
(973) 672-7701 • Fax (973) 677-7570
www.justusbooks.com

Kane/Miller Book Publishers
P.O. Box 310529
Brooklyn, NY 11231-0529
(718) 624-5120 • Fax (718) 858-5452
www.kanemiller.com

Alfred A. Knopf
(Imprint of Random House)

Lee & Low Books
95 Madison Avenue, Room 606
New York, NY 10016
(212) 779-4400 • Fax (212) 683-1894

Lerner Publications Co.
241 First Avenue North
Minneapolis, MN 55401
(612) 332-3344 • Fax (612) 332-7615
(800) 328-4929 • www.lernerbooks.com

Little, Brown & Co.
3 Center Plaza
Boston, MA 02108
(617) 227-0730 • Fax (617) 263-2864
(800) 759-0190 • www.littlebrown.com

Lothrop Lee & Shepard
(Imprint of William Morrow & Co.)

Macmillan
(Imprint of Simon & Schuster Children's Publishing)

McGraw-Hill Publishing Group
1221 Avenue of the Americas
New York, NY 10020
(212) 512-2000

Meredith Books
1615 Locust Street
Des Moines, IA 50309-3023
(505) 284-3000

Millbrook Press, Inc.
2 Old New Milford Road
Brookfield, CT 06804
(203) 740-2220 • (800) 462-4703
Fax (203) 740-2526
www.millbrookpress.com

Mindfull Publishing
177 W. Norfolk Road
Norfolk, CT 06850
(203) 831-0855 • Fax (203) 853-2943

William Morrow & Co.
(Imprint of HarperCollins)

Morrow Junior Books
(Imprint of HarperCollins)

National Geographic Society
1145 17th Street, NW
Washington, DC 20036
(800) 638-4077
www.nationalgeographic.com

Orchard Books (A Grolier Company)
95 Madison Avenue
New York, NY 10016
(212) 951-2600 • Fax (212) 213-6435
www.grolier.com

Penguin Putnam, Inc.
375 Hudson Street
New York, NY 10014
(212) 366-2000 • Fax (212) 366-2666
(800) 631-8571
www.penguinputnam.com

Philomel Books
(Imprint of Penguin Putnam, Inc.)

Pippin Press
Gracie Station, Box 1347
229 E. 85th Street
New York, NY 10028
(212) 288-4920 • Fax (732) 225-1562

Price Stern Sloan
(Imprint of Penguin Putnam, Inc.)

Puffin Books
(Imprint of Penguin Putnam, Inc.)

G.P. Putnam's Sons Publishing
(Imprint of Penguin Putnam, Inc.)

Random House
1540 Broadway
New York, NY 10036
(212) 782-9000 • Fax (212) 782-9452
(800) 200-3552
www.randomhouse.com/kids

Rising Moon
(Imprint of Northland Publishing)

Scholastic
555 Broadway
New York, NY 10012
(212) 343-7500 • Fax (212) 965-7442
(800) SCHOLASTIC • www.scholastic.com

Sierra Club Books for Children
85 Second Street, Second Floor
San Francisco, CA 94105-3441
(415) 977-5500 • Fax (415) 977-5793
(800) 935-1056
www.sierraclub.org/books

Silver Burdett Press
(Division of Pearson Education)
299 Jefferson Rd.
Parsippany, NJ 07054-0480
(973) 739-8000 • (800) 848-9500
www.sbgschool.com

Simon & Schuster Children's Books
1230 Avenue of the Americas
New York, NY 10020
(212) 698-7200 • (800) 223-2336
www.simonsays.com/kidzone

Sunburst
(Imprint of Farrar, Straus & Giroux)

Tricycle Press
(Division of Ten Speed Press)
P.O. Box 7123
Berkeley, CA 94707
(510) 559-1600 • (800) 841-2665
Fax (510) 559-1637
www.tenspeed.com

Viking Children's Books
(Imprint of Penguin Putnam Inc.)

Voyager
(Imprint of Harcourt Brace & Co.)

Walker & Co.
435 Hudson Street
New York, NY 10014
(212) 727-8300 • (212) 727-0984
(800) AT-WALKER

Watts Publishing
(Imprint of Grolier Publishing; see Children's Press)

Westcliffe Publishers, Inc.
2650 S. Zuni Street
Englewood, CO 80110-1145
(303) 935-0900 • (800) 523-3692

Yearling Books
(Imprint of Random House)

Multimedia Resources

AIMS Multimedia
9710 DeSoto Avenue
Chatsworth, CA 91311-4409
(800) 367-2467
www.AIMS-multimedia.com

Ambrose Video and Publishing
28 West 44th Street, Suite 2100
New York, NY 10036
(800) 526-4663 • Fax (212) 768-9282
www.AmbroseVideo.com

BFA Educational Media
(see Phoenix Learning Group)

Brittannica
310 South Michigan Avenue
Brittanica Center
Chicago, IL 60604-4293
(800) 621-3900 • Fax (800) 344-9624

Broderbund
(Parsons Technology;
also see The Learning Company)
500 Redwood Blvd.
Novato, CA 94997
(800) 474-8840 • www.broderbund.com

Carousel Film and Video
250 Fifth Avenue, Suite 204
New York, NY 10001
(212) 683-1660 • Fax (212) 683-1662
e-mail: carousel@pipeline.com

CBS/Fox Video
1330 Avenue of the Americas
New York, NY 10019
(800) 457-0686

Coronet/MTI
(see Phoenix Learning Group)

Direct Cinema, Ltd.
P.O. Box 10003
Santa Monica, CA 90410-1003
(800) 525-0000 • Fax (310) 396-3233

Encyclopaedia Britannica Educational Corp.
310 South Michigan Avenue
Chicago, IL 60604
(800) 554-9862 • www.eb.com

ESI/Educational Software Institute
4213 S. 94th Street
Omaha, NE 68127
(800) 955-5570 • Fax (402) 592-2071
www.edsoft.com

GPN/Reading Rainbow
University of Nebraska-Lincoln
P.O. Box 80669
Lincoln, NE 68501-0669
(800) 228-4630 • Fax (800) 306-2330
www.gpn.unl.edu

Hallmark Home Entertainment
6100 Wilshire Blvd.
Suite 1400
Los Angeles, CA 90048
(213) 634-3000 • Fax (213) 549-3760

LibraryVideo Company
P.O. Box 580
Wynnewood, PA 19096
(800) 843-3620 • Fax (610) 645-4040

Listening Library
A subsidiary of Random House
One Park Avenue
Greenwich, CT 06870-1727
(800) 243-4504 • www.listeninglib.com

Macmillan/McGraw-Hill
(see SRA/McGraw-Hill)

Marshmedia
P.O. Box 8082
Shawnee Mission, KS 66208
(800) 821-3303 • Fax (816) 333-7421
www.marshmedia.com

MECC
(see The Learning Company)

National Geographic Society Educational Services
P.O. Box 10597
Des Moines, IA 50340-0597
(800) 368-2728 • Fax (515) 362-3366
www.nationalgeographic.com/education

PBS Video
1320 Braddock Place
Alexandria, VA 22314
(800) 344-3337 • www.pbs.org

Phoenix/BFA Films and Videos
(see Phoenix Learning Group)

The Phoenix Learning Group
Phoenix/BFA Films & Video
2348 Chaffee Drive
St. Louis, MO 63146
(800) 221-1274 • Fax (314) 569-2834

Pied Piper (see AIMS Multimedia)

Rainbow Educational Video
4540 Preslyn Drive
Raleigh, NC 27615
(800) 331-4047 • Fax (314) 569-2834
www.rainbowedumedia.com

Social Studies School Service
10200 Jefferson Boulevard
P.O. Box 802
Culver City, CA 90232-0802
(800) 421-4246 • Fax (310) 839-2249
www.socialstudies.com

SRA/McGraw-Hill
220 Danieldale Road
De Soto, TX 75115
(800) 843-8855 • Fax (972) 228-1982
www.sra4kids.com

SVE/Churchill Media
6677 North Northwest Highway
Chicago, IL 60631
(800) 829-1900 • Fax (800) 624-1678
www.svemedia.com

Tom Snyder Productions (also see ESI)
80 Coolidge Hill Rd.
Watertown, MA 02472
(800) 342-0236 • Fax (800) 304-1254
www.teachtsp.com

Troll Associates
100 Corporate Drive
Mahwah, NJ 07430
(800) 929-8765 • Fax (800) 979-8765
www.troll.com

United Learning
1560 Sherman Avenue
Suite 100
Evanston, IL 60201
(800) 323-9084 • Fax (847) 328-6706

Zenger Media
(see Social Studies School Service)

UNIT 1

Selection	Vocabulary	Spelling			
The Lost Lake		Words with Short Vowels			
	brand-new	**drank**	hung	lift	swept
	compass	rest	trouble	flock	pleasant
	darted	**ahead**	**magazines**	trust	fist
	mug	**drink**	self	cousin	couple
	muttered	dock	deaf	cannon	wealth
	talker				
Amelia's Road		Words with long *a* and long *e*			
	accidental	cape	agree	crayon	**rusty**
	labored	**gray**	**teacher**	cable	tray
	occasions	station	secret	fail	raisin
	rhythms	rail	**family**	tea	bean
	shortcut	freight	cane	zebra	**tidy**
	shutters				
Sarah, Plain and Tall		Words with long *i* and long *o*			
	eerie	tiger	**crow**	tomato	pine
	huddled	**drive**	oak	**stove**	**overhead**
	overalls	reply	iron	below	chose
	pesky	roll	alike	groan	hollow
	reins	note	supply	title	file
	squall				
Seal Journey		Words with /ū/ and /ü/			
	assured	ruler	**continue**	**improve**	ruin
	horizon	avenue	gloomy	beautiful	bugle
	jagged	raccoon	unit	cube	argue
	mature	loose	whose	stool	community
	nursery	commute	humor	**movement**	tuna
	squealed				
Time for Kids: Open Wide, Don't Bite!		Words from Health			
	broad	**dentist**	**gums**	brain	ache
	fangs	crown	gland	cavity	**dental**
	patients	**hospital**	joint	disease	clinic
	healthy	**medicine**	fever	plaque	oral
	reptiles	diet	**chewing**	vitamin	**molars**
	skills				

Boldfaced words appear in the selection.

UNIT 2

	Vocabulary	Spelling			
Justin and the Best Biscuits in the World		Syllable Patterns			
	festival **guilt** **inspecting** **lingered** **pranced** **resounded**	**biscuit** clover public oven bandage	cabin plastic radar mitten **knapsack**	local mustard pupil sofa **welcome**	**razor** fancy limit **famous** item
Just a Dream		Words with Consonant Clusters			
	bulging **crumpled** **foul** **haze** **shrieking** **waddled**	blank daring claim **flour** crack	bridge **float** plank classified cradle	brand among flatter **clothesline** bridle	credit darling flutter clatter cruise
Leah's Pony		Words with Consonant Clusters			
	bidding **clustered** **county** **glistened** **overflowing** **sturdy**	thrill spruce **stand** speed stretch	sprint spare threw **stranger** springtime	stern spectacle strap thrifty street	stung sparkle stress special steak
Baseball Saved Us		Plurals			
	crate **ditches** **endless** **glinting** **inning** **mound**	cities **mistakes** foxes **babies** knives	engines **soldiers** ranches hobbies yourselves	eyelashes **uniforms** batteries calves **shovels**	**sunglasses** groceries loaves **mattresses** ferries
Time for Kids: Will Her Native Language Disappear?		Words from Social Studies			
	backgrounds **century** **communicate** **extinct** **generations** **native**	**language** **history** **pottery** **study** **spoken**	accent tribe human custom village	folktale practice **relatives** interview region	symbol guide totem colony **prints**

Boldfaced words appear in the selection.

UNIT 3

Selection	Vocabulary	Spelling			
The Hatmaker's Sign		Words with /ou/ and /oi/			
	admitted **brisk** **displaying** **elegantly** **strolling** **wharf**	oily annoy **around** growl disappoint	royalty bounce **bowing** moist enjoyment	**aloud** tower avoid employ **lookout**	**however** appointment scout powder noun
Pat Cummings: My Story		Words with /ů/ and /yů/			
	exist **image** **inspire** **loft** **reference** **sketch**	curious pure fully **sure** wooden	**should** furious cure handful crooked	**would** bulldozer soot tour butcher	woolen pudding goodness pulley overlook
Grass Sandals: The Travels of Basho		Work with Digraphs			
	chanted **nipped** **pouch** **restless** **scribbled** **stitching**	**changed** **watch** fresh shoulder **whatever**	south chimney scratch shove wheat	**cloth** **themselves** crunch batch harsh	whittle thoughtful birch switch theater
A Place Called Freedom		Adding *-ed* and *-ing*			
	fretted **gourd** **plantation** **settlement** **sunrise** **weary**	**freed** **hugged** **emptied** figured budding	**carried** **believed** dimmed studied providing	shedding sledding magnified wedged rotting	varied **arrived** plugging rising **celebrated**
Time for Kids: Twisted Trails		Words from the Arts			
	challenge **combine** **contained** **entertaining** **mazes** **requires**	**designs** **artist** **building** activity **museum**	art create **master** poster statue	assemble craft express arrange **professional**	mold easel plaster masterpiece exhibit

Boldfaced words appear in the selection.

UNIT 4

	Vocabulary	Spelling			
Scruffy: A Wolf Finds His Place in the Pack		**Words with /ô/ and /ôr/**			
	affection **climate** **clinging** **injury** **methods** **threat**	awful daughter roar order office	**toward** already brought **form** author	false jaw offer sauce **chorus**	dawn hoarse war board cough
Gluskabe and the Snow Bird		**Words with /är/ and /âr/**			
	confusion **freeze** **hilltop** **lodge** **messenger** **praised**	**apart** hardly yarn army marbles	repair **careful** scare somewhere wear	starve barber carnival carpet unfair	therefore dairy hare **prepare** pear
Meet an Underwater Explorer		**Words with /îr/ and /ûr/**			
	connected **endangered** **haul** **overcome** **poisonous** **sponge**	fern curve worst **shirt** **clear**	mere cheer serious germ burst	**worse** swirl **gear** sincerely volunteer	period insert purpose twirling spear
On the Bus with Joanna Cole		**Compound Words**			
	abandon **absorb** **available** **original** **research** **traditional**	**bedroom** **anymore** everybody **classroom** anyway	backyard railroad forever bathtub homemade	**outline** windowpane **evergreens** grandparents **photocopy**	**whirlwinds** loudspeaker northwest thunderstorm bedspread
Time for Kids: Earth's First Creatures		**Words from Science**			
	ancestors **disaster** **microscope** **snout** **spikes** **weird**	**shells** **crabs** liquid fact butterfly	**discovered** cast lobster **hatch** expert	mineral dolphin **systems** clam imprint	kelp caterpillar depth skeleton fungus

Boldfaced words appear in the selection.

UNIT 5

	Vocabulary	Spelling			
The Fox and the Guinea Pig		Words with /s/ and/f/			
	amazement **destroyed** **eldest** **fowl** **stake** **strewn**	**mess** sorry balance police classic	rough certain telephone **surprise** elephant	**laughter** citizen advice photograph cider	alphabet triumph careless tough **enormous**
Mom's Best Friend		Words with /ər/ and /chər/			
	clippers **errands** **instinct** **memorizing** **relieved** **sirens**	**brother** honor either popular number	**pictures** odor enter vinegar capture	member nature tender visitor polar	anchor pasture chapter suffer **furniture**
The Rajah's Rice		Words with /əl/ and /ən/			
	attendants **awkwardly** **celebration** **knowledge** **released** **spice**	final uncle **several** model terrible	pencil lion **taken** simple women	reason gentle total settle level	**medical** evil listen common cotton
Yeh-Shen: A Cinderella Story from China		Contractions			
	beloved **bid** **desire** **heaved** **marveled** **permit**	that's he'll **wasn't** what's I'd	there's couldn't he'd could've let's	they'll weren't here's she'd who's	it'll hadn't they'd where's wouldn't
Time for Kids: Can We Rescue the Reefs?		Words from Science			
	coral **damage** **loosened** **percent** **reefs** **ton**	**rescue** survive channel vessel expose	**dying** shelter extreme **danger** protect	**seaweed** **creatures** dissolve motion feature	adapt locate assist future **divers**

Boldfaced words appear in the selection.

UNIT 6

	Vocabulary	Spelling
Teammates	**circulated** **extraordinary** **launched** **opponents** **organizations** **teammate**	**Words with Silent Letters** **knew**, climb, calm, although, knight writer, knob, numb, delight, wren knead, plumber, chalk, midnight, wreck stalk, kneel, **sought**, thorough, wrestle
The Malachite Palace	**cultured** **feeble** **fragrance** **mingled** **resembled** **scampered**	**Homophones and Homographs** **seen**, great, **light**, beat, lean scene, beet, bowl, grate, fan peak, post, pail, bury, punch pale, grave, berry, **peek**, **dates**
The Toothpaste Millionaire	**brilliant** **commercials** **expensive** **gallon** **ingredient** **successful**	**Words with Suffixes** useless, entertainment, construction, adjustable, darkness motionless, description, measurement, adorable, breathless fairness, government, protection, dependable, sickness hopeless, **production**, enjoyable, greatness
Whales	**identify** **mammals** **marine** **pods** **preserve** **related**	**Words with Prefixes** redo, unkind, disappear, reread, nonfat inactive, **international**, unlucky, dislike, unpack nonstop, refill, uncertain, interstate, incomplete rewind, unsure, disagree, reheat, nonsense
Time for Kids: Saving the Everglades	**compares** **importance** **instance** **lurk** **soggy** **wildlife**	**Words from Math** **area**, **hundreds**, **size**, **billions**, weight minute, noon, cone, yard, edge **amount**, cylinder, zero, figure, calendar quart, decade, rectangle, era, length

Boldfaced words appear in the selection.

Listening, Speaking, Viewing, Representing

☑ Tested Skill
Tinted panels show skills, strategies, and other teaching opportunities

	K	1	2	3	4	5	6
LISTENING							
Learn the vocabulary of school (numbers, shapes, colors, directions, and categories)							
Identify the musical elements of literary language, such as rhymes, repetition, onomatopoeia, alliteration, assonance							
Determine purposes for listening (get information, solve problems, enjoy and appreciate)							
Understand and follow directions							
Listen critically and responsively; recognize barriers to effective listening							
Ask and answer relevant questions (for clarification; to follow up on ideas)							
Listen critically to interpret and evaluate							
Listen responsively to stories and other texts read aloud, including selections from classic and contemporary works							
Connect and compare own experiences, feelings, ideas, and traditions with those of others							
Apply comprehension strategies in listening activities							
Understand the major ideas and supporting evidence in spoken messages							
Participate in listening activities related to reading and writing (such as discussions, group activities, conferences)							
Listen to learn by taking notes, organizing, and summarizing spoken ideas							
Know personal listening preferences							
SPEAKING							
Uses repetition, rhyme, and rhythm in oral texts (such as in reciting songs, poems, and stories with repeating patterns)							
Learn the vocabulary of school (numbers, shapes, colors, directions, and categories)							
Use appropriate language, grammar, and vocabulary learned to describe ideas, feelings, and experiences							
Ask and answer relevant questions (for clarification; to follow up on ideas)							
Communicate effectively in everyday situations (such as discussions, group activities, conferences, conversations)							
Demonstrate speaking skills (audience, purpose, occasion, clarity, volume, pitch, intonation, phrasing, rate, fluency)							
Clarify and support spoken messages and ideas with objects, charts, evidence, elaboration, examples							
Use verbal communication in effective ways when, for example, making announcements, giving directions, or making introductions							
Use nonverbal communication in effective ways such as eye contact, facial expressions, gestures							
Retell a story or a spoken message by summarizing or clarifying							
Connect and compare own experiences, ideas, and traditions with those of others							
Determine purposes for speaking (inform, entertain, compare, describe, give directions, persuade, express personal feelings and opinions)							
Recognize differences between formal and informal language							
Demonstrate skills of reporting and providing information							
Demonstrate skills of interviewing, requesting and providing information							
Apply composition strategies in speaking activities							
Monitor own understanding of spoken message and seek clarification as needed							
VIEWING							
Demonstrate viewing skills (focus attention, organize information)							
Understand and use nonverbal cues							
Respond to audiovisual media in a variety of ways							
Participate in viewing activities related to reading and writing							
Apply comprehension strategies in viewing activities, including main idea and details							
Recognize artists' craft and techniques for conveying meaning							
Interpret information from various formats such as maps, charts, graphics, video segments, technology							
Knows various types of mass media (such as film, video, television, billboards, and newspapers)							
Evaluate purposes of various media, including mass media (information, appreciation, entertainment, directions, persuasion)							
Use media, including mass media, to compare ideas, information, and points of view							
REPRESENTING							
Select, organize, or produce visuals to complement or extend meanings							
Produce communication using appropriate media to develop a class paper, multimedia or video reports							
Show how language, medium, and presentation contribute to the message							

Reading: Alphabetic Principle, Sounds/Symbols

✓ Tested Skill

Tinted panels show skills, strategies, and other teaching opportunities

PRINT AWARENESS	K	1	2	3	4	5	6
Know the order of the alphabet							
Recognize that print represents spoken language and conveys meaning							
Understand directionality (tracking print from left to right; return sweep)							
Understand that written words and sentences are separated by spaces							
Know the difference between individual letters and printed words							
Understand that spoken words are represented in written language by specific sequence of letters							
Recognize that there are correct spellings for words							
Know the difference between capital and lowercase letters							
Recognize how readers use capitalization and punctuation to comprehend							
Recognize the distinguishing features of a letter, word, sentence, paragraph							
Understand appropriate book handling							
Recognize that parts of a book (such as cover/title page and table of contents) offer information							
PHONOLOGICAL AWARENESS							
Listen for environmental sounds							
Identify spoken words and sentences							
Divide spoken sentence into individual words							
Produce rhyming words and distinguish rhyming words from nonrhyming words							
Identify, segment, and combine syllables within spoken words							
Blend and segment onsets and rimes							
Identify and isolate the initial, medial, and final sound of a spoken word							
Add, delete, or substitute sounds to change words (such as *cow* to *how*, *pan* to *fan*)							
Blend sounds to make spoken words							
Segment one-syllable spoken words into individual phonemes							
PHONICS AND DECODING							
Alphabetic principle: Letter/sound correspondence	✓	✓	✓				
Blending CVC words	✓	✓					
Segmenting CVC words	✓						
Blending CVC, CVCe, CCVC, CVCC, CVVC words	✓	✓	✓				
Segmenting CVC, CVCe, CCVC, CVCC, CVVC words and sounds	✓	✓	✓				
Initial and final consonants: /n/n, /d/d, /s/s, /m/m, /t/t, /k/c, /f/f, /r/r, /p/p, /l/l, /k/k, /g/g, /b/b, /h/h, /w/w, /v/v, /ks/x, /kw/qu, /j/j, /y/y, /z/z	✓	✓					
Initial and medial short vowels: *a, i, u, o, e*	✓	✓	✓				
Long vowels: *a-e, i-e, o-e, u-e* (vowel-consonant-e)		✓	✓				
Long vowels, including *ay, ai; e, ee, ie, ea; o, oa, oe, ow; i, y, igh*		✓	✓				
Consonant Digraphs: *sh, th, ch, wh*		✓					
Consonant Blends: continuant/continuant, including *sl, sm, sn, fl, fr, ll, ss, ff*		✓					
Consonant Blends: continuant/stop, including *st, sk, sp, ng, nt, nd, mp, ft*		✓					
Consonant Blends: stop/continuant, including *tr, pr, pl, cr, tw*		✓					
Variant vowels: including /ů/*oo*; /ô/*a, aw, au*; /ü/*ue, ew*		✓	✓				
Diphthongs, including /ou/*ou, ow*; /oi/*oi, oy*		✓	✓				
r-controlled vowels, including /âr/*are*; /ôr/*or, ore*; /îr/*ear*			✓				
Soft *c* and soft *g*			✓				
nk		✓	✓				
Consonant Digraphs: *ck*	✓	✓					
Consonant Digraphs: *ph, tch, ch*			✓				
Short *e*: *ea*			✓				
Long *e*: *y, ey*			✓				
/ü/*oo*			✓				
/är/*ar*; /ûr/*ir, ur, er*		✓	✓				
Silent letters: including *l, b, k, w, g, h, gh*		✓	✓				
Schwa: /ər/*er*; /ən/*en*; /əl/*le*;			✓				
Reading/identifying multisyllabic words		✓	✓				
Using graphophonic cues							

✓ Tested Skill

Tinted panels show skills, strategies, and other teaching opportunities

Reading: Vocabulary/Word Identification

WORD STRUCTURE	K	1	2	3	4	5	6
Common spelling patterns							
Syllable patterns							
Plurals		✓					
Possessives		✓					
Contractions		✓					
Root, or base, words and inflectional endings (*-s, -es, -ed, -ing*)		✓	✓	✓		✓	
Compound Words		✓	✓	✓	✓	✓	✓
Prefixes and suffixes (such as *un-, re-, dis-, non-; -ly, -y, -ful, -able, -tion*)			✓	✓	✓	✓	✓
Root words and derivational endings				✓	✓	✓	✓
WORD MEANING							
Develop vocabulary through concrete experiences, word walls, other people							
Develop vocabulary through selections read aloud							
Develop vocabulary through reading							
Cueing systems: syntactic, semantic, graphophonic							
Context clues, including semantic clues (word meaning), syntactical clues (word order), and graphophonic clues	✓	✓	✓	✓	✓	✓	✓
High-frequency words (such as *the, a, and, said, was, where, is*)	✓	✓					
Identify words that name persons, places, things, and actions							
Automatic reading of regular and irregular words							
Use resources and references (dictionary, glossary, thesaurus, synonym finder, technology and software, and context)							
Classify and categorize words							
Synonyms and antonyms			✓	✓	✓	✓	✓
Multiple-meaning words			✓		✓	✓	✓
Figurative language			✓	✓	✓	✓	✓
Decode derivatives (root words, such as *like, pay, happy* with affixes, such as *dis-, pre-, un-*)							
Systematic study of words across content areas and in current events							
Locate meanings, pronunciations, and derivations (including dictionaries, glossaries, and other sources)							
Denotation and connotation							✓
Word origins as aid to understanding historical influences on English word meanings							
Homophones, homographs							
Analogies							✓
Idioms							

Reading: Comprehension

PREREADING STRATEGIES	K	1	2	3	4	5	6
Preview and predict							
Use prior knowledge							
Set and adjust purposes for reading							
Build background							
MONITORING STRATEGIES							
Adjust reading rate							
Reread, search for clues, ask questions, ask for help							
Visualize							
Read a portion aloud, use reference aids							
Use decoding and vocabulary strategies							
Paraphrase							
Create story maps, diagrams, charts, story props to help comprehend, analyze, synthesize and evaluate texts							

(continued on next page)

✓ Tested Skill

Tinted panels show skills, strategies, and other teaching opportunities

(Reading: Comprehension continued)

SKILLS AND STRATEGIES	K	1	2	3	4	5	6
Recall story details, including character and setting	✓	✓					
Use illustrations	✓	✓					
Distinguish reality and fantasy	✓	✓	✓				
Classify and categorize	✓						
Make predictions	✓	✓	✓	✓	✓	✓	✓
Recognize sequence of events (tell or act out)	✓	✓	✓	✓	✓	✓	✓
Recognize cause and effect	✓	✓	✓	✓	✓	✓	✓
Compare and contrast	✓	✓	✓	✓	✓	✓	✓
Summarize	✓	✓	✓	✓	✓	✓	✓
Make and explain inferences		✓	✓	✓	✓	✓	✓
Draw conclusions		✓	✓	✓	✓	✓	✓
Distinguish important and unimportant information				✓	✓	✓	✓
Recognize main idea and supporting details	✓	✓	✓	✓	✓	✓	✓
Form conclusions or generalizations and support with evidence from text			✓	✓	✓	✓	✓
Distinguish fact and opinion (including news stories and advertisements)				✓	✓	✓	✓
Recognize problem and solution			✓	✓	✓	✓	✓
Recognize steps in a process		✓	✓	✓	✓	✓	✓
Make judgments and decisions				✓	✓	✓	✓
Distinguish fact and nonfact				✓	✓	✓	✓
Recognize techniques of persuasion and propaganda							✓
Evaluate evidence and sources of information, including checking other sources and asking experts							✓
Identify similarities and differences across texts (including topics, characters, problems, themes, cultural influences, treatment, scope, or organization)							
Practice various questions and tasks (test-like comprehension questions)							
Paraphrase and summarize to recall, inform, and organize							
Answer various types of questions (open-ended, literal, interpretative, test-like such as true-false, multiple choice, short-answer)							
Use study strategies to learn and recall (preview, question, reread, and record)							
LITERARY RESPONSE							
Listen to stories being read aloud							
React, speculate, join in, read along when predictable and patterned selections are read aloud							
Respond to a variety of stories and poems through talk, movement, music, art, drama, and writing							
Show understanding through writing, illustrating, developing demonstrations, and using technology							
Connect ideas and themes across texts							
Support responses by referring to relevant aspects of text and own experiences							
Offer observations, make connections, speculate, interpret, and raise questions in response to texts							
Interpret text ideas through journal writing, discussion, enactment, and media							
TEXT STRUCTURE/LITERARY CONCEPTS							
Distinguish forms and functions of texts (lists, newsletters, signs)							
Use text features to aid comprehension							
Understand story structure							
Identify narrative (for entertainment) and expository (for information)							
Distinguish fiction from nonfiction, including fact and fantasy							
Understand literary forms (stories, poems, plays, and informational books)							
Understand literary terms by distinguishing between roles of author and illustrator							
Understand title, author, and illustrator across a variety of texts							
Analyze character, character's motive, character's point of view, plot, setting, style, tone, mood		✓	✓	✓	✓	✓	✓
Compare communication in different forms							
Understand terms such as *title, author, illustrator, playwright, theater, stage, act, dialogue,* and *scene*							
Recognize stories, poems, songs, myths, legends, folktales, fables, tall tales, limericks, plays, biographies, autobiographies							
Judge internal logic of story text							
Recognize that authors organize information in specific ways							
Recognize author's purpose: to inform, influence, express, or entertain							
Describe how author's point of view affects text				✓	✓	✓	✓
Recognize biography, historical fiction, realistic fiction, modern fantasy, informational texts, and poetry							
Analyze ways authors present ideas (cause/effect, compare/contrast, inductively, deductively, chronologically)							
Recognize literary techniques such as imagery, repetition, flashback, foreshadowing, symbolism							

(continued on next page)

✓ Tested Skill

Tinted panels show skills, strategies, and other teaching opportunities

(Reading: Comprehension continued)

VARIETY OF TEXT	K	1	2	3	4	5	6
Read a variety of genres and understand their distinguishing features							
Use expository and other informational texts to acquire information							
Read for a variety of purposes							
Select varied sources when reading for information or pleasure							
Know preferences for reading literary and nonfiction texts							
FLUENCY							
Read regularly in independent-level and instructional-level materials							
Read orally with fluency from familiar texts							
Self-select independent-level reading							
Read silently for increasing periods of time							
Demonstrate characteristics of fluent and effective reading							
Adjust reading rate to purpose							
Read aloud in selected texts, showing understanding of text and engaging the listener							
CULTURES							
Connect own experience with culture of others							
Compare experiences of characters across cultures							
Articulate and discuss themes and connections that cross cultures							
CRITICAL THINKING							
Experiences (comprehend, apply, analyze, synthesize, evaluate)							
Make connections (comprehend, apply, analyze, synthesize, evaluate)							
Expression (comprehend, apply, analyze, synthesize, evaluate)							
Inquiry (comprehend, apply, analyze, synthesize, evaluate)							
Problem solving (comprehend, apply, analyze, synthesize, evaluate)							
Making decisions (comprehend, apply, analyze, synthesize, evaluate)							

Study Skills

INQUIRY/RESEARCH AND STUDY STRATEGIES	K	1	2	3	4	5	6
Follow and give directions							
Use alphabetical order							
Use text features and formats to help understand text (such as boldface, italic, or highlighted text; captions; headings and subheadings; numbers or symbols)							
Use study strategies to help read text and to learn and recall information from text (such as preview text, set purposes, and ask questions; use SQRRR; adjust reading rate; skim and scan; use KWL)							
Identify/frame and revise questions for research							
Obtain, organize, and summarize information: classify, take notes, outline, web, diagram							
Evaluate research and raise new questions							
Use technology for research and/or to present information in various formats							
Follow accepted formats for writing research, including documenting sources							
Use test-taking strategies							
Use text organizers (book cover; title page—title, author, illustrator; contents; headings; glossary; index)		✓	✓	✓	✓	✓	✓
Use graphic aids, such as maps, diagrams, charts, graphs, schedules, calendars		✓	✓	✓	✓	✓	✓
Read and interpret varied texts, such as environmental print, signs, lists, encyclopedia, dictionary, glossary, newspaper, advertisement, magazine, calendar, directions, floor plans, online resources		✓	✓	✓	✓	✓	✓
Use print and online reference sources, such as glossary, dictionary, encyclopedia, telephone directory, technology resources, nonfiction books		✓	✓	✓	✓	✓	✓
Recognize Library/Media center resources, such as computerized references; catalog search—subject, author, title; encyclopedia index		✓	✓	✓	✓	✓	✓

Writing

✓ Tested Skill

Tinted panels show skills, strategies, and other teaching opportunities

MODES AND FORMS	K	1	2	3	4	5	6
Interactive writing							
Descriptive writing			✓				
Personal narrative			✓	✓	✓	✓	✓
Writing that compares		✓	✓	✓	✓	✓	✓
Explanatory writing			✓	✓	✓	✓	✓
Persuasive writing				✓	✓	✓	✓
Writing a story		✓	✓	✓	✓	✓	✓
Expository writing; research report		✓	✓	✓	✓	✓	✓
Write using a variety of formats, such as advertisement, autobiography, biography, book report/report, comparison-contrast, critique/review/editorial, description, essay, how-to, interview, invitation, journal/log/notes, message/list, paragraph/multi-paragraph composition, picture book, play (scene), poem/rhyme, story, summary, note, letter							
PURPOSES/AUDIENCES							
Dictate sentences and messages such as news and stories for others to write							
Write labels, notes, and captions for illustrations, possessions, charts, and centers							
Write to record, to discover and develop ideas, to inform, to influence, to entertain							
Exhibit an identifiable voice							
Use literary devices (suspense, dialogue, and figurative language)							
Produce written texts by organizing ideas, using effective transitions, and choosing precise wording							
PROCESSES							
Generate ideas for self-selected and assigned topics using prewriting strategies							
Develop drafts							
Revise drafts for varied purposes, elaborate ideas							
Edit for appropriate grammar, spelling, punctuation, and features of published writings							
Proofread own writing and that of others							
Bring pieces to final form and "publish" them for audiences							
Use technology to compose, revise, and present text							
Select and use reference materials and resources for writing, revising, and editing final drafts							
SPELLING							
Spell own name and write high-frequency words							
Words with short vowels (including CVC and one-syllable words with blends CCVC, CVCC, CCVCC)							
Words with long vowels (including CVCe)							
Words with digraphs, blends, consonant clusters, double consonants							
Words with diphthongs							
Words with variant vowels							
Words with r-controlled vowels							
Words with /ər/, /əl/, and /ən/							
Words with silent letters							
Words with soft *c* and soft *g*							
Inflectional endings (including plurals and past tense and words that drop the final *e* and double a consonant when adding *-ing, -ed*)							
Compound words							
Contractions							
Homonyms							
Suffixes such as *-able, -ly, -ful,* or *-less,* and prefixes such as *dis-, re-, pre-,* or *un-*							
Spell words ending in *-tion* and *-sion*, such as *station* and *procession*							
Accurate spelling of root or base words							
Orthographic patterns and rules such as *keep/can; sack/book; out/now; oil/toy; match/speech; ledge/cage;* consonant doubling, dropping *e,* changing *y* to *i*							
Multisyllabic words using regularly spelled phonogram patterns							
Syllable patterns (including closed, open, syllable boundary patterns)							
Synonyms and antonyms							
Words from Social Studies, Science, Math, and Physical Education							
Words derived from other languages and cultures							
Use resources to find correct spellings, synonyms, and replacement words							
Use conventional spelling of familiar words in writing assignments							
Spell accurately in final drafts							

(continued on next page)

☑ Tested Skill

Tinted panels show skills, strategies, and other teaching opportunities

(Writing continued)

GRAMMAR AND USAGE	K	1	2	3	4	5	6
Understand sentence concepts (word order, statements, questions, exclamations, commands)							
Recognize complete and incomplete sentences							
Nouns (common, proper, singular, plural, irregular plural, possessives)							
Verbs (action, helping, linking, irregular)							
Verb tense (present, past, future, perfect, and progressive)							
Pronouns (possessive, subject and object, pronoun-verb agreement)							
Use objective case pronouns accurately							
Adjectives							
Adverbs that tell how, when, where							
Subjects, predicates							
Subject-verb agreement							
Sentence combining							
Recognize sentence structure (simple, compound, complex)							
Synonyms and antonyms							
Contractions							
Conjunctions							
Prepositions and prepositional phrases							
PENMANSHIP							
Write each letter of alphabet (capital and lowercase) using correct formation, appropriate size and spacing							
Write own name and other important words							
Use phonological knowledge to map sounds to letters to write messages							
Write messages that move left to right, top to bottom							
Gain increasing control of penmanship, pencil grip, paper position, beginning stroke							
Use word and letter spacing and margins to make messages readable							
Write legibly by selecting cursive or manuscript as appropriate							
MECHANICS							
Use capitalization in sentences, proper nouns, titles, abbreviations and the pronoun *I*							
Use end marks correctly (period, question mark, exclamation point)							
Use commas (in dates, in addresses, in a series, in letters, in direct address)							
Use apostrophes in contractions and possessives							
Use quotation marks							
Use hyphens, semicolons, colons							
EVALUATION							
Identify the most effective features of a piece of writing using class/teacher-generated criteria							
Respond constructively to others' writing							
Determine how his/her own writing achieves its purpose							
Use published pieces as models for writing							
Review own written work to monitor growth as writer							

Index

Abbreviations, 157N, 369N

Activating and assessing prior knowledge, 20A, 41O, 44A, 65O, 68A, 93O, 96A, 117O, 120A, 127O, 129A, 134A, 157O, 160A, 189O, 192A, 215O, 218A, 241O, 244A, 251O, 258A, 281O, 284A, 297O, 300A, 331O, 334A, 359O, 362A, 369O, 376A, 405O, 408A, 423O, 426A, 443O, 446A, 471O, 474A, 481O, 488A, 515O, 518A, 535O, 538A, 567O, 570A, 599O, 602A, 609O, 616A, 631O, 634A, 663O, 666A, 691O, 694A, 713O, 716A, 723O

Activities for anthology and leveled books, 41D, 65D, 93D, 117D, 127D, 157D, 189D, 215D, 241D, 251D, 281D, 297D, 331D, 359D, 369D, 405D, 423D, 443D, 471D, 481D, 515D, 535D, 567D, 599D, 609D, 631D, 663D, 691D, 713D, 723D

Ada, Alma Flor, 632A, 634

Adjectives, 405M–N, 423M–N, 443M–N, 471M–N, 481M–N, 483G, 611G, 631M–N, 723M–N
- articles, 423M–N, 483G, 611G
- comparative form of, 443M–N, 471M–N, 481M–N
- proper, 405N, 443N
- sentence combining with, 723M–N
- superlative form of, 443M–N, 471M–N, 481M–N
- using *good* and *bad*, 481M–N, 631N

Adverbs, 253G, 631M–N, 653, 663M–N, 723M–N, 725G
- adding *ly*, 631M–N, 653
- sentence combining with, 723M–N
- that compare, 253G, 663M–N, 725G

Advertisements, 253A–B, 514, Unit 5: T61

Alexander, Sally Hobart, 516A, 531

Alliteration, 94E, 132E, 136, 158E, 692E, 714E

Almanac, 414, 421, 624, 629

Alternate teaching strategies, Unit 1–6: T60–T66

Altman, Linda Jacobs, 42A, 44

Amelia's Road, 44–65

Analogies, 93P, 372, 378, 405P, 535P, 723P

Antonyms, 65I–J, 93I–J, 127I–J, 157P, 297P, 308, 485, 663I–J, 691I–J, 723I–J, Unit 1: T65, Unit 6: T65

Apostrophes, 241M–N, 331N, 371I, 515N, 599N, 609N, 691N

"Arrow and the Song, The," 130–131

Articles, 423M–N, 483G, 611E

Art link, 30, 58, 249, 272, 284A, 302, 369O–P, 376A

Assessment
- checklist, 16H, 130H, 254H, 372H, 484H, 612H
- follow-up, 37, 61, 89, 113, 123, 153, 185, 211, 237, 247, 277, 293, 327, 355, 365, 401, 419, 439, 467, 477, 511, 531, 563, 595, 605, 627, 659, 687, 709, 719
- formal, 39, 63, 91, 115, 125, 155, 187, 213, 239, 249, 279, 295, 329, 357, 367, 403, 421, 441, 469, 479, 513, 533, 565, 597, 607, 629, 661, 689, 711, 721
- informal, 36, 37, 61, 88, 89, 112, 113, 122, 123, 152, 153, 184, 185, 210, 211, 236, 237, 246, 247, 277, 293, 327, 355, 365, 401, 419, 439, 366, 467, 476, 477, 510, 511, 530, 531, 562, 563, 594, 595, 604, 605, 626, 627, 658, 659, 685, 687, 718, 719
- performance, 17, 18E, 20A, 41L, 42E, 44A, 65L, 66E, 68A, 93D, 93L, 94E, 96A, 117L, 118E, 120A, 127L, 129F, 129, 131, 157L, 158E, 160A, 371D, 371F, 372E, 374A, 405L, 422E, 424A, 423L, 424E, 426A, 443L, 444E, 446A, 471L, 472E, 474A, 481L, 483F, 483, 485, 515L, 535L, 567L, 599L, 609L, 611F, 611, 613, 631L, 632E, 634A, 663L, 664E, 666A, 691L, 713L, 714E, 716A, 723L, 725F, 725
- portfolio, 41L, 65L, 93L, 117L, 127L, 157L, 189L, 215L, 241L, 251L, 281L, 297L, 331L, 359L, 369L, 405L, 423L, 443L, 471L, 481L, 515L, 535L, 567L, 599L, 609L, 631L, 663L, 691L, 713L, 723L
- scoring rubrics, 41L, 65L, 93L, 117L, 127L, 129J, 157L, 189L, 215L, 241L, 251L, 253H, 281L, 297L, 331L, 359L, 369L, 371J, 405L, 423L, 443L, 471L, 481L, 483H, 515L, 535L, 567L, 599L, 609L, 611H, 631L, 663L, 691L, 713L, 723L, 725H, Unit 1–6: T107–108
- selection, 39, 63, 91, 115, 125, 155, 175, 187, 213, 239, 249, 279, 295, 329, 357, 367, 403, 421, 441, 469, 479, 513, 533, 565, 597, 607, 629, 661, 689, 711, 721
- standardized test practice, 41, 65, 93, 117, 127, 157, 189, 215, 241, 251, 281, 297, 331, 359, 369, 405, 423, 443, 471, 481, 515, 535, 567, 599, 609, 631, 663, 691, 713, 723
- student self-assessment, 36, 60, 88, 112, 129J, 152, 184, 210, 236, 253F, 276, 292, 326, 354, 371F, 400, 418, 438, 466, 483F, 510, 530, 562, 594, 611F, 626, 658, 686, 725H
- unit resources for, 16G, 16H, 129K–M, 130G, 130H, 253I–K, 254G, 254H, 371K–M, 372G, 372H, 483I–K, 484G, 484H, 611I–K, 612G, 612H, 725I–K

Assonance, 94E, 194, 485

Audience response, 41D, 65D, 93D, 117D, 127D, 157D, 189D, 215D, 241D, 251D, 253D, 281D, 297D, 331D, 359D, 369D, 371F, 405D, 423D, 443D, 471D, 481D, 483D, 515D, 535D, 567D, 599D, 609D, 631D, 663D, 691D, 713D, 723D

"August 8," 252–253

Author's purpose and point of view. *See* Comprehension strategies.

Barlow, Alan, 370–371

Barry, David, 536A, 563

Baseball Saved Us, 218–241

Base words. *See* Root words, Vocabulary.

Book, parts of, 40, 64, 92, 116, 126, Unit 1: T61

Bose, Anruddha, 610–611

Brainstorming, 16J, 17, 20A, 25, 27, 35, 37, 53, 54, 55, 63, 65D, 65J, 65K, 75, 77, 89, 113, 115, 117K, 117L, 125, 127K, 128, 129F, 130, 131, 158E, 160, 189J, 189K, 189N, 192A, 213, 216E, 232, 241B, 241K, 244B, 245J, 249, 251F, 251K, 252, 254, 255, 261, 267, 279, 281K, 281N, 284A, 287, 291, 297K, 319, 323, 331K, 331L, 331N, 353, 357, 359K, 367, 369K, 370, 372J, 372, 376C, 390, 405J, 408C, 421, 423J, 423K, 457, 469, 471D, 481O, 482, 484J, 505, 513, 515K, 518A, 521, 523, 529, 533, 535J, 553, 567F, 567K, 591, 597, 599K, 610, 612, 618, 645, 653, 659, 661, 663F, 663J, 666A, 691J, 691K, 694A, 713F, 716A, 721, 723J, 723K, 724, 729F

Brandenburg, Jim, 374A, 376

Bruchac, Joseph, 406A, 408

Building background, 20A, 44A, 68A, 96A, 120A, 129A, 134A, 160A, 192A, 218A, 244A, 253A, 258A, 284A, 300A, 334A, 362A, 371A, 376A, 408A, 426A, 446A, 474A, 483A, 488A, 518A, 538A, 570A, 602A, 611A, 616A, 634A, 666A, 694A, 716A, 725A

Can We Rescue the Reefs?, 602–609

Capitalization, 41N, 65N, 93N, 129I, 157M–N, 215N, 297N, 359N, 369N, 405N, 423N, 443N, 535N, 567N, 713N, 723N

Card catalog, 630, 662, Unit 6: T61

Cause and effect, analyzing. *See* Comprehension strategies.

Challenge activities, 39, 63, 91, 115, 125, 155, 175, 187, 213, 239, 249, 279, 295, 329, 357, 367, 403, 421, 441, 469, 479, 513, 533, 565, 597, 607, 629, 661, 689, 711, 721. *See also* Meeting Individual Needs.

Character, analyzing. *See* Comprehension strategies; Story elements, analyzing.

Charts
- author's purpose and point of view, 299B, 299, 300, 301, 304, 311, 326, 331D
- cause and effect, 191B, 191, 192, 193, 198, 199, 204, 208, 210, 215D, 243B, 243, 244, 246, 615B, 615, 616, 617, 620, 621, 624, 626, 663H, 694A, 715B, 715, 716, 717, 718
- compare and contrast, 375B, 375, 376, 377, 384, 386, 394, 400, 405F, 422, 423H, 473B, 473, 474, 476, 538C, 574, 693B, 693, 694, 695, 699, 700, 708, 709
- draw conclusions, 425B, 425, 426, 427, 428, 430, 438
- fact and nonfact, 407B, 407, 408, 409, 411, 415, 417, 418, 471H
- fact and opinion, 283B, 283, 284, 285, 286, 290, 292, 333B, 333, 334, 335, 336, 340, 347, 350, 353, 354
- five-column, 443N, 705
- flowchart, 189B, 206, 296, 394, 443K, 446A, 471K, 474A, 483B, 483C
- four-column, 41D, 65D, 117D, 157D, 189D, 189N, 215D, 241D, 251D, 281D, 281N, 297D, 331D, 359D, 369D, 405D, 423D, 443D, 471D, 481D, 515D, 535D, 567D, 599D, 609D, 631D, 663D, 691D, 713D, 723D
- generalizations, 157H, 189H
- important and unimportant information, 517B, 517, 518, 519, 520, 522, 526, 530, 601B, 601, 602, 604
- inferences, 41H, 65H, 515H, 567H
- judgments and decisions, 257B, 257, 258, 259, 260, 269, 274, 276, 277, 361B, 361, 362, 363, 364, 665B, 665, 666, 667, 671, 675, 686, 713H
- K-W-L, 134A, 244A, 246, 390, 474C, 567C, 599A, 602A, 604, 716A, 718
- main ideas/supporting details, 95B, 95, 96, 97, 98, 102, 105, 112, 127F, 517B, 518, 519, 520, 522, 526, 530
- predictions, 20, 44, 61, 68, 89, 96, 120, 133B, 133, 134, 135, 140, 144, 152, 160, 185, 192, 211, 217B, 217, 218, 219, 222, 225, 230, 235, 236, 258, 277, 284, 293, 300, 327, 334, 355, 376, 401, 408, 419, 426, 439, 446, 467, 488, 511, 518, 537B, 537, 538, 539, 546, 547, 549, 550, 557, 558, 559, 562, 570, 616, 634, 666, 694, 716
- problem and solution, 43B, 43, 44, 45, 47, 53, 56, 60, 65D, 65F, 93H, 119B, 119, 120, 121, 122, 127D, 127K, 423D, 488A, 633B, 633, 634, 635, 636, 642, 650, 654, 658, 663F, 691H

sequence of events, 65K, 159B, 159, 160, 161, 167, 175, 184, 215H, 241D, 487B, 487, 488, 489, 492, 497, 504, 510, 569, 570, 571, 572, 575, 580, 584, 591, 594
steps in a process, 445B, 445, 446, 447, 449, 452, 455, 466, 666A
story elements, 19B, 19, 20, 21, 22, 28, 32, 36, 41D, 67B, 67, 68, 69, 73, 77, 88, 275, 611B–C
summary, 93H, 273, 297H, 517B, 518, 525, 611B–C
three-column, 16J, 93K, 129F, 130J, 142, 213, 254J, 279, 297H, 297J, 372J, 405N, 448, 484J, 515K, 533, 567H, 567M, 612J, 663F, 663N
two-column, 39, 59, 65H, 65N, 68A, 120B, 157K, 157N, 160A, 189K, 192A, 244B, 251L, 258B, 288, 320, 334A, 362B, 367, 369B, 376B, 408A, 426B, 437, 471H, 474B, 515H, 524, 535N, 538A, 599M, 602B, 631H, 663K, 691N, 694B, 713H
See also Graphic organizers, Study skills.

Ciardi, John, 484–485

Cole, Joanna, 444A, 446

Commas, 65N, 93N, 157K, 189N, 281N, 297N, 481N, 713N, 723N
between days and years, 65N, 297N, 713N
between names of cities and states, 65N, 297N, 713N
between words that separate, 189N, 281N
in a sentence combining, 93N
in a series, 189N, 281N
in letters, 65N, 297N, 713N
to set off words, 481N, 723N

Comparatives, 443M–N, 471M–N, 481M–N, 663M–N

Comparison and contrast. *See* Comprehension strategies.

Comparison in writing. *See* Writing activities.

Compound words, 33, 46, 87, 100, 140, 189I–J, 199, 241I–J, 251G–H, 405I–J, 463, 471O–P, 521, 585, 671, Unit 2: T65

Comprehension strategies
analyzing author's purpose and point of view, 298, 299A–B, 299, 330–331, 331A–C, 331E–F, 369A–C, 369E–F, Unit 3: T66
analyzing cause and effect, 173, 190, 191A–B, 191, 192–212, 215A–C, 215E–F, 242, 243A–B, 243, 244–248, 251A–C, 614, 615A–B, 615, 616–628, 631A–C, 631E–F, 663G–H, 666–688, 714, 715A–B, 715, 716–720, 723A–C, Unit 2: T66, Unit 6: T60
analyzing sequence of events, 158, 159A–B, 159, 160–186, 189A–C, 189E–F, 215G–H, 218–238, 251A–C, 486, 487A–B, 487, 488–512, 515A–C, 515E–F, 568, 569A–B, 569, 570–596, 599A–C, 599E–F, 609A–C, Unit 2: T64, Unit 5: T60
analyzing steps in a process, 296, 444, 445A–B, 445, 446–468, 471A–C, 471E–F, 481A–C, 481E–F, Unit 4: T66
analyzing story elements, 18, 19A–B, 19, 20–37, 41A–C, 41E–F, 51, 53, 66, 67A–B, 67, 68–90, 93A–C, 93D, 93E–F, 127A–C, 139, 163, 171, 268, 275, 291, 305, 306, 323, 337, 343, 345, 352, 509, 527, 560, 575, 577, 589, 643, 652, 670, 672, 673, 685, Unit 1: T60
character, 18, 19A–B, 19, 20–37, 41A–C, 41E–F, 51, 53, 66, 67A–B, 67, 68–90, 93A–C, 93D, 93E–F, 127A–C, 139, 163, 171, 268, 275, 291, 305, 306, 323, 337, 343, 345, 352, 509, 527, 560, 575,577, 589, 643, 652, 670, 672, 673, 685, Unit 1: T60
plot, 67A–B, 67, 68–90, 93E–F, 589
setting, 19A–B, 19, 20–37, 41A–C, 41E–F, 67A–B, 67, 68–90, 93B, 93E–F, 264, 348
comparing and contrasting, 181, 209, 374, 375A–B, 375, 376–402, 405A–C, 405E–F, 423G–H, 472, 473A–B, 473, 474–478, 481A–C, 692, 693A–B, 693, 694–710, 713A–C, 713E–F, 723A–C, 723E–F, Unit 4: T60, Unit 6: T66
distinguishing between fact and nonfact, 406, 407A–B, 407, 408–420, 423A–C, 423E–F, 443G–H, 471G–H, 474–478, 481A–C, 509, Unit 4: T64
distinguishing between fact and opinion, 282, 283A–B, 283, 284–294, 297A–C, 297E–F, 332, 333A–B, 333, 334–356, 359A–C, 359E–F, 369A–C, 393, 529, Unit 3: T64
distinguishing between important and unimportant information, 516, 517A–B, 517, 518–532, 535A–C, 535E–F, 600, 601A–B, 601, 602–606, 609A–C, Unit 5: T64
drawing conclusions, 29, 73, 129, 183, 253, 263, 371, 405G–H, 408–420, 424, 425A–B, 425, 426–440, 443A–C, 443E–F, 446–468, 481A–C, 483, 611, 651, 725, Unit 4: T62
forming generalizations, 157G–H, 160–186, 189G–H, 192–212, 241G–H, 244–248, 251E–F, 435, 453, 699, 705, Unit 2: T62
identifying main idea/supporting details, 94, 95A–B, 95, 96–114, 117A–C, 117E–F, 127A–C, 127E–F, 149, 188K, 216, 291, 307, 343, 371G, 429, 623, Unit 1: T66
identifying problem and solution, 42, 43A–B, 43, 44–62, 65A–C, 65E–F, 93G–H, 96–114, 118, 119A–B, 119, 120–124, 127A–C, 395, 411, 488C, 545, 632, 633A–B, 633, 634–660, 663A–C, 663E–F, 691G–H, 694–710, 723A–C, Unit 1: T64, Unit 6: T64
making inferences, 41G–H, 44–62, 65G–H, 66, 67A–B, 67, 68–90, 93F, 109, 117G–H, 120–124, 147, 197, 225, 495, 515G–H, 518–532, 535G–H, 538–564, 567G–H, 570–596, 619, Unit 1: T62, Unit 5: T62
making judgments and decisions, 256, 257A–B, 257, 258–281, 281A–C, 281E–F, 331G–H, 334–359, 360, 361A–B, 361, 362–369, 369A–C, 631G–H, 634–660, 664, 665A–B, 665, 666–688, 691A–C, 691E–F, 713G–H, 716–720, 723A–C, Unit 3: T60, Unit 6: T62
making predictions, 20, 21, 41A–C, 44, 65A–C, 68, 72, 85, 93A–C, 96, 117A–C, 120, 127A–C, 132, 133A–B, 133, 134–154, 157A–C, 157E–F, 160, 189A–C, 192, 215A–C, 216, 217A–B, 217, 218–238, 241A–C, 241E–F, 244, 251A–C, 258, 281A–C, 284, 297A–C, 297M, 300, 331A–C, 334, 359A–C, 362, 376, 405A–C, 408, 423A–C, 426, 443A–C, 446, 471A–C, 474, 481A–C, 488, 515A–C, 518, 535A–C, 536, 537A–B, 537, 538–567, 567A–C, 567E–F, 599A–C, 599G–H, 602–609, 609A–C, 609E–F, 616, 631A–C, 634, 663A–C, 666, 691A–C, 694, 713A–C, 716, Unit 2: T60, Unit 5: T66
summarizing, 27, 36, 47, 60, 77, 88, 93H, 97, 103, 112, 122, 152, 171, 184, 203, 210, 229, 236, 246, 258, 273, 276, 281G–H, 284–298, 297G–H, 300–331, 354, 359G–H, 362–369, 371A–D, 385, 400, 415, 418, 438, 461, 466, 476, 507, 510, 525, 530, 551, 562, 579, 594, 604, 626, 657, 664E, 683, 686, 707, 718, Unit 3: T62

Conclusions, drawing. *See* Comprehension strategies.

Conjunctions, 93M–N, 117M–N

Consonant clusters, 189O–P, 205, 215O–P, 223, 241A

Content area reading, 96–113, 120–123, 129A–D, 244–247, 253A–B, 300–327, 362–365, 371A–D, 483A–B, 602–605, 611A–B, 694–709, 716–719, 725A–B

Context clues. *See* Vocabulary and vocabulary strategies.

Contractions, 331N, 483G, 515N, 599O–P, 609M–N, 611G, 691N

Conventions of language. *See* Grammar, mechanics and usage, Oral language development, Writing process.

Cooperative learning. *See* Group work, Partner work, Writing activities: collaboration in.

Critical thinking, 38, 62, 90, 108, 114, 124, 138, 148, 154, 168, 169, 186, 212, 238, 278, 294, 315, 328, 356, 366, 402, 420, 440, 465, 468, 478, 489, 512, 532, 564, 596, 606, 628, 660, 688, 710, 720. *See also* Story questions.

Cross-curricular
art, 30, 58, 249, 272, 284A, 302, 369O–P, 376A
fine arts, 18, 42, 66, 94, 118, 132, 158, 190, 216, 242, 256, 282, 298, 332, 360, 374, 406, 424, 444, 472, 486, 516, 536, 568, 600, 614, 632, 664, 692, 714
health, 120A, 127P, 441, 513
language arts, 18E, 42E, 66E, 94E, 118E, 132E, 190E, 216E, 242E, 256E, 282E, 298E, 300A, 322, 360E, 374E, 406E, 424E, 444E, 446A, 472E, 486E, 533, 536E, 568E, 597, 632E, 664E, 692E, 714E
math, 34, 56, 80, 104, 115, 138, 155, 166, 198, 224, 239, 274, 279, 318, 344, 392, 421, 452, 490, 524, 538A, 554, 565, 586, 624, 654, 670, 678, 696, 711, 723O–P
music, 150, 158E, 332E, 357, 516E, 560, 576, 600E
science, 20A, 24, 39, 54, 74, 91, 96A, 102, 120A, 125, 142, 160A, 176, 180, 187, 206, 226, 264, 290, 295, 320, 338, 367, 371A–D, 394, 396, 403, 408A, 412, 426A, 430, 454, 469, 474A, 481O–P, 492, 506, 518A, 528, 550, 580, 602A, 607, 609O–P, 629, 636, 650, 661, 672, 694A, 700, 716A, 721, Unit 6: T60
social studies, 28, 44A, 48, 63, 68A, 72, 91, 98, 129A–D, 134A, 144, 170, 192C, 196, 213, 218A, 222, 232, 244A, 249, 251O–P, 258A, 268, 286, 324, 329, 334A, 340, 362A, 380, 414, 432, 448, 460, 479, 488A, 500, 526, 540, 548, 570A, 588, 614E, 616A, 618, 620, 634A, 638, 666A, 674, 680, 689, 702

Cultural perspectives, 22, 52, 82, 108, 148, 182, 208, 228, 266, 288, 314, 348, 390, 410, 428, 456, 494, 522, 542, 574, 622, 648, 668, 698

Cummings, Pat, 282A, 284–297

Daily language activities, 41M, 65M, 93M, 117M, 127M, 157M, 189M, 215M, 241M, 251M, 281M, 297M, 331M, 359M, 369M, 405M, 423M, 443M, 471M, 481M, 515M, 535M, 567M, 599M, 609M, 631M, 663M, 691M, 713M, 723M

"Decisions," 724–725

Decisions, making. *See* Comprehension strategies: making judgments and decisions.

Diagrams, 20A, 44A, 91, 117C, 120A, 125, 189L, 213, 218A, 239, 241K, 253B, 253E, 314, 319, 331H, 362A, 368, 423G, 441,471L, 476, 481L, 513, 625, 634A, 725B, 725D, Unit 3: T61, Unit 4: T60. *See also* Study skills.
Dialogue. *See* Fluency, Writing activities.
Dictionary, using, 137, 156, 214, 227, 251J, 443J, 465, 483A–B, 483E, Unit 2: T61
Digraphs, 319, 331A, 331O–P, 353, 359A
Directions, reading, giving, following, 371D, 405K–L, 423K–L, 443K–L, 470, 471K–L, 481K–L, 483A–F, 611A–B, 713N, Unit 2: T63, T65, Unit 3: T65, Unit 4: T61
Discussions, class and group, 16I, 16J, 16, 17, 20A, 37, 38, 41A–C, 61, 62, 65A–C, 68A, 68B, 89, 90, 93A–C, 96A, 113, 114, 117A–C, 123, 124, 127A–C, 128, 129, 129J, 130I, 130J, 130, 131, 153, 154, 157A–C, 173, 174, 185,186, 189A–C, 211, 212, 215A–C, 237, 238, 241A–C, 244A, 247, 248, 251A–C, 251D, 252, 253, 253B, 254I, 254, 255, 258A, 278, 281A–C, 284A, 293, 294, 297A–C, 327, 328, 331A–C, 355, 356, 359A–C, 362A, 365, 366, 369A–C, 371, 372I, 372J, 372, 373, 401, 402, 405A–C, 419, 420, 423A–C, 439, 440, 443A–C, 467, 468, 471A–C, 477, 478, 481A–C, 482, 484I, 484J, 484, 485, 511, 512, 515A–C, 531, 532, 535A–C, 563, 564, 567A–C, 595, 596, 599A–C, 605, 606, 609A–C, 610, 611, 612I, 612J, 612, 613, 627, 628, 631A–C, 659, 660, 663A–C, 687, 688, 691A–C, 695, 709, 710, 713A–C, 713F, 713L, 715, 718A, 719, 720, 723A–C, 723D
Drafting and drafting strategies, 41K, 65K, 93K, 117K, 127K, 129G, 157K, 189K, 215K, 241K, 251K, 253E, 281K, 297K, 331K, 359K, 369K, 371G, 405K, 423K, 443K, 471K, 481K, 483E, 515K, 535K, 567K, 599K, 609K, 611E, 631K, 663K, 691K, 713K, 723K, 725E

Earth's First Creatures, 474–481
Elaboration, 129H, 253F, 371H, 483F, 611F, 725E
Encyclopedias, using, 24, 44A, 63, 91, 98, 115, 125, 155, 213, 214, 222, 239, 240, 249, 279, 329, 357, 369D, 403, 443H, 483A–B, 490, 597, 607, 629, 638, 661, 689, 711, 712, 713K, 720, 721, 725B, Unit 2: T61
English as a Second Language. *See* Language support.
Explanatory writing. *See* Writing activities.
Expository writing. *See* Writing activities.
Extend activities. *See* Cross-curricular, Cultural perspectives, Leveled books, Meeting Individual Needs, Presentation ideas, Story activities.

Fact and nonfact, distinguishing. *See* Comprehension strategies.
Fact and opinion, distinguishing. *See* Comprehension strategies.
Figurative language, 81, 129, 131, 255, 320, 342, 373, 535I–J, 599I–J, 609G–H, 611, Unit 5: T65
Figurative meaning, 131
"Final Curve," 372–373
First person, 17
Flashbacks, 226, 673
Fleming, Candace, 256A, 258
Fluency
choral reading, 16, 254, 612
dialogue, 85, 151, 270, 498, 582
echo reading, 416, 472E
partner reading, 46, 130, 372, 484, 558, 686
personification, 612
reading haiku, 304
reading rate, 36, 60, 88, 112, 122, 152, 184, 210, 236, 246, 276, 292, 326, 354, 364, 400, 418, 438, 466, 476, 510, 530, 562, 594, 604, 626, 654, 686, 708, 718
reading with expression/intonation, 26, 88, 100, 204, 234, 290, 350, 386, 434, 520, 644, 684
repeated readings, 162, 464, 706
rereading for, 36, 60, 88, 100, 112, 122, 151, 152, 162, 184, 204, 210, 234, 236, 246, 276, 292, 304, 326, 350, 354, 364, 386, 400, 418, 434, 438, 466, 476, 510, 530, 558, 562, 594, 604, 626, 658, 686, 708, 718
Foreshadowing, 568E
Fox and the Guinea Pig, The, 488–515
Free verse, 253, 483
Freewriting, 129G, 405K, 481K, 599K, 611E
Friedrich, Elizabeth, 190A, 192

"Garden We Planted Together, The," 610–611
Generalizations, forming. *See* Comprehension strategies.
Genre, literary. *See* Literary genre.
Gifted and talented. *See* Challenge, Meeting Individual Needs.
Glossary, using, 20B, 41P, 44B, 65P, 68B, 93P, 96B, 117P, 120B, 127P, 134B, 157P, 160B, 189P, 192B, 215P, 218B, 241P, 244B, 251P, 258B, 281P, 284B, 297P, 300B, 331P, 334B, 359P, 362B, 369P, 376B, 405P, 408B, 423P, 426B, 443P, 446B, 471P, 474B, 481P, 488B, 515P, 518B, 535P, 538B, 567P, 570B, 599P, 602B, 609P, 616B, 631P, 634B, 663P, 666B, 691P, 694B, 713P, 716B, 723P
Gluskabe and the Snow Bird, 408–423
Golenbock, Peter, 614A, 627
Grammar, mechanics and usage, 41M–N, 65M–N, 93M–N, 117M–N, 127M–N, 129I, 157M–N, 189M–N, 215M–N, 241M–N, 251M–N, 253G, 281M–N, 297M–N, 331M–N, 359M–N, 369M–N, 371I, 405M–N, 423M–N, 443M–N, 471M–N, 481M–N, 483G, 515M–N, 535M–N, 567M–N, 599M–N, 609M–N, 611G, 631M–N, 663M–N, 691M–N, 713M–N, 723M–N, 725G
abbreviations, 157N, 369N
adjectives, 359M, 405M–N, 423M–N, 443M–N, 471M–N, 481M–N, 483G, 611G
adverbs, 253G, 631M–N, 663M–N, 723M–N, 725E
articles, 423M–N, 483G, 611G
capitalization, 41N, 65N, 93N, 129I, 157M–N, 215N, 297N, 359N, 369N, 405N, 423N, 443N, 535N, 567N, 713N, 723N
conjunctions, 93M–N, 117M–N
contractions, 331N, 483G, 515N, 599O–P, 609M–N, 611G, 691N
homophone/homographs, 117I–J, 609M–N, 663O–P
negatives, 691M–N
nouns, 157M–N, 189M–N, 215M–N, 241M–N, 251M–N, 359M, 371I, 405M–N, 423M–N, 599N
possessives, 241M–N, 253G, 371I, 599M–N, 609M–N, 725G
prepositions/prepositional phrase, 713M–N
pronouns, 253G, 515M–N, 535M–N, 567M–N, 599M–N, 609M–N, 611G, 725G
punctuation, 41M–N, 65N, 85, 93N, 117N, 129I, 157N, 189N, 241M–N, 253G, 281N, 297N, 331N, 359N, 481N, 515N, 567N, 609N, 691N, 713N, 723N
quotations, 117N, 359N, 423N, 567N
sentences, 41M–N, 65M–N, 93M–N, 117M–N, 127M–N, 129I, 281M–N, 297M–N, 331M–N, 359M–N, 723M–N
subject–verb agreement, 281M–N, 331M–N, 371I
titles, 359N
verbs, 253G, 281M–N, 297M–N, 331M–N, 359M–N, 369M–N, 371I, 405M, 483G, 515N, 567M–N, 725G
See also Abbreviations, Adjectives, Adverbs, Capitalization, Commas, Nouns, Pronouns, Punctuation, Sentences, Spelling, Verbs, Writing Process.
Grammar/spelling connections, 41K, 65K, 93K, 117K, 127K, 129I, 157K, 189K, 215K, 241K, 251K, 253I, 281K, 297K, 331K, 359K, 369K, 371I, 405K, 423K, 443K, 471K, 481K, 483G, 515K, 535K, 567K, 599K, 609K, 611G, 631K, 663K, 691K, 713K, 723K, 725G
Graphic aids/organizers
charts. *See* Charts.
diagrams, 20A, 44A, 91, 117C, 120A, 125, 189L, 213, 218A, 239, 241K, 253B, 253E, 314, 319, 331H, 362A, 368, 423G, 441, 476, 471L, 481L, 513, 625, 634A, 725B, 725D, Unit 3: T61, Unit 4: T60
flowcharts, 189B, 206, 296, 443K, 446C, 471K, 483B, 483C
graphs, 80, 318, 358, 404, 490, 654, 691L
maps, 28, 39, 41L, 58, 61, 63, 98, 99, 115, 155, 158, 189F, 222, 286, 324, 329, 330, 340, 359D, 359L, 376A, 403, 414, 423K, 423L, 518A, 528, 533, 540, 702, Unit 3: T61, Unit 6: T63
organizer for persuasive writing, 297K, 371F
sense star, 300A
summary organizer, 281H
timelines, 275, 442, 444E, 479, 567D, 588, 711, Unit 4: T61
webs, 215K, 258A, 281D, 284A, 297K, 405H, 405K, 426A, 432, 527, 535H, 535K, 570A, 616A, 643, 645, 673, 723K, 725D
See also Charts, Diagrams, Graphs, Maps, Study Skills, Webs.
Graphophonic cues, 27, 29, 47, 75, 110, 168, 230, 267, 291, 311, 317, 436, 505, 573, 623, 701
Graphs, 80, 166, 318, 358, 404, 490, 565, 654, 689, 691K, 691L, 711
bar, 80, 404, 565, 654, 689, 691L, 711
circle, 689
line graph, 358
pictograph, 318, 490, 691K
pie, 166
Grass Sandals: The Travels of Basho, 302–331
Group work, 16J, 16, 17, 41D, 41F, 41H, 43B, 56, 65D, 65H, 67B, 68C, 79, 85, 91, 93F, 96C, 115, 117D, 117F, 117H, 117J, 119B, 123, 125, 127J, 128, 129E, 129, 130, 131, 132E, 134C, 157F, 157H, 157L, 157M, 159B, 176, 189F,189H, 189J, 189K, 192C, 194, 204, 213, 215F, 215H, 217B, 236, 241F, 241H, 241J, 249, 251F, 251H, 252, 253C, 253, 254J, 254, 255, 268, 276, 281F, 281H, 281J, 284C, 291, 295, 297D, 297F, 297H, 297J,

299B, 319, 331B, 331D, 331F, 331J, 333B, 337, 357, 359J, 362C, 369F, 369H, 369J, 370, 371A, 371, 371E, 373, 375B, 403, 405D, 405J, 423H, 423J, 443C, 443F, 461, 466, 471F, 471L, 471N, 471P, 474C, 481F, 481J, 481N, 482, 483A, 484J, 485, 506, 508, 510, 513, 515F, 517B, 521, 535H, 535J, 535N, 553, 567F, 567J, 570A, 599F, 599H, 599J, 607, 609J, 610, 611C, 611D, 611, 612, 613, 614E, 616C, 626, 631N, 633B, 638, 663F, 663H, 663J, 665B, 666C, 680, 684, 691F, 691H, 691J, 694C, 698, 700, 711, 713F, 713J, 715B, 716A, 716C, 721, 723H, 723J, 725. *See also* Activities for anthology and leveled books, Alternate teaching strategies, Theme projects.

Handwriting, 65K, 117K, 157K, 215K, 281K, 297K, 405K, 443K, 535K, 567K, 691K, Units 1–6: T68–T71

Handwriting CD-ROM. *See* Handwriting.

Hatmaker's Sign, The, 258–281

Health link, 120A, 127P, 441, 513

Historical context in literature, 202, 219, 221, 271

Homophones/homographs, 117I–J, 367, 609M–N, 663O–P

Hopkins, Lee Bennett, 16–17

"How to Tell the Top of a Hill", 484–485

Hughes, Langston, 372–373

Humor, as literary device, 44, 484, 485, 508

"I Ask My Mother to Sing," 128–129

Idioms, 373, 413, 609G–H

Imagery, 298E, 371, 714E

Important and unimportant information, distinguishing. *See* Comprehension strategies.

Independent reading. *See* Meeting Individual Needs: leveled books, Self-selected reading..

Inferences, making. *See* Comprehension strategies.

Informal assessment. *See* Assessment.

Internet connection, 16J, 22, 39, 41D, 48, 63, 65D, 74, 91, 93D, 98, 115, 117D, 123, 125, 127D, 129, 130J, 148, 155, 157D, 176, 187, 189D, 208, 213, 215D, 226, 239, 241D, 247, 249, 251D, 253, 254J, 264, 266, 279, 281D, 290, 295, 297D, 318, 329, 331D, 334, 338, 357, 359D, 365, 367, 369D, 371, 372J, 396, 403, 405D, 410, 421, 423D, 430, 441, 443D, 454, 469, 471D, 477, 479, 481D, 483, 483A–B, 484J, 490, 506, 513, 515D, 522, 533, 535D, 560, 565, 567D, 597, 599D, 607, 609D, 611, 612J, 618, 629, 631D, 636, 661, 663D, 674, 689, 691D, 711, 713D, 721, 723D, 725

Interviews, 16J, 65D, 93D, 127L, 189L, 241L, 251K–L, 253F, 369C, 369L, 443L, 535C, 599L, 620, 631D, 648, 690, 691L, 713D, 725F, Unit 2: T62, Unit 6: T61

Johnson, Georgia Douglas, 612–613

Jordan, Norman, 252–253

Journal, 37, 41C, 41P, 61, 65P, 89, 93L, 93P, 113, 117P, 123, 127P, 153, 157A, 157B, 157L, 157P, 185, 189P, 211, 213, 215P, 237, 241B, 241C, 241P, 247, 251P, 258A, 277, 281A, 281P, 293, 294, 297A, 297C, 297P, 327, 331P, 355, 359A, 359P, 365, 369P, 401, 405P, 419, 423C, 423P, 439, 443P, 467, 471C, 471P, 477, 481P, 511, 515C, 515L, 515P, 531, 535P, 563, 567A, 567B, 567P, 595, 599P, 605, 609P, 616A, 619, 627, 631N, 631P, 659, 663A, 663B, 663P, 687, 691P, 709, 713D, 713P, 719, 723P

Judgments and decisions, making. *See* Comprehension strategies.

Just a Dream, 160–189

Justin and the Best Biscuits in the World, 134–157

Language Arts link. *See* Cross-curricular.

Language support, 20A, 21, 25, 32, 35, 41F, 41G, 41H, 41J, 41L, 41M, 41O, 43A, 44A, 45, 51, 55, 56, 57, 65E, 65F, 65H, 65J, 65L, 65M, 65O, 67A, 68A, 69, 70, 76, 79, 93F, 93H, 93J, 93L, 93M, 93O, 95A, 96C, 97, 101, 103, 107, 117F, 117H, 117J, 117L, 117M, 117O, 120C, 127E, 127F, 127H, 127J, 127L, 127M, 127O, 129G, 134C, 135, 136, 139, 157F, 157H, 157J, 157L, 157M, 157O, 159A, 160A, 161, 164, 167, 172, 179, 189F, 189H, 189J, 189L, 189M, 189O, 192A, 193, 195, 200, 207, 215F, 215H, 215I, 215J, 215L, 215M, 215O, 217A, 218A, 219, 220, 231, 233, 235, 241F, 241H, 241J, 241L, 241M, 241O, 244C, 245, 251F, 251H, 251J, 251L, 251M, 251O, 253E, 257A, 258C, 259, 262, 271, 275, 281F, 281H, 281J, 281L, 281M, 281O, 284A, 285, 289, 297F, 297H, 297J, 297L, 297M, 297O, 299A, 300C, 301, 306, 309, 323, 331F, 331G, 331H, 331J, 331L, 331M, 331O, 334A, 335, 337, 343, 352, 359F, 359H, 359J, 359L, 359M, 359O, 362A, 362C, 369F, 369H, 369J, 369L, 369M, 369O, 371C, 371G, 376C, 378, 381, 382, 393, 405E, 405F, 405H, 405J, 405L, 405M, 405O, 408A, 408C, 413, 415, 423F, 423H, 423J, 423L, 423M, 423O, 426A, 426C, 427, 435, 437, 443F, 443H, 443J, 443L, 443M, 443O, 445A, 446A, 446C, 447, 450, 453, 458, 471F, 471H, 471J, 471L, 471M, 471O, 474A, 475, 481F, 481H, 481J, 481L, 481M, 481O, 483E, 487A, 488A, 488C, 488, 493, 515F, 515G, 515H, 515J, 515L, 515O, 518A, 518C, 519, 520, 523, 525, 535F, 535H, 535J, 535L, 535M, 535O, 538A, 538C, 539, 541, 546, 567E, 567F, 567H, 567J, 567L, 567M, 567O, 570A, 570C, 571, 578, 589, 599F, 599H, 599J, 599L, 599M, 599O, 602A, 603, 609F, 609H, 609J, 609L, 609M, 609O, 611E, 616A, 616C, 617, 621, 625, 631F, 631H, 631J, 631L, 631M, 631O, 634A, 635, 641, 652, 655, 663F, 663H, 663J, 663L, 663M, 663O, 666A, 666C, 667, 669, 675, 677, 682, 691F, 691H, 691J, 691L, 691M, 691O, 694C, 695, 697, 704, 707, 713F, 713H, 713J, 713L, 713M, 713O, 716A, 716C, 717, 723F, 723H, 723J, 723L, 723M

Leah's Pony, 192–215

Learning styles
- auditory, 118E, 120C, 362C, 406E, 474C, 516E, 518C, 602C, 614E, 616C, 620, 714E, 716C
- bodily, Unit 1: T60–T63, T65, Unit 2: T60, T61, T64, T66, Unit 3: T60–T62, T64–T66, Unit 4: T62–T64, Unit 5: T64–T66, Unit 6: T61–T63, T65
- interpersonal, 20C, 22, 24, 48, 65H, 108, 119B, 132E, 133B, 142, 157F, 157H, 160C, 176, 180, 182, 189F, 189J, 215F, 226, 228, 232, 241H, 243B, 251F, 258C, 266, 268, 274, 288, 297H, 299B, 300A, 300C, 302, 314, 320, 322, 324, 361B, 369J, 376C, 380, 390, 408C, 410, 412, 414, 423F, 426C, 456, 460, 471J, 472E, 488C, 492, 500, 518C, 522, 536E, 538B, 538C, 540, 542, 560, 567F, 567H, 567J, 600E, 618, 620, 632E, 634D, 638, 648, 654, 663J, 668, 694B, 700, 713H, 723H
- intrapersonal, 58, 66E, 298E, 361B, 488C, 500, 550, 616C, 665B, 698, 714E
- kinesthetic, 18E, 30, 42E, 44C, 68C, 94E, 96C, 118E, 138, 148, 158E, 160C, 180, 215H, 232, 244C, 284C, 298E, 332E, 334C, 360E, 374E, 390, 406E, 412, 424E, 456, 486E, 515F, 516E, 518B, 518C, 570C, 599F, 614E, 623E, 634C, 691F, 694C, 713F
- linguistic, 19B, 20C, 22, 41J, 43B, 44C, 54, 65H, 65J, 68C, 93H, 94E, 96B, 96C, 117J, 120C, 127F, 127H, 127J, 133B, 134C, 142, 157H, 157J, 159B, 160C, 189J, 190E, 191B, 192C, 196, 208, 215F, 215H, 215J, 217B, 218C, 228, 241F, 241J, 244C, 251F, 251H, 258C, 268, 272, 282E, 284C, 297F, 297H, 297J, 300A, 300C, 322, 331J, 332E, 333B, 334C, 359H, 360E, 361B, 362C, 369F, 369H, 369J, 375B, 376A, 376C, 405F, 405H, 407B, 408C, 410, 425B, 426C, 430, 432, 443F, 443H, 443J, 445B, 446A, 446C, 448, 454, 460, 471J, 472E, 473B, 474C, 481F, 481H, 481J, 484C, 487B, 494, 500, 506, 515F, 515H, 515J, 518C, 528, 537B, 538A, 538C, 550, 567F, 567H, 567J, 568E, 569B, 570C, 599J, 601B, 602C, 609E, 609F, 609H, 609J, 616A, 616C, 618, 632E, 634C, 636, 650, 663H, 663J, 666A, 692E, 693B, 694A, 698, 700, 713F, 713H, 716C, 723F, 723H, 723J
- logical, 19B, 20A, 26, 28, 41F, 41H, 43B, 44A, 52, 56, 65H, 65J, 68A, 72, 93H, 102, 117H, 119B, 120A, 134A, 157F, 159B, 160A, 189F, 191B, 192A, 215J, 217B, 218A, 241F, 241H, 241J, 243B, 244A, 256E, 257B, 258B, 258C, 264, 281F, 281H, 283B, 284A, 297F, 331F, 333B, 334A, 348, 359H, 360E, 362A, 369H, 375B, 376A, 396, 407B, 408A, 423F, 423H, 425B, 426A, 443F, 443H, 443J, 444E, 445B, 446A, 448, 473B, 474A, 481F, 481H, 481J, 487B, 488C, 515H, 517B, 535F, 536E, 537B, 548, 554, 567B, 569B, 570A, 602A, 609F, 609J, 624, 633B, 634A, 636, 650, 663H, 666A, 674, 678, 680, 694A, 702, 716A, 723F, 723J
- mathematical, 56, 98, 102, 166, 222, 224, 274, 318, 338, 452, 490, 524, 554, 624, 654, 670, 678, 696
- musical, 158E, 533, 560, 622, 648
- oral/verbal, 37, 44C, 61, 89, 96C, 109, 113, 118E, 123, 132E, 134C, 148, 153, 192C, 211, 216E, 218C, 237, 244C, 247, 277, 293, 327, 334C, 355, 362C, 365, 376C, 380, 401, 419, 439, 446C, 467, 474C, 477, 486E, 506, 511, 517B, 518C, 531, 563, 570C, 595, 602C, 605, 614E, 627, 658, 666C, 687, 692E, 700, 709, 716C, 719
- spatial, 18E, 24, 28, 42E, 48, 58, 66E, 72, 95B, 98, 132E, 182, 226, 242E, 256E, 258C, 264, 272, 281H, 284C, 286, 290, 298E, 320, 324, 338, 348, 414, 424E, 430, 432, 486E, 487B, 490, 492, 506, 524, 540, 542, 632E, 638, 664E, 665B, 672, 680, 696, 702, 714E
- visual, 20A, 20C, 30, 41H, 44A, 44C, 52, 68A, 118E, 120A, 127F, 127H, 132E, 133B, 134A, 138, 154B, 160A, 170, 176, 190E, 192A, 206, 208, 216E, 218A, 222, 226, 242E, 244A, 251H, 266, 282E, 284A, 284C, 288, 297H, 297J, 298E, 299B, 300C, 302, 314, 318, 334A, 360E, 362A, 374E, 396, 405F, 405H, 406E, 423H, 426A, 444E, 452, 454, 474A, 486E, 516E, 522, 528, 568E, 569B, 570A, 600E, 601B, 602A, 609H, 616C, 633B, 634A, 666A, 670, 674, 692E, 715B, 716A

See also Alternate teaching strategies.

Lee, Li-Young, 128–129

Leveled books. *See* Meeting Individual Needs.

Library, using, 630, 662, 690, 712, 722, Unit 6: T61. *See also* Study skills.

Limited English Proficiency. *See* Language support.

Listening and speaking activities, 16I, 16J, 16, 17, 18E, 20A, 37, 41D, 41L, 42E, 44C, 61, 65D, 65L, 66E, 68A, 89, 93D, 93L, 94E, 96A, 113, 117D, 117L, 118E, 120A, 123, 127D, 127L, 129, 129J, 131, 132E, 134A, 153, 157D, 157L, 158E, 160A, 185, 189D, 189L, 190E, 192A, 211, 215D, 215L, 216E, 218A, 237, 241D, 241L, 242E, 244A, 247, 251D, 251L, 253H, 253, 255, 256E, 258A, 277, 281D, 281L, 282E, 284A, 293, 297D, 297L, 298E, 300A, 327, 331D, 331L, 332E, 334A, 355, 359D, 359L, 360E, 362A, 365, 369D, 369L, 371, 371J, 373, 374E, 376A, 401, 405D, 405L, 406E, 408A, 419, 423D, 423L, 424E, 426C, 439, 443D, 443L, 444E, 446A, 467, 471D, 471L, 472E, 474A, 477, 481D, 481L, 483H, 483, 485, 486E, 488A, 511, 515D, 515L, 516E, 518A, 531, 535D, 535L, 536E, 538C, 563, 567D, 567L, 568E, 570A, 595, 599D, 599L, 600E, 602C, 605, 609D, 609L, 611H, 611, 613, 614E, 616A, 627, 631D, 631L, 632E, 634A, 659, 663D, 663L, 664E, 666A, 687, 691D, 691L, 692E, 694A, 709, 713D, 713L, 714E, 716A, 719, 723D, 723L, 725H, 725, Unit 1–6: T60–T66. *See also* Speaking and listening activities, Speaking and listening strategies.

Listening library, 16, 42A, 44, 66A, 68, 94A, 96, 118A, 120, 128, 130, 132A, 134, 158A, 160, 190A, 192, 216A, 218, 242A, 244, 252, 254, 256A, 258, 272, 282A, 284, 298A, 300, 332A, 334, 360A, 362, 370, 372, 374A, 376, 406A, 408, 424A, 426, 444A, 446, 472A, 474, 482, 484, 486A, 488, 516A, 518, 536A, 538, 568A, 570, 600A, 602, 610, 612, 614A, 616, 632A, 634, 664A, 666, 692A, 694, 706, 714A, 716, 724

Lists, making, 16J, 23, 39, 41L, 41P, 53, 58, 63, 65C, 65D, 65P, 67B, 93P, 96, 99, 115, 117P, 127F, 127P, 129B, 130, 131, 157P, 160A, 168, 174, 189F, 189K, 189P, 205, 215P, 218A, 241H, 241L, 241P, 249, 251F, 251O, 251P, 252, 254J, 254, 255, 281L, 281P, 285, 287, 289, 295, 297D, 297P, 319, 331P, 345, 359K, 359P, 362A, 362C, 368, 369D, 369P, 370, 371C, 405P, 408A, 423P, 443P, 445B, 471D, 471P, 481P, 482, 483B, 483C, 484, 485, 515C, 515F, 515P, 535P, 567M, 567P, 569B, 570, 599F, 599M, 599P, 609P, 610, 612, 613, 622, 631H, 631P, 634A, 649, 651, 661, 663P, 666A, 691P, 694A, 701, 713D, 713F, 713P, 723P, 724, Unit 1: T64, Unit 6 : T63

Literacy support. *See* Language support.

Literal meaning, 131, 132E

Literary devices
- alliteration, 94E, 132E, 136, 158E, 692E, 714E
- analogy, 372, 378
- assonance, 94E, 194, 485
- figurative language, 129, 255, 342, 373, 611
- exaggeration, 664E
- first person, 17
- flashbacks, 226, 673
- foreshadowing, 568E
- free verse, 253, 483
- humor, 44, 484, 485, 508
- idioms, 373, 413, 609G–H
- imagery, 298E, 371, 714E
- irony, 44, 664E
- metaphor, 42E, 131
- nonsense, use of, 484, 485
- personification, 612, 613
- repetition, 17, 18E, 94E, 132E, 242E
- rhyme/rhyme patterns, 48E, 94E, 118E, 130, 131, 484, 485, 516E, 613, 614E, 664E, 725
- rhythm, 42E, 130, 131, 158E, 242E, 516E, 614E, 725
- sensory words, 612, 640
- symbolism, 254, 472E, 590, 600E, 656, 714E
- tone, 44, 118E, 260, 568E, 664E
- text features, 16, 372
- vivid words, 42E, 94E

Literary genre, 18E, 20, 21, 42E, 44, 45, 66E, 68, 69, 94E, 96, 97, 118E, 120, 121, 128, 132E, 134, 135, 158E, 160, 161, 190E, 192, 193, 216E, 218, 219, 242E, 244, 245, 252, 256E, 258, 259, 282E, 284, 285, 298E, 300, 301, 332E, 334, 335, 360E, 362, 363, 370, 374E, 376, 377, 406E, 408, 409, 424E, 426, 427, 444E, 446, 447, 472E, 474, 475, 482, 486E, 488, 489, 516E, 518, 519, 536E, 538, 539, 568E, 570, 571, 600E, 602, 603, 610, 614E, 616, 617, 632E, 634, 635, 664E, 666, 667, 692E, 694, 695, 714E, 716, 717, 724
- African-American spiritual, 332E
- autobiography, 284, 286, 424E, 444E, 447
- biographical story, 301, 370, 617
- biography, 256E, 616, 724
- creative autobiography, 285, 482
- fable, 190E, 486E, 494
- fairy tale, 360E, 568E, 570, 571, 593, 610, 632E, 634, 635
- fantasy, 161, 252, 460
- folk tale, 18E, 488, 489, 536E, 538, 539
- historical fiction, 66E, 69, 192, 193, 216E, 219, 252, 258, 259, 335, 370
- myth, 406E, 408, 409, 421, 423D
- narrative nonfiction, 97, 377, 519, 610
- nonfiction, 96, 128, 216E, 244, 362, 376, 426, 446, 474, 518, 602, 694, 716
- play, 666, 667, 669, 680, 724
- poetry, 42E, 94E, 118E, 128, 132E, 242E, 300, 372, 373, 374E, 482, 614E, 664E, 692E
- realistic fiction, 20, 21, 44, 45, 68, 128, 134, 135, 192, 193, 218, 282E
- science article, 121, 427, 475, 603, 609, 717
- science nonfiction, 694, 695, 716
- social studies article, 245, 362, 363
- song, 158E, 516E, 600E
- *See also* Poetry.

Literary genre, comparing and contrasting, 463

Literary response, 17, 37, 41A–C, 61, 65A–C, 89, 93A–C, 113, 117A–C, 123, 127A–C, 129, 131, 153, 157A–C, 185, 189A–C, 211, 215A–C, 237, 241A–C, 247, 251A–C, 253, 255, 277, 281A–C, 293, 297A–C, 327, 331A–C, 355, 359A–C, 365, 369A–C, 371, 373, 401, 405A–C, 419, 423A–C, 439, 443A–C, 467, 471A–C, 477, 481A–C, 483, 485, 511, 515A–C, 531, 535A–C, 563, 567A–C, 595, 599A–C, 605, 609A–C, 611, 613, 627, 631A–C, 659, 663A–C, 687, 691A–C, 709, 713A–C, 719, 723A–C, 725

Longfellow, Henry Wadsworth, 130–131

Lost Lake, The, 20–41

Louie, Ai-Ling, 568A, 595

MacLachlan, Patricia, 66A, 89

Main idea/supporting details, identifying. *See* Comprehension strategies.

Malachite Palace, The, 634–663

Maps, using, 28, 39, 41L, 58, 61, 63, 98, 99, 115, 155, 158, 189F, 222, 286, 324, 329, 330, 340, 359D, 359L, 376A, 403, 414, 423K, 423L, 518A, 528, 533, 540, 702, Unit 3: T61, Unit 6: T63

Math link. *See* Cross-curricular.

Mechanics and usage. *See* Grammar, mechanics and usage.

Medearis, Angela Shelf, 724–725

Media, reading, 253A–B

Meet an Underwater Explorer, 426–443

Meeting Individual Needs
- for comprehension, 19B, 41F, 41H, 43B, 65F, 65H, 67B, 93F, 93H, 95B, 117F, 117H, 119B, 127F, 133B, 157F, 157H, 159B, 189F, 189H, 191B, 215F, 215H, 217B, 241F, 241H, 243B, 251F, 257B, 281F, 281H, 283B, 297F, 297H, 299B, 331F, 331H, 333B, 359F, 359H, 361B, 369F, 375B, 405F, 405H, 407B, 423F, 423H, 425B, 443F, 443H, 445B, 471F, 471H, 473B, 481F, 487B, 515F, 515H, 517B, 535F, 535H, 537B, 567F, 567H, 569B, 599F, 599H, 601B, 609F, 615B, 631F, 631H, 633B, 663F, 663H, 665B, 691F, 691H, 693B, 713F, 713H, 715B, 723F
- for study skills, 40, 64, 92, 116, 126, 156, 188, 214, 240, 250, 280, 296, 330, 358, 368, 404, 422, 442, 470, 480, 514, 534, 566, 598, 608, 630, 662, 690, 712, 722
- for vocabulary, 20C, 41J, 44C, 65J, 68C, 93J, 96C, 117J, 120C, 127H, 127J, 134C, 157J, 160C, 189J, 192C, 215J, 218C, 241J, 244C, 251H, 251J, 258C, 281J, 284C, 297J, 300C, 331J, 334C, 359J, 362C, 369H, 369J, 376C, 405J, 408C, 423J, 426C, 443J, 446C, 471J, 474C, 481H, 481J, 488C, 515J, 518C, 535J, 538C, 567J, 570C, 599J, 602C, 609H, 609J, 616C, 631J, 634C, 663J, 666C, 691J, 694C, 713J, 716C, 723H, 723J
- for writing, 41L, 65L, 93L, 117L, 127L, 157L, 189L, 215L, 241L, 251L, 281L, 297L, 331L, 359L, 369L, 405L, 423L, 443L, 471L, 481L, 515L, 535L, 567L, 599L, 609L, 631L, 663L, 691L, 713L, 723L
- grouping suggestions for strategic reading, 20, 44, 68, 96, 120, 134, 160, 192, 218, 244, 258, 284, 300, 334, 362, 376, 408, 426, 446, 474, 488, 518, 538, 570, 602, 616, 634, 666, 694, 716
- leveled books, 41A–C, 65A–C, 93A–C, 117A–C, 127A–C, 157A–C, 189A–C, 215A–C, 241A–C, 251A–C, 281A–C, 297A–C, 331A–C, 359A–C, 369A–C, 405A–C, 423A–C, 443A–C, 471A–C, 481A–C, 515A–C, 535A–C, 567A–C, 599A–C, 609A–C, 631A–C, 663A–C, 691A–C, 713A–C, 723A–C
- resources for, 18B, 42B, 66B, 94B, 118B, 132B, 158B, 190B, 216B, 242B, 256B, 282B, 298B, 332B, 360B, 374B, 406B, 424B, 444B, 472B, 486B, 516B, 536B, 568B, 600B, 614B, 632B, 664B, 692B, 714B

Merrill, Jean, 664A, 666

Metaphors, 42E, 81, 131, 254, 255, 535I–J, 599I–J, Unit 5: T65

Minilessons, 23, 27, 29, 35, 47, 53, 55, 59, 75, 77, 81, 83, 99, 101, 103, 109, 137, 143, 147, 149, 163, 167, 169, 171, 173, 181, 183, 197, 203, 205, 207, 209, 223, 225, 227, 229, 261, 267, 273, 275, 287, 289, 291, 307, 309, 319, 323, 337, 343, 345, 347, 353, 385, 389, 393, 395, 399, 411, 413, 415, 417, 429, 433, 435, 437, 453, 457, 461, 465, 491,

495, 499, 507, 509, 521, 523, 525, 527, 545, 551, 553, 559, 575, 579, 585, 591, 619, 621, 623, 625, 643, 645, 649, 651, 657, 673, 677, 681, 683, 699, 701, 703, 705, 707

Mochizuki, Ken, 216A, 218

Modeling skills, 19A, 21, 22, 23, 41E, 41G, 41I, 43A, 45, 49, 65E, 65G, 65I, 67A, 70, 75, 78, 93E, 93G, 93I, 95A, 98, 104, 106, 110, 117E, 117G, 117I, 119A, 127E, 127G, 127I, 133A, 135, 136, 141, 157E, 157G, 157I, 159A, 162, 163, 165, 172, 189E, 189G, 189I, 191A, 194, 195, 201, 215E, 215G, 215I, 217A, 220, 227, 228, 229, 233, 241E, 241G, 241I, 243A, 251E, 251G, 251I, 257A, 269, 270, 274, 281E, 281G, 281I, 283A, 286, 287, 288, 297E, 297G, 297I, 299A, 302, 308, 313, 319, 331E, 331G, 331I, 333A, 336, 342, 344, 359E, 359G, 359I, 361A, 369E, 369G, 369I, 371A, 371C, 375A, 378, 379, 392, 397, 405E, 405G, 405I, 408A, 411, 412, 423E, 423G, 423I, 425A, 429, 432, 433, 434, 443E, 443G, 443I, 446A, 449, 456, 460, 471E, 471G, 471I, 474A, 481E, 481G, 481I, 483A, 487A, 492, 505, 515E, 515G, 515I, 517A, 520, 524, 535E, 535G, 535I, 538A, 540, 541, 549, 567E, 567G, 567I, 569A, 571, 584, 599E, 599G, 599I, 602A, 609E, 609G, 609I, 611A, 616A, 617, 623, 624, 631E, 631G, 631I, 633A, 636, 655, 663E, 663G, 663I, 666A, 667, 671, 675, 691E, 691G, 691I, 693A, 694A, 696, 703, 713E, 713G, 713I, 715A, 716A, 723E, 723G, 723I, 725A

Mom's Best Friend, 518–535

Moral or lesson in literature, 18E, 190E, 486E

Morfin, Jesus Carlos Soto, 254–255

Multiple–meaning words, 41I–J, 53, 117I–J, 127G–H, 177, 227, 260, 266, 287, 341, 353, 431, 461, 679, 705, Unit 1: T63

Music link. *See* Cross–curricular.

"My Poems," 370–371

Negatives, 691M–N

Newman, Mary Ann, 486A, 488

Nonsense, use of for humorous effect, 485

Note taking, 16J, 39, 41L, 127D, 157L, 163, 241D, 250, 251D, 254J, 295, 297L, 331L, 359L, 369D, 371H, 405K, 423L, 481D, 483E, 611H, 713C, 723D, 725A–B, Unit 4: T60

Nouns
and adjectives, 405M–N
common, 157M–N
irregular, 215M, 251M–N
plural, 189M–N, 251M, 371I, 423M–N, 599N
irregular, 215M–N
possessives, 241M–N, 251M–N, 371I, 599M–N
prepositions and, 713M
proper, 157M–N, 215N, 443N
singular, 189M–N, 215N, 241M–N, 371I, 423M–N, 599N

Online resources, reading, 483A–B

On the Bus with Joanna Cole, 446–471

Open Wide, Don't Bite, 120–127

Oral comprehension. *See* Read–alouds.

Oral language development, 20A, 44A, 68A, 96A, 120A, 134A, 160A, 192A, 218A, 244A, 258A, 284A, 300A, 334A, 362A, 376A, 408A, 426A, 446A, 474A, 488A, 518A, 538A, 570A, 602A, 616A, 634A, 666A, 694A, 716A

Oral tradition, 357, 494

Organizing information. *See* Graphic organizers, Lists: making, Research and inquiry, Story activities, Study skills, Summarizing.

Outlines, 129F, 149, 157L, 369K, 481K, 713K, 723D

Parallel construction, 704

Paraphrasing, 95B, 103, 200, 215I, 262, 275, 297, 524, 578, 579, 623, 663, 669, 707

Partner work, 20A, 26, 36, 39, 41F, 41J, 41K, 44A, 44C, 63, 65K, 65P, 68C, 91, 93K, 93P, 96A, 115, 117F, 117J, 117P, 118E, 120C, 125, 127F, 127J, 130, 157K, 189F, 189H, 189J, 189P, 192C, 213, 215F, 215P, 218A, 218, 241N, 241P, 244C, 246, 251F, 251H, 251K, 251P, 256E, 258C, 270, 279, 281A, 281F, 281J, 281N, 282E, 284C, 292, 297F, 297H, 297J, 297K, 297P, 326, 331K, 331P, 333B, 334C, 354, 357, 359J, 359K, 359P, 369J, 403, 405H, 405J, 405N, 405P, 423J, 426C, 443P, 446C, 469, 471J, 471L, 471P, 481J, 481P, 484, 485, 488C, 515F, 515K, 515L, 515P, 518C, 520, 535P, 538C, 567N, 599K, 607, 631B, 631F, 631H, 631M, 634C, 663F, 663J, 663K, 689, 691F, 691K, 691P, 706, 713F, 713J, 713N, 721. *See also* Alternate teaching strategies.

Pat Cummings: My Story, 284–297

Peer conferencing. *See* Group work, Partner work, Writing: collaboration in.

Penmanship. *See* handwriting.

Performance assessment opportunity. *See* Assessment.

Personal narrative, writing, 38, 41K–L, 62, 65K–L, 90, 93K–L, 114, 117K–L, 124, 127K–L, 129E–J

Personification, 613

Persuasive techniques, analyzing, 253A–B

Persuasive writing, 278, 281K–L, 294, 297K–L, 328, 331K–L, 356, 359C, 359K–L, 369K–L, 371E–J

Phonics and decoding, 29, 35, 41A, 41O–P, 47, 55, 65A, 65O–P, 75, 83, 93A, 93O–P, 101, 110, 117A, 117O–P, 127A, 143, 157A, 157O–P, 168, 169, 189A, 189O–P, 197, 205, 215A, 215O–P, 221, 223, 230, 241A, 251A, 251O–P, 261, 267, 281A, 281O–P, 287, 291, 297A, 297O–P, 311, 317, 319, 331A, 331O–P, 353, 359A, 359O, 369A, 399, 405A, 405O–P, 413, 423A, 423O–P, 436, 437, 443A, 443O–P, 465, 471A, 481A, 499, 505, 515A, 515O–P, 521, 535A, 535O–P, 559, 567A, 567O–P, 573, 591, 599A, 609A, 623, 625, 631A, 631O–P, 642, 645, 663A, 677, 705, 713A, 723A

Place Called Freedom, A, 334–359

"Poet Pencil," 254–255

Poetry, 16–17, 42E, 94E, 118E, 128–129, 130–131, 132E, 242E, 252–253, 254–255, 292E, 300A, 300, 370–371, 372–373, 482–483, 484–485, 518C, 610–611, 612–613, 614E, 664E, 692E, 714E, 724–725
alliteration, 94E, 692E, 714E
analogy, 372
assonance, 485
figurative language, 254
free verse, 253, 483
haiku, 298E
idioms, 373
imagery, 298E, 371, 714E
irony, 664E
nonsense and humor, 484
personification, 612
rhyme/rhyme patterns, 48E, 94E, 118E, 131, 242E, 484, 485, 516E, 613, 614E, 664E, 725
rhythm, 42E, 130, 131, 158E, 242E, 516E, 614E, 725
sensory words, 612
stanzas, 16, 42E, 118E, 472E
symbolism, 714E, 255
tempo, 16, 94E
text features, 16, 372
tone, 254
See also Literary devices, Literary genre.

Portfolio. *See* Assessment.

Position statement, 371B–371D

Possessives, 241M–N, 253E, 371E, 599M–N

Predictions, making. *See* Comprehension strategies.

Prefixes, 143, 267, 405I–J, 417, 443G, 471I–J, 481G–H, 621, 713O–P, Unit 4: T63

Prepositions/prepositional phrases, 713M–N

Prereading strategies. *See* Previewing literature.

Presentation ideas, for writing. *See* Publishing.

Prevention/intervention, 27, 29, 33, 46, 47, 53, 71, 73, 75, 87, 100, 105, 110, 140, 143, 145, 168, 174, 177, 194, 197, 199, 221, 227, 230, 260, 267, 273, 287, 291, 308, 311, 317, 339, 341, 353, 379, 383, 384, 431, 461, 463, 497, 501, 505, 521, 527, 529, 547, 553, 573, 581, 586, 619, 623, 642, 649, 653, 671, 676, 679, 699, 701, 706

Previewing literature, 19, 20, 41A–C, 43, 44, 65A–C, 67, 68, 93A–C, 95, 96, 117A–C, 119, 120, 127A–C, 129A, 133, 134, 157A–C, 159, 160, 189A–C, 191, 192, 215A–C, 217, 218, 241A–C, 243, 244, 251A–C, 253A, 257, 258, 281A–C, 283, 284, 297A–C, 299, 300, 331A–C, 333, 334, 359A–C, 361, 362, 371A, 375, 376, 405A–C, 407, 408, 423A–C, 425, 426, 443A–C, 445, 446, 471A–C, 473, 474, 481A–C, 483A, 487, 488, 515A–C, 517, 518, 535A–C, 537, 538, 567A–C, 569, 570, 599A–C, 601, 602, 609A–C, 611A, 615, 616, 631A–C, 633, 634, 663A–C, 665, 666, 691A–C, 693, 694, 713A–C, 715, 716, 725A

Prewriting and prewriting strategies, 41K, 65K, 93K, 117K, 127K, 129F, 157K, 189K, 215K, 241K, 251K, 253D, 281K, 297K, 331K, 359K, 369K, 371F, 405K, 423K, 443K, 471K, 481K, 483D, 515K, 535K, 567K, 599K, 609K, 611D, 631K, 663K, 691K, 713K, 723K, 725D
conducting a survey, 691K
dramatizing, 599K
focusing content, 93K
focusing questions, 41K, 331K, 481K
freewriting, 405K, 609K
listing ideas, 359K, 369K, 483D, 611D
researching a topic, 253D, 723K, 725D
visualizing, 41K, 117K, 535K
working with a partner, 443K

Problem and solution, identifying. *See* Comprehension strategies.

Pronouns, 17, 253G, 515M–N, 535M–N, 567M–N, 599M–N, 609M–N, 611G, 725G
contractions and, 515N, 609M–N
matching referents, 515M–N
object, 535M–N

plural, 515M–N
possessive, 253G, 599M–N, 609M–N, 725G
singular, 515M–N
subject, 535M–N, 567M–N
verb agreement, 253G, 567M–N, 725G

Proofreading, 41K, 41P, 65K, 65P, 93K, 93P, 117K, 117P, 127K, 127P, 129I, 157K, 157P, 189K, 189P, 215K, 215P, 241K, 241P, 251K, 251P, 253G, 281K, 281P, 297K, 297P, 331K, 331P, 359K, 359P, 369K, 369P, 371I, 405K, 405P, 423K, 423P, 443K, 443P, 471K, 471P, 481K, 481P, 483G, 515K, 515P, 535K, 535P, 567K, 567P, 599K, 599P, 609K, 609P, 611G, 631K, 631P, 663K, 663P, 691K, 691P, 713K, 713P, 723K, 723P, 725G

Publishing, 41K, 65K, 93K, 117K, 127K, 129I, 157K, 189K, 215K, 241K, 251K, 253G, 281K, 297K, 331K, 359K, 369K, 371I, 405K, 423K, 443K, 471K, 481K, 483G, 515K, 535K, 567K, 599K, 609K, 611G, 631K, 663K, 691K, 713K, 723K, 725G

Punctuation, 41M–N, 65N, 85, 93N, 117N, 129I, 157K, 157N, 189N, 241M–N, 281N, 297N, 331N, 359N, 423N, 481N, 515N, 567N, 609N, 691N, 713N, 723N
apostrophes, 241M–N, 331N, 515N, 599N, 609N, 691N
commas, 65N, 93N, 157K, 189N, 281N, 297N, 481N, 713N, 723N
exclamation marks, 41M–N, 85, 129I
letter, 65N, 297N, 713N
periods, 41M–N, 129I, 157K, 157N
question marks, 41M–N, 85, 129I
quotation marks, 117N, 359N, 423N, 567N

Questions/question marks, 41M–N, 85, 129I

Quotations/quotation marks, 117N, 359N, 423N, 567N

Rajah's Rice: A Mathematical Folk Tale, The, 538–567

Read-alouds, 18E, 42E, 66E, 94E, 118E, 132E, 158E, 190E, 216E, 242E, 256E, 282E, 298E, 332E, 360E, 374E, 406E, 424E, 444E, 472E, 486E, 516E, 536E, 568E, 600E, 614E, 632E, 664E, 692E, 714E

Reading comprehension. *See* Comprehension strategies.

Reading for information, 129A–D, 253A–B, 371A–D, 483A–B, 611A–B, 725A–B
reading directions, 611A–B
reading media, 253A–B
reading online resources, 483A–B
reading science, 371A–D
reading social studies, 129A–D
researching a report, 725A–B

Reading rate. *See* Fluency.

Reading strategies, 19, 43, 67, 95, 119, 129A–D, 133, 159, 191, 217, 243, 257, 283, 299, 333, 361, 375, 407, 425, 445, 473, 487, 517, 537, 569, 601, 615, 633, 665, 693, 715. *See also* Comprehension strategies.

Realia. *See* Cross-curricular, Cultural perspectives, Presentation ideas, Story activities.

Reference sources and materials, using, 156, 188, 214, 240, 250, 253B–D, 371B–C, Unit 2: T6. *See also* Internet connection, Research and inquiry, Study skills.

Reports, researching, 725A–B. *See also* Research and inquiry, Writing activities: reports.

Rereading for fluency. *See* Fluency.

Research and inquiry, 16J, 22, 24, 39, 41D, 48, 54, 56, 63, 65D, 72, 74, 80, 82, 91, 93D, 98, 102, 115, 117D, 123, 125, 127D, 129, 130J, 131, 148, 155, 157D, 170, 176, 187, 189C, 189D, 196, 206, 208, 213, 215D, 222, 226, 228, 232, 239, 241D, 249, 251D, 253, 253B, 254J, 264, 266, 268, 279, 281D, 286, 290, 295, 297D, 318, 320, 329, 331D, 338, 340, 348, 357, 359D, 367, 369D, 371, 371B, 372J, 380, 390, 396, 403, 405D, 410, 414, 421, 423D, 430, 432, 441, 443D, 448, 454, 456, 460, 469, 471D, 479, 481D, 483, 484J, 490, 494, 500, 506, 513, 515D, 522, 528, 533, 535D, 550, 554, 560, 565, 567D, 576, 580, 588, 597, 599D, 607, 609D, 611, 612J, 618, 624, 629, 631D, 636, 650, 661, 663D, 668, 674, 680, 689, 691D, 698, 700, 711, 713D, 721, 723D, 725, Unit 1, 2: T61

Research strategies, 16J, 130J, 254J, 372J, 484J, 612J

Retelling. *See* Speaking and listening activities.

Revising and revising strategies, 41K, 65K, 93K, 117K, 127K, 129H, 157K, 189K, 215K, 241K, 251K, 253F, 281K, 297K, 331K, 359K, 369K, 371H, 405K, 423K, 443K, 471K, 481K, 483F, 515K, 535K, 567K, 599K, 609K, 611F, 631K, 663K, 691K, 713K, 723K, 725F

Rhyme/rhyme patterns, 48E, 94E, 118E, 130, 131, 484, 485, 516E, 613, 614E, 664E, 725

Rhythm, 42E, 130, 131, 158E, 242E, 516E, 614E, 725

Root words, 41P, 99, 207, 267, 281I–J, 289, 297I–J, 331P, 359P, 369I–J, 423I–J, 423P, 443I–J, 457, 481I–J, 491, 553, 585, 691P

Sanders, Scott Russell, 332A, 334

Sarah, Plain and Tall, 68–93

Saving the Everglades, 716–723

Say, Allen, 18A, 37

Science link. *See* Cross-curricular.

Scruffy: A Wolf Finds His Place in the Pack, 376–405

Seal Journey, 96–117

Second-language support. *See* Language support.

Selection summary, 18A, 42A, 66A, 94A, 118A, 132A, 158A, 190A, 216A, 242A, 256A, 282A, 298A, 332A, 360A, 374A, 406A, 424A, 444A, 472A, 486A, 516A, 536A, 568A, 600A, 614A, 632A, 664A, 692A, 714A

Self-assessment. *See* Assessment.

Self-monitoring strategies, 31, 49, 78, 106, 144, 172, 201, 228, 269, 288, 313, 344, 397, 416, 434, 460, 505, 524, 549, 584, 624, 655, 675, 703
adjusting reading rate, 313
asking for help/asking questions, 106, 269, 313, 549, 703
paraphrasing, 524
rereading 31, 78, 144, 416, 584
searching for clues, 49, 172, 201, 228, 288, 344, 397, 460, 655, 675
visualizing, 434, 505, 624

Self-selected reading, 41E, 65E, 93E, 117E, 127E, 157E, 189E, 215E, 241E, 251E, 281E, 297E, 331E, 359E, 369E, 405E, 423E, 443E, 471E, 481E, 515E, 535E, 567E, 599E, 609E, 631E, 663E, 691E, 713E, 723E, Units 1–6: T78–79

Semantic cues, 33, 46, 53, 71, 73, 87, 100, 105, 140, 143, 145, 177, 194, 197, 199, 221, 227, 260, 287, 308, 341, 353, 379, 383, 429, 431, 461, 501, 521, 527, 543, 547, 553, 581, 619, 642, 649, 653, 671, 679, 699, 701, 705

Sentences
combining, 93M–N, 117M–N, 723M–N
complete, 41M–N, 65M–N, 129I, 129I
complex, 117M–N, 127M–N
compound, 93M–N, 117M–N, 127M–N
predicates of, 65M–N, 93M–N, 129I, 359M
run-on, 127M–N
sentence fragments, 41M–N, 65M–N, 129I
subjects of, 65M–N, 93M–N, 129I, 281M–N, 297M–N, 331M–N, 359M–N

Sequence of events, analyzing. *See* Comprehension strategies.

Setting, analyzing. *See* Story elements, analyzing.

Setting purposes
for reading, 19, 20, 41A–C, 43, 44, 65A–C, 67, 68, 93A–C, 95, 96, 117A–C, 119, 120, 127A–C, 129A, 133, 134, 157A–C, 159, 160, 189A–C, 191, 192, 215A–C, 217, 218, 241A–C, 243, 244, 251A–C, 253A, 257, 258, 281A–C, 283, 284, 297A–C, 299, 300, 331A–C, 333, 334, 359A–C, 361, 362, 371A, 375, 376, 405A–C, 407, 408, 423A–C, 425, 426, 443A–C, 445, 446, 471A–C, 473, 474, 481A–C, 483A, 487, 488, 515A–C, 517, 518, 535A–C, 537, 538, 567A–C, 569, 570, 599A–C, 601, 602, 609A–C, 611A, 615, 616, 631A–C, 633, 634, 663A–C, 665, 666, 691A–C, 693, 694, 713A–C, 715, 716, 725A
for writing, 129F, 253D, 371F, 483D, 611D, 725D

Silent letters, 625, 631O–P, 677, 691A, 705, 713A

Similes, 81, 129, 320, 464, 535I–J, 609G

Simon, Seymour, 692A, 709

Sobol, Richard and Jonah, 94A, 96

Social Studies link. *See* Cross-curricular.

Soto, Gary, 482–483

Speaking and listening activities
act it out, 18E, 20A, 25, 42E, 65D, 65L, 93D, 94E, 94, 108, 117L, 118E, 131, 132E, 157D, 157L, 166, 192A, 215L, 216, 241J, 241L, 254, 266, 281A, 297N, 334C, 359D, 359L, 373, 390, 405N, 406E, 423D, 424E, 471K, 488C, 502, 515L, 518C, 567A, 567F, 567L, 567N, 570A, 570C, 587, 599K, 599L, 614E, 615A, 632E, 663M, 694A, 714E, Unit 1: T60–T62, Unit 2: T60, Unit 3: T60, Unit 4: T62, 63, Unit 5: T61, T66, Unit 6: T62, T64
audiotaping, 251L
choral reading, 16, 254, 612
debate, 359D, 481L, Unit 3: T60
dialogue, 85, 145, 270, 471L, 486, 498, 535L, 567L, 611H, 634C
giving advice, 405L
giving directions, 713N
improvisation, 599L
interview, 16J, 65D, 93D, 127L, 215L, 249, 251K, 297L, 469, 535D, 631D, 620, 648, 691D, 713C, 725H, Unit 2: T60
oral presentations/reports, 16J, 41L, 42D, 65D,

65L, 93D, 93L, 117D, 117L, 127D, 127L, 129J, 135, 136J, 157D, 157L, 189D, 189L, 215D, 215L, 241D, 241L, 251D, 251L, 253H, 253, 254J, 256E, 281D, 281L, 297D, 297L, 331D, 331L, 359D, 359L, 362C, 369D, 369L, 371J, 371, 372J, 405D, 405L, 423D, 423L, 443D, 443L, 471D, 471L, 481D, 481L, 483H, 483, 484J, 506, 515D, 515L, 535D, 535L, 567D, 567L, 597, 599D, 599L, 609D, 609L, 611H, 611, 612J, 631D, 631L, 636, 663D, 663L, 691D, 691L, 713D, 713F, 713L, 723D, 723K, 723L, 725H, 725
pantomime, 20A, 25, 41D, 51, 65E, 68C, 79, 117L, 118E, 120A, 136, 164, 178, 209, 297N, 309, 332E, 388, 426A, 428C, 452, 471K, 513, 567N, 614E, 626, 632E, Unit 1: T62, T65, T66
poetry reading, 129, 373
read-alouds, 16, 41L, 42E, 65L, 77, 93L, 129J, 131, 157F, 157K, 253, 297K, 331L, 359K, 369L, 371J, 405L, 471L, 483G, 518C, 535J, 535L, 535N, 599K, 609L, 611H, 626, 631C, 635L, 637, 663K, Unit 5: T62
roleplaying, 18, 23, 28, 42E, 52, 54, 66, 75, 85, 106, 145, 148, 151, 166, 173, 203, 226, 231, 258C, 266, 267, 271, 309, 349, 360E, 393, 413, 469, 493, 498, 508, 526, 535L, 554, 576, 614, 619, 622, 634A, 637, 658, 673, 679, 684, 711
speech, 189L, 631L, 723L, 725
storytelling, 117L, 513, 538C, 597, 599L, 693B, 713N, Unit 1: T65, Unit 3: T66
summarizing/retelling, 36, 60, 88, 97, 103, 112, 117D, 152, 184, 203, 210, 229, 236, 246, 276, 292, 308, 326, 354, 364, 400, 415, 418, 438, 461, 466, 476, 507, 510, 525, 530, 562, 579, 594, 604, 626, 631D, 657, 658, 663D, 664E, 686, 691D, 714E, 718
television and radio scripts and ads, 127L, 241L, 253J, 281L, 297L, 397H, 423L, 471L, 535L, 631F, 631K, 725H, Unit1: T61, Unit 5: T61
video-taping, 91, 93L, 125, 196, 251L, 254J
See also Discussions, Paraphrasing.

Speaking and listening strategies, 16J, 41L, 42D, 42L, 65D, 65L, 93D, 93L, 117D, 117L, 127D, 127L, 129J, 135, 136J, 157D, 157L, 189D, 189L, 215D, 215L, 241D, 241L, 251D, 251L, 253, 253H, 254J, 281D, 281L, 297D, 297L, 331D, 331L, 359D, 359L, 362C, 369D, 369L, 371, 371J, 372J, 405D, 405L, 423D, 423L, 443D, 443L, 471D, 471L, 481D, 481L, 483, 483H, 484J, 515D, 515L, 535D, 535L, 567D, 567L, 599D, 599L, 609D, 609L, 611, 611H, 612J, 631D, 631L, 663D, 663L, 691D, 691L, 713D, 713L, 723D, 723K, 723L, 725, 725H

Spelling, 41O–P, 65O–P, 93O–P, 117O–P, 127O–P, 157O–P, 189O–P, 215O–P, 241O–P, 251O–P, 281O–P, 297O–P, 331O–P, 359O–P, 369O–P, 405O–P, 423O–P, 443O–P, 471O–P, 481O–P, 515O–P, 535O–P, 567O–P, 599O–P, 609O–P, 631O–P, 663O–P, 691O–P, 713O–P, 723O–P
adding *ed* and *ing*, 359P
changing *y* to *i*, 359O
compound words, 471O–P
contractions, 599O–P
double consonants, 359O
homophones and homographs, 117I–J, 609M–N, 663O–P
patterns, 41O, 65O, 93O, 117O, 127O, 157O–P, 189O, 215O, 241O, 251O, 281O, 297O, 331O, 359O, 369O, 405O, 423O, 443O, 471O, 481O, 515O, 535O, 567O, 599O, 609O, 631O, 663O, 691O, 713O, 723O
plurals, 241O–P
words from art, 369O–P
words from health, 127O–P
words from math, 723O–P
words from science, 481O–P, 609O
words from social studies, 251O–P
words with *är* and *âr*, 423O–P
words with consonant clusters, 189O–P, 215O–P
words with digraphs, 331O–P
words with əl and ən, 567O–P
words with ər and chər, 535O–P
words with *îr* and *ûr*, 443O–P
words with long *a* and long *e*, 65O–P, 251O
words with long *i* and long *o*, 93O–P, 251O
words with *ô* and *ôr*, 405O–P
words with *ou* and *oi*, 281O–P
words with prefixes, 713O–P
words with *s* and *f*, 515O–P
words with short vowels, 41O–P, 251O
words with silent letters, 631O–P, 705
words with suffixes, 691O–P
words with *ū* and *ü*, 117O–P
words with *u̇* and *yu̇*, 297O–P

Spelling/vocabulary connections, 20C, 44C, 68C, 96C, 120C, 134C, 160C, 192C, 218C, 244C, 258C, 284C, 300C, 334C, 362C, 376C, 408C, 426C, 446C, 474C, 488C, 518C, 538C, 570C, 602C, 616C, 634C, 666C, 694C, 716C

Spivak, Dawnine, 298A, 300

SQRRR strategy, 725A–B

Steps in a process. *See* Comprehension strategies.

Stereotypical characters in literature, 486E

Stories in Art. *See* Visual literacy.

Story activities, 39, 41A–C, 63, 65A–C, 91, 93A–C, 115, 117A–C, 125, 127A–C, 155, 157A–C, 175, 187, 189A–C, 213, 215A–C, 239, 241A–C, 249, 251A–C, 279, 281A–C, 295, 297A–C, 329, 331A–C, 357, 359A–C, 367, 369A–C, 403, 405A–C, 421, 423A–C, 441, 443A–C, 469, 471A–C, 479, 481A–C, 513, 515A–C, 533, 535A–C, 565, 567A–C, 597, 599A–C, 607, 609A–C, 629, 631A–C, 661, 663A–C, 689, 691A–C, 711, 713A–C, 721, 723A–C

Story elements, analyzing. *See* Comprehension strategies.

Story questions, 38, 41A–C, 62, 65A–C, 90, 93A–C, 114, 117A–C, 124, 127A–C, 154, 157A–C, 186, 189A–C, 212, 215A–C, 238, 241A–C, 248, 251A–C, 278, 281A–C, 294, 297A–C, 328, 331A–C, 356, 359A–C, 366, 369A–C, 402, 405A–C, 420, 423A–C, 440, 443A–C, 468, 471A–C, 478, 481A–C, 512, 515A–C, 532, 535A–C, 564, 567A–C, 596, 599A–C, 606, 609A–C, 628, 631A–C, 660, 663A–C, 688, 691A–C, 710, 713A–C, 720, 723A–C

Story words, 20B, 44B, 68B, 96B, 120B, 134B, 160B, 192B, 218B, 244B, 258B, 284B, 300B, 334B, 362B, 376B, 408B, 426B, 446B, 474B, 488B, 518B, 538B, 570B, 602B, 616B, 634B, 666B, 694B, 716B

Story, writing. *See* Writing activities.

Study skills and information resources, 40, 64, 92, 116, 126, 156, 188, 214, 240, 250, 280, 296, 330, 358, 368, 404, 422, 442, 470, 480, 514, 534, 566, 598, 608, 630, 662, 690, 712, 722, Unit 1–6: T61
graphic aids, 280, 296, 330, 358, 368, 404, 422, 442, 480, Unit 3: T61, Unit 4: T61
charts, 422, 480
diagrams, 368, Unit 3: T61
flowchart, 296, Unit 3: T61
following directions, 480, Unit 3: T65, Unit 4: T61
graphs, 358, 404, 480
bar graph, 404
line graph, 358
maps, 330, Unit 3: T61
signs, 280
time lines, 442, Unit 4: T61
library/media center, 630, 662, 690, 712, 722, Unit 2: T61, Unit 6: T61
card catalog, 630, 662, Unit 6: T61
encyclopedia index, 712
location of resources, 712
using the Internet, 690, 722, Unit 6: T61
parts of a book, 40, 64, 92, 116, 126, Unit 1: T61
captions/sidebars, 126, Unit 1: T61
glossary, 40, 64, Unit 1: T61
headings, 92, 126, Unit 1: T61
index, 40, 116, 712, Unit 1: T61
table of contents, 40, 92, Unit 1: T61
title page, 40, Unit 1: T61
using, 40, 64, 92, 116, 126, Unit 1: T61
reference sources, using, 156, 188, 214, 240, 250, Unit 2: T61
atlas, 214
choosing, 214
conducting an interview, 250
dictionary, 156, 214, Unit 2: T61
encyclopedia, 214, 240, 712, Unit 2: T61
Internet, 722
thesaurus, 188, Unit 2: T61
using various texts, 514, 534, 566, 598, 608, Unit 5: T61
advertisements, 514, Unit 5: T61
e-mail, 598
newspaper, 534
dateline, 534
headline, 534
news article, 534
recipe, 566
telephone directory, 608
See also Charts, Diagrams, Graphic organizers, Research and inquiry.

Subject
agreement with verb, 281M–N, 331M–N, 371I
complete , 65M–N
compound, 93M–N
plural, 281M, 331M
pronoun, 535M–N, 567M–N
simple , 65M–N, 93N
singular, 281M, 297M–N, 331M

Suffixes, 99, 207, 281I–J, 281P, 297I–J, 347, 369I–J, 423P, 433, 457, 497, 527, 553, 681, 691P, Unit 3: T63

Summarizing. *See* Comprehension strategies.

Syllable patterns, 65O, 143, 157A, 157O–P, 359O, 535O, 567O

Symbolism, 472E, 590, 600E, 656, 714E

Synonyms, 65I–J, 65P, 71, 93I–J, 120C, 127I–J, 134C, 188, 213K, 215P, 308, 523, 567P, 609P, 631P, 663I–J, 663P, 691I–J, 723I–J, Unit 1: T65, Unit 6: T65

Syntactic cues, 33, 46, 73, 87, 140, 174, 194, 199, 273, 341, 461, 497, 527, 543, 553, 619, 649, 653, 679, 699, 705

Teaching tips

instructional, 25, 28, 41E, 41I, 41K, 51, 65G, 65I, 70, 71, 80, 93E, 93I, 99, 109, 117E, 117I, 117K, 119A, 127G, 127I, 127K, 129A, 133A, 141, 146, 157E, 157G, 157I, 171, 189E, 189G, 189I, 193, 203, 206, 215E, 215G, 215I, 221, 226, 241G, 241I, 243A, 251E, 251G, 251K, 261, 266, 271, 281I, 283A, 289, 297E, 297G, 297I, 303, 312, 320, 331E, 331I, 331K, 333A, 349, 359G, 359I, 359K, 369E, 369G, 369I, 371A, 371H, 375A, 381, 388, 405G, 405I, 407A, 410, 423E, 423G, 423I, 423K, 425A, 426C, 428, 432, 443G, 443I, 448, 457, 463, 464, 471G, 471I, 473A, 481E, 481G, 481I, 481K, 490, 494, 502, 515E, 515I, 515K, 535E, 535G, 535I, 541, 550, 554, 567I, 573, 587, 589, 599E, 599G, 599I, 599K, 609G, 609I, 609K, 615A, 618, 631E, 631G, 633A, 644, 648, 663E, 663G, 663I, 663K, 665A, 669, 673, 677, 680, 691E, 691G, 691I, 693A, 696, 697, 704, 707, 713E, 713G, 713I, 713K, 715A, 723G, 723I, 723K

management, 20A, 44A, 54, 68A, 96A, 117E, 117G, 120A, 134A, 160A, 166, 189K, 192A, 218A, 223, 241E, 244A, 251I, 258A, 266, 281E, 284A, 297E, 300A, 306A, 334A, 334C, 359E, 362A, 376A, 388, 408A, 446A, 474A, 488A, 515K, 518A, 527, 528, 538A, 570A, 602A, 616A, 618, 622, 631I, 634A, 666A, 694A, 716A

organization, 129F, 253D, 371F, 483D, 611D, 725D

teacher conference, 129H, 253F, 371H, 483F, 611F, 725F

Teammates, 616–631

Technology resources. *See* Internet connection, Listening library, Study skills, Technology tips.

Technology tips, 41K, 65K, 93K, 117K, 127K, 157K, 189K, 215K, 241K, 251K, 281K, 297K, 331K, 359K, 369K, 405K, 423K, 443K, 471K, 481K, 515K, 535K, 567K, 599K, 609K, 631K, 663K, 691K, 713K, 723K

clip art, 423K

cutting and pasting, 251K, 423K, 609K

file and print preview, 41K

fonts and type styles, 281K, 631K, 691K

formatting, 65K, 117K, 241K, 297K, 369K, 443K, 471K, 481K, 535K, 691K, 713K, 723K

Internet as a resource, 157K

notes on the computer, 189K

quotations, 567K

save function, 127K, 157K, 359K, 599K

tools/tool bar, 93K, 331K, 515K, 663K

using computer thesaurus, spelling dictionary, 215K, 405K, 535K, 663K

Test–taking practice. *See* Assessment: standardized test practice.

Text connections, 16, 41D, 65D, 93D, 117D, 127D, 128, 129E, 157D, 189D, 215D, 241D, 251D, 253C, 254, 281D, 297D, 331D, 359D, 369D, 371E, 372, 405D, 423D, 443D, 471D, 481D, 482, 483C, 515D, 535D, 567D, 599D, 609D, 610, 631D, 663D, 691D, 713D, 723D, 724

Text features, 16, 40, 64, 92, 97, 110,116, 121, 124, 126, 129A–D, 245, 363, 371A–D, 372, 427, 483A–B, 611A–B, 695, Unit 1: T61

Theme bibliography, Units 1–: T78–79

Theme connections, 16I, 16J, 41D, 65D, 93D, 117D, 127D, 128, 129, 130I, 130J, 157D, 189D, 215D, 241D, 251D, 252, 253, 254I, 254J, 281D, 297D, 331D, 359D, 369D, 370, 371, 372I, 372J, 405D, 423D, 443D, 471D, 481D, 482, 483, 484I, 484J, 515D, 535D, 567D, 599D, 609D, 610, 611, 612I, 612J, 724, 631D, 663D, 691D, 713D, 723D, 724, 725

Theme projects, 16J, 129, 130J, 253, 254J, 371, 372J, 483, 484J, 611, 612J, 725

Thesaurus, using, 188, 214, 215K, 663J, Unit 2: T61

Time for Kids, 120–127, 244–251, 362–369, 474–481, 602–609, 716–723

Timelessness of literature, 489, 539

Timelines, 275, 442, 444E, 479, 567D, 588, 711, Unit 4: T61

Titles, 215N, 359N

"To," 16–17

Toothpaste Millionaire, The, 666–691

"Tortillas Like Africa," 482–483

Twisted Trails, 362–369

Universal theme in literature, 409, 489, 593, 635

Usage. *See* Grammar, mechanics and usage.

Van Allsburg, Chris, 158A, 185

Various texts, using, 16J, 253B, 373, 514, 534, 566, 598, 608, 613, 725B, Unit 5: T61. *See also* Study skills.

Venn diagram, 20A, 44A, 120A, 218A, 241K, 253B, 253E, 331H, 362A, 423G, 634A, Unit 3: T61, Unit 4: T60

Verbs

action, 281M–N, 567M–N

contractions, 331N, 515N

future tense, 297M–N, 371I

helping, 331M–N, 369M, 483G

irregular, 369M–N

linking, 359M–N, 405M, 483G

main, 331M–N

past tense, 297M–N, 371I

present tense, 281M–N, 371E, 567M–N

pronoun–verb agreement, 253G, 567M–N, 725G

subject–verb agreement, 281M–N, 331M–N, 371I

with object pronouns, 535M–N

Viewing and representing, 18, 32, 41L, 42, 50, 65D, 65L, 66, 76, 93D, 93L, 94, 117D, 117L, 118, 127D, 127L, 129D, 129J, 132, 157D, 157L, 158, 178, 189D, 189L, 190, 202, 215D, 215L, 216, 230, 241D, 241L, 242, 251D, 251L, 253H, 256, 281D, 281L, 282, 297D, 297L, 298, 310, 331D, 331L, 332, 346, 359D, 359L, 360, 369L, 371J, 374, 382, 405D, 405L, 406, 423D, 423L, 424, 436, 443D, 443L, 444, 458, 471D, 471L, 472, 481D, 481L, 486, 496, 515D, 515L, 516, 535L, 536, 567D, 567L, 568, 572, 599D, 599L, 600, 609D, 609L, 611F, 614, 631D, 631L, 632, 646, 663D, 663L, 664, 669, 691L, 692, 713L, 714, 723L, 725H

Viewing strategies, 93L, 117L, 189L, 251L, 281L, 369L, 405L, 443L, 471L, 515L, 535L, 609L, 713L

Visualization, 18E, 30, 41K, 42E, 66E, 93F, 94E, 117K, 117L, 118E, 127L, 129, 132E, 298E, 300A, 323, 371, 405K, 423L, 471L, 472E, 483F, 505, 535K, 567K, 600E, 609K, 611, 714E

Visual literacy, 18, 32, 42, 50, 66, 76, 94, 118, 132, 158, 178, 190, 202, 216, 230, 242, 256, 282, 298, 310, 332, 346, 360, 374, 382, 406, 424, 436, 444, 458, 472, 486, 496, 516, 536, 568, 572, 600, 614, 632, 646, 664, 669, 692, 714

Vocabulary and vocabulary strategies

analogies, 93P, 378, 405P, 535P, 723P

antonyms, 65I–J, 93I–J, 127I–J, 157P, 297P, 308, 663I–J, 691I–J, 723I–J, Unit 1: T65, Unit 6: T65

compound words, 33, 46, 87, 100, 140, 189I–J, 199, 241I–J, 251G–H, 405I–J, 463, 471O–P, 521, 585, 671, Unit 2: T65

context clues, 20B–C, 23, 44B–C, 59, 68B–C, 81, 96B–C, 105, 120B–C, 127I, 134B–C, 137, 145, 157I–J, 160B–C, 167, 192B–C, 194, 197, 215I–J, 218B–C, 227, 244B–C, 251I–J, 258B–C, 284B–C, 300B–C, 309, 331I–J, 334B–C, 359I–J, 362B–C, 369G–H, 369P, 376B–C, 383, 389, 408B–C, 426B–C, 446B–C, 474B–C, 488B–C, 501, 515I–J, 518B–C, 523, 538B–C, 547, 567I–J, 570B–C, 602B–C, 609I–J, 616B–C, 619, 631I–J, 634B–C, 643, 649, 666B–C, 676, 694B–C, 697, 703, 713I–J, 716B–C, 723G, 723H, Unit 2: T63, Unit 3: T65, Unit 5: T63, Unit 6: T63

contractions, 331N, 483G, 515N, 599O–P, 609M–N, 691N

discussing word meaning, 20B, 44B, 68B, 96B, 120B, 134B, 160B, 192B, 218B, 244B, 258B, 284B, 300B, 334B, 362B, 376B, 408B, 426B, 446B, 474B, 488B, 518B, 538B, 570B, 602B, 616B, 634B, 666B, 694B, 716B

figurative language, 81, 129, 131, 255, 320, 342, 373, 535I–J, 599I–J, 609G–H, 611, Unit 5: T65

metaphor, 81, 131, 255, 535I–J, 599I–J, Unit 5: T65

simile, 81, 129, 320, 464, 535I–J, 609G

homophones/homographs, 117I–J, 367, 609M–N, 663O–P

idioms, 609G–H

instructional, 41A–C, 65A–C, 93A–C, 117A–C, 157A–C, 189A–C, 215A–C, 241A–C, 281A–C, 297A–C, 331A–C, 359A–C, 405A–C, 423A–C, 443A–C, 471A–C, 515A–C, 535A–C, 567A–C, 599A–C, 631A–C, 663A–C, 691A–C, 713A–C,

multiple–meaning words, 41I–J, 53, 117I–J, 127G–H, 177, 227, 260, 266, 287, 341, 353, 431, 461, 679, 705, Unit 1: T63

prefixes, 143, 267, 405I–J, 417, 443G, 471I–J, 481G–H, 621, 713O–P, Unit 4: T63

root words, 41P, 99, 207, 267, 281I–J, 289, 297I–J, 331P, 359P, 369I–J, 423I–J, 423P, 443I–J, 457, 481I–J, 491, 553, 585, 691P

specialized vocabulary, 129A–D, 371A–D

suffixes, 99, 207, 281I–J, 281P, 297I–J, 347, 369I–J, 423P, 433, 457, 497, 527, 553, 681, 691P, Unit 3: T63

synonyms, 65I–J, 65P, 71, 93I–J, 120C, 127I–J, 134C, 188, 213K, 215P, 308, 523, 567P, 609P, 631P, 663I–J, 663P, 691I–J, 723I–J, Unit 1: T65, Unit 6: T65

word structure, 27, 73, 87, 168, 174, 221, 273, 339, 379, 384, 411, 429, 529, 543, 581, 587, 619, 642, 653, 699, 701

Vocabulary Puzzlemaker, 20C, 44C, 68C, 96C, 120C, 134C, 160C, 192C, 218C, 244C, 258C, 284C, 300C, 334C, 362C, 376C, 408C, 426C, 446C, 474C, 488C, 518C, 538C, 570C, 602C, 616C, 634C, 666C, 694C, 716C

Walter, Mildred Pitts, 132A, 153

Webs, word, 215K, 258A, 281D, 284A, 297K, 405H, 405K, 426A, 432, 527, 535H, 535K, 570A, 616A, 643, 645, 673, 723K, 725D

Whales, 694–713

Will Her Native Language Disappear?, 244–251

Woelflein, Luise, 424A, 439

Word choice, 18E, 1K, 42E, 66E, 81, 94E, 129, 129G, 131, 132E, 254, 255, 298E, 320, 342, 371, 371G, 372, 373, 374E, 472E, 484, 535I, 535J, 599I, 599J, 609G, 609H, 610, 611, 612, 614E, 640, 664E, 692E, 714E, 725E

Writer's craft, 86, 110, 136, 174, 194, 260, 308, 342, 378, 508, 590, 640, 656
- alliteration, 136
- analogies, 378
- assonance, 194
- descriptive writing, 308
- figurative language, 342
- humor, 508
- sensory language, 640
- sentence variety and fragments, 86
- symbol, 590
- text features, 110
- theme, 656
- tone, 260
- transitional devices, 174
- *See also* Literary devices.

Writing activities
- advertisements, 253B, 278, 281K, 331F, 405B, 666C, 691B, 713B, Unit 5: T61
- analogies, 378
- autobiographical piece, 127K
- award certificate, 241L
- biography, 241K, 241L
- books/booklets, 127L, 281J, 423A, 471L, 483B, 567C, 661, 663G, Unit 2: T62
- book review, 228, 231K
- brochure, 127L, 129D, 189L, 297L, 329, 331L, 405B
- business report, 688, 691K
- captions, 20C, 48, 65L, 66E, 96C, 157L, 189L, 190E, 213, 229E, 284A, 297L, 376A, 405B, 405D, 405L,423A, 426A, 471N, 609L, 631D, 631N, 663L, 691L, 713K
- character sketch, 515L
- class book, 17, 483B
- collaboration in, 39, 41K, 65H, 65K, 68C, 129D, 132E, 138, 157F, 189H, 189J, 215F, 239, 244C, 251F, 251H, 253D, 256E, 258C, 281A, 281F, 281K, 282E, 284A, 284D, 292, 297F, 331B, 334C, 359J, 362A, 371C, 371D, 376C, 405L, 408C, 446A, 471F, 471J, 481F, 483B, 483C, 483D, 488C, 513, 518C, 533, 535D, 535F, 535N, 538C, 565, 599F, 602C, 634C, 713J
- comic strip/cartoon, 20A, 127A, 127L, 284A, 359B, 461, 535L, 567L, 631D, 663L, 691L, Unit 2: T60, Unit 5: T60
- descriptions, 20C, 41K, 41L, 63, 65L, 93L, 127L, 134A, 157A, 241A, 253C, 281B, 281L, 307, 342, 367L, 405L, 430, 515A, 515L, 518A, 535K, 535L, 567L, 602A, 631A, 640, 716A
- dialogue, 41C, 86, 127L, 192C, 241L, 281A, 331L, 376C, 486, 564, 567K, 599L, 631C, 631L, 634C, 663C
- diary entry, 44A, 62, 65K–L, 134A, 215K, 215L, 225, 248, 251K, 359L, 631A
- directions and rules, 471L, Unit 2: T63, Unit 4: T61
- editorial, 281L, 356, 359K, 371B
- e-mail, 297L
- encouraging note, 297K
- encyclopedia article, 720, 723K
- essay, 114, 117K, 186, 189K, 253E, 468, 471K, 599C, 628, 710, 713K
- explanatory, 402, 405K–L, 420, 423K–L, 440, 443K–L, 468, 471K–L, 478, 481K–L, 483C–H
- expository, 628, 631K–L, 663K–L, 691K–L, 713K–L, 723K–L, 725C–H
- factual statement, 725B, 725D
- fairy tale/folk tale/fantasy/fable, 41L, 93F, 512, 515K, 599F, 606, 609K
- flyer, 426A
- how-to, 241K, 241L, 297L, 402, 405K–L, 420, 423K–L, 440, 443K–L, 468, 471K–L, 478, 481K–L, 483C–H, 612J, 688
- illustrated fact sheet, 403
- imaginative translation, 632
- interview, 93D, 189D, 189L, 241L, 248, 251L, 289, 295, 369L, 443L, 518A, 535C, 599L, 609L, 691L, 713C
- labels, 48, 65B, 66E, 91, 117L, 125, 155, 157L, 213, 266, 297L, 331L, 338, 348, 423L, 441, 481L, 483F, 631N, 634A, 663L, 691L, 723D
- letter, 90, 93K, 117L, 127B, 127K, 154, 157K, 215L, 241K, 241L, 251C, 258C, 281L, 297L, 366, 369K, 443A, 515L, 600, 691K, 713K
- myth, 215K–L, 408A, 423B, 423K
- newspaper/magazine article/column, 189D, 212, 215K, 228, 238, 241K, 251D, 369L, 371I, 402, 405K, 423L, 481L, 515L, 602A, 609B, 616C
- outline, 149, 127F, 157L, 481K, 713K
- paragraphs, 22, 41H, 41L, 44C, 63, 65B, 77, 82, 91, 93A, 96A, 127C, 127K, 157C, 171, 187, 189J, 215F, 215K, 218C, 241B, 241J, 244C, 251D, 260, 281B, 292, 297C, 297F, 307, 323, 331H, 331J, 331K, 369K, 405L, 418, 425B, 443F, 471F, 481F, 483, 488C, 494, 495, 515A, 515B, 517B, 518A, 519, 535B, 542, 567H, 567N, 590, 599A, 599J, 602A, 609F, 640, 656, 666A, 686, 691F, 691K, 713A, 723L
- personal narrative, 38, 41K–L, 65K–L, 90, 93K–L, 114, 117K–L, 124, 127K–L, 129D–J
- persuasive, 278, 281K–L, 294, 297K–L, 328, 331K–L, 356, 359C, 359K–L, 369K–L, 371C–J
- plan, 117L, 478, 481K, 691A
- play/drama, 241F, 359A, 488C, 567L, 609L, 691L
- poem, 17, 131, 241J, 244C, 255, 300A, 312, 322, 327, 329, 331B, 331F, 332, 369J, 373, 483, 485, 518C, 613, 694C, 714E
- postcard, 41L, 65A, 241K, 241L
- poster, 359L, 371J, 469, 533
- questions, 41K, 41L, 62, 93C, 117B, 187, 215C, 239, 241A, 247, 250, 359A, 359C, 369L, 518C, 599A, 599B, 599C, 663C, 691A, 691C
- quick write, 37, 61, 89, 113, 123, 153, 185, 211, 237, 247, 277, 293, 327, 355, 365, 401, 419, 439, 467, 477, 511, 531, 563, 595, 605, 627, 659, 687, 709, 719
- recipe, 155
- report, 63, 65D, 117A, 120A, 157L, 189C, 241K, 253C–H, 420, 423K, 428, 443L, 460, 528, 550, 660, 663K, 688, 689, 691K, 713L, 723L, 725C–E, Unit 2: T61
- review/critique, 251B, 328, 331K, 360, 481C, 723C, Unit 4: T60
- rhymes, 474C
- riddles/limerick, 331C, 666C, Unit 2: T66
- scene, script, 41C, 241F, 420, 423K, 471L, 535L, 612J, 713K, Unit 5: T61
- schedule, 20A, 44A, 157B, 192A, 331L, 446A, 634A
- science article, 481L
- sensory language, 640
- sentences, 36, 41J, 41M, 41N, 41P, 53, 55, 65M, 65N, 68C, 93M, 93N, 96C, 117L, 117M, 117N, 117P, 120C, 127J, 127L, 127M, 127N, 134C, 137, 157H, 157M, 157N, 167, 174, 189P, 192C, 210, 215J, 218D, 227, 244C, 251A, 251H, 276, 281M, 281P, 284C, 297F, 297N, 297P, 331M, 334C, 359J, 359L, 359P, 362C, 369N, 405F, 405M, 405P, 423J, 423M, 423N, 423P, 443J, 443N, 443P, 471J, 471P, 481M, 481P, 491, 497, 515J, 515M, 515P, 535M, 535N, 535P, 562, 567D, 567M, 568E, 621, 631M, 631P, 663P, 666C, 691P, 691N, 703, 713J, 723P, Unit 4: T63, Unit 5: T63, T65
- slogans, 132E, 600E, 711
- song, 155, 158E, 331A, 602C, 694C, 721, Unit 5: T65
- speech, 215L, 359C, 723L
- sports column, 238, 241K, 241L
- story, 38, 41F, 41K–L, 65H, 68C, 65L, 93F, 93L, 117F, 124, 127K, 127L, 133B, 157F, 160C, 215K, 244A, 251L, 258C, 281F, 281H, 282E, 300C, 331J, 331K, 333B, 334A, 359F, 359H, 359L, 423B, 423C, 474C, 488A, 512, 515K–L, 532, 535F, 535K–L, 538B, 538C, 551, 567K–L, 570C, 596, 599C, 599H, 599K–L, 606, 609K–L, 611C–H, 691L
- story problems, 392, 395, 629
- student self-evaluation of, 41K, 65K, 93K, 117K, 127K, 129F, 189K, 213K, 241K, 251K, 253F, 281K, 297K, 331K, 359K, 369K, 371F, 423K, 443K, 471K, 481K, 483H, 515K, 535K, 567K, 599K, 609K, 611F, 663K, 691K, 713K, 723K, 725F
- summaries, 36, 60, 88, 122, 152, 171, 236, 273, 276, 281D, 281H, 297H, 331D, 354, 359H, 364, 400, 415, 418, 438, 510, 530, 551, 562, 594, 620, 626, 658, 686, 723B
- that compare, 154, 157K–L, 186, 189K–L, 212, 215K–L, 238, 241K–L, 248, 251K–L, 253C–H
- theme, 656
- title, 91
- weather report, 420, 423K
- *See also* Journal, Lists, making.

Writing, connecting to literature, 129E, 253C, 371E, 483C, 611C, 725C

Writing, features of, 129F, 253D, 371F, 483D, 611D, 725D

Writing process, 41K–L, 65K–L, 93K–L, 117K–L, 127K–L, 129E–J, 157K–L, 189K–L, 215K–L, 241K–L, 251K–L, 253C–H, 281K–L, 297K–L, 331K–L, 359K–L, 369K–L, 371E–J, 405K–L, 423K–L, 443K–L, 471K–L, 481K–L, 483C–H, 515K–L, 535K–L, 567K–L, 599K–L, 609K–L, 611C–H, 631K–L, 663K–L, 691K–L, 713K–L, 723K–L, 725E–J. *See also* Drafting, Prewriting, Proofreading, Publishing, Revising.

Writing purpose and audience, 129F, 253D, 371F, 483D, 611D, 725D

Yeh-Shen: A Cinderella Story from China, 570–599

"Your World," 612–613

Scoring Chart

The Scoring Chart is provided for your convenience in grading your students' work.

- Find the column that shows the total number of items.
- Find the row that matches the number of items answered correctly.
- The intersection of the two rows provides the percentage score.

	TOTAL NUMBER OF ITEMS																													
NUMBER CORRECT	1	2	3	4	5	6	7	8	9	10	11	12	13	14	15	16	17	18	19	20	21	22	23	24	25	26	27	28	29	30
1	100	50	33	25	20	17	14	13	11	10	9	8	8	7	7	6	6	6	5	5	5	5	4	4	4	4	4	4	3	3
2		100	67	50	40	33	29	25	22	20	18	17	15	14	13	13	12	11	11	10	10	9	9	8	8	8	7	7	7	7
3			100	75	60	50	43	38	33	30	27	25	23	21	20	19	18	17	16	15	14	14	13	13	12	12	11	11	10	10
4				100	80	67	57	50	44	40	36	33	31	29	27	25	24	22	21	20	19	18	17	17	16	15	15	14	14	13
5					100	83	71	63	56	50	45	42	38	36	33	31	29	28	26	25	24	23	22	21	20	19	19	18	17	17
6						100	86	75	67	60	55	50	46	43	40	38	35	33	32	30	29	27	26	25	24	23	22	21	21	20
7							100	88	78	70	64	58	54	50	47	44	41	39	37	35	33	32	30	29	28	27	26	25	24	23
8								100	89	80	73	67	62	57	53	50	47	44	42	40	38	36	35	33	32	31	30	29	28	27
9									100	90	82	75	69	64	60	56	53	50	47	45	43	41	39	38	36	35	33	32	31	30
10										100	91	83	77	71	67	63	59	56	53	50	48	45	43	42	40	38	37	36	34	33
11											100	92	85	79	73	69	65	61	58	55	52	50	48	46	44	42	41	39	38	37
12												100	92	86	80	75	71	67	63	60	57	55	52	50	48	46	44	43	41	40
13													100	93	87	81	76	72	68	65	62	59	57	54	52	50	48	46	45	43
14														100	93	88	82	78	74	70	67	64	61	58	56	54	52	50	48	47
15															100	94	88	83	79	75	71	68	65	63	60	58	56	54	52	50
16																100	94	89	84	80	76	73	70	67	64	62	59	57	55	53
17																	100	94	89	85	81	77	74	71	68	65	63	61	59	57
18																		100	95	90	86	82	78	75	72	69	67	64	62	60
19																			100	95	90	86	83	79	76	73	70	68	66	63
20																				100	95	91	87	83	80	77	74	71	69	67
21																					100	95	91	88	84	81	78	75	72	70
22																						100	96	92	88	85	81	79	76	73
23																							100	96	92	88	85	82	79	77
24																								100	96	92	89	86	83	80
25																									100	96	93	89	86	83
26																										100	96	93	90	87
27																											100	96	93	90
28																												100	97	93
29																													100	97
30																														100

Persuasive Writing

6-Point Writing Rubric					
6. Exceptional	**5. Excellent**	**4. Good**	**3. Fair**	**2. Poor**	**1. Unsatisfactory**
• **Ideas & Content** devises a strong editorial that could persuade the reader to become involved in a school project; thoughtful details sharpen the argument. • **Organization** careful strategy moves a reader easily through clear stages of the argument; ideas, paragraphs and sentences are effectively connected. • **Voice** originality and deep involvement with the proposal enhance the argument; strong personal message reaches out to persuade a reader. • **Word Choice** resourceful use of new and everyday words strengthens the argument; advanced vocabulary makes the text clear and engaging. • **Sentence Fluency** crafts simple and complex sentences that flow naturally; writing is easy to follow and read aloud; fragments or other devices, if used, reinforce and add interest to the argument. • **Conventions** is skilled in most writing conventions; proper use of the rules of English adds to clarity, meaning, and style; editing is largely unnecessary.	• **Ideas & Content** crafts a cohesive, carefully detailed argument that could affect a reader's opinion; main idea and details are clearly stated. • **Organization** has a well-planned strategy; sequence helps a reader follow the argument's logic; ideas, details, and sentences are effectively tied together. • **Voice** shows originality and strong involvement with the topic; brings a focused personal message to the persuasive task. • **Word Choice** accurate, colorful words make the message clear and interesting; explores unfamiliar words, or uses everyday words in a fresh way. • **Sentence Fluency** well-paced simple and complex sentences flow naturally; a range of lengths, beginnings, and patterns fit together well. • **Conventions** is skilled in a wide range of conventions; paragraphs are placed correctly and effectively; little editing is needed.	• **Ideas & Content** presents a solid, clear argument, with details that help clarify the main idea. • **Organization** presents facts and ideas in a logical order; has a clear beginning and ending; ideas are linked within the structure. • **Voice** attempts to bring a personal touch to the editorial task; is involved with the topic; reaches out to the audience. • **Word Choice** uses a range of words that help clarify the argument; experiments with some new words, or makes fresh use of everyday words. • **Sentence Fluency** careful, easy-to-follow sentences vary in length, beginnings, and patterns; uses simple and complex constructions, with stronger control of simple sentences. • **Conventions** makes a few errors in spelling, capitalization, punctuation, or usage, which do not interfere with reading the text; some editing is needed.	• **Ideas & Content** attempts to present a position; may include ideas or details which are not clear, or do not fit the persuasive task. • **Organization** tries to structure a proposal, but the logic is sometimes hard to follow; ideas, sentences, and paragraphs may need more transition words. • **Voice** may not show involvement with the topic, or show who is behind the writing; opinion comes across, but may not be clearly linked to the purpose and audience. • **Word Choice** states the argument in a predictable way; may attempt to use a variety of words, but some do not fit; may overuse some words. • **Sentence Fluency** most sentences are readable, but limited in lengths and patterns; some rereading may be necessary to follow the meaning; some sentences may be choppy or awkward. • **Conventions** has basic control of conventions, but makes enough noticeable errors to prevent a smooth reading of the text; significant editing is needed.	• **Ideas & Content** has little control of the task to persuade, or seems unsure of the topic; facts and details are few, repeated, or inaccurate. • **Organization** lack of structure makes ideas hard to follow; few connections are made between facts and ideas; details don't fit where they are placed. • **Voice** is not involved in sharing ideas or opinions with a reader; writing may be lifeless, with no sense of who is behind the words. • **Word Choice** does not choose forceful words that convey an opinion; some words are overused, or may detract from the meaning or impact of the text. • **Sentence Fluency** sentences may be choppy or awkward; patterns are similar or monotonous; text may be hard to follow or read aloud. • **Conventions** makes frequent errors in spelling, word choice, punctuation, and usage; paper is difficult to read; extensive revision is needed.	• **Ideas & Content** does not state an opinion or a proposal; writer is unsure of what s/he wants to say. • **Organization** extreme lack of structure; ideas and details are disconnected; facts or details, if any, are irrelevant or vague. • **Voice** does not address an audience at all; does not have a sense of sharing a personal message or style. • **Word Choice** uses words that do not fit, or are vague and confusing; no new words are attempted. • **Sentence Fluency** uses incomplete, rambling, or confusing sentences that make the text hard to understand and read aloud. • **Conventions** makes severe errors in most conventions; spelling errors may make it hard to guess what words are meant; some parts of the text may be impossible to follow or understand.

0 Incomplete: This piece is either blank, or fails to respond to the writing task. The topic is not addressed, or the student simply paraphrases the prompt. The response may be illegible or incoherent.

8-Point Writing Rubric

Persuasive Writing

8-Point Writing Rubric

8	7	6	5	4	3	2	1
The writer • has presented an unusually well-organized, insightful, and convincing argument for a specific position. • adeptly uses different forms of research to bolster the argument with interesting facts and details. • has used varied transitions to create a fluid structure for the argument. • demonstrates an exceptional grasp of persuasive language. • uses numerous details from personal experience to strengthen the persuasive position. • has offered an argument that is likely to change the mind of the listener. • demonstrates a strong sense of audience and purpose.	The writer • has presented a highly convincing argument for a specific position. • uses many well-researched facts and thoughtful comments to elaborate on the main position. • uses many transition words to lead the reader from point to point. • employs some strong examples from personal experience to build a position. • demonstrates an excellent grasp of persuasive language. • offers an argument that could persuade readers to change their minds on an issue. • shows a persistent awareness of audience and purpose.	The writer • has presented a convincing argument for a clearly stated position. • uses interesting research to elaborate upon each idea in logical sequence, with a good use of transition words. • shows a capable overall structure, and good understanding of persuasive language. • has offered an argument that has the potential to change a reader's mind. • shows a good awareness of audience and purpose.	The writer • has presented a solid argument for a stated position. • has elaborated sufficiently on most points, using some facts from research. • shows an overall grasp of persuasive language. • exhibits minor organizational difficulties that do not distract from overall understanding. • demonstrates an awareness of audience and purpose.	The writer • has presented a somewhat convincing argument for a position. • states, but does not adequately explain, a position. • has elaborated on some points with basic facts from limited research. • uses some persuasive language. • may exhibit organizational difficulties that occasionally distract from readability. • sometimes demonstrates an awareness of audience.	The writer • has presented a minimally successful argument for a position. • may not have sufficiently elaborated upon important points, and uses sketchy facts. • demonstrates limited control of persuasive language and writing conventions. • may lose the focus of an idea after stating an initial position, or may include digres-sions serious enough to impair readability. • demonstrates a vague sense of audience and purpose.	The writer • has made a disorganized, unclear attempt at arguing a poorly stated position. • offers few supporting facts and details. • uses few examples of persuasive language. • exhibits problems connecting ideas meaningfully. • incorrectly uses or inconsistently applies writing conventions. • does not demonstrate a sense of audience or awareness of purpose .	The writer • does not develop a clearly stated position on an issue. • has not used supporting facts or details to elaborate an argument. • has not used persuasive language. • exhibits difficulties with language and organization that severely distract from understanding. • has not demonstrated a grasp of the criteria that comprise a persuasive argument.

0 Incomplete: This piece is either blank, or fails to respond to the writing task. The topic is not addressed, or the student simply paraphrases the prompt. The response may be illegible or incoherent.

Notes

Notes

Notes

Notes

Notes

Notes

Guided Reading Support

Macmillan/McGraw-Hill Leveled Books

TITLE	READING LEVEL
George Washington and the American Revolution	P
Ping's Pictures	P
Bookworm's Band	R
How Do They Do That?	R
Nonsense, Mr. Lear!	R
Paul Revere: Midnight Rider	R
Teeny's Great Inventions	R
Walking in Beauty	R
Bad Day, Glad Day	S
The Work of Many Hands: Writing the Declaration of Independence	S
Wynton Marsalis: Music Man	S
Aboard the Underground Railroad	T

Additional Leveled Books from The Wright Group

TITLE	READING LEVEL
Spreading the Word	J
Stories on Stage	K
Bad News, Good News	L–M
Platypuses	O
Careers-Day Surprise	P
Cultural Instruments	P
Making A TV Documentary	P
The School Newspaper	P
Storyteller Quilts	Q

To order these titles or other Wright Group Leveled Book titles, call 1-800-648-2970.

Guided Reading Lesson Plan

Before You Read

PREVIEW YOUR BOOK
- What is the title?
- What do you know about the author?
- What illustrations are on the cover and title page?
- Is this book fiction or nonfiction?

MAKE PREDICTIONS
- Think about what you noticed as you previewed.
- What do you think this book will be about?
- Record your prediction in your response journal and explain your response.

As You Read

BE A STRATEGIC READER
- Does what you are reading make sense to you? If not, what can you do to help yourself?
- How does what you just read fit in with what you have already read?
- Was your prediction about the book correct, or do you need to change it?
- Are there any important words that you don't know? Reread the sentence and listen to yourself read. Can you figure out the word? If not, look it up in a dictionary or ask your teacher.

WRITE IN YOUR RESPONSE JOURNAL
- Write any thoughts you have about what you are reading.
- Write words you might use in your own writing, or things the author says that you really like.
- Write a question you want to ask your group later. Make sure your question is related to the text.

After You Read

DISCUSS THE BOOK WITH YOUR GROUP (fiction)

Discuss the Characters
- Who is the main character? Is this person a perfect hero or someone with faults? Explain.
- Is there a villain? Is this person all bad? Explain.
- Do any characters change by the end? How?
- How do you feel about the characters? Find examples in the book to support your feelings.

Discuss the Plot
- What is the setting? Is it important to the story?
- What is the problem facing the main character? Is it solved? How?
- Is there a happy ending? How did you feel about the ending?

Discuss the Theme
- What important message do you think the author wants readers to think about?
- How do you feel about this message? Is it something important to you? Why or why not?

Rate the Author
- Do you think that the author did a good job delivering the message or idea of the story? Find examples in the book to support your position.
- Would you want to read another book by this author? Why or why not?

Share Response Journals
- Be a good listener when other group members share from their journals. Respect their responses.
- Look for any questions you had about the book. Ask group members. Maybe one of them has an answer.
- Decide whether there is anything else in your journal that you would like to share.

To the Teacher After modeling the following routine with your students for a while, have them use it in their literature circles. On the board, list the steps for students to follow.

Before You Read
- Preview Your Book
- Make Predictions

As You Read
- Be a Strategic Reader
- Write in Your Response Journal

After You Read
- Discuss the Book with Your Group
- Pick a Follow-Up Activity

DISCUSS THE BOOK WITH YOUR GROUP (nonfiction)

Discuss the Topic
- What is the book about? What is the main idea or topic? What information does the author tell you about this topic?
- Is this a topic that interests you?
- Is there something else about the topic that you still want to find out about?

Discuss the Author's Purpose
- Does the author just want to inform readers about the topic? Is that the only purpose?
- Does the author also want to persuade readers to do something or to feel a certain way about something? If so, are you persuaded? Find examples from the book to support your responses.

Rate the Author
- Is the book easy to follow?
- Is the information interesting?
- Do the illustrations help you to understand the information?
- Would you want to read another book by this author? Why or why not?

Share Response Journals
- Be a good listener when other group members share from their journals. Respect their responses.
- Look for any questions you had about the book. Ask group members. Maybe one of them has an answer.
- Decide whether there is anything else in your journal that you would like to share.

PICK A FOLLOW-UP ACTIVITY (fiction)
- **Compare and Contrast Characters** Write about similarities and differences between two characters in the story, or between one of the characters and a character from another story.
- **Draw Pictures** Find something in the story that is not pictured. It could be a place, an event, or a character. Get ideas from the story and draw a picture. Write a paragraph that tells what your picture is about.
- **Be an Author** Write a new ending for the story, add a character, or change the setting. Or write a new story for the same characters.
- **Look at the Language** Look for dialog in the story. Were quotation marks used correctly to set off the characters' exact words? Did the author always use *said* in dialog, or were other words used? If other words were used, make a list and turn it into a classroom poster. You can refer to the poster to make your own stories more interesting.

PICK A FOLLOW-UP ACTIVITY (nonfiction)
- **Make a Word Web** Use a word web to organize the information from the book. Write the topic of the book in a center circle and the most important ideas in circles around it. Then write interesting details from the book on lines extending from each main idea.
- **Find Out More** Think of something in the book that you would like to learn more about. Research your topic and report what you learned to group members.
- **Be a Teacher** Think of how you would retell what you read to make it interesting and fun for someone else (a younger child, a friend, a family member).

Additional Theme Resources

Contents

Theme Book
The Time to Choose **T120**

Theme Book
Grant Wood: Farm Boy With an Artist's Eye **T121**

Theme Book
Dear Dad **T122**

Theme Book
Go Free or Die **T123**

Trade Book
Sarah, Plain and Tall **T124**

SKILLS AND OBJECTIVES

Theme	Identify the theme
Character	Understand character motivation

The Time to Choose

Written by Michael Burgan
Illustrated by Ron Himler

A 10-year-old Boston girl chronicles in her diary confrontations between British soldiers and colonists before the Revolutionary War.

Before They Read

BUILDING BACKGROUND Discuss with students the American Revolution. Ask, *What were the causes of the Revolutionary War? What were the results?* Ask students to imagine that they were living in America just before the war. What might life have been like then?

INTRODUCING VOCABULARY Write these words on the board and read them. Have students use the words in a cumulative story in which each student contributes one sentence.

scold	scowled	harsh	squabbling
ruthless	raged	taunted	massacre

STUDENTS ACQUIRING ENGLISH

To help keep students focused on the theme, ask them to explain how each event relates to the theme of "taking a stand."

SETTING A PURPOSE Display the book cover and read the title. Ask, *Based on details in the illustration, what year do you think it is? What kind of choice do you think the title refers to?* Record students' predictions on a predictions chart.

While They Read

READING THE STORY

- Check students' understanding of character motivation by asking, *Why does Rebecca keep a diary?* (to record all that she sees, thinks, and does) *Why doesn't Rebecca's father want to take sides at first?* (He feels it is better to remain neutral than to squabble.) *Why does Rebecca's father later decide to take a stand?* (He can no longer tolerate the killing he has seen.)
- After students finish the book, discuss the theme by asking, *Do you think Rebecca's father is right or wrong in refusing to take a stand at first? Why?* Then ask, *What is the author's message, or theme, in this story?* (It is important to fight for your beliefs.)

After They Read

EXTENDING THE STORY Choose from the following activities to provide additional thematic support for the different modality needs of your students.

- **Pick a Side.** Focus on the theme by having students choose a controversy currently in the news. Divide students into two groups to debate the issue. Stress that each group should support its arguments with facts. After each side presents its argument, let classmates decide which side was more convincing. *(Verbal/Linguistic, Interpersonal)*
- **The Other Side.** Have students imagine that the story had been told by one of the "lobsters." Challenge students to write the redcoat's diary entry, explaining his motivations for his actions. *(Intrapersonal)*

MORE BOOKS TO READ Suggest to students that they read these other books about the Revolutionary War.

- *The Fighting Ground* by Avi
- *Samuel's Choice* by Richard Berleth
- *My Brother Sam Is Dead* by James and Christopher Collier

Theme Book

SKILLS AND OBJECTIVES

Theme	Identify the theme
Genre	Understand elements of biography

Grant Wood: Farm Boy With an Artist's Eye

Written by Jean Kinney

Artist Grant Wood discovers inspiration in Iowa farm country and builds his career as an American painter.

Before They Read

BUILDING BACKGROUND Talk with students about images they have seen in paintings. Point out that paintings show us how someone else sees the world. They can also remind us of times and places that have changed. Ask students what subjects they like to paint and what they like to look at in the land around them.

REVIEWING VOCABULARY Write these words on the board. Ask if any students who are interested in art can define the words. Provide definitions for the more challenging words.

transgressor	plaster	whimsical	portrait
manual training	Quaker	silhouettes	Gothic

STUDENTS ACQUIRING ENGLISH

To help students focus on the theme, ask them to explain how each event relates to Wood's development as a painter.

SETTING A PURPOSE Read the title and show students the last three paintings by Grant Wood in the book. Tell them that the book is a *biography*—a true story about his life. Ask students what they would like to find out about the time and place in the paintings. What would they like to know about the artist?

While They Read

READING THE STORY

- Discuss the importance of learning from other people's lives, and ask students to focus on time and place as they read. Ask, *Where and when did Grant Wood live?* (Iowa; early 1900s) *What did he like to paint as a boy?* (birds, animals, flowers) *Why did he want to paint in Paris?* (French painters were selling work.) *How did Grant feel about the people and land of his home? How can you tell?* (He loved them; it shows in his paintings.) *Why did Grant feel he had cheated people back home?* (because he was trying to be someone he was not)
- To check comprehension of theme, ask, *What advice would Grant give a young artist?* (Paint the things you know and love from your own experience.)

After They Read

EXTENDING THE STORY Choose from the following activities to provide additional thematic support for the different modality needs of your students.

- **Write an Interview.** Invite students to interview an artist or other adult friend or family member. Help them prepare courteous questions and plan to record the answers. Then ask students to write brief, illustrated biographies to share with the class. *(Verbal/Linguistic, Interpersonal)*
- **Paint a Mural.** Help students paint a mural with poster paints and butcher paper. Discuss how Grant Wood's paintings keep the memory of time and place alive. Encourage students to paint their favorite local scenes. *(Visual/Spatial)*

MORE BOOKS TO READ Suggest to students that they read these other artists' biographies.

- *Benjamin West and His Cat Grimalkin* by Wesley Dennis
- *From the Hills of Georgia: An Autobiography in Paintings* by Mattie Lou O'Kelley
- *Li'l Sis and Uncle Willie* by Gwen Everett

SKILLS AND OBJECTIVES

Theme	Identify the theme
Picture Clues	Understand how illustrations aid comprehension

Dear Dad

Written by Erica Silverman
Illustrated by Tom Leonard and Diane Paterson

In an exchange of letters with her father, a young girl learns that we don't always get what we wish for—but we sometimes discover wonderful things while pursuing our dreams.

Before They Read

BUILDING BACKGROUND Ask students to discuss the difference between a letter and a phone call. Which do they prefer and why? What other forms of communication are there?

INTRODUCING VOCABULARY Write each word on the board, pronounce it, and have volunteers look up each word's definition in the dictionary to share with the class. Challenge students to make up silly book titles using the vocabulary words.

allergies	rainbow	jungles	tarantula
octopus	Victorian	collage	

STUDENTS ACQUIRING ENGLISH

To check students' understanding of the story, have them describe Jenna's wishes.

SETTING A PURPOSE On the board, begin a story chart to help students recognize the theme. Label horizontal columns, *Letter #1, Letter #2, Letter #3,* and so forth. Have students copy the chart. Explain to students that after reading each letter, they will write a sentence or phrase that summarizes it.

While They Read

READING THE STORY

- As students read, have them focus on theme by asking themselves, *What is the point of this story?*
- Focus on the illustrations by saying, *Compare the photographs of Dad on page 9 and page 14. How do they change over time?* (The house and garden look better; he holds a phone instead of a guitar.)
- After students finish reading have them review their story charts. Then ask volunteers to state the themes in the story. (Writing letters is satisfying; wishes can lead to new discoveries.)

After They Read

EXTENDING THE STORY Choose from the following activities to provide additional thematic support for the different modality needs of your students.

- **Write a Letter.** Encourage students to write about a wish or goal they have for the future. Ask them to illustrate their letters. Provide class time for students to write letters to distant friends or relatives. International pen-pal addresses are available through the local library. *(Verbal/Linguistic)*
- **Make a Collage.** Give students old magazines, scissors, paste, and paper, and ask them to create collages about their personal wishes and dreams. Encourage them to add words, sentences, and original drawings to share ideas they can't find in photographs. *(Visual/Spatial)*

MORE BOOKS TO READ Suggest to students that they read these other books about families.

- *Julian, Dream Doctor* by Ann Cameron
- *A Job for Jenny Archer* by Ellen Conford
- *The Skirt* by Gary Soto

Theme Book

SKILLS AND OBJECTIVES

Theme	Identify the theme
Author's Purpose	Identify author's purpose

Go Free or Die

Written by Jeri Ferris
Illustrated by Karen Ritz

Harriet Tubman escapes from slavery and courageously returns to the South to guide many African Americans to freedom.

Before They Read

BUILDING BACKGROUND Ask students to share stories about favorite real-life heroes and heroines. Explain that thinking about a person's life can help us understand and appreciate their actions.

INTRODUCING VOCABULARY Write each word or term on the board, define it, and ask a volunteer to use it a sentence.

windowless	slave	slave gang
plantation	overseer	freedom
Underground Railroad		

STUDENTS ACQUIRING ENGLISH

To help keep students focused on the theme, ask them to explain how each event relates to courage.

SETTING A PURPOSE Read the title of the book and explain that Harriet Tubman was once a slave. Ask students what they know about slavery and discuss the somber mood of the cover illustration.

While They Read

READING THE STORY

- Ask students to think about the story's theme as they read. Remind them that the story is true, and have them ask themselves, *What decision did Harriet make? Why?* (to be free or die; slavery was cruel and inhuman)
- To help students understand the author's purpose, ask, *What is the author's purpose? To inform? To persuade? To entertain?* (to inform readers about Harriet's life)
- After students finish the story, ask them to discuss the themes of courage and fighting for your beliefs.

After They Read

EXTENDING THE STORY Choose from the following activities to provide additional thematic support for the different modality needs of your students.

- **Act It Out.** Ask students to act out scenes from the story. Encourage them to focus on scenes that illustrate the theme of the book. *(Interpersonal, Kinesthetic)*
- **Write a Letter.** Tell students to write letters from Harriet to her grandchildren. Ask them to express Harriet's beliefs. Students' letters might include Harriet's advice for her grandchildren. *(Verbal/Linguistic)*

MORE BOOKS TO READ Suggest to students that they read these other books about courageous Americans.

- *Young Frederick Douglass: Fight for Freedom* by Laurence Santrey
- *Walking the Road to Freedom: A Story About Sojourner Truth* by Jeri Ferris
- *Andrew Young: Freedom Fighter* by Maurice Roberts

Trade Book

SKILLS AND OBJECTIVES

Summarize/Retell	Summarize and retell story events
Fact/Opinion	Distinguish between fact and opinion

Sarah, Plain and Tall

Written by Patricia MacLachlan

Papa is looking for a new wife after the death of Caleb and Anna's mother. When Sarah comes from Maine to stay on the prairie, the children quickly grow to love her. They worry she won't stay, but in the end Sarah makes their family complete again.

Before They Read

BUILDING BACKGROUND Write the word *prairie* on the board and ask, *What is a prairie?* Help students understand that a prairie is a large area of flat or slightly hilly land that is mostly covered with tall grasses. Display a map of the United States and point out the states of Texas, Oklahoma, Kansas, Nebraska, South Dakota, and North Dakota. Explain that all these states once included large areas of prairie land.

Explain to students that pioneers from the eastern United States settled on the prairie in the 1800s. Have students tell what they think life on the prairie would have been like in the 1800s without electricity, running water, or vehicles such as cars and trucks.

INTRODUCING VOCABULARY Write the following words on the board and help students define them. Have students sort the words into two categories: *Things Found on the Prairie* (pitchfork, windmill, tumbleweed) and *Things Found in or Near the Sea* (flounder, gulls, scallop, conch, dune). Then invite students to use the words in sentences about the prairie and the sea.

flounder	gulls	conch	dune
pitchfork	scallop	windmill	tumbleweed

SETTING A PURPOSE Have students look at the cover of the book and read the title. Point out the woman on the cover. Explain that her name is Sarah and that she has just come to live on the prairie. Invite students to speculate on who the children on the cover might be and what happens to Sarah in the story. Invite students to read the story to find out.

STUDENTS ACQUIRING ENGLISH

As students read, stop after each chapter and have them summarize events. Check comprehension by asking questions about characters' actions and feelings; for example, *Who does Sarah write to in her letters? When does Sarah arrive at the children's home? How do Anna and Caleb feel about Sarah? How do you know?*

While They Read

READING THE STORY

Beginning Ask students to read the beginning of the story, stopping at the end of Chapter 3.

- Review that a fact is a statement that can be proved to be true or untrue; an opinion is a belief or a judgment. Then point out to students that when Sarah first writes to Papa, she asks him if he has opinions on cats. Have students think about what Papa says about Seal later in the story. Have them speculate on his opinion of cats. Students might say that he doesn't believe that cats should live in the house. He thinks that the best use for a cat is catching mice in the barn.
- Reread Sarah's second letter to Papa on page 15. Ask, *Does Sarah state facts or opinions in this letter to Papa?* (facts) *What does this tell you about her?* (She is honest and to the point.)
- Have students briefly summarize what happens in the beginning of the story. Then have them take turns retelling the scene in which Sarah arrives by wagon.

Middle Ask students to read the middle of the story by continuing from where they left off and stopping at the end of Chapter 6.

- Have students reread Sarah's description of seals on page 27. Ask, *Does Sarah give facts or opinions when she describes the seals? How do you know?* (Sarah gives facts about seals. Everything she says can be proved to be true or untrue.)
- Review the words that Sarah writes to William at the end of Chapter 5: "Sliding down our dune of hay is almost as fine as sliding down the sand dunes into the sea." Ask, *Is this a statement of fact or is it an opinion? Why do you think so?* (It is an opinion. Sarah judges sliding down the dune of hay and tells how she feels about it.)
- Ask students to briefly summarize what happens in the middle of the story. Then have them retell the scene in which Sarah and the children swim in the cow pond.

End Ask students to finish reading to the end of the story.

- Have partners look through the last three chapters of the book and find three examples that are statements of fact and three examples that are opinions. Have them share their findings with the class.
- Ask students to briefly summarize how the book ends. Then have them take turns retelling their favorite part of the story.

Summarize Have students recall their previous summaries of the beginning, middle, and end of the book and use them to write a summary of the entire story.

See Graphic Organizers Transparency 28.

After They Read

EXTENDING THE STORY Choose from the following activities to provide additional support for comprehension strategies for the different modality needs of your students.

- **Write a Description.** Have students go back and review the letters in which Sarah describes herself to Papa, Anna, and Caleb. Then ask students to write paragraphs in which they describe themselves. Tell students to include a description of what they look like and where they live. Have them add details about the things they like. Invite volunteers to read their descriptive paragraphs aloud. *(Verbal/Linguistic, Intrapersonal)*
- **Compose Diary Entries.** Invite students to imagine that they are Sarah and write a diary entry telling how she might have felt when she first came to the prairie in the spring. Then have them write a diary entry from Sarah's viewpoint at the end of the story. Encourage students to read both diary entries aloud and tell how Sarah's feelings changed. *(Verbal/Linguistic)*
- **Draw the Sea.** Remind students that Sarah brought colored pencils back from town so that she and the children could draw the sea. Provide students with blue, gray, and green colored pencils and invite them to draw their own picture of the sea. If colored pencils are not available, students can use crayons or markers. Invite volunteers to display their pictures and describe the sea to the class. *(Visual/Spatial, Kinesthetic)*
- **Compare Settings.** Have students use the descriptions in the story and their own knowledge to compare the prairie to the sea. Students can use a Venn diagram to record the ways the prairie and the sea are alike and different. Have students come together in small groups to share their comparisons with each other. *(Logical, Visual/Spatial, Interpersonal)*

  See Graphic Organizers Transparency 14.